Nations and Governments

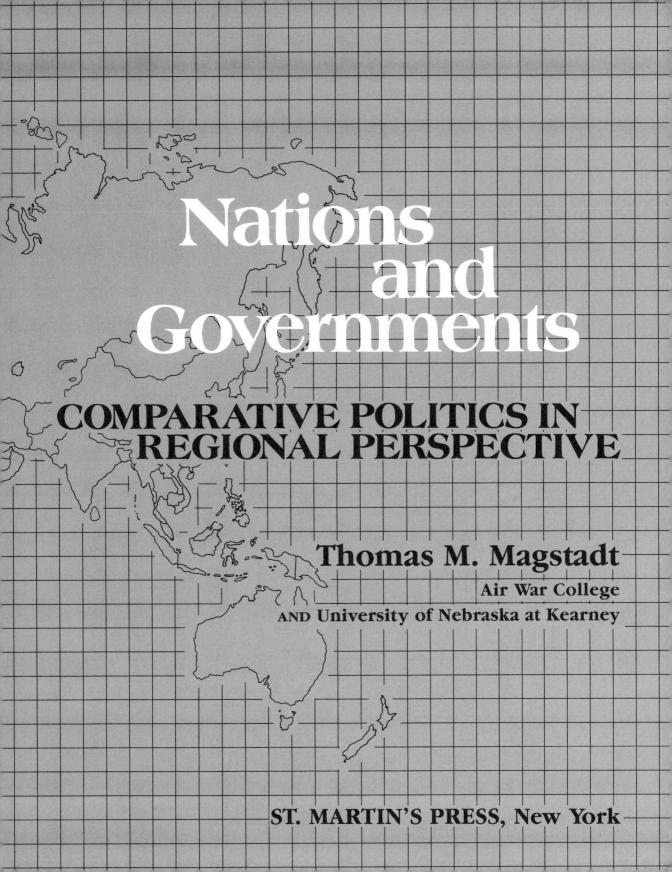

Nations
and
Governments

COMPARATIVE POLITICS IN
REGIONAL PERSPECTIVE

Thomas M. Magstadt

Air War College

AND University of Nebraska at Kearney

ST. MARTIN'S PRESS, New York

Senior editor: Don Reisman
Development editor: Bob Weber
Project management: Gene Crofts
Production supervisor: Alan Fischer
Text design: Gene Crofts
Maps: Jeane E. Norton
Cover design: Jeanette Jacobs

Library of Congress Catalog Card Number: 89-63917

Manufactured in the United States of America.
5 4 3   2   1
f e   d c   b

For information, write:
St. Martin's Press, Inc.
175 Fifth Avenue
New York, NY 10010

ISBN: 0-312-00404-4

For MJ
1946–1990

Preface

When first thinking about this book, the idea of using a regional perspective to introduce students to comparative politics seemed like a good one. But I had no right to expect that trends and events in the ensuing years would be so accommodating. Even a decade ago the rationale for taking a regional approach to comparative politics was less obvious than it is today. "Why look at *regions*?" one might have asked. Are there, in fact, regional characteristics, commonalities, outlooks, patterns, trends, interests? Do regions really provide a useful way of dividing up the world for purposes of comparison and analysis? Well, let's consider some cases.

During the 1980s a democratization movement swept across South America, as one military junta after another bowed out in favor of freely elected civilian governments. The retreat of the military from politics in this region of the world followed another regionwide phenomenon that had occurred in the preceding decade—a steady slide into what is now called the "debt crisis." Throughout the region the pattern was repeated: military rule, economic mismanagement, grossly uneven distribution of wealth and power, widespread human rights abuses, growing social unrest, huge external debt, and, finally, the voluntary handing over of power to civilians.

At the end of the 1980s another region—Eastern Europe—underwent remarkable transformations. In just one year virtually all Eastern Europe moved away from monolithic, one-party (Communist) rule and central planning toward pluralistic, multiparty rule and a free-market economy. What is most remarkable is not simply that these changes occurred but that they spread throughout the region. Significantly, the reforms did not spread beyond the region; Communist regimes in the People's Republic of China, North Korea, Vietnam, and Cuba did not relinquish power. Although the sinews connecting the fates of Poland, Hungary, East Germany, Czechoslovakia, Romania, Bulgaria, and Yugoslavia may be invisible, they are nonetheless real. Moreover, events in Eastern Europe were inseparably intertwined with events in the Soviet Union: The rise of reform-minded Mikhail Gorbachev to Kremlin leadership in 1985 is what set the stage for changes throughout the region once known as the "Soviet bloc."

In Western Europe regionalism is also apparent. The movement toward a unified (not merely integrated) economy among the twelve members of the European Community is a scintillating example of regional cooperation. In 1992 the EC will become a single market with unified Germany as the anchor. Will this serve as a model for other regions? Will European nationalism gradually give way to regionalism rather than to globalism, which the United States has championed since World War II?

It is axiomatic that economic interdependence has increased greatly in recent decades, and in all parts of the globe. But what many call "global interdependence" in fact conceals a high degree of regionalism—a point that gets too little attention. The most spectacular example of this has occurred within the European Community, but the United States and Canada have now signed a historic treaty to create a North American customs union. Similarly, the economically resurgent nations of the Pacific Rim have the potential (but not yet a strong inclination) to replicate the European experiment in integration. If the nations of Southeast Asia were included in an Asian common market, the result would be a powerful trading bloc that could rival the economic might of North America and the European Community.

Other examples of regionalism are not difficult to find. The OPEC oil embargo of the 1970s expressed Arab solidarity against the West following the Yom Kippur War, in which Israel defeated Egypt and occupied the Sinai. More recently, the strength of regional bonds was manifested in the response of many Arabs to Iraq's annexation of Kuwait in August 1990. Many Western observers had difficulty grasping that Saddam Hussein was a hero to many (perhaps most) Arabs. Such a manifestation of grass-roots "regionalism" is a sign of our times and possibly a harbinger of our future.

Sub-Saharan Africa has made no real move toward regional economic cooperation, but elements of a common outlook combine with a common colonial heritage and common problems to produce a political portrait and an economic predicament that are distinct to the region. The passing of apartheid in South Africa will remove one overarching issue on which all the nations and governments of this region could agree, but it remains to be seen whether they now will determine their own destiny. Possibly, regional interdependence will pave the way to meaningful independence for the individual nations.

Although the case for a regional perspective has become more obvious in recent years, regional factors have always influenced political patterns and interactions. Hence, the maps used in Imperial China reflected the notion that China was the Middle Kingdom—the center of the universe—and depicted the rest of the world, including Europe, as peripheral parcels of real estate too remote and insignificant to take seriously or treat ceremoniously. In hindsight, the Spanish Conquest can be viewed as a regional phenomenon, an encounter between one region (Europe) and another (Latin America) in which a particular regional power (Spain) happened to play the key role. Europe's colonization of Africa and Asia during the nineteenth century can also be seen as a series of encounters between regions.

In retrospect, the Cold War also had a distinctly regional dimension. How can its intensity and duration, its origins in Europe (whence it spread to other regions), and its peculiar ideological coloration of communism versus capitalism be explained apart from Europe's religious, ethical, philosophical, and political traditions? Is it any wonder that for most Asians, Africans, and Latin Americans the Cold War, East-West conflict was never a compelling paradigm for explaining world politics? On the contrary, in the Third World the North-South conflict has always taken precedence.

Still more recently, the world has witnessed the rise of two new regional powers. In Europe, the European Community is now a major economic force in the world. In Asia, Japan has emerged as an economic superpower and has been emulated by other Asian nations, possibly paving the way for a future Asian "common market."

Thus, looking at world history from a regional rather than national perspective reveals patterns of interregional as well as international politics. The existence of such patterns is not new; what's new is our growing recognition of them. The importance of historical and contextual differences among regions is reflected in the tripartite structure of this book. Each region is covered in a three-chapter sequence: the first focuses on history, geography, and other factors commonly known as the "political setting"; the second examines contemporary political institutions and processes; and the third looks at the problems and prospects of key countries in each region. To oversimplify slightly, the first chapter looks at the past, the second at the present, and the third at the future.

Acknowledgments

I owe a large debt of gratitude to many people, including past and present students, without whose efforts this project might never have been realized. Rebecca Hausmann, my graduate assistant in 1989–1990 and the author of the first draft of the Instructor's Manual, did an outstanding job. Joe Blankenau also ably assisted me in researching portions of the book. Admasu Shunkuri, a friend and colleague, wrote the first drafts of the three chapters on sub-Saharan Africa; his work was invaluable in laying the foundations for Part VI. Daniel Lang, who once sat in comparative politics classes I taught at Augustana College (Sioux Falls), made incisive suggestions that shaped the contours of the book in many ways. Stepanka Korytova read Parts II and III with the historian's eye for accuracy and detail. Bob Weber, Senior Development Editor at St. Martin's, is not only a gifted editor but also a trusted adviser and associate who once again lived up to his title. I also thank Richard Steins, Director of Editing at St. Martin's, whose reading of the edited manuscript was invaluable.

Many reviewers made helpful suggestions during the drafting and revision of manuscript, and I particularly want to acknowledge the help of W. Raymond Duncan, State University of New York, Brockport; Anthony Joes, St. Joseph's University; Paul Johnson, Florida State University; Kathleen McQuaid, Drexel University; Jack Parson, College of Charleston; and Donald Pienkos, University of Wisconsin, Milwaukee.

Finally, I owe a great deal to my family. My late wife, Mary Jo, always gave me moral support, even when the writing diverted my attention from matters that weighed heavily on her mind and heart. My sister, Barbara, has always given me encouragement and understanding. Finally, I owe much to my son, David, for helping me keep things in perspective and never letting me forget that there is more to life than writing books.

Thomas M. Magstadt

Contents

PART I

Introduction

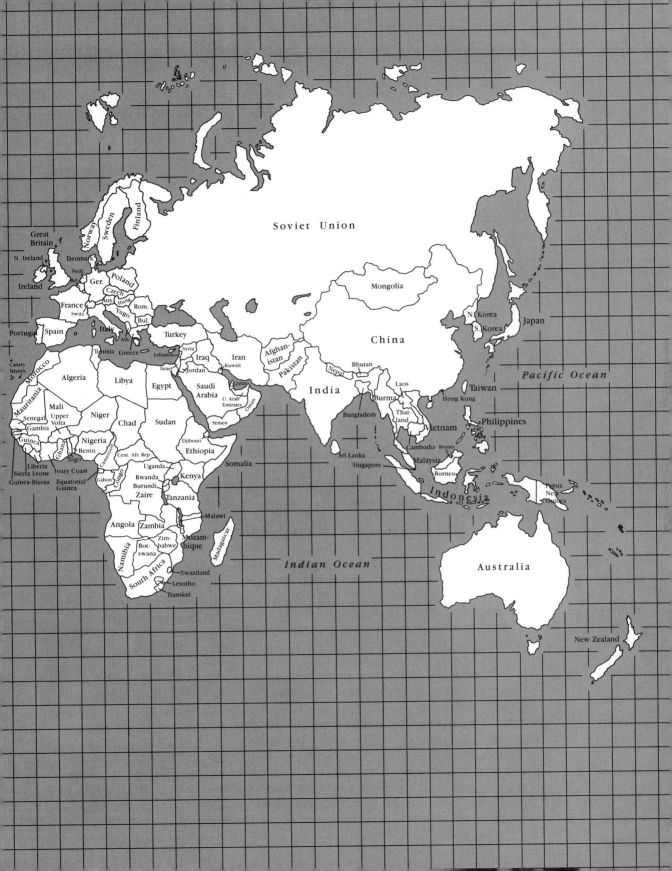

Chapter 1
Comparative Politics and the Regional Perspective

Lycurgus and the Founding of Sparta

"In the development of the city-state Sparta stands apart," according to Raphael Sealey, a distinguished scholar of Greek antiquity.[1] Indeed, Sparta was the great rival of Athens during Greece's Golden Age, and led one of the two grand alliances (the other was led by Athens) in the Peloponnesian Wars chronicled by Thucydides.

Plutarch, in his famous *Lives of the Noble Grecians and Romans*, told the intriguing story of Lycurgus, a heroic figure from Sparta. Lycurgus traveled widely, taking note of the features, fine points, and faults of different regimes (engaging in "comparative political studies"). On return to his homeland, he created a new political order, drawing on all that he had learned from his travels. He incorporated the region's particular circumstances (what some political scientists would today call the "political ecology") in reconstituting the Spartan regime. Above all Lycurgus kept self-defense and national security in mind. Because in Sparta slaves ("helots") vastly outnumbered citizens, there was constant fear of a mass insurrection. After the Messenians (a people enslaved by Sparta in 730 B.C.) revolted, Sparta became an armed camp. It engaged in little or no commerce with the outside world, stressed patriotism and battlefield valor, glorified physical prowess over intellectual or artistic pursuits, urged austerity and self-denial, and placed the good of the whole above that of the individual. Sparta consequently became the most powerful state in Greece.

Every aspect of life in Sparta—marriage, the birth and education of children, the economy—was geared to ensuring Sparta's physical security by keeping the citizenry "lean and mean." This siege mentality was a direct result of political ecology—in particular, the numerical superiority of the helots: "The citizens were, in fact, a garrison in their country; and the stability of their political institutions was due to their conscious knowledge that the numbers of that garrison, compared with the numbers of the Helot foe, were perilously small."[2] To this day the word *Spartan* is synonymous with strict (even severe) discipline, frugal living, and a martial spirit.

Although the Lycurgan system was seemingly well adapted to the unique circumstances of Sparta, "Her history illustrates how a rigorous training can turn a people, essentially no braver than the rest of mankind, into an invincible force; it shows, too, how conservatism can stagnate until it becomes a cruel selfishness determined to maintain a system no matter what the cost."[3] For students of comparative politics, what is of lasting importance in this story is the way in which Lycurgus went about founding the new Sparta: thought and analysis—*comparative* analysis—preceded action.

Just as Lycurgus is reputed to have built a political order on empirical observation and reason, so two centuries ago the founders of the United States claimed to have constructed a ''new science of politics.'' The theoretical underpinnings of the U.S. Constitution can be found in the *Federalist Papers*, written by James Madison, Alexander Hamilton, and John Jay shortly after the Philadelphia Convention.

Before reading on, try this mental exercise: Imagine yourself a Lycurgus or Madison. What sort of political system would you create? How would you go about it? What purposes would you want it to serve? What dangers would you want it to guard against? Ask yourself these questions as well: Is there one form of government that is best everywhere and always? Or is the best form of government relative to time and place?

Answering these questions should help you develop a sense of what you think good government is all about and how it might best be achieved under different sets of circumstances. Finally, discuss answers with a classmate. The best (and most enjoyable) way to learn is to engage in lively, informal discussions with peers. That's just what educated citizens in ancient Greece and colonial America did, with results that left an indelible imprint on world history.

Why Compare?

''Know thyself,'' admonished the oracle of Apollo at Delphi in the seventh century. These two words, probably the most famous words of wisdom to come out of Greek philosophy, suggest the value of making comparisons. ''An age-old idea of philosophers is that knowledge of the self is gained through knowledge of others.''[4] What is true of individuals is also true of societies. Mattei Dogan and Dominique Pelassy, two contemporary political scientists, make this point very clearly:

> Let us imagine a country encircled for centuries by an unbreachable wall. Which of its inhabitants would be in a position to describe such a confined nation? What could be the reference point; how could one measure what is perceived; moreover, what *could* be perceived? . . . the observer would be incapable of understanding most of the fundamental and pertinent traits of the environment. With what rigidity are social groups constituted, what features characterize the mentality of the populace, to what degree is power centralized? The simple formulation of these questions presupposes comparison; denied the possibility of looking beyond his or her own world, the analyst is virtually blind.[5]

Comparison is an excellent antidote to ethnocentrism (a narrow view of the world based on one's own culture, religion, nationality, and so on). Indeed, there is perhaps no better way to gain perspective on one's own society than to view it from afar, through the eyes of others.

Some of the most penetrating analyses of American political and social institutions have been made by foreigners. Few scholars would dispute that *Democracy in America*, an incisive two-volume study by Alexis de Tocqueville, a Frenchman who visited the United States in the 1830s, retains much of its relevance and validity in the 1990s. Similarly, in the early 1900s an Englishman named James Bryce showed in *The American Commonwealth* how the U.S. system of candidate selection tends to eliminate many of the best qualified individuals.

By the same token, American observers have made significant contributions to the knowledge of others about their own societies. In 1976, Hedrick Smith, then Moscow correspondent of the *New York Times*, wrote a best-seller (*The Russians*) on the people, culture, economy, and government of the Soviet Union at the time. Smith visited the Soviet Union several times in the years immediately following publication of his book. Many Soviet citizens inquired eagerly about it. A candidate-member of the Soviet Academy of Sciences who had seen parts of it expressed anger and dismay, and then related a personal experience that corroborated Smith's account of a privileged political, managerial, and artistic elite flourishing in the shadow of the Kremlin. "I have lived here all my life," said this academician, "and in Smith's book I discovered things about my own country that I did not know."

There are many such examples, leading us to ask, Why can outsiders so often see something that insiders cannot? And the answer? Precisely because it is obvious. What seems ordinary or natural to native dwellers may in fact be unique. As human beings we are often least objective about ourselves. We regularly err in evaluating our own strengths and weaknesses. Americans are often accused of moral arrogance, of exaggerating our own virtues and treating our own values, beliefs, ideas, and institutions as the embodiment of universal truth. Our belief in the superiority of our institutions paradoxically coexists with widespread cynicism about politics and politicians. In reality, our institutions are not so perfect nor our politicians so imperfect as we commonly suppose.

Almost everyone has a political viewpoint, but few have the time or inclination to pursue politics intensively. Myths and misconceptions thus abound. The same can of course be said about other fields of knowledge, but there is a crucial difference: Unlike the case with most other fields, *the way we think about politics can and does affect the way we conduct our public affairs*.

In contrast to, say, how the solar system works, or the life cycle of butterflies, politics is a human activity, and government is a human invention. The life cycle of a political system is not dictated or governed by cosmic laws, nor is the system, divinely ordained. Faulty understanding in the realm of politics can and frequently does produce faulty policies.

Why do we compare? Let's summarize our answers.

☐ Comparison is a very useful way to evaluate what we see and hear about the world beyond our shores, as well as about our own society.

☐ What the citizenry believes can have a significant impact on what government does, especially in democratic countries.

☐ Political myths, to the detriment of a nation (and possibly the world), may be used to prop up policies that have outlived their usefulness.

☐ An attempt to identify and explain the fundamental patterns of political behavior across different societies and cultures may help us to arrive at some useful theoretical generalizations.

☐ Finally, by comparing our own political institutions, processes, ideas, and traditions with those of others we can learn more about ourselves.

Methods of Comparative Politics

Comparative politics is as old as the discipline of political science itself. The Greek philosopher Aristotle (384–322 B.C.), a pioneer in the science of politics, set standards for the discipline that have survived to the present. Aristotle appreciated and demonstrated the importance of both theory and method.

The term *theory* refers to concepts, ideas, or bodies of thought that purport to explain, predict, or prescribe political systems, patterns, processes, and trends. *Political forms* are sets of institutions or systems that, taken together, constitute regimes; *political processes* include interest articulation and opinion formation, elections, coalition building, and bargaining.

References to methods (or methodology) can be confusing or even intimidating to students, but they need not be. The so-called scientific method has two aspects—induction and deduction. Regarding deduction John Locke, a seventeenth-century political philosopher, wrote, ''Reasoning is nothing but the faculty of deducing unknown truths from principles already known.'' Deduction involves abstract thought and logical reasoning. For example, that constitutional democracy is the best form of government is a premise that few Americans doubt. Most people would also agree that India is a democracy. Logically, if democracy is good and India is a democracy, then India must have good government.

Although the logic of this proposition is unassailable, the truth of it is not. Many observers of the Indian scene would argue that India does *not* have good government. The inference then is that either (a) the premise equating democracy with good government is false or (b) India is not a true democracy.

Such an example shows the need for *inductive* analysis: To know whether India does or does not have good government one must seek empirical (factual) evidence. To do this one can begin with a hypothesis (a proposition to be proven or disproven) and proceed to test it by (a) gathering all relevant data (information) possible, (b) classifying these data, (c) comparing them with similar data from other countries, and finally (d) drawing conclusions (this time from concrete facts, rather than from abstract reasoning).

Depending on the specific hypothesis being tested, one might subject the data to sophisticated statistical analysis in an effort to discover correlations (or relationships) among key variables. In our India example, an initial step would be devising a definition of good government that can be operationalized, that is, measured accurately. It would also be important to distinguish between dependent and independent variables. In this example, the form of government might be the independent variable and various measures of good government (such as education opportunities, availability of health care, and respect for human rights) might be the dependent variables. If one could show that India scores lower on a variety of measures than some other, nondemocratic countries, we might conclude that (a) India is not a true democracy or (b) the original premise equating democracy and good government is false.

The deductive approach is most often associated with normative political theory, while the inductive approach is preferred by modern behavioral scientists. Is one approach better or more fruitful than the other? Significantly, Aristotle did not choose between normative and empirical methods, but instead blended the two—with results that are still studied some 2300 years later. As a groundbreaking theorist, Aristotle made hypotheses about political life that he then tested for historical, factual, and logical validity. History provided many of the empirical data for his analyses, and he was also a practitioner of the art of comparative inquiry. The Lyceum where he taught kept a collection of all of the constitutions that were available at that time—158. In Aristotle's political thought, "The man of science appears again and again behind the student of politics."[6] At the same time, Aristotle's ultimate concerns were ethical (that is, normative). His empirical investigations were driven by questions such as, What is the good life? What form of government is best? What is the relationship between the type of political regime in a given place and the moral character of the people who live under it?

As we embark on this exploration of the contemporary world's major political systems, we should remind ourselves that others, following Aristotle, have been doing the same thing through the ages. Whether the purpose is to create a new science of politics (like the American founders), to better understand what makes a particular form of government tick (for example, Tocqueville's *Democracy in America*), or simply to "know thy enemy," the comparative study of politics is an essential part of the undergraduate political science curriculum.

Three Questions

This book adopts a commonsense approach. It combines the ancient Greek penchant for asking fruitful questions with an appreciation of the insights offered by modern-day students of human behavior—in particular, behavior relevant to the problem(s) of government of increasingly complex societies. Here we ask three questions that, taken together, serve as a conceptual framework for the book. The first question deals with political setting, the second with patterns of rule, and the third with problems and prospects. Beginning with Part II, the rest of the book is divided into six regions of the world, each section having three chapters corresponding to these three questions. Each section also presents specific case studies.

Political Setting   *How and why do political patterns and trends vary from one region of the world to another?*

Surprisingly, by viewing societies and governments in a regional perspective we can easily observe certain patterns that may be less than obvious if we merely focus on individual countries. For example, most people in the United States know that Great Britain, France, and Germany are democratic republics (governments in which political power is vested in popularly elected representatives). Fewer people know that since the mid-1970s *all* the nations of Western Europe are democratic. No doubt fewer still have ever given any thought to the significance of this remarkable fact. Moreover, following the dramatic events of 1989 in Eastern Europe, virtually all of Europe may soon feature pluralistic political systems and market economies (these terms are defined where discussed).

Other regions that show distinct patterns and trends include the Soviet Union (and until recently Eastern Europe), sub-Saharan Africa, the Middle East, Asia, and Latin America. Not all of these display the uniformity found in Europe; nations within a region sometimes have sharply contrasting political traditions and practices. We will note the most significant deviations in each region and attempt to account for them.

Although our main concern is the fundamentals of the form(s) of government found in a given region, we will not ignore important differences in the practice of a particular form. For example, Great Britain, France, and Germany are all democracies, but they show major differences in the way they conduct elections, organize the government, apportion political power, and choose their chief executives. The Middle East evidences a wide range of authoritarian forms of government: the theocratic Iranian state, the feudal monarchies of the Arabian Peninsula, the modern monarchies of Jordan and Morocco, the personal dictatorships of Syria, Iraq, and Libya, and the mixed regime of Egypt.

In sub-Saharan Africa, too, authoritarianism predominates. In some cases a military strongman runs the country; in others a civilian rules; in still others a civilian or military oligarchy wields power. In a few cases (Botswana, Mauritius, and Gambia), parliamentary democracy has been made to work. In Africa, as in the Middle East during the first two decades after World War II, governments are sometimes brought down by military coups. The political instability implicit in this method of changing rulers has been a persistent problem.

The contemporary Asian scene displays the greatest variety of regimes in the world—parliamentary democracies (Japan, India, Pakistan, Sri Lanka, and the Philippines), Marxist-Leninist regimes (the People's Republic of China, Vietnam, and North Korea), authoritarian regimes (Indonesia, Bangladesh, Nepal, and Thailand), mixed (or transitional) regimes (South Korea, Taiwan, Singapore, and Malaysia), and puppet regimes (Cambodia and Laos). Some of these political systems defy easy classification, and for the region as a whole it is not possible to discern a definite trend in one direction or another. The important point is that, despite the prevalence of authoritarian, patron-client political traditions throughout the region, Asia is no longer the breeding ground of "oriental despotism" it was once said to be.

In the 1980s a trend could be discerned in Latin America, particularly in South America. There one military dictatorship after another gave way to civilian democratic rule. In 1990 almost every country in South America was governed by civilians who had won freely contested elections. (The exceptions were Paraguay and Chile. In Paraguay the longtime military dictator, Alfredo Stroessner, was ousted in a military coup; in Chile another military strongman, Augusto Pinochet, stepped down to clear the way for free elections.) In conflict-ridden Central America, the democratization trend is far less evident, but Costa Rica continues to be a model republic and, farther north, Mexico has moved toward a more open, multiparty system.

Describing the patterns and trends of different regions of the globe is relatively simple; explaining them is not. Later chapters will attempt explanations, but clear-cut answers are not always possible.

Patterns of Rule   *Why do certain forms of government often flourish in one regional setting and not in another?*

We will answer this question by asking (and exploring) a series of related questions (called the "Socratic method"). First, how do environmental factors such as geography, climate, and natural resources affect political values, perceptions, traditions, and institutions in a given region or nation? This avenue of inquiry we will call *political ecology*—the relationship between political institutions and the physical (or natural) environment to which the societies of a given region have had to adapt.

Second, do religious, ethnic, and linguistic differences complicate the problems of governing? If so, how and to what extent? Do these factors preclude any particular form(s) of government? Do they necessitate a certain form? The concern here is with the *political culture* of a given society or collection of societies and with the process of *political socialization* (the ways in which political culture is transmitted from one generation to the next).

Third, are there any particularly traumatic, triumphant, or tragic events in the history of a region or nation that have left an indelible mark on the collective psyche of the people and their leaders? For example, was the region subjected to colonial rule? Was the now-dominant power the victim of foreign invasion, conquest, and subjugation? Did revolution play a role in bringing the present regime(s) into existence? If so, what was the nature of the revolution? Finally, is there danger of war in the region? If so, how long has this danger prevailed? Just as we must know something about an individual's history to understand his or her personality, so must we know something of a nation's history to understand its politics.

Two examples of how geography, climate, natural resources, land–population ratios, and of course history influence political institutions help to show the importance of these factors. Other examples are found throughout the book (see especially the opening chapter of each main section).

In Africa and Asia, resentments against the West occasioned by colonial exploitation have played a major role in shaping attitudes and foreign policies. Colonialism has also directly impacted the politics of former colonies. When the

European imperialist powers retrenched after World War II, little thought was given to whether the "nation-states" created by the colonizers would be viable. As a consequence they often were (and continue to be) a congeries of different ethno-linguistic groups, frequently lacking natural resources or arable land and having few or no common folkways, religious traditions, or other shared experiences to hold the people together. Given the poverty and population problems of these nations, it is not at all surprising that authoritarian regimes have sprung up throughout much of the Third World. These regimes can be seen as a response to pressing needs for internal order, social mobilization, and external security. Moreover, the rejection of Western-style parliamentary democracy may be a reaction to European imperialism; if we understand the indignity associated with colonial status (and as former colonies we should), we can easily see why many developing nations have not rushed to emulate Western institutions.

In the other example, Russia has been invaded repeatedly throughout its history. The invaders came from two directions—Mongols from the East, French (Napoleon) and Germans (twice in this century) from the West. The empire-building tendencies so evident in Russian history can be explained, in part, by this vulnerability. Because Russia has no natural barriers (mountain ranges, oceans, deserts) to invasion, Russian rulers have sought to insulate the country by grabbing adjacent lands as a buffer zone. The notion that the czars, at least since the time of Peter the Great, sought warm-water ports may also have some validity. The vast wilderness of Siberia, rich in natural resources but inhospitable to human habitation, has no doubt played a role in shaping the Russian psyche and Russian political traditions. Authoritarian patterns of rule probably evolved in response to the exigencies of a harsh climate, a far-flung territory dangerously exposed to attack from without, and a resulting obsession with security. Ironically, despite the heavy-handed authoritarianism that has always been the trademark of Russian rule, a streak of anarchism occasionally appears. The notion that Russians are innately unruly is, in fact, deeply embedded in the political culture. Having internalized the norms of a society that stresses security above all else, Russians not surprisingly tend to equate good government with order and discipline.

Problems and Prospects   *What are the human consequences of different political traditions, processes, and systems?*

Aristotle argued that the proper aim of politics is not simply to sustain life but to seek the good life. Philosophers since Aristotle who have contemplated this concept have differed greatly as to its meaning. What exactly is the "good life"?

For Thomas Hobbes, an English political philosopher writing in the seventeenth century, the good life was inconceivable apart from security and order. Anarchy, for Hobbes, was the great enemy of civilization. He watched in horror as the Puritan Revolution, during which Charles I was beheaded, shattered the established order and threatened to sweep away centuries-old customs, values, and institutions. *Leviathan*, his famous treatise on politics published in 1651, remains one of the classic defenses of authoritarian government. In the state of nature, Hobbes wrote, "Life would be solitary, poor, nasty, brutish and short." This unruly nature could be kept in check only by an omnipotent state that could "overawe" the great unwashed.[7]

For followers of Jean-Jacques Rousseau, the good life can be equated with the natural life. Rousseau believed that human beings are good and decent at birth and subsequently learn (through the "socialization" process) to be power hungry and money grubbing. Hence, Rousseau decried the institution of private property and imagined a "state of nature" in which people lived together harmoniously, were group oriented rather than greedy and egocentric, and respected nature rather than looking on nature as something to be exploited for personal, short-term gain.[8]

For disciples of Marx, the good life is a function of equality (human misery is a function of exploitation arising from capitalism). Marx agreed with Rousseau about the evils of private property. He went far beyond Rousseau with his theory of "dialectical materialism." According to Marx, slavery gave way to feudalism, which gave way to capitalism. Capitalism, Marx believed, is destined to give way in turn to socialism and eventually communism. The engine of change is "class struggle." For example, in France the middle-class "bourgeoisie," acting in its own class interests, overthrew the feudal aristocracy in the eighteenth century. Eventually the working class (or "proletariat") created by the capitalist-led Industrial Revolution will overthrow its capitalist oppressors and establish an egalitarian—and therefore just—society. Then everyone will enjoy the good life.

For Thomas Jefferson and the other founders of the United States of America, the good life is all about the pursuit of happiness, which, they fervently believed, necessitates liberty. Jefferson was heavily indebted to John Locke, the seventeenth-century English philosopher for whom liberty was the paramount political value. Locke, in turn, was a product of *his* age: The Puritan Revolution—which as we have seen also profoundly influenced Hobbes—occurred when Locke was an impressionable youth.

For Jeremy Bentham, the famous nineteenth-century English "utilitarian" philosopher, happiness—defined as the greatest good for the greatest number—was the true test of the goodness of a political system. (Utilitarianism holds that the value of anything is determined solely by its power to bring pleasure or happiness.) Bentham was not indifferent to liberty, but he judged all things political in relation to his utilitarian standard. Seen in this light, liberty is instrumental, a means to an end (happiness), rather than an end in itself.

Our study of comparative politics will take account of both the tangible and intangible "goods" implicit in the notion of the good life. Liberty is small consolation for people who are starving and destitute. By the same token, people who have adequate food and shelter may be miserable if they lack freedom of speech and religion.

The difficulty in making comparisons is not one of knowing where people are well off and where they are oppressed or wanting. Rather it is connecting their condition with a particular political order. To what extent is poverty in a given context a function of environment and to what extent is it a function of politics? Is a trade-off between political freedom and economic well-being a good bargain in some cases (for example, where great hardship has historically been the lot of the majority)? Does chronic instability require authoritarian (or repressive) remedies? Where freedoms are denied or curtailed, are popular sacrifices compensated by a steadily increasing standard of living? By greater security? By some other public good? Is social and cultural diversity compatible with democracy in a given context?

These questions defy simple answers. But as Socrates demonstrated long ago, it is worthwhile to grapple with puzzling questions even if the answers remain beyond our reach.

Politics in Regional Perspective

Domestic political patterns and political development often reflect transnational or regional traits and circumstances. The world can be divided into many relatively small regions or into a few large ones. For example, Latin America can be treated either as a single superregion or as two regions (Central America and South America). In turn, South America can be divided into three regions: Brazil, the Andean countries (Venezuela, Colombia, Ecuador, Peru, Bolivia, and Chile), and the Southern Cone (Chile and Argentina plus Uruguay and Paraguay). Similarly, Asia can be subdivided into South Asia, Southeast Asia, East Asia, and North or Northeast Asia. Unless *region* is defined very broadly (such as ''Asia,'' ''Europe,'' ''Latin America''), some states will be major players in more than one regional system (China, Japan, and the Soviet Union in Asia; the Soviet Union and Germany in Europe; and Brazil in Latin America are obvious examples).

Nor is there general agreement about how or where to draw boundaries for regions. Should Mexico be included in Central America? Should Japan be included in Southeast Asia? Depending on who is defining the region, Japan is considered part of the ''Pacific Rim,'' the ''Western Pacific,'' ''East Asia,'' and ''Northeast Asia.''

Drawing regional boundaries, then, is always difficult, and there is no ''right'' way to do it. This book takes the approach of dividing the world into six superregions:

- ☐ Western Europe (and the North Atlantic) (Part II)
- ☐ The Soviet Union and Eastern Europe (Part III)
- ☐ The Middle East (including North Africa and the Persian Gulf) (Part IV)
- ☐ Asia (China, South Asia, Southeast Asia, and Northeast Asia) (Part V)
- ☐ Sub-Saharan Africa (East Africa, West Africa, and southern Africa) (Part VI)
- ☐ Latin America (Mexico, Central America, and South America—Brazil, the Andean countries, and the Southern Cone) (Part VII)

These regions do not correspond precisely to continents, although continental boundaries provide a partial basis for the sixfold division. Geographic location and propinquity are important factors, but so are other commonalities, including history, culture, language, religion, population characteristics, climate, natural resources, economic structure, and quality of life.

Regions can also be viewed as subsystems, or subordinate systems, in which regional powers regularly interact. A subordinate system consists of "two or more proximate and interacting states which have some common ethnic, linguistic, cultural, social, and historic bonds, and whose sense of identity is sometimes increased by the actions and attitudes of states external to the system."[9] Another characteristic is that regional issues are often at the root of local conflicts (like Palestine in the Middle East) and of attempts at collaboration (such as the Common Market in Western Europe).

One scholar has argued that subordinate systems must meet the following conditions:

1. Their scope must be delimited, with a primary stress on a geographic region.
2. There must be at least three actors (or states).
3. Taken together, the members of the subsystem must be objectively recognized as constituting a distinctive community, region, or segment of the global system.
4. The members themselves are conscious of their regional identity.
5. The principal units of power (nation-states) are relatively inferior to the dominant units in the global system.
6. Changes in the global system have greater effect on the subordinate system than vice versa.[10]

This checklist emphasizes the importance of geography in comparative politics.

Much of the literature on political development assumes that national leaders can intentionally build institutions and modernize society to achieve some desirable future vision rather than passively submit to economic and political forces. In keeping with this, in the era of decolonization after World War II, various national governments and international organizations instituted programs to assist developing areas in the belief that durable, modern political institutions require economic development and social progress. Often, the hidden agenda was to establish democratic governments that would serve as bulwarks against revolution and would align themselves with the West. The Cold War that followed World War II thus formed the background for much economic and military assistance to the "Third World."

By the 1960s there was growing awareness that the pace of political development varied greatly from one region or country to the next. The forces of modernization were felt everywhere, but in many areas natural and cultural conditions posed formidable obstacles to socioeconomic change—as well as to political stability.

Theories of political development were initially influenced by such nineteenth-century thinkers as Max Weber, Karl Marx, and Emile Durkheim. The theories also borrowed from such fields as psychology and anthropology to explain processes like acculturation and social change. The notion of a world economically divided between north and south (rich and poor) as well as between east and west (communist and capitalist) was a common thread. In the 1970s, much of the literature on political development was based on *dependency theory*, which holds that progress in Third World countries is blocked by international capitalism (or "economic imperialism"). In this view, regimes and political elites in developing countries are manipulated by multinational corporations more interested in profits than in the welfare of the host nations. These corporations require indigenous regimes that can guarantee stability, even if that means supporting authoritarian rulers and working to undermine democratic forces. Chile under Allende in the early 1970s was often cited as the example par excellence.

In the 1980s, dependency theory lost many adherents. One reason is the extraordinary economic performance of several Asian nations that *did* rely on foreign investment and developed close ties to Western multinational concerns. Another is the replacement of military regimes by popularly elected civilian governments throughout Latin America. The bankruptcy of centrally planned economies and the sudden collapse of Soviet hegemony in Eastern Europe in 1989 also has discredited Marxist-Leninist theories of political development and has given market-oriented approaches new respectability throughout much of the Third World. Perhaps even more important is the crushing debt burden—over $1 trillion—that threatens many developing states, especially in sub-Saharan Africa and Latin America, and has forced them to accept economic policies set down by the International Monetary Fund (and, more generally, by the West).

Political Patterns and Trends: A Survey

In Western Europe and North America, liberal democracy is solidly established. In the Middle East, authoritarian regimes—mostly monarchies or personal dictatorships—prevail. Until recently, military juntas could be found throughout Latin America, and the coup d'état was the normal method of changing the guard. In the past decade democracy has flowered throughout South America—an extraordinary and unprecedented trend largely confined to the Western hemisphere.

In Eastern Europe and the Soviet Union, a long history of autocratic rule culminated in the highly centralized structures still in place there. In the 1930s the Soviet economy became centrally planned, agriculture was collectivized (that is, land and equipment are controlled by the state and production quotas are assigned by central planners), and development priority was given to heavy industry, particularly that related to defense. After World War II Stalin imposed this model on the East European "satellite states" (East Germany, Poland, Czechoslovakia, Hungary, Rumania, and Bulgaria) as well. In the late 1980s, a trend toward economic liberalization swept across the region. Surprisingly, the Soviet Union under Mikhail Gorbachev took the lead. Events soon outpaced the Kremlin, and in 1989 all the communist regimes of Eastern Europe (except for those in Albania and Yugoslavia) crumbled.

The long Soviet domination of Eastern Europe gave rise to a degree of uniformity unmatched in any other region. Until recently, Czechoslovakia alone in Eastern Europe had experienced democracy. All of the other Slavic nations have, like Russia, a tradition of authoritarian rule.

Trends and patterns are less clear-cut in Asia and Africa. Historically, a brand of extreme authoritarianism known as "oriental despotism" was the rule in China, India, Cambodia, Vietnam, and Japan. Authoritarian rule and an emphasis on patron–client relations (reciprocal obligations in which individuals of subordinate social status pay deference to a "superior" who assumes some responsibility for their welfare) continue to be common throughout Asia, with some notable exceptions. (We discuss these exceptions in Part V.)

Africa is somewhat ambiguous as a regional entity because it can be divided into two distinct parts. North Africa is largely Arab and Moslem; for this reason we include Morocco, Algeria, Tunisia, Libya, and the Sudan, as well as Egypt, in the Middle East. The sub-Saharan part of the African continent—known also as "Black Africa"—has a history of tribalism and ethnic conflict. When colonizing European powers dismantled their empires after World War II, they created new states into which they often incorporated ethnic groups hostile to one another. Chronic instability has been one legacy, and authoritarian rule has been another. There are frequent coups. Perhaps the most striking pattern has been the predominance, in one guise or another, of personal rule.[11]

One thing is clear: Democracy has fared even worse in Black Africa than in Asia. Indeed, a trivia question that would stump all but experts on African politics is the following: Name one country in sub-Saharan Africa in which a chief executive has handed over the reigns of government to an opposition leader through free elections. (Answer: Mauritania.)

Regional Influences on Politics

As was suggested earlier, many region-linked factors have a bearing on governmental structures and policies. For the sake of brevity we will group these factors into (a) history and culture and (b) resources and demographic characteristics. Then we will briefly consider how regions are affected by the interrelated processes of modernization and development. Not surprisingly, levels of development tend to vary by region (Asia being a notable exception).

History and Culture Professor Jurg Steiner pointed to the importance of region-linked factors when he wrote, "Europe is not only a geographical region, but a cultural concept." European nations, he added, "are bound together by a common culture based on centuries of close interaction."[12] This "common culture" is rooted in part in a common religious heritage. Before the twentieth century historians frequently referred to Europe as "Christendom"—a term that seemed appropriate because Christianity was officially enshrined (and popularly embraced) throughout the Continent as the one true faith. Indeed, monarchs even ruled by "divine right" (meaning that the church was used to legitimize the state).

Language is also an important part of Europe's common cultural heritage. The Romance languages of Western Europe—French, Italian, Spanish, and Portuguese being the major ones—derive their name from their common Latin (Roman) origin. In time, French emerged as the diplomatic language of Europe: French was spoken at diplomatic conferences, treaties were written in French, and fluency in French was de rigueur for all who aspired to a diplomatic career. Indeed, following the "westernizing" innovations of Peter the Great, the official language of the Russian royal court was French, not Russian! Even today, the ability to speak French is a mark of culture and sophistication throughout Western Europe.

In addition to religion and language, the nations of Western Europe share many common historical experiences. The Renaissance and Reformation, the Enlightenment, and the Industrial Revolution all left a strong cultural imprint on European art, architecture, music, philosophy, and literature. These experiences had a cumulative effect, helping to produce certain common "European" political values and norms—a kind of moral consensus grounded in humanistic values. One way this consensus manifested itself was in attempts at conflict management through treaties, the "balance of power" mechanism, and international organizations such as the Concert of Europe and the congress system of the nineteenth century.[13]

What is true of Europe is also true, in varying degrees, of the other regions encompassed in this book. In the Middle East, Islam and Arabic language impart a cultural unity that sets the nations of the Arab world apart from other nations. Similarly, in Asia the imprint of Chinese on the languages of Japan, Korea, and Vietnam is unmistakable, while Buddhism and patron–client relations have powerfully influenced the historical development of most of the nations of the region. In Latin America, Spanish (except in Brazil, where Portuguese is spoken) and Roman Catholicism provide elements of a common "Latin" tradition. The Spanish conquest, and later the hemispheric dominance of the United States, have also aided in the accretion of a common regional political culture.

Finally, even Black Africa, with its rich cultural diversity, exhibits some common historical and sociopolitical patterns. These include animism (a belief in spirits and demons) and tribalism (a form of political and social organization based on membership in a tribe). In addition, the nations of Black Africa—like those of the Middle East and Asia—were European colonies until well into the twentieth century, and thus acquired common colonial characteristics (see Chapter 3).

Resources and Demographic Characteristics   Oddly enough, the most obvious explanations of social and political differences are often the least emphasized. Certainly climate distinguishes the nations of the northern latitudes from those of the southern latitudes in highly significant ways. Montesquieu, in his famous book *L'Esprit des Lois* (*The Spirit of the Laws*), decried "the vices of climate." Climate is detrimental when it causes indolence, as it does (or appears to do) in extremely hot regions. This is particularly true, he believed, in a country like India, where the predominant religion (Hinduism) encourages passivity. Whether or not one agrees with Montesquieu on this point, one cannot deny that climatic factors affect food production and sometimes cause droughts and floods that imperil human life.

In Montesquieu's day, agriculture was the economic foundation of society. It is not surprising, then, that for Montesquieu, the more the climate induces individuals to shun physical labor, "the more the religion and the laws of the country ought to incite him to it." Thus Montesquieu criticized a law of India because it gave lands to the princes and destroyed the spirit of property (or free enterprise) within the popular masses, thereby augmenting "the evil effects of the climate, that is, the natural idleness."

Montesquieu went so far as to posit a connection between climate and form of government, arguing that despotism was more natural in hot climates than in cold, and that liberty was more natural to inhabitants of temperate and cold areas. He pointed out that Asia, with its political tradition of oriental despotism, has no temperate zone, in contrast to Europe (or North America), which has an extensive one.[14]

Differences in the type of crops grown account not only for differences in cultivation patterns, dietary preferences, and nutritional standards but also, in some cases, for differences in the type and level of economic development. Some scholars have even argued that such elemental factors as climate, soil, and water resources may account for contrasting forms of social, economic, and political organization.

In China, for example, where rice has been the staple food for centuries, a system of permanent agriculture based on elaborate, man-made irrigation networks both necessitated a centralized bureaucracy and reinforced the autocratic tendencies of the imperial court, according to Karl Wittfogel.[15] This "hydraulic" theory of Chinese civilization places primary emphasis on economic geography: China's autocratic political tradition, Wittfogel argued, grew out of a need to organize and regiment society for the purpose of taming China's great rivers. These rivers, combined with a conducive climate and at least adequate soil, made continuous rice cultivation possible.

Differences in climate and resource availability may also partly account for the dramatic inequalities in wealth from one region to the next. One of the most important natural resources (one we often take for granted) is fertile land. Since the early 1970s there has been a steady deterioration in the global land/population ratio. According to Lester Brown, founder of the World-watch Institute, the period since World War II "breaks into two distinct periods— before and after the 1973 oil price increase." Why 1973? Because that was the year in which "the age of cheap energy" came to an end. Prior to 1973 world food output had been growing at a pace of 3 percent per year, enough to keep food production ahead of population growth. Since 1973, however, the annual growth in food output has dropped below 2 percent, barely matching population increases.[16]

Even so, Brown noted, the true dimensions of the problem cannot be entirely appreciated without a closer look at the "wide variations in individual geographic regions." Specifically,

In North America, production has steadily outstripped demand, generating ever-larger surpluses. In the Soviet Union, output has fallen behind demand over the past decade, making the country the largest grain importer in history. And in Africa, which has a population of 512 million and which has to feed 14 million additional people each year, food production per person has fallen steadily since 1970. Despite a tripling of grain imports since then, hunger has become chronic, an enduring part of the African landscape.[17]

The political and economic implications of this food/population squeeze differ enormously from one region to the next. Africa, Asia, and Latin America are all food-deficit regions with huge foreign debts (see Tables 1-1, 1-2, and 1-3). In contrast, North America is the principal food-surplus area and, along with Western Europe, the major source of foreign aid and investment for the developing nations. As a consequence, low farm prices and a depressed rural economy resulting from overproduction have been major political issues in the United States at the same time that chronic food shortages and periodic famines have plagued Africa and Asia (see Table 1-4).

The Middle East has largely escaped the fate of Africa, Asia, and to a lesser extent Latin America. The reason can be stated in a single word: oil. The same oil crisis that precipitated the worldwide decline in food production also brought an economic windfall to many oil-rich Middle East countries. As we shall see in Part IV, the uses to which this newfound wealth was (and was not) put have had a profound effect on the region and the world.

Table 1-1 Wheat, Rice, and Corn Production, Selected Countries (millions of metric tons)

	Wheat		Rice		Corn	
	1984	1986	1984	1986	1984	1986
World	516	536	470	476	453	481
United States	71	57	6	6	195	210
Argentina	13	9	0.5	0.4	10	12
Brazil	2	5	9	10	21	21
China	88	89	181	177	74	66
Egypt	2	2	2	2	3	4
France	33	27	.04	.06	10	10
Great Britain	15	14	—	—	—	—
India	45	47	88	90	8	8
Japan	0.7	0.9	15	15	—	—
Mexico	5	5	0.5	0.5	13	12
Soviet Union	69	92	3	3	14	13
West Germany	10	10	—	—	1	1

Source: Food and Agriculture Organization of the United Nations, *1986 FAO Production Yearbook*, Vol. 40.

Table 1-2 External Debt and Debt Service of Developing Countries (expressed as percent of exports)

	1985	*1988*	*1991*
External Debt	150.5%	141.9%	118.4%
(billions of U.S. dollars)	($998.4)	($1,216.4)	($1,313,3)
Africa	188.0%	242.5%	226.7%
Asia	102.9%	79.2%	64.1%
Europe	149.8%	146.2%	135.0%
Latin America	295.6%	292.1%	250.3%
Middle East	89.5%	120.8%	104.4%
Debt Service Payments	20.8%	19.0%	15.4%
(billions of U.S. dollars)	($137.8)	($162.8)	($171.0)
Africa	26.7%	25.2%	29.0%
Asia	14.7%	10.7%	8.0%
Europe	22.3%	23.1%	17.5%
Latin America	41.3%	44.9%	36.1%

Source: World Economic Outlook (Washington, D.C.: International Monetary Fund, May 1990), Table A45.

Table 1-3 Population (1989) and Gross National Product (1987), Selected Countries

	Population (millions)	*GNP (billions)*
United States	248	$4,527
Argentina	32	77
Brazil	151	291
China	1,112	478
Egypt	55	71
France	56	868
Great Britain	57	667
India	833	246
Japan	123	2,369
Kenya	24	8
Mexico	86	139
Nigeria	115	23
Saudi Arabia	16	85
South Africa	39	77
Soviet Union	289	2,460
Venezuela	19	38
West Germany	61	1,126

Table 1-4 Food Insecurity in Selected African Countries, 1986
(insufficient food for normal health and activity)

	Millions of People	Percent of Population
Ethiopia	14.7	34
Nigeria	13.7	13
Zaire	12.0	38
Kenya	6.2	29
Uganda	6.1	40
Mozambique	5.9	42
Algeria	4.1	18
Sudan	3.4	15
Zambia	2.7	39
Chad	2.4	47
Somalia	2.3	42

Source: World Bank, *World Development Report 1988.*

Unfortunately, the regions that have the lowest per capita income levels tend to have the highest population growth rates (see Table 1-5). In Asia, two countries, China and India, account for roughly two-fifths of global population—approaching the 2-billion mark in the mid-1980s. Six of the ten most populous countries are in Asia, by far the most densely populated region with more than 3 billion people. Unlike many developing nations, however, China and India have made at least limited progress in bringing down population growth rates.

In Africa, with a population of about 661 million, the average annual population growth rate is 2.9 percent, the highest of any region in the world. At that pace, Africa's population will double in just twenty-four years. Kenya currently has the highest fertility rate in the world—eight children per mother—and a 4-percent net population increase per year.[18] Nigeria, Tanzania, and Uganda also have potentially disastrous birth rates (in excess of 3 percent per year).

These figures suggest that in many African countries development will have to take a back seat to mere survival—that African governments will find themselves in a defensive rather than an offensive posture in the years to come. In these lands a vicious cycle is at work, one that is extremely difficult to break. Poverty and malnutrition are pressing problems due to the absence of economic development and little or no new job creation. But the dynamics of rapid population expansion are such that an increasing percentage of society's members are young. As Table 1-5 indicates, 45 percent of Africa's population was under age 15 in 1987. In a country with high unemployment, the youth are inevitably the hardest hit. They are also the most rebellious. Lacking opportunities and having no hope for the future, they are like dry kindling waiting to be ignited. The potential for political instability in these circumstances is self-evident.

Table 1-5 Selected Population Data by Region

	Africa	Asia	Europe	Latin America	North America	Soviet Union
Population 1990 (millions)	661	3,128	499	450	277	291
Projected to 2000	890	3,712	511	540	296	312
Crude birth rate*	44	28	13	28	15	18
Crude death rate*	14	9	11	7	9	11
Annual growth rate	2.9%	1.9%	0.3%	2.1%	0.9%	0.9%
Life expectancy	53	62	75	67	76	69
Under age 15	45%	34%	21%	38%	22%	26%
Over age 65	3%	5%	13%	4%	12%	9%
Living in cities	39%	32%	73%	67%	74%	65%

*Crude rates = number during one year per 1,000 persons.

Sources: U.S. Bureau of the Census, *World Population Profile, 1989;* and Population Reference Bureau, Inc.

Latin America faces similar problems. The population of Costa Rica, El Salvador, Guatemala, Honduras, and Nicaragua doubled (to 27 million) in twenty-five years, according to the Latin American Demographic Center (a branch of the United Nations). The population is projected to reach 40 million by the turn of the century. In fact, the population growth rate in Central America is "one of the highest in the world," according to the executive director of a family planning agency in Guatemala. "Demographic factors," he asserted, "are tremendously important, and they will continue to play a major role not only in our social, economic and political situation, but also in the generation of violence."[19] Indeed, it seems likely that the flames of insurgency that engulfed Central America in the 1980s were fanned, in part, by the poverty and despair that accompanied this rapid population growth.

By contrast, the economic and social problems of Europe and North America are largely unrelated to overpopulation or underdevelopment. On the contrary, they are often part of a "postindustrial" syndrome characterized by the shift from a manufacturing to a service-based economy; an emphasis on capital-intensive, high-technology production methods; a tendency toward "stagflation" (economic recession combined with inflation); and a growth in trade relations and economic interdependence. Consumerism and commercialism are two other well-known attributes of postindustrialization. In addition, social and environmental problems such as a high crime rate, chronic traffic congestion, air pollution, and a dramatic rise in stress-related health problems generally accompany the urbanization process.

Although concepts like development and modernization are usually associated with the developing nations of Africa, Asia, and Latin America, they have universal validity. Nation-states are the building blocks of the modern international order. Levels of economic and political development vary from one nation or region to the next, but problems such as national integration (or disintegration) are not confined to any one nation or region.

Any broad overview of regional differences must by definition neglect the more subtle physical and cultural characteristics that distinguish one region from another. Such an overview does, however, show that major differences exist, and it suggests that a regional approach to comparative politics is likely to yield valuable insights into why governments differ and why certain *patterns* of politics are either unique to a particular region or clearly more prevalent in one region than another. The differences painted with broad brush strokes here are examined in greater depth and detail in subsequent chapters.

CONCLUSION

Although the boundaries of regions are difficult to define and can be drawn in various ways, a regional approach to comparative politics has advantages over other approaches. One such advantage is that it captures historical, cultural, and socioeconomic features common to all or most of the states within a given geographic area. Choosing key countries as case studies within each major region—Western Europe, the Soviet Union and Eastern Europe, the Middle East, Asia, sub-Saharan Africa, and Latin America—makes general patterns come alive and provides concrete examples of politics in action. We begin our tour in Europe.

STUDY QUESTIONS

1. What are the major regions of the world? What is a subordinate system? Do all of these "superregions" encompass smaller regional subsystems?
2. What are the most prominent patterns and trends in various regions of the world?
3. How do history and culture influence political traditions and practices from region to region?
4. To what degree do variables such as climate, resources, food, and population play a role in shaping political institutions?

SUGGESTED READINGS

Amate, C.O.C. *Inside the OAU: Pan-Africanism in Practice*. New York: St. Martin's, 1986.
Boyd, Gavin. *Regionalism and Global Security*. Boston: Heath, 1984.

Boyd, Gavin, and Feld, Werner J., eds. *Comparative Regional Systems.* New York: Pergammon, 1980.

Brecher, Michael. "The Subordinate System of South Asia," *Asian Survey*, vol. XV, no. 2 (January 1963).

Burgess, Michael. *Federalism and European Union: Political Ideas, Influences, and Strategies in the European Community, 1972–1987.* London: Routledge, 1989.

Cantori, Louis T., and Spiegel, Stephen L. *The International Politics of Regions: A Comparative Approach.* Englewood Cliffs, N.J.: Prentice-Hall, 1970.

Croan, Melvin. "Lands In-Between: The Politics of Cultural Identity in Contemporary Eastern Europe," *Eastern European Politics and Societies*, vol. 3, no. 1, (Spring 1989).

El-Ayouty, Yassin, and Zartman, William I. *The OAU After Twenty Years.* New York: Praeger, 1984.

Emmerson, Donald. "ASEAN as an International Regime," *Journal of International Affairs*, vol. 41, no. 1 (Summer/Fall 1987).

Haas, Michael. *The Asian Way to Peace: A Story of Regional Cooperation.* New York: Praeger, 1989.

Mazzeo, Domenico, ed. *African Regional Organizations.* Cambridge, Mass.: Cambridge University, 1984.

NOTES

1 Raphael Sealey, *A History of the Greek City States ca. 700–338 B.C.* (Berkeley: University of California, 1976), p. 68.
2 Cyril E. Robinson, *A History of Greece.* (New York: Crowell, 1929), p. 51.
3 Sealey, op. cit., p. 68.
4 Mattei Dogan and Dominique Pelassy, *How to Compare Nations: Strategies in Comparative Politics.* (Chatham, N.J.: Chatham House, 1984), p. 5.
5 Ibid.
6 *The Politics of Aristotle*, Ernest Baker, ed. and trans. (New York: Oxford University, 1958); see especially the introduction, pp. xxviii–xxix.
7 Thomas Hobbes, *The Leviathan* (London: Everyman's, 1965).
8 Jean-Jacques Rousseau, *First and Second Discourses*, Roger and Judith Masters, trans., Roger Masters, ed. (New York: St. Martin's, 1964).
9 Louis T. Cantori and Stephen L. Spiegel, *The International Politics of Regions: A Comparative Approach* (Englewood Cliffs, N.J.: Prentice-Hall, 1970), p. 6.
10 Michael Brecher, "The Subordinate System of Southern Asia," *Asian Survey*, vol. XV, no. 2, January 1963, p. 220.
11 See, for example, Robert Jackson and Carl Rosberg, *Personal Rule in Black Africa: Princes, Autocrats, Prophets, Tyrants* (Berkeley: University of California, 1982), p. 235.
12 Jurg Steiner, *European Democracies* (New York: Longmans, 1986), p. 1
13 See, for example, Hans Morganthau and Ken Thompson, *Politics Among Nations: The Struggle for Power and Peace* (New York: Knopf, 1985), pp. 233–240.
14 See, for example, Henry J. Merry, *Montesquieu's System of Natural Government* (West Lafayette, Ind.: Purdue University).
15 Karl Wittfogel, *Oriental Despotism: A Comparative Study of Total Power* (New Haven, Conn.: Yale University, 1957).

[16] Lester R. Brown, ''Putting Food on the World's Table,'' in *Global Issues 87/88* (Guildford, Conn.: Dushkin, 1987), p. 86. Reprinted from *State of the World 1984, Worldwatch Institute Report on Progress Toward a Sustainable Society* (New York: Norton, 1984), Chap. 10.

[17] Ibid.

[18] See Brian W. Walker, *USA Today*, July 1985, pp. 38–41.

[19] Larry Rohter, ''Central American Plight Is People in Abundance,'' *New York Times*, Sept. 6, 1987, p. 1.

Chapter 2
Comparing Political Systems

Political systems can be classified in a variety of ways. The most common classifications stress concentration (diffusion) of power or the level of economic and political development. Those based on power often make a threefold distinction among democratic, authoritarian, and totalitarian systems. For a long time those based on development featured just two types of nations—"developed" and "developing"; more recent development schemes identify a few nations (for example, South Korea, Taiwan, Hong Kong, Singapore) as new industrial countries (NICs). Still others subdivide the less developed countries (LDCs) into the poor nations and the poorest of the poor.

In this chapter we will explore the democratic-authoritarian-totalitarian scheme. Because constitutional democracies feature market or mixed economies and totalitarian states feature command economies, this type of economic classification will also receive some attention. The development paradigm will be examined in Chapter 3.

A common obstacle to clear thinking in any field of study is the confusion of models of reality with reality itself. This observation is especially pertinent to political science, partly because the stuff of politics is largely intangible. Thus a note of caution is in order at the outset. The political systems (or models) sketched in this chapter are *theoretical* constructs—they do not exist in "pure" form anywhere. Nonetheless it is useful to discuss governments in the abstract before moving on to description and analysis of concrete forms. Hence this chapter will rely more heavily on deductive reasoning than will subsequent chapters (which will be heavily inductive).

Two modern forms of government, constitutional democracy and totalitarian dictatorship, have left an indelible mark on world politics in the past half century. What are the historic forerunners of these two models? Is traditional authoritarian rule likely to supplant Stalinism in the Soviet Union and Eastern Europe, or will the forces of liberalism that burst onto the scene there in 1989 transform these societies into authentically pluralistic systems? Is democracy really on the march worldwide? Can totalitarianism now be relegated to the dustbin of history? Is military rule or some other form of authoritarian dictatorship inevitable in developing nations that have never experienced democracy? In general, are conditions in different regions of the world conducive to different types of regimes?

We take a closer look at these questions—and others that they raise—in the pages that follow.

Political Models: Yesterday and Today

For thousands of years political thinkers have tried to design the perfect government—or to dissect imperfect ones—by conceptualizing the relationships between rulers and ruled. Aristotle was perhaps the most gifted model builder of all time. His classic work, *The Politics*, was the first comparative study of political systems. Aristotle identified six possible forms of rule which, as we shall see, can be reduced to three practical forms: rule by one, rule by a few, and rule by the many. For Aristotle, however, the most important question was not *who* rules, but *in whose interest*: Rule by one can be the basis for the best or the worst regime, depending on whether the ruler is enlightened or tyrannical.

Although he abhorred tyranny, Aristotle was no great enthusiast of democracy, because he feared it would degenerate into mob rule. Such rule, Aristotle reasoned, would celebrate mediocrity and scorn excellence. Justice—a political condition in which society's members are rewarded in proportion to their individual merit—was regarded as incompatible with popular rule.

To his great credit, Aristotle did not get hung up on his own models. He recognized that reality is much more complex than any theoretical construct, that the range of possibilities is broader than any simplistic typology can encompass, and that, if avoiding the worst regime is difficult, creating the best is impossible.

Aristotle argued that a constitutional system combining elements of monarchy, oligarchy, and democracy is the best form of government possible under most circumstances. Such a "mixed" regime, he believed, would give the middle class a key role in government—that of mediating between the rich (whom they admire without resenting) and the poor (whom they pity without either fearing or embracing.) This type of regime would offer the best means of achieving equilibrium between the class interests of the two extremes, especially where the middle class was large. The middle class, he reasoned, was not so affluent as to lack all sympathy for the poor, nor so destitute as to revolt or seek to dispossess the rich—moderate wealth would produce moderate political opinions. (By the same token, extreme poverty would produce political extremism.) In this manner Aristotle made a logical connection between social class structure and political stability.

Aristotle's model of a mixed regime resembles many contemporary governments in which power and wealth are widely distributed (and, in the modern welfare state, redistributed). A strong executive somewhat similar in function to a monarch is often present even in the most democratic of these regimes. The strong presidencies built into the U.S. and French constitutional systems are two cases in point.

The secret of success of a mixed form of government lies in its realism. What Aristotle sketched was a kind of internal balance of power among competing interests. Although he did not elaborate a Madisonian theory of checks and balances like that found in the *Federalist Papers*, he provided the conceptual underpinnings for such a theory. Indeed, Aristotle drew up the blueprints for constitutional democracy as it is widely practiced today—a form of government in which power and wealth are broadly (albeit unequally) dispersed and the right to rule derives from set procedures, including, above all, periodic popular elections.

The other two common forms of government Aristotle identified, tyranny (rule by one) and oligarchy (rule by a few), are variations on the same theme: concentration of power and wealth. Today such regimes are normally described as authoritarian. They may be headed by a military or civilian strongman, a king, a military junta, or a party-based directorate (for example, the Soviet politburo).

Aristotle's models are quite germane to the modern world, in large part because of their elasticity. They can be stretched into an almost infinite variety of forms. In fact, before the twentieth century there was no political system that did not fit into one or the other model. The rise of totalitarian Soviet Russia and Nazi Germany, however, forced political thinkers to reevaluate the adequacy of the authoritarian model. Today it would appear that totalitarianism has receded and that a traditional form of paternalistic or authoritarian rule is the principal alternative to democracy.

Authoritarian Regimes

Authoritarian rule has been around as long as government itself. It is the most prevalent form of government in Africa, the Middle East, and Asia. Until the 1980s it was also the norm in Latin America and was present in Europe.

There are many forms of authoritarian government, but most share certain characteristics. First, there is usually an elite class closely linked to the ruler or rulers. In sharp contrast to totalitarian governments, no radical transformation, restructuring, or penetration of society is attempted, and the regime is often quite content to let the free market operate unmolested. It may even be closely allied with domestic business and banking interests. The ruling elite aims, above all, to maintain the status quo. In doing so it assumes a defensive posture: tolerate no challenges from opposition parties or autonomous interest groups, but otherwise let sleeping dogs lie. To this end, popular participation is often deliberately kept to a minimum (in contrast to Marxist-Leninist regimes that mobilize or manipulate the masses for particular economic and political ends). For this reason, too, political and sometimes civil liberties are curbed or denied. Finally, the military often has a key governing role, even where it does not rule directly.

Authoritarian systems can be classified in various ways, none of which can accommodate all relevant cases with equal precision. With this caveat we will identify the most common types of contemporary authoritarianism as follows:

1. Personal dictatorships (tyrannies)
2. Military oligarchies ("juntas")
3. Dynastic regimes (monarchies)

Personal Dictatorships

Personal dictatorships have long dominated the pages of history. Indeed, they were prevalent in Aristotle's day (he called them "tyrannies"—rule by a tyrant). The twentieth century has certainly been no exception. Totalitarian rulers like Hitler and Stalin appear in retrospect to have read and digested at least one passage from Aristotle. In *The Politics*, he noted that tyrants were famous (or infamous) for "the 'lopping off' of outstanding men, and men of spirit."[1] Some other methods of personal rule, according to Aristotle, included the following:

> . . . the forbidding of common meals, clubs, and anything of a like character—or, in other words, a defensive attitude against everything likely to produce the two qualities of mutual confidence and a high spirit . . . the adoption of every means for making every subject as much of a stranger as is possible to every other . . . requir[ing] every resident to be constantly appearing in public . . . endeavouring to get information about every man's sayings and doings. This entails a secret police. . . . (Men are not so likely to speak their minds if they go in fear of a secret police; and if they do speak out, they are less likely to go undetected.)[2]

In summary, according to Aristotle tyrants have three basic aims:

1. To break the spirit of their subjects
2. To breed mutual mistrust ("Tyranny is never overthrown until men can begin to trust one another. . . .")
3. To make their subjects incapable of action ("Nobody attempts the impossible.")

Not all personal dictators are equally tyrannical. Fortunately, few modern tyrants can hold a candle to Hitler or Stalin when it comes to brutality and an insatiable appetite for power.[3] Nonetheless, personal dictatorships are often associated with extreme political repression and arbitrary rule.

Personal dictators come in many different guises. They usually gain power through force or fraud, often by means of a coup d'état or a rigged election. They may start out as military officers, charismatic politicians, or even religious gurus. One of the first military officers to seize power and then establish a highly personalistic dictatorship was Egypt's Nasser. Other military officers who have become personal dictators include Muammar al-Qaddafi (Libya), Samuel Doe (Liberia), Jerry Rawlings (Ghana), Hafez al-Assad (Syria), Mohammad Zia ul-Haq (Pakistan), Mohammad Ershad (Bangladesh), Manuel Noriega (Panama), and Alfredo Stroessner (Paraguay). Uganda under Idi Amin and the Central African Republic under Jean-Bedel Bokassa are two recent cases of notoriously cruel and arbitrary tyranny at the hands of personal dictators who began as military officers. (Both were ousted in 1979.) General Trujillo of the Dominican Republic ruled as a brutal tyrant for thirty years until his assassination in 1961. General Somoza of Nicaragua, overthrown by the Sandinistas in 1979, is yet another example of a modern-day tyrant.

In recent times there have also been some notorious civilian tyrants. They are often demagogues or visionaries with a gift of eloquence and a lust for power.

Several of the charismatic Third World figures who led their nations to independence three or four decades ago were able to translate their popularity into a formula for personal rule, for example, Sukarno in Indonesia (1949–1965), Nkrumah in Ghana (1957–1966), and Sekou Toure in Guinea (1958–1984). Most are now gone. Sukarno and Nkrumah were ousted by military coups in the mid-1960s. Habib Bourguiba, who became president-for-life following the independence of Tunisia in 1956, remained in power for more than three decades, until he was finally overcome in a bloodless coup in 1987. Among living heads of state, only King Hussein of Jordan had ruled longer.

Several other civilian dictators have fallen in the past decade. The Shah of Iran was ousted in 1979; seven years later Ferdinand Marcos in the Philippines and the notorious Jean-Claude ("Baby Doc") Duvalier in Haiti met a similar fate.

Whether tyrants have military or civilian backgrounds, they must rely on a military ("praetorian") guard to keep them in power. As two observers of this phenomenon in Africa have noted, "The key to tyranny is the relations between the tyrant and his mercenaries without whom tyranny is impossible."[4] Personal dictatorships in which the military plays a key role should not, however, be confused with military rule, which is a distinct type of authoritarian system.

Military Juntas

Only where military rule has been institutionalized can a military regime be said to exist. In this type of authoritarian government there is almost always a person who is "first among equals," because someone must perform the ceremonial and symbolic functions of a chief executive. But one of the ways a typical military regime differs from a tyranny, even one dominated by a military strongman, is that rule is collegial, rather than personal.

Personalistic rule cannot be institutionalized. The reason is simple: A ruler cannot succeed himself—even the most absolute dictator is mortal. Furthermore, choosing an *heir apparent* is risky because the anointed one may become an impatient rival. Thus, a system dominated by a military strongman would fit the description of a tyranny better than that of a military regime.

Where the military rules *as an institution* there is seldom a charismatic or popular leader. The powers of the chief executive are shared by several high-ranking military officers who form a *junta*, or ruling oligarchy. Military juntas have a long history, particularly in Latin America where military intervention in domestic politics is a widespread tradition.

Political systems in which the army frequently intervenes and has the potential and disposition to dominate are often called "praetorian" systems.[5] Military regimes typically come to power in a coup d'état, which often are bloodless. In some parts of the world they occur with astonishing frequency. One scholar counted eighty-eight military coups in fifty-two countries between 1958 and 1969.[6] According to Eric Nordlinger, the military has intervened in every Latin American country except Mexico and Costa Rica in the last half century.[7] Nordlinger noted further:

Between 1945 and 1976, soldiers carried out successful coups in half of the eighteen Asian states. By 1976 the soldiers had made at least one successful or unsuccessful attempt to seize power in two-thirds of the Middle Eastern and North African states. They established military regimes in Egypt, Syria, Iraq, the Sudan, Libya, and Algeria. . . . By 1976 coups had occurred in more than half of the African countries, and in that year the military occupied the seat of government in half of them.[8]

The study of military regimes, Nordlinger concluded, "is the study of one of the most common, and thus characteristic, aspects of non-Western politics." One decade later there was still little reason to challenge this statement, at least not in relation to Africa and Asia.

In Latin America, however, the picture has changed dramatically in recent years. Until the 1980s, Latin America was the most coup-prone region in the world. Military juntas were the rule, representative democracies the exception. Only in Mexico, Costa Rica, Venezuela, and Colombia were democratic institutions well entrenched. One by one South America's military rulers have relinquished power to popularly elected civilian governments, beginning with Ecuador in 1979, followed by Peru (1980), Bolivia (1982), Argentina (1983), and Uruguay and Brazil (1985). Despite regional tensions arising from civil wars in El Salvador and Nicaragua, several Central American states that were previously under military sway (including El Salvador, Guatemala, and Honduras) also moved toward civilian, though highly fragile, government in the 1980s.

As a form of authoritarian rule, juntas appeared to be on the decline as the 1980s drew to a close. The same could not be said of dynastic regimes, which continued to demonstrate surprising resilience in one region (the Middle East) despite their increasingly anachronistic character.

Dynastic Regimes

Dynastic rule, or *monarchy*, was the most common form of authoritarianism (which, as already noted, has always been the most common form of government) nearly everywhere in the world until the present century. Monarchs have gone by different names in different places—kings, emperors, caliphs, sultans, emirs, moguls, and czars, among others. Whatever their title, monarchs exercise rule as a birthright—they inherit absolute power. In Europe and elsewhere, kings and emperors often reinforced this dynastic claim by asserting a "divine right" to rule (in other words, God had ordained them as temporal ruler). Only in parts of the Middle East has this form of authoritarianism continued to thrive. The Monarchs remaining in Europe may reign but they do not rule. Iran was under dynastic rule until 1979, when Shah Reza Pahlavi was overthrown by Islamic zealots and succeeded by their spiritual leader, the Ayatolla Ruholla Khomeini.

Monarchs continue to rule as well as reign in Jordan (King Hussein), Saudi Arabia (King Fahd), and Morocco (King Hassan II). In addition, the oil-rich "ministates" such as Bahrain, Oman, Qatar, and the United Arab Emirates are governed by autocratic rulers (sultans, emirs).

Beyond the Middle East, surviving monarchies are few and far between. Only in such obscure places as Swaziland, Nepal, Brunei, Bhutan, and Tonga can they still be found.

Is monarchy a vanishing species of authoritarianism? Certainly this particular type of dynastic rule has undergone a precipitous decline since the nineteenth century. In addition to Iran, countries in which monarchies have fallen or been displaced in recent decades include Afghanistan (1973), Burundi (1966), Cambodia (1955), Egypt (1952), Ethiopia (1974), Iraq (1958), Libya (1969), and Tunisia (1957). Unlike military regimes, which come and go, monarchs, once deposed, are seldom if ever restored to power.

Constitutional Democracy: Face of the Future?

If we look at broad historical trends over the past 100 years, we can reach a striking conclusion: The fading of monarchy has been accompanied by the coming of age of democracy. Whereas there were many monarchs and few republics in the nineteenth century, today the situation is reversed. As noted earlier, democracies flourish in Western Europe and have recently flowered in Latin America as well.

In the contemporary world there are two basic forms of democracy— presidential and parliamentary. The United States exemplifies the former, Great Britain the latter.

Presidential Democracy

In the presidential model, the chief executive is popularly elected by the nation as a whole (legislators are elected in local constituencies). The executive, legislative, and judicial branches are distinct structures with special constitutional functions, and a system of checks and balances is built in. No member of the government can serve in more than one branch at any given time.

In this system the president is both head of state and head of government. The president leads the nation at home and abroad, but must sell preferred policies and programs to the legislature, which has the power of the purse (final taxing and spending authority). In the United States, at least, constitutional questions, including those involving disputes between the executive and legislative branches, are decided by the Supreme Court exercising its power of judicial review.

Parliamentary Democracy

In the parliamentary system, the chief executive is usually a prime minister. To become prime minister one must have a seat in parliament, won by standing for election in a local constituency. There is no separation of powers in this type of democracy; rather there is a fusion of powers. The prime minister and cabinet are chosen by members of parliament from the leadership of the majority party or coalition in the parliament. They retain their legislative seats while they simultaneously serve in executive posts in the government.

A British-style parliamentary system has several advantages over the presidential system. First, the government rarely has great difficulty getting its budget approved by the legislature because it almost always has a legislative majority. Second, a government judged to be doing a poor job can be forced out at any time by a "no confidence" vote in the parliament (in Great Britain such a vote requires only a simple majority to pass). Third, the government can dissolve the parliament at any time and call for new elections. This power is important for two reasons: It helps maintain party discipline and it gives the party in power the opportunity to choose an auspicious time for new elections. (In the British system a government must call new elections at least once every five years.)

Many variations of both the U.S. and the British models exist. Some countries combine features of both. The most notable example is France, which has both a popularly elected president and a prime minister chosen by the majority party in parliament. Whether nations choose one model or the other or some combination of the two, the goal is always essentially the same: to have a government of laws, not of men and women. A sharper contrast with personal dictatorships or with authoritarian regimes of all kinds is difficult to conceive.

Today constitutional democracies can be found in nearly every part of the globe, although they continue to be vastly outnumbered by authoritarian regimes in the Third World. (Eastern Europe, sometimes called the Second World, is now undergoing transition.) Two of the largest democracies coexist harmoniously in North America; in fact, the United States and Canada share the longest unguarded border in the world. The most populous democracy, India, is located in Asia. In truth, Western-style government has not fared very well in the rest of Asia, although Japan has successfully adapted the parliamentary system imposed by the United States after World War II into a unique form of patron–client democracy. Sri Lanka (formerly Ceylon), an island neighbor of India, is the other notable exception. Australia and New Zealand have long been solidly democratic nations; the Philippines has also lurched toward democracy following the overthrow of Marcos in early 1986. Marcos' successor, Corazon Aquino, has vowed to preserve democracy despite continuing guerrilla warfare against the government by Communist insurgents.

Democracy has had the least success in Africa and the Middle East. Popularly elected civilian government has not taken firm root in any Arab state with the possible exception of Lebanon prior to onset of the civil war in the mid-1970s. Gambia is one of the few functioning democracies in Africa. The Ivory Coast and Kenya both have close ties to the West, hold periodic elections, and encourage free enterprise.

Modern Mixed Regimes

The reader will recall that Aristotle favored the mixed regime, one with elements of both democracy and oligarchy. In fact, what we normally sanctify as democracy is not pure democracy at all, but a watered-down version (known as a republic) in which elected representatives of the people, not the people themselves, make laws and decide policy. These elected officials form a kind of political class—a legislative oligarchy, if you will. Presidents and prime ministers typically possess some of the same powers as tyrants; in times of crisis they often become virtual dictators. A case in point is Indira Gandhi. As prime minister of India she declared a national state of emergency in 1975 and exercised dictatorial powers for nineteen months. General Charles de Gaulle as president of France from 1957 to 1969 is another example. Although a democratic constitution was in effect in France and free elections determined who held public offices, de Gaulle ruled as an imperial president. Among his many Bonapartist acts, he even changed the manner in which the president (himself) was elected. In the process he violated the constitution he had ordered tailor-made a few years earlier.

If democracies have elements of oligarchy and even tyranny, dictatorships may have elements of democracy. Elections are often held even though they may be rigged. Sometimes they are little more than plebiscites designed to demonstrate how much the masses adore the dictator. In many dictatorships at least limited civil liberties exist. In some instances there may even be token political opposition—perhaps a small maverick party in a rubberstamp legislature or a relatively independent newspaper that dares to criticize the government. The government of Egypt is an example: It is still more authoritarian than democratic, but many of the trappings of democracy are undeniably present.

This mingling of different forms of government is even more evident when we look at different types of the same form. Particularly in the case of authoritarian regimes, categorizing is often extremely difficult. South Korea is a case in point. In South Korea elections are held, some civil liberties are permitted, and people move about freely. But until 1987 South Korea was in reality part military junta and part personal dictatorship. Following a coup in 1961, General Park Chung Hee ran the country as a military strongman (although he was ''elected'' president in 1962). In 1972, a referendum allowed him to be elected for six-year terms unlimited times. He was assassinated by one of his own lieutenants in 1979 and was succeeded by another military strongman, General Chun Doo Hwan. In 1987, student-led popular demonstrations against the government, backed by pressure from the Reagan Administration to democratize, compelled Chun Doo Hwan to allow popular presidential elections. These recent developments are dramatic and could even break new ground in Northeast Asia. However, the tender shoots of democracy in South Korea will remain fragile, at best, for many years to come.

Market and Mixed Economies

Both democratic and authoritarian forms of government are typically associated with *market*, or *mixed*, economies. Market economies regard free enterprise as the key to self-sustaining growth and general prosperity. They feature a minimum of state interference in commerce, finance, industry, and agriculture (*laissez faire*). The forces of supply and demand are allowed to operate without extensive state regulation and subsidization. The profit motive provides the incentive for individuals to work hard, compete vigorously, improve the quality of the service(s) or product(s) they deliver, and strive for excellence. In theory, coercion and exhortation are unnecessary because everyone in a free-enterprise system is *self-motivated*.

In fact, the whole concept of laissez faire as originally expounded by Adam Smith in the late eighteenth century posited a natural harmony of interests in society. Individuals behaving rationally (that is, trying to get rich) would unwittingly serve the needs of society as a whole. By working hard, earning as much money as possible, spending some and saving the rest, investing soundly, and playing by the rules so as not to jeopardize the legal order on which contractual obligations ultimately depend, individuals would create a synergy that could be expected to maximize creativity, ingenuity, and productivity. It would do so, in part, by rewarding innovation and invention.

In reality, no pure market economies exist. All market economies are mixed free-enterprise systems, that is, the operation of market forces is regulated in varying degrees by government. For example, the money supply is generally controlled by a central bank (in the United States the Federal Reserve Board performs this function). Governments use fiscal as well as monetary policy to regulate the economy: They raise taxes and cut spending to cool down an "overheated" economy and they lower taxes and increase spending to resuscitate a slumping economy. They also typically give extensive subsidies to agriculture and tax breaks to business and industry. In many developing countries the government heavily subsidizes the general populace by providing food, fuel, and other necessities at prices well below actual cost. Subsidies are a major source of government indebtedness in Africa, Asia, and Latin America, but ruling elites in these regions are reluctant to discontinue them because of the hardships that would result and the danger of provoking riots and regime-threatening unrest.

Totalitarianism: Yesterday's Model?

The word *totalitarian* denotes a concept of relatively recent vintage. It was first used to describe the system established in the Soviet Union during the long and bloody reign of Joseph Stalin and the system in Germany under Adolf Hitler, in which millions of European Jews were killed in Nazi extermination camps. The word is appropriate because the political regimes created by Stalin and Hitler were characterized by *total* concentration of power at the center (in Stalin's case in the hands of a single individual).

A pivotal feature of the totalitarian model is an all-encompassing and monolithic party organization that functions like a state within a state. This party is controlled by an omnipotent dictator with the help of an oligarchic elite handpicked by the dictator. Members of the elite make decisions in secret and rely heavily on secret police to intimidate and mobilize the society. In the Stalinist variant, the party apparatus and state bureaucracy are inextricably intertwined; the bureaucracy implements policies while the party acts primarily as the dictator's whip hand and watchdog.

Carl Friedrich and Zbigniew Brzezinski listed the following as characteristics of all totalitarian regimes:

1. An official ideology covering all aspects of human existence to which every member of the society must adhere, not only by outer forms but also by inner convictions
2. A single mass party led by one person and consisting of relatively small proportions of the total population, which acts as the official ideology's priesthood
3. A system of terroristic police controls making full use of modern technology for spying and surveillance
4. Centralized state control of the mass media
5. Confiscation of all arms and explosives previously in private hands
6. Centralized state control of the economy through bureaucratic coordination of all productive enterprises[9]

In the full-blown totalitarian state, political liberties (and human rights in general) are nonexistent. Dissidence and nonconformity are not tolerated; those who do not submit often vanish in the night, dispatched to labor camps or the firing squad. The press is state controlled and the performing arts are tightly regulated. Newspapers, books, and movies, as well as radio and television programming, are censored. No independent group or association of any kind is permitted. The educational system is geared to the regime's political objectives and the curriculum is infused with ideological content.[10]

Totalitarian rulers, by definition, aim at a radical restructuring of society. To achieve such ambitious goals as rapid industrialization, social transformation, and territorial expansion, they must have mass mobilization. Passive obedience on the part of the masses is not enough; active participation is required. Ardor is an order. Sloth is treason. In true Orwellian fashion, society must be so infiltrated and controlled that no one can hide anything from the state—including subversive thoughts or feelings. Today air transportation systems, mass communications systems, computerized information management systems, electronic surveillance systems, and increasingly sophisticated internal security systems place formidable new means and methods of control at the disposal of the modern state.

The *potential* for totalitarianism would appear to be inherent in the processes of economic and political development. Has any tendency toward totalitarian rule been apparent in developing countries in recent decades? Are industrially developed and technologically advanced societies more susceptible to totalitarian blandishments under some circumstances than more traditional societies? The answers to questions such as these can be found only through comparative political analysis. For now it will suffice to note that the Stalinist example demonstrates the danger of totalitarianism in a largely agrarian, traditional setting, while the Nazi example shows clearly that advanced industrial societies are not immune from this contagion. Fortunately, by the end of the 1980s there were few regimes still around that precisely fit the totalitarian pattern described here. This does not mean, of course, that totalitarianism will not rear its ugly head again.

Marxist-Leninist Regimes

Prior to the sweeping political reforms of 1989–1990, the Soviet Union was the prototype for the Marxist-Leninist form of government. Lenin readily acknowledged his intellectual debt to Karl Marx, but he recast Marxism into an ideology suitable for use as a kind of state religion. Ever since the triumph of Lenin's *Bolsheviki* (as the original Russian Communists were known) in the October Revolution of 1917, a state-sponsored ideology (Marxism-Leninism) imposed on society by means of intimidation and censorship has been a trademark of Marxist-Leninist regimes.

During the heyday of Stalinist rule, these regimes were totalitarian in nature. In recent years, however, internal repression has been sharply curtailed, and the command economy is gradually being replaced by a more market-oriented economic system. At the same time, respect for human rights has greatly improved, and the structures of the totalitarian state are being dismantled piece by piece. What follows is a sketch of the Marxist-Leninist system as it was, not as it now is. (With certain modifications this system continues to operate in places like the People's Republic of China and Cuba.)

Power is concentrated in a single, all-encompassing party organization that rules through a subservient state bureaucracy. Elections are held regularly, but in the absence of a competitive party system they are little more than window dressing. Civil liberties (free speech, freedom of the press, freedom of association and assembly, freedom of movement, and so on) may not be entirely repressed but are severely restricted. Periods of relative leniency toward dissenters alternate with crackdowns on dissent.

Before World War II, the Soviet Union was the only Communist regime in existence. At the end of that war in 1945, with the Red Army in control of Eastern Europe, Stalin installed Soviet-type puppet governments in Poland, East Germany, Czechoslovakia, Hungary, Romania, and Bulgaria. These countries had been overrun and occupied during the war, first by Nazi Germany and then by Soviet forces. Only in Yugoslavia, which had liberated itself from Hitler's armies, was an independent—albeit Marxist—state established.

Marxist-Leninist regimes can now be found in nearly every region of the globe. In Asia the People's Republic of China, North Korea, Vietnam, Cambodia, and Laos are under various forms of Communist rule. In Africa the two conspicuous examples are Angola and Ethiopia. Benin is a self-proclaimed Marxist-Leninist state and Mozambique was ruled by a Maoist, Samora Machel, for a time in the 1980s. In Latin America Cuba (and until recently Nicaragua) falls into this category.

To call all of these governments totalitarian is to suggest a uniformity and continuity that does not stand up well under close scrutiny. Nonetheless, to include them with authoritarian regimes as discussed at the beginning of this chapter ignores the distinctive features they continue to display.

Command Economies

Marxist-Leninist regimes have all in varying degrees adopted the Soviet (or Stalinist) model of economic organization. In general, this model places public goods (and state interests) above private interests. Industry and commerce are state owned and operated. The marketplace is, at best, secondary to central planning as a means of regulating the economy. The state heavily subsidizes consumption: People live in subsidized public housing, depend on subsidized public transportation, and receive free education, medical care, and many other social needs. Nearly everyone works in the public sector (for state-run enterprises). Historically, the same government that has provided subsidies has also paid the low salaries that make subsidies necessary.

Command economies are so named because enterprises respond to instructions from above rather than consumer preferences (demand) from below. An overall plan is developed each year. It contains production targets for every sector of the economy, broken down into monthly quotas. Every factory, farm, and enterprise is expected to fulfill its quota(s). Rewards (in the form of bonuses) are given for overfulfillment; underfulfillment is not career enhancing for the plant manager who is ultimately held responsible.

This system maximizes state (or party) control, which is the chief reason why Stalin created it. It enables the ruler(s) to shape the economy, extract and allocate resources (including land, labor, and investment capital), and concentrate on a particular objective, such as military-industrial development. Stalinist political economy stressed the primacy of heavy industry, which meant everything from coal and steel production to hydroelectric power and machine tools for heavy construction and infrastructure (roads, bridges, dams, and the like). "Heavy industry" was also a euphemism for a major Soviet arms buildup, the genesis of a permanent wartime economy that eventually created an arsenal rivaled only by that of the United States.

The command economy is particularly well suited to crash industrialization based on forced labor—the model of economic development Stalin patented. The system has major liabilities, however. For example, it is increasingly cumbersome to administer as the economy modernizes and becomes more highly differentiated. Although Stalin proved that the initial stages of industrialization can be forced by *quantitative* inputs—massive amounts of conscript labor, capital squeezed from agriculture, and the export (for hard currency) of raw materials extracted without regard to human costs or future needs—it is now glaringly apparent that sustained economic growth in an age of rapidly advancing technology requires *qualitative* inputs (applied research, managerial skills, innovative ideas and attitudes, entrepreneurship, vision, investment strategies, risk taking). In the past two decades command economies have fallen farther and farther behind the most dynamic market economies. Economic decline was the major reason Mikhail Gorbachev launched the Soviet economic reform movement in the mid-1980s and that Eastern Europe has undergone even more dramatic changes recently.

CONCLUSION

In conclusion, Aristotle's ancient classification scheme accommodates all forms of modern government, for political systems from the most pluralistic democracy to the most autocratic dictatorship, with one notable exception—totalitarianism. In the next chapter we turn our attention to the processes and problems of nation-building (sometimes called state-building, institution-building, or political development).

STUDY QUESTIONS

1. What are some major differences between presidential and parliamentary democracies? What are the advantages and disadvantages of each? In your opinion, which system is better?
2. What is authoritarianism? What modern forms has it assumed? Where is it most prevalent, and why?
3. How does totalitarianism differ from authoritarianism? What principal forms has totalitarianism assumed, and where is (was) it found? Is totalitarianism a thing of the past, in your opinion? Why or why not?

SUGGESTED READINGS

Arendt, Hannah. *Totalitarianism*. New York: Harcourt, 1968.

Aristotle. *The Politics*. Ernest Barker, ed. and trans. New York: Oxford, 1962.

Bailey, Sidney. *British Parliamentary Democracy*, 3rd ed. Boston: Houghton Mifflin, 1978.

Conquest, Robert. *The Harvest of Sorrow: Soviet Collectivization and the Terror-Famine*. New York: Oxford, 1986.

Crick, Bernard. *Basic Forms of Government: A Sketch and a Model*. London: Macmillan, 1980.

Diamond, Martin. *The Founding of the Democratic Republic*. Ithaca, N.Y.: Cornell, 1955.

Dicey, A. V. *Introduction to the Study of the Law of the Constitution*. New York: St. Martin's, 1982, Liberty Fund. (A classic interpretation of the British political tradition.)

Friedrich, Carl. *Limited Government: A Comparison*. Englewood Cliffs, N.J.: Prentice-Hall, 1974.

Friedrich, Carl, and Brzezinski, Zbigniew. *Totalitarian Dictatorship and Autocracy*. New York: Praeger, 1965.

Hamilton, Alexander, Jay, John, and Madison, James. *The Federalist*. New York: Modern Library.

Latey, Maurice. *Patterns of Tyranny*. New York: Atheneum, 1969.

Machiavelli, Niccolo. ''The Prince.'' In *The Prince and the Discourses*. New York: Modern Library, 1950.

Macridis, Roy C. *Modern Political Regimes*. Boston: Little, Brown, 1986.

Menze, Ernest, ed. *Totalitarianism Reconsidered*. Port Washington, N.Y.: Kennikat, 1981.

Moore, Barrington. *Social Origins of Dictatorship and Democracy*. Boston: Beacon, 1966.

Orwell, George. *1984*. New York: New American Library, 1961.

Ponchaud, Francois. *Cambodia: Year Zero*. New York: Holt, 1978.

Rubin, Barry. *Modern Dictators*. New York: McGraw-Hill, 1987.

NOTES

[1] Aristotle, *The Politics*. Ernest Barker, ed. and trans. (New York: Oxford, 1962), p. 244.

[2] Ibid., pp. 244–245.

[3] For a discussion of the magnitude of the suffering and deaths caused by totalitarian dictators (Hitler, Stalin, Mao Zedong in China, and Pol Pot in Cambodia), see Thomas Magstadt and Peter Schotten, *Understanding Politics: Ideas, Interests, and Issues*, 2nd ed., (New York: St. Martin's, 1988). For a more detailed discussion see C. W. Cassinelli, *Total Revolution* (Santa Barbara, Calif.: Clio, 1976).

[4] Robert Jackson and Carl Rosberg, *Personal Rule in Black Africa: Princes, Autocrats, Prophets, and Tyrants* (Berkeley: University of California, 1982), p. 235.

[5] Amos Perlmutter, ed., *The Military and Politics in Modern Times*, (New Haven, Conn.: Yale University, 1977), p. 4.

[6] Samuel H. Finer, *Comparative Politics* (London: Penguin, 1970).

[7] Eric Nordlinger, *Soldiers and Politics: Military Coups and Governments* (Englewood Cliffs, N.J.: Prentice-Hall, 1977), p. 6.

[8] Ibid.

[9] Carl J. Friedrich and Zbigniew Brzezinski, *Totalitarian Dictatorship and Autocracy* (Cambridge, Mass.: Harvard University, 1956), p. 9.

[10] Any more-or-less systematic set of political beliefs can be called an ideology; in the totalitarian state there is an elaborate *official* ideology that is force-fed through propaganda and education.

Chapter 3

Nation-Building:
Dimensions of Development

No treatment of theories, patterns, and approaches in the study of comparative politics is complete without a discussion of development—a synonym for nation-building.[1] This chapter explores the many dimensions of development in the modern world. This topic is especially relevant to the Third World, where the stages and strategies of development are often used as a basis for classifying national political systems.

Putting Development into Perspective

Development can be defined as "the increasing capacity to make rational use of natural and human resources for social ends."[2] It is a key concept in nearly all the natural and social sciences.

Anthropologists and sociologists stress sociocultural aspects of development such as values, beliefs, taboos, attitudes, and orientations. They focus on group relations (families, clans, tribes or ethnic, religious, or other distinct groups). Economists stress changes in patterns of production and distribution, consumption, and investment. Political scientists focus mainly on changes in patterns of power and authority. As societies develop, how do power relationships change? What new institutions emerge? How is political stability affected? What is the relationship between political development and economic development? Are certain kinds of government more suitable for developing societies than others? Is there a close correlation between regime type and stage of economic development? These questions and others have been addressed since World War II.

Political economists examine development from a perspective that views power and wealth as inseparable. They emphasize structural features of the international politico-economic environment in which unequal nation-states compete and cooperate.

Historical Backdrop

In many ways World War II was a watershed. First, it ushered in a bipolar, global balance-of-power system that replaced the previous regional (European) system. Although Europe continued to be the focus of international tensions for a time, the once dominant powers of the Continent were now militarily, economically, and psychologically dependent on the United States. One reason was the menacing presence of the Soviet Union—half European and half Asian—in the East. Post-World-War II East-West rivalry became known as the *Cold War.*

A second (and closely related) change after the war was the breakup of the European colonial empires. Indeed, the dissolution of these empires was one sign that the former great powers of Europe were in decline. Internationally, this new state of affairs meant that Europe no longer controlled, and could no longer easily exploit, Asia, Africa, and the Middle East.

Third, the United States and the Soviet Union, which confronted one another across an ideological chasm symbolized by Winston Churchill's famous "iron curtain" metaphor, looked increasingly to other regions of the world for allies, trading partners, military bases, strategic minerals, and investment opportunities. The Third World became a new battleground in the East-West rivalry. Each "super-power" sought to have its politico-economic system adopted; each offered a variety of inducements including economic and military aid; finally, each pressured its aid recipients to choose sides. The developing nations often resisted this pressure, preferring to play one side against the other and insisting that the division between North and South was more important than any East-West division.

How Many Worlds?

Never have regions played a more prominent role in international affairs than after the Second World War. Europe and North America became synonymous with the First World; the Soviet Union and its allies, especially the satellite states of Eastern Europe, constituted the Second World; the former colonial areas (located mainly in the southern half of the globe) formed the Third World. These three "worlds" correspond to regions to some extent, but this way of dividing the globe is arbitrary and is less useful—especially since fading of the Cold War—than a regional approach that takes into account historic, geographic, religious, cultural, linguistic, and other similarities found among many nations in different regions of the globe.

In the 1950s, similarities among former colonies, irrespective of their location, were more apparent than differences:

> As the newly emergent states of Asia, Africa, and Latin America took their place in the international community, it rapidly became apparent that they were not states in the Western sense of the word. They were desperately poor. Their economies were based upon subsistence agriculture and the export of raw materials to the industrial powers of the West. Their political systems were fragile and subject to frequent coups d'etat. More often than not, they were ruled by narrow elites whose strength came from tribal support or large landholdings. Socially, they were fragmented into a multitude of poorly integrated ethnic and religious factions. Culturally, their populations, largely illiterate, clung to the ways of the past.[3]

Although this description is becoming increasingly oversimplified (witness the success of Asia's newly industrialized countries South Korea, Taiwan, Hong Kong, and Singapore), a great economic divide remains between the North (actually the West) and the South. The seven most prosperous developed countries (the United States, Great Britain, Germany, France, Italy, and Japan) comprise only about one-seventh of the world's population but consume two-fifths of its energy, garner half of all export earnings, and take over half of total goods and services every year. Poverty plagues much of the rest of the world:

> Three hundred million 6–11-year-olds in developing countries do not go to school. Fifty percent of all children who actually enter elementary school will not stay to the end of the second year. Only 25 percent will finish elementary school. Only 10 percent . . . . are immunized against the six basic childhood diseases.[4]

From the perspective of those who were formerly under European colonial rule, the blame for these dire straits rests squarely with the West (and particularly the United States as the leading Western power).

This common perspective should not obscure the fact that there is enormous diversity within developing nations and within religions. This diversity is both old and new in origin. Increasingly pronounced economic differentiation tends to be new; geographic, historical, cultural, racial, ethnic, social, religious, and linguistic differences are obviously very old.

In following chapters the substance of these differences in perspective will be elucidated. Here our aim is to set the stage for that in-depth discussion. Accordingly, we now consider some competing theories and approaches in the study of political development.

Political Development in Classic Political Theory

The idea of political development can be traced back at least as far as Plato. In *The Republic*,[5] Plato posited that the highest form of political order would be rule by a philosopher-king, a person who understood the good and had the moral character to act on that understanding. The key to Plato's *Republic* was education, both for the ruler(s) and the ruled. Philosopher-kings would need elaborate moral and intellectual preparation for their lofty vocation. The auxilliaries (the warrior class that would ensure order and security) would also need special training in the military arts. Finally, the masses (artisans and farmers) would receive an education designed to socialize them into acceptance of their station in life. This education would be based on a myth (Plato called it a "noble lie"):

> . . . I shall try to convince, first the Rulers and the soldiers, and then the whole community, that all that nurture and education we gave them was only something they seemed to experience as if it were in a dream. In reality they were the whole time down inside the earth, being molded and fostered while their arms and all their equipment were being fashioned also; and at last, when they were complete, the earth sent them up from her womb into the light of day. So now they must think of the land they dwell in as a mother and a nurse, whom they must . . . defend against any attack, and of their fellow citizens as brothers born of the same soil. . . . It is true, we shall tell our people in this fable, that all of you in this land are brothers; but the god who fashioned you mixed gold in the composition of those among you who are fit to rule, so that they are the most precious quality; and he put silver in the auxiliaries, and iron and brass in the farmers and craftsmen. . . . They will appeal to a prophecy that ruin will come upon the state when it passes into the keeping of a man of iron or brass.[6]

Plato's conception may seem quaint to us, but over the centuries the notion of a ruling class has been entertained in many different guises and settings. Moreover, it is often associated with progress or development. Historically, monarchs frequently claimed to be "enlightened," and political elites were often drawn from a landed aristocracy. The idea of rule by a scientific-technological elite has also been broached. As early as the sixteenth century Francis Bacon wrote about such an elite in a book entitled *The New Atlantis*. More recently the concept of "technocracy"—rule by technocrats—has been popularized in many countries.

Plato's idea of rule by the wise and gifted has a present-day echo in the theory of Steven Chilton.[7] Chilton posits the evolution of a universal moral philosophy. As people mature, their capacity to engage in abstract moral reasoning increases (an argument supported by the research of developmental psychologists). Some individuals, however, have a greater innate ability to engage in such reasoning than do others. Political systems that manage to put these gifted individuals into leadership and policy-making positions are most likely to develop in accordance with universal moral values.

Karl Marx provided the basis for another theory of political development. His concept of the "withering away of the state" held that as societies evolve and go through developmental stages, government will eventually become superfluous. The need for coercive political institutions to control society will disappear. Under socialism (and then communism), society's members will internalize the values of the collective rather than the individualistic values associated with capitalism. What we know as government will be replaced by the "administration of things."

A contemporary version of this idea has been espoused by sociologist James Davies. In his view, the best developed societies are those whose members most universally and thoroughly internalize rules associated with sharing and fair play. Davies argued that governments arose to combat anarchy and will be replaced by mere administration as societies evolve to a level where everyone internalizes the rules of the road, so to speak.[8]

Other political philosophers have embraced ideas, especially about human nature, that have far-reaching implications for theories of political development. Thomas Hobbes believed that life in the state of nature would be "solitary, poor, nasty, brutish, and short." An imposing state (or "Leviathan," as he called it in his book of the same name) was thus necessary to "overawe" the masses and maintain order and stability. Societies that lacked such a strong state were, by definition, politically underdeveloped.

Rousseau took quite the opposite view. He believed that the modern state represents political degeneracy, not progress. "Man is born free," he declared, "and everywhere he is in chains." In particular, Rousseau decried the institution of private property and viewed political systems as elaborate devices for perpetuating inequality based on property ownership. Remove the political and social props that at once support the existing system and create a culture of greed and self-aggrandizement and the natural goodness of human beings would blossom.

Darker views of human nature can be extracted from (political) science fiction such as George Orwell's *1984* and Alduous Huxley's *Brave New World* (sometimes called "dysutopias"). Orwell presented a stark picture of totalitarian rule in which propaganda replaces information, love and other human emotions are manipulated for political purposes, lies are institutionalized as truth, and obedience to authority is ensured by constant surveillance and total denial of privacy. Huxley painted a portrait of a future technological society in which human beings are enslaved in a totalitarian system they cannot resist. Through genetic engineering even mental capacities are determined by the state, so that individuals have no greater abilities than their prescribed social role requires. Drones, for example, are reproduced in large numbers and have very limited intelligence.

Another popular novel, B. F. Skinner's *Walden Two*, stresses behavior modification rather than biogenetics as the means for creating a new and presumably higher form of society. The setting for the novel is a self-contained community of carefully selected members who are part of an experiment. In this community no violence, greed, or egoism—in short, no antisocial behavior—is permitted. Love and gentle persuasion are used to reinforce desired behavior. Disciplinary measures consist of shame rather than physical abuse.

In a later book, *Beyond Freedom and Dignity*, Skinner argued that intangible "goods" (for example freedom and dignity) are not nearly as important as living standards or the satisfaction of physical needs. The state (or society) that is best able to satisfy these needs and attain a high standard of living is the most politically developed. It stands to reason, given Skinner's belief in the efficacy of behavior modification, that in a society free of poverty and want, the need for coercion to keep people in line would diminish. But would it?

Finally, John Herz propounded the theory that political units enlarge in response to the changing security needs of society.[9] When these needs could be satisfied by the family, clan, or tribe there was no need for the modern state. When, however, traditional forms of socio-political organization were no longer adequate for protection, they were replaced by the modern nation-state. Herz argued that the nation-state is also now inadequate, owing to new threats such as nuclear war and ecological disaster. Only world government can deal effectively with these new challenges.

Although the argument that whatever is necessary in human affairs is possible has some appeal, one can question whether world government is, in fact, necessary. Evidence is mounting that nation-states are becoming increasingly interdependent. Evidence also suggests that the most plausible alternative to the nation-state at this historical juncture may be regional rather than global government. The most obvious case in point is the European Community, but others are the Association of South-East Asian Nations (ASEAN) and the new U.S.-Canadian customs union.

The fact that regionalism provides an intermediate step between the nation-state and world government may partially account for the current trend toward regional integration. The success of the European Community—underscored by its economic unification in 1992—can be expected to act as a spur to efforts at regional integration in other parts of the world. This possibility makes a regional approach to the study of comparative politics especially appropriate at this time.

Evolutionary Development Theory

More than two centuries ago the French philosopher Montesquieu (1689–1755) argued that complete understanding of a political system would require a careful examination of the environmental and cultural context of politics.[10] Such an approach would look at geography, population, climate, resource endowments, the economy, and cultural characteristics.

Incorporating all of these variables into one theory is, of course, easier said than done. Nonetheless, Montesquieu's argument still serves as a foundation for traditional approaches to development. These approaches all view development as an *evolutionary process*, one that occurs in increments over an extended period of time. Various conceptual schemes have placed countries on a developmental continuum, classifying them according to their level of economic development or the prevailing mode(s) of production (agriculture, industry, services). Different studies share the common assumption that economic development leads to physical well-being derived from the increasingly efficient organization and mechanization of production. This process is usually viewed as inseparable from social and political modernization.[11]

Development theorists often attempt to compare different political systems by looking at goal-attainment capabilities and success in extracting and distributing resources or in regulating social, economic, and political activity. Societies are then said to be developed and ''modern'' to the degree that the successfully perform such functions. Not surprisingly, political instability and economic stagnation are often cited as evidence that Third World nations are underdeveloped, that is, incapable of managing society so as to extract and distribute resources efficiently.[12]

But it is one thing to describe the end result of development and quite another to prescribe how, when, and where it should occur. Every society is unique, and generalizations that ignore the context of development (culture, physical environment, and so on) are hazardous. We examine two variants of evolutionary development theory here.

The Perspectives of Sociology and Psychology

Some theorists stress that economic development reflects a state of mind more than anything else, that it is essentially psychological and cultural. Explanations of this kind are found in the works of sociologists Talcott Parsons, Daniel Lerner, and Amatai Etzioni; psychologist David McClelland; anthropologist C. Geertz; and political scientist Edward Banfield.[13] In different ways these authors have suggested that personality structures conditioned by social and cultural norms must change from within for development to be possible.

Daniel Lerner observed the traditions of Middle Eastern society and concluded that lack of empathy (inability to put oneself in another's place) is the key factor inhibiting economic development in Arab societies. Lerner's thesis is that this lack stifles individual and group motivation.[14]

McClelland, on the other hand, studied individuals in Western societies, using a psychological measure of the need to achieve. McClelland discovered that individuals with low scores had a low ambition for acquiring wealth or other attributes of success, and concluded that for this reason societies vary in achievement levels, the principal expression of this variation being economic development or underdevelopment.

> In a century dominated by economic determinism in both communist and Western thought, it is startling to find a concrete evidence for psychological determinism, for psychological developments as preceding and presumably causing economic changes.[15]

From a study of a traditional village in Southern Italy, Edward Banfield attempted to explain backwardness in terms of specific behavior patterns of individuals and families of the village. Banfield attributed backwardness to the villagers' orientation toward life and society. He described them as now-oriented, self-centered people who feared death, exhibited lack of interest in outside affairs, and embraced a world view bounded by self or family.[16]

The Perspective of Political Science

In political science, development theory often stresses the political prerequisites for economic development: political order and stability, which in turn are a function of viable institutions and enforceable rules. Development thus entails an increase in the capability of the political system to expand the range of individual freedoms, opportunities, and choices.[17]

According to input–output theorists, the political system receives inputs in the form of public demands, supports, and pressures from its various environments and converts them into outputs expressed as policies, programs, and priorities. This view holds that institutionalization of the functions of the political system (expressed by universality of rules and regularity and reliability of operations) will create a climate conducive to domestic peace and prosperity.

For evolutionary theorists, a solution to the problem of underdevelopment is to be found primarily in changing the psychology and culture, as well as the political rules, of the society. To induce such changes these theorists often call for stepped-up foreign aid, trade, and investment and introduction of modern technology. A country that absorbs Western products and capital, so the theory goes, will modernize not only its modes of production but also its patterns of consumption and its life-style. Greater popular participation is also likely to follow. This in turn will both galvanize the society and spur the government to higher standards of performance.

Judgmental Versus Descriptive Approaches

Political development means different things to different people. One reason is that concepts of development are often judgmental. If, for example, order is given the highest priority, states capable of suppressing dissent or socializing citizens into cooperative rather than competitive behaviors could be considered the most developed. If liberty is prized most highly, states that encourage individuality, private enterprise, and self-expression might be deemed the most mature.

Approaches of this kind tend to be not only normative but also prescriptive. Proponents make moral choices—freedom over order, equality over liberty, and so on. On the basis of these choices they prescribe developmental models and policies designed to produce the type of society they prefer. Political systems that manifest the traits they value are labeled progressive or developed; regimes that show opposite traits may be given labels like "primitive," "regressive," "despotic," or "reactionary."

An alternative to the judgmental approach is one that is descriptive in nature. It spurns moral or ethical judgments in favor of careful observation and analysis. Often espoused by behavioralists, this approach sticks to the facts, stresses scientific objectivity, conscientiously seeks to verify its findings, and avoids sweeping generalizations.

A third approach is deterministic. Marx, for example, argued that one historical stage would follow another inexorably. Free choice plays little or no role here. But Marxists are not the only ones who tend to be deterministic. Many developmental theorists stress forces and factors beyond human control.

The approach used in this book combines normative and prescriptive elements with description and analysis. It acknowledges the claims of determinism, but recognizes that determinism can too easily become an excuse for defeatism and self-fulfilling prophecies. The persistent appeal of determinism does serve to remind us that powerful impersonal forces *are* at work in the world and that there are limits to politics.

Politics and Economics: Two Sides of One Coin

The study of comparative politics on a global scale has benefitted from the work of scholars who look at the world through the prism of political economy—politics and economics as two sides of the same coin. From this perspective, economic inequality among nations and regions is a stark fact of international political life. Three patterns are particularly noteworthy.

First, as already noted, the world's material wealth is grossly maldistributed between the North and the South, especially between the nations of North America, Western Europe, and much of the Pacific Rim on the one hand and the nations of South and Southeast Asia, sub-Saharan Africa, and much of Latin America and the Middle East, on the other.

Second, economic growth rates have declined in many regions of the world over the past three decades, but the decline has hit the Third World the hardest. The full impact of declining growth rates can be gauged only by comparing these rates with population growth rates, which gives the average annual per capita GNP growth rate. By this measure, many low-income countries in Asia, Africa, and Latin America experienced *negative* growth between 1965 and 1985 (see Table 3-1).

Table 3-1 Per Capita Gross National Product of Developing Countries
(annual changes, in percent)

	1985	1988	1991
By Region			
Africa	1.4%	−0.5%	0.1%
Asia	5.0%	7.2%	4.0%
Europe	1.8%	0.5%	2.1%
Latin America	1.3%	−1.8%	2.2%
Middle East	−3.6%	0.4%	—
Miscellaneous Groups			
Sub-Saharan Africa	1.1%	−0.7%	—
12 major oil exporters	−1.9%	0.3%	0.5%
4 newly industrializing Asian economies	3.2%	8.3%	5.8%
15 heavily indebted countries	1.6%	−1.4%	2.1%

Source: World Economic Outlook (Washington, D.C.: International Monetary Fund, May 1990), Table A6.

Third, unequal distribution of wealth is greater within developing than within developed nations and regions. For example, the top 10 percent of the population owns 50 percent of the wealth in Brazil and 40 percent of the wealth in Kenya, Zambia, Peru, and Mexico. In the United States and Japan, by contrast, the top 10 percent owns considerably less than 25 percent of the wealth. The economic problems endemic throughout Africa, Latin America, and much of Asia are exacerbated by—and reflected in—the world debt crisis. This phenomenon, which grew to ominous proportions in the 1980s, accentuated the inequalities between North and South. In the late 1980s, the debt burden on the developing nations reached $1.3 *trillion*! The biggest debtor nations, Mexico and Brazil, owed over $100 billion each, while Argentina (over $50 billion), Indonesia ($40–45 billion), and Venezuela ($30–35 billion) were also major debtors. Other countries as far apart as Poland, Nigeria, and the Philippines shouldered debt burdens that far exceeded their capacity to repay.

The causes of the debt crisis can be separated into two categories: proximate (immediate) and systemic. The proximate causes were skyrocketing oil prices in the 1970s (rising from $2.50 per barrel to $34.00 per barrel), the availability of foreign loans (due in large part to huge OPEC oil profits), and, at the beginning of the 1980s, a sharp rise in interest rates (reaching a high of 21 percent) in the United States coupled with a global recession that cut export revenues.

The systemic causes are more difficult to identify, and more controversial. The International Monetary Fund (backed by the U.S. government) has pointed to structural problems within many of the debtor nations' economies—hyperinflation and chronic budget deficits due to state subsidies, high arms spending, capital flight, and a porous tax-collection system. It urges a combination of economic austerity measures such as spending cuts, contraction of the money supply, new incentives for domestic and foreign investment, and general policies aimed at encouraging free enterprise and reducing the role of the state.

The Third World perspective is quite different from that of the IMF. It draws from the writings of Marx and Lenin and from more recent works by scholars who subscribe to a school of thought known as *dependency theory*.

Dependency Theory: A Regional Perspective

Dependency theory starts with the proposition that the world's resources are finite. The rest of the argument flows from certain assumptions and observations about the nature of the global political economy.

Dependency theorists have adapted Marxist class analysis. The world, they contend, is divided into three basic classes: the *industrial core* (the United States, Western Europe, and Japan); the *semiperiphery* (or so-called New Industrial Countries such as South Korea, Taiwan, Singapore, and Brazil); and the *periphery* (the vast majority of countries in the former colonial areas of Asia, Africa, and Latin America). The states of both the periphery and semiperiphery are dependent on the industrial core for markets, capital, and technology. The industrial nations have a vested interest in maintaining this state of dependency.

The dependency system has a number of salient features. First, the core states export expensive manufactured goods and the peripheral states export cheap raw materials (foodstuffs and minerals). (The price structure is manipulated by the dominant economic powers.) The terms of trade thus heavily favor the core states.

A closely related feature is that commodity prices fluctuate widely from one year to the next, and many developing countries are dependent on the export of one or two commodities (for example, sugar, coffee, bananas, jute). Thus, export revenues are extremely sensitive to price fluctuations beyond the control of the exporting countries. The developing countries must continue to import, however, and must pay for imports with hard currency (foreign reserves). They thus must borrow, and must pay whatever interest rates international financiers in the core states choose to charge. Further, they are forced to accept foreign aid, and they must also accept the strings attached to it. Finally, in a crisis, they have little choice but to accept the conditions imposed by the IMF for short-term loans. Called *conditionality*, this practice of demanding austerity measures has been a major bone of contention in the North-South conflict.

An especially insidious aspect of this whole system, according to dependency theorists, is the collusion between capitalists in the core states and a small economic elite in the peripheral states. This elite typically profits enormously from the arrangement, but it is mutually beneficial: The core states back "anti-communist" regimes that maintain order and stability and ensure access to domestic markets. Grants of military and economic aid, seen in this light, are payoffs and props that reap larger dividends for the donor nations than for the citizens of the recipient countries, in part because corrupt rulers siphon off most of the monies.

Not all political economists embrace dependency theory. Particularly in the West, development scholars tend to blame the developing nations themselves for most of their problems and argue that these nations must find their own solutions. Typically, they stress that many developing nations are plagued by weak institutions, corrupt or incompetent leaders, and chronic sociopolitical instability. Hence, the path to economic development is essentially political in nature.

Conditions for Economic Development

Political instability is the bane of economic health and social progress. Instability takes a variety of forms, including military coups, riots, and insurgencies; it is especially prevalent in Africa, Asia, and Latin America. Its economic consequences are myriad, including disruption of communications and transport, diversion of scarce resources to internal security needs, and large-scale capital flight. Instability is anathema to investors. In the mid-1980s, *Business Week* estimated that without capital flight Argentina's foreign debt would have been $1 billion rather than $50 billion, Mexico's would have been $12 billion rather than roughly $100 billion, and Venezuela would have had no debt.[18]

If it is true that political failure leads to economic failure, the reverse is also true. Poverty begets instability by undermining economic development.

Political factors that impinge on the pace and direction of economic development include (a) the quality of leadership, (b) the capabilities of existing political structures, (c) the availability of necessary resources, (d) the "quality" of the citizenry, and (e) the threats and opportunities presented by a changing regional and international environment.

The quality of leadership refers to the attitudes and attributes of political elites. Are they progressive or tradition bound? Do they want economic development even if it is accompanied by other changes that might be destabilizing? Are they more concerned about income distribution or economic growth? Is social justice important to them, or are they interested only in feathering their own nests? In short (from Aristotle), do the leaders rule in their own interest or in the interest of all?

In addition to their moral character, the skills and abilities of political elites—those who implement policy as well as those who formulate it—are of key importance. Do these elites understand basic principles of economics? Are they familiar with appropriate technologies in agriculture, industry, and the service sector? Do they have administrative experience and skills? Answers to these questions are crucial to the economic prospects of developing nations and regions.

The concept of institutional capacity is particularly important in the comparative study of politics. Are viable institutions already in place, or do they have to be built from the ground up? Can these institutions perform essential functions? For example, can they facilitate the processes of controlling, extracting, and mobilizing human and material resources? Institutionalization of the functions all governments must perform is one measure of political development.

The availability of resources may appear at first blush to be unrelated to political leaders and institutions. But such is not the case. Here one must distinguish between potential and actual resources. Some political systems are more effective than others in extracting and developing resources. A nation with oil reserves will not benefit from this resource unless or until the oil is discovered. Even then the financial and technological wherewithal for development must be available. In addition, the infrastructure—canals, harbors, bridges, railroads, storage facilities, pipelines, and communications systems—must be built. Clearly, such an effort requires a great deal of planning, coordination, and expertise.

Equally important, human resources must be developed. Education and training, as well as fulfillment of basic human needs, are essential. In their absence human potential will be wasted and population growth will become a liability.

By "quality" of citizens is meant values, attitudes, and behaviors that, taken together, help or hinder economic growth, social harmony, and political stability. One crucial variable is the presence or absence of the "work ethic." Are people highly motivated or nonchalant on the job? Do people feel a sense of responsibility to the state and society or are they sullen and cynical? The quality of citizens is no less vital to the future of nations and regions than the quality of leaders.

Finally, the regional and international environment gives rise to certain political possibilities and constraints. The ability to coordinate foreign policies regionally so as to present a united front to the rest of the world can be critical. The success of the Organization of Petroleum Exporting Countries (OPEC) in the 1970s is one example. Constraints to regional cooperation arise in various forms, but nationalism is the most prevalent and persistent. Leaders and citizens continue to identify primarily with national symbols, interests, and causes, even though knowledge is growing that regional and global action is needed to solve or even alleviate many common problems.

The Strains of Development

Economic development alleviates some causes of instability, but it also creates new stresses and strains. The dislocations (urbanization, anomie, unemployment, and so on) that accompany economic development typically give rise to social conflict as well as to feelings of personal alienation. Governments must be able to mediate between and among new social groups (students, workers, professionals), accommodate competing demands, and in general manage conflict. Examples of countries that have not been able to deal with the forces unleashed by the processes of modernization are all too many. A classic case is Iran both before and after the fall of the Shah, an ardent modernizer, in 1979. Nicaragua, El Salvador, the Philippines, and South Korea all experienced domestic upheaval in the 1980s.

One further example is in order. In the spring of 1989, Communist China, thought by most observers to be nearly immune to political instability, was rocked by a massive student-led rebellion. Over a million protesters gathered in Tiananmen square in Beijing, demanding an end to press censorship and official corruption. They also wanted new leadership and broad democratic reforms. The government eventually ordered a bloody crackdown. In the end the regime proved once again its ability to deal with internal conflict.

In sum, the capacity to mobilize resources and to manage social conflict are necessary (but probably not sufficient) conditions of economic development. The revolt in China demonstrates that no developing nation is immune to political instability, but that some governments are more capable of coping with conflict—either managing or suppressing it—than others. In contrast to the experiences of Second and Third World nations, the First World also experiences occasional unrest, but domestic tensions rarely exceed or even seriously strain the capacity of political institutions to absorb or accommodate conflict.

The Role of the State in the Economy

There are two basic approaches to the role of the state in the economy: (a) the free market and (b) state intervention. Market economies are typically associated with the United States, Western Europe, and Japan, whereas central planning (the ultimate form of state intervention) is associated with the Soviet Union and Eastern Europe. Elsewhere both approaches can be found, market economies in South Korea, Taiwan, Hong Kong, Singapore, the Ivory Coast, and Chile, to name a few, and command economies in the People's Republic of China, Vietnam, Ethiopia, Angola, and Cuba. The majority of developing nations combine free enterprise with varying degrees and kinds of state intervention.

The free-enterprise model places primary emphasis on private incentives and private investment. The profit motive is the engine of economic growth. The marketplace sets prices and allocates profits—competition is the key. The most efficient producers prosper by being able to offer a quality product at a relatively low price.

In most developing nations, political goals are given primacy. National pride and self-reliance are important and sometimes have economic implications. Building a large steel mill or a sports stadium, starting a national airline, or acquiring sophisticated jet fighters can have more to do with politics then economics or defense. Above all, most developing nations want to escape the external dependence they associate with colonialism. In practical terms this desire translates into state policies aimed at economic self-reliance.

State intervention has taken three principal forms: etatism (state socialism), export promotion, and import substitution. Etatism involves an effort by the state to form a partnership with private capital with the aim of spurring and guiding economic development. Turkey in the interwar years and Mexico more recently are two prime examples of this strategy. Export-led growth is a strategy most often associated with Japan's "economic miracle." It has also been adopted and adapted by South Korea, Taiwan, Hong Kong, and Singapore. Import substitution is especially attractive in the early stages of industrialization. The United States followed this strategy in the early nineteenth century when it protected its infant industries. Ultimately, import substitution must be accompanied by export promotion because most countries do not have adequate internal markets to support sustained economic growth.

Development and Regime Type

Are some regime types more adept than others at implementing policies aimed at rapid economic development? Common sense and experience both suggest that regimes in which power and authority are centralized or concentrated are more effective at mobilizing society and dealing with conflict (most often by crushing opposition). Such regimes are sometimes called *mobilization systems*. They may be authoritarian or totalitarian in form. If the leadership fastens onto economic development as its supreme goal, a mobilization regime, by definition, is well equipped to do the job. By the same token, if the leaders set some other goal(s), such as military conquest or international prestige, they can divert resources and postpone purely economic priorities indefinitely (for example, Germany and Japan in the interwar period).

Democratic governments place social harmony and individual liberty above rapid economic development. They typically seek to accommodate competing interest groups. Public policy is the result of compromises cobbled together on an ad hoc basis rather than of rational plans predicted on clearly articulated goals. Regimes of this type are sometimes called *reconciliation systems*.

The conventional wisdom that mobilization regimes are more likely to succeed economically than reconciliation regimes has been seriously questioned in recent times. It may be true that in the early stages of economic development mobilization regimes can accomplish rapid growth; it now seems clear, however, that beyond a certain point, reconciliation regimes are at least as successful and sustainable as their authoritarian counterparts.

The Time Crunch

Whatever the type of regime in power, its leadership will face a dilemma. What is needed to ensure stability, in the long run, is a prosperous society in which the benefits of economic growth are widely enjoyed. The austerity policies urged on developing nations by the IMF are aimed at achieving this result. These policies, however, are often at odds with the short-run objectives of staying in power and avoiding destabilizing and disruptive social conflict. Cutting subsidies for food and other basic needs, for example, is one way to divert scarce resources from unproductive (but popular) social programs to growth-sustaining development projects. In countries where the government has done this (examples include Egypt, Sudan, Tunisia, Morocco, and Zaire), massive food riots have erupted, and austerity measures have had to be softened or rescinded to quell the unrest.

Latin American governments have faced a similar dilemma. For example, in 1985 Peru's newly elected president, Alan Garcia, blamed the country's economic and political problems (hyperinflation, widespread poverty, and a ferocious insurgency movement) on the IMF and the United States. And when Venezuela, one of South America's most stable democracies, became the scene of major riots in early 1989, the new president, Carlos Andres Perez, attributed them to the country's heavy foreign-debt burden and IMF-authored austerity.

Hence time is not always on the side of economic development. In poverty-stricken developing countries, urgent immediate needs are likely to take precedence over longer range goals and objectives. If the government decides to cut short-term consumption when many or most citizens live on the edge of starvation, the moral and political consequences are dire. But if the government takes care of basic human needs, there may be little or nothing left over for long-term investment. Even in affluent countries, high-consumption policies are always more popular than high-investment policies. More than a half century ago this tendency toward immediate gratification was noted by Alexis de Tocqueville, who considered it a defect peculiar to democratic governments. In truth, it may be a "defect" inherent in the very nature of the development process.

The Causes of "Underdevelopment"

Most experts agree that development is a complex phenomenon with many dimensions—economic, social, cultural, psychological, and political. Most probably agree as well that developing nations and regions have certain characteristics in common. For example, developing countries typically lack investment capital, have small domestic markets, depend on one or two cash crops (produced for export rather than local consumption), and lack infrastructure (schools, hospitals, roads, communications networks, and the like). There are other stereotypes: Their populations grow too fast, engage primarily in subsistence agriculture, and cannot read or write. They are, moreover, tied to tradition, village, and family; resistant to change; and mired in myth and superstition. They do not understand the idea of private property, and the profit motive is alien to them.

In contrast to the Madisonian model of constitutional democracy, developing countries are plagued by reinforcing rather than cross-cutting cleavages. As Mittleman has noted, "In most parts of the Third World, the receding colonial power sought to graft Western parliamentary and party institutions on to indigenous cultures, which are based on other historical realities." The result "often aggravated existing class and ethnic rivalries." Not surprisingly, spasmodic repression, accompanied by burgeoning bureaucracies in which loyalists are rewarded with government jobs, has been the pattern. The riots, insurgency, secessionist movements, and civil wars seemingly so endemic to the Third World are symptomatic of the popular discontent bred by these conditions.[19]

Developing nations are not, however, all alike, nor have their leaders all pursued the same ends, used the same means, or embraced the same strategies. There are three basic patterns. Some developing nations, such as the People's Republic of China, North Korea, Cuba, and Vietnam, have pursued egalitarian policies (equitable income distribution) more avidly than economic growth. Others, such as Brazil, Mexico, and Argentina, have pursued high-growth policies with scant regard for equality or equity. Finally, some have been able to achieve both high growth and a high general standard of living (equity). The shining example is Taiwan, but South Korea, Hong Kong, and Singapore also fall into this charmed category.

These patterns will be discussed in greater depth in Parts IV through VII. For now it is enough to note that the Third World encompasses scores of nations in four geographically and culturally distinct regions, all at different stages of economic and political development. Some experts now contend that a Fourth World, comprising the poorest of the poor, can be identified. By definition, Fourth World nations lack the resources needed for development. In practice, however, this distinction is difficult to make. Indeed, ''resources'' can be almost anything, and very few developing nations lack at least one vital resource, namely human beings.

Nations and Regions: The Challenge of Integration

In this chapter we have discussed the regional context of politics and the problems of nation-building, which cut across regional boundaries, particularly in the Third World. Despite noting similarities we have suggested that patterns vary not only from nation to nation, but also from region to region. Hence, the nation-building tasks and problems confronting most of sub-Saharan Africa are not identical to those facing most East European countries, and the development issues that are most pressing in Latin America are very different from those facing Western Europe.

The very idea of economic and political development may seem irrelevant to the technologically advanced nations of the West. But development is an ongoing, never-ending process, and the challenges of postindustrial development are widely recognized in countries like Great Britain, France, and the United States whose economic achievements were once the envy of the world. Some scholars assert that there are ''limits to growth,'' which many of the advanced industrial nations are approaching. The general thrust of their arguments is that failure to recognize these limits will lead to overdevelopment and eventually to social, economic, and political decline. The merits of this argument will not be explored here, but its proponents do raise an important question for students of comparative politics: What is the future of the industrial democracies? Have they exhausted their potential? Do affluent, mass-consumption societies face inevitable decline?

We will examine these questions in the next section. For now, we note that the nations of Western Europe are moving toward greater regional integration through the European Community. In the 1960s and 1970s the nations of Central and South America, Southeast Asia, and other regions or subregions took cautious first steps in this direction as well. In the late 1980s the United States and Canada moved toward a common market in North America. Finally, there are even rumors of an impending Western Pacific common market involving Japan and the ''four little dragons'' (South Korea, Taiwan, Hong Kong, and Singapore).

These and other initiatives around the globe at least hint at the possibility that the twenty-first century will be the age of regionalism, much as the nineteenth and twentieth centuries have been the age of nationalism. It is still too soon to predict how far attempts at regional integration will go. But one thing seems certain: Success in Western Europe will prompt efforts to duplicate that success in other regions. In politics, as in fashion, trends are often set by the rich and power-ful, and imitation is the sincerest form of flattery.

CONCLUSION

Political development is a universal phenomenon—it occurs in varying degrees and at differential rates of change in the most advanced (or modern) societies as well as in the most traditional (or least modern) societies. In the next chapters we begin our in-depth look at many of these societies.

STUDY QUESTIONS

1. What is nation-building (or state-building)?
2. What are the various theories and approaches in the study of political develop-ment? Which one(s) is (are) the most illuminating?
3. What is dependency theory? Is it valid?
4. What is the relationship between economic development and the state?
5. What are the causes of underdevelopment? What are some of the symptoms? Are the major causes internal or external? Are natural circumstances or human beings to blame?
6. Can the maladies of underdevelopment be treated? What prescriptions, if any, are likely to work on the causes and not merely the symptoms?

SUGGESTED READINGS

Almond, Gabriel and Coleman, James. *The Politics of Developing Areas*. Princeton, N.J.: Princeton, 1960.

Apter, David. *The Politics of Modernization*. Chicago: University of Chicago, 1965.

Banfield, Edward. *The Moral Basis of Backward Society*. New York: Free Press, 1958.

Caporaso, J. S., ''Dependence, Dependency, and Power in the Global System: A Structural and Behavioral Analysis,'' *International Organizations, 32*, (1) (Winter) 1978, pp. 14–43.

Chilcote, Ronald. *Theories of Development and Underdevelopment*. Boulder, Colo.: West-view, 1984.

Chilton, Stephen. *Defining Political Development*. Boulder, Colo.: Lynne Reinner, 1988.

Easton, David. *The Political System*. New York: Knopf, 1977.

Huntington, Samuel. *Political Order in Changing Societies*. New Haven, Conn.: Yale, 1968.

Jaguiribe, Helio. *Political Development: A General Theory and a Latin American Case Study*. New York: Harper, 1973.

Lerner, Daniel. *The Passing of Traditional Society: Modernizing the Middle East*. New York: Free Press, 1958.

McClelland, David. *The Achieving Society*. New York: Halstead, 1976.

Mittelman, James H. *Out from Underdevelopment*. New York: St. Martin's, 1988.

Palmer, Monte. *Dilemmas of Political Development*. 4th ed. Itasca, Ill.: Peacock, 1989.

Pye, Lucian. *Aspects of Political Development*. Boston: Little, Brown, 1966.

Rostow, W. W. *The Process of Economic Growth*. 2nd ed. New York: Norton, 1962.

NOTES

[1] See Thomas M. Magstadt and Peter M. Schotten, *Understanding Politics: Ideas, Institutions, and Issues* (New York: St. Martin's, 1988), Chap. 2, "The Nation-State," pp. 29–54.

[2] James H. Mittelman, *Out from Underdevelopment* (New York: St. Martin's, 1988), p. 22.

[3] Monte Palmer, *Dilemmas of Political Development*, 4th ed. (Itasca, Ill.: Peacock, 1989), p. 2.

[4] *World Development Forum 2*, Nov. 15, 1984.

[5] Plato, *The Republic of Plato*, Francis MacDonald Cornford, trans. (London: Oxford, 1945).

[6] Ibid., pp. 106–107.

[7] Stephen Chilton, *Defining Political Development* (Boulder, Colo.: Lynne Reinner, 1988).

[8] Palmer, op. cit., p. 10.

[9] John H. Herz, *International Politics in the Atomic Age* (New York: Columbia University, 1959).

[10] Melvin Richter, *The Political Theory of Montesquieu* (Cambridge, Mass.: Cambridge University, 1977), pp. 98–100.

[11] See, for example, W. W. Rostow, *The Stages of Economic Growth: A Non-Communist Manifesto*, 2nd ed. (London: Cambridge University, 1966). Rostow delineated five stages of growth: (1) traditional, (2) precondition for take-off, (3) take-off, (4) drive for maturity, and (5) high mass consumption. See also A. F. K. Organski, *The Stages of Political Development* (New York: Knopf, 1967).

[12] Robert A. Nisbet, *Social Change and History: Aspects of the Western Theory of Development* (New York: Oxford, 1969).

[13] Talcott Parsons, *The Social System* (New York: Free Press, 1964), especially pattern variables, pp. 46–51 and 58–67; see also Daniel Lerner, *The Passing of Traditional Society: Modernizing the Middle East* (New York: Free Press, 1958), pp. 47–52; Amatai Etzioni, *The Active Society* (New York: Free Press, 1968); David C. McClelland, *The Achieving Society* (New York: Halstead, 1976); Clifford Geertz, *Islam Observed* (New Haven, Conn.: Yale University, 1968), p. 107; and Edward Banfield, *The Moral Basis of Backward Society* (New York: Free Press, 1958).

[14] Lerner, op. cit., pp. 47–52.

[15] McClelland, op. cit., pp. 103–105.

[16] Banfield, op. cit., pp. 10–11, 83–101, 139, 155–158.

[17] Among the most highly respected developmental approaches in political science are the following: David Easton, *The Political System* (New York: Knopf, 1977) and "An Approach to the Analysis of a Political System," *World Politics*, April 1957; Gabriel Almond and James Coleman, *The Politics of the Developing Areas* (Princeton, N.J.: Princeton University, 1960); Gabriel Almond and G. Bingham Powell, *Comparative Politics: A Developmental Approach* (Boston: Little, Brown, 1966); Samuel Huntington, *Political Order in Changing Societies* (New Haven, Conn.: Yale University, 1973); Lucian Pye, *Aspects of Political Development* (Boston: Little, Brown, 1966).

[18] *Business Week*, Apr. 21, 1986.

[19] Mittleman, op. cit., p. 16.

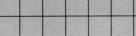

GREAT BRITAIN

Area: 94,247 square miles
Population: 57 million
Density per square mile: 606
Languages: English, Welsh, Gaelic
Literacy rate: 99%
Religions: Churches of England, Ireland,
Scotland (Presbyterian), and Wales;
Roman Catholic, Methodist,
Congregational, Baptist, Jewish
Monetary unit: pound sterling
GNP: (1988) $758 billion;
$13,329 per capita

FRANCE

Area: 211,208 square miles
Population: 56 million
Density per square mile: 266
Language: French
Literacy rate: 99%
Religion: Roman Catholic (76%)
Monetary unit: franc
GNP: (1987) $868 billion;
$15,500 per capita

GERMANY

Area: 137,777 square miles
Population: 78 million
Density per square mile: 566
Language: German
Literacy rate: 99%
Religions: Protestant, Roman Catholic
Monetary unit: Deutsche mark
GNP: (1988) West—$1.12 trillion;
$18,370 per capita
(1986) East—$188 billion;
$11,300 per capita

PART II

Western Europe

Chapter 4
The Western Political Heritage

During the heyday of the Cold War, Europe was divided into two parts—"Western Europe," rooted in classical Greek and Roman civilizations, and "Eastern Europe," a commingling of Slavic, Scandinavian, Mongolian, and Byzantine cultures. This division resulted from a specific set of circumstances, in particular the mistrust and enmity between the United States (the bastion of capitalism) and the Soviet Union (the citadel of communism).

In 1989, forty-plus years after the beginning of the Cold War, momentous events took place on the Continent, and the "two camp" conception of Europe began to fade. With the breaching of the Berlin wall, the rapid move toward German reunification, the toppling of Communist regimes in Eastern Europe, Gorbachev's allusion to a "common European house," and prospects for major conventional force reductions in Europe, the Cold War apparently is coming to an end. At the same time, however, the "North-South" split within the European Community (EC), the reemergence of the Balkan states as independent actors with potentially interdependent economies, and the presence of historic, geographic, and economic antecedents for a distinct Mediterranean region or subregion in Europe all point to the conclusion that (a) Europe in the twenty-first century may more appropriately be viewed as a single region with several subregions, and (b) future obstacles to the creation of a common European house are likely to appear in forms other than those associated with the Cold War.

The East European nations—Poland, Czechoslovakia, Hungary, Romania, Bulgaria, and Yugoslavia—are all engaged in sweeping reform movements aimed at ending decades of political repression, foreign (Soviet) domination, and (more recently) economic decline. In 1990 many of these countries held free elections, and the new governments vowed to end the rigid central planning system imposed by Stalin after World War II and to institute market reforms. Only time will tell whether these reforms will succeed, whether a new pattern of authoritarian rule will emerge, or whether a crazy-quilt of political forms will take shape in Eastern Europe. One thing seems certain: Stalinism is dead, and the era of Soviet hegemony is gone forever. The processes of change in Eastern Europe now appear to be irreversible. This does not mean, however, that Western-style political and economic pluralism is just around the corner. What it does mean is that Europe will no longer be artificially divided by an ideological "iron curtain."

This book is being written at this time of transition, and it is most tempting to treat the East and West European nations as a single region. But this would be premature. For a host of cultural, historical, economic, and psychological reasons,

Europe will continue to be divided into the "Roman" West and the "Slavic" East for years to come. Differences remain not only in language, history, and culture but also in living standards. Economically, Eastern Europe is more like the Third World than like the West. The division may become less important with the passage of time, however, particularly if Western Europe gives the new democratic governments of Eastern Europe easy access to their Common Market.

The similarities among contemporary West European nations are so striking that they can only be attributed to a certain cross-fertilization and overlapping of linguistic, cultural, religious, literary, and intellectual experiences. Today the most obvious of these similarities is democratic government. Another related similarity is that all embrace market-oriented capitalism as opposed to the state-centered economic planning long associated with Soviet-style command economies. Moreover, all boast large, well-educated, relatively affluent urban middle classes employed increasingly in the service sector (law, medicine, public administration, education, management, banking, and so on) as opposed to agriculture or manufacturing.

Urbanization and economic diversification throughout Western Europe have been accompanied by the growth of materialism and secularism. Reliance on human potential rather than on divine providence has been a salient feature of Western civilization since at least the Renaissance in the fifteenth century. Religion is still important to many, but it is no longer the chief determinant of public and private morality. Ever greater faith has been placed in the power of technological innovation to solve human problems and make life longer and better.

Western Europe also has a distinctive intellectual tradition. The Renaissance and Reformation, as well as the Enlightenment, belong almost exclusively to the West. These events, which were so formative in modern European history, rippled only the surface of Russian society, culture, and politics. The overthrow of czarist rule in 1917 brought to power a band of revolutionaries who espoused a Western ideology (Marxism), but the institutions that replaced czarism were far removed from the ideal of a liberal democracy inspired by the Enlightenment.

The broad patterns just noted are familiar to anyone who has grown up in a Western country. What is not familiar is how these patterns evolved, and why they are unique to the West. In the following section we will survey the main features of this evolution. Later in the book we will do the same for every region of the world and every cluster of historical and cultural experiences, in order to gain a better understanding of the context of politics in each.

Environmental Influences

The great peninsula of Western Europe is not separated from the continental interior by any obvious natural barrier; the topographic grain of the region runs east-west rather than north-south. A crescent of low mountains (the Carpathians), however, "present their convex front to the Russian plain in the form of steep slopes," while north of the Carpathians a vast plain extends to the Baltic Sea. "In this belt lies a huge morass, the Pripet Marsh, a barrier equal to or surpassing the mountains.'' Nonetheless, ''wide-open gateways'' of firm ground flank it.[1]

The significance of this geography for European history is something of a paradox. On the one hand, there has been intermittent communication and contact between the two parts of Europe—peninsular and interior—for many centuries; on the other hand, the parts developed along separate lines, even though Russia has imitated and borrowed from Western Europe in many areas. According to one expert:

> The distinction between the two worlds appears when the natural and cultural character of Europe is compared with that of interior Eurasia. . . . The marked contrast between typical European geography and the equally typical inland geography then appears. It follows that any division *line* drawn through the border zone is arbitrary. More properly the frontier is a belt through which run several kinds of transitions: the break between Roman-German culture and Greek-Slavic culture; the broad span where hill-bordered lowlands on or near salt water give way to featureless inland plains; the coarse versus fine mesh of transport routes; the dominance of continental over marine climate; the political boundary of Russia.[2]

For most of the modern era, Western Europe has been a kind of nursery in which new ideas and institutions in science, technology, and politics have germinated, grown to maturity, and spread, first to surrounding lands and peoples and then, through imitation or imposition by colonial administrators, far and wide.

> Beginning with very small areas, uniform in climate and resources, and isolated from neighbors, the western tradition has moved into larger spaces, adapted itself to varied climates and landforms, and learned to use a multiplicity of resources. In the process, isolation has given way to a worldwide net of communication. Possessing a unique combination of favorable natural conditions, Europeans maintained political dominance and economic leadership in the successive worlds of which they have been a part.[3]

Although the metaphor of Western Europe as nursery may overstate European influence and understate indigenous developments in other regions of the world, the concept holds more than a grain of truth. From the beginning of the great European explorations during the fifteenth-century Renaissance, to the ''Age of Imperialism,'' which coincided with the late stages of the Industrial Revolution in the nineteenth century, Europe made a deep imprint on every region of the world. Why did it display such enormous vigor during this protracted period? Could physical, geographic, or climatic factors have contributed to this burst of creative energy?

Western Europe does enjoy certain inherent advantages over most other regions of the world. Its climate displays an enviable variety of types, without climatic extremes. ''No area of equal size on earth is so favored in climate—both in its variety and in its suitability for human life under conditions of the present day.''[4] Its soils and climates are generally conducive to agriculture, but a great variety of minerals are also abundant:

Two of the three most critical soil fertilizers are present in large quantities, and the third can be manufactured from local resources. Rich coal fields occur from Scotland to Poland, and ample iron ores for steelmaking lie not far from coal. The Western economic order since the Industrial Revolution has been based on these two minerals.[5]

Northwestern Europe thus became the center of the Industrial Revolution. In particular, its coal deposits, rivers, and access to the sea were crucial. According to a scholar of the 1920s:

> Modern industry is based upon the use of coal and to a less [sic] degree on "white coal," or waterpower. Coal is necessary in the making of iron and steel and for the operation of the machines in factories. Since coal is bulky and expensive to transport, it is usually easier to bring raw materials that are to be converted into manufactured articles to the vicinity of the mines than vice versa. As a consequence, many of the great manufacturing centers, particularly those of Germany, England, and Belgium, cluster near the coal fields. . . .
>
> It is a very important fact that there is almost no coal at all in the Alpine-Mediterranean Region. This circumstance, perhaps no less than the reorientation of the world's trade routes to the Atlantic which followed the discovery of America and the sea route to the Indies, helps explain why the Mediterranean countries have not experienced the tremendous industrial development and the growth of huge cities so characteristic of Northwestern Europe.[6]

It was no accident, for example, that a half century ago twenty-seven of Great Britain's forty major cities were situated alongside coal deposits, and that eleven of Germany's forty-seven cities of 100,000 population were on coal beds.[7]

Rivers were important as a source of hydroelectric power, and both rivers and the sea as a means of commerce, communication, and transport. The main waterway of modern Europe has been along the Atlantic coast of the Continent rather than the Mediterranean. With only a few exceptions, the principal seaports are located on or near the mouths of rivers. Thus, "The accessibility which many districts of Northwestern Europe have acquired through their nearness to river and sea routes was a powerful stimulus to commerce, to movements of people, to the spread of institutions, and to the exchange of ideas for centuries before the Industrial Revolution.[8]

Historical and Cultural Factors

Western Europe is distinct from Russia and the Balkans not only in terms of geography and climate but also relative to history, culture, language, ethnicity, religion, and seminal intellectual developments. Throughout Western Europe, the Romance languages (those based on Latin, the language of the Roman Empire) predominate; in Russia and bordering areas, Slavic languages are predominant. The alphabets used in these two distinct linguistic families differ markedly, as do their rules of grammar, syntax, and the like.

French, Italian, Spanish, and Portuguese are more closely related to one another than to the languages of northwestern Europe (English, German, Dutch, the various Scandinavian tongues). All, however, have a common alphabet and Latin roots. Moreover, there has been much mutual borrowing among these languages, so that their vocabularies have many common derivatives and many similar (or identical) words.

As regards religion, all of Western Europe has been part of Christendom since the days of the Holy Roman Empire. Until the Reformation in the sixteenth century, Roman Catholicism was the universal religion. The Reformation was a revolt against Rome, not against Christianity. Quite the opposite: It was a revitalizing of Christianity as the one true faith. Luther, Calvin, Zwingli, and the other great church reformers were determined to rescue the church from a corrupt papacy. The Reformation, then, was a time of tumult and change, both spiritual and temporal, but it reaffirmed the dominance of Christianity in the moral and spiritual life of the West. It also, ironically, set the stage for the Scientific Revolution and the Age of Enlightenment, which led to the secularization prevalent in the modern era.

It would be a mistake to regard the Reformation as the sole, or even the primary, cause of secularization. One must instead look at the antecedents of the Reformation. Certainly the Renaissance and the subsequent ''Age of Exploration'' paved the way for the spirit of adventure, free inquiry, iconoclasm, and intellectual ferment that lay at the core of the Reformation.

The Renaissance, with its origins in Italy, was revolutionary in its implications. Why? Above all, because of its emphasis on human beings as the center of all things. Christianity stressed that divine providence sets the shape and course of history, the giants of the Renaissance (exemplified by Leonardo da Vinci in art, science, and technology; Michelangelo in art and architecture; and Machiavelli in political philosophy) believed in the surpassing powers of the human will and intellect.

The Renaissance and Reformation together fed into powerful new intellectual, economic, and political undercurrents that emerged in the form of mercantilism, the Scientific Revolution, the Age of Enlightenment, the Industrial Revolution, and most recently the Age of Imperialism.

Mercantilism refers to the means devised by England and France to deal with the economic challenge posed by Holland in the seventeenth century. As formulated in France under Colbert (Louis XIV's famous minister), mercantilism was a policy aimed at impeding or preventing importation of Dutch products by the imposition of high tariffs, bans on the use of third-country ships in foreign trade and commerce, and subsidies to one's own shippers and manufacturers. Mercantilism equated wealth with money and considered a country to be richer or poorer according to the size of its balance-of-trade surplus or deficit.[9] Mercantilism also reflected the desire to promote domestic producers and manufacturers (an early version of the ''infant industries'' development strategy).

In Holland, England, and France, mercantilism provided the impetus for the acquisition of colonial empires. The instruments of this early empire-building rivalry were the great merchant companies, notably the Dutch East India

Company and the English East India Company. (Later in the seventeenth century a French Company of the Indies was also established.) "It was the company, not its members, which conducted the business, sent out its ships—the great *East Indiamen*, bought and sold beyond the seas, and exercised rights of sovereignty in its colonial possessions by delegation from its own government."[10]

The urge to conquer new worlds in the sixteenth and seventeenth centuries was no less evident in domestic than in international economic affairs. The *Scientific Revolution*, as this period has come to be known, was a time of tremendous intellectual vitality. Leonardo da Vinci, Copernicus, Galileo, Kepler, Descartes, Francis Bacon, Robert Boyle, and Sir Isaac Newton gave new meaning to the humanistic impulses associated with the Renaissance. In little more than a century and a half, they revolutionized our understanding of the physical world and laid the foundations of the natural sciences, including physics, astronomy, chemistry, and biology. In so doing, they also laid the foundations of modernity, with all that this term implies for good or evil. In fine, they gave future generations the tools to conquer nature and they paved the way for the *secular humanism* of the present day—a philosophy that stresses the potential of humankind, using scientific as well as political means to solve social and economic problems and build a better world in the here and now.

The *Enlightenment* of the eighteenth century may be regarded as following naturally on the heels of the Scientific Revolution. And the Industrial Revolution developed side by side with the Enlightenment. The two had a kind of symbiotic relationship.

As an intellectual movement, the Enlightenment was "a significantly new way of looking at man and the world"—one that emphasized human reason over blind faith.[11] The morality linked to Enlightenment ideas and ideals was readily identifiable in the Judeo-Christian tradition and the ethical systems of Greek and Roman antiquity: the Golden Rule of the Old Testament, the Golden Mean of the Greek philosophers, the emphasis on honesty and other conventional virtues. Two elements of Roman Catholic dogma, however, were rejected. One was the role of the holy sacraments as the path to salvation; the other was the importance of ascetism, self-deprivation, and resistance to temptation (broadly defined as worldly pleasures).

In place of the notion that one must endure suffering and self-sacrifice to get to heaven, Enlightenment thinkers developed the doctrine of "ethical hedonism," which held that ordinary human desires were natural and good, not something to be ashamed of or denied. The orthodox Christian teaching of evil inherent in human beings (the doctrine of original sin) was replaced by a belief in innate goodness.

> The ultimate dream of the Enlightenment thinkers, although they disagreed on many points and seldom set forth their aspirations for the future in a fully explicit picture, focused on a world without conflict, without harshness, with men of intelligence and goodwill working independently, each for his own welfare, yet all together for common interests as well.[12]

The French *philosophes*—most notably Montesquieu, Voltaire, Diderot, and Rousseau—set about doing for the social sciences what the giants of the Scientific Revolution did for the natural sciences. They emphasized the empirical world (fact and experience) and sought the truth about human nature and society through introspection. By this method the *philosophes* developed trenchant critiques of established social values and political institutions. Their overriding aim, however, was not to disparage existing customs and beliefs but, in Jeremy Bentham's felicitous phrase, to seek "the greatest good for the greatest number."

Politically, the *philosophes* seem surprisingly moderate (and modern) by today's standards. In general they did not advocate anything so radical as the dismantling of the nation-state system or even the overthrow of Europe's absolute monarchs. Instead they envisioned a new social order in which the rule of law bound rulers and ruled alike, and all citizens were guaranteed equal rights. They did not favor a leveling type of economic equality or common ownership of property. In fact, they seldom called for abolition of noble titles and ranks, but they did favor withdrawal of aristocratic powers and privileges.

The reader will recognize in the prescription of the *philosophes* the general outline of liberal democracy as it now exists throughout Western Europe. But the transformation the rational thinkers of the eighteenth century sought, though temperate in its ends and means, was brought about on the Continent only after protracted civil strife. Appropriately enough, the first European upheaval occurred in France.

The Revolutionary Tradition

The French Revolution of 1789 was the product of complex social, economic, and political difficulties. It was not the inevitable result of the intellectual dissent associated with the Enlightenment. It began as a rebellion of the nobility against what this class regarded as unfair and onerous taxation imposed by King Louis XVI. The execution of this monarch was a turning point in French (and European) history. The revolution progressed through several stages. First a limited, constitutional monarchy was created by charter. Then the monarchy was abolished altogether. Next radical Jacobins, led by Maximilian Robespierre, set about creating a "Republic of Virtue"—a thinly veiled tyranny run by ideological zealots with a vision of a utopian society. In the Orwellian politics of this phase, the Revolution turned bloody and bizarre. Opponents of the Jacobins were sent to the guillotine in droves; prices of essentials were set by the state; public revenue and supplies were obtained by ruthless requisitioning (payment was made in inflated paper currency); and mass conscription provided France's mushrooming armies with a steady influx of recruits.

The "fever" stage of the French Revolution did not last long: it soon gave way to the "Thermidorean reaction." The Thermidoreans rejected the idea of popular government (they saw it as synonymous with mob rule) and the idea of absolute monarchy based on a social system rooted in heredity and privilege.

Under the guise of republicanism, they set up an oligarchical mechanism known as the Directory. The Thermidorean regime lasted about five years and then gave way to the personalistic dictatorship of Napoleon Bonaparte.

The twists and turns of the French Revolution—and its ultimate failure—make for a fascinating study in themselves. The important point here is that this upheaval was a presentiment of the far-reaching demands for political liberalization that would accompany the social and economic changes wrought in eighteenth- and nineteenth-century Europe by a revolution of a different sort.

The Industrial Revolution and Its Consequences

The rise of liberalism in nineteenth-century Europe was facilitated by the application of science to production. The new economic frontiers being opened could best be explored and exploited by parliamentary government, or so it seemed. At the same time, new technologies and the factory system they spawned had enormous socioeconomic implications. The emergence of an urban, industrial class of wage laborers transformed the structure of previously rural, agriculturally based, aristocratic societies, with consequences that could hardly have been imagined at the time.

The use of mechanical energy in manufacturing as a means to increase labor productivity was a key feature of the Industrial Revolution. Textile manufacture and mining were the first industrial sectors to be mechanized, with all others following. One of the first social consequences was the exploitation of labor (including that of children) for profit; another was the concentration of labor. In time this concentration precipitated new forces and formations in Western European politics.

The widespread industrial application of mechanical energy provided an impetus for construction or refurbishing of roads and canals. The availability of such energy revolutionized the modes of transportation and communication. It also made farming far more efficient and productive than previously, even as farming became vastly less labor intensive.

Today we can see the results of the Industrial Revolution, good and bad, all around us. Big cities, elaborate highway systems, mammoth shopping malls, a depopulated countryside, agricultural surpluses, air and water pollution, urban sprawl, traffic congestion, and high crime rates—these are just a few of its economic and social consequences.

Along with socioeconomic changes came changes in political thinking—in particular, the rise of liberalism. This philosophy represented a middle way between the extreme egalitarianism of the Jacobins and the inherited wealth, power, and privilege of the old aristocratic order. It was ideally suited for the emerging middle class for whom liberty ranked above equality in the hierarchy of political values. Politically, liberalism decried arbitrary and repressive rule, press censorship, laws conferring special privilege on hereditary aristocracies, and discrimination against individuals on the basis of race or religion. Economically, it stressed property rights and other middle-class interests.

Following the teachings of Adam Smith, Thomas Malthus, and David Ricardo, nineteenth-century liberals embraced the view that free competition among nations and individuals, unrestrained by tariffs and monopolies, would inevitably produce the greatest prosperity for the largest number; that unemployment, hunger, and deprivation were nature's way of regulating population growth; and that wages are determined not by capitalists seeking to maximize profits and minimize costs but by an "iron law" of supply and demand. In theory, wages must neither fall below the subsistence level nor rise to a level at which the toiling masses increase in number so rapidly that the labor market is glutted (thus driving down wages to the subsistence level). How provident for the budding capitalists of the day!

Because liberalism represented rather narrow economic interests (by contemporary standards nineteenth-century liberalism was, in fact, stiffly conservative), advocates of democracy and republicanism stepped forward (in England they were called radicals!). And as the Industrial Revolution came of age, the working class also came of age. For the champions of this underclass, "bourgeois" democracy was too cautious and too compatible with capitalism. Charles Fourier, Louis Blanc, Robert Owen, and of course Karl Marx considered socialism the answer.

Socialism is an ideology that views private ownership of the means of production as the root of all evil in society. It disdains the profit motive and advocates extreme equality in the distribution of material goods. It takes an optimistic view of human nature and blames greed, envy, corruption, and crime on injustices built into the nature of capitalistic society. Remove the social causes of antisocial behavior and domestic tranquility will surely follow.

While liberalism, republicanism, and socialism were vying for the allegiance of newly emerging social forces in Great Britain and on the Continent, the advocates of conservatism were trying to preserve traditional values and protect the old order. The most important (and prescient) of the conservative thinkers was Edmund Burke (1729–1797). In his book *Reflections on the French Revolution*, written in 1790, Burke warned that nations that discard customs, beliefs, and institutions rooted in the past in their endeavor to build a perfect society in the future risk chaos and political catastrophe. No doubt the victims of the Jacobin terror would have agreed.

Against the background of the advancing Industrial Revolution, these crosscurrents—liberalism, republicanism, socialism, and conservatism—competed for primacy in Western Europe during the nineteenth century. They continue to compete there today.

Social Class and Politics

As the foregoing discussion suggests, the political spectrum in Europe is much broader and more diversified than in the United States. The American students are often astonished by the range of the spectrum. Further, our conventional American understanding of "class" can be misleading when applied in the European setting. There, social class has played a major role in defining ideological positions and creating political parties. To a much greater extent than in the United States, class consciousness is a motive force in politics, and ideological divisions are hardly less important in election campaigns and outcomes than more pragmatic policy differences.

Historically, European political parties have reflected the evolving class structure of European society. Center-right parties (the Christian Democrats in West Germany, the Gaullists and neo-Gaullists in France, and the Tories [Conservatives] in Great Britain) have represented conservative farming and business interests—the middle class. The far-left Communist has represented the working class and intellectuals. Center-left parties (notably the Social Democrats and Socialists) have sought broad popular appeal among both blue-collar and white-collar classes as well as among enlightened elements in the business sector. Center-right parties have sought to broaden their political base and often support (or do not oppose) ''welfare state'' policies of the kind most conservative U.S. Republicans consider anathema. Social Democratic parties are ideologically similar to our Democratic party, but tend to be oriented more to the left.

Why would some Europeans identify with the Communist party? First, throughout Europe this party historically has fought for the rights of workers, as have the Socialists and the Social Democrats. Second, in World War II the Communists generally put up the strongest resistance to the Nazis and Fascists, and many voters in France and Italy, including non-Communists, showed their appreciation by voting for Communist party candidates in the first elections held after the war. Third, the Communist parties of Europe are not subversive or revolutionary organizations. In most cases they disavow violence and participate in elections like any responsible political party. Nonetheless, Communist parties have fallen on hard times in Europe, both East and West. The reasons are not difficult to discern: (a) The industrial work force, the Communists' main constituency, has dwindled in proportion to service-sector jobholders in recent decades; (b) throughout Western Europe measures protecting workers from exploitation or abuse at the hands of profit-minded ''capitalists'' are in force; and (c) the Communist parties have failed to broaden their base or build lasting coalitions with other parties.

Two other examples will suffice to illustrate the class character of many European political parties. In Great Britain, the Labour party emerged as the champion of the working class around the turn of the last century. The party was closely linked to the trade union movement from the start (it still is). The absence of a significant Marxist party in Great Britain is due partly to the rise of the Labour party and partly to the fact that the British ruling elite pursued relatively progressive policies, making both economic and political concessions to workers. On the Continent, Socialist and Communist parties competed with each other (and with Social Democratic parties) for the allegiance of the workers.

The Christian Democratic party in West Germany exemplifies another ideological strand in European politics. Throughout Europe, religion has long been a politically potent force. In Germany both Roman Catholics and Protestants historically have viewed Marxism with alarm, in part because of its atheistic bent. At the same time, Christian Democrats, as the name implies, are strong advocates of democracy and free enterprise. Hence, Christian Democrats represent a coalition of middle-class elements (farming, business, banking, and the professions) and working-class people for whom religion is, or at least was, more important than bread-and-butter issues. Today, with the fading of the "Communist threat," the religious dimension of politics in West Germany is no longer of great significance. Instead, both Christian Democrats and Social Democrats are essentially centrist parties, the former stressing free enterprise and the latter advocating welfare state measures aimed at sharing the nation's considerable wealth more equitably.

Finally, new problems have produced new parties, the best example being the Greens. Green parties sprang up throughout Western Europe in the 1960s and 1970s in response to a growing fear of nuclear war and nuclear accidents (like the one that did happen in 1986, in Chernobyl, in the Soviet Ukraine). In the 1970s and 1980s the Greens became increasingly concerned with environmental pollution. In West Germany, where they have had some electoral success, they continue to oppose nuclear weapons and nuclear power plants but have begun to focus more and more on air and water pollution. Their support is drawn largely from the universities—both professors and students—and from white-collar workers. Their main opponents are farmers (who use large quantities of pesticides and chemical fertilizers), industrialists, bankers, and developers (who tend to place commercial gain ahead of environmental protection). Green parties have also appeared in Eastern Europe and the Soviet Union in recent years.

Imperialism and the European System

The second half of the nineteenth century is often called the *Age of Imperialism*, for at this time began the second wave of European colonial expansion. Earlier in the century there was disillusionment with empires and colonies, no doubt partly due to successful revolutions in the Americas against England, Spain, and Portugal. In addition, the industrialization taking place diverted attention from external expansion to internal development, and the new emphasis on free trade appeared to remove much of the rationale for global empire-building. A famous British prime minister, Benjamin Disraeli, expressed the tenor of the times in 1852. "These wretched colonies," he said, "will all be independent too in a few years and are a millstone around our necks."

As industry grew, however, Europe's economic and political leaders began to seek new sources of raw materials and new markets for their products. After 1870 free trade gave way to protectionist policies, and soon began a race for new colonies. Theories defending colonial expansion were numerous. Alfred T. Mahan's geopolitical concepts were used to "prove" that great powers could not survive without overseas possessions. Charles Darwin's concept of the survival of the fittest was used to "prove" that colonialism was in accordance with the inexorable laws of nature. Rudyard Kipling wrote about the "white man's burden" (to spread civilization to a benighted world). Even President McKinley claimed that God had spoken to him on the eve of the Spanish-American War (1898), commissioning the United States to take the Philippines and to Christianize "our brown brothers."

By the end of the nineteenth century all of Asia and Africa had been colonized. Even China had lost its sovereign status: It was subjugated through a series of "unequal treaties" that gave the various European powers rights and prerogatives. Africa in 1914 was under the colonial sway of no fewer than seven European nations—Belgium, France, Germany, Great Britain, Italy, Portugal, and Spain.

Paradoxically, as Europe approached the zenith of its power it was also reaching the end of its preeminence in world affairs. For centuries the international system had been synonymous with the European system. Since the Treaty of Westphalia in 1648, the rulers of Europe had recognized the existence of a "balance of power" system that preserved at least a modicum of order and prevented the hegemony of any one state over the others. This system resulted from shared values forged over the centuries. In 1871, Edward Gibbon, author of *The Decline and Fall of the Roman Empire*, proposed:

> . . . to consider Europe as one great republic, whose various inhabitants have attained almost the same level of politeness and cultivation. The balance of power will then continue to fluctuate, and the prosperity of our own or the neighboring kingdoms may be alternately exalted or depressed; but these events cannot essentially injure our general state of happiness, the system of arts, and law, and the manners which so advantageously distinguish, above the rest of mankind, the Europeans and their colonies.[13]

During the heyday of the European balance-of-power era, many of the great thinkers made implicit reference to the intellectual and moral foundations that undergirded a de facto political unity. For example, Fenelon noted, "Christendom forms a kind of general republic which has its common interests, fears, and precautions"; Rousseau asserted, "The nations of Europe form among themselves an invisible nation . . ."; and Vattel, the great Enlightenment philosopher of international law, wrote that "Europe forms a political system, a body where the whole is connected by the relations and different interests of nations inhabiting this part of the world. . . ."[14] In sum, the fuel that kept "the motor of the balance of power moving," according to this thesis, "is the intellectual and moral foundation of Western civilization, the intellectual and moral climate within which the protagonists of eighteenth-century society moved and which permeated all their thought and action."[15]

Beyond a common world view, the main features of the European balance-of-power model can be briefly summarized as follows:

1. Five to ten significant state actors are present at any given time.
2. Flexible alliances—state actors are pragmatic and unencumbered by ideological baggage.
3. Limited objectives—state actors do not pursue goals that threaten the existence of other states.

4. Limited means—strategies, tactics, and armaments employed in pursuit of national interests are circumscribed by both the state of technology and moral constraints.

5. A keeper (or holder) of the balance—as an island power aloof from the affairs of the Continent, England was ideally situated to play this role.

Ironically, the demise of this eurocentric international system was hastened and facilitated by the globalization brought about by European imperialism. In the years leading up to World War I, the European system showed signs of decrepitude: Alliances turned rigid, an unrestrained arms race occurred, ideological divisions sharpened, and nationalism spread. After the war, power shifted dramatically from Europe to North America and Asia. Europe was no longer ascendant, and the European system was a shambles.

The new League of Nations, designed by U.S. President Woodrow Wilson, was proposed as an alternative to nationalism and the European balance-of-power system. Although it never worked, it prefigured the emergence of a new global system in which the United States and Japan (later the United States and Soviet Russia) were the major non-European powers.

The Totalitarian Interlude

One other legacy has shaped the political landscape of Europe in the twentieth century: totalitarianism. A left-wing ideology, Marxism-Leninism, triumphed in Russia in 1917, and a right-wing ideology, Fascism, gained ascendancy in Italy a few years later. But it was in Germany in the 1920s and 1930s that the battle lines between extremist ideologies of the right and left were drawn most sharply and fatefully.

Germany's defeat in World War I was humiliating, and harsh peace terms were imposed. In 1919 Germany was forced by the Treaty of Versailles to accept a "war guilt" clause—in effect an admission of responsibility and liability for the death and destruction caused by the war. The treaty assessed heavy reparations and indemnities against Germany and called for permanent and unilateral German disarmament.

Understandably, this treaty was never popular in Germany. Nor was the Weimar Republic, which emerged after the collapse of the German monarchy in 1918 and carried the stigma of Versailles. But it was the draconian economic burdens imposed by the treaty that proved to be the undoing of the Weimar government and the making of Adolf Hitler's Nazi party.

In the early 1920s, hyperinflation hit Germany and left the middle class impoverished. The worldwide stock market crash of 1929 was the coup de grace. Foreign banks called in their loans to Germany, and a wave of protectionism brought international trade to a near standstill. Depression spread across the industrialized countries, and unemployment grew to epidemic proportions. In the chaos and despair that ensued, extremism found fertile soil. Germany became a hothouse for radical ideologies, in particular for National Socialism.

National Socialism had much in common with other extreme right-wing (fascist) ideologies. It was ultranationalistic, glorifying the German "Volk" as a chosen people and enshrining a mythical "Volksgeist" (popular spirit) as the force that defined, unified, and guided the German nation. Among its highest values were loyalty to the leader, obedience to authority, and courage in the face of danger. The Nazis glorified power; for true believers violence was a virtue, not a vice, and war would bring triumph rather than tragedy.

Hitler came to power legally; indeed his Nazi party had a larger popular following in the early 1930s than any of its competitors. The Nazi leader was popular in part because he told the German people what they wanted to hear. For example, he attributed Germany's defeat in World War I not to German failings but to a stab in the back by Communists and Jews (he tended to equate the two). He also pandered to German prejudices, in particular to anti-Semitism. Jews became a convenient scapegoat for nearly everything that was wrong with German society. In sum, National Socialism was a doctrine of hatred, prejudice, violence, and revenge.

Such dark sentiments were not confined to Germany. The roots of European Fascism were in Italy, and the branches reached far and wide. Fascism triumphed, in a relatively mild form, in Spain in the 1930s. It also took hold in Eastern Europe; fascist regimes in Hungary, Romania, and Bulgaria collaborated with Hitler in the early stages of World War II. Even where Fascism failed to become dominant, its sympathizers occasionally made their presence felt. In southern France, for instance, the Vichy Regime headed by Marshal Petain collaborated with Hitler during the war. Finally, a militaristic, expansionist, and fanatically nationalistic regime closely resembling the fascist model came to power in Japan in the 1930s.

War and Revolution: An Ambiguous Legacy

Critics of the European balance-of-power system are wont to call it the "war system." If its purpose was to prevent war and bloodshed, they argue, it failed miserably. Wars have been a recurring phenomenon in Europe since the nation-state system emerged from the morass of the Middle Ages.

Defenders of the European system argue that in the absence of a balancing mechanism wars would likely have been more frequent and less restrained. They point out that before this century (when the classic balance-of-power system broke down), wars were generally limited in scope if not in duration. By contrast, several all-out wars have been fought in the twentieth century, suggesting that once the old European order collapsed there was nothing equally efficacious to take its place.

Wherever the truth may lie, one thing is certain: War has played a major role in shaping the modern history of Western Europe. As we have already seen, revolution—the domestic equivalent of war—has also been an integral part of European history during the past two centuries. The unmistakable conclusion is that collective violence is a political tradition in Europe, Christianity and the humanizing influences of the Renaissance and the Enlightenment notwithstanding.

The implications of this dark side of Europe's heritage are far from obvious. One could easily assume that a violent history predisposes individuals or societies to violence. But this is not necessarily the case. Indeed, the cataclysmic events that have torn Europe asunder in this century could just as well have the opposite effect: to make succeeding generations determined not to repeat the mistakes of their elders.

Similarly, the nations of Western Europe have firsthand experience with the burdens of imperialism and the pitfalls of unrestrained nationalism. It may be that these lessons will be forgotten (or that they were never properly learned). From the vantage point of the 1990s, however, it appears that Western Europeans, chastened by the sanguinary episodes of their recent past, are determined to find a different pathway to the future.

World War II sealed the fate of the European system and, for a time at least, relegated the former great powers of Europe to second-rate status. As a result of two devastating wars on the Continent, France, Germany, and Great Britain—today the core countries of Western Europe—were forced to turn to the United States for succor and security. The Marshall Plan and the North Atlantic Treaty Organization, two American initiatives, symbolized the decline and fall of Western Europe on the world stage.

As we shall see in the following chapters, obituaries for Western Europe were premature. The recovery of the countries on the Continent, highlighted by twin economic miracles in West Germany and Italy; the resurgence of freedom and democracy; the integration of national economies into a single trading bloc called the European Community (popularly known as the Common Market); and the recent democratization movements in Eastern Europe have spurred a dramatic revival and set the stage for the emergence of a third superpower.

Case Studies: The United Kingdom, France, and Germany

In the late 1980s, the United Kingdom, France, and Germany had a combined population of more than 191 million and a combined gross national product just shy of $3 trillion. These three countries form the inner core of the European Community, which is the world's largest trading bloc. In addition, they are the major West European military powers: France and Great Britain boast their own nuclear weapons, and West Germany has been the key to the West's major collective security structure, the North Atlantic Treaty Organization.

Great Britain

Roughly the size of Oregon, Great Britain (also called the United Kingdom) is a relatively small island nation that has played a disproportionately large role in modern European history. The distance from the northern tip of Scotland to the southern coast of England is slightly less than 600 miles. Because Great Britain is long and narrow, the ocean is never very far away; even in the so-called Midlands, the coast is less than a two-hour drive. (By contrast, the Nebraska ''midlands'' are a two-*day* drive from either coast!)

The United Kingdom comprises four distinct regions and national groups: England in the center, Scotland in the north, Wales in the south, and Northern Ireland. By far the majority of the population lives in England (about 47 million, or 84 percent of the total). Given the small land mass involved, Great Britain is one of the most densely populated countries in the world—the density is greater than India's and ten times that of the United States. In England proper there are more than 900 people per square mile, 50 more than Japan. As we shall see in Chapter 6, overcrowding is now a fact of life that has serious implications for politics and public policy.

The political, financial, and cultural center of Great Britain is London (in this respect few nations are more highly ''centralized''). With a population in excess of 7 million, London is among the largest cities in the world. Not only is London the capital, but most of the major banks, corporations, newspapers, and television networks are located there. So too are the British equivalents of Wall Street, Broadway, and Hollywood. Finally, most of Britain's most famous historical and cultural landmarks (and tourist attractions)—Buckingham Palace, the Tower of London, Westminster Abbey, Big Ben, the British Parliament, St. Paul's Cathedral—are in London.

The historical domination of Great Britain by England and of England by London would presumably have created strong pressures toward homogenization, and can easily give rise to the impression that the British people are, in fact, all alike; that there is an extremely high degree of social harmony; and that, whatever political problems the nation might have, disunity is not one of them. All of these are false. Although English is spoken throughout the country and the political system is a unitary one, each of the four regions comprising Great Britain has its own identity, including language, history, customs, and folkways. There is no large non-white minority in Great Britain, but the influx of immigrants from former British colonies has led to racial tensions and tighter restrictions on immigration in recent times.

Great Britain's storied political stability derives in part from its geography. Separated from the Continent by the English Channel, its internal boundaries have changed little for centuries. Wales has belonged to England since the thirteenth century and was formally united with England in 1535; Scotland was joined to England in 1707; Ireland accepted union with England in 1800. Religious differences (Ireland is Roman Catholic, England is Anglican) and economic disparities made the marriage of Great Britain and Ireland unworkable: in 1922, following years of bloody civil war, Ireland, minus the six northeastern counties of Ulster (also known as Northern Ireland), became independent. (The majority of Ulster's population is Protestant, but a militant Roman Catholic minority has been fighting for a reunited Ireland.)

Historically speaking, the absence of frequent boundary changes means that Great Britain has in general avoided the destabilizing effects of having to digest new chunks of territory or assimilate new populations. Equally, problems arising from the presence of disaffected or displaced minorities have been relatively few and far between. These internal circumstances, combined with favorable external circumstances, have created an environment conducive to the comparatively peaceful evolution of the British political system from a monarchy to a parliamentary democracy.

Externally, the English Channel, a mere 20 miles wide at its narrowest point, has played a major role in shaping British political history. For centuries it was a geographic barrier to invasion (the last successful invasion was the Norman Conquest in 1066). It also enabled England to remain aloof from many of the conflicts on the Continent. England's advantageous geopolitical position meant that the British Crown could act as the "keeper of the balance," choosing when (and when not) to get involved in the game of power politics on the Continent.

Because the threat of invasion was minimal, the British never had to maintain a large standing army and the military was never a serious threat to civilian rule. Instead, Great Britain concentrated on building a powerful naval force, which enabled it to dominate the seaways in the eighteenth and nineteenth centuries. One consequence of the "small army, large navy" system was that the absolute power of the monarchy was never so absolute in England as on the continent. Navies, unlike armies, are useful only against *external* challenges. Internally, the British monarchy had to negotiate power.

Great Britain's geography thus goes far toward explaining its historic rise to economic prowess. A strong maritime tradition and an auspicious location at Europe's gateway to the North Atlantic placed England in an ideal position to establish a foothold in the New World. The opening of new Atlantic trade routes made Great Britain a major international financial and commercial center. The need to protect these routes in both war and peace in turn provided every incentive to build a strong navy. Sea power made possible the growth of a colonial empire, which counteracted any temptation to lapse into the isolationism of an island fortress.

Even so, the British have traditionally been self-reliant and independent in both domestic and foreign affairs, setting their own agenda and viewing the entanglements on the Continent with a mixture of disinterest and disdain. This tradition of aloofness helps to explain why Great Britain did not become a member of the Common Market until 1973, fifteen years after it was formed. Furthermore, it explains why the British people continue to be wary of the Common Market and question whether the benefits of membership outweigh the burdens. Very likely this issue will stir controversy in British politics for years; simultaneously, the current construction of a tunnel under the English Channel will be at least a symbol of the tie between Great Britain and the Continent.

Another legacy of Britain's strong maritime tradition is an attachment to the doctrine of free trade. Tariffs were steadily reduced in Great Britain, and by the middle of the nineteenth century British agriculture was largely unprotected. The existence of overseas colonies, British naval supremacy, and the cost-effectiveness of oceanic transport encouraged the importation of food, and this in turn freed up domestic resources for industrialization. Today the United Kingdom is highly dependent on agricultural imports.

Not surprisingly, the British have also long paid close attention to their balance of payments. Imports of food must be balanced by export of manufactured goods; fluctuations in exchange rates, domestic inflation, foreign competition, and changes in consumer habits at home and abroad can all have serious political and economic ramifications in a country so deeply enmeshed in the international economy. If British industrial goods lose their competitive edge, the impact on the economy (and on the consumer) will be profound. Similarly, if the price of food imports increases, the impact will be direct and immediate. Thus, whether the Conservative or Labour party is in power, governmental intervention in the economy—through price-and-wage regulation, budget measures, taxation, currency controls, and the like—is likely to be needed, if for no other reason than to manage external trade and maintain adequate foreign reserves.

British history has clearly been influenced by geography, but it also exerts a force of its own on contemporary British politics and government. The "British" are not, as one might suppose, descendants of the island's original inhabitants. Rather, their ancestors were Angles, Saxons, and Jutes from the mainland (more precisely, Germany) who invaded the island after the Romans withdrew and seized it from the Celtic Britons (ancestors of the Welsh, Scots, and Irish).

Until the eleventh century Great Britain was invaded repeatedly—after the Angles, Saxons, and Jutes came the Danes. In 1066 William the Conqueror invaded from Normandy (known as the Norman Conquest), established a monarchy, and introduced the feudal system. Under this system, a hereditary nobility was granted certain rights and privileges (entitlement to land, access to the royal court, and others) in exchange for loyalty to the king and acceptance of various duties and obligations (paying taxes, defending the realm, keeping the peace). Disputes over these rights and duties were settled in a council of lords convened by the king. From these humble origins evolved the concepts of constitutionalism and parliamentary government.

The years 1100 to 1135 saw a great expansion of royal administrative power during the reign of Henry I. In 1215 the Magna Carta was signed at Runnymede. Contrary to popular opinion, this document had nothing to do with government by the people. Rather, it was the instrument by which the barons enforced their rights under feudal contract (or "magna carta") with King John. From this point forward, the lower nobility had the right to be represented in decisions (especially tax levies) directly affecting them. As early as 1265 ("De Montfort's Parliament"), townspeople were also given the right to representation in the great council (which was called Parliament by this time).

But the right to be represented is not the same as the right of consent. The king was not obligated to heed the wishes of any of his subjects, including the nobility, and he did not have to convene the Parliament at regular intervals. Nor were the representative bodies truly representative—the idea of popular elections was still centuries away. Representatives of commoners were not allowed to meet with the king and nobles or take any direct part in decision making. By the

fifteenth century (the reign of Henry V), commoners were able to elect a "speaker" and to put their views in the form of a petition to the monarch (an early version of a legislative bill).

Hence, in the beginning Parliament was a kind of royal sounding board and advisory council. It was never intended to be a check on the monarch's power and authority. In time, the right of barons to approve taxes became the right of Parliament to originate all revenue and spending bills. Along the way there were occasional battles between the Parliament and the king—none more fateful than the one begun in 1629 when Charles I dissolved the Parliament and proceeded to rule as a tyrant. In 1650 Oliver Cromwell led a revolution that overthrew the monarchy (Charles I was beheaded) and established a short-lived republic.

The issue of religion was also a factor in the revolution. The Anglican Church had replaced the Roman Catholic Church as the established church in England more than a century earlier, but controversy over the break with Rome still raged. When James II, a Roman Catholic, tried to revisit the religious question, forcing a showdown between the Parliament and the monarchy, he was deposed in a bloodless coup. Rather than abolish the monarchy, Parliament invited the king's Protestant daughter, Mary, and her husband, William, to share the Crown. By accepting, they implicitly recognized the supremacy of Parliament. Since 1689, no British monarch has challenged this constitutional principle.

In the nineteenth century the franchise was gradually extended. Whigs (liberals) and Tories (conservatives) evolved from factions in the seventeenth century into full-fledged political parties. Finally, the idea of "cabinet" rule, in which the leaders of the majority party in Parliament form a kind of board of directors (called the "government") to set policy and manage the bureaucracy, emerged as an integral part of the British constitutional system.

France

The largest country in Western Europe (about the size of Texas), France is located in a pivotal position on the Continent. Although sharing a common border with six other countries (Spain, Italy, Switzerland, Germany, Luxembourg, and Belgium), France is nonetheless geographically well defined and well protected (except, as we shall see, in one border zone). To the north is the English Channel; to the west the Bay of Biscay; to the southwest the Pyrenees Mountains; to the south the Mediterranean; and to the southeast the Alps.

In the northeast, however, France has often engaged in confrontation and conflict with Germany over territories along the southern Rhine River (particularly in a resource-rich region known as the Saar) and in Alsace-Lorraine. There are no insurmountable barriers to invasion in this region. Even Belgium, which never posed a direct military threat, was a geostrategic liability for France before World War II because Belgium could (and did) serve as a springboard for German armed aggression.

Internally, France has no formidable geographic barriers to communication and transportation. A well-developed network of navigable rivers, canals, and railways, combined with a compact geography and natural land and sea boundaries, has contributed to a strong sense of national identity and a high degree of political and economic integration. French is the national language and Roman Catholicism is the religion of the overwhelming majority of the church-going population.

Even so, the French are far from homogeneous. Customs, attitudes, and opinions vary significantly from region to region. Historically, the south of France was heavily influenced by Roman civilization, the north by Germanic culture. Economically, too, there is an important division: the south (and west) is rural, conservative, and relatively poor, whereas the north (and east) is industrially developed, growth oriented, and relatively prosperous.

France has remained a nation of shopkeepers, artisans, and small farmers longer than most of the Western industrial democracies. Although the actual numbers of self-employed producers and proprietors in traditional sectors of the economy have declined sharply since the 1950s, the vaunted individualism of the French citizenry lingers on.

Paris is to France as London is to Great Britain. The Paris metropolitan region has a population of 10 million, nearly one-fifth of France's total population. Even more than in Great Britain, Paris dominates the political, economic, cultural, and intellectual life of the country. It is the banking center and industrial hub of the nation. More than one-third of all commercial and financial profits are earned in Paris, which also accounts for over half of France's domestic wholesale and retail trade. Paris is also one of Europe's most popular tourist attractions, with its rich historical heritage, magnificent architecture, world-famous art museums, beautiful parks, and fine restaurants. The Louvre, the Cathedral of Nôtre Dame, the Eiffel Tower, Montemarte, and the Champs d'Elysee are only a few of the many Paris landmarks every visitor must see.

The division between Paris and the provinces is etched deeply into French culture, society, and politics. The contrast between the hustle-bustle of Parisian life and the rustic and relatively relaxed pace of life in the provinces is made all the more significant because French society, as noted, remains less urban in nature than other industrialized countries. France has only six or so cities with populations over 500,000—half as many as Germany and only a third as many as Great Britain. About one-third of the French live in such cities, compared with one-half of the British population. France has an abundance of arable land and a variety of climates conducive to farming, and farmers still make up about 8 percent of the labor force. As a consequence, France is not only agriculturally self-sufficient but also a major food exporter, accounting for no less than a quarter of the European Community's total agricultural output. France's desire to protect its farm producers and buttress its position as the Continent's paramount food exporter has long been a source of tension within the Common Market.

Although France kept pace with industrialization elsewhere on the Continent during the nineteenth century, the French economy (and society) stagnated in the first half of the twentieth century. One reason is that, unlike Great Britain, which stressed free trade and welcomed competition, France instituted protectionist policies to *prevent* competition, both foreign and domestic. Tariffs, quotas, cartels, and subsidies were the chosen instruments of France's autarkic development strategy. Before the formation of the Fifth Republic in 1958, roughly one-third of the French national budget was allocated to direct or indirect subsidies.

French business practices also impeded growth and change. The family firm (along with the family farm) was the foundation of the French economy. Turning a bigger profit, capturing a larger market share, opening up new product lines, modifying consumer habits, expanding, diversifying, modernizing—these were not primary considerations. In fact, competition itself was viewed as unethical. A business was inseparable from family tradition, it was a way of life. Many businesses were owned and operated by the same family for generations, even centuries.

Unfortunately, respect for tradition is often accompanied by resistance to change; until the 1960s French business practices were a superb illustration of this truth. Profits were seldom reinvested; quality was stressed over quantity, which meant limited production and high unit costs; and concentration of capital into research and development, aggressive marketing, and technological retooling was rare.

The resulting stagnation was not overcome until recently. After World War II the French government took the lead in directing the reconstruction effort and revitalizing the economy. Through "indicative planning" and "modernization commissions," the state set targets for growth in specific industries. Consultation, as well as carrot-and-stick methods, were used to persuade the private sector to go along.

The results were spectacular! A French "economic miracle" only slightly less impressive than West Germany's occurred. Industrial production doubled between 1952 and 1963, then grew by another 70 percent in the next decade. By the early 1980s France had left Great Britain in the dust and was giving the West Germans a run for their money. France's GNP per capita was higher than Japan's, and the French economy was growing faster than all other major industrial democracies except Japan.

In a world where overpopulation is an enormous concern, France has had the opposite problem. Between 1860 and 1940 France's population growth was near zero (long before this was fashionable). This fact was alarming for economic, military, and even psychological reasons. After all, France was the only Roman Catholic nation in the world with almost static population growth. Between the world wars the population actually started shrinking.

After 1945 the population began to rebound; still, the current fertility rate in France remains low, probably below replacement level. Paradoxically, nearly a third of France's population is under age 20, which means considerable pressure on educational facilities at present and the prospect of serious unemployment or underemployment problems in the future.

That France is today a predominantly Roman Catholic society speaks volumes about French history but says little about the role of religion in France. Religion has long been at or near the center of civil strife here. In the sixteenth century French Protestants ("Huguenots"), who wanted to bring the Reformation to France, fought church loyalists, who wanted to preserve Catholicism as the one true faith. The Edict of Nantes (1598) brought religious toleration and a peaceful interlude, but the struggle resumed in the next century. It culminated in the decree of King Louis XIV that all of France would be Roman Catholic. Religion was also a factor in the French Revolution (1789), but this time it was Catholics against anticlericals (those who denounced the church) rather than against Protestants. Historically, the Church has been a conservative force in French society, opposed to republicanism and allied with the monarch, its protector. Religious controversy in general and anticlericalism in particular thus have deep roots in French political history. This fact helps explain why both Communist and Socialist parties have, at different times, enjoyed a large popular following in postwar France, despite the incompatibility of Marxist and Christian doctrines.

Thus the appearance of religious unity in present-day France is deceptive. The overwhelming majority of the French people may be Roman Catholic (over 76 percent are baptized in the Church), but most are, at best, nominal Catholics.

As the discussion so far suggests, to understand French politics it is necessary to know something about French history. France was ruled by a monarchy for approximately 800 years, until the French Revolution. This long stretch of royal absolutism, which reached its zenith during the reign of Louis XIV (1643–1715), is one reason why France developed a strong sense of national identity.

The French political system began to degenerate after the long, despotic reign of Louis XIV, and French society became increasingly polarized. A kind of representative assembly, the Estates General, had been in existence since the fourteenth century, and judicial bodies called *parlements* occasionally served—at the pleasure of the monarch, of course—as sounding boards or advisory councils. Thus, the mechanisms for political accommodation were available but were little used; unlike their British counterparts, French monarchs were loath to compromise with the aristocracy or the rising middle class.

One event that precipitated the French Revolution was Louis XVI's decision to suspend the *parlements*. The privileged classes sided with the *parlements*, never dreaming that the "Third Estate," which represented middle-class commoners and peasants, would eventually seize the initiative. This is not the place to recount the story of the French Revolution. We will simply note again that this political event was a watershed in European history. Its impact went far beyond France and outlasted the tyrannical regime the revolution brought to power, as well as its successor under Napoleon. The revolution was the prelude to a century of political turmoil and started a tradition of division and disunity.

The First Republic gave way to the First Empire under Napoleon Bonaparte. Napoleon continued to do lip service to the republican ideal but in reality he established a personal dictatorship similar in practice to the style of rule associated with absolute monarchy.

After Napoleon's defeat, the House of Bourbon was restored to the throne. The Bourbons are said to have learned nothing and forgotten nothing. In 1848 a revolt again toppled the monarchy and led to the short-lived Second Republic. Louis Napoleon, the nephew of Napoleon Bonaparte, emerged as the new popular leader; following in his famous uncle's footsteps, he crowned himself emperor in 1852.

The Second Empire lasted until 1870, when France was defeated by Germany in the Franco-Prussian War. This defeat and the election of a large number of reactionary monarchists to the National Assembly alarmed progressive elements of all persuasions. Radicals violently opposed to the monarchy and also to the Church, perhaps influenced by Marxism, set up a rival government in the capital, the so-called Paris Commune. A bloody civil war ensued in which 20,000 people died during the last week of fighting alone.

The Third Republic came into being in 1876 and lasted until World War II—the longest-surviving political structure in France since the French Revolution. It was, however, plagued by divisive party politics and a weak executive.

World War I brought great war damage to France, but the political system somehow survived. World War II sounded its death knell.

We will look at France's Fifth Republic in the next chapter. For now we note that France has tried a dozen different political systems since 1789, including five republics. The contradictory political legacy of modern French history can be summed up as follows:

1. A belief in republicanism combined with a mistrust of government expressed in the insistence on a weak executive under the Third and Fourth Republics
2. A susceptibility to "Bonapartism" expressed in the occasional emergence of a man-on-horseback (for example, Napoleon Bonaparte, Louis Napoleon, and General Charles de Gaulle) and the use of periodic plebiscites to renew the leader's popular mandate
3. A tendency toward polarization expressed in the historic dichotomies of reactionary versus revolutionary, Royalist versus Socialist (and Communist), the Church versus anticlericalists, and republican versus *dirigiste* (an advocate of strong central government and broad executive powers)
4. A durable, efficient, and centrally run system of law courts and public administration combined with a tendency toward governmental paralysis and drift
5. A high level of patriotism and national pride combined with a tendency toward popular revolt against the symbols and substance of national authority

Compared with Great Britain, France has been far less stable or cohesive and has lacked the continuity that is the hallmark of British parliamentary rule. France's economic policies have, until rather recently, been autarkic and protectionist, in contrast to the British stress on free trade and competition.

Germany

A century ago, Germany was the preeminent military power on the Continent. After World War II it was divided into two distinct parts—the Federal Republic of Germany (FRG) and the German Democratic Republic (GDR). Beginning with the opening of the Berlin Wall and the intra-German border in 1989, the movement toward reunification reached such momentum so quickly that it culminated in a united Germany on October 3, 1990.

Germany's geographic position on the Continent places it at the crossroads between East and West. Unlike Great Britain and France, Germany does not have natural boundaries, and this fact has influenced Germany's fate in several ways. For centuries, whenever wars were fought in Europe, the territory of Germany was apt to be the battleground. Why? Because Germany is centrally located; because until the latter part of the nineteenth century Germany was divided into many principalities, most of them diminutive; and because the absence of geographic barriers made German lands accessible to the armies of neighboring states.

That Germany had no natural boundaries, however, also meant that Germans could spread out and settle in adjacent territories without being cut off from their homeland. As a result, the German nation (and language) became disseminated well beyond Germany proper. When Hitler seized the Sudetenland (historically part of Czechoslovakia), he justified the seizure on the grounds that most of the people there were Germans. He justified Nazi aggression in general on the grounds that Germany needed *Lebensraum* (living space). This argument was specious, but it made sense to a nation long accustomed to migrating into neighboring areas.

Germany's lack of natural boundaries and subsequent vulnerability influenced German history in other ways as well. If, as is often said, the best defense is a strong offense, then one logical response to the danger of invasion is to go on the offensive. For centuries a fragmented "Germany" was unable to follow this type of strategy. In the eighteenth century, however, Prussia emerged as a major power under Frederick the Great, (1740–1786). Frederick enlarged Prussia considerably (he took Silesia from Austria in 1742, and thirty years later he acquired another large chunk of territory in the first partition of Poland). From this time forward, the ideal of the military state was a prominent part of the German *Weltanschauung* (world view).

Due largely to the struggle against Napoleon, the concept of Germany as a nation began to emerge. The German Confederation created at the Congress of Vienna in 1815 was a precursor of the modern German state, but very modest—rivalry between Austria and Prussia, distaste for reform, and the claims of German princes combined to block any move toward German unification. The loose Confederation, which recognized Vienna as the permanent presidency, encompassed thirty-nine sovereign entities running the gamut from the formidable Austrian Empire and Prussia to four free cities. For example, the diet that was supposed to meet at Frankfurt was more a council of ambassadors than an elective assembly, and a unanimous vote was required on important matters. Also, the Confederation's legislative powers were severely restricted. In practice the league was important in German politics only on the rare occasions when Prince Metternich, the great Austrian statesman, found it convenient.

Metternich used the Confederation, for example, to suppress student protests inspired by pan-German nationalism and liberalism, both anathema to the ruling elites. After the assassination of a reactionary writer, the Confederation was the vehicle used to launch the Carlsbad Decrees of 1819. These measures intensified censorship, banned radical professors and students (including Karl Marx), and outlawed political clubs. They also required each member-state to appoint commissioners to monitor and certify the universities for ideological reliability.

Although there was considerable ferment in intellectual circles, German society as a whole, still largely rural but with a growing urban-industrial labor force, remained rather more tranquil than elsewhere in Europe. In Prussia, the Junker land-owning nobility was allied to the Crown. The Junker class supplied most of the officers for the royal army and for the top posts in the state administration:

> Sons of burghers filled state posts in the lower echelons and shared in decision making on municipal affairs. The skillful and efficient bureaucracy of Prussia set standards that other German states sought to imitate. The peasant masses in overwhelmingly rural ''Germany'' seemed content to allow public business to be conducted by their social betters.[16]

Prussia was an efficient monarchy. Under the enlightened rule of Frederick William III, the state continued to support education and promote economic growth. A common tariff, established in 1818 in all its territories, lowered duties (discouraging smugglers as well as opening up the economy to competition) and allowed free entry to raw materials (a spur to industrial development). These progressive measures worked remarkably well, so well that nearly all the German states except Austria soon joined Prussia's customs union, the *Zollverein*. Indeed, ''by 1834 over 23 million Germans, living in an area larger than New York, Pennsylvania, and New England combined, were exchanging goods freely.''[17] Revenues were collected by Prussian inspectors, shared by all *Zollverein* members, and used primarily to build roads (creating essential infrastructure for a future German state). In retrospect, the Prussian experiment in economic integration can be seen as an early forerunner of the European Community.

The *Zollverein* was a tonic to commerce; by midcentury, manufacturing and trade were also stimulated by an intricate railroad network built and subsidized mainly by Prussia. It is noteworthy that economic integration facilitated political unification, that is, new economic relationships preceded political change. (Is it not possible that the new Europe of the 1990s, under the impetus of the European Community [which began as a customs union in 1958], will repeat that pattern? At the very least there may be a parallel between the role Prussia played in the formation of the modern German state and the key role Germany is now playing in Europe.)

Economic development inevitably brought social dislocations. Modern factories, both foreign and domestic, displaced the old trades. Growing signs of popular discontent and even political disturbances were rooted in a newly emerging commercial-industrial class structure. Some elements demanded what were then radical reforms, including a graduated income tax and guarantees of the right to work.

Limited concessions to liberalism (mainly in the guise of constitutional reform) were made in some parts of the Confederation. In Prussia, Frederick

William IV, the most liberal of the Prussian monarchs, convened a United *Landtag* (a representative assembly) in 1847, but soon had second thoughts. The revolutionary turmoil that occurred throughout much of Europe in 1848 brought class conflict to the surface in German society. Landed gentry were pitted against the middle class (factory owners, bankers, lawyers, professors), the middle class against the workers, and peasants against liberals of all stripes. The revolts in the German states (and in Austria) failed to depose the rulers, who were supported by loyal armies.

The clamor for constitutional change in Prussia and elsewhere mingled with nationalistic fervor. Talk of German unification in time became commonplace to the point where even the Hohenzollern (Prussia) and Hapsburg (Austria) rulers paid it lip service. Ironically, dreams of a single German state—a "superpower"—continued to be associated with a desire for liberal democratic government.

Otto von Bismarck unified Germany in 1871, having gained wide popular support following impressive military victories first over Austria (in 1866) and then France (in 1870). The formation of the German Empire (the so-called Second Reich) was the product of triumph and the prelude to tragedy for the German people. Under Bismarck Germany came to play a dominant role in Europe. In 1878 Bismarck masterminded the Three Emperors' Alliance (German, Austria-Hungary, and Russia) at the Congress of Berlin, as a bulwark against liberal reform.

Over the next seventy-five years Germany fought and lost two world wars, underwent a tumultuous revolution, and embraced the totalitarian designs of Adolph Hitler. Whether or not German aggression was the real cause of World War I, the victorious powers placed this stigma on Germany when they insisted on a "war guilt" clause in the Versailles Treaty.

Woodrow Wilson spoke for many when he blamed the war on two prominent features of prewar German politics: nationalism and autocracy. He believed that one way to prevent future wars in Europe was to remake Germany (and other autocratic regimes) in the image of a parliamentary democracy. Where there are popular controls on government, Wilson theorized, war is likely to be a last resort; if people are given a choice they will choose not to fight and die unless it is a matter of self-defense.

The Weimar Republic, Germany's first constitutional system, was born in these inauspicious circumstances. The new German government had several strikes against it from the start. First, it was a symbol of Germany's humiliating defeat in World War I. Second, it was un-German: Germany had no prior experience with republican government and there was little in German history or culture to underpin any kind of democracy. Third, it was associated with a draconian peace that included onerous (and highly punitive) war reparations and indemnities levied against Germany. Fourth, it was powerless to protect legitimate German interests against continuing foreign encroachments. For example, Germany was required to finance an allied army of occupation in the Rhineland for fifteen years. Not surprisingly, when the economy went into a tailspin (as it did at least twice in the 1920s), popular disenchantment with the form of government opened the door to demagoguery and dictatorship.

Hitler's Third Reich was an aberration made possible by the impact of a worldwide depression on an already beleaguered German economy and society. Although Hitler came to power legally, he had no respect for laws and constitutions. As Chancellor, he quickly obtained an Enabling Act from the German *Reichstag* (parliament). Thus armed with the power to rule by decree, Hitler instituted one of the most repressive and brutal tyrannies in history.

At the Munich conference in September 1938, Hitler demanded that the Sudentenland be ceded to Germany. The following year Hitler and Stalin made an infamous deal, known as the Molotov-Ribbentrop Pact. Ostensibly a nonaggression pact, it was the device by which the two dictators divided up Poland and Hitler "conceded" the Baltic states and Bessarabia (now called Moldavia, then part of Romania) to the Soviet Union. The Holocaust—the genocidal murder of nearly 6 million Jews and a like number of others (including Poles, Gypsies, and Magyars)—stands as the most heinous symbol of Nazi totalitarian rule.

A lively academic debate about Germany's role in the outbreak of World War I continues, but there is little question that Germany was the aggressor in World War II. Nonetheless, the Allies (except for the Soviet Union) did not seek a punitive peace after Germany's defeat in 1945. In fact the United States and Great Britain *shielded* West Germany from Soviet and French demands for huge reparations payments.

CONCLUSION

Europe is a mix of many cultures and nations with distinct languages, historical experiences, and political traditions. Nonetheless, Western Europe has a foundation of common values and beliefs due to the pervasive and enduring influence of the Christian religion, the Renaissance and Reformation, the Scientific Revolution, the Enlightenment, the Industrial Revolution, and the Age of Imperialism. In Chapter 5 we explore contemporary patterns of politics and government, which are the fruits of this heritage.

STUDY QUESTIONS

1. What are the seminal features of European civilization relative to the shaping of the political cultures of the Continent?
2. In what sense has totalitarianism shaped both the history and the political landscape of Europe in the twentieth century?
3. Why was Europe so prone to war in the first half of the twentieth century? Why has it been immune from war during the second half?

SUGGESTED READINGS

Carr, Edward Hallett. *The Twenty Years' Crisis, 1919–1939*. New York: Harper, 1964 (originally published in 1939).

Cipolla, Carlo M. *Before the Industrial Revolution: European Society and Economy, 1000–1700*. New York: Norton, 1976.

Dehio, Ludwig. *Germany and World Politics in the Twentieth Century*. New York: Norton, 1959.

Dehio, Ludwig. *The Precarious Balance: Four Centuries of the European Power Struggle*. New York: Vintage, 1962.

Kissinger, Henry. *A World Restored: The Politics of Conservatism in a Revolutionary Age*. New York: Grosset, 1964.

Plumb, J. H. *The Italian Renaissance*. New York: Harper, 1961.

Slavin, Arthur J. *The Way of the West: The Era of World Dominion, 1760–Present*. Lexington, Mass.: Xerox, 1974.

NOTES

[1] Derwent Whittlesey, *Environmental Foundations of European History* (New York: Appleton, 1949), p. 140.

[2] Ibid., p. 141.

[3] Ibid., p. 132.

[4] Ibid., p. 138.

[5] Ibid.

[6] John Kirtland Wright, *The Geographical Basis of European History* (New York: Holt, 1928), pp. 78–79.

[7] Ibid.

[8] Ibid.

[9] Bryce Lyon, Herbert H. Rowen, and Theodore S. Hamerow, *A History of the Western World* (Chicago: Rand McNally, 1969), p. 443.

[10] Ibid., p. 444.

[11] Ibid., pp. 508–509.

[12] Ibid., p. 509.

[13] Quoted in Hans Morganthau and Kenneth Thompson, *Politics Among Nations: The Struggle for Power and Peace*, 6th ed. (New York: Knopf, 1985), pp. 233–234.

[14] Ibid., p. 235.

[15] Ibid., p. 238.

[16] Arthur J. May, *The Age of Metternich* (New York: Holt, 1963), p. 40.

[17] Ibid., p. 44.

Chapter 5
The Triumph of Pluralism and the Marketplace

In Chapter 4 we explored the overlapping cultural and religious traditions of the West European nations. Here we will look more closely at some contemporary political systems—in particular Great Britain, France, and Germany. We note at the outset that the similarities in these systems far outweigh any differences. Indeed, in the late 1980s every country in Western Europe was democratically governed by civilian rulers who came to power through free elections. The governments of Western Europe display a remarkably clear and consistent pattern, a pattern too uniform to result from mere coincidence.

It is probably not an exaggeration to say that, before the 1980s when many Latin American nations converted from military to civilian rule, fully half of all existing constitutional democracies could be found in Western Europe. The list is impressive: Great Britain, France, West Germany, Italy, Belgium, the Netherlands, Luxembourg, Denmark, Norway, Sweden, Austria, Switzerland, Spain, Portugal, and Greece. Although the governments of these nations are not identical, and their differences are not insignificant, they have three characteristics in common: They are all based on clearly defined principles (constitutional), elected by universal suffrage (democratic), and ruled by representatives of the people rather than the people themselves (republican).

Most European countries have been democratically governed for the major part of the twentieth century. The exceptions were West Germany and Italy, which became democratic after World War II; and Spain and Portugal, which were dictatorships until the mid-1970s. Greece is a partial exception: It was under military rule from 1967 to 1974 and has had democratically elected civilian rulers since then.

Some of the governments of Western Europe can be called constitutional monarchies. Those of Great Britain, Spain, Belgium, Luxembourg, the Netherlands, Denmark, Norway, and Sweden are in this category. In these countries the monarch "reigns but does not rule"—the king or queen is the ceremonial head of state, while a democratically elected prime minister is the head of the government (the chief executive responsible for policymaking and public administration). A constitutional monarch could theoretically intercede in the political process, but this might place the institution of the monarchy itself at risk.

Great Britain is a parliamentary democracy and might also be characterized as a constitutional monarchy, with one caveat: Great Britain does not have a written constitution. The British do, however, have a "constitution," which happens to be more deeply entrenched than most written ones.

Great Britain: The Mother of Parliaments

In contrast to the United States, where the founding fathers developed elaborate theoretical foundations for the political system, in Great Britain the political tradition is an outgrowth of centuries of history, experiment, and legal precedent. A theory of British democracy can be found in the late eighteenth-century writings and speeches of Edmund Burke, who celebrated the role of continuity and stability in the development of British constitutionalism. Burke stressed the importance of Great Britain's long unbroken chain of political development, during which economic equality and political liberty evolved side by side.

The Unwritten Constitution

Great Britain's constitution is not recorded in any single document. Rather it is the product of four elements: statutory law, common law, custom and convention, and works of authority. Today the normal method of amending and augmenting the British Constitution is by means of *statutory law*. This law originates from acts of Parliament and the subordinate legislation spawned by such acts. The Parliament Act of 1911, which greatly curbed the legislative role of the House of Lords, is an example of a statutory law that amended the Constitution. Other examples include the Bill of Rights of 1689 and the European Communities Act of 1972. Statutory law is made by legislators, called members of Parliament (MPs) if they sit in the House of Commons or lords if they sit in the House of Lords.

Common law is judge-made law. It is based on rulings and decisions that have been passed on through generations and that are generally upheld in the courts. At one time common law played a crucial role in the evolution of the British system. For example, it is the basis for the principle of parliamentary sovereignty. A. V. Dicey, the great nineteenth-century British political thinker, considered this principle one of the two main pillars of the British Constitution (the other being the rule of law). Common law now has a secondary role.

Custom and convention refer to long-standing practices not based on statutory or common law. They are rooted in nothing but the perceived logic of the system itself: They must be observed for the government to run smoothly and efficiently, or so the British believe. For example, it is important for symbolic reasons that the British Crown give its royal assent to Acts of Parliament. A law that did not have the royal stamp of approval would somehow seem not legitimate. The last time a British monarch refused to give assent to an Act of Parliament was in the 1700s. Another example is the practice by which the monarch, at the prime minister's request, dissolves the parliament and calls for new elections if the government receives a vote of no confidence.

A final source of constitutional law can be found in *works of authority*. These works derive their authority from the quality of reasoning they exhibit and from the reputation of the scholars who produce them. Prominent British constitutional authorities include, in addition to A. V. Dicey, John Austin, Walter Bagehot, Sir Ivor Jennings, Sir Kenneth Wheare, O. Hood Phillips, and E. C. S. Wade.

In contrast to the United States, there is no power of judicial review in Great Britain. Government ministers, judges, and administrative officials can interpret the Constitution in specific instances, but in general, Acts of Parliament are supreme. And, as we have just seen, there are no extraordinary procedures for amending the British Constitution; statutes and common law comprising the Constitution are changed by ordinary legislation (that is, they require only a simple majority in the House of Commons).

Two seminal ideas undergird British democracy—parliamentary sovereignty and the rule of law. Dicey defined *parliamentary sovereignty* as "the right to make or unmake any law whatever; and, further, that no person or body is recognized by the law of England as having a right to override or set aside the legislation of Parliament." The *rule of law*, according to Dicey, means two things. First, "no man is punishable . . . except for a distinct breach of law established . . . before ordinary courts of the land." Second, "no man is above the law . . . whatever his rank." Dicey also observed that "the constitution is pervaded by the rule of law" in the sense that "the general principles of the constitution [are themselves] the result of judicial decision determining the rights of private persons in particular cases brought before the courts."[1]

The British parliamentary system has four salient characteristics. First, the British system is *unitary*, in contrast to the federal system found in the United States and Germany. Another term for unitary is *centralized*—the central government possesses all the powers of government and delegates only that measure of authority to the local governments that it deems necessary and proper. Consequently, London has complete power over the local authorities; the concept of reserved powers has no relevance whatever in the British system.

Second, a *fusion of powers* obtains at the national level rather than the *separation of powers* found in the United States. The U.S. presidential system bars members of Congress from holding a cabinet office concurrently. In contrast, the British *cabinet* comprises the leaders of the majority party in the House of Commons. Thus, under normal circumstances, election to the Parliament is a prerequisite to becoming a cabinet member. After an election, the head of the victorious party in Parliament (the prime minister) names the other members (ministers) of the new cabinet; following a pro forma vote of approval by the party's majority in the House of Commons, a government is formed. (In a multiparty system, the government will often be formed by a coalition of two or more parties.) The cabinet, headed by the prime minister, is responsible for formulating and initiating legislation. Although all members of Parliament, including the opposition, are free to question and criticize the government, the majority party is virtually assured that its legislative proposals will pass.

A third key feature is *collective ministerial responsibility*. The prime minister and cabinet (the government) are members of the Parliament and exercise executive power only so long as they are supported by a parliamentary majority.

The government must be prepared to answer questions about government policies before both houses of Parliament. The "collective" aspect of ministerial responsibility relates to the fact that cabinet members are expected to support all policies, actions, and decisions of the government in public; they may dissent in private. Governing thus is a team sport in Great Britain, and the prime minister is the coach, team captain, and head of the cheering section. Grandstand plays by individual cabinet members are frowned on, and prime ministers do not like being circumvented or upstaged. Prime ministers can make cabinet changes any time they wish.

Fourth, the system is a *two-party system*. This does not mean that there are never more than two parties in existence, but rather that typically two major parties tend to alternate in power. Furthermore, these two parties represent relatively clear programmatic alternatives to the electorate, much more so than the two major parties in the United States. Also, British political parties display considerably more party discipline in Parliament than do their counterparts in the United States. (The reasons are discussed later in this chapter.) As a consequence, when one party wins the election and forms a government, it can put its program into effect expeditiously.

The British Parliament

Great Britain's Parliament has managed to fuse the political symbols, ceremonies, and conventions of the past with the changing realities of the present. It has retained an element of British aristocracy in the House of Lords, but it has lodged virtually all legislative power in the House of Commons. The gradual ascendancy of the elected House of Commons over the hereditary House of Lords was completed early in the twentieth century, when the Lords were reduced to little more than an aristocratic (and anachronistic) debating society.

In 1990 the House of Commons had 650 members, each elected in single-member districts by plurality vote. England accounted for 531, Scotland for 71, Wales for 36, and Northern Ireland for 12. The House of Commons approves or rejects legislation and provides an "oratorical battleground" where the Opposition can and often does go on the offensive, forcing the prime minister and cabinet to defend their public statements, actions, and policies and sometimes their private behavior as well.

The Parliament alone can make new laws and repeal or revise old ones. This power gives the majority party enormous leverage. Theoretically it could reshape the entire political system by one simple parliamentary act. But the political obstacles to drastic structural change are formidable. The existing system has broad national support. Any attempt to reorder the system would risk a tumultuous outpouring of public indignation. In Great Britain, when the government loses public support it is expected to resign.

Moreover, the opposition party would join the public in protesting any fundamental change in the system. The role of the Opposition is, quite simply, to oppose—if it does not do so, it is acting irresponsibly. Thus, both major parties, no matter which one is in office, have vital roles in the British system. This point is underscored by the traditional name given to the party out of power—Her Majesty's Loyal Opposition.

Despite opposition, the government is in firm control of the legislative process. After a bill is formally introduced in the House of Commons, the government decides when it will be debated. Except for the nineteen "Opposition Days" during each session of Parliament, the government has control of the legislative agenda. Bills go through three readings—one when they are introduced, another when they are debated, and a third when they are voted on. Floor debate occurs after the second reading. This is a crucial point in the process: Bills approved at this stage usually have clear sailing the rest of the way. Following debate, bills go into standing committees.

In contrast to the committee system in the U.S. Congress, British committees are often very large (up to fifty members) and not all are specialized. Their powers are narrowly circumscribed as well: They refine the language of legislation, they do not redefine the legislation itself. They rarely pass amendments unless the minister of the affected department proposes them. The majority party always controls the committees by the same margin that it enjoys in the full House.

Next comes the report stage, when amendments can be approved or rejected. The government's amendments are almost always passed; any individual member's amendment at this stage is generally rejected unless it has the blessing of the government.

Bills dealing with constitutional issues are handled differently: They go to a Committee of the Whole, meaning that the entire House of Commons is the "committee." If a bill of this nature is passed without amendments it does not have to go through the report stage.

The third reading in the House of Commons is when a bill is voted up or down in final form. If it passes, it goes to the House of Lords. The Lords can amend it, but only if the House of Commons approves. The final step is the granting of royal assent by the Crown, a mere formality but one that preserves the symbolism so important to the legitimation of government in Great Britain.

It may sound as though the legislative process is cut and dried, with the government holding all the trump cards. In point of fact, however, the Opposition has ample opportunity to criticize, embarrass, and call the government to account. The most important device used by the Opposition is question time. Each day, Monday through Thursday, government ministers must answer questions on the floor of the House of Commons, and twice a week the prime minister must answer questions as well. Question time makes politics something of a spectator sport in Great Britain. It places a premium on debate skills and forces policymakers to justify their actions and decisions continually—not just to Parliament, but to the British people as well.

If the government loses its popular support it may either resign or risk a vote of "no confidence" in Parliament. If Parliament passes such a motion or defeats a government bill with a "vote of confidence" attached, the government must, by convention, resign and either permit another party leader to form a government or ask the monarch to dissolve Parliament and call new elections. This procedure was last followed in 1979 when the Labour party lost on a vote of confidence, resigned, and opened the door to the Conservative party, which subsequently won the elections and has held power ever since.

Under normal circumstances the government need not worry about losing important votes in Parliament. The majority party members are led by the government's chief whip, which is a salaried position. The chief whip helps the government set the schedule in Parliament and keeps the cabinet briefed on developments there. Above all, the chief whip is responsible for party discipline, which in the British context means ensuring that majority-party MPs support government policy and vote to pass government bills. (The Opposition and minor parties also have whips who perform the same disciplinary function.)

The House of Lords merits only brief attention here because the Parliament Acts of 1911 and 1949 reduced its role to that of a reviewing and recommending body. Unlike MPs, the Lords are not elected; they hold hereditary titles of nobility or, in some cases, are "life peers" (that is, ennobled by the Queen in recognition of special achievement). In general, the Lords scrutinize legislation, refine the language, and occasionally offer an amendment to reinforce rather than weaken a bill's original intent. They can also obstruct and delay, within limits: They can hold up money bills for up to one month and all other legislation for up to one year.

As noted earlier, the British system features a fusion of powers. This fusion is particularly evident in the judicial functions of the Lords. The House of Lords is the highest court of appeals in Great Britain. In effect it plays a role similar to that of the U.S. Supreme Court, with one important caveat: Unlike the Supreme Court, the House of Lords does not have the power to declare legislative acts unconstitutional.

Some critics argue that the House of Lords is an anomaly in the modern world and should either be abolished altogether or replaced by a democratically elected upper house. One proposal would reconstitute Parliament so that representation would be based on geographic areas or regions in one house and on population in the other, something like the federal-style bicameral legislatures found in the United States and Germany.

The British Cabinet System

The British system has sometimes been called "cabinet" government. Without a doubt, the prime minister holds the most powerful position in the system. The prime minister is chief executive, majority party leader, and principal adviser to the Crown. The prime minister appoints and dismisses cabinet members, sets the legislative agenda, decides major policy issues, directs the bureaucracy, and manages the nation's diplomatic affairs. Being both head of government and leader of the parliamentary majority, the prime minister has enormous constitutional authority. Some critics have asserted that the British prime minister is a virtual dictator. However, no prime minister exercises as much actual political power as the system appears to concentrate in this position. Any prime minister who attempted to govern autocratically would soon encounter resistance both from Parliament and the public.

Further, the cabinet system has inherent liabilities that tend to offset a prime minister's constitutional powers. For instance, a prime minister cannot blame the Parliament for failed government policies the way U.S. presidents frequently blame the Congress. For British prime ministers, the more power the chief executive wields, the more responsibility he or she must bear for the outcome.

British voters do not vote for the prime minister in national elections the way American voters vote for the president; rather, the majority party in Parliament chooses the prime minister. The choice is always a foregone conclusion, however, because each party selects a leader at its party convention before a general election. This part of the process in Great Britain is similar to the nominating conventions in the United States, except that future prime ministers do not have to face grueling primaries.

Parliamentary elections must be held at least every five years in Great Britain. Prime ministers, however, have the prerogative of calling elections sooner if they so choose. Negative circumstances, for example, a vote of no confidence or a scandal, can force early elections. More often the prime minister will try to capitalize on a momentary surge in public approval to win another five-year term. For example, in 1983, after the British had defeated Argentina in the Falkland (Malvinas) Islands, Prime Minister Margaret Thatcher called early elections to take advantage of the resulting rise in her personal popularity.

The British cabinet illustrates the fusion of powers between the executive and legislative branches. The prime minister chooses leading MPs to serve in the cabinet. The main functions of this body were defined in 1918 by the Haldane Committee on the Machinery of Government as follows: (a) final determination of the policy to be submitted to Parliament, (b) supreme control of the national executive, and (c) continuous coordination of the administrative departments.

The cabinet is not synonymous with the government, but is rather like the steering committee of the government. In common usage, references to the British ''government'' may mean either the political system as a whole or the specific set of leaders (prime minister and cabinet) who happen to be in power. There is no set limit on the size of the cabinet; rather it is up to each prime minister to decide which departments will have cabinet representation. Nonetheless, there are certain ministers—for example Chancellor of the Exchequer (treasury), Foreign Secretary, and Home Secretary—who are always included.

As already noted, the cabinet operates under the principle of collective responsibility. Publicly, all cabinet members must support the government's policies without reservation, even if they disagree among themselves in closed cabinet meetings or in private. A cabinet member who cannot support a decision is expected to resign.

The cabinet generally convenes once a week in the cabinet room at 10 Downing Street. The chief whip normally attends cabinet meetings, and the meetings are chaired by the prime minister. Votes are rarely taken, the prime minister preferring instead to seek consensus or to listen to the discussion and then declare a decision. The precise nature of cabinet meetings is shrouded in mystery: Tradition, self-restraint, and the Official Secrets Act have combined to keep leaks to a minimum.

There are two schools of thought regarding the extent of the prime minister's powers in the cabinet. One school views the prime minister as a dictator who makes the final decisions and can appoint or dismiss cabinet members at will. The other school stresses that any politician who gets a cabinet post is powerful in his or her own right. Creating a cabinet is a political act: The prime minister must placate the party's power brokers in Parliament and in some instances faction leaders as well. According to this view, the prime minister must mediate and mold a consensus, rather than dictate.

Coordination and communication between the cabinet and the subordinate levels of the government is done through cabinet committees and the Cabinet Office. Originally the committees were created to deal with particular issues; today there are about twenty-five permanent cabinet committees responsible for interdepartmental coordination and oversight in various issue areas. There are also over 100 ad hoc committees set up to handle specific issues and facilitate two-way communication between the cabinet and the appropriate government departments.

The Cabinet Office also houses a Secretariat that handles the administrative affairs on the cabinet. It assists in coordinating the operations of government, keeps noncabinet ministers informed of cabinet decisions, prepares and circulates the agenda for cabinet meetings (and cabinet committee meetings), and the like. With the growth of the powers, functions, and responsibilities of the executive, the Secretariat has become an indispensable part of the government's administrative apparatus.

The Administrative Departments

The cabinet is the keystone in the arch of the central government, but the departments are the building blocks. The departments run the day-to-day business of the government; they are headed by a minister or by a secretary of state (not all departments enjoy cabinet status). Each departmental minister is assisted by at least one junior minister called a parliamentary secretary. The largest departments may also have parliamentary undersecretaries. All of these officials are members of the majority party, and all are appointed by the prime minister (about 100, plus the cabinet posts).

Department ministers are in charge of the main administrative units of the government and must perform a variety of managerial functions, including motivating and monitoring the large number of civil servants who staff the department. The minister's chief aid is the permanent secretary, a senior civil servant who has the broad administrative experience and substantive expertise that a politically appointed minister may lack. Notwithstanding, ultimate responsibility for departmental performance rests squarely on the minister's shoulders.

Perhaps the ministers' most important (and difficult) task is to persuade, bully, cajole, and otherwise induce the civil servants at the working levels of government to implement policy according to the government's wishes. As a professional class, civil servants are notoriously resistant to change and cynical about the "amateurs" who make the policy decisions they (the bureaucrats) must carry out. Foot-dragging is a time-honored form of bureaucratic resistance, one that has been the bane of many a British minister, from junior to prime.

Parties and Elections

Traditionally Great Britain has had a two-party system, but throughout most of the twentieth century there has been at least one minor political party as well. Even so, only two parties have won control of the government since the early 1900s—the Conservative party (presently in power) and the Labour party. (The small Scottish Nationalist party did help to bring down the Labour government in 1979 with a vote of no confidence.)

In the late 1980s the Conservatives had dominated British politics for a decade. In 1987 Margaret Thatcher became the first British prime minister in this century to lead her party to three consecutive election victories. In terms of doctrine, the British Conservative party can be loosely compared with the Republican party in the United States. Margaret Thatcher shared with Ronald Reagan a belief in the benefits of the free-enterprise system. Both advocated a strong national defense and embraced "containment" as the best way to deal with Soviet Communism. Prime Minister Thatcher was instrumental in winning NATO support for the Intermediate Nuclear Force (INF) treaty negotiated by the two superpowers in 1987. In general, the two leaders—Thatcher and Reagan—were highly compatible in matters of both principle and policy.

Thatcher's Conservatives have sought to reduce the size of government, curb spending, denationalize (or reprivatize) industry, cut taxes, maintain a strong independent nuclear strike force, and remain in the European Community (EC). The government also has endeavored to break the grip of trade unions on domestic economic policy. In pushing their ambitious program of government retrenchment and economic revitalization, Thatcherites have been helped by the fact that the Conservative party is highly cohesive—there are no deep divisions or warring factions. At most, certain "tendencies" are discernible—for example, some Conservatives focus on social change and ways to resist it, while others stress economic change and ways to promote it.

The Labour party, by contrast, is a coalition of disparate interests. Originally an outgrowth of the British trade union movement, it was founded as the party of the working class. It became the main opposition party in the 1920s. From the outset, it distanced itself from the once-powerful Liberal party by embracing Socialism (but not necessarily Marx and definitely not Marxism-Leninism).

Today the Labour party is no longer simply a working-class party. It is an "umbrella" organization directing its appeal not only to blue-collar workers but also to middle-class civil servants, teachers, housewives, peace activists, welfare recipients, students, pensioners, the jobless, the homeless, and in general the poor and downtrodden. Because the Labour party's constituency is so diverse and unity is lacking, the party's programs cannot easily be summarized. Some policies advocated in recent years include renationalization of industry, unilateral nuclear disarmament, withdrawal from the EC, closing of U.S. military bases, expansion of the social welfare system, higher taxes for the wealthy, and concessions to organized labor.

The Labour party lost control of the government in 1979, and a struggle between left-wing and moderate factions ensued. The moderates were opposed to the party's stance favoring British withdrawal from the EC, and to a change in the party's method of selecting its leader. The new Social Democratic party, founded by disaffected Labourites, is the bitter fruit of this struggle. The defection weakened the Labour party but so far has not given rise to a viable alternative.

For the 1983 elections, the Social Democrats and Liberals formed a coalition named the Alliance. The two parties kept their campaign finances separate but issued a joint manifesto calling for government action to relieve unemployment (borrowing to fund public works programs), scuttling of the Trident nuclear submarine project, redoubled arms control efforts, expanded welfare programs, continued membership in the EC, and ending of nationalizations or denationalizations of industry coupled with new incentives for private enterprise. The Alliance was designed to offer the British voters a middle-of-the-road alternative to the right-leaning Conservatives and left-leaning Labourites.

The Alliance met with little success at the polls, but the idea did not die. Neither did it thrive. There is always a possibility that a new political party will come along to challenge the old established ones, and perhaps the Alliance or an offshoot is destined to be that party. In the early 1990s, however, it is still premature to write the obituary for Great Britain's celebrated two-party system.

There are other minor parties in Great Britain—The Greens, the Scottish Nationalist party, the Unionist Party, the Nationalist Front party, and the Communist Party. They are all marginalized by one or more of the following factors: extremism, a narrow popular base, a lack of resources, poor leadership, or internal bickering.

In addition, minor parties face two systemic obstacles—tradition and the "first-past-the-post" electoral system: Candidates run in single-member districts and whoever gets the most votes wins. On tradition, Sydney Bailey's observation is apposite: "There is nothing sacred in the number two, but the fact is that for by far the greater part of the three centuries during which parties in the modern sense have existed in Britain there have been two major parties, a Government party and an Opposition party."[2] On the electoral system, some elaboration is necessary.

Elections in Great Britain are short and simple compared with those in the United States. In the United States, president, senators, and representatives are elected to terms of different lengths and national elections are staggered, taking place every two years. As a result, campaigns are frequent and it seems like one election barely ends before the next begins. In Great Britain there is normally but one national election every four or five years.

Elections are held when the prime minister formally asks the monarch to dissolve Parliament, a procedure that usually takes about ten days. Next, a royal proclamation summons a new Parliament. The election must be held within three weeks of the proclamation. As a rule, the prime minister dissolves the Parliament before the five-year term is up. Since the government can decide precisely when the next election is to be held, the party in power has an advantage over the Opposition. Elections are most often held in May or October, but no law says this must be so.

All British subjects or citizens 18 years of age or older may vote, provided they have registered. Because voting registers are now produced only once a year, it can take up to sixteen months for a voter to qualify! Currently there are 650 seats in the House of Commons, each seat representing a local constituency. Every fifteen years the Boundary Commission redraws the boundaries of the constituencies to reflect population changes.

The electoral system is based on the first-past-the-post principle. The successful candidate does not have to win a majority of the votes. If there were ten candidates, for example, the winner might have only 25 percent of the votes.

This system has been widely criticized on the grounds that it distorts the actual voting results. To cite one example, in 1979 the Conservative party won 339 seats in Parliament, a clear majority. If the seats had been distributed in proportion to the votes, however, the Conservatives would have won only 279, well short of a majority. In fact, only in 1900, 1906, 1931, and 1935 would the government have won a working majority in Parliament if the seats were distributed in direct proportion to the votes.[3]

There has been considerable debate in Great Britain over changing the way MPs are elected. The advocates of change want a proportional representation system of one kind or another. Tradition is a formidable obstacle to such a change. Another is the logic of the British two-party system, which ensures that one party or the other will have a working majority in the Parliament. The electoral system magnifies the top-vote-getting party's winning margin. Hence the Conservatives received about 43 percent of the popular vote in the June 1987 elections but ended up with a 100-seat majority in Parliament. (In 1983, they won a 144-seat majority—again with well under half the popular votes.)

Changing the system would reduce the odds that any single party would win a working majority. For a new government to be formed, parties would be forced to enter into coalitions. This outcome is greatly desired by struggling parties like the Liberals or Social Democrats. Others, however, fear that it would undermine the stability and capacity to act that have been the hallmarks of the British system.

Thus, British elections are like those in the United States with regard to the method of election (plurality vote/single member districts). But that is where the similarity ends. British elections are much shorter, and much less expensive. National elections in Great Britain are more party oriented than in the United States, where the personality, reputation, and charisma of the individual candidate are so often paramount. Because the government can put its programs into effect in the British system, the party in power is held strictly accountable for the condition of the country. Thus in 1979, when the British economy was in the doldrums, the voters ousted the Labour party and put the Conservatives in power. The Conservatives can look forward to a similar fate if and when Great Britain falls on hard times again.

Public Opinion and Pressure Groups

The role of public opinion in the British system has already been mentioned. Prime ministers often decide when to call new elections on the basis of opinion polls. Conversely, when the popular approval rating falls, the government may be forced to resign. Thus, public opinion has a far greater impact on government in Great Britain, where the prime minister and cabinet have an indefinite term of office, than in the United States, where the president and administration have a fixed term.

Pressure groups have gained influence since World War II in Great Britain. In fact, prior to the Thatcher revolution the trade unions—in particular the Trades Union Congress (TUC)—and the business interests—especially the Confederation of British Industry (CBI)—had become so powerful that some political scientists began to describe the system as "corporatist." The heralds of corporatism argued that Parliament was losing its relevance because the new triple alliance of big government, big business, and organized labor was shaping policy and, in effect, dominating the political system.

The corporatist model as it applies to postwar British politics has some merit, but there is little reason to believe that the parliamentary system itself is in jeopardy. Indeed, Prime Minister Thatcher has greatly *reduced* the influence of organized labor in economic policy formulation. Labor's loss of political clout is reflected in the fact that union membership declined by more than 20 percent between 1979 and 1986.[4]

British pressure groups find that they are most effective when they can establish lines of communication with the civil service. In contrast to the United States, where lobbying the Congress is as important as establishing contacts within the bureaucracy, in Great Britain, where policy emanates almost exclusively from the cabinet and the various ministries and departments, pressure groups generally bypass Parliament altogether.

France's Fifth Republic

The fact that France has been governed by five different republics in two centuries (during which time the United States has had but one) is indicative of the political turmoil that has characterized so much of modern French history. Actually, France has had no fewer than *fifteen* constitutions since the French Revolution (late eighteenth century). The most recent one has lasted over three decades—itself a noteworthy achievement. Its predecessor, adopted in the wake of World War II, endured only twelve years. During that time French governments lasted an average of about six months! Small wonder that political instability was both the cause of the Fourth Republic's early death and the principal malady the Fifth Republic's Constitution was designed to cure.

A Hybrid System

The Constitution of the Fifth Republic is a composite of France's earlier constitutions. It incorporates authoritarian, plebiscitarian, parliamentary, and republican features, and also certain innovations insisted on by the Fifth Republic's founder and first president, General Charles de Gaulle.

The hallmark of the current Constitution is the majestic presidency, which contrasts sharply with its predecessors. Under the Third and Fourth Republics the president was little more than a figurehead who rubberstamped measures passed by the French parliament. The president was chosen by the legislature acting as an electoral college, and thus tended to be a captive of that body. French parliaments were notoriously fragmented and ineffectual, which meant that the government was often adrift. Presidents had the power to appoint prime ministers (with legislative approval) and to dissolve parliament. The latter power was negative; positive power, to the extent that it existed at all, was lodged in the prime minister and cabinet, who, in turn, were often handicapped by a perpetually divided parliament.

General de Gaulle stressed the need for a strong and dignified president who would be aloof from fractious party politics and could guide the nation; mediate between and among the parties; discipline—and if necessary circumvent—the parliament in the interests of unity, stability, and efficiency; and embody the general will as opposed to the particularism of petty politicians. De Gaulle himself was both admired for his leadership abilities and reviled for his Bonapartist (dictatorial) tendencies.

The plebiscitarian aspect of the Constitution has its roots in the populist nature of Napoleon Bonaparte's rule and, more specifically, in the French Constitution of 1852. A plebiscite is a direct vote by the people on some issue of political importance to the nation. The idea of taking issues directly to the people sounds democratic, but in the hands of a charismatic leader it can be an instrument of dictatorship. Hence a popular president can use plebiscites to circumvent parliament, in effect establishing a personalistic (and deliberately antirepublican) form of rule.

An example of how President de Gaulle used (and abused) this power was the 1962 referendum on the direct election of the president. De Gaulle decided somewhat belatedly that it would strengthen the hand of the French president (namely de Gaulle) to be directly elected to a seven-year term of office. (At the time the president was indirectly elected to a shorter term by an electoral college.) The referendum passed after de Gaulle announced that he would resign if it failed. Thus he gave French voters the choice of granting his wish or losing his leadership. The referendum had the effect of amending the Constitution by clearly unconstitutional means! (French presidents since de Gaulle have been considerably less highhanded.)

The republican facet of the French system is evident in the National Assembly, whose members are directly elected by secret ballot on the basis of universal suffrage. This body reflects the notion of popular sovereignty found in the writings of the French philosopher Jean Jacques Rousseau. Rousseau argued that all legitimate political authority flows from the people. The people can, if they so choose, delegate that authority to a legislature, which must in turn take its cues from the sovereign citizenry. The Fifth Republic's Constitution would probably be found wanting by Rousseau, however, because the legislative branch, while not powerless by any means, can nonetheless be circumvented by a popular and willful president, as de Gaulle often demonstrated.

Finally, the quasi-parliamentary nature of the system can be seen in the presence of a cabinet-style executive in which the leader of the majority party in parliament (or of a coalition) chooses a cabinet and forms a government (à la Great Britain). The Constitution does not clearly delineate which executive functions fall within the purview of the prime minister and which are assigned to the president. This ambiguity may have been deliberate, but it gives rise to a potential constitutional crisis if the two executives are not on parallel tracks.

The present Constitution was approved by 70 percent of the French voters and has now weathered three decades of storm and stress. It has thus gained some legitimacy by virtue of its longevity alone. The mix of authoritarian, populist, republican, and parliamentary characteristics mirrors both the complexities of France's political history and the ideological diversity of the French electorate.

Who Rules? President and Prime Minister

France has a unique dual executive: a president with ample constitutional prerogatives to act and a prime minister who is the head of the government. This arrangement may seem impracticable, but it has worked surprisingly well in the French context.

Almost all West European governments are of the parliamentary variety in which the executive is chosen by the parliament and cabinet members are also party leaders in the legislature. Parliamentary rule can lead to governmental instability, especially where a multiparty system and an ideologically fragmented or polarized electorate prevent any single party from gaining a clear majority. Coalition governments are often vulnerable to votes of no confidence on controversial issues. Under some conditions they can even produce the expectation of instability, which may in time become a self-fulfilling prophecy.

In a presidential system, the chief executive is chosen by the people rather than the legislature and is elected for a fixed term. Except in extraordinary circumstances using cumbersome procedures, the legislative branch cannot oust the president. Thus in one sense the presidential system has greater stability than the parliamentary system. On the other hand, presidential government lacks the flexibility of the parliamentary system. In the former, if a scandal occurs or public support wanes, the government cannot simply resign and call for new elections as can the latter.

The French system attempts to have the best of both worlds: a strong president and a parliamentary form of government. Both fusion and separation of powers are present: The prime minister and cabinet (the government) are linked by party ties and constitutional logic to the National Assembly, but the president is elected separately and is not directly affected by the vicissitudes of parliamentary politics. The government can be censured and forced to resign; the president can dissolve parliament as often as once every twelve months. (This power has been used very sparingly.)

Today, thanks to de Gaulle, the French president possesses in practice all the powers the Queen of England exercises in theory. These include the power to appoint the prime minister (although the president must carefully weigh the balance of power among the parties in parliament in making this choice). The president can dissolve the National Assembly. He also can exercise emergency powers (which make him a virtual dictator) by simply declaring a state of emergency after consultation with the Constitutional Council. His power to call a national referendum on issues dealing with the organization of public powers, agreements in the European Community, and treaties also places him in a strategic position to manage political conflict and manipulate the system to produce a desired outcome.

In dealing with the National Assembly, the president has several constitutional weapons at his disposal. For example, he can ask for broad ''decree'' powers and combine this request with a vote of confidence. The National Assembly must then either grant the request, which means the president can make laws by fiat (without parliamentary approval), or face dissolution. Or the president can put a controversial bill into a bundle with other legislation expected to win easy approval, and demand a ''package vote.'' This tactic forces the National Assembly either to approve a measure many members may oppose or to vote down legislation the majority favors.

In general, the Constitution positions the president as an arbitrator charged with settling differences among conflicting interests. This has led to assumption by the presidential office of preeminent power in both domestic and foreign policy. Elected for a seven-year term and eligible to run for reelection, a popular president may dominate the political system for many years without facing the rigors of frequent campaigning or the vagaries of party politics. To win an election, the candidate must gain an absolute majority of the votes cast; lacking this, a run-off election is held. This two-ballot system ensures that whoever is elected will be the first or second choice of the majority of voters—the president will have a national mandate. Having a president endorsed by only a minority of the electorate would be an inauspicious start for a new government, especially in a country like France with a tradition of divisive politics.

In France, prime ministers have played a clearly subordinate, supporting role. Even so, the current power of the prime minister would have been the envy of prime ministers under the Third and Fourth Republics. The prime minister typically takes the lead in policy areas of little interest to the president, supervises and coordinates the work of the cabinet ministers, acts as the principal liaison between the executive and legislative branches, and, in the absence of a parliamentary majority, mediates between or among the different parties in the governing coalition.

The president and prime minister in cooperation can push legislation through the National Assembly or block measures they oppose. For the most part, cooperation has been the rule: During the past thirty years, the four presidents together have had only eleven prime ministers.

The power of the French cabinet, along with that of the prime minister, was reduced by the de Gaulle Constitution. As a rule, cabinet members owe their positions and the scope of their power to the president. The number of cabinet members has ranged from twenty-four under President de Gaulle (1958–1969) to forty-three under Prime Minister Chirac (1986–1988). Cabinet members are drawn from diverse walks of life; many come from the universities and the civil service. Unlike their British counterparts, members of the National Assembly must relinquish their seats in the Assembly to take a cabinet position. This requirement ensures a separation of powers (similar to that in the United States), and puts the president and government on the same side, so to speak.

Ministers act under the direction of the president and prime minister. Their primary duty is to oversee the implementation of policy by that part of the bureaucracy for which they are responsible. The French government has traditionally been highly centralized, although the main thrust of current President Mitterand's administrative reforms has been to decentralize the system.

France's Technocracy: The Civil Service

The civil service has three basic components: the Ministry of Interior (center), the prefects (territorial departments), and the mayors (local government). The Ministry of Interior is charged with monitoring implementation of the government's decisions, policies, and programs. It is run mostly by career civil servants (technocrats) and it has sweeping police and supervisory powers.

Prefects are unique to France. They provide the linkage between Paris and the provinces, connecting the ministries in the capital with local governments around the country. Their powers are far reaching. Historically, they have often kept the country functioning even when the government has been paralyzed by partisan politics.

Locally elected mayors are responsible both to the people and to the prefect of the department in which they are located. They may act only with permission of the prefect. If they fail to observe this top-down line of authority they can be dismissed.

In general, French technocrats are among the most sophisticated and professional in the world. Extremely important at all levels of government, they play a large policy role, not only enforcing policy but also formulating and interpreting it.

The Taming of Parliament

Under the Third and Fourth Republics (1871–1940; 1946–1958), the French parliament wielded most of the power. The instability and paralysis of the government during that often turbulent era led directly to the curbing of the powers of parliament by the present Constitution. The fulcrum of the French government moved from the parliament to the presidency under the Fifth Republic.

The legislature comprises an upper and a lower house—the National Assembly and the Senate, respectively. Until 1981, deputies to the National Assembly were elected in single-member districts, the two receiving the most votes on the first ballot then competing in a run-off election. After Mitterand's election in 1981, the Socialists changed the system to election in multimember districts on the basis of a complex system of proportional representation. Following elections in 1986 the earlier system of *ballotage* was reinstituted. This system has an interesting twist: Parties can form alliances for the second vote, in effect dividing up a voting district according to which party's candidate has the best chance of winning. One practical consequence of this system is impedance of extremist parties (they cannot find alliance partners). Even the French Communist party, which abandoned extremism long ago, has been hampered by this system. Deputies to the Assembly in 1987 numbered 577.

The Senate is indirectly elected by an electoral college consisting of members of the Assembly and representatives of local governments. Its members, numbering around 300, serve nine-year terms. Elections to the Senate are staggered at three-year intervals. The Senate is autonomous and cannot be dissolved by the president.

The National Assembly and the Senate share power equally, with two exceptions: The Assembly has the right to examine the budget first, and the cabinet is responsible to the Assembly rather than to the Senate. Almost all legislation originates in the executive branch; private members may not even introduce budget measures.

The Senate gives disproportionate representation to rural areas and thus acts as a counterweight to the urban-oriented National Assembly. Although it is weaker than the Assembly, the Senate may reject government bills. (The Assembly can override a Senate veto, however.) The Senate's chief role is to keep the government honest by using question time to challenge those responsible for policy and decision making.

In many respects, the French parliament is more interesting for the powers it does *not* have than for the powers it has. First, it cannot meet for more than six months each year. Second, it has no power to introduce financial bills—if it fails to approve the government's budget by a certain deadline, the budget can be enacted by executive decree. Moreover, as already noted, it can be compelled by the executive branch to cast a *package vote* on several pieces of legislation at once. Also, the government can make any particular vote a vote of confidence; in such a case, a negative vote in the National Assembly forces the resignation of the government and may lead to the dissolution of parliament. Although this device may seem to be one way for the legislature to control the government, the president, as we have seen, is beyond the reach of parliament. The upshot is that the Assembly penalizes itself by triggering new elections.

President de Gaulle creatively combined different provisions of the Constitution to maximize presidential leverage over the parties in parliament. For example, he was not above calling for a package vote on some part of his overall program and then making the vote itself a matter of confidence! De Gaulle's successors have treated the National Assembly with considerably less disdain.

The committee system in the Fifth Republic is a cross between those found in the U.S. Congress and the British House of Commons. Like the British system, there are only six standing committees; like the U.S. system, the committees are specialized. Most have more than 100 members. Membership on committees is apportioned according to party strength in the parliament. Unlike their counterparts in the U.S. Congress, committees in the French parliament cannot change the substance of government bills. Investigative committees can be created to probe government actions but they have limited powers. The length of time they may investigate is set, they cannot investigate matters that are being handled by the judiciary, their findings must be reported to a standing committee for approval or rejection, and they can meet only in closed sessions, to plug any leaks. Committees are generally used as a means to distribute power among the parties and to give the opposition a formal role, albeit highly limited, in the political process.

A Multiparty System

France continues to have a panoply of political parties, although the tendency has been toward consolidation around center-right and center-left poles. Traditionally, the Socialists and Communists have comprised the two main parties on the left. From the end of World War II until the late 1970s, the Communist party generally received at least 20 percent of the popular vote. In the 1980s there was a steady erosion of Communist party strength: In the 1986 legislative elections the party's fortunes fell to an all-time low—Communist candidates garnered about half the number of votes normally cast in their favor. The downward trend continued in the presidential and parliamentary elections in 1988–1989.

The Socialist party has been the major beneficiary of this moderating trend on the left. In 1981 it not only won the presidency but also gained a clear majority in the National Assembly. Although support for the Socialist party dropped in the 1986 elections, France's Socialist President François Mitterand easily won reelection to a second term in 1988. (Mitterand won 54 percent of the popular vote on the second ballot to Jacques Chirac's 46 percent). In that year, Socialists in the Assembly fell short of the majority that pollsters were predicting; nonetheless, the 276 seats they won gave them the largest block of votes (only 13 short of the 289 needed for an absolute majority in 1988). Moderate Socialist leader Michel Rocard formed a minority government and sought the cooperation of an autonomous group of fifty deputies known as the Center for Social Democrats (CDS).

The Socialists became the preferred party of the French left because of their pragmatism and the popularity of their leadership, for policies favoring expanded social welfare programs, for concessions to free-market forces (especially business and banking interests), and for strong support for the Western alliance system (NATO). After the 1988 elections, President Mitterand outlined a series of goals for the new government: working toward a united Europe, supporting further superpower nuclear arms reductions, investing more in research and education, accelerating modernization of French industry, and protecting France's elaborate social security system. There appeared to be a national consensus behind this mix of liberal and conservative measures.

On the political right, Gaullist parties under various names have predominated during the last four decades. De Gaulle himself never founded a party; indeed, he was contemptuous of political parties in general. Nonetheless, today his followers continue to keep the Gaullist legacy alive under the banner of the Union of French Democracy (UDF), a center-right party headed by Raymond Barre that stresses greater European cooperation and integration. There is also a more conservative neo-Gaullist party, the Rally for the Republic, headed by former Prime Minister Jacques Chirac, and an Independent Republican party led by former President Valéry Giscard d'Estaing. These two parties share a common political philosophy, both favoring strong presidential government, a centralized administrative system, and free-market economic policies. However, personal differences among their leaders have prevented full cooperation.

Splinter parties on both the left and right have arisen from time to time. The most recent ''flash in the pan'' party was the reactionary National Front, whose leader, Jean-Marie Le Pen, did surprisingly well in his presidential bid in 1988. In the subsequent legislative elections, however, his party—which espouses nationalistic, antiimmigration policies—made a very poor showing.

The 1980s: Testing the System

In 1964, Prime Minister Georges Pompidou described the delicate institutional balance of the Fifth Republic:

> France has now chosen a system midway between the American presidential regime and the British parliamentary regime, where the chief of state, who formulates general policy, has the basis of authority in universal suffrage but can only exercise his function with a government that he may have chosen and named, but which in order to survive, must maintain the confidence of the Assembly.[5]

The Fifth Republic has provided France with unprecedented political stability. The personality of de Gaulle was certainly a factor in the early years. De Gaulle's influence extended well beyond his presidency. His opposition to domestic Communism, his emphasis on France's sovereign independence (symbolized by the French nuclear strike force), his concern with enhancing French prestige in Europe and beyond, and his desire for economic growth without extensive nationalization of industry—all were continued by his two successors, Georges Pompidou (1969–1974) and Valéry Giscard d'Estaing (1974–1981). The National Assembly and French voters have also broadly supported these policies.

But in 1981 this national consensus was challenged. For the first time the Socialist party won a clear majority in the Assembly, and a Socialist was elected president. These victories portended a turn to the left in the form of expanded welfare programs, deficit spending on a grand scale, new nationalizations of French industry, worker participation in management ("autogestion"), and administrative decentralization. As it happened, the realization of this agenda was hampered by deepening domestic difficulties, in particular higher unemployment and economic stagnation, which adversely affected the Socialists' popularity.

While France was experiencing these political changes, the system itself came under fire. The president was seen as being too aloof from political pressures and public opinion, and the system was attacked for being overly politicized. Because the president was elected every seven years and the National Assembly was chosen at least every five years, elections—and preparations for them—came to dominate French politics. Legislative or presidential elections were held in 1962, 1965, 1968, 1969, 1973, 1974, 1978, 1981 (two), 1986, and 1988 (two). One authority asserted that "long-range programs gave place to expediency, and party alignments obeyed the logic of electoral tactics rather than policy making."[6]

The severest test of the system came in 1986, when the center-right parties won the legislative elections by a narrow majority (291 of 577 seats) in the National Assembly. By the logic of the system, President Mitterand was compelled to choose a conservative prime minister. He asked Jacques Chirac, leader of a neo-Gaullist party, to form a new government. The Fifth Republic had been created with a built-in time bomb that seemed about to detonate: a *divided executive* was in power. The president and prime minister belonged to different political parties, had different agendas, and looked to different constituencies.

This predicament produced *cohabitation*, a term used to describe how France's two chief executives managed to coexist for two years without bringing the system down. There were tensions at times, and the machinery of government did not run as smoothly as it might have, but Mitterand and Chirac both displayed enough flexibility and mutual tolerance to avert a major constitutional crisis. The fact that the system faced this challenge and survived suggests something of historic importance to the French nation: Both major political configurations—left and right—have a commitment to the Constitution that transcends ideologies. The Fifth Republic has perhaps acquired a legitimacy no other French republic has known.

West Germany's Federal Democracy

On October 3, 1990, West Germany and East Germany were united as one country. Unification meant that, in effect, the West German system of government was extended into the former East German territory under Article 23 of West Germany's Basic Law (see below).

Despite a tradition of autocratic and sometimes dictatorial rule, Germany today is a thriving democracy. The Federal Republic of Germany (FRG) consisted of ten states, or *Laender* (singular *Land*), not counting West Berlin. United Germany consists of sixteen *Laender*, including the united city of Berlin, which is both the capital of the nation and a federal state.

The following discussion focuses on the German system of government from 1949 to 1990, when its authority extended only over West Germany.

The *Laender* are the building blocks in a system designed to ensure a high degree of political decentralization. *Land* governments have the primary responsibility to enact legislation in specific areas such as education and cultural affairs. They alone have the means to implement laws enacted by the federal government, to command most of the administrative personnel to accomplish this task, to exercise police power (taking care of the health, welfare, and moral well-being of the people), to direct the educational system, and to ensure that the press plays by the constitutional rules.

Impressive though the power of the *Laender* may be, the federal government is the main repository of political authority in the constitutional system. The federal government is given exclusive right to legislate in foreign affairs, citizenship matters, currency and coinage, railways, postal service and telecommunications, and copyrights. In other areas, notably civil and criminal law and laws relating to the regulation of the economy, the central government and *Laender* share power.

The German system is probably more federal than is that of the United States; that is, its *Laender* run more of their own affairs and receive a larger proportion of taxes than do American states. For example, individual and corporate income taxes are split between the federal government and the *Laender* in equal 40-percent shares; the cities get 20 percent. The *Laender* also receive one-third of the value-added tax, the large but hidden sales tax used throughout Europe. As a result, while some additional funds are transferred from the federal government to the *Laender* and cities, the *Laender* do not have to beg the national government for money, as their counterparts in the United States so often do.

The Basic Law

West Germany's charter is called the "Basic Law" rather than the "Constitution," because it was designed as a temporary document to be supplanted by a true constitution at some point after the unification of the two Germanys. The last article states, "This Basic Law loses its validity on the day on which a Constitution comes into effect which has been freely decided upon by the German people."

The drafting of the Basic Law was extraordinary, in part because it was done under the watchful eyes of the powers occupying Germany after World War II. The United States, Great Britain, and France served as models from whom the West Germans borrowed freely. From the United States they took the principles of federalism and bicameralism. From Great Britain they adapted the parliamentary system. They imitated the French electoral system, using proportional representation to fill some of the seats in the *Bundestag* (lower house). The preamble to the Basic Law proclaims West Germany's right of self-determination, and there is nothing in the Law that mentions the Occupation. Remarkably, a few short years after World War II, a sovereign, independent, and democratic government became fully operational in West Germany.

The Basic Law and Individual Rights   Significantly, the first nineteen articles of the Basic Law deal with the inalienable rights of every citizen. As one student of German politics has observed, "The relevant historical experience was that of the Third Reich with its oppressive flouting of all human liberties."[7] The Weimar Constitution allowed the government to suspend constitutional rights during times of emergency. Abuse of this emergency power by the Nazi regime eventually led to the revocation of the Constitution itself. Accordingly, Article 19 of the present "constitution" proclaims that "In no case may the essential content of a basic right be encroached upon." The guarantees contained in the first nineteen articles are entrenched: no act of the executive, legislative, or judicial branch of government can revoke or abridge them. If a question arises as to whether a statutory law conflicts with the Basic Law, the issue is resolved by the Federal Constitutional Court.

The rights guaranteed under the Basic Law include equality before the law; freedom of speech, religion, assembly, and the press; academic freedom; freedom of association; freedom from unlawful searches; private property rights; the right of asylum; freedom from discrimination based on race, sex, or political convictions; and the right to refuse military service as a matter of conscience. Article 18 attaches a caveat to these rights, stipulating that they cannot be used "to attack the democratic order." This proviso was clearly aimed at the two extremes of left and right, Communism and Nazism, which have so afflicted German life in the present century. Doubtless it reflected most of all the postwar preoccupation with Soviet

Communism that prevailed throughout the Atlantic Community and was particularly pervasive in West Germany. However, fear of the reawakening of neo-Nazi ultranationalism has never been far beneath the surface in the FRG, as evidenced by the fact that neo-Nazi activity generally has been interpreted as constituting an "attack [on] the democratic order."

The Amendment Process   Amending the Basic Law requires a two-thirds majority vote in both houses of parliament, but, as stated, the fundamental principles and guarantees cannot be revoked or amended. In addition to the civil liberties enumerated in the first nineteen articles, the federal, republican, democratic, and welfare-state features of the political system are deliberately set in stone to prevent a recurrence of the Nazi nightmare.

Article 23   From its inception, the Basic Law of the Federal Republic looked ahead to a time when Germany would be united. Under Article 23, the German Democratic Republic (GDR) could be reunited with the FRG at any time, the only proviso being that the GDR had to accept the Basic Law. Prior to 1989, this part of the West German constitution seemed irrelevant in the context of the Cold War. With the overthrow of Communist rule in East Germany in 1989, however, Article 23 became the vehicle by which the two German states were united in 1990.

The Chancellor

West Germany has a parliamentary form of government with a divided executive. The President is a figurehead, indirectly elected and endowed with ceremonial powers exclusively. The chancellor is the true chief executive; a person receives this office in the same way that the British prime minister does—by being leader of the majority party in the lower house (the *Bundestag*). If no one party enjoys an absolute majority, as has often been the case in West Germany, the leader of the major party in the ruling coalition becomes the chancellor.

The chancellor, with parliamentary approval, appoints and dismisses cabinet members. Together with the cabinet, he (she) sets policy guidelines and proposes legislation. As the head of government he is responsible for translating paper policies (words) into operational programs (deeds). The chancellor has the power to veto budget measures that do not meet his approval. In case of a national emergency, the chancellor becomes commander-in-chief. In short, the chancellor, like the British prime minister, is the lynchpin in the system.

The position of chancellor has been reinforced by a novel constitutional rule that makes it difficult to remove a person in this position. In contrast to the British prime minister, a chancellor cannot be ousted by a vote of no confidence unless the *Bundestag* simultaneously chooses a new chancellor. This procedure is known as a *constructive vote of no confidence*; it was designed as a safeguard against the governmental instability of the Weimar Republic. It has served this purpose well. Konrad Adenauer served as chancellor for the first fourteen years of the

FRG's existence (1949–1963). In 1982, Chancellor Helmut Schmidt was replaced by opposition leader Helmut Kohl through a constructive vote of no confidence—the first and only time since the founding of the West German state that a chancellor has been dismissed in this manner.

As mentioned, the chancellor handpicks his cabinet members. They usually number about seventeen. Most West German governments have involved coalitions between one of the two major parties and a minor party. As a consequence, West German cabinets typically reflect the need to allocate several key posts to the coalition partner. The chancellor heads the cabinet; members are responsible directly to him.

Almost all cabinet members are also active members of the *Bundestag*. Appointed because of their political stature, cabinet members are seldom specialists in their respective departments. (These tend to be small [in contrast to British departments], since the Land governments administer most federal programs and enforce federal as well as state laws.) The most prominent cabinet members are the ministers of finance, foreign affairs, defense, and interior. Cabinet members participate in decision making, advise the chancellor on policy matters, direct the formulation policy proposals and legislation within their own departments, and oversee the implementation of policy by their subordinates.

Directly below the chancellor and his cabinet are the parliamentary secretaries (who are members of the Federal Diet) and state secretaries (career civil service employees). The parliamentary secretaries are considered junior ministers—they leave office when the term of the cabinet member they serve ends. The state secretaries, professional bureaucrats, provide continuity from one government to the next—they stay on after cabinet members leave office.

The West German Parliament

Unlike Great Britain, Germany lacks a great parliamentary tradition. Bismarck largely ignored the *Reichstag* (the forerunner of the *Bundestag*), and during the Weimar period it was ineffectual. Even after 1949 the *Bundestag* lacked prestige and was treated with a certain disdain by Chancellor Adenauer (who resembled France's authoritarian President Charles de Gaulle in this respect).

The West German parliament is bicameral, consisting of a lower house, the *Bundestag*, and an upper house, the *Bundesrat*. The *Bundestag*, whose members are directly elected, is the primary law-making body. Most bills are initiated by the chancellor, but before any bill can become law the *Bundestag* must vote its approval. Thus it functions as one of the principal mechanisms in the constitutional system of checks and balances. The Basic Law underscores the independence of the *Bundestag* by stipulating that its members are ''not bound by orders and instructions and shall be subject only to their conscience.''

In addition to choosing the chancellor, the *Bundestag* acts as a watchdog over the government. As we have already seen, the *Bundestag* has the power to oust a chancellor with a constructive vote of no confidence at any time. On its own initiative, it can also enact legislation binding on the government, conduct public debates on government policy, investigate government actions, and directly question the chancellor and cabinet members. (The latter can be summoned to appear before the *Bundestag*, but they cannot be forced to disclose information.)

Voting patterns within the *Bundestag* reflect a strict party discipline. Parliamentary parties are organized into *Fraktionen* (factions). The *Fraktionen* meet frequently to decide how to vote on upcoming bills and discuss legislative strategy. Indeed, they go so far as to determine the specific responsibility each deputy will assume on each piece of legislation. The assignments and instructions include even the precise arguments deputies will make. The *Fraktionen* are built into the parliamentary structure: Only parties with a large enough block of deputies to form a *Fraktion* (at least 5 percent of the total membership) can be represented in committees.

In Germany, as in the United States, committees are a principle source of legislative power. Most committee meetings are held in private, and the opposition has ample opportunity to participate. There are currently nineteen standing committees; nearly all have identical counterparts in the cabinet, an arrangement that facilitates the flow of communications between the government and the *Bundestag*. Normally, committees in the FRG do not have the kind of investigatory powers found in the U.S. Congress, but the *Bundestag* can establish special committees of inquiry on the recommendation of one-fourth of the deputies.

The *Bundestag* elects a presiding officer through a secret ballot. In practice, the majority party decides who will be the president. There are also three vice presidents selected from opposition parties. Together with other party leaders, these officials form a Council of Elders that acts as an advisory board to the president of the *Bundestag*, schedules debates on pending legislation, and allocates speaking time to the parliamentary parties.

The *Bundesrat*, or Federal Council, is the main institutional mechanism for adjusting and regulating relations between the *Bund* (federal government) and the *Laender*. It is perhaps the most distinctive feature of the West German system. Unlike the relatively powerless British House of Lords, the *Bundesrat* is a powerful body with exclusive constitutional functions. Directly responsible to the state governments, it has wide-ranging influence on federal policies and procedures.

Members of the *Bundesrat* are not popularly elected. Rather the *Land* governments appoint representatives, apportioned on the basis of population. *Laender* with over 6 million inhabitants are allowed five seats, those with over 2 million get four seats, and the rest receive three seats. There are forty-five members in all, including four nonvoting observers from West Berlin. The representatives of each *Land* government must vote as a block, a provision that heavily reinforces the federal character of the West German parliament.

The *Bundestag* is constitutionally required to submit the legislation it passes to the *Bundesrat*. All bills that directly affect the *Laender* must be approved by the *Bundesrat* to become law—in other words, the *Bundesrat* can veto such legislation. Other bills do not require its approval, but any objections raised by the

Bundesrat must at a minimum be debated in the *Bundestag* before the bill becomes law. With the passage of time, the influence of the *Bundesrat* over federal policy has increased considerably. This, in turn, has given the *Laender* a role in the political system far exceeding that of their counterparts in the United States.

Because the composition of the *Bundesrat* is not affected by national elections, this house has a special aura of stability. It is also more streamlined and efficient than the lower house, since most of its members hold ministerial posts in their respective *Land* governments and can use their own administratives staffs to help them prepare legislation. In general, *Bundesrat* members tend to have more technical expertise than do *Bundestag* deputies, and they can be more specialized. Finally, there is little party influence in the *Bundesrat*. Members are expected to represent the interests of their respective *Land* without regard for party preference. The strict party discipline found in the *Bundestag* is matched by the tight control *Land* governments exercise over their representatives in the *Bundesrat*. In sum, the *Bundesrat* gives the German states a powerful weapon to protect themselves against federal encroachment.

The Basic Law divides legislation into three categories—exclusive, concurrent, and framework law. Article 30 lodges state legislative authority firmly in the *Laender*, and Article 70 stipulates that the *Laender* have all legislative powers not expressly conferred on the Federal Parliament. Exclusive legislative authority, that is, authority assigned solely to the *Bund* (federal government), is limited to foreign affairs, defense, currency, and trade. Concurrent legislative authority applies in such areas as criminal and civil law, trade and commerce, and public roads. The *Laender* may legislate in these areas so long as the *Bund* has not already done so. (All federal legislation in this category must be approved by the *Bundesrat* to become law.) Framework legislative authority limits the *Bund* to providing outline bills only, leaving the details to the *Laender*. This category includes public services, the environment, and regional planning. Although the most important legislation is given to the *Bund*, administration of programs and implementation of policy are left largely in the hands of the *Laender*.

Bills in the Federal Parliament run a familiar gauntlet: formal introduction, committee review, several readings, debate, and final vote. Measures may be introduced by individual members of the *Bundestag*, by the government, or by the *Bundesrat*. Most legislation is drafted by the executive branch. All government bills must be sent to the *Bundesrat* first, and any changes to a bill must accompany it to the *Bundestag*. Since the *Bundesrat* has veto power over all concurrent legislation, the government normally works closely with this body in the drafting stages to avoid potential problems.

After a bill has been introduced, it goes to the *Bundestag* where it is debated. Next it is sent to a standing committee, where most of the detail work is done. A committee member is usually assigned to prepare a report on the bill, which then goes back to the full house for further debate. This stage is called the "second reading." A third reading usually follows shortly thereafter, and the measure is voted on. If it passes, it is sent to the *Bundesrat*.

In the case of legislation introduced by the government, the *Bundesrat* gets two reviews. If the *Bundesrat* and the *Bundestag* do not agree on the form or substance of a particular bill, the bill goes to a Conference Committee, much like the practice in the U.S. Congress. The Conference Committee has twenty-two members, half from each of the two houses of parliament. Differences in language are usually reconciled through this mechanism. Once a bill has been passed by both houses and signed by the president and chancellor, it becomes law.

Parties and Elections

National elections normally occur every four years in West Germany. Two different electoral systems are used to choose the *Bundestag's* 496 deputies. Half are elected by the first-past-the-post system in effect in Great Britain and the United States, that is, single-member districts, plurality vote. This is called the "first vote." The other half are elected by proportional representation, called the "second vote." In the first vote, the individual candidate is featured; in the second vote, the party is paramount. Thus, each voter casts two votes, one for an individual and one for a *Land* list put together by the party. The second (or party) vote is crucial because it determines the total number of seats a party receives in each *Land*. The party decides who is at the top of the list and who is at the bottom, a practice that enhances the role and importance of political parties in West Germany.

Under the Weimar Republic, the left- and right-wing parties were separated by a yawning ideological chasm that produced the instability that led Germany down the path to totalitarian rule. Today, the vast majority of West German voters crowd around the political center—moderation is in and extremism is out.

Since 1949, West Germany has had just two major parties—the center-left Social Democratic party (SPD) and the conservative Christian Democratic party (CDU). The latter has formed a permanent alliance with the Bavarian Christian Social Union (CSU). In addition, the relatively small Free Democratic party (FDP) has shown remarkable staying power and, most of the time, has played a strategic role by striking a balance midway between the evenly matched SPD and CDU/CSU. Because the two major parties have frequently been almost perfectly balanced in the *Bundestag*, the Free Democrats often have held the decisive votes. Their influence thus has been disproportionate to their small following, and they have enjoyed "junior partner" status in most coalition governments.

Although the SPD is a socialist party and the CDU/CSU is a free-enterprise party, both are relatively moderate. Indeed, the two parties shared power from 1966 to 1969 in what was known as the Grand Coalition.

Smaller parties have a better chance of surviving in West Germany than in Great Britain because half the *Bundestag* is chosen by proportional representation. Even so, the party system was consciously designed to keep the number of parties at a reasonable level and to prevent small extremist groups from disrupting the orderly democratic process. Thus, parties must receive a minimum of

5 percent of the national vote or win seats in a minimum of three electoral districts to gain *Bundestag* representation.

The most successful "fringe" party in West Germany has been the Greens—a leftist party that focuses almost exclusively on environmental and antinuclear issues. In the spring of 1987, the Greens led an amorphous counterculture coalition in a protest against a nationwide census. The ostensible issue was the right to privacy; the real issue was the authority of the state, which the Greens generally regard with fear and loathing.

In the January 1987 elections a coalition of the CDU/CSU and the FDP won 53.4 percent of the popular vote and 266 (of a possible 496) seats in the *Bundestag*. The CDU/CSU actually dropped from 48.8 percent of the popular vote in 1983 to 44.3 percent in 1987. The little parties were the big winners: the FDP went from 7.0 percent in 1983 to 9.1 percent, while the Greens gained the most, going from 5.6 percent to 8.3 percent. Later in the year, the CDU suffered heavy losses in Schleswig-Holstein and Bremen *Land* elections. The Greens, however, were hampered by internal wrangling (historically the curse of left-wing parties in Western Europe and elsewhere).

As noted previously, the issue of German reunification was taken off the shelf and put on the front burner following the dramatic events that toppled the Communist regime in East Germany at the end of 1989. The conservative East German Christian Democratic Union, which won a plurality (41 percent) of the votes in elections held in March 1990, campaigned on a platform calling for rapid merger of the two German states.

When that merger occurred—on October 3, 1990—the population of the FRG increased by 17 million overnight. No one can say for certain what the political implications of suddenly incorporating so many people who have never lived under constitutional democracy or coped with a free-enterprise system might be.

A Limited Government

If we weigh the cumulative effects of West Germany's key constitutional provisions (federalism, the unique organization of the legislature, the carefully structured party system, the independent judiciary, the explicit guarantees of civil liberties), it becomes apparent that one of the principal purposes behind the Basic Law was arrangement of the institutional furniture in the "new Germany" so as to preclude a repeat performance of the "old Germany." Limited government, more than any other facet of constitutional democracy, was central to the drafters of the Basic Law. They deliberately sought to create safeguards against the concentration of power that had caused so much turmoil in the interwar years.

The democratic performance of the West German government since World War II has indeed been impressive. The experience of Weimar has not been repeated. While the Weimar Republic was largely undone by severe economic distress, West Germany's rapid postwar recovery and sustained industrial growth since 1949 have frequently been described as an economic miracle. Spurred on by a remarkable economic resurgence and a firm commitment to constitutional government, the present generation of West Germans has given democracy a new lease on life in a land where it was once thought to be unworkable. Moreover, West German economic success no doubt spurred East Germans' dissatisfaction with a Communist regime that was unable to match West Germany's performance or come close to providing a comparable standard of living. Germany was a microcosm of the Cold War for over forty years; the collapse of Communism in the GDR symbolizes the end of an era in international politics and a new beginning for Germany.

The European Community: Political Structures

Any discussion of contemporary political systems in Western Europe would be incomplete without a look at the quasi-government of the European Community (EC). Since its inception as a ''common market'' (or customs union) in 1958, the EC has moved steadily toward full-scale economic integration. Efforts toward political integration have been less successful, but not inconsequential. The framework for a new European superpower comprising the twelve current EC member states— Germany, France, Great Britain, Italy, Belgium, the Netherlands, Luxembourg, Denmark, Greece, Ireland, Portugal, and Spain—has been constructed.

The EC encompasses three separate legal entities: the European Coal and Steel Community (ECSC), the European Economic Community (EEC or Common Market), and the European Atomic Energy Community (Euratom). It is governed by institutions common to all, including a Parliament, Council of Ministers, Commission, Court of Justice, and Court of Auditors. The Economic and Social Committee performs an advisory role.

The Council of Ministers has the final decision-making authority. The Council is composed of the foreign ministers of the member states, which in practice means that these states have not given up their right of self-determination or sovereignty. The Commission is the administrative arm of the EC. It is accountable to the European Parliament, which can dismiss it by a vote of censure. It initiates proposals, but must obtain the prior approval of the Council of Ministers before taking action on any new measures. Parliament shares the power of the purse with the Council of Ministers, and has the right to reject the budget—a power it exercised in 1979 and 1984 because it disagreed with the Council's spending priorities.

An ''Assembly'' (named the European Parliament in 1962) was envisioned in the original treaties setting up the Community, but the first election of members of the European Parliament (MEPs) did not take place until 1973. For several years, delegates were appointed from their national parliaments; in 1979 MEPs were directly elected for the first time. In 1984 the second EC direct elections involved 120 million voters in ten countries—60 percent of eligible voters (a slight drop from the 1979 elections). The turnout varied greatly, ranging from a high of 92 percent in Belgium (where voting is compulsory) to a low of 32 percent in the Great Britain (where the electorate has always been lukewarm at best).

With the inclusion in the EC of Greece in 1981 and Spain and Portugal in 1986, the number of MEPs rose from 410 to 518. The largest member states—Germany, France, Great Britain, and Italy—have eighty-one members each; the smallest—Denmark, Ireland, and Luxembourg—have sixteen, fifteen, and six, respectively.

The members of the European Parliament in 1984–1989 represented a broad political spectrum. The largest political groups were the Socialists (165) and the Christian Democrats ("European People's Party") (115). The bloc of center-right groups and Conservatives retained their majority despite losing a few seats in the 1984 elections.

To give the EC a genuinely supranational character, Parliament's activities are located in three different cities: administration is in Luxembourg; week-long plenary sessions take place monthly in Strasbourg; and the eighteen specialized committees normally meet for two weeks each month in Brussels. The proceedings in full sessions and in committees are simultaneously translated into the nine official languages of the Community—English, Danish, Dutch, French, German, Greek, Italian, Spanish, and Portuguese.

Besides budgetary and economic matters, the special committees deal with a wide range of public policies in such areas as agriculture, energy, transport, and the environment. They also focus on economic relations with nonmember countries, unemployment, women's rights, and consumer protection, among other issues.

Parliament does not have the power to legislate, but in recent years it has become more assertive in dealing with the Commission. In particular, it has applied the powers of delay (effectively a veto) in drafting laws as a means of compelling the Commission to respond to its concerns before proposals go forward for final decision by the Council of Ministers. In 1984 the European Parliament adopted a blueprint for the Community's future organization. This plan for "European Union" sought to enhance the legislative powers of Parliament, streamline decision making, and reduce the ability of the individual member states to impede the progress of the Community. Not surprisingly, the twelve individual governments considered the plan too radical. Instead, in February 1986 they signed the Single European Act, which called for greater use of majority voting in the Council and a limited increase in Parliament's powers. The Act also set 1992 as the deadline for the full integration (or unification) of the EC economies.

The Act went into effect in 1987 following approval by the national parliaments. The Council of Ministers now adopts most legislation by qualified majority, rather than unanimous, voting. EC members have a total of seventy-six votes apportioned as follows: Germany, ten; France, ten; Italy, ten; the United Kingdom, ten; Spain, eight; Belgium, five; Netherlands, five; Greece, five; Portugal, five; Denmark, three; Ireland, three; and Luxembourg, two. It takes fifty-four votes for a qualified majority, and twenty-three to block a measure. In practice this new procedure means that EC decision making has been streamlined—"the equivalent of upgrading the community's motor from steam power to gasoline."[8] Whereas before adoption of the Single European Act any member state could veto any measure, now a minimum of three member states is needed. Six of the seven small states would have to join forces to block a measure. Furthermore, three of the "big four"—Germany, France, Italy, and Great Britain—are needed to defeat a proposal.

Under the new law, Parliament has the right to reject or amend legislation and the Council of Ministers can override its decisions only by a unanimous vote. Also, the importance of coordinating policy in two salient areas, foreign affairs and environmental protection, was formally recognized, giving higher visibility to Parliament's debates than in the past.

"Nevertheless," notes journalist Stephen Brookes, "Europe still lacks a genuine government; decisions are made through a cumbersome process that might be described as bureaucracy tempered by diplomacy, and national governments are holding firmly to the reins of their sovereignty."[9] Moreover, the executive branch—which, as we have seen, gives the seventeen-member Commission power to propose legislation and the Council of Ministers final authority to approve it—is widely criticized as nondemocratic, especially by parties of the left.

In the late 1980s a great debate raged in Europe between the center-right and the left over the future of the EC. The issue was not whether a European Union is desirable, but rather what kind—one embracing the liberal, free-market policies associated with Margaret Thatcher and Helmut Kohl or one featuring bureaucratic, welfare-state policies typically favored by Socialist parties. The Commission President, Jacques Delors, a former French finance minister, advocated a tight economic unity with a "social dimension," including a "platform of guaranteed social rights" for workers. British Prime Minister Thatcher denounced Delors' "Marxist" vision, declaring in 1988 at the College of Europe in Bruge, Belgium, "We have not successfully rolled back the frontiers of the state in Britain only to see them reimposed at a European level, with a European superstate exercising new dominance from Brussels."[10]

But even Margaret Thatcher's eloquence and iron will may not be enough to prevent the birth of a new technocratic superstate in Europe. Having spurned the Common Market in 1957, Great Britain has always been somewhat isolated within the EC. For a host of historical reasons, the British remain somewhat aloof from the Continent and continue to be viewed by other Europeans as less than fully committed to Europe. Economically, London has always objected to the protectionist Common Agricultural Policy (CAP), which places tariffs on agricultural imports and heavily subsidizes European (especially French) farmers. Only the Danes share British ambivalence toward political unification.

Elsewhere in the EC, public opinion now strongly favors a European Union. This widespread acceptance of the idea of a united Europe represents a sea change in popular attitudes and suggests that the EC's economic benefits are eroding the strong nationalistic tendencies that have so long been the hallmark of European politics.

In conclusion, Western Europe is on the verge of unification in the economic sphere and has made significant, though halting, progress toward political integration. The obstacles to a full-fledged United States of Europe, however, remain formidable. If Europe is ever ruled by a single political authority, the impetus will come from the economic dynamism of the "common market," a topic discussed in the next chapter.

CONCLUSION

At present, the political systems of Western Europe display a remarkable consistency: All are based on the principle of government by consent of the governed, all are ruled by civilians who came to power by free elections based on universal suffrage and the secret ballot, and all protect personal freedoms and civil liberties from infringement by the state. This consistent pattern is no doubt one reason why the West has been able to move farther and faster toward economic unity (and perhaps political union) than any region of the world. In Chapter 6 we explore the challenges Western Europe will face in the 1990s and we assess the future of the European Community as a response to these challenges.

STUDY QUESTIONS

1. Given a choice between serving as the president of the United States or the prime minister of Great Britain, which job would you prefer, and why?
2. How do the electoral systems of Great Britain, France, and Germany differ, and with what consequences?
3. In comparing and contrasting the constitutional powers of the French president and the British prime minister, what features should be stressed most heavily, and why?
4. To what extent is the German political system based on the U.S. model? To what extent is it based on the British model? To what extent is it unique?

SUGGESTED READINGS

Conradt, David P. *The German Polity.* New York: Longmans, 1986.

Jacobs, Dan N., et al. *Comparative Politics: United Kingdom, France, Germany, Soviet Union.* Chatham, N.J.: Chatham House, 1983.

Norton, Philip. *The British Polity.* New York: Longmans, 1984.

Steiner, Jurg. *European Democracies.* New York: Longmans, 1986.

Rodes, John E. *The Quest for Unity: Modern Germany, 1848–1970.* New York: Holt, 1971.

Safran, William. *The French Polity.* New York: Longmans, 1985.

Willis, F. Roy. *France, Germany and the New Europe, 1945–1967.* New York: Oxford, 1968.

NOTES

[1] Sydney Bailey, *British Parliamentary Democracy*, 3rd ed. (Greenwood, 1978), pp. 4–5.

[2] Ibid., p. 131.

[3] Punnett, *British Politics and Government*, p. 68.

[4] *The Economist*, "One More Defeat On Long Retreat," May 7, 1988, pp. 51–52.

[5] Cited in Suzanne Berger, *The French Political System*, 3rd ed. (New York: Random House, 1974), p. 368.

[6] Roy Macridis, ed., *Modern Political Systems:: Europe*, 6th ed. (Englewood Cliffs, N.J.: Prentice-Hall, 1986), p. 120.

[7] Guido Goldman, *The German Political System* (New York: Random House, 1974), p. 56.

[8] Stephen Brookes, "Juggling the Scepter in a Unified Europe," *Insight*, June 19, 1989, p. 9.

[9] Ibid., p. 8.

[10] Ibid., p. 9.

Chapter 6
A Common European House?

Western Europe emerged from World War II exhausted and supine. The physical destruction was devastating; the psychological damage was almost as bad. Clearly the Old World was dead—the Great Powers that had so recently colonized the world were now reduced to supplicants.

With the ending of one nightmare, another loomed on the horizon. No sooner had the smoke cleared from the battlefields than a new, "cold" war broke out. This time the antagonists were not the continental powers of Europe, but instead the United States and the Soviet Union. The main battleground, however, was Germany. The Soviet Union, which during the war had seized Eastern Europe and part of Germany, appeared to threaten Western Europe as well. The war-weary United States had quickly demobilized, which left the Soviet Red Army in a dominant position on the Continent. If Stalin's armies suddenly began to roll westward, who could stop them?

The only answer—the United States—created a predicament for Western Europe. It meant that European security now hinged on decisions made outside of Europe and that at the very least, the nations involved had lost a large measure of control over their own destinies (as well as some of their sovereignty and independence).

To make a bad situation worse, several West European countries had strong Communist parties, most notably Italy and France. These parties, closely linked to Moscow, enjoyed wide popularity because they had fought valiantly against fascism. (In France, for example, the Communist party won the largest vote totals in the 1946 elections.) Anywhere the Communists gained control of a government, the Soviet Union gained another "satellite"—or so it appeared at the time.

In sum, the war had left the economies of Western Europe shattered and bereft of the capital (and human resources) needed for reconstruction, and the specter of Communism seemed about to envelope the Continent. As the period between the two world wars had so clearly shown, fear and despair can predispose societies to political extremism.

Despite the bleak outlook for Western Europe in 1946, today it is one of the most prosperous regions in the world. The explanation for this "miracle" has two parts: American economic and security assistance and West European self-help.

Western Europe's Economic Miracle

Immediately after World War II, the Truman Administration made several key decisions regarding the future of Europe. First, it abandoned all of the preceding isolationist tendencies and assumed primary responsibility for stimulating economic recovery on the Continent. This decision took the form of the European Recovery Program (better known as the Marshall Plan), approved by the Congress in 1948. Second, it determined on a course of reconciliation rather than retribution toward West Germany. The decision to include Germany in the Marshall Plan was a crucial step in this direction. Third, it made a long-term commitment to West European security by creating the North Atlantic Treaty Organization (NATO). This initiative removed any lingering doubts in Europe as to whether the United States would risk war to defend democracy and freedom on the other side of the Atlantic.

Fourth, and perhaps least appreciated at the time, the United States encouraged economic cooperation among the West European democracies from the very start. The first fruit of this policy was the Organization of European Economic Cooperation (OEEC) set up to administer Marshall Plan aid. The OEEC countries pledged themselves "to combine their economic strength, to join together to make the fullest collective use of their individual capacities and potentialities, to increase their production, to develop and modernise their industrial and agricultural equipment, reduce progressively barriers to trade amongst themselves, promote full employment and restore or maintain the stability of their economies and general confidence in their national currencies."[1] As things turned out, this lofty diplomatic rhetoric foretold developments that would transform Western Europe from a blighted region into the world's most dynamic trading bloc.

The OEEC was followed by the European Coal and Steel Community (ECSC) in 1952. The ECSC, which established the framework for a sharing of strategic resources, set the stage for formation of the European Economic Community (EEC) in 1958. The resulting "Common Market" was, in reality, a customs union, meaning that the six members (France, West Germany, Italy, and the Benelux countries Belgium, Holland, and Luxembourg) removed tariffs on trade among themselves and set common tariffs on trade with others. More important, it was the nucleus of a larger, more complete European Community (EC) that now includes Great Britain, Denmark, Ireland, Spain, Portugal, and Greece.

Meanwhile, France, West Germany, and Italy were all undergoing an "economic miracle" during the 1950s. The miracle was not that they recovered, but that they did so faster than anybody expected. Within a decade of the war's end, industry was up and running again, granaries were bulging, and roads, railways, and bridges were rebuilt. Furthermore, the rising tide lifted all the boats—the resurgence of the bigger nations boosted economic growth in the smaller ones.

But along with prosperity came new problems. From the 1960s onward, as industry became increasingly automated and the work force shifted from manufacturing to the service sector, the challenges facing the governments of the region changed rapidly, and the very pace of the change itself became a major challenge. Simultaneously, the Common Market came of age as the European Community, creating new opportunities for the member nations but also bringing new tensions and necessitating sometimes painful adjustments.

We will return to the EC later in this chapter when we assess the prospects for Western Europe, but first we will discuss some problems associated with the postindustrial stage of development in Great Britain, France, and West

Germany. In many respects, the problems these countries are encountering typify the whole region.

The Problems of Postindustrial Society

Students in the United States will have little difficulty relating to the concept of "postindustrial society." The Industrial Revolution brought a major shift in the economic foundations of European (and American) society. The transition from farming to manufacturing entailed a massive demographic shift from rural to urban settings, a shift accompanied by secularization, breakup of the extended family, and a sharp rise in the need for governmental regulation and intervention (particularly in such areas as public utilities and social services). The problems associated with this "revolution" were offset by major advances in living standards owing to general affluence, political gains by organized labor (for example, the right to strike), and consumer-related technological innovation.

Economically, postindustrial society is characterized by a shift (a) from the manufacturing to the service sector (banking, insurance, advertising, marketing, management, and so on), (b) from domestic to international markets, (c) from a cash-and-carry economy to one based on credit and installment buying, (d) from one-income to two-income families (which means that a very high percentage of adults under the age of 65 are, or wish to be, gainfully employed), and (e) from a saving culture to a consuming culture. Postindustrialism also brings overdevelopment—a concept that deserves a place alongside underdevelopment in the economic textbooks of the future.

Overdevelopment is exemplified by the "megalopolis." London, Paris, Rome, Milan, Essen (West Germany), Madrid, and Athens are a few examples of urban overdevelopment in contemporary Western Europe. The dynamics of economic growth in postindustrial nations lure people to big cities in search of high-paying jobs, professional opportunities, social status, and popular (as well as high) culture. Cities become more and more crowded, and population growth typically outruns the capacity of local government to maintain adequate police and fire protection, sanitation, schools, hospitals, streets, parks, and the like.

Overcrowding leads to a host of social problems, including traffic congestion, air pollution, increasing crime, juvenile delinquency, drug abuse, high divorce rates, domestic violence, and homelessness. Some of these problems are no doubt exacerbated (if not caused) by the difficulties many urban dwellers have in coping with high levels of everyday stress. An issue related to crowding is immigration: People are more likely to resent "foreigners" if they already feel cramped for space.

Politically, postindustrial nations face problems arising from their past economic and technological successes (and excesses.) As society changes, new circumstances give rise to new political forces. For example, the increase in life expectancy (combined with an early retirement option for many employees) has created a powerful new interest group demanding more and better social services. The fact that most households now have two breadwinners means that even an expanding economy is no guarantee against unemployment (and underemployment). Minorities and people entering the work force for the first time tend to be hardest hit by joblessness. University-educated youth may be forced to take low-paying menial jobs for which they are vastly overqualified. The inevitable consequence is disillusionment and an urge to rebel (often in self-destructive ways). Thus, educational opportunity can be destabilizing if it does not lead to something more.

Threats to the environment give rise to a variety of new policy problems: air and water pollution, noise pollution, chemical and nuclear waste disposal, deforestation, and species decimation are but a few examples. Air pollution is largely an urban scourge—it is caused by emissions from the automobile, mass transit vehicles, and smokestack industries. But the cost of clearing the air, and of other environmental regulation, must in the end be borne by all taxpayers and consumers no matter how or where they happen to live. One of the most fundamental political questions in any society is who gets what, when, and how; another equally fundamental question is who pays what, when, and how.[2]

A fundamental issue facing postindustrial states is how to define the role of the state in the economy, environment, and society—where to draw the line between government intervention and free enterprise, public needs and private rights. The recent free-market trend in Western governments began with the election of Margaret Thatcher's Conservative government in 1979 and of U.S. President Ronald Reagan in 1980. In 1982 conservative leader Helmut Kohl became Chancellor in West Germany.

The political pendulum seemed to be swinging the other way in France, however. As noted in the previous chapter, a Socialist, François Mitterand, was elected President of France in May 1981, running on a pro-labor, anti-business platform. Mitterand moved quickly to nationalize industrial firms and banks, pushed for wage hikes, and deliberately ran up large budget deficits. The results were high inflation, trade deficits, a stagnating industrial sector, and falling economic growth. In 1986 a center-right coalition won control of the Assembly from the Socialists. By that time the government had abandoned its profligate ways and had instituted a tough austerity program. In 1988 Mitterand ran (successfully) for a second term—on a platform that was barely distinguishable from that of the center-right!

The ''taming'' of the French Socialists points to one final feature of postindustrial politics: the blurring of the differences between parties of the right and parties of the left. Extremist parties on both ends of the political spectrum fall by the wayside. Ideology is downplayed. Government and opposition alike take a moderate, businesslike approach to economic and social problems. These trends, in turn, appear to reflect a middle-of-the-road popular consensus. So long as postindustrial societies remain basically prosperous, this general movement toward the middle will likely continue.

The Core Countries

The problems faced by Great Britain, France, and Germany are not all directly attributable to their stage of economic development. Nonetheless, many of these problems are present in one form or another in all three countries (and elsewhere on the Continent), which suggests that they are rooted in certain general conditions rather than in circumstances unique to a particular society.

Great Britain

The most persistent policy problem in Great Britain for the past four decades has been the disappointing performance of the economy. While France, West Germany, and Italy experienced economic miracles, Great Britain stagnated. When OPEC (Organization of Petroleum-Exporting Countries) oil prices skyrocketed in the early 1970s, inflation soared in Western Europe. In Great Britain the inflation rate exceeded 20 percent a year at one point. British voters began wondering whether any government, Conservative or Labour, could revive the economy from its decades-long doldrums. Loss of public confidence in existing institutions is potentially destabilizing for any society. Fortunately for the British, the tremendous force of tradition, like a great reservoir, has always sustained the system even in times of ''drought'' and recession.

One windfall that saved the British economy from calamity in the 1970s was the discovery and development of oil and gas reserves in the North Sea. By 1980 Great Britain was basically self-sufficient in oil and natural gas, whereas France and West Germany continued to be heavily dependent on energy imports. However, a new economic phenomenon pundits called ''staglation'' appeared—a combination of stagnating growth and high inflation. According to Keynesian economic theory, market economies can be expected to go through ''boom and bust'' business cycles. In periods of rapid growth, inflation is a problem (prescribed cure: budget cuts, higher taxes and interest rates); in periods of recession, unemployment is a problem (prescribed cure: deficit spending, lower taxes and interest rates). But in the 1970s, the British economy was hit by inflation and recession *at the same time.*

Full employment has been a top priority of British public policy since the worldwide depression of the 1930s. Indeed, the jobless rate is a key measure of governmental performance in Great Britain. Since the 1970s, unemployment has inched steadily upward. By the mid-1980s a record 3.2 million Britons were unemployed. Public opinion polls reinforced the impression that the state of the economy was a potential time bomb for the Thatcher government.

Even so, the British economy bounced back in the 1980s under the free-market policies of Prime Minister Margaret Thatcher's Conservative government. In June 1987, British voters gave the ''Iron Lady'' a record third consecutive term as prime minister, in part because Conservative economic policies seemed to be working. Following the Conservative victory, *The Economist* stated that the ''warning lights are flashing.'' The problem was now not a stagnant economy but one showing "advanced symptoms of overheating."[3] The overall picture, however, was bright: housing starts at a record level and the economy was growing at an annual rate of 3.5 percent (compared with less than 1 percent from 1960–1982). Moreover, a widely publicized survey of manufacturers suggested growth could accelerate: Order books were bulging and many firms were expecting output in the following months to rise rather than fall. Also, the official index of leading economic indicators (stock prices, interest rates, housing starts) rose faster during the six months leading up to the election than at any time since the early 1970s.[4]

Under Conservative rule, all economic policy issues in Great Britain boil down to one fundamental question: What is the proper balance between government intervention and free enterprise? Margaret Thatcher ran on a reprivatization (or denationalization) platform in 1979 and did not waver from this position throughout her eleven years in power. She blamed Great Britain's sagging economy on the excesses of a cradle-to-grave "welfare state" in which an ever-expanding public sector encroached on and undercut the private sector.

Under Mrs. Thatcher's firm leadership the Conservatives kept their promises. Industry has been denationalized, business has gotten investment incentives, taxes have been cut, and welfare spending has been curtailed. Whether or not these acts are responsible, one thing is certain: The British economy has recovered from its prolonged slump.

As for the quality of life in Great Britain, however, things are not so rosy. "Amid a revivified economy, Britain's decaying inner cities are the worst blot on eight years of Tory government," proclaimed *The Economist*.[5] The original Thatcher agenda included the following: rehabilitate the inner cities; correct chronic housing problems; free public schools from stultifying local-authority controls; reform local taxes. None of these items has much sex appeal, but taken together they provide a glimpse of the nettlesome postindustrial problems facing the country in the waning years of the twentieth century.

In addition, violence and civil strife in Northern Ireland continue to divert attention, energy, and resources away from domestic ills. In that troubled corner of the country, militant Irish nationalists, claiming to represent the Roman Catholic minority, have been waging a guerrilla war against British rule (and the Protestants who comprise a majority of the population in the six northern counties of Ulster). The Provisional Irish Republican Army (IRA) uses terrorist tactics to achieve its objective of separation from Great Britain and union with the Republic of Ireland. If such a union were indeed effected, the Protestant majority in Ulster would become a minority in Ireland. Thus a bloody deadlock between Protestants and Catholics—and between the British government and the IRA—has developed. No end is yet in sight.

Finally, foreign and defense policy fuels a good deal of controversy in Great Britain. For many years, other European nations (particularly France) denounced Great Britain's "special relationship" with the United States. The fact that London chose not to join the EEC in 1958 underscored the British desire to remain aloof from the Continent. When Great Britain applied for membership in the early

1960s, French President Charles de Gaulle vetoed it, alleging that London would be a Trojan horse for Washington. Not until de Gaulle was gone from the scene was Great Britain finally admitted, along with Ireland and Denmark, in 1973. But lingering doubts about British loyalties and London's own ambivalence toward the Common Market continued to obstruct efforts to build bridges (figuratively speaking) across the English Channel. By 1990 Prime Minister Thatcher's opposition to many aspects of European economic union eroded support within her own Conservative party. After a challenge to the leadership—in which she received a less-than-expected majority of votes from the Conservatives in the House of Commons—she resigned. On November 28, 1990, she was replaced as prime minister by John Major, the chancellor of the exchequer.

The Thatcher government's defense policies were also controversial. The left wing of the Labour party calls for unilateral nuclear disarmament, while Mrs. Thatcher was staunchly committed to maintaining and modernizing Britain's nuclear strike force. To this end the government began replacing the Polaris fleet (of early-1960s vintage) with the advanced Trident nuclear submarine system. The program will cost more than 10 billion pounds and is certain to create severe budgetary strains.[6]

Behind this debate over nuclear weapons and defense spending is a more fundamental question: What is the proper allocation of resources between national security and domestic programs? The Conservative party emphasizes the need for a strong national defense to protect British institutions and national interests. The Labour party stresses domestic programs and argues that a nation's security cannot be measured by the size of its military forces alone: Stability and social cohesion are tied to the general welfare, which in turn necessitates a compassionate and benevolent government.

France

The French postwar economic miracle gave way to a time of troubles in the 1980s. By odd coincidence, the French economy started to sputter just when the British economy began to get cranked up. It was probably not a mere coincidence that France's difficulties deepened under Socialist economic reforms aimed at enlarging the role of the state and cutting the size of the private sector.

In February 1982 the Socialist government nationalized nine major industrial groups and thirty-six banks and lending institutions. (The previous November the government had taken over two failing steel companies.) The nine industrial groups represented 20 percent of the French market and 15 percent of the export market. They employed 760,000 workers. After the new nationalizations, the public sector accounted for 30 percent of industrial sales and nearly a quarter of the French work force. In addition, the state gained near-total control of France's banking and credit systems. The cost of this expensive "rupture with capitalism" was a tidy sum: 43 billion francs!

The theory behind the nationalization program was enhancement of the power of the state vis-à-vis the economy—not as an end in itself, presumably, but as a means to several interrelated ends, including rapid capital formation, economic modernization, and state-managed growth. The plan foundered when the government allowed state-owned enterprises to pursue their own strategies rather than conforming to a central plan. At the same time, the Mitterand government, anxious to avoid embarrassment, poured money into the newly nationalized industries through budget allocations and loans from state-owned banks. These transfusions depleted the treasury but did not revive the "patient," as one industry after another sank into a rising sea of red ink.

To his credit, President Mitterand then encouraged state enterprises to seek private investment capital by creating special "stock" certificates that could be sold on the open market without jeopardizing public ownership. Private capital flowed into public firms in torrents (20 billion francs in 1985). By the 1986 elections the Socialist government had, for all practical purposes, abandoned its love affair with *dirigiste* (state-centered) economic policies.

But the consequences of President Mitterand's false start in 1981 could not be swept under the rug. The budget deficit rose from 0.4 percent in 1981 to 3.0 percent of gross domestic product (GDP) the following year. Inflation remained high at a time when it was falling elsewhere in Western Europe, and a sudden trade deficit mushroomed to 94 billion francs in 1982. In the face of these rapidly deteriorating conditions, Mitterand bit the bullet: In 1983 the government reversed engines and adopted a tough austerity program (called "rigor" by crow-eating Socialist politicians).

The austerity measures involved holding down wages, curbing budget increases, and strictly controlling the money supply. This program, still in effect in 1986 when a new National Assembly was elected, did not bring quick results. France's growth rate fell below that of most other West European nations, while inflation stayed above the norm. At the same time France endured several consecutive "double deficits" (simultaneous budget and trade shortfalls). The chronic trade deficit was particularly troubling because it suggested a loss of French competitiveness in the world market.

To make matters worse, unemployment climbed steadily under Socialist rule. Even a state-mandated job creation program had little effect. If the Socialist party, with its strong commitment to the working class, could not even guarantee jobs for those who wanted to work, French voters were almost certain to punish them at the polls.

The Socialists indeed lost the 1986 elections to a center-right coalition headed by Jacques Chirac. The French Constitution, with its unique dual executive, was now put to one of its most severe tests: how power could be shared by two leaders with completely different political philosophies (called "cohabitation" in France). Prime Minister Chirac was interested in denationalizing firms and banks that the Socialists had brought under state control in 1981–1982. His more general aim was to deregulate the economy and return the initiative to the private sector.

To no one's surprise, cohabitation proved to be just a stopgap until the 1988 presidential election. The government was more or less on hold for these two years. In 1988 President Mitterand campaigned for reelection on a pragmatic, market-oriented platform that closely resembled that of his center-right opponent, Prime Minister Chirac. He promised voters that there would be no repeat of the failed "socialist" experiment of 1981—no nationalizations, no new corporate taxes, no quixotic measures like his earlier attempt at shortening the work week.

The voters responded. In May Mitterand won a second term with an impressive 54 percent of the popular vote. Pollsters predicted that the Socialists would win a clear majority in National Assembly elections the following month. But they were wrong. The center-right parties captured 271 seats to the Socialists' 276 seats (13 less than the 289 seats needed for a majority).

At first glance the results appeared to be ambiguous, even contradictory. According to one interpretation, there was a postindustrial logic at work in these elections. "Forget the razor-close results and confused political maneuvering," wrote a close observer, "...the clear message [is that] France wants to be governed from the center."[7] An overwhelming majority of French voters "rejected both extreme-right fascism [Jean-Marie Le Pen's National Front] and extreme-left Marxism [the French Communist party]." Further:

> Although they split right down the middle with no party gaining an outright majority, experts say voters do not want renewed right-left dueling. They are instead calling for a bipartisan approach on major issues, a pro-European, pro-Atlantic alliance foreign policy, and a free-market economic policy checked by a strong social system.
>
> This message is spreading not just in France, but through Europe. With nuances, both socialist Spain and conservative Britain promote the virtues of NATO and capitalism. The old ideological battles between a collectivist and individualistic vision of the world slowly is slipping into history's dustbin.[8]

Indeed, it did appear that business was not upset by the prospect of a new Socialist-led government. After the Socialist victory in 1981, share values fell so fast that trading had to be suspended; after the 1988 elections, the stock market rose!

With full economic integration of the EC slated for 1992, President Mitterand's highest priority was to prepare France for a competitive future, one without the protectionism and state intervention that have been trademarks of the French economy. (It is one of history's ironies that this job fell to a Socialist leader; it is a sign of the times that he seemed to relish the prospect.)

Despite the resounding vote for moderate parties and policies, the surprising (but short-lived) popularity of a right-wing extremist named Jean-Marie Le Pen in the 1988 presidential race struck a discordant note. Le Pen, leader of the National Front party, won 14.4 percent of the vote on the first ballot. He campaigned on a nationalistic and racist platform that critics denounced as a new form of fascism. The target of Le Pen's demagoguery was the influx of immigrants from France's former colonies in Africa and Asia; his vehement antiimmigration stance appealed to an odd assortment of conservatives and reactionaries. But the Le Pen phenomenon was not just an aberration. As *The Economist* noted:

> The National Front has a mixed ancestry: interwar fascists, wartime collaborators, monarchists, Catholic ultras, Algerie Française diehards, smalltown populists. Yet today's extreme right is also a product of modern France.[9]

Table 6-1 Immigrants in Western Europe, Late 1980s

Country	Situation
West Germany	4.4 million foreigners (just over 7% of population); Frankfurt population 24% foreigners
Netherlands	During 1987 Asian refugee wave, 300 of 700 towns refused government requests to accept them; 85% of Dutch polled wanted limits set
Great Britain	Antiimmigration sentiment subsiding (influx of immigrants from former colonies declined after mid-1970s)
Italy	Illegal immigrants arriving at rate of 50,000/yr for total of 750,000; 100,000 legally registered non-EEC immigrants (40,000 from Libya, Tunisia, Morocco, and Ethiopia)
Norway	In 1988 antiimmigration party led by Carl Hagen climbed to 31% in opinion poll (from 3.1% in 1985 elections)
Switzerland	In 1988 right-wing ''Automobilists'' gained popular following; 24,000 foreigners (mostly Asian) sought asylum

The rise of the National Front is a reflection of the social and economic troubles facing France in the early 1990s. Unemployment and underemployment continue to aggravate racial and ethnic tensions in French society, as do urban overcrowding, rising crime rates, drug abuse, and traffic congestion. There is probably a connection between the jobless rate and the rise of racial bigotry and xenophobia in France as well as in other West European countries (see Table 6-1).

President Mitterand's moderation in domestic policy has been matched by prudence in foreign policy featuring firm support for NATO (in contrast to the Gaullist tradition that stresses strategic self-reliance and France's unique role between the two superpowers). Mitterand has also pursued policies long popular in France, bolstering France's independent nuclear strike force (the world's third largest) while promoting strategic and conventional arms reduction in Europe and beyond. Under Mitterand, France has played a leadership role in the European Community as well.

Both NATO and the EC are vital to France, in part because they ensure against a resurgence of German nationalism. A Germany militarily dependent on NATO and economically tied to the EC poses little threat to its neighbors. Ingrained fear of Germany might well have led to Franco-German tensions in 1989 when the opening of the intra-German border and the fall of the Communist regime in East Germany pointed to German reunification. But Mitterand, calm and reassuring in demeanor, did much to counteract any alarmism.

West Germany

In 1982, the center-right Christian Democratic Union–Christian Social Union (CDU–CSU) formed a coalition government with the Free Democrats (FDP), who broke a thirteen-year alliance with the left-leaning Social Democrats (SDP).

Six months later, German voters gave a solid mandate to Helmut Kohl's conservative government.

The victory of Chancellor Kohl's *Koalition der Mitte* (center coalition) followed Germany's worst economic slump since the Great Depression of the 1930s. Many voters blamed the slump on the expensive welfare-state programs favored by the SDP. Kohl and the Christian Democrats promised to reverse the course with a combination of tax cuts, investment incentives, and budget reductions. Kohl's approach closely resembled "Reaganomics" and the supply-side prescriptions of Britain's Prime Minister Thatcher.

Kohl's economic program produced generally positive results: Economic growth stopped declining (growth reached an impressive 3.5 percent in 1986), inflation was brought down to a thirty-four-year low (from over 5 percent in 1982 to 1 percent), and budget deficits were reduced from about $30 billion in the last year of Social Democratic rule to about $8 billion in 1987. In addition, spending for social welfare programs was curbed significantly.

In this auspicious climate, business and industry rebounded. By mid-1986 German factories were operating at 85 percent of capacity; in some sectors (for example automobiles and machine tools) output could not keep pace with demand. Capital investment perked up as well: after lagging from 1982 to 1984, it increased by 10 percent. Plant modernization, particularly the use of computers and robots, accelerated rapidly. To top it all off, the balance of payments harvested a record surplus in 1986. The one low mark on Kohl's report card was unemployment, which remained at 9 percent.

In the 1987 parliamentary elections, West Germans reaffirmed their support for Kohl and his coalition, giving them a combined total of 53.4 percent of the popular vote (44.3 percent for the CDU–CSU and 9.1 percent for the FDP). The vote was not a resounding triumph for Kohl and his party, however; the CDU–CSU lost twenty-one seats while the FDP gained twelve.

Of particular concern to conservatives was the fact that the Greens—an antinuclear, environmental party—garnered a million votes more than they had four years earlier. Environmentalists and peace activists got a boost in West Germany from the Chernobyl nuclear accident in the Soviet Union in April 1986. The Greens called for Bonn's immediate withdrawal from NATO, unilateral disarmament, and the dismantling of all nuclear power stations in the FRG. Their relatively strong showing in 1987 (forty-two seats in the *Bundestag* on 8.3 percent of the vote) was still not enough to make them a major force in West German politics. Nonetheless, opinion polls showed that over 80 percent of the voters opposed construction of new nuclear power plants in the FRG and nearly half the voters saw the Greens as the party best qualified to deal with environmental issues.

Although Germany is an affluent society, the struggle over how wealth and power are (or ought to be) distributed continues unabated. Organized labor charged the Kohl government of being blatantly partial to business, pointing in particular to a 1986 labor law that tightened the rules on payment of unemployment compensation to striking workers.

A related problem is the growing incidence of poverty amidst plenty. Especially hard hit by what Germans call the "new poverty" are the long-term employed, divorced women with children, elderly pensioners, and refugees seeking asylum. Some citizens see a relationship between poverty and policy. For example, the percentage of long-term unemployed rose sharply in the 1980s.

United Germany

The unemployment issue was greatly exacerbated at the end of the decade when the reform movement sweeping Eastern Europe caught fire in the German Democratic Republic. In a few short weeks, the hard-line regime of Erich Honecker, a man widely regarded as one of the most repressive figures in the Eastern bloc, was toppled. The fall of Communism in East Germany led straightaway to the opening of the intra-German border and made the Berlin Wall—symbol par excellence of the East-West conflict—an anachronism. One consequence of this drama was an immediate surge in unemployment in West Germany.

Germans always longed for a united Germany, but before 1989 this seemed a hopeless dream. The Kohl government, like its immediate predecessors, sought close relations with East Germany. The FRG extended loan guarantees worth billions of dollars, encouraged bilateral trade expansion, and concluded the first-ever cultural exchange accord between the two German governments. In return, the German Democratic Republic (GDR) allowed more travel to West Germany and, in the late 1980s, let record numbers of East Germans emigrate.

In the fall of 1989, a flood of refugees poured out of the GDR through Hungary, Poland, and Czechoslovakia, countries in which democratic reform movements were either well under way or about to burst onto the scene. This mass exodus created a political crisis in East Germany and, as noted, ended over forty years of Communist rule in the GDR. Democratic elections were held in the spring of 1990; unsurprisingly, the reformed (and renamed) Communist party was handed a resounding defeat. The expected winner, the left-of-center Social Democrats (SPD), garnered less than 22 percent of the popular vote. Instead, a conservative alliance, the Christian Democratic Union (CDU), won nearly 41 percent. The outcome was widely interpreted as a mandate for unity, in part because West German Chancellor Kohl, an unabashed advocate of rapid reunification, had gone to East Germany and campaigned for the CDU. Suddenly, making Germany whole again was at the top of the agenda in both the FRG and the GDR.

The pace of reunification, not its desirability, was the primary issue. The CDU on both sides of the border favored a merger "as soon as possible" via Article 23 of the West German Basic Law, which allows regions of prewar Germany to reunite with the FRG on acceptance of the Basic Law. The SPD, however, called for a new constitution. Drafting such a constitution would obviously take time and involve careful negotiations between the two German governments. The timetable for unity was thus a key question. A closely related issue was how much the FRG would compromise with the GDR in negotiating the precise terms of reunification.

Having dreamed of a united Germany for four decades, West Germans quickly discovered that the dream had a price tag. Absorbing the influx of East Germans and financing modernization of the GDR's outmoded factories turned out to be an expensive proposition. In addition to unemployment, adjustments associated with the quick monetary union that occurred in July 1990 (that is, using one currency—West German Deutschmarks—throughout both Germanys) would bring the risk of inflation and recession. Inflation, in turn, was likely to drive official interest rates up at the same time that the government's annual borrowing doubled. Economists predicted that a tax increase of at least DM25 billion would also be needed to cover the costs of aiding East Germany and cushioning the impact of economic reform.[10]

West Germany faced dilemmas in foreign policy as well. The reunification issue brought old fears of German megalomania to the surface in both Eastern and Western Europe. In the Soviet Union, Mikhail Gorbachev declared that Moscow would not interfere with East Germany's reform efforts, including movement toward unification, but warned that a united Germany must not be part of the North Atlantic Treaty Organization (NATO). The Kohl government, however, was steadfast in its commitment to the Western alliance. In August 1990 Gorbachev reversed himself and agreed to let the united Germany be part of NATO. In return, Germany agreed to reduce the size of its army, to pay for the upkeep of Soviet forces on German soil, and to pay the Soviets $7.5 billion in addition to an economic-aid package.

Similarly, the European Community (EC) was concerned about the impact of a German merger on the Common Market. Currency analysts predicted that "the potential for a weakened Deutschmark, a West German current-account deficit, and rising inflation and interest rates in Germany will severely strain the European Monetary System, a delicately balanced basket of nine currencies intended to be the basis for a future European Monetary Union."[11]

The question of nuclear weapons is no less nettlesome. When West Germany joined NATO in 1954, it pledged never to acquire nuclear weapons. But it has allowed the United States to deploy such weapons on its soil under the aegis of NATO. In one respect, West Germany had the worst of both worlds: Nuclear weapons within its borders were targets for Soviet rocket forces, but any decision to use these weapons depended on concurrence by a foreign government. At the same time, however, U.S. nuclear forces in the FRG served as a deterrent to Soviet attack and symbolized the firm U.S. commitment to West Germany's freedom and independence.

The FRG's perennial dilemma was illustrated recently by the Intermediate Nuclear Force (INF) accord. Agreeing to accept the Pershing IIs and cruise missiles in the first place was controversial (the Soviet Union objected vehemently); agreeing to their removal reopened the wound. Did it mean that the American nuclear guarantee was about to end? Would the United States now expect Germany to up its NATO contribution to compensate for the loss of nuclear clout? What to do about short-range (tactical) nuclear weapons was also a source of tension. The psychological impact of nuclear arms control is often poorly understood in the

United States. Not so in Germany, where people are acutely aware that their country would be the main battlefield in any future war in Europe.

The European Community

The economic prospects for Western Europe are closely tied to the future of the European Community (EC). Since its founding in 1958 the EC has grown from "the Six" to "the Twelve" (member-states) with a combined population of 320 million people. In 1992, all remaining barriers to internal trade will be removed, and the economic unification of Britain, France, Germany, Italy, Spain, Portugal, Greece, Ireland, Belgium, Denmark, Luxembourg, and the Netherlands will become a reality.

The nucleus of the original Common Market was the European Coal and Steel Community (ECSC). From the standpoint of economic geography, the ECSC's core was the so-called Heavy Industrial Triangle, an area bounded by the Nord, the Ruhr river, and Lorraine. According to Geoffrey Parker, there is a "logic of unity" behind the evolution of the EC:

> The countries of the Community originally decided to enter into an economic merger for a variety of reasons, but, particularly in the case of those five of them [France, West Germany, and the Benelux countries] which are part of trunk Europe, their motivation was based on a very real geographical unity. The shatter belt of political frontier which extends through its centre from the Rhine delta to the Alps coincides only in one place with a linguistic boundary, and frequently divides areas which are physically, economically, and frequently culturally single units. Most basic of all is the essential unity of the Triangle and its associated areas which has been, in the words of the Schuman Declaration, "Always prescribed by geography, always prevented by history," and the Community has given this formal expression.[12]

The benefits of "economic integration" were demonstrated first and foremost in the area of external trade: In 1966, the Common Market overtook the United States to become the world's largest exporter. Total exports to outside countries had risen over 85 percent since the Community's inception in 1958. Four-fifths of these exports were manufactured goods, mostly machinery and transport equipment. (The other 20 percent were food exports.) By 1984, the enlarged EC's share of the world export market had surpassed the United States' share by a wide margin, nearly matching that of Japan, Canada, and the Soviet Union combined.

In 1992, the European Community will reach a historic milestone:

> Physical barriers for shipping goods will be abolished. Technical barriers will end on everything from the contents of food to government procurement. Value added taxes will be coordinated. Banking, insurance, and capital movements will flow freely. Doctors and other professionals will be able to practice where they please.
> It will be a giant step toward an economically united Europe.[13]

The impetus behind this "giant step" is the same as that behind previous, smaller steps—economic self-interest. Unifying the market will, by itself, boost the European Community's gross domestic product by 4.5 to 6.5 percent, according to a 1988 EC study. In addition, it will create as many as 2 million jobs and pare down consumer prices by an average of 6 percent. Lord Cockfield, vice-president of the EC Commission, characterized it as "the greatest development that has happened since the end of World War II."[14]

In short, a unified "supereconomy" of the kind presently envisaged should present unprecedented opportunities for expansion of trade and industry throughout the European Community. Without any barriers to the movement of goods, labor, or capital, the EC should, in fact, be one massive and highly lucrative market—an economic Leviathan that will dwarf the Soviet Union and Japan and rival the United States. If, that is, it can overcome the chauvinism and cultural particularism that are still prevalent in Western Europe after three decades of "integration."

Assuming that the dream of a unified Europe becomes a reality, there will still be serious challenges ahead for the societies and governments involved. For starters, not all West Europeans will benefit equally from the coming union. The countries of the north will benefit more than the countries of the south because of their comparative advantage in manufactured goods. The EC is attempting to deal with this problem in part by doubling its regional development aid (which goes primarily to the southern-tier members) in the years leading up to 1992. But the potential for north-south conflict within the Community will not disappear until intraregional disparities between rich (north) and poor (south) do.

Nor is the European Community equally popular among all groups *within* member-states. Generally speaking, urban industrial areas have more to gain from economic unification than do rural areas. Most Europeans do not live in cosmopolitan cities, where pro-EC sentiment typically runs high. Millions still live in rustic surroundings; their attitudes are conditioned by relative isolation and they instinctively distrust both big business and big government. "We risk an increasing polarization in European societies," one expert has noted. "There is a large part of society that remains in its little village, insular."[15]

"Personally, I do not feel European at all." This sentiment, candidly expressed by the Communist mayor of a town near Marseilles, France, captures the way many people, especially those living outside big cities, no doubt feel. Moreover, "the European Community is a community of capitals, of the interests of capital cities."[16] This assessment has at least a grain of truth, if not more, and it is likely to color the perceptions of many provincials for whom antibusiness and antigovernment populism always has strong appeal. Claude Cheysson, a former French foreign minister and currently an EC commissioner, has warned, "A Europe that would become too much a Europe of the traders and the bankers will give birth to very deep social and cultural reactions."[17]

The intensified competition that a single, unified market will bring is seen as a boon by most of the EC's biggest companies, but it is threatening to smaller firms and workers who stand to lose their jobs if some of these firms cannot compete. The companies most likely to fail, in many cases, are the family-owned ones.

Some have been around for centuries. Their demise could signal the disappearance of a way of life in rural Europe.

The road to European Union has other obstacles as well. For example, politicians realize that the concept of nationalism and pride in one's own cultural heritage always sells in the provinces, where the market for "Europeanism" is likely to remain soft for some time to come. In France, Le Pen's surprising popularity underscored that point in the 1988 presidential election. In West Germany at the end of 1989, reunification mania raised the possibility that the government's previous commitment to Europe would be eroded by the new opportunities for investment in the GDR. By the same token, the movement for democracy throughout Eastern Europe promised to give the FRG access to a potentially lucrative market closed to Western trade and investment since World War II.

The fact that the EC is a collection of democracies does not necessarily facilitate the politics of integration. One example of the nationalistic impediments to a unified market: It took EC members thirteen years to agree on lawn-mower noise standards. The difficulties went beyond technical questions such as allowable noise levels: "What actually constitutes a lawn mower and other imponderables kept governments, corporations and gardeners at daggers drawn."[18] If details like these can stir up controversy, one can only imagine what obstacles lie in store for the "Eurovisionaries" and "Eurocrats" who are trying to lead Western Europe into the brave new world of 1992!

In 1985, an EC white paper estimated that some 300 directives were necessary to bring about a unified market. This task would be daunting enough without the political complications that inevitably intrude. Much attention has been paid in the West to the economic restructuring (*perestroika*) going on in the Soviet Union. Now, however, the EC countries face a restructuring hardly less painful:

> . . . the merging of companies, the elimination of redundant jobs and the lifting of barriers that protect uncompetitive industries. The force of change will be felt most heavily at the bottom of the pyramid, especially in companies that, because they existed in backwaters, were slower to reduce labor costs and increase investment in mechanization than companies that have been competing internationally for years. In the short run, that means more conflict, more anguish, and perhaps a fatal backlash against the European ideal that the corporate bigwigs have been touting."[19]

Despite these obstacles, the twelve members of the EC will merge into a single economy in 1992. Economic unification will not be easy. Historical precedents do not exist. Indeed, the EC countries are engaged in a pioneering effort, an experiment in international relations on a scale never before attempted in Europe (or anywhere else for that matter). The trial-and-error method of problem solving, by definition, involves risks. Even so, the prospects for a prosperous new European superstate are so alluring, and the incentives for further integration so powerful, that no problems or risks, however large they may loom, are likely to derail the EC locomotive.

CONCLUSION

Western Europe emerged from the ashes of World War II like a phoenix. The West German "economic miracle" overshadowed the remarkable recovery of the entire western portion of the Continent. The United States played a key role in shaping Europe's postwar destiny by providing generous reconstruction aid (the Marshall Plan); perhaps equally important, the United States encouraged aid recipients to coordinate their recovery efforts. Mechanisms of institutionalized cooperation—the Organization for European Cooperation and Development (OECD), the European Coal and Steel Community (the ECSC), the European Atomic Energy Agency (Euratom), and the European Economic Community (EEC)—set the stage for the economic unification planned for 1992—the most spectacular "economic integration" success story in modern history. Will other regions follow suit? The chapters that follow shed light on this question.

Ironically, Eastern Europe, homogenized by Soviet military might after World War II, came unglued at the very time when integration was bringing Western Europe ever closer together. In Chapter 7 we examine the context of politics in the Slavic world, the Soviet Union, East Central Europe, and the Balkans.

STUDY QUESTIONS

1. What forms did U.S. assistance to Western Europe take after World War II? What motives, interests, and objectives drove the Truman Administration's foreign policy vis-à-vis the Continent during this period?

2. What are the economic characteristics of postindustrial society? What problems developed in Western Europe as a result of postindustrialism? How have the governments in the region dealt with these problems?

3. What is Thatcherism? Is Great Britain better or worse off than it was at the beginning of the 1980s when Margaret Thatcher became prime minister? Is the British economy likely to dominate the Continent in the 1990s?

4. In 1982, the Socialist government led by French President François Mitterand attempted to revive a sagging economy by nationalizing several industries. What was the theory behind this program? Was it successful? Is France under Socialist rule dismantling its market-based economy? Is the French Socialist party a threat to democracy and free enterprise?

5. Are there "limits to growth" in Western Europe? Has Germany, the Continent's leading economic power, exhausted its growth potential? Have the other Common Market countries?

6. What is the European Community, who belongs to it, and how does it work? How did it get where it is today, and where is it going? Does it have a bright future, or has it outlived its usefulness?

SUGGESTED READINGS

Burgess, Michael. *Federalism and European Union: Political Ideas, Influences, and Strategies in the European Community, 1972–1987*. London: Routledge, 1989.

Laurent, Pierre-Henri. "The European Community: Twelve Becoming One," *Current History*, November 1988, pp. 357–360, 394.

Price, Roy. *The Dynamics of European Union*. London: Croom-Helm, 1987.

Yemma, John. "Europe 1992," *Christian Science Monitor* (two-part series), "Setting Sights Boldly on Unity" (subtitle), June 27, 1988; and "European States Weigh the Costs of Uniting" (subtitle), June 29, 1988.

NOTES

[1] Cited in John Paxton, *The Developing Common Market: The Structure of the EEC in Theory and in Practice* (Boulder, Colo.: Westview, 1976), p. 7.

[2] Harold Lasswell, *Who Gets What, When And How* (Peter Smith).

[3] *The Economist*, June 27, 1987, p. 60.

[4] Ibid.

[5] Ibid., p. 57.

[6] *The Economist*, January 26, 1985, pp. 57, 60; see also "Political Development in Britain," *Current History*, November 1986, p. 268.

[7] William Echikson, "French United Despite Divided Parliament," *Christian Science Monitor*, June 14, 1988, p. 1.

[8] Ibid.

[9] *The Economist*, Apr. 30, 1988, p. 46.

[10] Terence Roth, "East German Winners in Election now Seek Fast Monetary Union," *Wall Street Journal*, Mar. 20, 1990, p. 1

[11] Ibid., p. A11.

[12] Geoffrey Parker, *An Economic Geography of the Common Market* (New York: Praeger, 1969), p. 127.

[13] John Yemma, "'No Going Back' for EC, Biggest Market in the World," *Christian Science Monitor*, May 27, 1988, p. 15.

[14] Ibid.

[15] Danielle Pletka, "The Supereconomy Stirs in a Web of Self-interest," *Insight*, June 20, 1988, p. 10.

[16] Ibid., p. 12.

[17] Ibid., p. 17.

[18] Ibid., p. 15.

[19] Ibid., p. 17.

SOVIET UNION

Area: 8,649,489 square miles
Population: 289 million
Density per square mile: 33
Republics (by 1986 population):
Russia, Ukraine, Uzbekistan, Kazakhstan,
Byelorussia, Azerbaijan, Georgia,
Tadzhikistan, Moldavia, Kirghizia,
Lithuania, Armenia, Turkmenistan, Latvia,
Estonia
Languages: Russian, Ukrainian, Uzbek,
Byelorussian, Kazak, Tatar
Literacy rate: 99%
Religions: Russian Orthodox, Muslim,
Roman Catholic, Jewish, Lutheran, atheist
Monetary unit: ruble
GNP: (1988) $2.5 trillion;
$8,700 per capita

ROMANIA

Area: 91,700 square miles
Population: 23.2 million
Density per square mile: 251
Languages: Romanian, Magyar
Literacy rate: 98%
Religions: Romanian Orthodox (80%),
Roman Catholic (6%)
Monetary unit: leu
GNP: (1986) $138 billion;
$6,030 per capita

YUGOSLAVIA

Area: 98,766 square miles
Population: 23.7 million
Density per square mile: 240
Languages: Serbo-Croatian, Slovene,
Macedonian
Literacy rate: 90%
Religions: Eastern Orthodox (50%),
Roman Catholic (30%), Muslim (10%)
Monetary unit: dinar
GNP: (1986) $145 billion;
$6,220 per capita

HUNGARY

Area: 35,919 square miles
Population: 10.6 million
Density per square mile: 294
Language: Magyar
Literacy rate: 99%
Religions: Roman Catholic (67%),
Protestant (25%), atheist (7%)
Monetary unit: forint
GNP: (1986) $84 billion;
$7,910 per capita

POLAND

Area: 120,727 square miles
Population: 38.2 million
Density per square mile: 316
Language: Polish
Literacy rate: 98%
Religion: Roman Catholic
Monetary unit: zloty
GNP: (1987) $151 billion;
$3,998 per capita

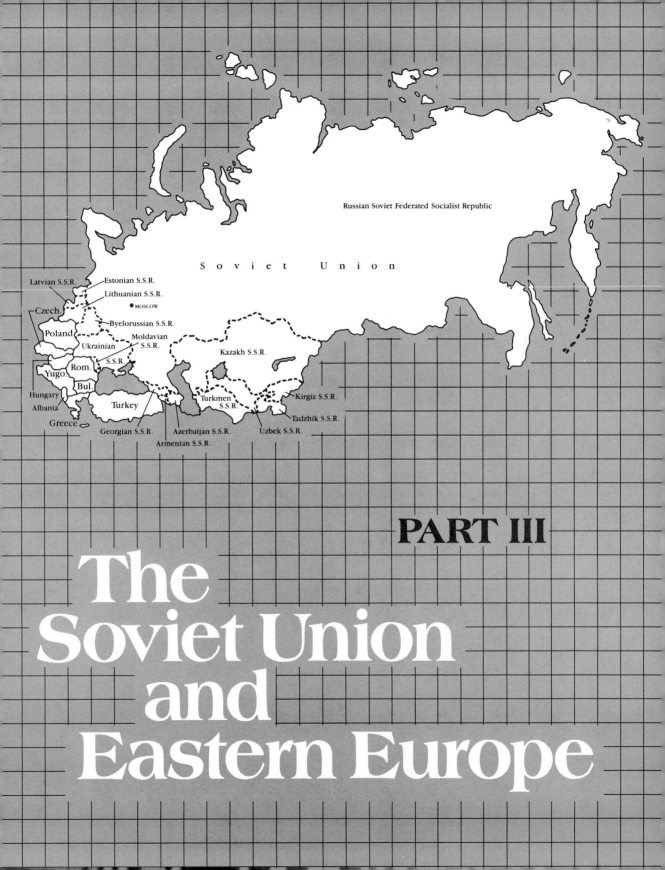

Russian Soviet Federated Socialist Republic

Soviet Union

Latvian S.S.R.
Estonian S.S.R.
Lithuanian S.S.R.
● MOSCOW
Czech.
Byelorussian S.S.R.
Poland
Moldavian
Ukrainian   S.S.R.
Kazakh S.S.R.
Rom.   S.S.R.
Yugo.
Hungary   Bul.
Albania   Turkey   Turkmen
S.S.R.   Kirgiz S.S.R.
Greece   Tadzhik S.S.R.
Georgian S.S.R.   Azerbaijan S.S.R.   Uzbek S.S.R.
Armenian S.S.R.

PART III
The Soviet Union and Eastern Europe

Chapter 7
The Marxist-Leninist Heritage

On March 5, 1946, Winston Churchill gave an address at Westminster College in Fulton, Missouri, in which he spoke darkly of the danger posed by Soviet Communism:

> From Stettin in the Baltic to Trieste in the Adriatic, an iron curtain has descended across the Continent. Behind that line lie all the capitals of the ancient states of Central and Eastern Europe. Warsaw, Berlin, Prague, Vienna, Budapest, Belgrade, Bucharest, and Sofia, all these famous cities and the populations around them lie in what I must call the Soviet sphere, and all are subject in one form or another, not only to Soviet influence but to a very high and, in many cases, increasing measure of control from Moscow. . . . [1]

Whether one regards Churchill's chilling words as alarmist or prophetic, the political geography he traced can hardly be faulted. This region included the Union of Soviet Socialist Republics (USSR), more commonly known as the Soviet Union or Russia. Its European part encompasses not only Russia proper, including the Ukraine, but also the Baltic states (Lithuania, Latvia, and Estonia) as well as Georgia, Armenia, and Azerbaijan in the Caucasus, along with the nations of Eastern Europe—Albania, Bulgaria, Czechoslovakia, Hungary, Poland, Romania, and Yugoslavia.

Most (two-thirds) of the inhabitants of Russia and Eastern Europe are of Slavic origin. The Slavs have been the predominant group at least since the seventh century A.D. They can be divided into three major groupings: Eastern Slavs (Great Russians, Ukrainians, White Russians, and Ruthenians); Western Slavs (primarily Poles, Czechs, and Slovaks); and Southern Slavs (Serbs, Croats, Slovenes, Montenegrins, Bulgars). The principal non-Slavic groups in Eastern Europe are the Magyars (Hungarians) and the Romanians.

The Slavic nations are extremely diverse. Both physical traits and cultural traditions vary considerably, as does language. Christianity spread throughout the region but took different forms: Eastern and Southern Slavs embraced the Eastern Orthodox rite, whereas Western Slavs looked to Rome. The Reformation did not penetrate most of Eastern Europe. As to language, two different alphabets are found: the Latin alphabet, used by Western Slavs, and the Cyrillic alphabet, used by Eastern and Southern Slavs.

While the peoples of the Soviet Union and Eastern Europe are diverse in many ways, their fates have been interwoven. In addition to the political fortunes (or misfortunes) that have fused them together in one empire or another at different junctures, in some cases they have shared religious and cultural experiences.

143

Above all, the forces of history and geography have intruded on these nations and shaped a destiny that is uniquely Slavic.

The Influence of Geography

The Soviet Union dominates the map of Eastern Europe. Indeed, it dominates the map of Europe and Asia combined. Occupying more than 8.6 million square miles (one-sixth of the earth's total land mass), it is by far the largest country in the world (more than twice the size of the United States). Only about 25 percent of the USSR is in Europe.

If Eastern Europe has been dominated by the Soviet Union, the Soviet Union, in turn, is dominated by Russia. There can be little doubt that geography has played a major role in shaping the political traditions of the Russian people. One authority on Soviet politics has written:

> It is indeed easy to see how Russia's geography has influenced the course of its history. To begin with, Russia's original location on the East European plain contributed directly to many of its important historic events. Being relatively close to Byzantium, for example, influenced Russia's choice of Eastern (Greek) Orthodoxy as its state religion (988). Two and a half centuries later, because of its location, Russia fell prey to the Mongol invasion and remained for several centuries almost completely isolated from Europe, which was then going through the Renaissance and Reformation. A result of this isolation was Russia's lagging behind Europe in technology and industrialization.[2]

Three facts of life determined by Russia's geography have been especially crucial in the shaping of Russian history and culture. First, it lies in northern latitudes and is thus cold much of the year. Second, it is mostly flat (much like Kansas and Nebraska in the United States) and thus presents no natural barriers to invasion or expansion. Third, it is vast, especially the Siberian wilderness: "The immensity of Russia, the absence of boundaries, was expressed in the structure of the Russian soul...the same boundlessness, formlessness, reaching out into infinity, breadth."[3]

Russia has been blessed with an abundance of fertile soil, mineral resources, and mighty rivers. However, Nature has always yielded bounties grudgingly to the Russians, given the relatively short growing season and the long, cold winters. The Ukraine is Russia's breadbasket, but if it were located in North America it would be in Canada rather than in the United States! The storied resilience of the Russian people in the face of adversity no doubt owes much to the rigors of the climate.

The sheer size of Russia, resulting in a need to protect boundaries thousands of miles long, and the absence of natural barriers, which leaves Russia open to attack from any direction except north, have contributed to a pervasive sense of insecurity. In the thirteenth century the Mongols invaded, pillaged, and plundered Kievan Russia. The Mongol yoke was not removed for nearly 250 years. In the early sixteenth century, danger came from the opposite direction: Poland. The result was another humiliating defeat and another foreign occupation, this time a short one.

In 1709 Sweden attacked, under the direction of Charles XII, a military genius. Russia's Peter the Great, soon to become an empire builder in his own right, rose to the challenge. Under his command the defending Russian forces defeated the Swedes at Poltava in the Ukraine.

A century later Napoleon invaded and marched all the way to Moscow. The onset of winter was a major factor in forcing his army to retreat. Russia's sheer physical size came into play as well. According to historian Nicholas Riasanovsky, ''More soldiers of Napoleon died from hunger and epidemics than from cold, for the supply services, handicapped by enormous distances, insecure lines of communication, and bad planning, failed on the whole to sustain the military effort.''[4]

Germany has invaded what is now Soviet Russia twice in the present century. In World War II Hitler conquered and occupied most of Old Russia. Kiev was destroyed, Leningrad was besieged for two and a half years, and Moscow came perilously close to falling (the invading forces were finally stopped at the outskirts of the city). In all, some 20 million Russians died; cities, towns, and villages were reduced to rubble and ash; and the foundations of the economy were obliterated.

The same geography that has made Russia vulnerable to invasion has also afforded opportunities for expansion. Thus, ''when not being invaded, Russia itself was often invading neighboring countries, annexing them, building an empire, and pursuing territorial expansion in the quest for greater physical security.''[5] Russian rulers themselves thus created stability problems in peripheral areas by incorporating non-Russian groups into the empire. The Russian czars never fully achieved ''Russification'' of these groups.

Aside from the quest for security, there were powerful economic and commercial inducements to engage in empire-building, many of them also affected by geography. The desire to gain access to warm-water ports, long a major motif of Russian foreign policy, can be traced directly to Russia's geographic predicament.

Geography has also influenced Russian culture. A famous Russian historian, Vasili Klyuchevsky, once wrote that ''the forest, steppe and river are . . . the basic elements of Russian nature in terms of their historical significance [which] played an active and unique part in the formation of the life and ideas of the Russian man.''[6] Another Russian scholar, Nicholas Berdyaev, argued that ''the immensity of Russia'' has also left a deep imprint on the culture, society, and general outlook of the Russian people. What is particularly fascinating is the way Berdyaev linked geography and politics:

> A difficult problem presents itself ceaselessly to the Russian—the problem of organizing his vast territory. The immensity of Russia, the absence of boundaries, was expressed in the structure of the Russian soul. . . . Russian historians explain the despotic character of Russian government by this necessary organization of the boundless Russian plain. Klyuchevsky, the most distinguished of Russian historians, said, ''the state expands, the people grow sickly.'' In a certain sense this remains true

also of the Soviet-Communist government, under which the interests of the people are sacrificed to the power and organization of the soviet state.[7]

Geography and environment have not predetermined Russia's history, but these physical factors have undoubtedly conditioned and constrained the development of Russian institutions, traditions, and values. The great "constants" in Russian history are environmental in the broadest sense of the word: its location on the globe; its vast space and daunting distances; its smooth, flat plains; and its harsh winter climate.

The Imprint of Recent History

Just as geography influences history, so the legacy of the past, the history of a nation's finest and darkest moments, leaves a deep imprint on political culture. A historical event is relevant to politics for however long it is remembered. For reasons that will soon become apparent, many of the Slavic nations would probably like to forget much of their history.

Decline of the Romanov Dynasty

When Czar Nicholas II abdicated the throne in 1917 amid the turbulence of war and revolution, he brought to an end three centuries of Romanov rule in Russia. Nicholas II and his predecessor, Czar Alexander III (1881–1894) had been obsessed with unification of the multinational empire they inherited. However, unlike their illustrious ancestors, Peter the Great (1682–1725), Catherine the Great (1762–1795), Alexander I (1801–1825), and Nicholas I (1825–1855), the last two Romanov rulers were unequal to the challenges they faced.

And challenges blossomed like crocuses in spring. First, there were external threats on two sides: to the west a united Germany, to the east Japan. Twice in the recent past Germany had demonstrated its aggressive tendencies and military prowess in victories against Austria (in 1866) and against France (in 1870). Japan's emergence as a great power caught Russia by surprise. In the Russo-Japanese War of 1904–1905, Japan destroyed Russia's Far Eastern fleet with a surprise attack in the outer harbor of Port Arthur. When Czar Nicholas II ordered the Baltic fleet to sail around the globe to save the day, the Japanese fleet was ready and waiting: Japan dealt Russia's antique armada a crushing blow at the battle of Tsushima Strait in 1905.

The Far Eastern debacle set the stage for the second challenge, this one internal: Russia's first revolution. Like the October Revolution twelve years later, the Revolution of 1905 was precipitated by defeat in war. But war alone does not explain Russia's revolutions. In truth, the forces of rebellion and violence had been stirring within Russian society for several decades before the eruption of 1905. They first appeared in the 1870s, when anarchism and nihilism mixed with populism to produce an explosive ideology called *narodnichestvo* (the Russian word for people is *narod*). The chief ideologists of this movement came to be known as *narodniki*; some of the most prominent were Alexander Herzen, Michael Bakunin, Nicholas Chernyshevsky, Peter Lavrov, and Nicholas Mikhailovsky.

The *narodniki* inspired a group of fanatical revolutionaries, the *Narodnaya Volya* (''People's Will''), who launched an offensive against the government of Alexander II. Members of this group believed that ''because of the highly centralized nature of the Russian state, a few assassinations could do tremendous damage to the regime, as well as provide the requisite political instruction for the educated society and the masses.''[8] Alexander II had the misfortune to become their chief target: The ringleaders of *Narodnaya Volya* condemned him to death and began what has been described as an ''emperor hunt'':

> The Executive Committee of the ''Will of the People'' included only about thirty men and women. . . . Although the police made every effort to destroy the revolutionaries and although many terrorists perished, the ''Will of the People'' made one attempt after another to assassinate the emperor. Time and again Alexander II escaped through sheer luck. Many people were killed when the very dining room of his palace was blown up, while at one time the emperor's security official refused to let him leave his suburban residence, except by water![9]

Alexander II was killed in 1881. Several years later an attempt was also made on the life of Alexander III. The plot failed, but one of the conspirators arrested by the *Okhrana* (the Czar's secret police) was Alexander Ilyich Ulyanov, the brother of Vladimir Ilyich Ulyanov, who became known to the world as Lenin. Without Lenin there would probably have been no October Revolution; without the October Revolution there would certainly not be a Soviet Union.

Lenin and the October Revolution

Lenin's ideas on revolution were a mixture of Russian populism, anarchism, and Marxism. As a self-styled champion of Russia's oppressed masses he had a certain kinship with the old *narodniks*; as an advocate of violence (though not assassination) he was a soulmate of the anarchists; and as the founder of the Communist Party of the Soviet Union he was a disciple of Marx.

Lenin split the Russian Social Democratic party in 1903 over the issue of revolution. One faction of the party opposed subversion and revolution, arguing that socialism and democracy could be achieved in Russia without violence. Lenin's faction insisted that only the efforts of a conspiratorial ''vanguard'' party, which could secretly lay the groundwork for an all-out revolution, could bring the corrupt czarist order down. Lenin outlined this fundamental tenet in his famous 1902 essay, *What Is to Be Done?*:

> The working class exclusively by its own efforts is able to develop only trade union consciousness. . . . Modern social consciousness can be brought to them only from without . . . [it] can arise only on the basis of profound scientific knowledge. The bearers of science are not the proletariat but the bourgeois intelligentsia. It is out of the heads of members of this stratum that modern socialism originated . . . . Pure and

> simple trade unionism means the ideological subordination of the workers to the bourgeoisie. . . . Our task is to bring the labor movement under the wing of Social Democracy.

Lest anyone miss the point, Lenin added that "Aside from the influence of Social Democracy, there is no conscious activity of the workers."[10]

Marx and Engels had said that "The emancipation of the working class is the task of the working class itself." Lenin's amendment to this proposition was to have momentous consequences for Russia and the world. The Communist party (which Lenin called the "vanguard of the proletariat") would supplant the proletariat (working class) as the key to the future. An elite corps of "professional revolutionists" would move front and center on the stage of history; the workers would fade into the background. Here, then, are the seeds of the totalitarian Soviet state sown in the fertile revolutionary soil of a society in decay.

Of course without World War I Lenin's ideas on revolution would not have borne fruit. The defeat of the Russian army at the hands of the Germans, like the defeat of the Russian navy by the Japanese a decade earlier, created a crisis of confidence in the whole czarist system. The extreme hardships, the death and destruction, and finally the national humiliation associated with Russia's failing war effort the national humiliation associated with Russia's failing war effort focused the widespread discontent and sparked rebellion. Actually there were two revolutions in 1917: A moderate socialist named Alexander Kerensky led the first one; the Bolsheviks (Lenin and Trotsky, in particular) led the second one. The October Revolution actually occurred in the month of November; the Gregorian, or new-style, calendar used in the West was officially adopted by the Bolshevik regime on January 31, 1918.

It was Lenin (helped by Leon Trotsky) who masterminded the October Revolution. Lenin could hardly be accused of moderation. He quickly moved to consolidate his power by gutting the elected soviets, banning or suppressing all opposition groups, and putting Bolsheviks (members of the Communist party) in control of the military, the police, the state administration, and the economy. He also established his own dreaded secret police, called the *Cheka*. The *Cheka* imitated the czarist *Okhrana* but went further in perfecting a system of state terrorism that included purges against real or imagined counterrevolutionaries, expropriations of property, and tight control of all mass communications (radio, newspapers, journals, and publishing houses). Thus did Lenin and Leninism set the stage for Stalin and Stalinism.

The Bolsheviks faced a variety of challenges during the period of "war communism" (1917–1921). During this time the Soviet government was embroiled in a civil war with the so-called white (anti-Bolshevik) armies supported by the Western Allies. The latter, including the United States, Great Britain, and France, intervened directly, if somewhat half-heartedly, on the pretense of recovering war supplies given earlier to the czarist government. The main aim, however, was to assist the "whites" in overthrowing the "reds."

Lenin's government managed to survive the civil war and the allied intervention, but the harsh policies of war communism alienated many former supporters of the October Revolution. In 1921, when sailors (who had played a key role in the revolution) mutinied at Kronstadt, a naval base near Leningrad in the Gulf of Finland, Lenin crushed the rebellion in bloody fashion. This incident apparently made a deep impression on the Bolshevik leader, who subsequently relaxed the stringent measures imposed earlier. The result was the New Economic Policy (NEP), which allowed limited private enterprise, involvement of foreign managers in industry, farming for profit, and considerable literary and artistic freedom.

The Stalin Era: Totalitarianism in Full Swing

In the minds of most objective observers, Stalinism and totalitarianism are synonyms. At the height of the Stalin terror in the mid-1930s, nobody was safe. Nearly all the party's "old guard"—comrades of Lenin—fell before Stalin's firing squads. Most of the Soviet military high command met a similar fate. Guilt by association became the order of the day. Anyone who was connected in any way with the old czarist government—anyone who had ever held a position of responsibility in the economy or been recognized in any professional field (science, education, literature, and so on) before the revolution—was purged.

Stalin even invented subversive groups (for example, "Prom party"—industrial managers accused of trying to sabotage the Plan) as a pretext for purging whole categories of "enemies." Finally, a class of prosperous peasants (*kulaks*) was completely wiped out—either killed or sent into Siberian exile. In addition, millions of peasants perished in the early 1930s in a famine that was exacerbated, if not caused, by Stalin's brutal policy of squeezing capital from agriculture to boost industry. The state confiscated crops in the Ukraine and elsewhere, in effect starving the country to feed the city. Worse still, despite the famine, Stalin actually exported grain to the West to earn hard currency during this period.

Why did Stalin wage war against his own society? What did the resulting bloodbath accomplish? Was there a method in his madness?

When Lenin became incapacitated by a stroke in 1922, a succession struggle was inevitable. On Lenin's death in 1924, Stalin almost immediately began maneuvering against the other top Bolshevik leaders. His first victim was Trotsky, whom he condemned for advocating "permanent revolution" and expelled from the party with the support of Lenin's other lieutenants. Then he cut the Bolshevik old guard to pieces, cleverly playing one faction against another; denouncing first the leftists, then the rightists; until in the end he had vilified and discredited them all.

By 1928 Stalin had succeeded in turning the obscure position of general secretary into a vehicle of autocratic power. But achieving personal sway over a weak nation did not satisfy Stalin's lust for power, nor did it assuage his obsessive insecurity. Russia was weak, he reasoned, because it was economically backward. It would never be strong until it industrialized. In the modern age, industrial development is the key to military prowess and national glory: That was the lesson to be learned from Japan, Germany, and of course the United States. In Stalin's own words: "We are fifty or a hundred years behind the advanced countries. We must make good this lag in ten years. Either we do it or they crush us."[11] But how could Soviet Russia industrialize? It was, after all, poor and agrarian. Worse, it was surrounded by hostile capitalist states.

Trotsky's policy of permanent revolution (that is, working for the overthrow of bourgeois capitalist governments) was all wrong, Stalin asserted, because the Soviet Union was alone in the world. Trying to foment revolution would provoke Soviet Russia's enemies and jeopardize the future of the only Socialist state then in existence. Under these unfavorable circumstances, Stalin argued, a policy of "socialism in one country"—a euphemism for his highly nationalistic economic development strategy—made more sense than did Trotsky's adventurism.

Stalin's solution was simple but brutal: If the West would not provide the capital for Soviet industry, Stalin would squeeze it out of Soviet society. Since that society was largely agricultural, the Soviet farmer would have to bear the brunt of the industrialization drive. Stalin knew that the peasants would resist confiscatory taxes or forced deliveries to the state, and so he decided to *collectivize* agriculture, not out of ideological conviction so much as economic expediency. The collectivization, then, was Stalin's way of extracting capital from agriculture for investment in industry—collectivization and forced industrialization were two sides of the same coin.

Stalin's bloody campaign against the *kulaks* was also prompted by his economic development strategy. The *kulaks*, he reasoned, were the most successful farm producers. As such they had the most to lose from collectivization, and therefore were the most likely to resist or obstruct. Stalin's "dekulakization" campaign thus appears to have been launched because the hapless *kulaks* were inconvenient (not, as Stalin claimed, because they were capitalist bloodsuckers). The need to impose party control over the majority of the population (the peasantry) was another reason for collectivizing agriculture.

It is no accident that the first Five-Year Plan and the collectivization of Soviet agriculture were inaugurated in the same year: 1929. Henceforth Stalin would let nothing (and nobody) get in the way of his crash industrialization program.[12]

Even the Great Terror of the 1930s can be seen as part of Stalin's mad dash for modernization. Millions were arrested on the flimsiest of pretexts and sent off to labor camps run by the secret police. A major part of the USSR's industrial infrastructure (roads, canals, bridges, railroads, dams, power grids) was built by forced labor. In Siberia such labor opened new mines and built new towns. The Moscow subway was built by forced labor.[13]

Forced labor is slave labor. Much of the terror Stalin unleashed in the 1930s was in reality an excuse for enslaving much of the Soviet work force in order to industrialize the nation without paying for it. Too diabolical to be true? No one familiar with the show trials in which the old Bolsheviks who had been Lenin's comrades-in-arms publicly "confessed" to heinous crimes and denounced themselves as spies and traitors would doubt Stalin's capacity for cruelty. (Only after they had confessed were Stalin's rivals taken out and shot.)

In sum, Stalin created a rigidly centralized system of rule in which state terror was used to mobilize society and enforce strict conformity with his will. The entire economy was brought under a central plan that consistently gave top priority to industrial development. In particular, heavy industry was favored over agriculture or production of consumer goods. This dogmatic insistence on the "primacy of heavy industry" became one of the hallmarks of Stalinist economic policy, not only in the Soviet Union but also in East European satellite states.

World War II and the Soviet Phoenix

In Egyptian mythology, the phoenix is a beautiful bird that lives for 500 or 600 years before being consumed in flames, only to emerge from the ashes and start a new life cycle. The legendary rebirth of the phoenix takes place in the Arabian desert, not on the Russian steppe. Nonetheless, the phoenix is an appropriate metaphor for the Soviet experience in World War II.

June 22, 1941, is a black day in Soviet history. It is the day Hitler's army invaded the Soviet Union and rolled relentlessly toward Moscow. By October, German forces encircled Moscow on three sides along a perimeter just 20 miles from the city. Although Hitler's troops did not actually enter Moscow, they came much too close for comfort.

Without question the Soviet Union was the major victim of German aggression in World War II. The Red Army did emerge victorious but, as Isaac Deutscher noted:

> Against this backdrop must be set the price Russia paid for the victory: the seven million dead, officially counted—the losses may in fact have been much larger [most estimates put the number of Soviet war deaths at 20 million]; the uncounted millions of cripples; the devastation of most cities and towns, and of much of the countryside in European Russia; the destruction of industry, exemplified by the total flooding of the coal-mines of the Donets; the complete homelessness of twenty-five million people, living in caves, trenches, and mud huts, not to speak of the latent homelessness of many more millions of evacuees in the Urals and beyond.[14]

Soviet industry, bought at such a dear price in human suffering in the 1930s, was in a shambles. Between 1941 and 1945, Soviet industrial might was cut nearly in half; despite the Stalinist emphasis on steel production, the USSR was producing only about *one-eighth* as much steel as the United States in 1945. Furthermore, Soviet agriculture, too, had to be reequipped "almost from scratch" after the war.[15]

But for all the death and destruction, the Soviet Union did not disintegrate. On the contrary, the war undoubtedly strengthened Soviet patriotism and made the survivors determined to do whatever was necessary to rebuild the country. And rebuild they did. Much is made of West Germany's postwar reconstruction (often called the German "economic miracle"). Similar "miracles" occurred in Italy and Japan. What is more remarkable (though less frequently remarked upon) is the Soviet economic miracle. The Soviets, unlike the Germans, Italians, and Japanese, had to rebuild without economic aid from the United States.

Most of the Soviet recovery is attributable to two factors: (a) Stalin's draconian system of labor conscription (the war and its aftermath provided a steady flow of fresh recruits to the *gulags*, or labor camps); and (b) a centrally planned economy that permitted all resources and energies to be concentrated on strategic industries (coal, steel, electricity, machine tools, armaments).[16]

In sum, by 1950 the Soviet Union had consolidated its hold on Eastern Europe, successfully tested an atomic bomb, and rebuilt much of its heavy industry. The subjugation of Eastern Europe had been accomplished with clocklike precision—occupation by the Soviet Army, appointment of Communist quislings to key posts, forced union with Socialist parties, arrest of prominent opponents on false charges, and rigged elections. Moreover, Stalin had amassed the largest standing army in Europe (indeed, the largest in the world), and the Soviet Union was less than a decade away from entering the space age. (In 1957, the USSR became the first country to put a satellite—"Sputnik"—into orbit.)

Stalin's Heirs: From Khrushchev to Gorbachev

Stalin's death in 1953 caused a succession crisis. Following several years of bitter infighting, Nikita Khrushchev emerged as the winner. He lost little time in distancing himself from the deceased dictator.

It was at the historic Twentieth Party Congress in 1956 that Khrushchev delivered his famous "secret speech." The marathon address (it lasted four hours) contained a blockbuster: an announcement that Stalin had made serious errors in the 1930s. He had committed excesses in the name of building communism. Of course, everyone who heard this shocking "revelation" already knew about the Stalin terror. But prior to Khrushchev's "crimes of Stalin" speech nobody in the Soviet Union dared whisper a word about it.

Khrushchev's de-Stalinization drive was his most significant contribution to the development of the contemporary Soviet state. He not only denounced government by fear and Stalinist terror, but he also emptied the labor camps and dismantled most of the vast camp system (the "gulag archipelago" in Solzhenitsyn's memorable phrase).

Other attempts Khrushchev made at reforming the Stalinist state were destined to fail, however. In agriculture he launched the "virgin islands" campaign under which millions of acres of land in Kazakhstan and the eastern Russian SSR were plowed and planted for the first time. It seemed like a good idea at the time, and at first even appeared to be working. But within a decade it turned to disaster as the fragile topsoil was blown away by fierce winds. In the spring of 1963, according to one account:

> Dust clouds hid the sun for several days, irrigation canals were choked, and along some stands of trees drifts of soil more than two meters high were formed. Many towns and villages were covered with dirt, and from thousands of hectares [a hectare equals about 2½ acres] the arable layer was so completely removed by the winds that the underlying bedrock was exposed. Precise data on the damaged areas were not

published, but millions of hectares were involved. . . . It will take at least one to two centuries before the arable layer is restored to these areas.[17]

Khrushchev's other attempts at economic and administrative reform were equally ill-fated. In an effort to decentralize the cumbersome state bureaucracy, he abolished most of the Moscow-based economic departments, creating regional economic councils (*sovnarkhozy*) in their place. This radical reorganization was resisted by officials with a vested interest in preserving the power and status of the "center" (as Moscow is widely known to Soviet citizens). He also introduced a plan for the regular rotation of party personnel (thus threatening the job security of party bosses) and tried splitting *oblast*-level party committees into agricultural and industrial sectors, again in the name of increased efficiency. (Soviet republics are divided into *oblasts*, or regions, of various sizes.)

What resulted was increased confusion and probably no little sabotage by disgruntled *apparatchiki* (party functionaries) and administrators. When Khrushchev was ousted in 1964, his successors cited his "hare-brained schemes" as justification. His detractors also accused him of trying to create a "cult of personality" (a Stalinist sin), and thus violating the Leninist principle of collective leadership. Accordingly, Leonid Brezhnev, Khrushchev's successor as general secretary, did not assume the post of premier. (Khrushchev, like Stalin, had simultaneously held both the top party and government posts.) Alexei Kosygin became the new premier, and Nikolai Podgorny became the new president. Thus a kind of triumvirate, with Brezhnev as "first among equals," replaced one-man dictatorship for the first time in Soviet history. (Brezhnev ousted Podgorny and assumed the post of president, as well as party chief, in 1977.)

Brezhnev's eighteen-year tenure (1964–1982) brought a return to the structures and methods (minus state terror) of the Stalinist era. This neo-Stalinism, as it is sometimes called, was evident in both cultural and economic policy.

In the economic sphere, the Brezhnev regime briefly toyed with market-oriented reforms. This short-lived dalliance with decentralization was based on the proposals of a Soviet economist named Evsei Liberman. But the "Liberman reforms" were soon abandoned in favor of a return to the familiar Stalinist system of central planning with its emphasis on quotas, artificial prices, top-down management, and the like.

In the cultural sphere, the relaxation of censorship that Khrushchev had allowed in the early 1960s ceased. In 1968 two writers, Andrei Sinyavsky and Yuli Daniel, were put on trial and convicted of "anti-Soviet agitation," a political crime that typically carries a penalty of seven years in prison. The trial of Sinyavsky and Daniel sent a chill throughout artistic and literary circles in the Soviet Union.

Two events led to the emergence of the human-rights movement in the USSR in the late 1960s: the Israeli victory in the Six-Day War in 1967 and the Soviet invasion of Czechoslovakia in 1968. The first event inspired Soviet Jews to seek permission to emigrate to Israel (or the West); the second focused attention on repressive Soviet policies both at home and abroad and gave rise to protests (even from devout Communists) throughout Eastern and Western Europe. In the Soviet Union a small but vocal group of dissidents took up the cudgels for liberalization of Soviet politics and culture.

The human-rights movement was given a boost by the Soviet signing of the Helsinki Accords in 1975. Part of the agreement obligated the signatories to respect personal rights and civil liberties. Undoubtedly, the rapprochement between the two superpowers ("detente")—crowned by the Strategic Arms Limitation (SALT I) treaty of 1972 and a new trade agreement—was a major factor. But Soviet-American relations, always tense and tentative, soured in the late 1970s. The Soviet invasion of Afghanistan in 1979 brought relations between Washington and Moscow to their nadir. (The SALT II treaty, which subsequently stalled in the U.S. Senate, was one of the casualties.)

One manifestation of the hardening Soviet attitude toward the West and internal liberalization (the two policy tracks tend to move in tandem) was a crackdown on dissent. Several prominent human-rights activists and *refuseniks* (Soviet Jews who were refused permission to emigrate) were arrested and put on trial. The most famous, Anatoly Shcharansky, was both a human-rights activist and a *refusenik*, thus symbolizing everything the Brezhnev regime sought to suppress. He was accused not only of anti-Soviet agitation but also of being a spy. The punishment for treason in the Soviet Union is death. Shcharansky was "lucky"—he was sentenced to thirteen years in a labor colony! (In 1986 Shcharansky was exchanged for several East German spies; he now lives in Israel and continues to speak out against Soviet human-rights abuses.)

After 1979 Jewish emigration was reduced to a trickle, and the political climate discouraged open manifestations of dissent or nonconformity. The Kremlin's neo-Stalinist social and cultural policies were matched by a strict, orthodox approach to economic problems. The prescribed remedies for inefficiency continued to have one common denominator: hierarchical management within the rigid framework of economic planning. In the early 1980s, the ossified Soviet system, like its geriatric leaders, showed clear signs of old age.

Brezhnev died in 1982. His successor as general secretary was Yuri Andropov, former head of the KGB (the State Security Committee). Andropov moved quickly to revitalize the Soviet economy, relying primarily on exhortation and admonition; the watchword of the brief Andropov interregnum was discipline. Anyone caught skipping work ("absenteeism"), avoiding work or malingering on the job ("parasitism"), getting drunk or causing a public disturbance ("hooliganism"), dealing on the black market ("speculation"), or engaged in other corrupt practices (for example, committing economic crimes such as theft of state property or taking bribes) would be punished to the limits of the law. (Stealing from the state can lead to a death sentence in the Soviet Union.)

Many Soviet citizens greeted Andropov's accession to power with a mixture of optimism and apprehension. There was widespread recognition that stagnation had set in and that only a strong leader with a clear vision of the future could pull the nation out of its doldrums. But there was also unspoken fear that Andropov might resurrect the Stalinist police state.

These hopes and fears were for naught—Andropov fell ill and died in the spring of 1984. His successor, Konstantin Chernenko, old and frail from the start, died after only about one year in office. The Soviet Union now had been without energetic leadership for years. Between 1917 and 1964, three such leaders—Lenin, Stalin, and Khrushchev—had held sway in the Kremlin. Now, between 1982 and 1985, three men—Brezhnev, Andropov, and Chernenko—had died in office. Clearly, something had to be done about the Soviet gerontocracy. Rejuvenation could not be accomplished by stodgy old leaders whose jaded views and enfeebled bodies precluded initiative and innovation.

Enter Mikhail Gorbachev. Gorbachev was in his mid-50s when he took over the reins of power—a youngster by Soviet standards. He lost little time in changing the guard. Young party and state officials replaced older ones. Loyalty to Gorbachev was, of course, an important criterion. But it was not the only one. Sympathy with Gorbachev's reformist policies was also of critical importance.

The Gorbachev reforms are summarized and assessed in Chapter 9. For now it suffices to note that Gorbachev moved boldly on two fronts: cultural and economic. In the area of culture he proclaimed the advent of *glasnost* (openness). The precise meaning of *glasnost* was left rather vague by Soviet spokesmen, but it was widely interpreted to mean that the Soviet Union henceforth would be less secretive and more tolerant of dissent than in the past. In the economic sphere Gorbachev's reforms were dramatic and potentially far-reaching. Under the banner of *perestroika* (restructuring), market-type measures were introduced for the first time since Lenin instituted his New Economic Policy in the early 1920s. In the political sphere, Gorbachev began moves toward democratization that led in 1990 to the party's surrendering its monopoly on power. As the Soviet regime celebrated its seventieth anniversary in 1987, the USSR seemed poised on the edge of a new era.

The Cold-War Roller Coaster

The Cold War had a major impact on Soviet and Eastern European politics after World War II. The tenor of relations between the United States and the Soviet Union set the limits of East-West cooperation in all areas, including arms control, trade, technology transfers, and tourism as well as scientific, educational, and cultural exchanges. For this reason we need to look at the general pattern of superpower relations since 1945.

In retrospect, the Cold War began before the Great Patriotic War (as the Soviets call World War II) ended. The "Big Three"—Churchill, Roosevelt (and Truman), and Stalin—met several times as the war wound down, at Teheran, Yalta, and Potsdam. On the surface, these meetings were conducted in a spirit of mutual trust, as befits allies in a great and noble cause. Below the surface, mistrust guided the maneuvers of both Stalin and Churchill. Only Roosevelt appears to have entertained illusions about the possibilities for postwar collaboration between the Soviet Union and the West.

President Roosevelt did not live to see the end of World War II or the visible outbreak of the Cold War. (He died suddenly in April 1945.) His successor, Harry Truman, took a dim view of Stalin from the start. When the United States dropped the atom bombs on Hiroshima and Nagasaki in August 1945, Truman's desire to stop the Russian advance into Manchuria (northern China) may have been a factor (although defeating Japan without having to invade the main islands was no doubt the primary consideration).

The United States cut off lend-lease aid to the Soviet Union abruptly and turned down a Soviet loan request. Stalin reneged on war-time promises to allow free elections in Soviet-occupied Eastern Europe, especially Poland. He moved to consolidate Soviet control over Poland, East Germany, Romania, Hungary, Bulgaria, and, finally, in early 1948, Czechoslovakia.

Stalin's actions in Poland and Czechoslovakia were particularly galling to public opinion in the United States. There was (and still is) a sizable Polish community in the United States—Chicago at one time boasted the second largest concentration of Polish people in the world (only Warsaw was larger). Stalin had assured Roosevelt that the Soviet Union would respect Polish sovereignty. Czechoslovakia was a special case because it had been a showcase of democracy between the two world wars. In early 1948, leaders of the Czech Communist party, subservient to Stalin, staged a coup—undoubtedly with Stalin's backing and very likely on his orders. In the course of the Communist takeover, President Thomas Masaryk, the son (and namesake) of the beloved first president of Czechoslovakia during those interwar years died under mysterious circumstances—he fell or was thrown from a window. President Truman, capitalizing on the furor created by this latest Soviet land grab, asked Congress to approve the multibillion dollar Marshall Plan for Europe. Although it was by far the biggest foreign-aid package ever proposed, the funds were approved in short order.

The year 1948 also saw the first Berlin crisis. Before World War II, Berlin was the capital of Germany (as it is again now). Located inside East German territory, after the war Berlin was divided into zones: The eastern half of the city was under Soviet control, the western half under British, French, and American control. Stalin wanted all of Berlin under East German (that is, Soviet) jurisdiction, and he decided to force the issue by blockading Berlin. The United States responded with an airlift that kept West Berlin viable. Stalin was checkmated: Either he could shoot down the U.S. supply planes, which would touch off a new hot war, or he could back off. He backed off.

In 1949 the United States established the North Atlantic Treaty Organization (NATO), the first peacetime U.S. alliance in 150 years. The Soviet Union responded by forming the Warsaw Pact. In 1949, two other landmark events occurred: The Soviet Union conducted its first successful atomic bomb test, and the pro-Western Chinese government of Chiang Kai-shek was driven off China's mainland by the forces of Chinese Communist leader Mao Zedong.

The Cold War continued in the 1950s, despite a so-called thaw after Stalin's death in 1953. The Soviet Union faced major challenges both at home and abroad. Following Khrushchev's renunciation of Stalin in 1956, uprisings against Communist rule occurred in Poland and Hungary. Khrushchev sent troops into Hungary in 1956; in Poland the Communist government weathered the storm without direct Soviet intervention. The lessons were clear: For the Eastern European satellites, Moscow would not permit defection from the Warsaw Pact; for Moscow, the price of empire was eternal vigilance.

Between 1958 and 1961 the issue of Berlin heated up again, resulting in an on-again, off-again crisis that culminated in August 1961 with the building of the Berlin Wall to stop the flood of escapees to the West. Another crisis was brewing, however, on the other Soviet flank. In the early 1960s a rift in relations between the USSR and its erstwhile Communist ally, the People's Republic of China (PRC), escalated into a war of words. Throughout the 1960s the two Communist behemoths traded insults. The divorce took an ugly turn in 1969 when fighting broke out along the border demarcated by the Amur and Ussuri rivers. There were relatively few casualties, but Sino-Soviet relations remained frigid, and Moscow now found itself engaged in two "cold wars" at once.

The year 1968 brought another disturbance on the western flank, this time in Czechoslovakia. The "Prague spring" saw the flowering of a democratization movement ("socialism with a human face"). Led by Alexander Dubcek, the Communist regime proposed to open up the political system to opposition parties. Moscow would have no truck with such "bourgeois" heresy. Soviet troops rolled into Prague and crushed Dubcek's government before the planned liberalization could be implemented. Brezhnev justified the intervention on the grounds that socialist states have an obligation to come to the aid of another socialist state threatened by counterrevolution. In other words: Once a socialist state, always a socialist state—particularly in the contiguous territories of Eastern Europe. Outside Eastern Europe, the "Brezhnev Doctrine" was widely decried and condemned.

There were a few positive developments in Soviet-American relations in the 1960s. In 1963, a "hotline" agreement (a direct crisis-line telephone link between the Kremlin and the White House) and the Partial Nuclear Test Ban Treaty were signed. In 1967, the Nuclear Non-Proliferation Treaty (NPT) was also signed. But events in places like Vietnam and Czechoslovakia continued to underscore the obstacles to peaceful coexistence.

The early 1970s witnessed the opening wedge of a dramatic realignment, when the United States and Communist China buried the hatchet after more than two decades of nonrecognition and mutual hostility. Moscow looked on in dismay, but should not have been surprised: One of the oldest principles of international politics—the enemy of my enemy is my friend—was working to bring these strange bedfellows together. In retrospect, what is amazing is that it took so long to happen.

The Soviet Union decided it was time to seek accommodations with the United States. In 1972 the two superpowers signed the SALT I agreement. They also moved to improve trade relations. It should be noted, however, that East-West trade developed outside the bilateral Soviet-American relationship. In the early 1970s, West Germany, under the center-left government of Chancellor Willy Brandt, pursued an independent foreign policy (*Ostpolitik*) that bore fruit in the form of sharply increased trade and other ties between East and West Germany and, more generally, between Eastern and Western Europe.

The record of superpower relations in the 1970s is uneven and contradictory. Progress in strategic arms limitation was not matched by a warming trend in relations in other areas. The decade ended on a discordant note with the Soviet invasion of Afghanistan, the punitive grain embargo imposed on the Soviet Union by the Carter Administration, and the boycott of the Moscow Summer Olympics (by the United States, Communist China, Japan, and others). The election of Ronald Reagan, a staunch anti-Communist, seemed likely to bring a resurgence of the Cold War as the 1980s unfolded.

The "double-trouble" of an American president who deeply distrusted Moscow and a procession of Soviet leaders who lacked vision and vigor (due to old age or failing health or both) ruled out any real progress in superpower coexistence between 1980 and 1985. Gorbachev's accession to power (and Reagan's desire to finish his second term with a flourish) changed the mood: In November 1987, after a false start at the Iceland summit one year earlier, the INF treaty (eliminating intermediate-range nuclear forces in Europe) was signed. Auspiciously, Moscow had made several "uncompensated" concessions to get a treaty. This conciliatory attitude in matters of arms control, combined with appealingly "liberal" domestic reforms, already mentioned, raised the possibility of a new thaw in the Cold War.

Ideology and Political Culture

Until 1989 generalizations about ideology in the Soviet Union and Eastern Europe came easily: Marxism-Leninism prevailed everywhere. Even before communism collapsed in Eastern Europe, however, political culture was less homogeneous throughout the region. *Ideology* refers to the official belief system that, in the case of Soviet-type Communist states, was an amalgam of ideas and teachings associated primarily with Marx and Lenin. *Political culture* is broader and encompasses not only ideology per se but also values, attitudes, myths, fears, prejudices, perceptions, and preferences that permeate and condition the political thoughts and actions of society's rank-and-file members. This distinction was especially crucial with regard to Communist states because the ideology was so obtrusive that it could (and often did) become a smokescreen which concealed the values that truly motivated political behavior.

Marxism-Leninism: A Secular Religion

Volumes have been written about Soviet ideology, and almost every political science textbook devotes pages to this subject.[18] Here we will sketch only the basic outlines of Marxism-Leninism.

Marxism is not simply a blueprint for revolution. Instead, it combines a philosophy of history with an elaborate theory of social development. Karl Marx claimed to have discovered the laws of sociopolitical evolution. The driving force in history, he believed, is economics (that is, organization of the means of production). Social and political institutions are mere "suprastructure," edifices built on economic foundations and nothing more or less than manifestations of the underlying relationships of production. Control (or ownership) of the means of production determines political power and social status as well as economic well-being. According to Marx, this iron law of history applies at all times in all places.

It is easy to see how capitalism, in Marx's eyes, is simply the latest stage in this evolutionary process. Capitalism is a system by which the few ("monopoly capitalists") control the means of production (land, labor, buildings, machines, and, of course, money) and use this control to exploit the many (who have no choice but to work for meager wages). The *law of capitalist accumulation* operates through fierce, dog-eat-dog competition to squeeze out little producers and create constant opportunities for big ones to get bigger. A Darwinian survival of the fittest means that producers must either "get big or get out" of the market.

Profit is the engine that drives capitalism, according to Marx. Even non-Marxist economists generally agree with this proposition, but Marx believed that profits are a form of legalized robbery. Under capitalism, workers toil long hours for subsistence wages. The difference between the income their labor generates and the pay they receive for that labor is what Marx called *surplus value* (profit based on exploitation).

As the rich get richer, the poor get poorer. The rich also get fewer, while the ranks of the poor swell as industrialization shifts the economy from rural to urban and from farm to factory. A new underclass, the proletariat, is thus created by a relentless process Marx called the *law of pauperization*. As machines replace human labor, unemployment grows, poverty spreads, and domestic markets shrink. The resulting business recession leads to even greater unemployment and, eventually, economic depression. Here, in a nutshell, is the Achilles' heel of the free-market system—the inevitable and recurrent "crisis of capitalism" that will eventually cause its total collapse.

The concept of *alienation* plays a central role in the Marxist theory of revolution. As part of an impersonal wage-labor force, workers are estranged from the means of production. Their labor is owned by someone else. They have no voice in how things are run. Their jobs are monotonous and menial. They take no pride in their work (mass consumption means quality is less important than quantity; producers and consumers do not know each other). Workers are cogs in a machine. Capitalism, in a word, is dehumanizing.

The *Communist Manifesto* opens with these prophetic words: "A spectre is haunting Europe—the spectre of Communism." Marx wrote this pamphlet to elucidate his thesis that "The history of all hitherto existing society is the history of class struggle." The final class struggle, between the proletariat and the bourgeoisie, would result in spontaneous revolution and usher in socialism, a system of productive relations characterized by public ownership and a fair though not equal distribution of goods ("from each according to his ability, to each according to his work"). In time, the state would simply wither away. The ultimate form of society would evolve gradually and naturally from socialism to communism ("from each according to his ability, to each according to his needs"). For Marx, equality was the supreme moral value.

Lenin was less interested in theory than practice. He wanted to make a revolution, not philosophize about history. Marx had called for a *dictatorship of the proletariat* as a temporary measure to forestall counterrevolution. It was an unfortunate turn of phrase: Lenin used it as an excuse to create a dictatorship *over* the proletariat. In addition, as noted earlier, Lenin coined a new term for the Communist party, exalting it as the *vanguard of the proletariat*. Without the vanguard, the revolution would never get rolling, Lenin argued. In this way, Lenin set the stage for making party dictatorship the hallmark of the Soviet state.

Two other Leninist precepts deserve mention. First, Lenin invented *democratic centralism* that, to this day, governs the organization and operation of the party. Under this rule, lower-level discussion within the party must cease as soon as a decision is announced. Decisions on important issues are made behind closed doors at the highest level and are strictly binding on all subordinate levels. Second, Lenin placed a *ban on factionalism* within the party, meaning that any opposition to the party line—no matter how loyal—can be suppressed whenever the leadership finds it expedient to do so. Also, any party leader guilty of factionalism risks demotion or expulsion.

Leninism evolved into a state religion. "Despite all the museums of atheism that have taken the place of Russian Orthodox churches throughout the country, the Soviet Union is now less an atheistic country, than a Leninist country," wrote a close observer of contemporary Soviet culture.[19] Every day thousands of Soviet citizens stand in long lines waiting to file past Lenin's open coffin in the granite mausoleum on Red Square. Pictures, statues, and busts of Lenin are everywhere. Graven images of Lenin set against a background of scarlet to symbolize the Great October Revolution and bathed in a soft halo of light have replaced the traditional icons that once adorned special corners in factories and schools. "Even the most casual visitor to the Soviet Union is overwhelmed by evidence of the religion of Leninism."[20]

Soviet Political Culture: Old Wine, New Wineskins

Understanding of other cultures requires a certain ability to suspend one's own ingrained values and habits of mind. Failure to do so inevitably leads to misconceptions. To cite one example, a journalist named Hedrick Smith, posted to Moscow in the 1970s, expected to find that most Soviet citizens remembered Stalin with fear and loathing. He discovered, that on the contrary, "So essential was Stalin to the concept of how Russia should be ruled for many middle-aged and elderly people that they no longer recall their panic at the time of his death."[21] Many (if not most) ordinary Soviet citizens displayed nostalgia for a strong boss!

Smith's observations comparing Soviet (and especially Russian) attitudes toward authority with Western (in particular, American) views are worth quoting at some length:

[There is] a fundamental difference between Russians and Americans, who are often moved to seek similarities in their national characters. They may share an openness of spirit, but Russians and Americans differ sharply in their attitudes toward power and authority—and not just because of Soviet Communism. Inbred mistrust of authority is an American tradition. We are wary as a people of bigness when it is accompanied by unchecked power—Big Business, Big Labor, big anything. . . .

Not so the Russians. Bigness and power are admired almost without qualification. Size inspires awe—huge Kremlins, cannons, churchbells under the czars; huge dams, missiles, atom smashers under the Communists. Marxism-Leninism has provided a rationale for large-scale production and concentrated power in the hands of Party leaders and central planners. But six centuries of authoritarian rule from Ivan the Great and Ivan the Terrible forward had made Russians monarchists in their bones long before Lenin and Stalin came along. . . .

So much has been inherited from the past, that a Russian takes for granted elements of political despotism that are instantly an affront to a Westerner. History has conditioned Russians differently. The cruel tyranny of Stalin was prefigured by the bloody reign of Ivan the Terrible in the 16th century and the iron rule of Nicholas I in the 19th century. Peter the Great, celebrated for opening Russia to the West and administration, is well known abroad for having also improved the efficiency of authoritarian controls, some of which survive today. It was Peter who set up the first political police administration and who officially instituted censorship and the practice of issuing internal passports to keep Russians from traveling away from their permanent homes without special permission.[22]

The easy assumption that the virtues of democracy are as obvious to Russians as they are to Americans turns out to be a delusion. It appears that most Russians value security more than freedom (which they have never known); at the same time they seem to fear disorder more than tyranny.[23] Part of the Russian aversion to overt forms of disobedience can probably be explained by the aforementioned history of draconian rule, the resulting absence of democracy, and a natural fear of the unknown. People accustomed to stern discipline are bound to feel insecure and perhaps disoriented when that discipline is reduced or removed. Of course, not all Soviet citizens fear freedom or equate democracy with disorder. But the consensus among scholars, emigrants, and casual observers alike is that most do.

One way Russians deal with embarrassing facts is by hiding them. Western observers are often struck by the Russian penchant for *pokazukha*, which translated means ''snow job,'' or putting up a false front. The practice of deliberately disguising unpleasant realities is time-honored and highly perfected in Russia. One of the most famous examples occurred in the eighteenth century, when a prince named Potemkin erected fake villages along the route used by Catherine the Great to impress her with the wealth of his region. The ''Potemkin trick'' is still used—for example, by the Soviet travel agency, Intourist, which packages tours of the Soviet Union for foreigner groups, provides guides (who are also supervisors), and keeps visitors' schedules so packed with excursions, museums, ballet performances, and the like that there is no time to poke around and see the darker side of Soviet life. Asked to justify this deception, Soviet interlocutors will give a standard answer: "We are proud of our achievements and have accomplished much in the face of tremendous adversity; why should we go about airing our dirty linen in public?"

Russians have long believed that Western nations view them as crude and uncultured. "You like to laugh at our misfortunes" is a common sentiment Russians express toward Americans. The deep-rooted Russian inferiority complex—manifested, for example, in the Soviet proclivity to challenge American visitors to impromptu poetry-reciting contests!—is reinforced by Soviet propaganda. The upshot is a kind of reflexive Soviet patriotism that often shows up even in non-threatening, interpersonal "confrontations" with the West. When it happens it may seem offensive, paranoiac, or just plain bizarre to Westerners, but it is a natural response to what Russians since at least Peter the Great have regarded as the "challenge of the West."

Patriotism is a universal emotion, but the "blood-and-soil" Soviet variety startles many Western visitors. Signs of patriotism are everywhere; some are transparently contrived by the regime for foreign consumption, but many are spontaneous and heartfelt. Hedrick Smith quoted a young Soviet economist as follows: "We learned from our history that, to survive, we must band together." Smith also noted that Suvorov, the great Russian military commander who defeated both Frederick the Great and Napoleon, used to say, "*Pust khuzhe, da nashe*" ("Let it be worse, but let it be ours").[24]

This attitude is akin to "My country, right or wrong," and Smith explained the concept as follows:

> Like so many essentials of Russian life, the phrase does not readily lend itself to translation, for one has to know that kvas is a fermented peasant drink made from water dripped through burnt bread. Kvas has a malty flavor, and cheap kvas can be like cold coffee—bitter, the color of muddy water, with grounds at the bottom. In cities all over Russia, white-coated women serve up glass mugs of kvas from large, saffron-colored, mobile metal kegs in the summertime. Foreigners usually pass up a second mug, but Russians swear by it, and peasants produce their own home brew of kvas. So kvas patriotism represents the earthy, peasantry, intensely Russian brand of patriotism.[25]

No survey of Soviet or Russian political culture is complete without some mention of *blat*—a generic term for the pervasive corruption, cheating, and dishonesty that permeates everyday life in the USSR. *Blat* assumes myriad forms: theft of state property, bribery, embezzlement, moonlighting, dealing on the black market, and so on. It involves bending, evading, or breaking the rules in all sorts of subtle and not-so-subtle ways. Everybody does it, largely out of necessity, because consumer goods and services are always scarce (and therefore precious) and because prices fixed by the state do not reflect true (market) value. Thus the distortions introduced into the Soviet economy by the system of central planning—in particular, the emphasis on heavy industry and (until recently) defense production at the expense of consumer needs—has created a morally ambiguous climate in which widespread dishonesty and underhandedness are rewarded (and tacitly accepted) while honesty and integrity appear foolish. Moreover, the rigidities of central planning make it expedient for plant managers to cheat, lie, and falsify records on a vast scale—including the use of *tolkachi* (illegal go-betweens) to obtain essential materials on the black market—in the never-ending struggle to fulfill the monthly production quotas.

Does the foregoing mean that Marxist-Leninist ideology has had little or no impact on Soviet political culture? On the contrary, public morality in the USSR reflects the *collectivism* that constitutes the core of Marxist ethics. This moral propensity contrasts sharply with the individualism so prevalent in the West, especially in countries like France and the United States. In the Soviet Union, the paramount importance of the *kollektif* is rarely questioned. Schoolchildren are taught both overtly and covertly to place group rights above individual rights. They are also taught to take responsibility for the performance and conduct of their classmates. Similarly, teachers generally hold parents responsible for the attitudes and actions of their children in school. In addition, adults are expected to take responsibility for the conduct of other adults—especially family members, neighbors, and coworkers—to an extent that seems odd, perhaps even unfair and oppressive, to Westerners.

Eastern Europe

Geopolitically, Eastern Europe is overshadowed by the Soviet Union. The geography of Eastern Europe, like that of the USSR, has been an important factor in shaping the history and political culture of the region. Located between two civilizations, the Graeco-Roman in the West and the Byzantine-Ottoman in the East, the nations of Eastern Europe—Albania, Bulgaria, Czechoslovakia, Hungary, Poland, Romania, and Yugoslavia—have been influenced by both East and West to varying degrees.

The area of Eastern Europe (minus the Soviet part) is roughly equivalent to that of the Great Plains of North America (North and South Dakota, Minnesota, Nebraska, Kansas, Iowa, and Missouri). Unlike the Great Plains, however, it is a densely populated region. About 120 million people inhabit an area one-seventh the size of the United States. Poland (about the size of New Mexico) is the largest of the Eastern European countries; its population is nearly equal to that of California and New York combined. Yugoslavia and Romania are next in size, followed by Czechoslovakia, Bulgaria, and Hungary. Albania is by far the smallest.

Generalizations about Eastern Europe are not easy to make because of the diversity of the region. Perhaps the most impressive sweeping theory is the concept of Eastern Europe as a "shatter zone" in which boundary lines were, for centuries, broken to pieces and redrawn by one power or another. It is certainly true that Eastern Europe has historically been coveted (and carved up) by rival powers from outside the region. Not counting the Mongol invasion, Eastern Europe has been the object of aggression by the Ottomans, the Hapsburgs, the Germans, and, in recent times, the Soviets. In 1904, Sir Halford Mackinder, the great geopolitical thinker, argued that "whoever controls Eastern Europe controls the Heartland of Europe . . . and thus controls the world."[26] One thing is certain: Self-determination for the native peoples of Eastern Europe has seldom been more than a distant dream or pious incantation.

Poland on the eve of World War II epitomized the historical predicament of the countries of Eastern Europe. Caught between Nazi Germany to the east and Stalinist Russia to the west, Poland could do nothing to avert catastrophe. Poland has always been vulnerable to foreign invasion and subjugation because it lacks natural boundaries. As with Russia, this insecurity has no doubt helped to shape not only the history of Poland but also the national character of the Polish people. Unity and perseverance in the face of adversity were expressed in various forms in Communist Poland: steadfast allegiance to the Roman Catholic church by the vast majority, despite the disapproval of the party; refusal of Polish farmers to go along with collectivization; and the rise of the Solidarity movement, which defied a government ban and demanded greater rights and benefits for Polish workers, and ultimately overthrew communism. Poland's history—in particular, the futile Polish quest for independence over the past two centuries—is a metaphor for many of the other nations of Eastern Europe as well.

Political Ties Before 1945

All the countries of Eastern Europe are newcomers to the ranks of nation-states, most of them having gained their independence only in the past century. Romania became independent in 1878, Bulgaria in 1908, and Albania in 1912. Poland, Czechoslovakia, and Yugoslavia gained their independence after Germany and Austria-Hungary lost World War I.

Before World War I, four great empires dominated Eastern Europe. All were located on the periphery of the region, and only one (Russia) was anchored in a Slavic culture. By the mid-nineteenth century, the Russian Empire encompassed all the Ukraine, part of Poland, and Bessarabia. The German and Austrian Empires partitioned and ruled Poland from the end of the eighteenth century until 1918. Austria's domain encompassed the territories of what is now Czechoslovakia, Hungary, and northern Yugoslavia from the fifteenth century until its defeat (and dissolution) in World War I. The Ottomon Empire (Turkey) ruled present-day Bulgaria, Romania, central and southern Yugoslavia, and Albania.

The most important political distinction among East European countries is between those once ruled by Austria and Germany (Poland, Czechoslovakia, Hungary, and northern Yugoslavia) and those once ruled by the Ottoman Turks. Although all had limited autonomy, the northern-tier Slavic nations were generally less oppressed and abused than their neighbors to the south, who endured religious persecution and heavy taxation while benefiting from little or no economic and political development.

In the turbulent twenty-year period between World War I and World War II (1918–1939), many East European governments had a democratic veneer, but only Czechoslovakia was a true republic. For the others, inexperience in the art of self-government was an obstacle to democracy. Unlike Czechoslovakia, the other East European countries also lacked statesmanlike leadership and faced enormous economic and social problems. Antisemitism and extreme nationalism were prevalent throughout the region, as were divisions over religion, social reform, and nationalism. The leaders of Hungary, Romania, and Bulgaria saw the Nazi totalitarian model as a solution to their desperate domestic circumstances. (They later joined the Hitler-led Axis.) Widespread hostility to both the Soviet Union and communism also reinforced this perverse inclination to embrace Nazi Germany.

All the nations of Eastern Europe lost their independence in World War II. Poland, Czechoslovakia, and Yugoslavia were conquered by Nazi Germany. Hitler and Stalin signed a nonaggression pact in 1939, under which they split Poland. Two years later Hitler tore up the agreement and attacked the Soviet Union. Later, when Stalin turned the tide, the advancing Red Army waited on the eastern bank of the Vistula while German troops crushed the Polish underground. (The non-Communist Polish government-in-exile had called for the Warsaw uprising in the belief that it would hasten the defeat of the Germans; rather than helping the Polish fighters, Stalin kept his army on the sidelines.) In due time Soviet troops crossed the Vistula and pursued Hitler's retreating forces into Germany. Thus, in an ironic twist, Hitler ended up giving the USSR a golden opportunity to dispatch Soviet troops into Poland.

The story of Poland in World War II is tragic but is not without historical antecedent. Most notably, in 1772 Prussia and Russia annexed major portions of Polish territory in the First Partition of Poland. According to Ivan Volgyes, "Poland then tried to re-create its former greatness by reforming the obsolete working of its government." In the Second Partition, in 1793, Poland was further reduced. "Even though the Poles, under the brilliant general Tadeusz Kosciuszko, fought valiantly against partition," Volgyes commented, "the dream of Polish independence was brutally crushed by the invading Prussian and Russian armies." A Third Partition, now including the Austrians, occurred in 1795 and was "the end of Poland as a political entity, as a state."[27]

Hungary, Romania, and Bulgaria were first seduced and then subjugated by Hitler. As accomplices of Nazi Germany, they could expect little sympathy after the war from the Allies. Ironically, the postwar Soviet land grab in Eastern Europe was facilitated by the very nations that eventually fell victim to Stalin's megalomania.

One of the most important consequences of World War II was the unification of Eastern Europe into a military and political bloc known as the Warsaw Pact, led, of course, by the Soviet Union. Thus, one Slavic nation, Russia (the nucleus of the USSR), succeeded in bringing Eastern Europe's Slavic peoples under a single political authority for the first time. To appreciate the magnitude of this accomplishment, we must look at the rise of the USSR from ignominy at the opening of the twentieth century to superpower status as the century draws to a close.

Adjusting to the Soviet System

Up until 1989 the Soviet impact on the political culture of Eastern Europe was apparent—perhaps more apparent than real. The norms of Marxism-Leninism, discussed earlier, were also the official norms of political life throughout Eastern Europe. A traveler to any East European capital would see banners, signs, and placards sporting the same slogans and shibboleths that adorned the buildings, parks, and streets of every Soviet community, no matter how large or small. The following basic elements of the Soviet system were evident in the political culture of all these states:

1. The leading role of the party
2. The duties and obligations of socialist construction
3. The superiority of socialism to the old order
4. The imperatives of socialist internationalism (loyalty to Moscow as the leader of the Communist bloc)
5. The value of socialist morality[28]

The concept of socialist morality merits brief explanation. As Lenin saw it, morality was not general but particular. Hence, the morality of Communists was determined by particular class interests—those of the proletariat. The overriding aim of the proletariat, Lenin reasoned, was dictated by the ongoing class struggle. The "final victory" over capitalism could only be achieved by revolution. Anything that advanced the cause of revolution, therefore, was good; anything that impeded revolution was bad. As Volgyes wrote in his textbook on Eastern European politics:

> This ideology relegates universal ethical and moral values to a secondary role. Thus the generalizable ethical commandments regarding one's parents, for example, had to give way to particularism: "Betray your father and your mother if you suspect them of opposing Stalinist policies" in order to preserve your life and position and to foster the development of socialism. The harm done by this moral-ethical particularism in all of these societies cannot be measured; the only mitigating factor in the region appears to be the traditional cynicism of its people.[29]

The "traditional cynicism" of the East Europeans was manifested in a number of ways. First, they seldom gave the official ideology more than lip service (they often gave it much less). This ideology was the subject of jokes and sarcasm in private, even as it was treated with mock reverence in public. Second, anti-Russian sentiment flowed just beneath the surface in most Eastern European countries. The fact that the populace resented Soviet domination (and, as they saw it, exploitation) was hardly surprising.

This anti-Russianism was reinforced by another universal element in Eastern Europe: ethnic particularism, or nationalism. Poles were very conscious of their cultural heritage, as were Romanians and Hungarians and all the others. When the Soviet Union interfered (or worse, intervened) in the internal affairs of these countries, it stirred strong nationalistic impulses.

Nationalism also played and still plays an important role in relationships among the states of Eastern Europe. Historic rivalries have not been dissolved by ideology or alliance ties: "Witness . . . the pressures for military intervention in Poland in 1981 expressed by the East Germans and Czechoslovaks, or the problems between Hungary, on the one hand, and Czechoslovakia and Romania, on the other, regarding the presence of significant Magyar minorities in the latter two states."[30] Ethnic nationalism has worked at cross-purposes with the ideology of Marxism-Leninism in general, and with the Soviet-inspired ideal of "socialist internationalism" in particular.

In sum, the political culture of Eastern Europe exhibited a kind of schizophrenia: an external ideology superimposed on societies with rich cultural and political traditions of their own. One commonality that may have helped ease the pain of adjustment to the Stalinist system after World War II was the tradition of authoritarianism. Only in Czechoslovakia in the interwar period was democracy successful. Everywhere else, monarchy and hierarchy had been the twin pillars of the political order.

Communism at the Crossroads: Back to the Future?

In 1986, one year after Mikhail Gorbachev took charge in the Kremlin, the American scholar Seweryn Bialer published an incisive analysis of the Soviet political system entitled, significantly, *The Soviet Paradox: External Expansion, Internal Decline.*[31] According to Bialer, "When Stalin died in March 1953, the leaders of the Soviet Communist Party and government appealed to the population not to panic." But Brezhnev's death in November 1982 was a different story:

> The leaders who survived him had no reason to issue such an appeal. . . . Stalin's death threatened chaos; Brezhnev's promised a return to efficiency and order.
>
> Yet the death of Brezhnev may prove to have been as important to the future of the Soviet Union—and the United States—as the death of Stalin. And this may be so not only if the new leaders bring major changes to Russia, but also in the more likely event that the forces of inertia and continuity remain dominant. Both Western observers and members of the Soviet establishment are coming increasingly to the conclusion that the domestic system reached its peak under Brezhnev, and that without sweeping changes it will decline in its effectiveness in serving the goals of the Politburo.
>
> The troubles that the Soviets face at home constitute a crisis of the system. . . .
>
> On the domestic scene, the Soviet paradox is expressed in the following dilemmas: First, military growth is one of the chief sources of the internal problems besetting the Soviet Union and makes more difficult their resolution; at the same time, military growth is regarded by the leadership as a supreme value to which the economy and the society must be subordinated. Second, economic revitalization of the system would require a devolution of political power; yet the paramount goal of the leadership, from the regime's inception, has been the centralization and concentration of political power.[32]

If this thesis is correct, and the Soviet Union really is experiencing a period of decline—the underlying problem is probably more spiritual than material, more psychological than physical. In the final analysis, the success or failure of a society or an economy (especially one endowed with the natural resources and population that could sustain growth and prosperity) is the nation's heart and soul, the intangible factors that alone can account for the vigor and vitality of a China or Germany or Japan or United States in its heyday. Indeed, Japan has achieved its postwar economic miracle *without* the natural resources that seem to be a prerequisite.

In 1978 David Shipler quoted Katya Polikanov, a Moscow youth, at the tender age of 17: "Nobody believes in anything." What is so striking about this comment is not that it reveals disillusionment, for every society has its disillusioned people. But teenagers are not expected to be jaded; most of us associate optimism with youth. Most of us also associate hard work with faith in something—God, country, humanity, or perhaps the future itself. For an individual, belief in nothing is enervating, dispiriting, and depressing. For a society, disbelief is a wellspring for malaise, sloth, and stagnation.

To Shipler, who lived in and studied Soviet society for several years, "The ideology, once active, has grown passive. It no longer shapes the direction of change inside the country but merely molds analysis of the outside world. . . . The ideology has atrophied into a convenient cant, a set of symbols, often used to camouflage anti-Marxist practices and to elicit stereotyped interpretations of events at home and abroad."[33]

Shipler's insight into the "loss of faith [which] leaves a hollow mood in Russia" led him to this jarring conclusion:

> A yearning stirs. . . . [It] is not a lurch forward but a reaching back, back into the suffering and glory of World War II to nourish national honor and heroism, back into the tight authoritarianism of Stalinist times, back into the ethnic purity and nobility of what was "Russian," back into the simplicity and mythical honesty of Russia's village life, back into the church.[34]

This analysis, of course, reflects the late 1970s, before Gorbachev's accession to power. But it sheds light on important questions today: Will Gorbachev be able to revitalize Soviet society? Can he breathe new life into a moribund ideology or find some substitute for it? Will he be able to inspire and motivate a society that apparently has lost its optimism?

Such questions apply to Eastern Europe, too, where similar ailments afflict the countries of the region—all with the legacy of Stalinism. The "crisis of Communism," then, which led to the downfall of Soviet-style rule, can be seen as a *regional* problem that is more than skin deep.

Many years ago, Chiang Kai-shek, the pro-West leader of Nationalist China whose government survived Japanese occupation during World War II but was ousted by the Maoist insurgency in 1949, described Communism as a disease of the heart; in contrast, he said, Japanese imperialism had been only a disease of the skin. Today's Communist leaders, ironically, are forced by mounting domestic problems to ask whether Communism, as they have practiced it, is, in fact, suffering from a disease of the heart.

CONCLUSION

The Soviet Union ruled most of the Slavic world for four decades after World War II; Russia, in turn, has dominated the USSR. The other nations of Eastern Europe have almost always been dominated by an imperial power—Russia, Germany, Austria-Hungary, the Ottomans. In 1989 one Communist regime after another fell in a wave of popular discontent. We turn in the next chapter to consider the new political patterns and trends evident on the other side of Europe's vanishing East-West divide.

STUDY QUESTIONS

1. How has geography influenced the Soviet Union's history, political traditions, economy, and political culture (its attitudes, beliefs, myths, prejudices, hopes, fears, and the like)?
2. What impact did the Cold War have on East-West relations in such areas as arms control, trade, investment, and conflict management?
3. What, if anything, is distinctive about the geography and cultures of Eastern Europe? How have these factors influenced the region's history? Has a sense of Slavic solidarity been present throughout the region in modern times, or is today's nationalism more particularistic?

SUGGESTED READINGS

Berdyaev, Nicholas. *The Origin of Russian Communism*. Ann Arbor, Mich.: University of Michigan, 1960.
Conquest, Robert. *V. I. Lenin*. New York: Viking, 1972.
Conquest, Robert. *The Harvest of Sorrow*. New York: Oxford, 1986.
Crankshaw, Edward. *Khrushchev: A Career*. New York: Viking, 1966.
Halle, Louis. *The Cold War as History*. New York: Harper & Row, 1967.
Palmer, Alan. *The Lands Between: A History of East-Central Europe Since the Congress of Vienna*. New York: Macmillan, 1970.
Riasanovsky, Nicholas. *A History of Russia*, 3rd ed. New York: Oxford, 1977.
Rothschild, Joseph. *Return to Diversity: A Political History of East Central Europe Since World War II*. New York: Oxford, 1989.
Smith, Hedrick. *The Russians*. New York: Ballantine, 1976.
Ulam, Adam B. *Stalin: The Man and His Era*. New York: Viking, 1973.

NOTES

1. Quoted in Louis J. Halle, *The Cold War as History* (New York: Harper & Row, 1967), pp. 103–104.
2. Vadim Medish, *The Soviet Union* (Englewood Cliffs, N.J.: Prentice-Hall, 1987), p. 23.
3. Nicholas Berdyaev, *The Origin of Russian Communism* (Ann Arbor, Mich.: University of Michigan Press, 1937), p. 9.
4. Nicholas Riasanovsky, *A History of Russia*, 3rd ed. (New York: Oxford, 1977), p. 347.
5. Medish, op. cit., p. 22.
6. Quoted in Medish, op. cit., pp. 23–24.
7. Berdyaev, op. cit., pp. 8–9.
8. Riasanovsky, op. cit., pp. 425–426.
9. Ibid., p. 426.
10. See Robert Conquest, *V. I. Lenin* (New York: Viking, 1972), p. 32.
11. Quoted in Isaac Deutscher, *Stalin: A Political Biography* (New York: Vintage, 1960), p. 550.
12. See, for example, Robert Conquest, *The Harvest of Sorrow* (New York: Oxford, 1986); and Adam B. Ulam, *Stalin: The Man and His Era* (New York: Viking, 1973).
13. See especially Edward Crankshaw, *Khrushchev: A Career* (New York: Viking, 1966).
14. Deutscher, op. cit., pp. 550–551.
15. Alexander Werth, *Russia at War 1941–1945* (New York: Avon, 1964), pp. 904–906.
16. On the question of forced labor, one eyewitness estimates that at least a million Russian refugees were ''perfidiously returned by Allied authorities into Soviet hands'' in 1946 and 1947. The same writer records many other instances of mass arrests and banishment to the *gulags* during this period. See Alexander Solzhenitsyn, *The Gulag Archipelago 1918–1956* (New York: Harper & Row, 1973), p. 85.
17. Roy A. Medvedev and Zhores A. Medvedev, *Khrushchev: The Years in Power* (New York: Norton, 1978), p. 121.
18. See, for example, Thomas M. Magstadt and Peter S. Schotten, *Understanding Politics: Ideas, Institutions, and Issues*, 2nd ed. (St. Martin's, New York, 1987).
19. Stanley Meisler, ''For Kremlin Rulers, Lenin Is Only God,'' *Los Angeles Times*, Sunday, October 25, 1987.
20. Ibid.
21. Hedrick Smith, *The Russians* (New York: Ballantine, 1976), p. 332.
22. Ibid.
23. See David K. Shipler, *Russia: Broken Idols, Solemn Dreams* (New York: Penguin, 1983), p. 200.
24. Smith, op. cit., pp. 410–411.
25. Ibid.
26. Cited in Ivan Volgyes, *Politics in Eastern Europe* (Chicago: Dorsey, 1986), p. 15.
27. Ibid., pp. 29–30.
28. Ibid., pp. 287–289.
29. Ibid., p. 288.
30. Ibid., p. 297.
31. Seweryn Bialer, *The Soviet Paradox: External Expansion, Internal Decline* (New York: Vintage, 1986).
32. Ibid, p. 2.
33. Shipler, op. cit., p. 264.
34. Ibid., p. 265.

Chapter 8
Communism in Transition

As discussed in Chapter 7, the Soviet political system is the result of two inter-related processes: revolution and evolution. Although the Soviet regime even before the recent wave of dramatic reforms was not identical to the one Lenin founded in 1918, or the one Stalin later built on those foundations, many elements of both Leninism and Stalinism survived and continue to influence political patterns in the USSR and Eastern Europe. Although the policies and principles associated with Mikhail Gorbachev's "new thinking"—including *glasnost* (openness), *perestroika* (restructuring), and *demokratizatsiia* (political pluralism)—are transforming the Soviet Union, it is not yet clear what sort of political order will supplant the Stalinist system.

As noted in Chapters 5 and 6, sweeping changes also occurred in Poland, Hungary, East Germany, Czechoslovakia, and Romania in 1989–1990. (Reforms moved somewhat more slowly in Bulgaria.) By mid-1990 the reform movements had succeeded in democratizing the political processes and reorienting domestic policies in the former satellite states. Foreign policies followed suit. As a consequence, the East-West conflict was fading from the vernacular of European politics.

Nonetheless, new policies cannot be institutionalized over night, nor can failing or disrupted economies be stabilized easily. Given the obstacles to the integration of Eastern and Western Europe and the distinctive historical, ethnic, and cultural experience of the various Slavic nations, it is still appropriate to consider the Soviet Union and Eastern Europe as a distinct region separated from its neighbors by factors other than geography, including linguistics and psychology.

Since World War II and until the watershed events of 1989, Moscow sought to impose the Soviet model of "scientific socialism" on its client-states in Eastern Europe. Although in the 1980s Moscow began to question that model, and in 1989 Gorbachev declared unequivocally that the nations of Eastern Europe were free to determine their own domestic affairs, it is appropriate for us to examine the model in some depth, since it shaped the region's approach to politics, government, and the economy for so many decades.

We begin with a look at the nature and functions of the Soviet Communist party, which, according to Article 6 of the 1977 Constitution, was the "leading and guiding force of Soviet society and the nucleus of its political system." This party monopoly, long the keystone of Communist rule, was renounced in February 1990 at a historic meeting of the Central Committee. The implications of this momentous decision will be considered later. For now, suffice it to say that the Communist party was, until very recently, the sole repository of political power in the Soviet Union and Eastern Europe.

The Communist Party: A Retrospective View

The Soviet Constitution of 1977 proclaimed the Communist Party of the Soviet Union (CPSU) as the ''leading and guiding force of Soviet society.'' These were not empty words, for the CPSU has been an all-pervasive presence in Soviet society. Above all, its tentacles have reached deeply into four structures that implement party policy: the state bureaucracy, the secret police (KGB), the system of enterprise management, and the military.

This principle of the party's leading role is rooted in Leninist ideology, which stresses the surpassing importance of the party as the *vanguard of the proletariat*. Lenin believed that party leadership was necessary to galvanize the masses into revolutionary action. These two seminal ideas—that revolution is the path to working-class power and that the Communist party is the necessary catalyst—are the basic tenets of Marxism-Leninism. No Soviet leader before Gorbachev had dared (or cared) to renounce them.

Party Organization

Centralization of power and authority has always been the hallmark of the Soviet political system. Despite recent changes, the CPSU remains the epitome of centralization. Imagine a huge pyramid with a wide base: At the apex of the pyramid are the Politburo and the central party apparatus, including the Secretariat and the Central Committee; in the middle are the regional party organizations; closer to the base are the local party organizations; finally, at the very bottom are the so-called primary party organizations (or PPOs). We will discuss this system from the top down.

The Politburo   The Politburo was preeminent in the Soviet system up to February 1990. The changes announced at that time raised questions about the future role of the Politburo, but it is still too soon to say whether it will be eclipsed as the supreme decision-making body by some other entity.

The Politburo consists of eleven to fifteen full (voting) members and six to eight candidate (nonvoting) members. In theory these members are elected by the Central Committee; in practice the members are co-opted—that is, they are chosen secretively by the voting members of the Politburo itself. Politburo leaders thus constitute a self-perpetuating oligarchy. Until recently this elite group enjoyed a monopoly of decision-making power in the Soviet Union. Moreover, it hand-picked the Central Committee, one of two bodies to which it was theoretically accountable (the other being the Party Congress). In early 1990 Gorbachev unveiled plans to enlarge the Politburo, possibly a move to downgrade its decision-making role.

The internal workings of the Politburo have always been a mystery. Its meetings are chaired by the general secretary, who has been the single most powerful figure in the Soviet system from the beginning of Stalin's rule in the 1920s. In the late 1980s, however, Gorbachev elevated the presidency to a point where it rivaled the post of general secretary (he held both positions at the time). The premier (chairman of the Council of Ministers) and the president (chairman of the Supreme Soviet) have traditionally held seats on the Politburo as well. (The Council of Ministers and the Supreme Soviet are state, as opposed to party, organizations. They are discussed under "The Soviet State.") In addition, the Politburo's ruling group has usually included influential ministers such as the minister of defense, minister of foreign affairs, minister of agriculture, and chairman of the KGB (the Committee for State Security—secret police), plus one or two senior members of the Secretariat and several first secretaries of the major territorial subdivisions of the USSR.

Little is known about decision-making within the Politburo. Former General Secretary Leonid Brezhnev once said that "99.99 percent of the time" decisions were reached by consensus; in other words, voting was rare. Although party rules strictly forbid "factionalism," power struggles have sometimes burst into the open, especially when the death or ouster of one supreme leader made it necessary to choose another. Lacking a clear procedure for a changing of the guard, the danger of a succession crisis has always been present.

The General Secretary   The Soviet Union might be compared to a large corporation, with the general secretary playing the dual role of chairman of the board and chief executive officer. There is a crucial difference, of course: The Board of Directors of the USSR, Inc., unlike that of General Motors or IBM, is not subject to higher authority.

Although the office of general secretary has been the paramount position in the Soviet system, it is not mentioned in party statutes, the Constitution, or Soviet textbooks. The general secretary, no matter what his limitations, has always been glorified in the Soviet press as "heroic" but "modest."

Collective leadership was a tenet of Lenin's plan for the Soviet state. Stalin violated this principle and established a "cult of personality," ruling as dictator without regard for the opinions of Politburo cohorts. Stalin's successor, Nikita Khrushchev, on his ouster in 1964, was accused of trying to establish a new personality cult. The next general secretary, Leonid Brezhnev (1964–1982), was careful not to make the same mistake. Indeed, in 1966 the Central Committee resolved that no individual should ever again hold the two top positions of party chief (general secretary) and head of government (chairman of the Council of Ministers) simultaneously, as had both Stalin and Khrushchev.

No one knows whether Yuri Andropov, Brezhnev's successor and a former KGB chief, would have ruled in accordance with Leninist or Stalinist prescriptions, for his tenure was cut short by an early death. Konstantin Chernenko, who succeeded him, survived in office for only thirteen months, during most of which he was gravely ill and unable to exercise leadership. Chernenko died in 1985 and was succeeded by Mikhail Gorbachev.

Gorbachev launched a bold campaign aimed at economic reform ("restructuring," he called it), but not until he was assured of a Politburo majority. To this end he moved quickly to replace aging, Brezhnev-era party oligarchs (who could be expected to resist change) with younger, reform-minded leaders like himself.

The Secretariat and the Central Committee Apparatus   The general secretary is so named by virtue of his formal position as "first among equals" (and presiding officer) in the Secretariat, the executive committee of the CPSU. In some cases, party secretaries (usually ten or so) are also members of the Politburo; joint membership on the Politburo and Secretariat indicates that an individual is firmly entrenched in the inner circle of Kremlin decision-makers. It follows that major policy initiatives have been unlikely without consensus within this inner circle.

The existence of two top policymaking bodies within the Communist party often confuses students. How is power divided? What are the functions of each? Which body is more prestigious? Although there are no simple answers, it may help to distinguish between the party itself and the political system. On the one hand, the Secretariat runs the party, and each secretary heads one or more departments of the Central Committee apparatus (described below). The Politburo, on the other hand, has held supreme political power and thus traditionally has dominated the Secretariat as well as every other part of the political system. Such distinctions, however, are somewhat artificial and even misleading, because the membership of these two bodies overlaps, virtually ensuring agreement.

As for prestige, Politburo membership has carried more clout than membership in the Secretariat. A leader who holds positions on both bodies can survive being removed from the Secretariat, but being dropped from the Politburo for reasons other than health (or possibly old age) has been a form of political disgrace and has usually been the kiss of death for the fallen leader's career.

The nerve center of the CPSU is the party *apparat* (apparatus). The *apparat* is really the tip of the iceberg: Beneath it lurks a huge party bureaucracy that parallels (and duplicates) the vast state bureaucracy created by Stalin. The exact roles and functions of the party bureaucracy have been the subject of much debate. The main function has been to act as watchdog for the party leadership, to supervise the state bureaucracy and ensure against the emergence of independent power bases from which "enemies of the people" might obstruct or oppose party-endorsed policy.

The organization of the Central Committee apparatus illuminates this role, for every aspect of Soviet government and society is covered by one department or another. Individual secretaries oversee such key areas as ideology and culture, cadres, party affairs, agriculture, foreign policy, foreign relations, heavy industries, and defense. Other important concerns reflected in the structure of the *apparat* include science and education, construction, light industry and consumer goods, transport and communications, trade and domestic services, and machine building. (The *apparat* was reorganized by Gorbachev in 1988; the details of that reorganization are discussed later in this chapter.)

Politically sensitive functions of the *apparat* have always been hidden. For example, personnel matters—such as who gets promoted to high-level positions—are handled by a department whose name ("Organization Party Work") sounds innocuous; yet this party organ can make and break careers. Similarly, the department that acts as watchdog over the military—ensuring, for example, that coup plotting and disloyalty will be detected quickly—is known as the "Main Political Administration."

The Central Committee and Party Congress So far we have looked only at the apex of the party pyramid, the bodies that make and implement policy. In theory, the Politburo and Secretariat are elected by a party assembly known as the Central Committee, which, in turn, is elected by a much larger elective assembly, the Party Congress. In reality, however, "elections" are rigged; there is only one "candidate" for each position, and candidates are selected by party committees. Voting is simply a ritual.

Central Committee membership is a great status symbol, a sign of achievement not only in the party but also in the arts, sciences, technology, diplomacy, the mass media, the economy, and the armed services. Membership is a reward, a form of recognition, as well as a measure of political influence. The small size of the Central Committee indicates the elite social status that its members enjoy; there are fewer than five hundred members (about three hundred full members, with the rest being candidate members).

The Central Committee is, in theory, the party's supreme decision-making body; in practice it acts largely as a rubber stamp for Politburo policies. It thus plays an important role in legitimating the Politburo. Beyond this symbolism, it is possible that—if the Politburo were deadlocked—the committee might vote on an issue. (In 1957, for example, Khrushchev used the Central Committee to overcome an attempt by Politburo opponents to oust him; this is the only evidence that the Central Committee acts as a policy-making body). Now, as the Soviet leadership moves to more democratic methods, the Central Committee is likely to be one vehicle it will use.

By the same token, the impetus for democratization will almost certainly come from within the party itself. Party congresses are held at irregular intervals, but there is usually one every four or five years. In 1989–1990 there were signs of movement away from "democratic centralism" and toward a more open, participatory model of decision-making.

Before 1990, when party elections were cut and dried, delegates (about five thousand) were hand-picked from all over the Soviet Union. When a party congress was called, delegates gathered in Moscow to hear, with great pomp and ceremony, boring speeches by an assortment of "heroic" workers and long-winded party leaders. Eventually the speech making would end (congresses usually lasted about ten days), and the delegates would go home—but not before they voted unanimously to adopt the new party program, a blueprint that indicated the outlines of things to come. They also elected the Central Committee, a mechanical process of approving the "candidates" on a predetermined list.

Intermediate Party Organizations Below the central party apparatus in Moscow are several levels of bureaucracy that mirror the territorial subdivisions of the state bureaucracy. These levels, beginning at the bottom, are the rural and urban district (*raion*); the city (*gorod*) or autonomous area (*okrug*); the province (*oblast*) or territory (*krai*); and the union-republics (fifteen in all).

The arrangement of party organs on each level reflects the central party organization. All levels have conferences (analogous to a congress), committees, bureaus, secretariats, and first secretaries (analogous to the general secretary). Theoretically, rank-and-file members elect delegates to the conference, and the delegates elect a committee, which, in turn, elects a bureau (analogous to the Politburo) and several secretaries. The exact opposite actually occurs: Lists are made in advance by party bosses, and "elections" are so much window dressing.

Primary Party Organizations   At the bottom of the party pyramid are primary party organizations, or PPOs. Every party member, from highest to lowest, belongs to a PPO. Normally set up at places of employment, a party cell must have at least three members to be recognized as a PPO. All together, several million workers thus serve in leadership roles as members of PPO committees and bureaus or as PPO secretaries. These party cadres (workers) are released from their regular jobs to perform party work. Only PPOs with 150 or more members can have full-time paid workers.

Most PPOs are relatively small: 40 percent have 15 or fewer members, and 80 percent have less than 50. Only a few hundred of the more than 425,000 PPOs have 1,000 or more members. Generally, the larger the PPO, the more complex its organization, and the more active its leadership. In theory, all PPOs are supposed to hold general meetings at least once a month—another rule that is widely ignored.

Principles of Party Operation

Lenin himself established the doctrine of *democratic centralism* as the set of operational principles governing the CPSU. Today the party has its own constitution (or "Rules"), which enshrines and elucidates the following: (a) the election of all executive party organs, from lowest to highest; (b) the binding nature of decisions by higher organs on lower ones; (c) strict party discipline and subordination of the minority to the majority; and (d) periodic reports to members and to higher party bodies. In practice, the second rule has always overshadowed the others. Obedience and discipline are enforced from above: Party elections are rigged, majorities are produced on command, and accountability is a one-way street. In the Soviet system, bosses rule their bureaucratic fiefdoms, however large or small, like medieval lords.

Reinforcing this hierarchical pattern is the long-standing Leninist ban on factionalism. The preamble to the Rules states that:

> Ideological and organizational unity, monolithic cohesion of its ranks, and a high degree of conscious discipline on the part of all Communists are an inviolable law of the CPSU. All manifestations of factionalism and group activity are incompatible with Marxist-Leninist principles and with Party membership.[1]

Finally, the CPSU Rules refer several times to "criticism and self-criticism"—the obligation of party members to watch and judge fellow members as well as to confess their own shortcomings. Both watching and confessing are integral to the ethics of party membership, which is particularly poignant in the context of Soviet party history, because Stalin used show trials and public "confessions" to justify purging (and in many instances executing) real or imagined opponents. Today, party members are rarely required to denounce themselves publicly, but criticizing one's own conduct and that of one's peers remains a standard part of proceedings at closed party meetings.

Party Membership

Given the prominence of the CPSU in the Soviet system, the question of party membership takes on major importance. Since the founding of the Soviet state in 1917, the CPSU has grown from a handful of professional revolutionaries into a massive organization encompassing some 19 million members, or about 6.5 percent of the population. Despite its large membership, the CPSU constitutes a political (and some would say a socioeconomic) elite.

The Rules of the CPSU set strict admission standards and rather elaborate rites of initiation. Anyone 25 years of age or older may join the party. Applications must be supported by recommendations from at least three party members of five or more years' standing who have known the applicant for at least one year. Presumably, recommendations are not made lightly, for the Rules state that members may be held responsible for the character and conduct of anyone they endorse. Initiates are on probation for one year as candidate members before they gain full membership.

Party membership brings burdens as well as benefits. According to the Rules, Communists are expected to "master Marxist-Leninist theory," to epitomize "a conscientious and creative attitude toward labor," to follow the party line "firmly and steadfastly," and in general to be exemplary Soviet citizens. High expectations are evident in the Rules. For example, Article 12 states: "A party member bears a double responsibility to the state and to the party for the violation of Soviet laws. Persons who have committed indictable offenses are expelled from the CPSU." In fact, expulsion is automatic and typically precedes a verdict of the court. No wonder party bosses can boast that members are never convicted of serious crimes!

Nomenklatura

Soviet politics has no upstarts. The only way to the top is to begin at the bottom, and party bosses all have at least one thing in common: They have all paid their dues, all persevered for decades, and all made the long, slow climb up the ladder of the party bureaucracy. As a result, with few exceptions, Soviet leaders seem dull and colorless, having all been acculturated within a system that demands loyalty and frowns on individual efforts to curry popular favor. How sharply this contrasts with U.S. political culture, which often makes more of politicians' personalities than of their qualifications!

How, then, do party members become party bosses? The answer lies in *nomenklatura*, a system based on lists of positions for which approval is required before an incumbent can be removed or a replacement named. All party organs beyond the grass-roots level have *nomenklatura* lists, and the most important positions, naturally appear on the lists of the highest organs. But *nomenklatura* positions are not confined to party posts; on the contrary, they exist in all Soviet economic, social, and cultural organizations, as well as in the CPSU itself. Although not all coveted positions are filled by Communists, party members do hold most of the top jobs.

The consequences of this system are, first, that it gives the party control over all aspects of society. The central party apparatus holds the keys to virtually all high-level positions. Lenin once said that the ultimate issue in politics is *kto kogo*—"who decides the fate of whom." The Secretariat, as the chief administrative directorate of the CPSU, decides the fate of nearly everyone who aspires to high position—a monopoly that explains in part why the general secretary, not the president or the premier, is always the highest-ranking Soviet.

A *nomenklatura* appointment guarantees a kind of tenure, for appointees may be removed from a position only for incompetence (they are usually reassigned to a position of similar rank and status). Just as tenure is often blamed for the presence of "dead wood" on a university's faculty, so has the *nomenklatura* system been criticized for granting job security to incompetents in the Soviet system.

Other negative aspects of *nomenklatura* are still not discussed openly. According to one observer, the system has several additional disadvantages:

> The fact that the CPSU functions more as a simple "transmission belt" than as a political party in the accepted sense: the ability of one man with authority over a *nomenklatura* to build a power base in the party or elsewhere and consequently the necessity for purges; and the tendency of Soviet leadership as a whole to become inbred and conservative.[2]

We will examine the Gorbachev reforms in Chapter 9, but we must note here that the built-in inertia of *nomenklatura* can work against reform, not least because resistance to change is often expressed as deliberate foot-dragging by the very officials who are charged with putting policy into effect. On this point, one writer who emigrated from the Soviet Union has asserted:

> Only an outside observer could suppose all power in the Soviet Union to be in the hands of the Politburo. . . . In fact, the Politburo, though immensely powerful, has only a limited field of action. This limitation of its power has nothing to do with democracy and everything to do with the division of labor inside the nomenklatura class.[3]

Most *nomenklatura* lists are controlled by district and local party organs, and the Politburo rarely interferes at these levels. As a result, the system generally guarantees that incumbents will hold their positions for a long time and thus is a barrier to those who are younger, more energetic, and perhaps less jaded. This is one reason why the Soviet Union, especially under Brezhnev, has been perceived as a "gerontocracy"—rule by the aged.

The Soviet State

If the Communist party has monopolized power in the Soviet Union, what is the purpose of the state? Briefly put, the state implements policies and enforces rules while the party sets policy and makes rules. The Soviet system thus features a symbiotic relationship between the party and the state. The party wields the power, while the state exercises bureaucratic authority through the Council of Ministers.

The Council of Ministers

The Council of Ministers appears to be analogous to the cabinet in Western parliamentary or presidential systems. Nominally elected by the Supreme Soviet (discussed below), the Council of Ministers is the executive branch of the Politburo for the state bureaucracy (much as the Secretariat is the party's executive). The head of the Council of Ministers is the premier and is analogous to the prime minister in British-style parliamentary systems. Nikolai Ryzhkov currently holds this position.

Throughout most of Soviet history, the position of premier has been a highly coveted post, second only to that of general secretary (at least until recently). The premier is both head of the Council of Ministers and a member of the Politburo. Usually several other ministers hold Politburo seats as well, which ensures continuous communication between the two governing bodies and minimizes the likelihood of serious friction. The overlapping also blurs the boundaries between the party and the state at the pinnacle of the Soviet political system.

Similarities between the Council of Ministers and Western-style cabinets can easily be exaggerated. For example, the British cabinet, headed by the prime minister, *is* the government; other than Parliament itself, no supreme body instructs the cabinet. In the Soviet systems, the Council gets its marching orders from the Politburo, and Article 128 of the Constitution calls it "the highest executive and administrative organ" of the USSR. No reference is made to a "guiding" or "leading" (decision-making) role. As we have seen already, that role is reserved for the highest party organs.

Another major difference is size. The Council of Ministers, unlike cabinets in parliamentary systems, is huge, with more than a hundred members. Perhaps because it is so unwieldy, the Council rarely meets. Instead, the true executive functions of government are conducted by a much smaller group known as the Presidium. The chairman (premier), first deputy chairman, and deputy chairman of the Council of Ministers are members of this body; it normally numbers around fifteen. Under current Soviet law, the chairman of the Council, acting no doubt on Politburo authority, may make decisions in the Council's name when an urgent need arises. In addition, the chairman draws up the slate of ministerial candidates for Supreme Soviet approval and also may recommend the hiring and firing of individual ministers.

There are two principal reasons for the immense size of the Council of Ministers: the vastness of the Soviet Union and the large number of economic ministries (more than sixty!) necessitated by the system of central planning. Economic ministries cover everything from coal production to chemicals and automobiles. Some are highly technical and specialized, covering such things as the gas industry, the cellulose-paper industry, electronics, food processing, and the like.

Finally, the sheer size of the USSR necessitates subdividing it into a "federal" administrative system containing fifteen union-republics. Each union-republic has a council of ministers analogous to the national one, and their chairpeople are also members of the state Council.

Two types of ministries exist in the Soviet system. All-union ministries are found only at the national level; thus, in theory at least, they have *direct* administrative control of a particular economic sector throughout the country. Examples of all-union ministries include the defense industry (armaments), the oil industry, and foreign trade. In contrast, union-republic ministries do have counterparts below the republic level. Examples include defense, foreign affairs, justice, finance, and health, as well as some economic ministries (such as the coal industry).

The rationale for putting ministries in one category or another is not clear, but in general it seems that such "traditional" ministries as defense, justice, and foreign affairs are often of the union-republic type, whereas economic ministries tend to be all-union. Since the Khrushchev era (1956–1964), all-union ministries have proliferated, suggesting an expanded role for the central government in running the economy. Gorbachev has vowed to decentralize economic management as part of his reform program, but it remains to be seen how far and how fast the Soviet leadership can move in this direction.

Finally, the Council of Ministers subsumes the so-called USSR state committees, whose heads sit on the Council and thus enjoy "cabinet" rank. In contrast to ministries, which are officially responsible for "branch administration," state committees are assigned responsibility for "interbranch administration." The State Planning Committee (*Gosplan*) is a good example: All ministries have a vital planning function, and the myriad plans must be coordinated. Today there are over twenty such committees and agencies, including the State Bank of the USSR (*Gosbank*), the Central Statistical Administration (*Tserka*), the State Committee for Material Supplies (*Gossnab*), and the Committee for State Security (KGB).

The Pyramid of Government

The administrative machinery of the state, like the Communist Party of the Soviet Union, resembles a pyramid, with the Council of Ministers at the top and local units of government at the bottom. In between are intermediate levels that link Moscow's central government and the seemingly countless cities, towns, villages, and settlements that dot the country's vast landscape. Before 1989–1990, federalism in the Soviet context was an empty shell, but the nationalistic reform movements that have now taken many of the non-Russian republics by storm are giving new meaning to this concept.

Soviet Federalism From its inception, the Soviet Union has had a federal structure. (Federations typically comprise a number of states that are subordinate to a central political authority.) Below the all-union (national) level are political-administrative subdivisions known as union-republics (also called Soviet Socialist Republics, or SSR): autonomous republics (Autonomous Soviet Socialist Republics, or ASSR): autonomous provinces; and autonomous districts. Despite their names, these entities are *not* autonomous and, instead, have been politically subservient to the central government in Moscow. This situation appears to be changing, however, as several union-republics—most notably the Baltic states of Lithuania, Estonia, and Latvia—boldly demand independence.

The Bolsheviks opted for a federal system for two reasons: administrative convenience and propaganda. The need for convenience arose from the great size of the Soviet state, while propaganda helped hide the extreme centralization of power beneath a veneer of democracy. Under Article 72, union-republics are given the right ''freely to secede from the USSR.'' But Article 75 of the 1977 Constitution seems to contradict this provision by declaring that the USSR is ''a single territory and comprises the territories of the union-republics'' and that ''the sovereignty of the USSR extends throughout its territory.'' Today, Article 72 has become more than window dressing.

Federal units in the USSR generally reflect the predominant nationality groups within their territories, such as the Ukrainian SSR, Georgian SSR, Armenian SSR, Baltic SSRs (Latvia, Lithuania, and Estonia), and Soviet Central Asian SSRs (Kazakhistan, Uzbekistan, and Turkmenistan). The ASSRs represent concentrations of nationalities within union-republics and include the Buriats and Kalmyks in the Soviet Far East, the Iakuts in northern Siberia, the Tatars 500 miles east of Moscow, the Komi (related to the Lapps of Scandinavia), and the Karelians (along the border zone with Finland).

State administration in the union-republics and autonomous republics is a mirror image of the setup on the all-union level. Each republic has its own constitution; each has a presidium and council of ministers nominally chosen by an ''elected'' supreme soviet; and, of course, each has administrative counterparts for the myriad departments, agencies, and state committees that compose the state Council of Ministers.

As just noted, Estonia, Latvia, and Lithuania have led the way in demanding independence from Moscow. These union-republics have made significant progress toward economic autonomy and multiparty democracy. Even the Communist parties in the Baltics have demanded independence from Moscow. The Lithuanian Communist party formally broke away from the CPSU, and Latvia abolished the party's monopoly in December 1989—more than a month before the CPSU Central Committee voted to do so itself. In 1989 Estonia had seven organizations that were political parties in all but name; Lithuania had four. In local elections held in

Estonia and Latvia late in that year, non-Communist candidates won convincing victories. Latvia's Popular Front, for example, captured 60 percent of the vote.[4] In March 1990 elections to the Supreme Soviets in these two republics, independence-seeking Popular Front "parties" won decisive victories. Meanwhile, in Estonia nationalist leaders created a government based on a democratically elected congress in which only native Estonians were allowed to hold seats.

Independence was also demanded in the Moldavian republic and in the Transcaucasus (Georgia, Armenia, and Azerbaijan). In November 1989 Georgians declared their right to secede under Article 72. And in the Ukraine, latent tendencies toward nationalism and separatism were rekindled.

Local Governments: A Unitary System Hidden in a Federal Structure?
Below the union-republics and autonomous republics are provincial (*oblast*) governments that often encompass relatively large territories and populations. Party and state officials on the *oblast* level are a vital political and administrative link between the center and the grass-roots level of Soviet society. One scholar has gone so far as to compare officials at this level with the powerful prefects in the French administrative tradition.[5]

Nonetheless, the concentration and centralization of political power are still the keys to understanding the Soviet system and preclude anything like true federalism as it exists in Germany, Canada, or the United States, where some powers and autonomy are reserved for the subunits. In the Soviet Union, despite its "federal" structure, the relationship between the center and the provincial governments more closely resembles a unitary system as found in Great Britain and France.

The Supreme Soviet: How Supreme?

The neon lights above a Leningrad factory proclaim, "The soviets plus electrification equal communism." While this is less than a stirring slogan for most Westerners, it happens to be one of Lenin's best-known one-liners. Had his original blueprints been followed, the "soviet" in Soviet Union would be the master key to the system; in fact, it is little more than a museum piece.

The word *soviet* in Russian means "council" (as a verb it means "to advise"). Soviets played a key role in Lenin's prerevolutionary promise to establish a worker's democracy following a Bolshevik takeover. The idea was to base governmental power on elected councils (or soviets) of peasants, workers, and soldiers. Hence, the new Soviet government would derive its authority and legitimacy from grass-roots organizations made up of the proletariat (wage earners, landless peasants, the down-trodden).

This talk of "workers' democracy" made good propaganda, but Lenin quickly jettisoned the idea once he and his Bolshevik party seized power. He continued to pay lip service to the soviets—indeed, he went so far as to create an elaborate set of soviet institutions—but the real power passed to the Bolshevik party, which later became the CPSU.

Before the political restructuring of 1988–1989, the highest legislative body in the Soviet Union was the Supreme Soviet, which functioned like a parliamentary system; its 1,500 members were elected to two chambers (750 each), the Soviet of Nationalities and the Soviet of the Union. The Supreme Soviet chose the Council of Ministers, which implemented the laws it passed. As we have seen, this pattern was replicated on lower levels, all the way down to local soviets. (The head of a municipal soviet is the equivalent of a mayor in the United States; but the real political boss is the party secretary.)

Elections to the Supreme Soviet and to the 50,000 soviets at subordinate republic, provincial, and local levels have always been heralded with fanfare. Before 1989 everyone was required by law to vote; supposedly, 99.99 percent of eligible voters cast ballots in national elections. (According to official figures, one election in the Turkmen republic was almost perfect: Only 1 voter out of 1.5 million failed to vote!)

Paradoxically, because these "elections" were so empty, the party has used artificial (even garish) means to create the appearance that something truly significant was happening. In fact, things were just the opposite, and elections became a sterling example of *pokazukha*—the art of putting on a show for gullible onlookers, especially foreigners.

In truth, until recently soviets—including the Supreme Soviet—have been mere window dressing. Gorbachev's attempts to make elections more meaningful (see Chapter 9) underscores an important point: Elections are fraught with symbolism; they help legitimate a political system as "popular" and "democratic." Beyond symbolism, of course, *real* legislatures are powerful agents of change in democratic societies. Just how far the new Soviet parliament will be allowed to go, however, remains to be seen. It's possible that the elections of 1989 have set the stage for reforms more far-reaching than any undertaken since the stormy inception of the Soviet Union in 1917.

Gorbachev's Democratization Campaign

Any reform is risky in a country accustomed to repressive rule. Pushing for political change threatens the power and privileges of the rulers and their minions. By 1990 Gorbachev's democratization campaign had gone further than most Western experts had thought possible. Gorbachev was making dramatic efforts to reconstitute the Soviet parliament and to allow the first truly meaningful elections in Soviet history, at the same time breaking the Communist party's monopoly and permitting a modicum of pluralism.

Before the Nineteenth Party Congress in June 1988, there was speculation in both the Soviet Union and the West that Gorbachev would propose overhauling the political system. Several developments added to the anticipation. In late April Boris Kurashvili, a Soviet lawyer and scholar at the prestigious State and Law Institute of the USSR Academy of Sciences, called for a new mass organization—a "democratic union"—to represent the vast majority of citizens who do not belong to the CPSU and to coordinate new "social-action" groups.[6]

Even one of Gorbachev's key advisers, Tatyanna Zaslavskaya, endorsed the concept of a "popular front" alternative to the Communist party. She envisioned an organization that would perform such party functions as nominating candidates, proposing legislation, and suggesting issues for national referendums; but she also made it clear that this concept would not be an official opposition.[7]

In mid-1988 an alliance of seventeen independent political clubs met in Moscow, with approval, and adopted a platform calling for new across-the-board freedoms—from religion and emigration to education and labor unions.[8] The clubs also demanded that prisoners of conscience be released, and they even called for a review of political convictions "from the 1920's to the 1980's." Perhaps the most threatening decision that emerged from this meeting was an agreement in principle to create a "popular front"—the very idea sent up as a trial balloon by Zaslavskaya a month earlier.

The idea of a political alternative to the Communist party was more than a trial balloon in Estonia, where authorities permitted the formation of a non-Communist "front"—the first of its kind in Soviet history. The Estonian front reportedly had reached 45,000 to 50,000 members by July 1988.[9]

Like the Estonian initiative, the unprecedented assembly of non-Communist political groups in Moscow was obviously timed with the upcoming party conference in mind. But unsolicited proposals were apparently not part of Gorbachev's script, for at the conference he simply ignored them.

Politburo Reshuffle

Late in September 1988, Gorbachev called suddenly for a meeting of the Central Committee—catching his rivals unaware and apparently greatly strengthening his hand. At the meeting four aging Politburo members were dropped: Andrei Gromyko, Mikhail Solomentzev, Vladimir Dolgikh, and Pyotr Demichev. This made room for younger members who were more sympathetic to reform. In a move that surprised nearly all observers, Yegor Ligachev was demoted (it was probably no accident that he was on vacation when the meeting was called). He lost his powerful positions as chief ideologist and "second secretary" on the Politburo and instead was made responsible for agriculture—an unenviable post, given the disappointing performance of Soviet agriculture and Gorbachev's intention to reprivatize farming. There is both poetic justice and political cunning in putting Ligachev, the Kremlin's leading hard-liner, in charge of implementing free-market reforms in agriculture. If the reforms falter, Gorbachev can blame Ligachev; at the same time he gives Ligachev a strong personal incentive to make the rural *perestroika* work.

Other leadership changes were also significant, most notably, Gorbachev's own elevation to the presidency. In addition, several of his protégés were promoted to the Politburo: Vadim Medvedev became a full (voting) member, and Anatoly Lukyanov, Alexander Vlasov, and Alexandra Birykova became candidate (nonvoting) members.

As part of Gorbachev's promised party reorganization, a decision reportedly was made to cut in half the size of the Central Committee apparatus. Six new commissions were created within the Secretariat: Party Building and Cadre Policy (headed by Georgi Razumovsky); Ideology (Vadim Medvedev); Social and Economic Policy (Nikolai Slyunkov); Agricultural Policy (Yegor Ligachev); International Policy (Alexander Yakovlev); and Legal Affairs (Viktor Chebrikov). In return for his new post, Chebrikov, like Ligachev, was forced to relinquish his old one: He was replaced as KGB chief by Vladimir Kryuchkov.[10]

In sum, Gorbachev has assembled a new team consisting of Yakovlev (foreign policy), Medvedev (ideology), Razumovsky (cadres or personnel), and Lukyanov (first vice-president of the Politburo). Foreign Minister Eduard Shevardnadze, a close ally of Gorbachev's, completes this group. The reformers could barely conceal their euphoria following the Central Committee plenum. With Ligachev removed from his number-two position, it appeared that the "chief spoiler" was gone. But this reshuffling of party leadership, however dramatic, is not necessarily a giant step toward democracy, and most observers agree that Gorbachev's primary motive was to get the stalled economic reforms moving.

Gorbachev's Dilemma

The fact that Gorbachev so far has chosen to ignore independent political voices does not mean that political reform is anathema to him. Indeed, he appears to see political restructuring as necessary for economic restructuring. A greater measure of free-wheeling popular participation is the price the party must pay to get the country out of economic doldrums. How much "democracy" is too much? Where will Gorbachev draw the line? The party conference of June 1988 provides some clues.

Gorbachev's political reforms involve reconstituting the Supreme Soviet— the USSR's rubber-stamp legislature—into a 2,250-member Congress of People's Deputies; this, in turn, would elect a smaller full-time parliament and a president (who thus would be elected indirectly). In this new system the president would assume the power exercised by the leader of the Communist party. But Gorbachev was "elected" president by the Central Committee at the end of September; hence, the party preempted the planned "parliament"—a move all too familiar to students of Soviet political history.

Another reform shifts power away from party committees to local governing bodies (known as soviets). When the promised multicandidate elections were held in the spring of 1989, an open process of nominating candidates for national as well as local soviets was allowed for the first time. Throughout the country, public nominating meetings were held—enthusiastically and at times raucously. Given its superior organization, resources, and experience, the CPSU not surprisingly managed to nominate most of its favorite candidates. But in many electoral districts, non-Communist candidates also were nominated. Although the Communists won a majority of seats, amazingly enough many "independents" also won. Moreover, some highly placed Communist officials were defeated. And such outspoken "opposition" figures as Andrei Sakharov and Boris Yeltsin (who had been removed as Moscow party chief for criticizing Gorbachev) were elected by large majorities. Yeltsin, running as at-large candidate for all of Moscow, won by a landslide.

The election to the Congress of People's Deputies was followed by a second election within the Congress to determine the membership of the smaller Supreme Soviet, which, of course, is the real parliament under the new system. At first, Yeltsin was *not* seated in the Supreme Soviet, but such a hue and cry arose that he was quietly given the seat. Thus, popular opinion now seems to play a significant role in Soviet politics. (Yeltsin was later elected president of the Russian SSR; shortly after that he quit the Communist party.)

Incipient pluralism also is evident, even at the all-union level in Moscow. Besides the addition of two non-Communists to the Council of Ministers (in charge of ecology and culture), formal opposition has appeared in the form of a parliamentary faction—the so-called interregional group—made up of 400 to 500 radical deputies. This group has its own agenda, including a demand to end the Communist party's monopoly on power by abolishing Article 6, which guarantees the CPSU's "leading and guiding" role in Soviet society. A vote to abolish Article 6 was surprisingly close (1,138 to 839), despite Gorbachev's heavy-handed efforts to derail the movement. A commission established to write a new constitution will probably scrap Article 6 quietly, for Gorbachev conceded on this issue at the CPSU Central Committee plenum in February 1990.

Support for abolishing Article 6 has not been confined to the opposition. Communist deputies from the Far East, the Baltics, and elsewhere favored ending the CPSU's monopoly on the grounds that only by actually competing with non-Communists in free elections could the party win and keep the people's confidence. No doubt many are troubled by signs that popular support for the party has eroded. In the first half of 1989, for example, party membership fell by 600,000, and an opinion poll by the Academy of Social Sciences found that only 4 percent of party members believed the moral authority of the CPSU was still high; 50 percent said it was low, and one-third felt the party was incapable of reform.[11] Meanwhile, deputies from the Baltic states have created their own parliamentary group and have strong incentives to join forces with counterparts from Central Asia and other non-Russian republics, especially concerning economic matters and perhaps even political autonomy.

The precise relationship between local party organization and elected soviets remains unclear, but proposed changes may have far-reaching effects on how power will be distributed. The general reduction of party power below the regional level could benefit union-republics that have indigenous non-Russian majorities who seek greater autonomy from Moscow. As Vladimir Bukovsky, the dissident Russian author, sees it, "there is nothing suggested which will structurally reduce [the party's] power." On the contrary, under Gorbachev's plan local party bosses would head local soviets. The net effect, says Bukovsky, is to "submerge the soviets in the party machinery."[12]

Finally, Gorbachev has proposed limiting the tenure of senior officials to two 5-year terms. This would help prevent the aging of Soviet leadership, which was so prevalent under Brezhnev.

What Gorbachev means by "democratization" remains a mystery. Indeed, from the outset he has made it clear that Western-style democracy is not what he has in mind. At the party conference in June 1988 he denounced attempts to "use democratic rights for undemocratic purposes," specifically mentioning efforts aimed at "redrawing boundaries" or "setting up opposition parties."[13] Gorbachev's failure to spell out what he means by "democratization" is apparently calculated.

The Soviet Economy

The central importance of economics in Soviet ideology is evidenced in the name, the Union of Soviet Socialist Republics. Under socialism, of course, the means of production (land, capital, and labor) are not privately owned or controlled but rather are placed at the disposal of the state, which in theory acts as the agent of society. In contrast, under capitalism the primary form of property ownership is individual rather than collective.

Marxism Versus the Marketplace

According to Article 10 of the Soviet Constitution, the Soviet economy is "based on the Socialist ownership of all the means of production," including the land. Two forms of ownership are recognized in the USSR at present: state ownership and collective (or cooperative) ownership. The former is the "higher stage" because it encompasses the entire society; the latter form of ownership is a "lower stage" because it is limited to relatively few people. This distinction in ownership is clearly evident in agriculture, where land is divided into state farms (*sovkhozy*) and collective farms (*kolkhozy*). Historically, state farms have received preferential treatment (greater state investment funds, better equipment, and so on).

State farms are owned by society at large and are run by the government, whereas collective farms technically are owned by the farmers themselves. State farms are huge, averaging some 92,500 acres (five or six times larger than the average collective farm). They are operated like an assembly line in an industrial enterprise and are managed by professionals trained in such fields as agronomy, animal husbandry, and horticulture. State farm workers are specialized by function and, like their industrial counterparts, earn hourly wages. Thus, in many ingenious ways and despite disappointing results, the Soviet government has sought to industrialize agriculture.

The state also owns all industrial enterprises, public utilities, banks, transportation systems, and mass-communication facilities as well as most retail outlets and repair shops. One result of this system of ownership is that nearly every employed person (approximately 85 percent of the work force) is employed by state-owned enterprises. The other 15 percent belong to cooperatives (or collectives), which are tightly controlled by the state though, technically speaking, not state owned.

Obviously, this monopoly over employment opportunities gives the state enormous control over the individual, for one needs to make a living. But there is another consideration for Soviet citizens: "Anti-parasite" laws make it a crime *not* to work! If you are fired for any reason (including unauthorized political activity), where can you go to find another job? The same "employer" who dismissed you can bar you from another job and, at the same time, can put you on the wrong side of the law. This gives new meaning to the term "double jeopardy."

The Concept of Central Planning

For Marx and his adherents, capitalism is to be abhorred because it leads to exploitation of the many by the few. Capitalism, of course, is based on the economics of the marketplace. So if an alternative to the evils of capitalism is to be found, according to Communist orthodoxy, an alternative to the marketplace must also be found. In the Soviet Union, that alternative has been central planning.

The concept of central planning is simple enough: Decide what should be produced on the basis of society's needs; assign duties, responsibilities, and tasks; enlist the efforts of all able-bodied workers; and distribute rewards based on the value of each person's work. (Under full Communism the formula eventually would be "From each according to his abilities, to each according to his needs.") Prices, too, are set by the government and do not fluctuate in response to the market forces of supply and demand, as they do under capitalism. Thus, the entire Soviet economy is planned and managed from the top, whereas a market economy is driven from the bottom—by consumers.

The State Planning Committee (*Gosplan*) has the primary responsibility for charting the course of the Soviet economy, but it must coordinate its efforts with other bureaucratic entities. These include the State Committee on Prices, the State Bank (*Gosbank*), the Ministry of Finance, the State Committee on Material and Technical Supplies (*Gossnab*), and nearly 50 central ministries (as well as 750 in the fifteen union-republics) that oversee various branches of the economy (electronics, chemicals, metallurgy, machine-tools, and so on).

The complicated planning process leads to both long-range (five years) and short-range (one year) plans. These set production *growth targets* for economic sectors, which then are translated into *output quotas* for individual enterprises. The short-range plan contains aggregate growth targets for the whole economy for the current year. In turn, this general blueprint is broken down by the various ministries into monthly plans and quotas for every factory, plant, enterprise, and association in the Soviet Union. The plan always reflects the political priorities of top leadership—that is, the interlocking directorates of the Politburo, Secretariat, and Council of Ministers.

Such detailed economic planning is daunting under any circumstances. To keep factories humming and assembly lines moving it is necessary to determine *in advance* how many components of every size will be needed to turn out the quota of, say, tractors at a given plant; how many train cars, trucks, or barges will be needed to deliver the right quantities of iron, steel, and other resources on schedule; how much energy will be needed to run the plant during different times of the year; and on and on. Countless calculations must be made for every item manufactured or processed.

Under the Stalinist system of economic management, the state planning mechanism made no fewer than *83 million* supply-and-demand calculations each year. Simultaneously, it set prices for 200,000 industrial and consumer products.[14] Gorbachev has ordered streamlining of this system, but most of it was still operating as this decade opened. Indeed, attempts to link suppliers, producers, and consumers more directly—and thus to imitate market economies— have so far failed miserably. And as the number, variety, and complexity of products increase, so does the magnitude of planning. Bottlenecks and breakdowns have plagued the Soviet economy, and at their root is a deep-seated ideological antipathy to the whole idea of economics.

Anti-Economics: Stalin's Ghost

It can be argued that the Soviet system suppresses politics as we know it and, in that sense, is antipolitical. It can also be argued that the Stalinist model of central planning has created a system antithetical to economics. Perhaps the most prominent feature of Stalinist economic planning was the "primacy of heavy industry"—meaning that the rapid building of a vast military-industrial complex took precedence over consumer-oriented investment aimed at improving the standard of living and developing new technologies.

Stalin's first Five-Year Plan (1928) set the stage for the muscle-bound Soviet economy of the recent past. Under Stalin's "crash industrialization" program, "Consumer production all but ceased as every available resource was pressed into the program of rapid industrial expansion in capital-intensive heavy industries (e.g., steel, coal, and machinery)."[15] The entire society was mobilized through a massive combination of propaganda and police-state (terror) tactics.

However brutal, Stalinism brought seemingly impressive results, for a while at least. Most scholars now agree that the economic strategy was, at best, a quick fix for the industrial revolution that had largely eluded Czarist Russia; that it was purchased at a terrible human cost; and that it contained the seeds of its own demise. It worked temporarily for the following reasons:

> The Stalinist economic policies favored extensive growth, that is, growth by increasing inputs: labor, raw materials, factories and plants, and investment capital. With a large pool of unemployed or underemployed workers, seemingly endless supplies of oil, gas, coal, and other raw materials, ample land for cultivation, and capital squeezed from the rural sector through collectivization, Soviet planners during the 1930s and 1940s treated inputs as virtually infinite and inexhaustible.[16]

The Stalinist planning model no longer works anywhere—not in the USSR and not in Eastern Europe, where Soviet client-states at the time (Bulgaria, Czechoslovakia, East Germany, Hungary, Poland, and Romania) emulated "Big

Brother." We turn now to a brief discussion of several problems that were endemic in the Soviet economy (and, by extrapolation, in the Soviet-type economies of Eastern Europe and elsewhere).

Problems of Economic Planning

Of the many problems facing Soviet planners, some are primary and some are secondary. Some are root causes, while others are derivative. Some are not causes at all, but rather symptoms of underlying distortions. Certainly, the *absence of market mechanisms* appears to be at the root of many, if not most, Soviet economic problems. Other problems, in turn, can be traced to this defect.

Let us take performance indicators as an example. Output quotas (rather than the profits that drive capitalism) were long used to measure success in the Soviet economy. Every factory was expected to fulfill its quota every month. If a factory overfulfilled its quota for the year, its workers and managers were rewarded with pay bonuses. Underfulfillment was not career enhancing for plant managers and dashed workers' hopes for a year-end windfall. Thus the primary objective of every plant manager was not to improve efficiency but to overfulfill the assigned quotas by a small margin (overfulfilling by a large margin would have meant higher quotas in the following year, thus creating new pressures).

Plan fulfillment became an all-consuming end. To achieve it plant managers typically hoarded supplies and deliberately inflated labor requirements in order to have a cushion in case vital materials were not delivered or in case "storming" (accelerating production) was necessary to fulfill the monthly quota. Because these practices were so widespread, severe distortions and materials-supply problems could result.

Moreover, as performance indicators, quotas themselves were a problem. Imagine that a factory produced nails. Nails of all sizes, weights, and types were needed, of course, so it was necessary either to micromanage the nail factory from afar or to use more general quotas and give the plant manager some discretion. But if the quota were based on gross weight, the manager would have an incentive to produce large, heavy nails rather than small, light-weight ones. And if the quota were based on quantity, the "rational" manager again would adopt a strategy to produce lots of small nails. (The Soviet humor magazine *Krokodil* illustrated this point with a cartoon: A plant manager, bursting with pride, congratulated his workers for overfulfilling the plan—as a single, huge nail rolled off the assembly line!)

Another economic fact of life in the USSR has been productivity. But is this a cause or a symptom of the economy? In the past, it related to a general defect, namely, the paucity of incentives for workers and managers alike to achieve greater efficiency. Workers all got about the same pay, regardless of how much or how little they produced. Everyone was guaranteed a job, and rarely did anyone get fired (except, perhaps, for political reasons). And since salaries were not tied to profits, the system did little to encourage efficiency.

Soviet attempts to address these problems are outlined in Chapter 9. Here we should note that, although economic solutions may seem obvious, the political obstacles were formidable. The economy was so tightly and intricately interwoven, like a heavy woolen sweater, that tugging on one strand could unravel the entire fabric. Thus the profit motive could not be introduced without revamping prices, which, in turn, reflected long-standing political priorities of the party leadership. The best way to ensure a rational pricing system, of course, is to let supply and demand take over, which would mean taking a giant step toward a market economy. For the Soviet leadership, that course was fraught with ominous possibilities.

Eastern Europe: From Stalinism to Pluralism

After World War II, the Red Army occupied most of Eastern Europe with the notable exception of Yugoslavia. By 1948 Stalin had imposed the "Soviet model" on all these nations except Yugoslavia, where Marshall Tito rejected Stalin (even though, in many respects, he imitated Stalinism). Monolithic rule prevailed for four decades, until the avalanche of popular demands for democratization in 1989 buried it in sweeping socioeconomic reforms.

Stalin insisted that the governments of his "outer empire" in Eastern Europe be created in his own image. Until recently, a survey of these regimes was a refresher course on Stalinist rule—dictatorship by the Communist party; a government apparatus that appeared democratic but was highly centralized and hierarchical; a Socialist command economy in which production and consumption reflected political priorities; and a foreign policy based on fraternal relations with other Communist states. All this changed dramatically after the deluge of 1989.

The Communist Party before the Deluge

Throughout Eastern Europe the Communist party dominated politics. In some cases other political parties existed (for example, in Poland and Hungary), but they were only part of an effort to construct a democratic facade, to hide the fact that the party was all-powerful. As in the Soviet Union, the party dominated all major institutions and organizations, from state bureaucracies, educational systems, and armed services to trade unions, youth and professional associations, and even sports clubs. Moreover, monopolistic one-party rule operated through a Soviet-style "interlocking directorate" of top party and state officials and was perpetuated by a *nomenklatura* system of high-level personnel management.

Party organization in Eastern Europe also mirrored Soviet practice. Party membership in each country was kept within 6 to 12 percent of the population, ensuring that the party remained an elite organization. Paradoxically, elitism was needed for party morale, political recruitment, ideological integrity, and internal discipline.

The Soviet operating principles also applied throughout the Eastern bloc. Leaders were co-opted rather than elected to top positions, where they enjoyed tenure and often grew old and eventually died in office. Thus, many Eastern

European regimes, like the Soviet Union before Gorbachev, were gerontocracies. Finally, because abject obedience to higher authority within the party was the rule everywhere, accountability was virtually nil.

Communist parties in Eastern Europe also imitated the Soviet's insistence on political and intellectual conformity. Like the CPSU, they were intolerant of dissent and used censorship, surveillance, intimidation, coercion, and incessant propaganda to suppress artistic and literary freedom as well as political free speech.

The Hierarchical State

Governmental structures in Eastern Europe were also highly centralized. Some cosmetic differences existed between the Soviet executive and those in some Eastern European states. Even so, executive authority was centralized, and the state apparatus served the party.

Heads of state in Czechoslovakia and Romania in theory were chosen by the legislature but, in practice, were co-opted by top party bosses. Poland, East Germany, Bulgaria, and Hungary had a collective chief executive called a state council. (Yugoslavia still has a collective presidency.) Only in Romania was the presidency a position of great power; Nicolae Ceausescu—before being ousted, "tried," and executed in 1989—was both president and the party chief. (Brezhnev, Andropov, Chernenko, and Gorbachev in the Soviet Union also held both posts.)

Whatever specific form the head of state assumed in these countries, responsibility for daily administration rested, as in the Soviet Union, with the premier and a council of ministers who were hand-picked by the party. Rubber-stamping was the primary function of East European parliaments, much as the Supreme Soviet merely legitimated Politburo decisions in the Kremlin before 1989.

Central Planning in Eastern Europe

Following World War II, Moscow imposed not only Stalinist political structures and methods on Eastern Europe but also Stalinist economic practices. Hence, the entire region saw the advent of central planning, the nationalization of industry, and the collectivization of agriculture. Only in Poland did most land remain in private hands, due to stiff peasant resistance to collectivization.

In terms of organization and operation, then, the "command economies" of Eastern Europe became more or less carbon copies of the Soviet economy. Developmentally, however, they lagged behind even the Soviet Union. Moscow was content to buy raw materials from, and sell manufactured goods to, Eastern Europe. But this arrangement, with good reason, made Eastern European "satellites" feel exploited. As long as they continued to provide grist for the mill of Soviet industry, they would remain dependent and backward industrially. Furthermore, Soviet manufactures were relatively expensive, and the quality was generally poor.

The main problem with central planning, however, was that as years passed it became clear that the system was not working. First Hungary, and then other countries, began experimenting with market mechanisms. Their experiments were cautious and highly controlled, but they suggested that the Stalinist model was a major impediment to economic growth and technological progress.

Central planning was swept away in the flood of reforms that hit Eastern Europe in 1989–1990. As discussed in Chapter 9, it remains to be seen whether Western-style free enterprise will now be embraced and, if so, whether market economies can succeed where the discredited command economies have failed.

The Crumbling of the "Outer Empire"

Although several Eastern European states had displayed a measure of independence from Moscow in economic matters before 1989, there had been little corresponding movement for political independence. Undoubtedly, East Europeans remembered all too well the Soviet invasion of Hungary in 1956 and of Czechoslovakia in 1968, as well as Soviet pressures on the Polish government to crack down on dissent in 1956 and again in 1980–1981.

Among the bitter lessons of Hungary, Czechoslovakia, and Poland were the following:

1. Moscow would not allow any East European member-state to withdraw from the Warsaw Pact. Imre Nagy of Hungary tried and failed.
2. Moscow would not allow genuine opposition parties to be formed. The government of Czechoslovakia under Alexander Dubcek vowed to move in this direction (thus jeopardizing the party's monopoly of power); Dubcek's heresy led to the Soviet invasion and the enunciation of the Brezhnev Doctrine, which claims that Moscow and its allies have a right to intervene in Eastern Europe to defend socialism.
3. Moscow would not allow independent power centers (such as the Solidarity trade-union movement in Poland in the early 1980s), which threatened or challenged the party's monopoly of power. Under the Brezhnev Doctrine, the Soviet Army would intervene against "counterrevolution" if necessary.

Ceausescu's Romania: Stalinism with a Twist

Romania represented a partial exception to these rules. Specifically, Moscow allowed President Ceausescu considerable independence in foreign policy as long as Romania stopped short of withdrawing from the Warsaw Pact or the Council of Mutual Economic Assistance (Comecon).

Romania began to pursue an independent foreign policy in the 1960s, when Ceausescu refused to go along with Moscow's efforts to isolate Peking. Romania also opposed the Soviet invasion of Czechoslovakia in 1968, and it took the lead in responding to West Germany's *Ostpolitik* (reconciliation with the Communist states of Eastern Europe in the late 1960s). Romania also refused to sever diplomatic relations with Israel following the 1967 Arab-Israeli war, and in 1968 it became the first Warsaw Pact member to restore diplomatic ties with Bonn.

During all this, Romania successfully sought to expand trade with the European Community (Common Market). President Ceausescu visited the United States in 1970 and 1973, and President Ford went to Bucharest in 1975. Ceausescu's efforts paid off in the 1970s: The United States made a number of trade concessions to Romania, including most-favored-nation status so long denied to Communist countries.

Although Romania never threatened to withdraw from the Warsaw Pact and Comecon, it frequently criticized them as tools of Soviet foreign policy. Romania went so far as to call for the dissolution of both major military alliances in Europe, and it refused to participate in Warsaw Pact maneuvers. Comecon had always encouraged economic specialization, a policy that ran counter to Ceausescu's strategy of reducing Romania's economic dependence on the Soviet Union.

The price Romanians paid for Ceausescu's heterodox foreign policy was strict Communist orthodoxy in domestic policy. Over the years the Romanian regime remained rigidly Stalinist—perhaps more so than any other in Eastern Europe, including the Soviet Union. The fact that the Communist party played it so straight at home may explain why Romania got away with pursuing "deviant" policies abroad. It may also explain why Romania was the last country to experience a popular revolt against communism in 1989 and why, when revolt came, it was bloodier and more violent than elsewhere.

1989: The Great Counterrevolution

The year 1989 will stand out in history as a turning point in the long struggle between two irreconcilable ideologies—communism and capitalism—and Eastern Europe will be remembered as the setting for this drama. The year began with steps toward free elections in Poland and Hungary; it ended with the ouster of party chief Erich Honecker in East Germany, the opening of the intra-German border (and the symbolic dismantling of the Berlin Wall), the resignation of Communist leadership in Czechoslovakia, and the overthrow of Ceausescu in Romania.

During 1989 Poland and Hungary introduced a series of political reforms aimed at democratization. In Poland the independent trade union Solidarity was legalized after being banned for eight years, and the government allowed partially free elections to a new parliament in June. Solidarity was allowed to contest all the seats for the Senate (upper house), and it won an overwhelming majority (92 percent). It also won all 161 seats it was allowed to contest in the 460-seat *Sejm* (lower house). Although the Communists (PUWP) enjoyed a guaranteed majority in the *Sejm* (nearly two-thirds of the seats), the elections were a ringing mandate for Lech Walesa's opposition Solidarity "party." In August the Polish parliament confirmed Tadeusz Mazowiecki as the first non-Communist prime minister in a Soviet-bloc country.

The Hungarian parliament voted to allow freedom of association and assembly in January 1989, and the following month the Hungarian Socialist Workers' party (HSWP) (more commonly known as the Hungarian Communist party) approved formation of independent political parties. Hungary thus became the first East European state since the Stalinist takeover to relinquish the Communist party's monopoly position and to embrace in principle a competitive multiparty system. In May, Hungary dismantled the barbed-wire fence separating it from neutral Austria.

The pace of change accelerated in the fall, when the government announced it would allow East Germans on holiday in Hungary to emigrate to the West and when it reestablished diplomatic relations with Israel (suspended at the time of the Six-Day War in 1967). Next came a series of measures to institutionalize a multiparty system, a unicameral legislature, and free elections in 1990. In early October delegates to a special congress changed the party's name to the Hungarian Socialist party, enlarged the ruling presidium from four to twenty-four members, and renounced Marxism in favor of democratic socialism. The congress also voted to divest the party of property, disband the Workers' Militia, and disestablish party cells in factories. In mid-October the Hungarian National Assembly voted to make ninety-four changes in the constitution—deleting all references to the "leading role" of the Communist party; allowing independent political parties; establishing separation of powers; codifying civil and human rights; and changing the country's official name from "People's Republic of Hungary" to "Republic of Hungary." The Assembly also formally legalized opposition parties and disbanded the Workers' Militia.

On November 26, 1989, voters in a national referendum opted for parliamentary rather than popular election of the president. The outcome was widely viewed as a victory for the liberal Alliance of Free Democrats and a setback for Imre Poszgay, the most outspoken "liberal" within the ruling circle. Poszgay was the first Communist leader in Eastern Europe to advocate a multiparty system and competitive elections.

By the end of the year, Hungary's Communist party leaders had set the stage for a peaceful transfer of power to a non-Communist government. (Again, Poszgay had been the first Communist leader to say unequivocally that the party ought to relinquish power if it failed to win in free and fair elections.) Voters went to the polls in the spring. No fewer than eighteen political parties contested the elections, and so no single party won a clear majority. Even so, the newly enfranchised electorate gave two non-Communist groupings, the conservative Democratic Forum and the liberal Alliance of Free Democrats, strong endorsements (24.9 percent and 19.7 percent, respectively). The independent Smallholders party, which had won the last free elections in Hungary back in 1945, came in third. The parties of the left, including the orthodox Socialist Workers party (heir to the old Communist party), were the big losers.

The movement toward multiparty democracy proceeded relatively quietly in Poland and Hungary. Not so in East Germany, Czechoslovakia, and Romania, where Communist regimes toppled like dominoes. The crisis in the German Democratic Republic began with the flight to the West (to the Federal Republic of Germany) of East Germans vacationing in Hungary. Soon East Germans were clamoring for freedom to emigrate, freedom of speech, freedom of assembly—in a word, for freedom. Some fled from Poland; others sought refuge in the West

German embassy in Prague, Czechoslovakia. Throughout the fall of 1989 spectacular mass demonstrations occurred in Leipzig, East Berlin, and other East German cities. Under intense popular pressure and increasingly isolated (even Gorbachev offered no support), the Communist party replaced its hard-line chief, Erich Honecker, with Egon Krenz, who proved unable to slow the popular groundswell. Only Hans Modrow, one of the few East German Communists reputed to be a ''liberal,'' had any credibility.

In an effort to placate a society now in open revolt, the Krenz regime gave the Czech government permission to allow thousands of East Germans in Czechoslovakia to go west. With pressure mounting, the beleaguered GDR government lifted emigration restrictions and opened the intra-German border. East Germans, for the first time since 1961, were allowed to travel freely between the GDR and West Germany.

The Berlin Wall came tumbling down—not physically, although parts of it were dismantled, but symbolically. Berliners from both sides of the city divided since 1961 celebrated day and night atop the wall. People came from all over the world to celebrate with them, and television allowed everyone everywhere to join the party. German youths danced and sang, laughed and cried. Strangers embraced. For anyone who had grown up during the heyday of the Cold War, it was an unforgettable scene.

In short order the Krenz government resigned, and an interim cabinet headed by Hans Modrow prepared the country for free elections. In March 1990 East Germans went to the polls and gave the conservative Christian Democrats a mandate to rule. The Social Democrats came in a distant second, and the renamed SED (Communist party) suffered a humiliating defeat. East Germans thus endorsed an early merger of the two German states, for that was the key plank in the Christian Democrats' platform. Indeed, West German Chancellor Helmut Kohl had campaigned in East Germany for reunification, and the process was completed faster than most observers expected. Germany was united on October 3.

In neighboring Czechoslovakia the conservative Communist government of Milos Jakes steadfastly resisted major economic and political reforms until it was swept away by popular discontent in late 1989. In an amazing role reversal, Vaclav Havel, a dissident writer who had been jailed earlier in the year, accepted the presidency in December, after aging hard-liner Gustav Husak resigned. Havel's chief rival for the presidency was Alexander Dubcek, the fallen hero of the 1968 uprising (the so-called ''Prague Spring''). One of Husak's last official acts as president was to name a new cabinet whose twenty-one members were mostly non-Communists.

Although the new prime minister, Marian Calfa, was a Communist, it was Havel—the conscience of the nation—who was hailed both at home and abroad as the hero of the ''velvet revolution.'' As leader of a coalition of opposition groups called Civic Forum, Havel played a key role in negotiating the terms by which Czechoslovakia's beleaguered Communists relinquished power. At the beginning of 1989 Havel was a playwright and pariah; at the end he was the nation's president. His personal triumph is rich in symbolism both for Czechoslovakia and for the region as a whole.

Romania was the last domino to fall. As noted earlier, it was the most repressive regime in Eastern Europe—in many ways more medieval than modern. For Nicolae Ceausescu, governing the country was a family affair; he practiced nepotism shamelessly and lived in royal splendor. His opulent lifestyle contrasted sharply with the impoverished conditions afflicting the Romanian people. Even electricity was rationed, so that most apartments in Romania were dark and cold throughout the winter.

In December of 1989 Ceausescu's security forces staged a bloody crackdown against demonstrators in Timisoara and Bucharest. The army, refusing to fire on civilians, fought a series of battles with the security police, who remained loyal to Ceausescu. Their clashes ended when the army captured Ceausescu in flight, staged a perfunctory trial, and quickly executed the hated dictator and his wife. Later, mass graves containing the bodies of hundreds of demonstrators were discovered in Timisoara.

Romania's new leaders—so-called reform Communists—set up a Council of National Reconciliation to run the country until free elections could be held. Critics denounced the new government for including former members of Ceausescu's inner circle and for operating too much like the old government. If the elections did not resolve the situation, at least Ceausescu was gone, and so was the era of monolithic Communist rule.

In the string of elections in Eastern Europe during the first half of 1990, voters rejected not only the Communists but other parties of the left and center-left (most notably the Social Democrats). As *The Economist* noted: "In one country after another, 'reform communism' proved empty. Once the Soviet veto on change was withdrawn, there was suddenly no stopping point halfway. Communist power collapsed."[17] The surprising popularity of center-right parties touting free enterprise pointed to the main reason why Communist power toppled in Eastern Europe—the disappointing performance of economies still saddled with Stalinist central planning. But the rising expectations associated with market reforms may quickly put the new leaders "under the gun," for failure to produce results could be politically destabilizing. Throughout the region, fragile democratic reforms might be the first casualties of lackluster economic performance.

Communism in Yugoslavia: To Be or Not to Be?

Tito's decision to break with Stalin in 1948 was a watershed in the history of both world communism and Yugoslavia. It ensured that Moscow would use its control over Eastern Europe to try to isolate Belgrade and force Tito out. This left Tito with little choice but to turn to the West for trade, aid, and, in a roundabout way, protection.

Yet how could Tito, a fervent Communist, expect sympathetic hearing from the leaders of industrial democracies, particularly the United States? After all, communism and capitalism are antithetical, and Europe in 1948 was feeling the gathering chill of the Cold War. Tito's solution was to complicate the internal picture enough so that leaders of the ''Free World'' could consort with Yugoslavia and not seem to be consorting with the enemy.

In addition, Tito no doubt wanted to show the Soviets that he could find a third way—one between communism and capitalism—that would be a model (and an alternative to Stalinism) for the emerging nations of Africa and Asia. Indeed, Tito established himself as an early leader of the nonaligned movement (NAM)—Third World nations that sought to avoid choosing sides in the East-West conflict and to define global issues along North-South lines.

So Tito improvised, and in the process he created one of the most complex political and economic systems in the world. In this respect Yugoslavia stands out even among Communist countries, in which bureaucratic redundancies are a long-standing hallmark of party rule.

Upstaging Moscow: Democracy in the Workplace

In theory Tito's reforms were aimed at decentralization of decision-making authority—the antithesis of the highly centralized Stalinist system. One of the first and most dramatic steps in this direction was the introduction of *workers' self-management*. The idea was to give workers control over production, and therefore responsibility for it, via freely elected workers' councils and management boards. Even the boss (enterprise manager) was to be elected by the workers.

Workers' self-management, Tito reasoned, would remove a major obstacle to productivity, namely, workers' alienation. On the positive side, workers would take greater pride in their work, leading to improved quality of goods; they would better understand the problems of management, and thus avoid unreasonable demands and expectations; and they would develop greater loyalty to the ''collective'' (both to the enterprise and to their coworkers).

Within this system there evolved a form of ''indicative planning,'' by which overall targets were set for the various sectors of the economy. These targets were guidelines but did not exert tyranny over individual enterprises. The state also relinquished direct control in agriculture: Collectivization was halted, and most farmland was reprivatized in the 1950s. Today more than 80 percent of the land in Yugoslavia and nearly 90 percent of the livestock are privately held.

In the 1960s Yugoslavian leadership gave greater autonomy to plant managers and further reduced the role of central administrators. Prices were set by market forces of supply and demand, and profitability became the test of efficiency. There is still a state planning agency in Belgrade, but production targets are now set at the republic level, with the national planning agency acting as coordinator. Under these reforms the Yugoslav economy, not surprisingly, became more consumer oriented than elsewhere in Eastern Europe.

How well have the reforms worked? Results are mixed at best. In the 1980s Yugoslavia experienced several problems, including mounting external debt, a falling standard of living, and rising unemployment (roughly 15 percent in 1985). In addition, low productivity led to higher prices (although workers' self-management was supposed to avoid that), and energy costs were high. Yugoslavia seemed headed for even harder times. The question was: Would Tito's legacy sustain the nation in its time of troubles?

The Limits of Democracy

Economic reforms in Yugoslavia have been accompanied by changes in the formal organization of the government. The changes were designed to create the appearance of true federalism (decentralization) and democratic republicanism.

Present-day Yugoslavia is a monument to the leadership and vision of one man, Josip Broz Tito. While he was living, it did not matter much who held what official position in the government or the Communist party (formally named the League of Yugoslav Communists). As founder and chief architect of the nation, Tito called the shots; everyone knew that, and most people accepted it. This extraordinary consensus enable Tito to experiment with various forms of power sharing without having to relinquish any personal power.

When Tito died in 1980, he had already put the finishing touches on power-sharing arrangements that remain in effect. Under this unique system (sometimes called "consociational"), Yugoslavia has a collective chief executive that consists of nine persons—one from each of the six republics and the two autonomous provinces, and one ex officio member representing the Communist party. A chairman is elected by the Federal Assembly (in theory, the Yugoslav legislature) and serves on a rotational basis for one year. Tito always held this post until his death.

The thirty-three members of the Federal Executive Council (the cabinet) function like the Council of Ministers in the USSR. The Council is "the source of legislative proposals [and] represents the most important governmental body in terms of the day-to-day government operations."[18] The collective presidency nominates a member of the Federal Assembly to be president of the Federal Executive Council, and the Assembly then votes confirmation. The Yugoslav "premier" is thus chosen in a manner that, though more convoluted, resembles the procedure in many parliamentary democracies.

Perhaps the most that can be said in praise of Yugoslavian "democracy"—at least on the federal level—is that its institutional furniture has been arranged to promote some measure of regional pluralism. To find more authentic democracy one must look to the bottom of the political pyramid: "The decentralization of both political and economic power, which allegedly represents the basis for Yugoslavia's different approach to communism, is nowhere better illustrated than in local government."[19]

The basic unit of local government, called a commune, has considerable administrative authority and enjoys at least limited autonomy (in matters not expressly delegated to the federal government or to the republics and autonomous provinces). At the commune level government is characterized by extensive citizen participation, for the communes and workers' councils appear to be linked:

> The communes have become key local units that have several primary concerns. One of these is economic, including planning, investments, internal trade, and supervision over economic enterprises. Another concern is municipal services, such as water supply, sewers, streets, and public utilities. A third comprises the area of "social management," that is, citizen control over public utilities.[20]

Although municipal services and public utilities are certainly relevant to the quality of life, such matters are not the most momentous issues that confront a society. Despite Yugoslavia's democratic trappings, then, the Communist party cannot be said to have relinquished its control. Indeed, the party maintains its monopoly by denying competition from other political parties, and within the party dissent is kept to a minimum. Outside the party, Marxist-Leninist dogma still prevails in the press, the arts, and, of course, propaganda. In sum, Yugoslavia remains a Communist state that, politically speaking, resembles the Soviet Union more than the United States.

Nearly a decade after Yugoslavia split with the Soviet Union, Milovan Djilas—Tito's former comrade-in-arms and perhaps the most famous "inside" critic of Soviet-style communism—published a book called *The New Class*. (Djilas was in prison at the time for expressing the ideas in this book.) "The greatest illusion," he wrote, "was that industrialization and collectivization in the USSR, and destruction of capitalist ownership, would result in a classless society." Instead, he argued, a "new class" replaced the old one:

> The roots of the new class were implanted in a special party of the Bolshevik type. Lenin was right in his view that his party was an exception in the history of human society, although he did not suspect that is would be the beginning of a new class. . . .
>   This is not to say that the new party and the new class are identical. The party, however, is the core of that class, and its base. . . . The new class may be said to be made up of those who have special privileges and economic preference because of the administrative monopoly they hold.[21]

Nonetheless, thanks to Tito the Yugoslav Communist party has a stronger bias toward collective leadership than its Soviet counterpart has. To wit:

> Tito reorganized the League of Yugoslav Communists in order to provide both for continuity and for representation of the various nationalities in the Politburo. . . . Under this reorganization, there is a rotating collective party presidency with eight full Presidium members, elected by the Central Committee. Of these, six members represent each of the six Republican Central Committees; the Provincial Committees of the Autonomous Provinces of Vojvodina and Kosovo each send one full ex officio member to the Presidium. Together they make up the highest policy-making level of the Yugoslav party.[22]

Thus, Tito balanced regional and ethnic interests in the top party organs, much as he did in the collective presidency and the Federal Executive Council. This system may ensure that all major parts of Yugoslavia's diverse society are "represented" in the nation's decision-making apparatus; but it does not add up to anything even approaching liberal democracy.

CONCLUSION

The Soviet political system—based on a combination of Marxist, Leninist, and Stalinist principles—served as the model for the East European "satellite" states until the revolutions (delayed counterrevolutions, really) of 1989. After spearheading the reform movement under the banner of Mikhail Gorbachev's "new thinking," the USSR suddenly fell behind, as the rest of Eastern Europe plunged into the building of free-market economies and pluralistic societies. In Chapter 9 we explore the problems of transition from autocracy and central planning to democracy and the marketplace, and we assess whether the region can evolve into pluralistic, prosperous societies from its legacy of repression and stagnation.

STUDY QUESTIONS

1. Is the concept of the "vanguard of the proletariat" still relevant in Eastern Europe? If so, where? What does this phrase mean? Who invented it? For what purpose? Why is it now controversial in the USSR?
2. What are the principal political, economic, and social features of the "Soviet model"? Has Mikhail Gorbachev succeeded in reforming the Soviet system, or are his changes mostly cosmetic?
3. Why did the founders of the Soviet state opt for federalism, and what does the term mean in the Soviet context? How has federalism been affected by Gorbachev's reforms? (Hint: Focus on the role of the new Soviet legislature.) How have recent events threatened to reshape the Soviet federal system?
4. What is the traditional relationship between ideology and economics in Soviet-type systems? What leader most left his imprint on the Soviet economy? (Identify specific ideas and institutions associated with this leader.) What are the comparative advantages and disadvantages of central planning (versus market economies)?
5. In what sense is 1989 a watershed in the political history of Eastern Europe? What were the major events of that year, and how have those events transformed the region's politics?

SUGGESTED READINGS

Bialer, Seweryn. *The Soviet Paradox: External Expansion, Internal Decline.* New York: Vintage, 1986.

Goldman, Marshall I. *Gorbachev's Challenge: Economic Reform in the Age of High Technology.* New York: Norton, 1987.

Gorbachev, Mikhail. *Perestroika: New Thinking for Our Country and the World.* New York: Harper & Row, 1987.

Laquer, Walter. *The Long Road to Freedom: Russia and Glasnost.* New York: Scribners, 1988.

Lovenduski, Joni, and Jean Woodall. *Politics and Society in Eastern Europe.* Bloomington, Ind.: Indiana University, 1988.

Rothschild, Joseph. *Return to Diversity: A Political History of East Central Europe Since World War II.* New York: Oxford, 1989.

Smith, Gordon. *Soviet Politics: Continuity and Contradiction.* New York: St. Martin's, 1987.

Starr, Richard F. *Communist Regimes in Eastern Europe,* 5th ed. Stanford, Calif.: Hoover Institution, 1988.

Vozlensky, Michael. *Nomenklatura: The Soviet Ruling Class.* New York: Doubleday, 1984.

NOTES

[1] See Gordon B. Smith, *Soviet Politics: Continuity and Contradiction* (New York: St. Martin's, 1987), appendix B, p. 365.

[2] Bohdan Harasymiw, "*Nomenklatura*: The Soviet Communist Party's Leadership Recruitment System," *Canadian Journal of Political Science,* 2, no. 4 (December 1969), p. 506.

[3] Michael Vozlensky, *Nomenklatura: The Soviet Ruling Class* (New York: Doubleday, 1984), p. 71.

[4] *The Economist,* Dec. 16, 1989, p. 47.

[5] Jerry F. Hough, *The Soviet Prefects* (Boston: Cambridge University Press, 1969).

[6] V. Telegin, "A Scholar Looks at Restructuring—A Democratic Union of Social Forces: Utopia? Possibility? Necessity?" *Kommunist,* Apr. 28, 1988, p. 3.

[7] Bill Keller, "A Gorbachev Adviser Urges a Political Alternative to the Communist Party," *New York Times,* May 24, 1988, p. 8.

[8] Bill Keller, "Moscow Political Clubs Issue Call for Expanded Freedoms," *New York Times,* June 13, 1988.

[9] Bill Keller, "Setting Precedent, Estonia Allows a Non-Communist Front to Form," *New York Times,* June 29, 1988, p. 1; see also Paul Quinn-Judge, "New Element on Soviet Political Scene: Choice," *Christian Science Monitor,* July 7, 1988, p. 1.

[10] Paul Quinn-Judge, "Gorbachev's Stronger Hand," *Christian Science Monitor,* Oct. 3, 1988, p. 1; and "How Ligachev Lost Out in Kremlin Shuffle," *Christian Science Monitor,* Oct. 6, 1988.

[11] *The Economist,* Dec. 16, 1989, p. 48.

[12] Quoted in Jonas Bernstein, "Glasnost Benefits Gorbachev," *Insight,* July 25, 1988, p. 39.

13 See Paul Quinn-Judge, "Gorbachev Presses for a Rollback of Party's Power," *Christian Science Monitor*, June 29, 1988, p. 1.

14 Robert Gillete, "Perestroika: Bold Shift in Economy," *Los Angeles Times*, Oct. 27, 1987.

15 Smith, op. cit., p. 190.

16 Ibid.

17 *The Economist*, Mar. 24, 1990, p. 21.

18 Richard F. Starr, *Communist Regimes in Eastern Europe* (Stanford, Calif.: Hoover Institution, 1977), p. 194.

19 Ibid.

20 Ibid.

21 Milovan Djilas, *The New Class* (New York: Praeger, 1957), pp. 37–40.

22 Ivan Volgyes, *Politics in Eastern Europe* (Chicago: Dorsey, 1986), p. 147.

Chapter 9
Perestroika or Disintegration?

Across the Soviet Union and Eastern Europe the winds of reform are uprooting economic structures that undergirded Communist rule for four decades. The allure of the marketplace, evident in Yugoslavia and Hungary for many years, has become increasingly irresistible to all but the most incorrigible Stalinist regimes in the Communist world.

Economic liberalization has been accompanied by cultural and political democratization. Gorbachev apparently believes that economics, culture, and politics are inseparable—that economic revitalization is impossible without relaxing the cultural and political controls that were the hallmark of Communist rule under Lenin and Stalin. Eastern Europe has now renounced communism, while the Soviet Union pays at least lip service to Marxism-Leninism.

For Moscow, "market Marxism" has momentous implications, not least because of the extremely intimate relationship between politics and economics in the USSR. In daring to embrace market-type reforms, Gorbachev has sailed into uncharted waters. From the outset, hard-liners in the Kremlin have wondered how far economic reforms can go without toppling party rule, and the events of 1989 in Eastern Europe can hardly reassure them. Allowing capitalism to sprout is bound to bring into being an entrepreneurial class whose interests are at odds with those of the privileged party elite, who are determined to perpetuate their monopoly on power.

The Soviets' dilemma can be expressed as a paradox: The more effective the economic reforms (as measured by commercial success in the reborn private sector), the shorter the likely life span of the Stalinist party-state. Heidi and Alvin Toffler, who interviewed Gorbachev early in his drive for economic change, put it this way:

> An advanced economy requires incessant technological innovation. But the technological advance in today's world is ever more closely tied to culture and to social structure. To generate a lot of new ideas, even technological ideas, the system must permit the expression not simply of alternative scientific theories and hypotheses, but of "crazy" social notions, off beat art, controversial economic theories, errors, and even ideological dissent.[1]

According to the Tofflers, many Soviet scientists and intellectuals favor *glasnost* (cultural and political openness) and "want even more freedom" precisely for the reason just stated. Moreover, "it will be necessary [for Gorbachev] to think the apparently unthinkable—that many of the Soviet Union's most critical 'contradictions' arise from the monopoly of political power by a single party."

An American journalist assessing *glasnost* in the fall of 1987 cut to the core when he observed that

> For decades, Communist authorities have treated Soviet citizens like children who . . . could not be trusted with the truth [but] that is changing—in the belief that treating the people more like responsible adults is the only way to break through their apathy and enlist them in the enormous job of social and economic reconstruction.[2]

In other words, *perestroika* (economic and administrative restructuring) cannot succeed without *glasnost*.

Since the risks of reform did not stop at the Soviet border, Gorbachev also had to consider the ramifications of reform in Eastern Europe. When Khrushchev launched his de-Stalinization drive in 1956 (see Chapter 8), the repercussions in Eastern Europe were nearly disastrous from Moscow's standpoint. Rebellion against Soviet domination and Stalinist rule in Eastern Europe created a crisis that required military intervention in one case (Hungary) and a concerted effort to prop up a tottering regime in another (Poland).

Before 1989 some observers considered Eastern Europe to be Gorbachev's "acid test":

> You can't have *perestroika* in the Soviet Union and nothing in Eastern Europe. It won't work. . . . But once he [Gorbachev] releases the forces of reform in Eastern Europe, they can run faster than in the Soviet Union. And then the pressures in Eastern Europe could reach the point where they can't be controlled any more.[3]

In a crisis like the one in Hungary (1957) or Czechoslovakia (1968), Gorbachev would be forced to choose between intervening or losing control. But "once he intervenes militarily to crush one of the East European countries, his credibility is . . . shattered to pieces."[4] When the worst-case scenario occurred in 1989, Gorbachev chose not to intervene.

The decision to let the Soviet "outer empire" go indicated clearly that Gorbachev's make-or-break priority was to revitalize stagnant economies—his own and those of the East European partners in the Council of Mutual Economic Assistance (Comecon). To bring about this renaissance and relieve Moscow's burden in propping up the Eastern bloc's economies, Gorbachev had to find new means to motivate workers, new incentives for farm and factory managers, and new technologies to improve products. He adopted a three-pronged approach: restructuring the economy (*perestroika*), relaxing censorship and cultural controls (*glasnost*), and allowing a modicum of political pluralism (*demokratizatsiia*).

Will the latest Soviet reform movement produce lasting results? To do so, at least four obstacles must be overcome: public wariness, bureaucratic resistance, a possible reawakening of ethnic nationalism, and the danger that Moscow will lose influence over reform processes in Eastern Europe. Given the risks, why did Gorbachev venture into the unknown? The answer may lie in the predicament he inherited, along with his power, in 1985.

Stalin's Legacy: Reform or Decline?

Economists have long debated the relative merits of free-market and centrally planned economies. Even Soviet observers who contend that the Stalinist system achieved an unprecedented rate of industrialization in the 1930s often hasten to add that its human costs—estimates put the death toll at 6 million or more—were also unprecedented (and unacceptable).[5] Others stress that the Soviet Union's economic growth has been unbalanced, pointing to its chronic agricultural shortfalls.

A profound issue for Communist regimes as the century closes is whether centralized economic planning is appropriate for "mature" (that is, industrially developed) socialist nations. The image of a dying workers' state has haunted the Soviet Union since at least the early 1960s. Following Khrushchev's ouster in 1964 (in part because of his failure to revitalize agriculture and reorganize industry), Moscow's leaders have launched their own programs to rejuvenate the economy. Their efforts have been guided by the theoretical writings of Soviet economist E. G. Liberman.

The "Liberman reforms" aimed to decentralize economic decision making for the first time since Stalin instituted central planning in 1929. Now managers were to be given considerable discretion in making a variety of decisions about production and investments. Their enterprises were even to be charged interest on the amount of capital they used. "With this new-found latitude, managers were expected to take risks, innovate, reduce costs, and thereby increase the sales and profits of their enterprises."[6] Had this approach triumphed, Soviet managers would have operated much like Western entrepreneurs. But the embryonic reform movement was quickly aborted by the entrenched bureaucracy, at whose expense the reforms would have come.

In 1973 Leonid Brezhnev's regime announced a new approach: merging related enterprises into large industrial and production associations. Patterned after corporate conglomerates found in market economies, the purpose of the new groups was to cut costs and better use technology. Thus, for the second time in a decade, Soviet leadership imitated Western economic practices without adopting Western economic principles. Once again the undertaking smashed against the rock-hard resistance of the bureaucracy.[7]

The Brezhnev era ended with the economy as ossified and arthritic as its aging leaders. Brezhnev's successor, former KGB chief Yuri Andropov, apparently intended to address the perennial problem of low productivity through a mixture of intimidation and new incentives, but he died soon after ascending to power. And his successor, Konstantin Chernenko, was ailing from the start of his very short term as party secretary general. In 1985 it thus fell to Mikhail Gorbachev—at 54 the youngest leader since Stalin—to deal with the economic ills that Stalin had created when Gorbachev was only an infant.

The urgency of economic reform was obvious years before Gorbachev assumed power. By 1985 economic growth had declined to only 2 percent, about half what it had been a decade earlier. One of every nine industrial enterprises and nearly a third of farms were losing money, and such essentials as food, housing, medicine, and transportation were being subsidized to the tune of about 75 billion rubles per year.

At about 1 percent a year, growth in food production was barely keeping pace with population growth, and despite the heavy investment in agriculture (some 600 billion rubles over twenty years), the government continued to spend billions for imported meat and grain. Even so, the supply of meat and butter was so far short of demand three years after Gorbachev's rise to power that rationing remained in force in many provincial cities: as little as 1 kilogram (2.2 pounds) of meat and 200 grams (less than a quarter-pound) of butter for each adult per month![8]

Meanwhile, the USSR's investment priorities in agriculture reflected terrible planning. Farm-to-market roads and facilities for storage, food processing, packaging, and retailing were woefully neglected. Up to 30 percent of farm output was rotting or eaten by rodents, including a quantity of grain equal to what the government was buying each year on the world market. In 1987 an estimated 60 percent of the potato crop rotted in the fields when heavy rains disrupted the harvest.

The general standard of living was abysmal compared with life in Western industrial democracies. One-fifth of the people in cities were living in "communal" apartments, sharing bathrooms and kitchens. First Brezhnev had postponed the promised end to the housing shortage, from 1980 to 1990; then Gorbachev pushed it back another decade.

The most critical problem was the technology gap, which widened into a gulf during the 1970s and 1980s as the computer revolution eluded the East (and transformed the West). The consequence, in Gorbachev's own words, was to create "pre-crisis conditions." Either the USSR must change how it works or fall into decline and decay. Soviet economists have conceded that "no more than about 10 percent of the country's industrial production measures up to world standards of quality and technological advancement."[9]

Poor quality is only one side of the coin; the other side is low productivity. Some 20 percent of Soviet industrial capacity is currently idle—in some branches the figure is twice as high—due to labor shortages, while 25 percent of the labor force is redundant or underemployed. Many plant managers inflate their labor needs and even falsify the number of workers to ensure that they will not be short-handed during harvest season, when factory workers are temporarily redeployed to farms, or at the end of the month, when "crashing" is frequently necessary to fulfill quotas. Thus a major problem is how to redistribute and retrain Soviet labor without creating unemployment. Perhaps a more difficult question is how to motivate workers—to make them more dependable, more meticulous, and more efficient.

Defenders of the Soviet model usually point to Moscow's meteoric rise to superpower status under Stalin. In the early 1970s one scholar wrote:

> The Soviet Union has advanced from a relatively backward and predominantly agricultural country to an economic power second only to . . . the United States. . . . It is probably fair to say that in spite of all the shortcomings of the Soviet economic system one can point to, the annals of no other country show such rapid industrialization and such high growth rates sustained for so long a period of time.[10]

As noted, this assessment was made before the USSR's current economic situation was so clear. Recent trends strongly support the view long held by many Western students of economic development: Whatever successes may have been achieved in the Soviet Union by forced industrialization during the 1930s, the utility of the Stalinist approach is *at best* inversely related to the level of development that already exists in a given economy. Stalinist methods are likely to apply—if at all—only until an economy reaches a certain level of industrial and technological sophistication; after that, they increasingly become a drag on efforts to achieve sustained growth.

A study authored by William U. Chandler in 1986 under the auspices of the Worldwatch Institute revealed striking differences between the recent economic performance of free-market nations and that of nations run by central planning.[11] The indicators of economic efficiency in this study included agricultural productivity, energy conservation, and pollution control.

"Until recently, centralized planning served as a model for almost half the world," according to Chandler, but there is now growing reliance on free-market principles. Among the reasons for this reversal are the disastrous failure of Mao Zedong's all-out mass mobilization ("heaven storming") to develop China's economy, the debt crisis in Latin America, famine and stalled development in Africa, chronic underdevelopment in South Asia, and burgeoning deficits in Western Europe and elsewhere.[12] "The issue is not socialism vs. capitalism; it is the efficacy with which economic systems achieve their intended ends," wrote Chandler, who compared the resource-use efficiency in free-enterprise economies (including the United States, Japan, and West Germany) and in state-run economies (including the Soviet Union and Czechoslovakia). The study found that agricultural productivity in Western Europe was often double that of Eastern Europe, and that U.S. farmers were twenty times more efficient than their Soviet counterparts. The study also demonstrated that free-market economies enjoy a comparative advantage in energy conservation and pollution control.

These disparities may surprise some Western observers, but leaders of such Communist states as Yugoslavia, Hungary, and, to a lesser extent, Poland have for many years had misgivings about central planning—and expressed their misgivings by deviating from the Stalinist model. The mounting evidence that market-oriented systems are superior has no doubt played a major role in influencing the Soviet Union (and Communist China) to pursue economic reforms.

Early Reformers: Yugoslavia and Hungary

Yugoslavia was the first Eastern European country to experiment with market-oriented reforms, while Hungary was the pioneer within the Soviet bloc. The Yugoslav experience suggests that half-hearted reforms are no panacea—and may be worse than no reform at all.

Yugoslavia

Led by Josip Broz Tito, Yugoslavia broke with Moscow in 1948 and looked westward for friendship and assistance. Yugoslavia was the only East European state that was not occupied by Stalin's armies in World War II, having had the good fortune not to share a border with the Soviet Union.

Yugoslavia's pioneering efforts to decentralize administration and to institute workers' self-management—as well as its welcoming approach to trade with the West—are widely acknowledged.[13] The so-called workers' councils have been the cornerstone of Yugoslavia's "socialist democracy" since 1950, when Tito promised "factories to the workers" as the first step toward repudiating the Stalinist model. The workers' councils were intended to ensure democratic self-management at the enterprise level, in order to avoid the stultifying effects of party-state control.

But in the 1950s reality failed to catch up with Yugoslavia's rhetoric of self-management, and in the 1960s reformers made repeated attempts to achieve economic liberalization. They aimed at nothing less than ending "arbitrary political intervention in the economy in order to allow the market to work freely."[14] Self-management finally came of age in the 1970s, and in theory Yugoslav workers now manage the means of production and decide how the fruits of their labor will be distributed. The social and political significance of this system has been described as follows:

> Within Yugoslavia, self-management provides the foundation for the "democratization of social life" and "the construction of a political system" that expresses the plurality of interests in society and allows contradictions inherent in such a society "to be resolved democratically by dialogue and consultations." . . . Self-management affects almost every facet of Yugoslav life. Its application to the government and administration is reflected in the 1974 Constitution.[15]

Yugoslavia's 1974 Constitution was its fourth since the end of World War II (others were adopted in 1946, 1953, and 1963). A document unique in the Communist world, it introduced a new representational system and gave each of the six republics an equal number of delegates in the federal parliament. Yet the 1974 Constitution has done little to undercut the party's monopoly on power.

Without question, Yugoslavia has been the most innovative (and the least illiberal) state in Eastern Europe. For all its experimentation with market-oriented, pseudodemocratic reforms, however, Yugoslavia has not revitalized its lethargic economy or solved its festering political problems. Attempts to combine a free-market economy (including free emigration and free trade) with socialism and a one-party state have foundered. Efforts to close unprofitable factories threatened workers with unemployment even as soaring inflation reduced purchasing power. In 1987 austerity measures including price increases and a wage freeze led to widespread strikes.[16]

Nor is social unrest—often spurred by ethnic tensions—anything new in Yugoslavia. Enduring rivalry has existed between Serbs and Croats, but more recently tensions have involved the Albanian minority in Serbia. About a year after Tito's death, in 1981, thousands of them demonstrated in the Serbian province of Kosovo, chanting anti-Yugoslav slogans and demanding emancipation from Serbia. Such subnational particularism is always just beneath the surface of Yugoslav politics, but the upheaval in Kosovo also had economic causes, including a $20.5-billion foreign debt, a 40-percent inflation rate, and double-digit unemployment.[17]

Yugoslavia's economic plight has not improved much since then, although it did reduce its foreign debt through trade surpluses and in 1986 achieved a respectable 3.5-percent growth rate. But evidence of structural problems was also easy to find: Inflation rose above 90 percent, unemployment reached 14 percent, and state control of the economy has increased.[18]

Almost predictably in this economic climate, ethnic tensions reached crisis level again late in 1988. Milovan Djilas, Yugoslavia's most famous dissident, aptly summed up the situation: "We now face a choice. Either we go forward, become freer and join the rest of Europe, or we will fall backward and become the underdeveloped state we were before World War II."[19]

The urgent need for economic and structural reform in Yugoslavia well illustrates why countries throughout Eastern Europe and the Soviet Union itself decided to "go forward." At the time, even the Soviet bloc's foremost success story, East Germany, was sinking under the weight of structural rigidity and over-centralization.[20]

Hungary

Unlike Yugoslavia's reform movement, Hungary's came at the behest of a leader who had been hand-picked by the Kremlin. Following an abortive coup against Moscow in 1956, Hungary was forced back into the Communist fold. Under Janos Kadar, who ruled for three decades, a package of reforms known as the New Economic Mechanism (NEM) was created. Begun in 1968, halted in 1972, and reactivated in 1978, the NEM's features included greater reliance on prices and profits, decentralized industrial management, incentives for "worker entrepreneurism," and supports for private farming and small business—all under Communist domination of Hungarian politics.[21]

The revival of the NEM in 1978–1979 was necessitated by Hungary's growing foreign debt and stagnant productivity.[22] The renewed reliance on market forces helped make Hungary something of a showcase in Eastern Europe, even though worldwide recession in the late 1970s was causing many nations in both the East and the West to reevaluate their economic policies. An emphasis on consumerism supported by partial reprivatization of agriculture was one of the NEM's most conspicuous (and successful) departures from Stalinist norms:

> What proved decisive [for meeting consumer demand] was the priority accorded to the modernization of agricultural production and the green light given to the development of rural second economy. The result was adequate food supplies for the domestic consumer (with substantial amounts left for export) and the availability of

basic foodstuffs at subsidized prices (at least until 1983). [The revivified NEM] also helped dim the memory of the regime's often brutal recollectivization campaign of 1958–60 and created a basically reform-supportive consensus in the countryside.[23]

Hungary's economy slumped in the 1980s, and by 1985 the country had the lowest growth rate in Eastern Europe. The Central Committee of the Hungarian Communist party reportedly engaged in vigorous debate over the future of the NEM at the end of 1986; earlier market reforms were castigated for having been too cautious, and critics argued for more radical reforms.

But Hungary's experience appeared to mirror Yugoslavia's. With reform came higher prices and taxes, closed factories, and lost jobs. Party leaders even considered imposing the Communist world's first income tax! "The type of reform Gorbachev is talking about is turning out to mean austerity, not prosperity," wrote Pierre Kende, editor of a Hungarian exile magazine in Paris; "It's no magic recipe."[24] Against this backdrop of unsolved economic problems and uncertain prospects, Hungary's reform Communists relinquished the reins of power to a democratically elected government in 1990.

Poland's Solidarity Movement

Poland's economy stands out as an example of selective Stalinization. Although the state had long owned and operated all industry, Poland retreated from agricultural collectivization in the 1950s. Over the next two decades the government, disdainful of the "private enterprise" it had spawned in the farm sector, neglected agriculture and instead invested heavily in turnkey industries; that is, it purchased factories in package form from the West, financed with Western credits. But these industries did not function efficiently, and Poland was hard hit by the worldwide recession and high interest rates that followed the 1973 Arab oil embargo. Bad management and bad luck combined to create an economic crisis that was only made worse by Poland's huge foreign debt to the West.

Polish workers have been the most rebellious in Eastern Europe. When the government raised food prices in 1970, they staged a major strike, forcing the resignation of Communist party leader Wladyslaw Gomulka. In 1976 they struck again, charging that Gomulka's successor, Edward Gierek, had failed to keep promises of more food, higher wages, and a role for workers in factory management. Both these revolts were triggered by bread-and-butter issues.

In 1980 the most serious challenge to the Polish government came when a new independent labor union movement, Solidarity, burst onto the scene. Led by a charismatic shipyard worker named Lech Walesa, Solidarity was backed by the Roman Catholic church, an especially powerful force in Poland. Even Pope John Paul II—Polish born and a political activist—used his "bully pulpit" to focus international attention on events in Poland. The pressures on Communist leaders grew so great that on August 31, 1980, they signed the Gdansk Agreement, giving legal status to Solidarity. This was the first time since World War II that an independent mass organization (one not controlled by the Communist party) was enfranchised anywhere in Eastern Europe.

Poland's new leader, General Wojciech Jaruzelski, declared martial law in December 1981, and the following year he banned and arrested the leadership of Solidarity and other independent trade unions that had sprung up. Solidarity fell silent and went underground, but it was not crushed. Poland's economic ills continued, and the plight of workers worsened.

In 1987 the government took an unprecedented step, putting the issue of economic restructuring to a referendum vote. But the government cleverly stacked the deck by including huge price increases (up to 200 percent), and Polish voters rejected the proposal. Hard pressed to make ends meet, many Poles voted ''no'' out of desperation, not conviction. But since they were thus given a chance at ''democratic'' decision making (*glasnost*), Jaruzelski could use the defeated referendum to justify foot-dragging on reforms if Moscow applied pressure.

Faced with a $40-billion foreign debt and massive budget deficits, General Jaruzelski announced austerity measures in 1988. Polish workers again revolted. Solidarity resurfaced, and Lech Walesa again took the spotlight and demanded the relegalization of Solidarity. Ensuing popular unrest toppled Prime Minister Zbigniew Messner's government—a first in Eastern Europe. Messner's successor, Mieczyslaw Rakowski, refused to legalize solidarity but did quickly implement market-oriented policies that resembled Gorbachev's *perestroika*.

Few observers had any illusions. At best, Poland had embarked on a long, slow road to recovery; at worst, it faced another winter of discontent. Steep inflation, wage cuts, and continued shortages of food and other essential goods seemed to be setting the stage for another revolt. But when the economy tottered on the verge of collapse in the fall of 1989, Jaruzelski finally ''bowed to the inevitable'' and gave the nod to a non-Communist government intent on market remedies.

As noted in Chapter 8, Poland was the first East European country to make major democratic changes. Solidarity won the elections, capturing all seats in the Senate (upper house); it was limited by law to about one-third of the seats in the *Sejm* (lower house). The first non-Communist cabinet in four decades, headed by Tadeusz Mazowiecki, took charge in September, ''committed to sweeping market reforms more reminiscent of Latin America than Sweden.'' Market-minded liberals set Poland's economic course thereafter. The new finance minister, Leczek Balcerowisc, imposed a harsh stabilization program, made the zloty convertible (at least in theory), freed prices, tightened credit, and pushed privatization.[25]

These measures were music to the ears of free-enterprise enthusiasts, but the public feared rising prices, vanishing pensions, and dwindling subsidies for food, housing, and transportation. Bureaucrats and industrial workers—accustomed to job security and little pressure to produce—feared whip-cracking new bosses. Despite all efforts, the Polish economy remained a shambles at the beginning of the 1990s. Critics maintained that Warsaw depended too much on Western subventions and not enough on its own resources. The nation's foreign debt in 1989 stood at roughly $40 billion, and servicing the debt (or getting Western creditors to reschedule or forgive it) has become an on-going issue for Poland.

Romania

The hard-line regimes of Eastern Europe displayed little enthusiasm for Gorbachev's "new thinking" before 1989. If Hungary and Poland were most amenable to market-type reforms, Romania was least interested. Long the most independent of Moscow's satellites, Romania continued its unreconstructed Stalinist approach until Ceausescu's execution at the end of 1989 (see Chapter 8). Soviet-type industrialization had resulted in huge but obsolescent factories and widespread food shortages—in a country that was once the breadbasket of Eastern Europe.

The system failed in other ways as well. Romanians' much-touted social and economic rights (a guaranteed job, subsidized housing, free medical care, and the like) had become hollow substitutes for the political and cultural freedoms enjoyed in the West. By the winter of 1987–1988 they were not even substitutes, for the government reduced power supplies by at least 30 percent, limiting households to 40-watt lightbulbs for several hours a day. This spectacle of families shivering in dimly-lit apartments was not unique to Romania; the situation was similar in several other Eastern European countries.[26]

Perestroika: Making a Virtue of Necessity

Within the Soviet bloc, conventional wisdom has long held that Moscow is the model for other socialist countries. A small country like Hungary could not assume this role. But with the advent of Gorbachev's "new thinking," the Soviet Union has shown a willingness to learn from other socialist states, especially Yugoslavia, Hungary, and the People's Republic of China. One Hungarian expressed this change, tongue in cheek, to an American journalist: "We just have to succeed now. If our ideas let Gorbachev down, we'll be in real trouble!"[27]

At a Communist party conclave early in 1986 Gorbachev endorsed calls for a radical restructuring of Soviet society (*perestroika*). Later in the year the Supreme Soviet, the nominal legislature, published a list of thirty-eight measures to be implemented before the end of 1990; the new laws' concerns ranged from voting and plebiscites to economic incentives, pricing, the press, governmental reorganization, and even the activities of the KGB.[28] In November the Supreme Soviet approved a law allowing citizens to moonlight for extra cash—many of them had been doing this illegally for decades. Finally, in January 1987, the Communist party's Central Committee gave its imprimatur to Gorbachev's reform package.

The moonlighting law, which took effect in the spring of 1987, was the first to ease the ban on free enterprise since Lenin's short-lived New Economic Policy in 1921. Any Soviet citizen may now ask local authorities for permission to start what amounts to a small business, and the officials decide whether there is a need for the applicant's products. A Soviet spokesman stated that the moonlighting law does not sanction "free enterprise activities"; its ostensible aim is to tap the energies of citizens who are not already in the workforce.[29]

The service sector of the Soviet economy is woefully underdeveloped, and the moonlighting law attempts to alleviate this. It also can be seen as a first step toward recognizing an individuals' economic rights—by a regime long hostile to the idea of private property. But jealousy has proved to be a problem, for many Soviets resent entrepreneurs who make lots of money. Here is an excellent example of how Marxist ideology impedes economic reforms.

The main instrument of *perestroika* is the 1987 Law on Soviet Enterprise, which mandated three major changes by 1990. First, it slated about 37,000 industrial enterprises for "managerial decentralization," meaning they are to operate on a strict profit-loss basis rather than depending on state financial support.

Second, the law permitted some state firms to deal directly with foreign companies rather than working through the bureaucratic maze. It also allowed a small number of enterprises to negotiate joint ventures with Western firms, which may hold up to 49 percent of the equity. Since 1987 many such agreements have been signed, but few have borne fruit. Foreign companies find it difficult to repatriate profits, since the ruble is not convertible, and bureaucratic inefficiency continues to be a problem.

Third, the law increased the autonomy of the nation's 49,000 collective and state farms. For the first time in fifty years, collective farms are encouraged to organize around "family brigades" (apparently inspired by the highly successful Chinese moves to reprivatize agriculture in the early 1980s). Farmers can lease land from the state for fifty years or more, retaining profits in return for paying taxes and passing their holdings on to their children.

In late March 1987, the shutdown of a Leningrad construction trust—the first state-run company in the Soviet Union to "go bankrupt"—dramatized Gorbachev's commitment to economic revitalization. Although the shutdown temporarily displaced about 2,000 workers, it also served notice to the managers of inefficient enterprises that the reformers in Moscow meant business, literally and figuratively.[30] Since 1987 the state may liquidate any business that shows "long-time losses and inability to pay its debts."

In 1988 the Soviets unveiled the so-called Law on Cooperatives, which encourages a thinly disguised form of private enterprise by allowing individuals to produce and sell consumer goods for a profit at free-market prices. Within a year some fifty thousand businesses were operating—a burgeoning "private sector" that employed about 2 million Soviets. Although these cooperatives produced consumer goods of better quality than those made by state-run enterprises, shoppers complained that prices were prohibitively high. In turn, the cooperatives complained that government policies (for example, high taxes) made it impossible to lower prices.

Gorbachev also moved to decentralize the economy by changing regulations over external trade. As a result, about seventy industrial enterprises and twenty government departments were empowered to make deals with foreign firms. (Previously all international commerce was conducted through a state monopoly.) Moreover, these enterprises and departments were to retain some of their profit instead of turning it all over to the government for reallocation.[31]

Gorbachev has rewritten the Kremlin's long-standing claim that the Soviet Union is the proper economic model for the rest of the Communist world. The teacher now appears to be taking lessons from former students. As one observer has put it:

> What seems to have contributed to Moscow's changed thinking is that fact that an even bigger communist nation—China—is also drawing on Hungarian and Yugoslav experience and seems to be succeeding. Gorbachev's Russia must not be seen to be trailing Deng Xiaoping's China![32]

The Perils of *Perestroika*

Despite Gorbachev's shock treatments, Soviet economic performance has remained bleak. During the first half of 1989, for example, productivity rose only 2.7 percent, according to official figures. Against a backdrop of inflation and empty store shelves, consumers have complained bitterly that shortages are worse than under Brezhnev, worse (some say) than at any time since the war! Largely unnoticed by frustrated Soviet shoppers was the additional burden of a foreign trade deficit. In mid-1989 the Kremlin announced that the national debt stood at $500 billion. Gorbachev responded to this growing debt by reordering priorities, which among other things entailed cuts in military spending. The aim was to reduce defense outlays by 8.3 percent (about $10 billion) in 1990.

Another challenge for Gorbachev in 1989 was a crippling nationwide strike by coal miners, on the heels of other damaging strikes. Some made dark predictions that Gorbachev would resort to force or would be ousted; instead he negotiated. The miners won unprecedented wage concessions as well as an impressive package of benefits, while Gorbachev displayed a new tolerance for labor protest.

The strikes in 1989 were a presentiment of the social unrest that is likely to result from dislocations and adjustments associated with economic reform. Will the Soviets be willing to take the risks connected with allowing prices to seek their own level in the marketplace? Will they dare to cut state subsidies, which swallow 15 to 20 percent of the budget each year? With an estimated 300 billion rubles stashed in savings accounts, efforts to decontrol prices could lead to runaway inflation, unless the supply of consumer goods can be brought into line with demand. That will not be easy, for the Soviet economy grossly favors heavy and defense-related industries, and there is a tremendous backlog of demand for consumer goods.

Indeed, the extent of deprivation for consumers in the Soviet Union has long been treated as a state secret. Soviet comparisons between the standard of living in the United States and the USSR typically stress the seamy side of life in the former and the superior social benefits offered by the latter. This myth was exposed in 1989, when a Soviet scholar named Zaychenko published an article showing that U.S. living standards are far superior in virtually all areas of comparison.[33] Looking at everything from nutrition to medical care to housing to transportation, Zaychenko challenged official propaganda. He asserted, for example, that "the cost of housing in our country is 41 percent higher" than in the United States and that the means of transportation are ten times greater in the United States than in the USSR. He calculated that the average Soviet worker toils ten to twelve times as long as an American to buy a kilo of meat, and ten to fifteen times as long to buy a dozen eggs. More daringly, Zaychenko observed that "in the last 80 years the difference in the economic accessibility of foods in the US and the USSR has become particularly pronounced." He also cited other quality-of-life indicators, such as the availability of desirable consumer goods; the number of shopping centers, restaurants, and telephones; and even government outlays for education. In all areas, he said, the Soviet Union trails far behind. His message was unmistakable: "Let's face it, comrades, under Communism the East-West gap has grown steadily."

The comparison of living standards makes it clear that the greatest challenge for Soviets is to reverse the trends that threaten to make their country a second-rate power in the next century. There is also a more immediate threat—political instability in the form of labor unrest, food riots, and other economically motivated protests. Gorbachev's reforms are a double-edged sword: They are needed to get the economy moving, but they have also created higher expectations even as *glasnost* has increased public awareness of social and economic ills that once were cloaked in secrecy.

Glasnost: The Human Side of *Perestroika*

Perestroika was overshadowed in the late 1980s by *glasnost* and by democratization (see Chapter 8). Democratization has eased some of the political controls that were so tight under Communist party rule, and even before the landmark reforms of 1989–1990 Gorbachev had allowed greater candor in such areas as Stalin's purges and Soviet social and economic shortcomings. Certainly Soviets enjoy more artistic, literary, and cultural freedom than at any time since the short-lived liberalization that accompanied Lenin's dalliance with a marketplace economy in the early 1920s. Now freedom of expression is part of the strategy for economic revitalization, but it too carries considerable risks.

Gorbachev apparently has realized that "to unleash the latent human potential necessary to make national restructuring a success, each citizen must undergo a 'personal *perestroika*.'"[34] In fact, Soviet leadership is calling for a fundamental change in the nation's social psychology—a nation unaccustomed to personal freedom or individual initiative, a nation encumbered and inhibited by centuries of political and religious oppression. There remains a "cultural fear of spontaneity here dating back to the czars, a tendency to see Western-style individual freedom as the first, inevitable step toward anarchy."[35] Breaking this pattern without breaking up the political system is what *glasnost* is all about. Far from abandoning the system, Gorbachev hoped to breathe new life into it.

The Soviets have been deliberately vague about the outer limits of *glasnost*. Lacking any clear boundaries, Soviet society has become a giant laboratory to test new forms of cultural expression and even political activity. Writers and books long banished—among them Boris Pasternak (*Dr. Zhivago*), Vasily Grossman (*Life and Fate*), and Yevgeny Zamyatin (*We*)—have been "rehabilitated." The poetry of Joseph Brodsky, the Nobel laureate who spent eighteen months in a labor camp for "social parasitism," appeared in *Novy Mir* in 1988. Many films and documentaries that had been blocked by the censors for decades were cleared for at least limited showings in 1987–1988. Even such U.S. films as *Platoon*, *Amadeus*, and *One Flew Over the Cuckoo's Nest* began appearing in Soviet movie theaters.

The Soviet press also enjoyed a new openness, publishing articles on previously taboo subjects such as prostitution, drug abuse, homosexuality, and even the appalling misuse of psychiatry to punish dissidents. Embarrassing statistics about infant mortality and life expectancy, withheld for years by thin-skinned authorities, were again published. Other negative news—crime statistics, industrial accidents, traffic mishaps, and official corruption—began to transfigure Soviet media: The old formula combining Pollyanna and propaganda gave way to greater concern for accuracy, honesty, and realism.

The greatest potential challenge to the Kremlin's authority spawned by *glasnost* was the proliferation of informal groups with no connection to the party or state. Many of these involved activities with no political overtones, such as chess, rock music, or soccer. But some were less innocuous:

1. A Moscow group called Memorial urged the government to build a monument and information center in honor of Stalin's victims.
2. Green World in Leningrad opposed on environmental grounds a government flood-control project to dam part of the Gulf of Finland.
3. Press Club Glasnost, composed mainly of former political prisoners, monitored human rights and the progress of *glasnost*.
4. The Moscow Jewish Association, created as "an umbrella and support organization" for Soviet Jews, was allowed to hold a rally outside Moscow in 1987 commemorating the victims of Babi Yar (it was nonetheless denounced in the Soviet news media as a "Zionist conspiracy").[36]

Many informal groups now circulate uncensored newsletters. In the 1970s, an underground press known as *samizdat* ("self-publishing") flourished, but toward the end of the decade it was smashed in a crackdown on dissent. The new unofficial "press" is different from *samizdat* in at least one crucial respect: In keeping with the new spirit of "openness" it is openly published, distributed, and discussed. Whether or not this is the harbinger of a free press in the USSR remains to be seen.

Obstacles to Change

As noted earlier, four major obstacles impede political and economic change in the Soviet Union: (1) public wariness, (2) bureaucratic resistance, (3) ethnic nationalism, and (4) Eastern Europe's anti-Russia tendencies. Any one of these could impede the interrelated processes of *perestroika*, *glasnost*, and *demokratizatsiia*; together, they easily could cause the whole reform movement to collapse.

Public Wariness

Westerners often assume that Gorbachev's economic reforms are popular in the Soviet Union, but the reality is not so simple. Given their history of political oppression, the Soviet people have reason to be skeptical of government, pessimistic about the likelihood of change for the better, wary of promises, and indifferent to the idea of democracy. In fact, fear of anarchy is probably much closer to the surface (and deeper) than any yearning for the kind of individual liberties enjoyed in the West.[37] "Their history," wrote David Shipler, "as they repeatedly remind a foreigner, is replete with illustrations that their authority cannot be eroded only a little but is swept away completely when weakened and overwhelmed. . . . And in the milieu of Russia's upheaval and chaos, revolutions have been made."[38]

There are also pragmatic reasons why the rank and file might be cynical about *perestroika*. As we noted earlier, previous Soviet reformers have always failed. Furthermore, the surface changes associated with *glasnost* have "failed to bring any substantial change in the everyday life of people or the functioning of the system."[39] On the contrary, the early effects of *perestroika* included a cut in pay for many workers, price increases for food and other essentials subsidized by the state, and the disturbing possibility of unemployment. Suddenly the great advantage of state-centered socialism—security—gave way to a new and nagging sense of insecurity.

Given the premium that Russo-Soviet culture places on security—again, for reasons that history best explains—and the relative indifference or even hostility to liberty, it is small wonder that *perestroika* was greeted with less than wild enthusiasm. To succeed in revitalizing the economy, the Soviets must revitalize society; and to revitalize society, they must overcome widespread skepticism, suspicion, and fear.

Bureaucratic Resistance

Even more than the general public, the nation's 18-million party and state bureaucrats know that they have little to gain and much to lose from change, at least in the short run. In the proposed restructuring almost half of these functionaries stand to lose their jobs as ministries are cut back and merged in order to streamline administration and keep Kremlin officials from interfering with daily management of factories and farms.

Perestroika threatens not only careers but also the role of the party in Soviet society. Its power is inseparable from its watchdog function—a function that has given party officials at all levels a kind of veto power over any decisions which the hierarchy has not already reserved for itself. The pervasive surveillance system that the party nurtured and maintained since 1917 is glimpsed in this sardonic (and thoroughly Russian) condensation of the Soviet Constitution: ''Whatever is not forbidden, is compulsory.''[40]

Clearly, then, any reforms that relax party and state controls threaten the party itself. And the threat was only underscored by Gorbachev's deemphasis of dogmatism. (''We should seek the truth together,'' he has said.) The party functionary's nightmare is that the spell of *perestroika* will cause Soviet leadership to decide it no longer needs an ideological watchdog, turning the party into a dinosaur instead. Although this possibility seems farfetched, Russians—conditioned by their cruel history—take worst-case scenarios more seriously than most Westerners do.

The danger is not so much that bureaucrats will revolt openly against the leadership but that they will derail the reform drive by administrative footdragging and inertia. ''We fight for abstractions—democracy, truth, and freedom,'' said Vitaly Korotich, the liberal editor of the weekly magazine *Ogonyok*; ''They [opponents of *glasnost*] fight for quite normal, concrete things, like their own privileges.''[41]

Ethnic Nationalism

Former U.S. National Security Advisor Zbigniew Brzezinski called it ''the Achilles' heel of the Soviet system''—referring to the ethnically diverse Soviet state, which encompasses eleven time zones, one-sixth of the world's surface, 120 official languages, and over 100 separate nationalities. Great Russians now constitute a bare majority of the total population (52.4 percent, in the last census).

Expressions of cultural and linguistic particularism have been suppressed for decades by the Russian-dominated and highly centralized Soviet government. To some degree, contempt for ethnic traditions was an outgrowth of Marxist-Leninist ideology and of the need to fuse a multinational empire into a unified state. The ideology became a substitute for the various cultures.

In the Baltic states, Latvians, Estonians, and Lithuanians are nostalgic for the period before World War II, when they were self-governing. In Transcaucasia, Azerbaijanis, Georgians, and Armenians retain a strong sense of national identity. In the Ukraine, whose population nearly equals France or Great Britain, nationalism and even separatism are reinforced by a rich history that predates the Muscovite era—and by long-standing resentment of Great Russian dominance. Finally, in Soviet Central Asia, Turkmen, Kirghiz, Uzbek, Kazakh, and Tadzhik nationalities continue to observe their customs and practices, despite Soviet efforts to ''modernize'' them; all except the Tadzhiks speak Turkic languages, and all are Muslim.

Gorbachev was reminded of the power of ethnic nationalism early in 1987, when violence broke out in Kazakhstan after he replaced its regional party chief, a Kazakh, with an ethnic Russian. But in the late 1980s militant nationalism and internal turmoil were most manifest in two other regions: the Baltic states and the Caucasus (especially in Armenia and Azerbaijan).

Protests in Armenia in 1988 illustrated the dangers and dilemmas Gorbachev faced in pressing reforms. Long-standing tensions between Armenians and Azeris (the indigenous population of Azerbaijan) worsened when Armenian activities launched a campaign to transfer the Armenian enclave of Nagorno-Karabakh from predominantly Muslim Azerbaijan to Armenia. The situation took an ugly turn in February, when rioting erupted in the Azerbaijani city of Sumgait, where the two groups had previously lived peacefully. When the rampage was over, twenty-six Armenians and six Azeris were dead.

The shock of these events brought a lull that was short-lived. Huge demonstrations in Yerevan, the capital of Armenia, culminated in a strike that paralyzed the city by mid-June. Despite repeated warnings from Moscow, the unrest reached the boiling point when the Presidium of the Supreme Soviet declared that the transfer of the contested land was "contrary to the interests of the Azerbaijani and Armenian population of the republic." Yerevan was again rocked by massive rallies in early September. Calling *glasnost* a fraud, demonstrators denounced Gorbachev; Armenian leaders, under the banner of a new Armenian National Front, redoubled their efforts to unite Nagorno-Karabakh with Armenia. In November, demonstrations and rioting erupted again in both Armenia and Azerbaijan, and the crisis atmosphere in the Caucasus continued. When fighting broke out in Azerbaijan in 1990, Gorbachev sent Soviet troops to restore order. Many casualties were reported by both sides.

The Caucasus was not the only region where nationalism posed a problem. In the summer of 1988, demonstrations rocked the Baltic states when thousands of Latvians marched in Riga, the capital, to mark the anniversary of mass deportations from Latvia under Stalin. The chief Soviet press agency, Tass, reported the march and noted that a monument to the deportees would be built. (In the past, Soviet authorities had forbidden exhibitions of Latvian nationalism.)

Late in June Latvian leaders representing the local Writers' Union and other official bodies issued a proclamation calling for "a sovereign state" within the Soviet Union. The proclamation also asked that Latvia be allowed to have separate representation at the United Nations and the Olympic Games and that it be permitted to control its own press, set its own foreign travel policy, establish links with Latvians abroad, and reduce the intrusive presence of the military and secret police. Asserting that Latvians were threatened with becoming "a minority within their ethnographic borders," the statement urged that Lettish be made the primary language and asked that local authorities be allowed to limit the influx of Russians (who make up about 33 percent of Latvia's population; about 54 percent is Latvian).

In Estonia, authorities set a precedent by permitting creation of the first large-scale political group outside the Communist party. The new organization, the People's Front of Estonia, was reported to have 40,000 members within two months. Its platform combined support for Gorbachev's reforms with calls for greater political and economic independence for Estonia.

In late August 1988, mass demonstrations in the capitals of all three Baltic republics marked the anniversary (August 23) of the infamous 1939 Nazi-Soviet pact—the dark symbol of the Baltic states' subjugation. Some of the marchers demanded independence from Moscow, and speakers repudiated the Soviet version of history, which claims that the Baltic states joined the Soviet Union of their own free will in 1940. In Vilnius, the capital of Lithuania, no fewer than 100,000 people (roughly one-sixth of the city's population) turned out. In keeping with the new norms of *glasnost*, Soviet authorities granted permits for the rallies—a precedent-setting show of solicitude in a region where Moscow has long been particularly vigilant against nationalist yearnings.

Authorities made the greatest concessions yet to nationalism in Estonia, whose press for the first time was allowed to publish the secret protocols of the Nazi-Soviet deal. These protocols, which Moscow had always refused to acknowledge, raise obvious questions about the (preposterous) Soviet claim that the Baltic states entered the "union" freely. Other concessions, both symbolic and substantive, were also made. Estonia's Communist party agreed to legalize the national colors of the Estonian flag (an emotionally charged issue) and to switch to Estonian time (one hour later than Moscow). The party also agreed to consider demands that Estonian, rather than Russian, become the official language and that the republic establish a separate and distinct citizenship (Estonians make up 65 percent of the population).

Estonian nationalists also managed to get Moscow to endorse an extraordinary plan for the republic's economic autonomy. The plan called for cutting Estonia's links to the central ministries in Moscow and instituting market reforms in industry and agriculture. Given that only 10 percent of Estonia's industry is under local control, the plan adds a regional wrinkle to *perestroika* and has enormous implications for a multinational society like the Soviet Union.

The most dramatic challenge to Soviet authority in the Baltic states came in mid-November 1988, when the Estonian parliament unanimously rejected Gorbachev's proposed changes in the Soviet Constitution, claiming these "reforms" would further restrict the rights of republics. Instead, the Estonian chamber voted to amend the Estonian Constitution, allowing the republic to exempt itself from Soviet legislation. This seemed to put Estonia on a collision course with the Kremlin, which at the same time dispatched three high-level emissaries to the Baltic states to warn against rebellion. The Supreme Soviet lost little time in declaring the Estonian action unconstitutional, but Gorbachev conceded that certain unspecified changes in his proposed constitutional amendments were in order.[42]

In nearby Lithuania, developments were hardly more reassuring to Moscow. Nonetheless, the Lithuanian Reform Movement was allowed to hold a national convention in late October. Boasting a membership of 180,000 in grass-roots organizations, the movement (known locally as *Sajudis*) was nearly as large as the Lithuanian Communist party. The October meeting produced demands for sweeping reforms aimed at national autonomy and democratization.[43] However, Latvia and Lithuania backed away from confrontation in November, when their leaders decided not to follow Estonia's lead.

The Baltic states increasingly demanded independence from Moscow. In August 1989 Estonia passed legislation setting residency requirements of two years for voting and five years for holding local elective office—legislation that was transparently anti-Russian. Later that month Lithuania declared the 1940 Soviet annexation of Lithuania and its status as a republic illegal. The Baltic nations staged huge demonstrations throughout the fall; at one point as many as 1 million people formed a human chain 400 miles long, stretching from Estonia's capital (Tallinn) through Latvia's (Riga) to Lithuania's (Vilnius).

In December 1989 the Lithuanian Supreme Soviet raised the ante by voting overwhelmingly to abolish the Communist party monopoly and to legalize opposition parties. Next, the Lithuanian Communist party declared itself independent of party leadership in Moscow. Finally, the head of the Lithuanian Communist party, Algirdas Brazauskas, called for ''an independent democratic Lithuanian state.'' Gorbachev viewed this with ''alarm'' and warned that it would ''sow discord, bloodshed, and death.'' The crisis turned into confrontation in the early months of 1990, when Lithuania formally declared its independence (and Estonia followed suit).

In response to the Lithuanian declaration, Gorbachev imposed economic sanctions, including an embargo on oil and electric power. In addition, the Soviet army was put on display in the streets of Vilnius to remind Lithuanians that Moscow could crush the independence movement at any time.

Lithuania appealed to world public opinion for support but got little in return except rhetorical assurances. Realizing that the United States would not jeopardize its relationship with Gorbachev, the Lithuanians withdrew their formal declaration of independence later in 1990 and began to negotiate with Moscow. The immediate crisis had passed without force having been used.

Did Gorbachev's handling of the nationalities problem pass the *glasnost* test? Yes and no. That these protests were permitted, that no police repression was reported, and that the Soviet press was allowed to publish stories about the rallies are departures from how the Soviet government formerly dealt with such problems. Nonetheless, foreign journalists are still banned from troubled areas. Apparently, *glasnost* still does not mean that the Soviet press will be allowed (much less encouraged) to tell the whole truth and nothing but the truth in every case. But the slogan on the masthead of the *New York Times*—''All the news that's fit to print''—is now a realistic goal of publishers in the USSR.

A Resurgent Russia?

Ironically, ethnic nationalism has been sustained and perhaps even strengthened by heavy-handed Soviet policies aimed at ''Russianization'' and ''Russification'' of the various nationality groups. These twin policies have sought to extend the Russian language and culture throughout the Soviet empire. Not surprisingly they have been met with almost universal resentment and resistance, although public discussion of the nationality question has, until recently, been taboo.

All other pools of ethnic nationalism, however, pale in comparison with the resurgence of Great Russian nationalism. Many observers agree that the most likely upshot of *glasnost* will be an outpouring of old-fashioned "blood and soil" nationalism, rather than any groundswell in favor of Western-style liberalism.[44]

A nineteenth-century Slavophile poet, Fyodr Tyutchev, wrote:

> Not by the mind can Russian be understood,
> Nor measured by the common yardstick.
> She has a special character.
> One must simply believe in Russia.

This elemental, mystical, maudlin, and, above all, unreasoning love of the Motherland (*rodina*) is something few Russians, including the most disillusioned and "anti-Soviet," can escape. It is the most pervasive and potentially powerful cultural force in Russian (and Soviet) society. If it could be harnessed in the cause of *perestroika* as it was harnessed in the Great Patriotic War (against Nazi Germany), Russian nationalism might propel Soviet society into a new era of prosperity. But is seems more likely that it will work in the opposite direction, because it looks to the past rather than to the future; it emphasizes spiritual rather than material values, and it disdains technology as much as it reveres tradition.

If *perestroika* produces results, it seems likely that Moscow and the Russian heartland will benefit disproportionately, leading to even greater regional disparities in living standards. In this event, the resentments of minority nationalities may reach the boiling point. Undoubtedly, any uprising would be forcibly put down. A crackdown anywhere would have chilling effects everywhere and might strengthen the hard-liners who have been skeptical of reform all along.

Glasnost and Eastern Europe

Gorbachev's reforms could have been shipwrecked in Poland, Hungary, or Czechoslovakia, as well as in places like Armenia and Estonia. Nationalism remains a powerful force throughout Eastern Europe, as is anti-Russian and anti-Soviet sentiment.

Along with Roman Catholicism, anti-Soviet sentiment has been a unifying element in Poland, where a spirit of rebellion led to sporadic demonstrations, strikes, and demands for expanded rights even before the wave of protest movements rippled across the region in 1989. In August of 1988, Solidarity resurfaced as a broad-based popular movement demanding satisfaction on bread-and-butter issues and wrapping its demands in a call for "talks" with the government. Talks did take place in fact, with Lech Walesa, the personification of Solidarity, in his familiar role as the Polish workers' point man. Again, Walesa took charge; again, the Jaruzelski government felt impelled to negotiate with him.

But there were differences between the 1988 revolt and the revolt that occurred in 1980–1981. This time Polish workers did not all strike (nor did all strikers go back to work immediately when Walesa urged it). There were no large street demonstrations, no major confrontations between workers and government security forces. Police and soldiers reciprocated the workers' own restraint. Finally, backstage talks began before the crisis got out of control.[45] Like the situation in Armenia, however, the Polish unrest continued to simmer, the problems that caused it remained unresolved, and the crisis of confidence in the Jaruzelski government continued.

Significantly, Gorbachev's visit to Poland in July 1988 may have been instrumental in rekindling the rebellion among Polish workers. The Soviet leader's deafening silence on the issue of Solidarity was profoundly disappointing to many Poles; like others elsewhere in Eastern Europe, they had come to expect that they too would benefit from Gorbachev's much-touted commitment to democratization, as well as from *perestroika* and *glasnost*. In the words of Solidarity leader Konrad Bielinski, ''Gorbachev's visit dissipated our illusions.'' According to one view, Gorbachev needs Solidarity as much as Solidarity needs Gorbachev, because only Solidarity can get the Polish workers to accept the sacrifices associated with *perestroika*.[46]

As noted earlier, Poland's prime minister, Zbigniew Messner, faced a vote of ''no confidence'' in the *Sejm* and resigned in mid-September 1989. Although it was an unprecedented event in any Soviet-bloc country, the vote did not jeopardize General Jaruzelski's personal power. It did, however, underscore an important fact: Sooner or later, a stalemate between a popular movement that demands the right to be recognized in law and an unpopular government that views any ''free union'' as a threat to the Communist party's leading role must be broken.

Nor was Poland the only troubled state in the region on the eve of the 1989 deluge. In Hungary, several hundred coal miners went on strike in the fall of 1988—an action with symbolism far greater than its political or economic impact. This was the first independent strike in Hungary since the uprising in 1956.[47] Indeed, Hungary was poised to leap ahead of Moscow in the realm of political reform. Karoly Grosz, a Communist party leader who represented a new generation of reform-minded leaders, replaced the aging Janos Kadar (who had picked up the pieces after the Soviet invasion in 1956).

Another of Hungary's new leaders was Imre Pozsgay, who epitomized Eastern Europe's emerging model of pluralistic communism. Pozsgay outspokenly supported an independent press and the right of ''free association'' (freedom to organize for political and social action, including independent trade unions like Solidarity in Poland). Removed from top leadership in the summer of 1987, Pozsgay was reelected to the Politburo in May of 1988. In the belief that Hungary's ''economic stagnation is not economic in nature as much as social and political,'' he advocated political pluralism, insisting that ''our country must provide for emergence of interest groups, groups which have autonomy.'' Pozsgay was the first Communist leader in Eastern Europe to talk openly of a time when Hungary would ''no longer . . . have one alternative in political life.''[48]

Even in Czechoslovakia, a bastion of repressive neo-Stalinist rule, a taboo-breaking event occurred in the fall of 1988. Some 10,000 demonstrators in Prague marked the August 20 anniversary of the Soviet-sponsored Warsaw Pact invasion, which crushed the ''Prague Spring'' and ushered in two more decades of neo-Stalinist rule. Fraught with symbolism, this rally was the boldest act of public defiance in Czechoslovakia since the Soviet intervention. Unlike Hungary, though, Czechoslovakia had no rising young stars waiting to challenge the rigid rule of Milos Jakes. The likelihood that popular pressures would build and lead eventually to a showdown, as has happened so often in Poland, loomed larger as the gap between expectations and actual conditions grew wider.

In East Germany the Honecker government held firm against any liberalization until the fall of 1989. Bulgaria and Romania also resisted change. The situation was especially deplorable in Romania, under President Nicolae Ceausescu's Stalinist regime. In early 1988 demonstrations in the Soviet Union and Eastern Europe on behalf of persecuted Romanian dissidents marked the first ''coordinated'' human-rights action in Soviet-bloc history.

Despite this checkered pattern, the spirit of *glasnost* was spreading across Eastern Europe, and unofficial or ''nonformal'' political groups sprang up in profusion—especially in Poland, Hungary, and Czechoslovakia. Many of these groups focused on specific issues like pollution, feminism, and the environment; others stressed nationalism. In Hungary the independent Democratic Forum called attention to the persecution of over 2 million Hungarians living in Romania. In Czechoslovakia a group called Democratic Initiative revived the memory of Thomas Masaryk, the nation's founder and first democratic president. And in Poland an ardent defender of independence, Josef Pilsudski, became a cult figure.

Thus Eastern Europe posed a dilemma for Gorbachev. He could not encourage reforms without jeopardizing party rule (and with it Moscow's dominant position in the region). He could not relax the party's grip without risking instability and even rebellion. He could not advance economic and political reforms without opening the floodgates of nationalism. Finally, he could not continue to speak with moral authority about the ''new thinking'' needed to revitalize the Soviet Union while remaining silent on the need for similar reforms in Eastern Europe.

Except in Hungary, there was a notable lack of enthusiasm for Gorbachev's reforms. One possible explanation is that East European leaders decided to take a prudent, wait-and-see attitude. Why jump on the bandwagon until it was clear whether Gorbachev could avoid the fate of Khrushchev, who was ousted in part for attempting to reform the system?

It is not surprising that Communist leaders in Eastern Europe were reluctant to begin a process that might start a chain reaction of political and social change. Indeed, Gorbachev's restraint in not foisting *perestroika* on Eastern Europe may have reflected the same concern. He was also mindful of the repercussions that Khrushchev's ''secret speech'' had had at the Twentieth Party Congress in Hungary (1956); of the episodes of political instability in East Germany (1953), Czechoslovakia (1968), and Poland (1980–1981); and of the likely fate of any Soviet leader who is responsible for the disintegration of the Eastern Europe alliance.

This was the state of affairs in Eastern Europe on the eve of the cataclysmic events of 1989. As we have seen, the Communists bowed out quietly in Poland

and Hungary, while the end of Communist rule in East Germany and Czechoslovakia was more turbulent. And if change in Romania turned ugly and violent, all in all the instability associated with such momentous events was minimal. Dire predictions of chaos and war turned out to be overblown, at least in the short run.

Nonetheless, the risks and dangers of reversing the Communist revolution in the Soviet Union and Eastern Europe should not be dismissed lightly. Nor can we discount the limits of reform in a region that has never known the kind of freedom which flourishes in the West.

The Limits of Reform

Economist Milton Friedman has observed, "History suggests only that capitalism is a necessary condition for political freedom. Clearly it is not a sufficient condition." Pointing to Italy, Spain, Germany, and Japan between the two world wars (and Russia before the October Revolution), Friedman said, "It is therefore clearly possible to have economic arrangements that are fundamentally capitalist and political arrangements that are not free."[49]

Lenin proclaimed the need for "creative" interpretations of Marx's writings, and Khrushchev long ago stripped the mystique from the memory of Stalin (just as the Chinese leadership has demystified Mao). In retrospect it seems inevitable that, to move beyond half-hearted market reforms, the Soviet Union must reinterpret Leninism much as Lenin reinterpreted Marxism. In particular, the USSR must overcome Lenin's aversion to "bourgeois democracy," a process that is under way.

Democratization in the nations under Communist rule came suddenly, in a revolution or a counterrevolution. Yugoslavia—long a pariah in the Communist world—is the only East European country where limited freedoms have been granted gradually, and despite continuing Communist domination, it is a relatively open state and society. Foreign travel and freedom of movement are largely unrestricted—many Yugoslavs became *Gastarbeiter* (guest workers) in West Germany during the 1970s. Moreover, foreign journalists can get entry visas in minutes (rather than weeks to gain entry to, say, Czechoslovakia or Poland). Cultural controls on free speech and on academic and artistic expression are considerably less oppressive in Yugoslavia than in any other Eastern European nation. When six dissidents were arrested in Belgrade several years ago "for defaming the state," critical articles appeared in the Western press, and the dissidents were released.

In contrast, although Hungary's Kadar regime allowed plural candidatures in elections for the first time in 1985 and bookshops in Budapest were no longer filled with "agitrop trash," the Hungarian government suppressed open dissent with an iron hand until 1989. Likewise, despite several popular uprisings in Poland since 1956, the Jaruzelski regime crushed Lech Walesa's Solidarity movement in 1981 and stifled opposition before 1989. Elsewhere in Eastern Europe, democratization did not recover from the setback that Moscow dealt it by invading Czechoslovakia in 1968—not, that is, until the great revolt against communism in 1989.

It is too early to tell whether democratization will create viable representative governments, just as it is uncertain how pluralism will work, but Eastern Europe cannot afford the ''luxury'' of weak governments at present.

CONCLUSION

The steady decline of the Soviet economy indirectly precipitated the downfall of Communist regimes in Eastern Europe and created the danger of political and social upheaval throughout Moscow's multinational inner empire as well. Will the USSR still be intact in the year 2000? Will Eastern Europe move into a new era of peace and prosperity? The answers to these questions will have major consequences not only for the region but for Europe as a whole.

STUDY QUESTIONS

1. What is the essence of *perestroika*, and how successful has it been so far? What obstacles stand in the way of radical economic reform in the USSR? Are the Soviet people in favor of *perestroika*? Why or why not?
2. Besides *perestroika*, what are the other two major elements of Gorbachev's reform strategy? Are these policies compatible or contradictory? Did Gorbachev open a Pandora's box that unleashes chaos, or does the Soviet Union seem to have a master plan?
3. What is the relationship between Gorbachev's reforms and the revolutions of 1989 in Eastern Europe? Why did Gorbachev let Moscow's ''satellite empire'' disintegrate? Is the end of communism in Eastern Europe entirely good for the West? If not, why not?
4. What are the most urgent problems facing the new popularly elected governments of Eastern Europe? What are the prospects for economic revival in the short run, and what dangers do you see if living standards are not improved soon in Poland, Czechoslovakia, Hungary, and Romania?

SUGGESTED READINGS

Abel, Aganbegyan. *The Economic Challenge of Perestroika.* Bloomington, Ind.: Indiana University, 1988.

Bialer, Seweryn, ed. *Politics, Society, and Nationality Inside Gorbachev's Russia.* Boulder, Colo.: Westview, 1988.

Brzezinski, Zbigniew K. *The Grand Failure: The Birth and Death of Communism in the Twentieth Century.* New York: Scribners, 1988.

Goldman, Marshall. *Gorbachev's Challenge: Economic Reform in the Age of High Technology.* New York: Norton, 1987.

Hough, Jerry F. *Opening Up the Soviet Economy.* Washington, D.C.: Brookings, 1988.

Rothschild, Joseph. *Return to Diversity: A Political History of East Central Europe since World War II*. New York: Oxford, 1989.

Tismaneanu, Vladimir. *The Crisis of Marxist Ideology in Eastern Europe*. New York: Routledge, 1988.

NOTES

[1] Heidi Toffler and Alvin Toffler, "Society on the Move Has Far to Go," *Christian Science Monitor*, Jan. 6, 1987, pp. 1, 6.

[2] Dan Fisher, "*Glasnost*—Soviets Try to Open Up," *Los Angeles Times*, Oct. 29, 1987.

[3] Dan Fisher and William J. Eaton, "Rumbles of Change Stir Soviet Union," *Los Angeles Times*, Oct. 25, 1987.

[4] Ibid.

[5] See Alec Nove, *Was Stalin Really Necessary?* (London: Allen & Unwin, 1964); and *An Economic History of the USSR* (London: Allen & Unwin, 1969).

[6] Stanley Rothman and George W. Breslauer, *Soviet Politics and Society* (St. Paul, Minn.: West, 1978), p. 242; for a general discussion, see E. G. Liberman, *Economic Methods and Effectiveness of Production* (White Plains, N.Y.: International Arts and Sciences Press, 1971).

[7] Rothman and Breslauer, op. cit., pp. 213–244.

[8] Robert Gillete, "Perestroika: Bold Shift in Economy," *Los Angeles Times*, Oct. 27, 1987.

[9] Ibid.

[10] Harry G. Shaffer, "Economic Performance Under the Plan: The Soviet Union and East Europe," *Revue de l'Est* (Paris, 1972); excerpted in *The Soviet Crucible: The Soviet System in Theory and Practice*, ed. Samuel Hendel (Belmont, Calif.: Duxbury, 1973), pp. 271–277.

[11] William U. Chandler, "The Changing Role of the Market in National Economics" (Washington, D.C.: Worldwatch Institute, September 1986).

[12] Ibid.

[13] See Bogdan Denitch, "The Relevance of Yugoslav Self-Management," in *Comparative Communism: The Soviet, Chinese and Yugoslav Models*, eds. Gary K. Bertsch and Thomas W. Ganschow (New York: Freeman, 1976), pp. 268–279.

[14] April Carter, *Democratic Reform in Yugoslavia: The Changing Role of the Party* (Princeton, N.J.: Princeton University, 1982), p. 5.

[15] Wayne S. Vucinich, "Major Trends in Eastern Europe," in *Eastern Europe in the 1980's*, ed. Stephen Fischer-Galati (Boulder, Colo.: Westview, 1981), p. 5.

[16] See Darko Bekic, "Yugoslavia's System in Crisis: Internal View," *Problems of Communism* (November–December 1985), pp. 70–76; and William Echikson, "Soviet-Style Reform: First Step Is the Hardest," *Christian Science Monitor*, Dec. 17, 1987, p. 1.

[17] Bekic, op. cit., p. 71.

[18] Jackson Diehl, "Yugoslavia's New Leader Has Yet to Take Hold," *Washington Post*, Dec. 8, 1986, p. A17.

[19] Quoted in William Echikson, "Top Dissident Now Free to Go Abroad: Yugoslavia 'Faces a Choice'," *Christian Science Monitor*, Jan. 22, 1987, p. 12.

[20] Elizabeth Pond, "The Irony of East Germany's Relative Economic Prosperity," *Christian Science Monitor*, Jan. 2, 1987, p. 11.

21 Eric Bourne, "Thirty Years Later Hungary Still Yearns for Reform," *Christian Science Monitor*, Oct. 30, 1986, p. 9.

22 Rudolf C. Tokes, "Hungarian Reform Imperatives," *Problems of Communism*, September–October 1984, p. 2.

23 Ibid., p. 4.

24 Quoted in William Echikson, "Soviet-Style Reform," op. cit., p. 1.

25 *The Economist*, Mar. 24, 1990, pp. 21–22.

26 William Echikson, "Soviet-Style Reform," op. cit., p. 1.

27 Eric Bourne, "Gorbachev's Reforms: Old Hat, and Good News, for E. Europe," *Christian Science Monitor*, Dec. 29, 1986, p. 7.

28 Serge Schmemann, "Soviet to Codify Gorbachev's Social Changes," *New York Times*, Oct. 7, 1986, p. 21.

29 "Soviets Give OK to Moonlighting for Extra Cash," Associated Press, *Omaha World-Herald*, Nov. 20, 1986, p. 4.

30 Mark D'Anastasio, "Soviets Declare the Bankruptcy of a State Firm," *Wall Street Journal*, Mar. 27, 1987, p. 11.

31 "American Touts Trade with Soviets," Associated Press, *Omaha World-Herald*, Dec. 30, 1986, p. 2.

32 Bourne, "Gorbachev's Reforms," op. cit.

33 Institute of USA–Canada Studies, 1989.

34 Dan Fisher and William J. Eaton, "Rumbles of Change Stir Soviet Union," *Los Angeles Times*, Oct. 25, 1987.

35 Ibid.

36 For a discussion of the Moscow Jewish Association and Press Club Glasnost, see Alex Goldfarb, "Testing Glasnost: An Exile Visits His Homeland," *New York Times*, magazine, Dec. 6, 1987, p. 47.

37 On this point see Hedrick Smith, *The Russians*, (New York: Ballantine, 1976), pp. 320–362; and David Shipler, *Russia* (New York: Penguin, 1983), pp. 301–346.

38 Ibid., p. 326.

39 Goldfarb, "Testing Glasnost," op. cit., p. 49.

40 Quoted in Shipler, op. cit., p. 324.

41 Quoted in Dan Fisher and William J. Eaton, "Rumbles of Change Stir Soviet Union," *Los Angeles Times*, Oct. 25, 1987.

42 Paul Quinn-Judge, "Gorbachev Tactics Backfire in Baltics," *Christian Science Monitor*, Nov. 29, 1988, p. 1.

43 Philip Taubman, "Moscow's Baltic Thorn," *New York Times*, Oct. 25, 1988, p. 1.

44 See, for example, Shipler, op. cit., pp. 323–346; and Smith, op. cit., pp. 557–586.

45 Joseph C. Harsch, "The Polish Story," *Christian Science Monitor*, Aug. 30, 1988, p. 12; see also William Echikson, "Whither Poland's Independent Trade Union . . . Eight Years Later," *Christian Science Monitor*, Sept. 2, 1988, p. 9.

46 William Echikson, "Bubble, Bubble, Toil and Trouble in Eastern Europe," *Christian Science Monitor*, Aug. 26, 1988, p. 9.

47 William Echikson, "East Europeans Break Political Taboos," *Christian Science Monitor*, Sept. 12, 1988, p. 1.

48 William Echikson, "Outspoken Hungarian Communist Calls for Radical Reform," *Christian Science Monitor*, Oct. 13, 1987, p. 14; and William Echikson, "Winds of Change Pick Up Speed in Hungary," *Christian Science Monitor*, Nov. 28, 1988, p. 9.

49 Milton Friedman, *Capitalism and Freedom* (Chicago: University of Chicago Press, 1962), p. 10.

ISRAEL

Area: 8,020 square miles
Population: 4.5 million
Density per square mile: 559
Languages: Hebrew, Arabic, English
Literacy rate: 92%
Religions: Jewish (82%), Muslim (14%), Christian (2.3%), Druze and others (1.7%)
Monetary unit: shekel
GNP: (1988) $36 billion; $8,400 per capita

EGYPT

Area: 386,900 square miles
Population: 54.7 million
Density per square mile: 142
Language: Arabic (English and French, often understood)
Literacy rate: 43%
Religions: Muslim (94%; mostly Sunni), Coptic Christian and others (6%)
Monetary unit: Egyptian pound
GNP: (1987) $34 billion; $655 per capita

SAUDI ARABIA

Area: 865,000 square miles
Population: 16 million
Density per square mile: 18
Language: Arabic
Literacy rate: 52%
Religion: Muslim
Monetary unit: riyal
GNP: (1988) $74 billion; $5,480 per capita

IRAN

Area: 636,293 square miles
Population: 53 million
Density per square mile: 85
Languages: Farsi (Persian), Kurdish, Arabic
Literacy rate: 48%
Religions: Shiite Muslim (93%), Sunni Muslim (5%)
Monetary unit: rial
GNP: (1987) $86 billion; $1,756 per capita

LEBANON

Area: 4,015 square miles
Population: 3.3 million
Density per square mile: 822
Languages: Arabic, French, English
Literacy rate: 75%
Religions: Muslim (75%; 5 sects), Christian (25%; 21 sects)
Monetary unit: Lebanese pound
GNP: (1985) $1.8 billion

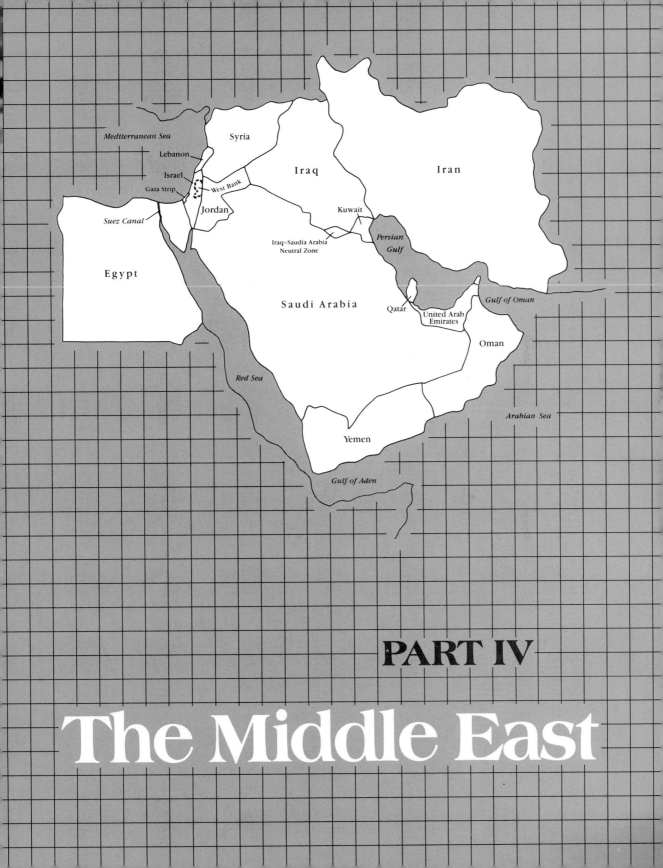

PART IV

The Middle East

Chapter 10
The Imprint of Religion

In the mass media and in diplomatic parlance, the Middle East is also called both the "Near East" and the "Arab world." The three names are used interchangeably to identify a region where even the boundaries defy precise definition, depending on one's vantage point. Generally, however, the Middle East encompasses all the Arabic-speaking countries—Morocco, Algeria, Tunisia, Libya, Sudan, and Egypt in North Africa; Jordan, Lebanon, Syria, Iraq, Saudi Arabia, Yemen, and Djibouti at the eastern end of the Mediterranean Sea; and Kuwait, Bahrain, Qatar, the United Arab Emirates, and Oman on the Persian Gulf. The only non-Arab nations in this region are Iran, Turkey, Afghanistan, and Israel (where, it must be noted, Palestinian Arabs make up approximately 15 percent of the population).

Like other regions, the Middle East can be subdivided in several ways. For example, the countries of North Africa—Morocco, Algeria, Tunisia, Libya, Sudan, and Egypt—can be grouped into a subregion known as the *Maghreb*. Israel, Lebanon, Jordan, Syria, Iraq, Saudi Arabia, Yemen, and the Persian Gulf ministates are often referred to as the *Near East*. And Turkey, Iran, and Afghanistan are sometimes called the *Northern Belt* (or *Northern Tier*).

North Africa is separated from the rest of the continent by the vast Sahara Desert, and the Near East is separated from North Africa by the Persian Gulf and the Mediterranean. A language barrier separates the Arabic-speaking Near Eastern states from the Northern Belt (Turkish is spoken in Turkey, Farsi in Iran, and Pushtun in Afghanistan).

Turkey and Iran constitute a buffer zone separating and protecting the Near East from the Soviet Union. Seen from this perspective, the Near East can be subdivided into the Fertile Crescent (which includes Egypt along with Iraq, Syria, Lebanon, Israel, and Jordan) and the Red Sea region (also known as Arabia or the Arabian Peninsula).

The "Arab core" of the Fertile Crescent has 80 to 85 million people who share a political culture based on religion (most are Sunni Muslims), language (Arabic), and memories of colonial rule. Regardless of their common heritage, however, conflict has been as prominent a feature of their relations as cooperation.

The Red Sea region—that vast, arid expanse of the Arabian Peninsula—is very thinly populated but contains the world's largest oil reserves. Saudi Arabia occupies most of the peninsula; its neighbors are tiny sheikdoms that, like Saudi Arabia, depend on oil exports for their livelihood. The surrounding waters and the forbidding desert isolate Saudi society from the world—even from the Arab

233

world. Consequently, the Saudi monarchy has not been influenced by regular contact with Europe, and it was never effectively colonized.

Egypt, one of the cradles of civilization, is sustained by the world's longest river, the Nile. Among its many natural assets are the lush delta of the Nile, where three crops a year are produced; an abundant supply of water, until recently; and a propitious location astride a great commercial route. On the negative side, Cairo's 12.5 million people make it one of the most overcrowded cities in the world, and Egypt is the only Arab country in which the population explosion has become a pressing problem. Yet, even with its grinding poverty, Egypt is the most economically advanced country in the Arab World.

Geostrategic Considerations

The term *Middle East* is appropriate insofar as the area it describes is located at the crossroads of Europe, Africa, and Asia. The strategic importance of the region results partly from its proximity to international waterways and "chokepoints" such as the Turkish Straits and the Suez Canal. During the nineteenth century, "the Near Eastern question . . . was essentially a rivalry on the part of the big powers for control of the Turkish Straits until the Isthmus of Suez was pierced by a canal in the latter part of the century."[1] Furthermore:

> Since time immemorial the Turkish Straits have been a vital trade route between the Black Sea shores and the Mediterranean. The prosperity of many a Mediterranean state, such as Genoa or Greece, has been largely dependent upon its ability to trade with the Black Sea hinterland. And, conversely, the Straits have played an increasingly important role in the foreign trade of Russia ever since the latter obtained an outlet to the Black Sea. The commercial significance of the opening of the Suez Canal, which replaced the old Cape route, is so obvious that it does not require elaboration.[2]

The military importance of the Middle East's waterways was amply demonstrated in World War II. Germany and Italy launched various offensives toward Egypt in an effort to seize the Suez Canal; the British, in turn, tenaciously defended the canal. Meanwhile, Allied efforts to get arms and equipment to the Soviet Union were hampered when Turkey closed the straits. Even in peacetime, "control of these waterways may prove decisive so far as the political independence of Turkey and the diplomatic alignment of Egypt are concerned."[3]

Outside powers have long cast a covetous eye on the Middle East. As dominant naval forces in different eras, Great Britain and the United States have both sought preeminence in the region and intense rivalry developed there after World War II between the United States and the Soviet Union. The USSR made inroads in the 1950s and 1960s, especially in Algeria, Egypt, and Syria. Soviet influence declined dramatically in the 1970s, but it has been partly restored recently by the statesmanship of Mikhail Gorbachev. Both superpowers have tried to secure a strategic grip on the eastern Mediterranean, seeking access to the Suez

Canal and Middle East oil. Up to 90 percent of the oil used in Western Europe and Japan comes from the Middle East, while the Soviet Union has its own vast reserves—a fact that has tipped the balance of interest toward the West.

Surrounded by the waters of the Mediterranean, the Red Sea, the Persian Gulf, and the Indian Ocean, much of the Middle East has been vulnerable. It is more accessible by sea than by land—another reason why the West, with its superior naval and merchant marine fleets, has been successful in gaining and keeping a foothold in the region.

Birthplace of Three Great Religions

Geography is not all that makes the Middle East so pivotal. This region is the cradle of three great monotheistic religious traditions: Islam, Judaism, and Christianity. As the center of the Islamic world—which comprises 825 to 850 million souls from Morocco to Malaysia, Indonesia (90 percent Muslim), and the Philippines—it claims the holiest places of Islam, above all Mecca in Saudi Arabia, the birthplace of the Muslim faith. The Dome of the Rock in Jerusalem, less well known in the West, is another of the three holiest Muslim shrines. Thus Muslims, as well as Christians and Jews, look upon Jerusalem as a "holy city."

The Muslim religion and the culture that grew up around it have permeated the entire Arab world, including the countries of the periphery—Turkey (98 percent Muslim) and Iran (90–95 percent Shia, a major Muslim sect). Although Islam has spread beyond the Middle East proper, it is first and foremost the religion of the Arabs:

> In many ways, the Arab world today is a religious empire. It encompasses eighteen countries and 4.6 million square miles, an area 25 percent larger than the United States. The largest country, Sudan, is more than three times the size of Texas; the smallest, Bahrain, would fit neatly inside the boundaries of New York City. Except for a small, aged generation of Jews and a relative handful of Christians . . . 94 percent of the people are Muslim.[4]

For the faithful, Islam is more than a religion; it is a way of life. Its writ (the Koran) includes "politics, law, social behavior, and is so exacting in detail that [it] even prescribes procedures for divorce, loans and wills."[5]

Two other major religious traditions, Judaism and Christianity, have their roots in the Middle East. Like Muslims, both groups consider Jerusalem the holiest of holy places, and both view Palestine (in which Israel is located) as the Holy Land. Palestine is the setting for the action in the Old Testament and encompasses biblical Judea and Sumaria (today the West Bank which Israel has occupied since its 1967 victory over Egypt and Syria). It is also the setting for the New Testament; Bethlehem, Nazareth, and Galilee, for example, are located in historical Palestine. Jews everywhere look to Israel as the embodiment of the long-awaited Zionist state, a refuge from political and religious persecution. Because Jews and Christians share the Old Testament, and because the West is steeped in the Judeo-Christian tradition, most Westerners can relate more easily to Judaism and Jews than to Islam and Arabs.

Ironically, religion has played a central role in the conflict of the Middle East. Arabs (especially Palestinians) and Jews have fought tooth and nail for control of the territory that both claim as their own. In truth, the conflict is about territory more than religion, but religious issues have inflamed passions on both sides. As we will see later, religion played an even more direct role in the Iranian Revolution and in the subsequent war between Iran and Iraq. The war pitted Arab against Persian, Shiite against Sunni (the two main branches of Islam).

Judaism and Christianity

Judaism and Christianity have common origins. Both are monotheistic, and both regard the books of the Old Testament (or at least some of them) as sacred texts. Judaism traces its origins to Abraham and then to Jacob, who took his sons (including Judah) to Egypt. According to legend and biblical history, Moses led the Hebrews out of Egypt and through the wilderness to the Promised Land (modern Israel). The religion of the Hebrews became monotheistic by the acceptance of Yahweh, the god of the patriarchs Abraham, Isaac, and Jacob, as the one true God. This monotheism was symbolized by a covenant between Yahweh and Abraham, confirmed by the rite of circumcision, and reiterated to Moses on Mount Sinai when the Decalogue (Ten Commandments) was handed down from on high, according to Jewish and Christian teachings.

The foundations of Judaism are contained in the Pentateuch (the first five books of the Old Testament) and in the Torah and the Talmud, which record the decisions and opinions of Jewish rabbis concerning civil and religious law. Far from forming a monolithic religious community, Jews divided into several groups, the two most prominent being Orthodox and Reform. Judaism has an elaborate set of rites and religious holidays that differ from those of Christianity, and its places of worship are called synagogues (not churches or cathedrals, as in Christianity, and not mosques, as in Islam).

Christianity is an offshoot of Judaism. It dates back nearly two thousand years to the birth of Christ, which has since become the great divide in world history, separating time into B.C. ("Before Christ") and A.D. (*anno Domini*, Latin for "in the year of our Lord"). In Christian teaching, Jesus Christ is the Son of God, born of a virgin, Mary, through a miracle known as the Immaculate Conception. The teachings of Jesus, such as the Sermon on the Mount, are recorded in the New Testament, written primarily by Jesus' Twelve Apostles.

Judaism and Christianity differ most sharply about whether Jesus was the Messiah (Savior). From that, many doctrinal differences follow. For example, Christians believe that Jesus died on the Cross to save humanity from eternal damnation (the doctrine of Original Sin and, hence, the idea of Jesus as Savior); for Jews, the Messiah is yet to come.

Oddly enough, the tensions between Christians and Jews have been most apparent in Europe. In the Middle East the religious differences that have led to extremism, zealotry, and terrorist violence have involved Zionism, on the one hand, and Islam, on the other.

Islam

Historically, in the Middle East more blood has been spilled between Christians and Muslims than between Muslims and Jews. The hostility seemed endless during the Crusades, three centuries of Christian expeditions to recover the Holy Land from the Muslims. Islam dates back to the seventh century A.D., when Muhammad, a merchant from Mecca in southwestern Arabia (now Saudi Arabia) received revelations from God through the Angel Gabriel, according to Muslim belief. Thus fortified, Muhammad founded Islam; his teachings are recorded in the sacred text of Islam, the Koran.

Muhammad's revelations were passed along to his followers over twenty-two years (A.D. 610–632) and constituted the way (*Sharia*, in Arabic). Muhammad taught belief in one God—Allah—and in the received Word of God. His own role was simply that of messenger; he was thus the Prophet of Islam.

Islam's five basic tenets, or Five Pillars, can be summarized as follows:

1. The confession of faith: "I testify that there is no God but God, and Muhammad is the Messenger of God."
2. Prayer (required five times daily) facing in the direction of Mecca, the holy city.
3. Fasting during the daylight hours in the month of Ramadan (the time of Muhammad's revelations).
4. Alms giving (at least $2^{1}/_{2}$ percent of one's income) to the community for relief of the poor.
5. A pilgramage to Mecca at least once in one's lifetime.

Muslims have much in common with Jews and Christians—belief in one God, in the power of prayer, and in an ethic of compassion. They believe that God revealed Himself to prophets before Muhammad, including Abraham and Moses. Muslims do not accept the divinity of Jesus, the Resurrection, or the Trinity. Islam, like Judaism, has strict dietary rules and relies on an authoritative body of religious scholarship to interpret divine law.

Muhammad was not only a religious figure but also a powerful political leader. Forced to flee Mecca in 622 (his escape is called the *Hegira*), he went to Medina and there established a power base from which he came to rule Arabia. Muhammad mixed politics and religion and even created a kind of theocracy—a pattern that can still be discerned in parts of the Middle East (most notably, in Iran).

Muslims consider Muhammad's life a model. His decisions and revelations constitute the *Sunna* ("Beaten Path"), which was not followed by all Muslims after Muhammad's death. Muhammad did not have an heir apparent. Although the majority of his followers favored an elective *caliph* ("successor"), some believed that Muhammad had meant for his cousin Ali, his closest male relative, ultimately to be a successor. This minority was adamant that only someone of the same bloodline could succeed Muhammad. In this sense they were purists, and so these *Shiite Muslims* originated as the "partisans" of Ali. (*Shia* in Arabic means "sectarian.") The majority are called Sunni Muslims.

Sunni Versus Shiite   The division between Sunni and Shiite Muslims is almost as old as Islam itself. About 90 percent of Muslims are Sunni; most of the rest are Shiite, and most of these are Iranian. The split in the seventh century was a bloody affair. Ali was eventually elected caliph, only to be murdered; one of his sons was poisoned; another was ambushed and killed on the orders of Ali's rival, who established his own dynastic rule. Through it all, the Shia Muslims, though outwardly obedient, never changed their beliefs.

Shia Muslims generally recognize a line of twelve direct descendants of Muhammad as their *imams* (spiritual leaders). Most Shiites believe the twelfth imam is hidden. They further believe he will return (or reveal himself) on the Day of Judgment. Until the "hidden imam" reappears, the religious leaders have the right and duty to interpret God's will and guide Shiite true believers in the Way. Thus, the Shiite tradition gives religious leaders like the late Ayatollah Khomeini more power over Shia Muslims than Sunni religious leaders have over Sunni Muslims.

To some degree the ferocity of the Iran-Iraq War (discussed later) reflected Islam's religious schism and the mutual enmity it has spawned. A majority of Iraqis (55 percent) are actually Shiite Muslims, but the Sunni minority (40 percent) are politically dominant. Saddam Hussein, Iraq's ruler, feared the spread of Khomeini-style Islamic revolutionary fervor within Iraq, and he believed that Khomeini was out to conquer Iraq for Islam (for Shia, that is). The two leaders loathed one another. This example demonstrates the difficulty of disentangling religious, political, and even personal factors in the conflicts that have rocked the Middle East since World War II.

Jihad and Islamic Fundamentalism   The concept of *jihad* is now well known to Westerners, who equate it with holy war and terrorism. One meaning of the word *is* "holy war," but it also can mean "sacred struggle" or simply personal "striving" to carry out God's will. In its violent form, jihad can be directed against external or internal enemies. The assassins of Anwar Sadat (the president of Egypt) claimed at their trial that they had acted out of religious principle, insisting that Egyptian laws were incompatible with Islamic law and that Sadat's 1979 peace treaty with Israel betrayed the Palestinians, whose cause is the cause of Muslims everywhere. Similarly, Muslim militants who seized the Great Mosque in Mecca in 1979 did so in the name of God—in their view, the secular Saudi monarchy was illegitimate and only halfheartedly Islamic.

Although the West has come to associate jihad primarily with the Shiites of Iran, Sunni Muslims also embrace the concept. For example, the Muslim Brotherhood is a militant Sunni secret society that seeks to establish a single Islamic state in place of the existing Arab regimes. The society has been especially active in Syria, where it is the main opposition to the Alawi Shia minority rule of President Hafez al-Assad. It has assassinated Alawi officials and has even seized an entire city (Homs) on one occasion.

The concept of jihad that lies at the root of some terrorist acts in the Middle East is the one that stresses individual striving to carry out God's will. For example, in July 1989, a Palestinian seized the steering wheel of a crowded bus in Israel and caused it to plunge into a ravine, killing or injuring civilians. Witnesses said that the terrorist shouted ''Allahu Akbar,'' the battle cry of the *intifada* (the Palestinian uprising in Israeli-occupied territories).

The Shia tradition emphasizes martyrdom, a trait that scholars trace back to the murder of Ali's son. As a result, some Shiite terrorist attacks have been carried out by individuals on ''suicide missions.'' Similar motives led Iranian children to walk through minefields ahead of soldiers in the Persian Gulf war: the Ayatollah Khomeini assured them that martyrdom in the jihad against Iraq would give them immediate entry into heaven.

The Challenges of Modernity   Many of the conflicts in the Middle East are rooted in religious and ethnic animosity, but the state of war that has characterized the politics of the region since the late 1940s is perpetuated by another, equally divisive issue: How should Arabs and Muslims respond to the challenges of modernity? Should they embrace Western ideas of individual rights and democracy? The secularized and bureaucratic state? Modern science and technology?

The different responses of various Arab leaders and ruling elites to some degree account for the grouping of Arab states as either moderate and ''traditional'' or radical and ''revolutionary.'' Thus, for example, Egypt under Nasser (1954–1970) clearly chose the radical course by following the path of Arab nationalism, non-Marxist socialism, and a secularism that denied any special role for Islam in political life. In contrast, the ruling dynasty of Saudi Arabia chose the traditional path of hereditary monarchy, fidelity to Islamic law, and rejection of Western modernization. Among the Arab states that followed the Egyptian model are Syria, Iraq, Algeria, and Libya. Jordan, Morocco, and the Persian Gulf sheikdoms have chosen the traditional path—all are moderate regimes that respect Islamic law, spurn association with revolutionary doctrines (whether Soviet-style communism or Khomeini-style fundamentalism), and show little enthusiasm for an Arab superstate.

Iran illustrates the fury generated by these alternative responses to the West. Its modernizing elite led by Muhammad Reza Shah Pahlavi (1941–1979) hastened the pace of change and borrowed unashamedly from the West. The Shah accepted massive military aid and economic investment from the West (especially from America), attempted to change Iranian society along Western lines, reduced the role of the imams, and vigorously pursued a pro-West foreign policy. Reaction came in 1979, when the exiled Ayatollah Khomeini led an uprising and toppled the Shah's regime, forcing him to flee Iran. He left a power vacuum that was filled quickly by devoted followers of the Ayatollah. Their revolutionary government arrested opponents (many of whom were executed) and imposed a regime that strictly observed Islamic law. Iran then became embroiled in the bloody war with Iraq, which raged throughout the 1980s. Perhaps more than any country in the Middle East, Iran epitomizes the conflicts posed by Western intrusion into Arab-Islamic societies.

A Brief History of the Middle East

Relatively little is known about the prehistoric origins of the Middle East and the people who inhabited it. David Lamb has noted:

> Some anthropologists say man himself originated in the Nile and the Tigris-Euphrates valleys. Others believe the first inhabitants of the Middle East were the black-skinned Nubians who emigrated northward up the Nile Valley and across the Red Sea. What seems most likely is that life evolved in different places at about the same time and that at some point the Arabian Peninsula—an area one third the size of Europe—became a junction of migrating populations. The nomads of the peninsula were to become known as Bedouin, a term Westerners incorrectly used for a long time as a synonym for Arab. Their society was based on the clan, a group of united families in which individual rights were subordinate to those of the majority, blood ties were through the male line, and story-telling provided the only entertainment for the adults and the primary source of education for the young.[6]

The Arab world's Golden Age dates back to the seventh century, when Muhammad founded Islam. (One of his successors was Ali, his cousin and son-in-law, who became the fourth caliph.) Subsequent caliphs conquered new territories and welded disparate tribes into a single state inspired by Islam. The tide of Arab conquests rolled over Iraq, Persia (Iran), Syria, Egypt, Cyprus, and North Africa during the seventh century. In 711 the Arabs surged into Spain, and in 717 they nearly seized Constantinople (now Istanbul, Turkey).

At its fullest extent the Arab Empire extended from the Pyrenees to India. In contrast to prejudiced stereotypes of Islam as a bloodthirsty, proselytizing creed, Arab rulers showed considerable religious tolerance and permitted conquered peoples to practice their own religions under certain civil arrangements. Arabs everywhere established themselves as the ruling aristocracy and absorbed the flourishing cultures of Persia, Syria, and Egypt. Arabic became the dominant language of a brilliant new culture.

The empire was doomed to be short-lived, for it expanded too fast and—like a meteor's spectacular display—soon burned itself out. The empire was torn apart by internal forces, especially sectionalism and schism, which are still apparent in the Arab world. One fundamental weakness was the lack of an accepted rule of succession to the caliphate. The Abbasid dynasty replaced the Umayyads in 750, and the seat of government was transferred from Damascus to Baghdad. By the ninth century the empire was no longer cohesive but a commonwealth of independent, often contentious states. Attacks from external enemies hastened its disintegration after the eleventh century.

In sum, the Arabs created a flourishing Islamic civilization that was concurrent with the Christian medieval period in Europe. Arabic culture made significant contributions to world literature, philosophy, historiography, art, and science, as well as to religious-law disputation.[7] The fact that today's Arabs and Muslims are aware of this former grandeur may help to explain Islamic resistance to the West.

The Ottoman Intrusion

The history of the Middle East before World War I was dominated by the Ottoman Empire and European colonialism. By the late fifteenth century the Black Sea had become a "Turkish lake," for the tentacles of the empire reached into three continents. Yet the Ottomans had to contend with "involvement of practically every great European power in its foreign and domestic affairs in the course of the last three hundred years."[8] Under Suleiman I, the Magnificent (1520–1566), the Ottoman Turks expanded their domain well into the Balkans, Armenia, and Mesopotamia. A formidable navy allowed Suleiman to conquer Aden and the southeastern coast of Arabia and to project his power into the Mediterranean and Adriatic seas, including North Africa. It was quite a performance:

> At the time of Suleiman's death the Ottoman Empire stretched from the Danube to the Persian Gulf and from the Ukrainian steppes to the Tropic of Cancer in upper Egypt. It included the mastery of the great trade routes of the Mediterranean, of the Black and Red seas, and of parts of the Indian Ocean. It had an estimated population of fifty million as against some four million in England and embraced some twenty races and nationalities.[9]

The Ottoman Empire declined following a failed attempt to defeat Austria and conquer Vienna in 1683. After that, Russia pushed southward toward the Near East, and the British established a toehold in Egypt. France, too, under Emperor Napoleon Bonaparte (1804–1815), made a play for the land of the Nile at the end of the eighteenth century, but without success.

European Colonialism

Imperialism characterized the second half of the nineteenth century, when the major powers of Europe scrambled for colonial territories in Africa and Asia. The Middle East was not spared. The French were interested in the region before the British were, mainly because France looked on the Ottoman Turks as natural allies against their arch-rival, Austria. But as imperial Russia encroached on the periphery of the Middle East in the second half of the eighteenth century, British interest in the region grew.

Napoleon's misadventure in Egypt drew British attention even more strongly. As the preeminent naval and trading power during the eighteenth and nineteenth centuries, Great Britain was anxious to control strategic waterways and chokepoints, including the Straits of Gibralter (Atlantic Ocean–Mediterranean Sea); the Turkish Straits (Aegean Sea–Black Sea); Isthmus of Suez (land bridge between the Near East and North Africa); Bab el-Mandeb (Red Sea–Indian Ocean); and the Straits of Hormuz (Indian Ocean–Persian Gulf). Furthermore, the waterways of the Middle East were the shortest route to India, the ''Jewel of the British Empire.'' It thus became ''an axiom of British foreign policy to uphold the independence and integrity of the Ottoman Empire, in order to prevent the undue strengthening of Russia and to protect the imperial life line.''[10]

Despite British goodwill the Ottoman Empire continued to decline during the nineteenth century, and Russia was the main beneficiary. Britain (allied with France) and Russia came to blows in the Crimean War (1854–1856), after Russia and France quarreled over control of holy sites in Palestine. The British won the war, with difficulty, and so Russian encroachment on the Ottoman Empire and the Middle East was stopped. For the next half-century Western imperialism eroded Ottoman rule in the Near East, until it finally displaced it after World War I.

The two main rivals for colonial control of the Middle East were Great Britain and France. The French were able to annex large territories in North Africa, directly across the Mediterranean from France's south coast, taking Algeria (1830), Tunisia (1883), and Morocco (1906–1912). France also had formal ties to the Levant (Syria and Lebanon). But the British gained the upper hand in Egypt and Palestine. Meanwhile, on the eve of World War I, Germany made inroads in the Porte (the seat of the decaying Ottoman Empire), and Italy managed to obtain control of Libya. Finally, Great Britain acted (against Russia) as the patron saint of Persian independence:

> Britain's Persian policy was dictated primarily by her concern for India, and Persia was to be an independent buffer state or neutral zone between the Indian and Russian empires. Britain sought unimpeded commercial opportunity in Persia, and to this extent she was interested in exercising moderate influence in the area.... It was, therefore, in her interest to see Persia relatively strong and capable of withstanding Russian pressure. It was largely due to this British policy that Persia succeeded in maintaining her independence instead of falling under Russian domination.[11]

An Arab Awakening?

No consideration of modern history in the Middle East can discount what some have called ''the Arab awakening.''[12] One reaction to foreign subjugation by both Ottomans and Europeans was the articulation of Arab nationalism. The rhetorical basis for Arab unity is rooted in this history, as is reaction to the establishment of

Israel (in which, to Arabs, the West was an accomplice); this history has led Arabs to adopt the Palestinian cause as their own.

Because Egypt is so prominent in the Middle East today and because its experience as a Western "dependent" somewhat typifies that of other Arab countries, it might serve as an example to help us link the legacy of foreign domination with the persistent urge to create a single Arab superstate. Consider that foreign domination of Egypt can be dated from at least the Persian conquest in 525 B.C. Then came the Greeks (Alexander the Great), the Romans, the Byzantines, and in the seventh century the Arabs, who introduced Islam and the Arabic language. Large numbers of nomadic Arabs settled in the Nile valley under the rule of the caliphs. In the tenth century a Shia group split with the Sunnis, and in the desert south of Alexandria, the ancient capital, they established a new capital, al-Qahira (literally, "City of War"—modern Cairo).

The Ottoman Turks annexed Egypt in the sixteenth century. The Ottoman overlords allowed the Mamluks, former Egyptian slaves or war prisoners who converted to Islam, to administer the area in return for occasional tribute and taxes. The leaders eventually became slaveholders themselves, formed a military aristocracy, and, as powerful warlords, fought for supremacy. Thus the Ottoman Empire encompassed Egypt but never penetrated Egyptian society and culture the way the Arabs had under the caliphate.

Egypt emerged as virtually autonomous under the rule of a powerful and visionary Albanian officer, Muhammad Ali, in the Ottoman garrison at Cairo. Appointed governor by the sultan in 1805, Ali eased Egypt into the modern world. His successors—called *khedives* (viceroys)—were nominally under the Ottoman sultan but ruled as autocrats in their own right.

The Suez Canal was opened in 1869 under Khedive Ismail. Not surprisingly, the British were keenly interested in the canal, not least because it offered a short-cut to India. An attempted military coup against the khedive in 1882 precipitated British intervention and formation of a "protectorate," which interrupted Egypt's movement toward independence.

The British protectorate lasted until 1922, but in the early part of this century an Egyptian national movement emerged, advocating an Islamic revival as a means of resisting European incursions. During World War I Great Britain promised Egypt's leaders that it would back their independence after the war, but London subsequently reneged on the grounds that Egyptians were not ready for self-rule.

A nationalist party, the *Wafd*, led the fight against British colonialism, and in 1922 Great Britain formally ended its protectorate. Egypt was given nominal independence under a new king, Faud, but London continued to control Egypt's foreign policy, armed forces, and some internal affairs.

Obviously, this brief historical survey omits a great deal. But it does set the stage to examine the twentieth-century history of two Middle East countries, Israel and Egypt. In addition, the next two chapters will look more closely at Saudi Arabia, Iran, and Lebanon.

Case Studies: Israel and Egypt

Westerners, especially Americans, often entertain negative images of Arabs. Ignorance and prejudice can be blamed:

> Once Jews, blacks and other minorities were subjected to similar degradation; today only Arabs and homosexuals are still fair game for media bashing. The Arabs, I think, are singled out primarily because, unlike most other peoples of the developing world, they have resisted assimilating Western ways or capitulating to Western values. Thus they are seen as a threat and, armed with oil and the ability to make war or peace with Israel, are thought to be in a position to translate that threat into actions that affect the industrialized world.[13]

Whatever its basis, prejudice against Arabs often evokes images of sheiks and harems and nomadic bedouins with towels on their heads forever roaming the scorched desert, riding camels, living in tents, and so on. It is a short step to seeing Arabs as barbaric and cruel, treacherous and warlike, fanatical and feudalistic (particularly in their attitudes toward women). Although most Americans are vaguely aware that the Middle East has nurtured highly advanced civilizations (Egyptian, Sumerian, Babylonian, Assyrian), many remain ignorant of Arabic culture and are indifferent or unsympathetic to Arabs.

Western prejudice against Middle Easterners includes a long history of anti-Semitism, as well. Hatred of Jews reached a fever pitch in Nazi Germany, of course, but anti-Semitism has also been a recurring element in American life. Extremist groups like the Ku Klux Klan and the American Nazi party espouse virulently anti-Semitic doctrines.

Besides breeding suspicion and hostility, prejudiced stereotypes can affect public policy. Thus many critics contend that U.S. policymakers have been systematically biased against one side or the other in the many Arab-Israeli conflicts since World War II. Without expecting or even trying to resolve this controversy, let us examine the politics of the Middle East as impartially and as objectively as possible.

Israel

Proclaimed a Jewish state on May 14, 1948, Israel was founded under extreme duress. On this date the British mandate over the territory of Palestine, which had been established after World War I under the auspices of the League of Nations, formally ended.

At its inception, Israel was a small country about the size of New Jersey, surrounded by hostile Arab neighbors—Lebanon to the north, Syria and Jordan to the east, and Egypt to the west. Only the Mediterranean Sea prevented Israel from being completely encircled by enemies. The fact that many charter members of the new Zionist state, including some of its leaders, were survivors of the Holocaust reinforced the fierce determination that marked the Jewish struggle for Palestine.

Nothing has made a deeper imprint on the Israeli psyche than the nation's precarious geography. As a consequence of its exposure to attack on all sides, and given the sizable Palestinian population within its borders, Israel's political life has been permeated by security considerations. Before the 1967 Six-Day War, Israel shared a jagged 50-mile border with Lebanon; a 48-mile border, which included the Golan Heights, with Syria; and a meandering 335-mile border with Jordan. Israel's frontier with Egypt in the blistering Sinai Desert provided a buffer zone that nonetheless did not prevent them from fighting three wars over seventeen years (in 1956, 1967, and 1973). In 1967 the country's length from Metulah in the north to Eilat in the south was 280 miles, while its width from the border of the Gaza Strip on the west to the Dead Sea on the east was a mere 70 miles. At about its midpoint, just north of Tel Aviv, it was only 12 miles wide, and at the southern end a mere 9 miles separated Israel's Port of Eilat and Jordan's Port of Aqaba.

In the age of air power the proximity of Israel and its Arab neighbors is especially threatening. Flying time between Cairo, Aman, or Damascus and Tel Aviv or Jerusalem is measured in minutes—scant warning time in an attack. Arabs, too, are concerned about their vulnerability and feel threatened by what they consider to be Israeli expansionism—with good reason after 1967. In the Six-Day War Israel mounted simultaneous air attacks against Egyptian, Jordanian, and Syrian bases. It tripled its territory, adding about 20,000 square miles by occupying the Sinai (returned to Egypt in the 1979 peace treaty), the Gaza Strip, the West Bank (part of Jordan), and the Golan Heights (belonging to Syria); Israel also seized the eastern half of Jerusalem.

The new middle East map seemed to make Israel secure at last. But these occupied territories were populated predominantly by Arabs, and so Israel now had a major *internal* Palestinian problem. (Including the West Bank and the Gaza Strip, Israel has a Palestinian population of about 1.5 million.) In addition, the seizure of Arab lands made future jihad inevitable. To appreciate the situation, it is necessary to consider Israel's origins.

The Idea of Israel   Israel was established as a Jewish state in 1948, following a bitter and bloody struggle with Palestine's native population ("the Palestinians"). The state of Israel is the culmination of Zionism—a Jewish national movement dating from the late nineteenth century. Jews had dreamed of being reunited in the Promised Land since their flight from Palestine (called the Diaspora) after a rebellion against Roman rule in A.D. 137 failed. The fact that Jews were persecuted in their adopted lands no doubt helped to sustain the dream. For example, although Jews in Eastern Europe and Russia were legally emancipated by the late nineteenth century, they continued to suffer from anti-Semitism, pogroms, and cultural isolation. Between 1882 and 1914 several million European Jews immigrated to the United States, and tens of thousands went to Palestine, which was still part of the Ottoman Empire.

In 1896 a young Viennese journalist named Theodor Herzl published a pamphlet entitled *Der Judenstaat* (*The Jewish State*), advocating the creation of a self-governing community for Jews. In 1897 he convened the First World Zionist Congress in Basel, Switzerland. The delegates declared that their goal was to create a "home for the Jewish People in Palestine to be secured by public law," and they created the World Zionist Organization to pursue their aim.

Herzl died in 1904, the same year in which Chaim Weizmann, a Zionist and a brilliant chemist, emigrated from Russia to Great Britain. Weizmann's scientific discoveries contributed to the Allied war effort and gave him access to British political elites. He used these connections to persuade the British government to back the cause of a Jewish homeland in Palestine. On November 2, 1917, the British foreign secretary, Lord Balfor, declared that Great Britain favored "the establishment in Palestine of a national home for the Jewish people" and pledged to "facilitate the achievement of this object, it being clearly understood that nothing shall be done which may prejudice the civil and religious rights of the existing non-Jewish communities in Palestine or the rights and political status enjoyed by Jews in any other country."

Because the British had replaced the Ottoman Empire in Palestine after World War I (Palestine became a British mandate under the League of Nations), London was in a position to make good on this promise. The League mandate expressly provided for a Jewish home in Palestine, incorporating the Balfour Declaration into its text almost verbatim. It also authorized Jewish immigration into Palestine, while it sought the cooperation of the Jewish Agency in laying the groundwork for a future Jewish state. In 1921 it divided Palestine, designating the territory east of the Jordan River the Transjordan. In the truncated Palestine that remained, the British intended to set up the promised Jewish homeland. To Arabs who lived in the area, however, the British were promising independence and an Arab State.

Between the two world wars, Jews immigrated to Palestine in great numbers. Some were in search of the Promised Land; others, especially from the Soviet Union and Central Europe, were fleeing oppression and persecution. On the eve of World War II, the exodus from Europe turned into a hemorrhage, as Jews sought refuge from the intolerable conditions created by the Nazis.

In Palestine a different tempest was stirring. The indigenous Arabs finally lost their trust in the British and revolted, culminating in the Arab Rebellion of 1937. The influx of Jewish immigrants into lands that had been promised to Arabs was the central issue. The Arabs attacked both mandate authorities and Jews. In this crucible, enmities formed and coalesced into the violence that continues to this day.

The War for Palestine   Israel's birth was violent. Palestinian Arab attacks on Jews in the 1930s were answered in the 1940s with Jewish terrorist acts by such groups as *Irgun* and the "Stern Gang." Jewish militants during this period included at least two future prime ministers: Menachem Begin and Yitzak Shamir. The British could not find a solution that was acceptable to both sides, and their vacillation led to rising levels of frustration. The British were committed to the idea of a Jewish state but seemed to envision a federation in which Jews and Palestinian Arabs would participate equally.

World War II and the Holocaust gave new impetus to Zionism. The Nazi's genocide against Jews naturally steeled the resolve of Zionist leaders to win the struggle over Palestine; Palestinian Arabs, however, were equally determined to resist.

The British finally brought the issue before the United Nations, and the General Assembly approved a plan to partition Palestine into an Arab state and a Jewish state. It also stipulated that Jerusalem was to become an international city. The Arabs in Palestine and the surrounding states rejected this plan, warning that "any attempt by the Jews or any other power or group of powers to establish a Jewish state in Arab territory is an act of oppression which will be resisted in self-defense by force."[14]

Ironically, the General Assembly's attempt at a peaceful resolution of the Palestinian problem precipitated the war, which did not reach full intensity until the British had left and the Jewish state was proclaimed on May 14, 1948. The war lasted about eight months. When the smoke cleared, Israel had prevailed over the armies of Egypt, the Transjordan, Syria, Lebanon, and Iraq; it now occupied 30 percent more territory than the United Nations had granted it. The war left a bitter legacy:

> The war drove nearly one million Arabs out of their homes. This flight was partly due to the fear of Jewish reprisals and partly to the urgings of Arab political leaders to evacuate probable battle areas. The refugees fled to the surrounding Arab countries or to the Arab-occupied parts of Palestine. In the spring of 1949 the number of Arab displaced persons eligible for relief was officially estimated at 940,000. At the beginning of the war there were 1,320,000 Arabs and 640,000 Jews in Palestine. The establishment of Israel resulted in the displacement of nearly 70 percent of the Arab population, which the Israeli government refused to readmit.[15]

Israel Ascendant and Besieged: 1949–1973 David Ben-Gurion led Israel through the crucial early years, serving as both prime minister and defense minister. (Weizmann was Israel's first president.) In the 1950s the Israeli government was made up of coalitions dominated by Ben-Gurion's Socialist Mapai party. Through its "Declaration of Independence" and "Law of Return," Israel welcomed Jewish immigrants with open arms. The population, which had been about 900,000 in 1948, nearly doubled by the end of 1955. Jews came from all parts of Europe and also from the Middle East, an influx that created serious tensions within the new state. For example, the Shepardi Jews (Spanish, Portugese, and Middle Eastern, or oriental) had a cultural background different from Ashkenazi Jews (Central and East European). By the mid-1950s, over half of Israel's population consisted of Shepardi, but Ashkenazi continued to dominate Israeli politics and business.

The war for Palestine led to a reshuffling of the population of the Middle East. Palestinian Arabs made a mass exodus to surrounding Arab states, while oriental (Middle Eastern) Jews fled to Israel. Palestinian Arabs who remained in Israel (about 300,000) became second-class citizens. For example, under the Land Acquisition Law of March 10, 1953, they were deprived of much of their property. Jewish discrimination against the Arab minority took other forms as well: Arabs were denied freedom of movement, their economic opportunities were limited, and they were shut out of government.

But the treatment of Arabs in Israel was only one grievance of the Arab states. After the war, Israel refused to relinquish territories occupied by its army, arguing that the Arab states had invalidated the U.N. resolution on Palestine by invading Israel on May 15, 1948. Israel also spurned the U.N. stipulation that "refugees wishing to return to their homes and live at peace with their neighbors should be permitted to do so at the earliest practicable date, and that compensation should be paid for the property of those choosing not to return . . . ." While Israel's stand may appear harsh, remember that it was greatly outnumbered and faced constant threats because Arab states refused to recognize its right to exist.

During the period leading to the 1956 Suez Crisis (really the second Arab-Israeli war), both sides perpetrated terrorist acts. Ben-Gurion advocated a policy of retaliation, while Moshe Sharett, his trusted lieutenant who served as prime minister during his temporary retirement (1953–1955), advocated a policy of accommodation. Sharett spoke Arabic and understood Arabic culture, which may explain why he believed it was possible to make peace. But Ben-Gurion's school of thought has prevailed since 1955; Golda Meir, Moshe Dayan, Menachem Begin, and Yitzak Shamir have been its most notable advocates. (The Sharett position has not died, however. Disagreements between hardliners and moderates continue to form a fault line in Israel's internal politics.)

As Israel's position hardened, so did the Arabs' position, especially in Egypt. In 1956, President Nasser nationalized the Suez Canal. Viewing this as one more in a series of provocations, Israel attacked, with British and French backing. America, however, condemned Israel's action (which, oddly enough, briefly put the United States on the same side as the Soviet Union). Although Israel won on the battlefield, its victory was hollow, for in effect the superpowers came to Egypt's defense by creating a United Nations Emergency Force to act as a buffer.

The U.N. peacekeeping force did its job, but for Arabs the Suez Crisis had added insult to injury. Egypt, in particular, felt humiliated. From 1956 to 1967, when the next war broke out, an arms race occurred in the Middle East, with the United States supplying Israel and the Soviet Union supplying Egypt. When Egypt attacked in 1967, Israel was ready. In the Six-Day War (yes, it was over in less than a week) Israel scored one of the most impressive military victories of modern times. As noted earlier, it defeated both Egypt and Syria and seized territories from them as well as from Jordan. The "occupied territories" thereafter included the West Bank and the Sinai, the Gaza Strip, and the Golan Heights.

There were to be other wars: in 1973 (the Yom Kippur War); in 1983 (in Lebanon); and from 1988 to the present (the *intifada*, or "uprising" of Palestinians in the West Bank and Gaza Strip). These events will be discussed in the next chapter.

Egypt

The core territory of Egypt is located in the extreme northeast of Africa. The Sinai Peninsula, a virtually uninhabitable wasteland, connects Africa and the Near East (or Southwest Asia). Egypt's territory is as large as Texas, Arkansas, and Oklahoma combined, but 96 percent of it is desert. The vast majority of Egypt's 55 million people are concentrated in a narrow strip along the Nile River—nearly the only area conducive to farming and settlement. Population density along the Nile is a serious problem. For example, Cairo, the capital, teems with 12.5 million people. Moreover, along with rapid population growth in the country as a whole, urbanization has accelerated: almost half the population lives in urban areas.

Egypt is a Muslim nation (90 percent Sunni) and since the mid-1950s has played a key role in the Arab world, particularly under President Nasser (1954–1970). The nation's relatively sparse natural resources are offset by more human resources—teachers, doctors, nurses, engineers, agronomists—than any other Arab country. Egypt has supplied much of the Arab world with professionals, specialists, and skilled workers of all kinds.

The Nile River is Egypt's greatest natural resource. Its waters sustain the teeming urban population as well as the country's vital agricultural sector. Without irrigation, Egypt would be forced to import most of its food; instead, the rural economy employs over 40 percent of the labor force and produces crops for export (especially cotton), even though only 4 percent of land is fit for cultivation.

In its modern form, Egypt is a young nation, being fully independent only since World War II. But Egyptians have formed a distinct nation since about 4000 B.C.; indeed, its Golden Age preceded Rome's by thousands of years.

As noted already, Egypt has been coveted and controlled by various foreign powers, most recently by Great Britain. The Suez Canal was once an essential link between Europe and Asia, and Egypt's control of it gave the country strategic importance. The war in North Africa from 1941 to 1943 underscored this, when Axis powers (Germany and Italy) tried but failed to take Egypt.

Although the Suez Canal is no longer as vital a link as it was, Egypt is still in a pivotal position, given its proximity to Israel. Before President Sadat's decision in 1978 to sign a separate peace with Israel (the so-called Camp David Accords), Egypt was the leader of the Arab world. Since the treaty, Egypt's stance has changed from confrontation with Israel to mediation (discussed in Chapter 11).

The Egyptian Revolution   The Egyptian national movement, a reaction to Ottoman rule and subsequent European colonialism, was energized and agitated by developments in Palestine. In 1952 popular unrest precipitated a military coup, planned by a secret organization calling itself the Society of Free Officers. The Free Officers persuaded King Farouk to abdicate and set up a Revolutionary Command Council (in effect, a military junta) let at first by Major General Mohammed Naguib.

But the power behind the scenes was a young lieutenant colonel named Gamal Abdel Nasser, who within a short time emerged as the junta's leader; in 1954 he deposed Naguib and became president and prime minister. Nasser ruled as a popular autocrat (he was overwhelmingly ''elected'' president in 1956) and created a cult of personality. During the Nasser era, Egypt became a leader not only in the Middle East but also in the Third World. Along with Nehru of India and Tito of Yugoslavia, Nasser was one of the founders of the so-called Non-Aligned Movement.

The Egyptian Revolution had three major aspects. It was first and foremost a nationalist affair. Egyptians wanted to be free of foreign interference for the first time in thousands of years. Second, it was a socialist revolution: Nasser was anti-Communist (he outlawed and persecuted the Egyptian Communist party), but he was also anticapitalist and antiimperialist. He railed against everything associated with European, particularly British, domination. This posturing against the West was immensely popular in Egypt at the time. Third, the revolution embraced the goal of Arab unity, or Pan-Arabism. Nasser recognized that, as long as the Arab world was a ''house divided,'' Arabs could not win the struggle against imperialism and Zionism.

The Egyptian Revolution and Nasser's role in it became a model for many other developing countries, especially in the Middle East and Africa. Nasser never made himself a general. He chose a civilian title—switching from colonel to president—but retained his military position and appeared in uniform at national celebrations. Although he was a dictator, Nasser staged elections to demonstrate his popularity and thus his legitimacy. His methods were adopted in Algeria, Libya, Syria, and Iraq. In Libya, for example, Colonel Qaddafi, having led a coup in 1969 that ousted King Idris I, established an authoritarian regime based on Islam, socialism, and personal charisma. Like Nasser, Qaddafi also had visions of a Pan-Arab superstate and tried to unite Libya with its neighbors, including Tunisia and Algeria. He also emulated Nasser in forging close ties with the Soviet Union and launching vitrioloci propaganda against Israel and the United States.

Although Nasser was committed to Egypt's modernization and economic development, his preoccupation was foreign affairs, and above all, Israel. As noted earlier, the Suez Crisis in 1956 was triggered by Nasser's decision to nationalize the canal; only U.S. diplomatic intervention saved Egypt from humiliation at the hands of Israel. Although Egypt claimed a moral victory, it clearly had suffered a crushing defeat.

To develop Egypt's economy, Nasser sought whatever outside aid he could find. When the United States refused to help finance the Aswan Dam project, he turned to the Soviet Union. Moscow not only helped to build the dam but supplied military equipment and advisers to train the Egyptian army.

The Six-Day War in 1967 was the nadir of Nasser's political life. Israel invaded Egypt in a preemptive attack after Nasser asked the United Nations Emergency Force to withdraw; Egypt's defenses were demolished in a matter of days. For the next few years hostilities with Israel continued to smolder, and Nasser once again had to turn to the Soviet Union to rebuild his shattered military.

Nasser's Legacy and His Successors   Nasser died of a heart attack in 1970, before he could redeem himself for ''The Catastrophe'' (as he called it). Besides making an indelible mark on Egypt and the Middle East, he also left a legacy of defeat. In internal politics he had never trusted political parties and had outlawed even the venerable *Wafd*, which had been so instrumental in resisting British rule after World War I. He created instead the Arab Socialist Union, (ASU), his own political organization—a one-party monopoly. Until his death Nasser was the undisputed leader of Egypt, known to his few close advisers simply as *El-Rais* ("The Boss").

Anwar Sadat succeeded Nasser and lost little time making his own mark. In 1972 he surprised the world by ordering 15,000 Soviet "advisers" to leave Egypt because he believed dependency on a single outside power raised the specter of a new form of colonialism. On October 6, 1973, Sadat again surprised everyone by attacking Israel on Yom Kippur, the Jewish high holy day. The Egyptian army crossed the Suez Canal and broke through Israel's forward defenses in the occupied Sinai; but Israel quickly recovered and counterattacked, retaking most of the territory it had lost. As in 1967 and 1956, only outside intervention appears to have stopped the Israelis from marching all the way to Cairo.

Nonetheless, Sadat claimed a moral and psychological victory. The Egyptian army had proved, he said, that Arabs could operate sophisticated military equipment and that Israel was not invincible.

In 1977 Sadat made another bold foreign-policy move when he addressed the Israeli parliament (the Knesset), breaking not only precedent but also the logjam in Egyptian-Israeli relations. There followed the fateful meeting at Camp David, where U.S. President Jimmy Carter brokered an agreement that became embodied in the 1979 peace treaty. Israel agreed to give the Sinai back to Egypt in return for Egypt's recognizing Israel's right to exist. Although Israel may appear to have given away more than it got, it was Sadat who went out on a limb. Throughout the Arab world he was denounced as a traitor to the Palestinian (and Arab) cause. Egypt was the first Arab state to recognize Israel—an unenviable distinction in the Arab world.

Sadat's actions also rankled Arab nationalists and Islamic fundamentalists in his own country. The fact that he was awarded the Nobel Peace Prize in 1978, along with Menachem Begin, meant little to his compatriots; to many Egyptians the peace treaty was a sellout, and Sadat had betrayed a sacred trust. On October 6, 1981, he was assassinated by Islamic extremists who called themselves "Repentance and Flight from Sin."

Like Nasser, Sadat left an ambiguous legacy. On the one hand, he had taken a historic step toward peace in the Middle East. On the other, he had alienated the Egyptian people and made his country something of a pariah in the Arab world. In internal politics he had continued in Nasser's footsteps, ruling with a personal flair and a firm hand. Although always attentive to the trappings of democracy, Sadat was hardly less authoritarian than Nasser. He often displayed an imperial contempt for public opinion, as when he pursued the extremely unpopular economic policy of *Infitab* ("Opening"); designed to attract foreign investment and spur an economic miracle, the policy succeeded only in making a few Egyptians very rich, including members of Sadat's family.

Vice-President Hosni Mubarak, another strongman with a military background, immediately succeeded Sadat and has ruled Egypt ever since. As Chapter

11 will explain, he has embroidered on Sadat's democratic reforms, but in essence Egypt remains a one-party authoritarian regime.

CONCLUSION

More than in other regions of the world, the history of the Middle East is dominated by religion. Judaism, Islam, and Christianity all have their roots in the Middle East, and the cultures of the region are strongly influenced by the aesthetics and ethics associated with these religions. Ironically, religion has not engendered peace and brotherly love in the Middle East. In fact, political systems in this area are authoritarian and in many cases repressive, while the foreign policies of several powerful players in the region at times reflect a militancy and uncompromising spirit often associated with religious zealotry. Chapter 11 will look more closely at the forms of government found in the Middle East today.

STUDY QUESTIONS

1. What are the major religions of the Middle East, and in what ways has religion shaped the region's history and culture?
2. Why do Muslims, Christians, and Jews all view Jerusalem as the Holy City? Has this common element in all three religious traditions contributed to greater mutual understanding, or has it done the opposite?
3. What inspired the Iranian Revolution? In what sense (if any) was the revolution the cause of the Iran-Iraq War?
4. What role did colonialism and foreign intrusion play in setting the stage for Middle East conflict? When and how did colonialism end in the region?
5. How have international relationships in the Middle East evolved since World War II? How many instances of war and revolution can you cite? How many successful efforts at peacekeeping and conflict resolution?

SUGGESTED READINGS

Bligh, Alexander. *From Prince to King: Royal Succession in the House of Saud in the Twentieth Century.* New York: New York University, 1984.

Cooper, Mark. *The Transformation of Egypt.* London: Croom Helm, 1982.

Eickelman, Dale F. *The Middle East: An Anthropological Perspective.* Englewood Cliffs, N.J.: Prentice-Hall, 1981.

Lamb, David. *The Arabs: Journeys Beyond the Mirage.* New York: Vintage, 1988.

Lenczowski, George. *The Middle East in World Affairs.* Ithaca, N.Y.: Cornell University, 1980.

Mackey, Sandra. *The Saudis.* Boston: Houghton Mifflin, 1987.

Marsot, Alfia L. *Egypt in the Reign of Muhammad Ali*. Cambridge, Mass.: Cambridge University, 1985.

Mattehedeh, Roy. *The Mantle of the Prophet: Religion and Politics in Iran*. New York: Simon & Schuster, 1985.

O'Brien, Conor Cruise. *The Siege: The Saga of Israel and Zionism*. New York: Simon & Schuster, 1986.

Pryce-Jones, David. *The Closed Circle: An Interpretation of the Arabs*. New York: Harper & Row, 1989.

Sivan, Emmanual. *Radical Islam: Medieval Theology and Modern Politics*. New Haven, Conn.: Yale University, 1985.

Viorst, Milton. *Sands of Sorrow: Israel's Journey from Independence*. New York: Harper & Row, 1987.

NOTES

[1] George Lenczowski, *The Middle East in World Affairs* (Ithaca, N.Y.: Cornell University, 1980), p. 694.

[2] Ibid.

[3] Ibid.

[4] David Lamb, *The Arabs: Journeys Beyond the Mirage* (New York: Vintage, 1988) p. 7.

[5] Ibid., p. 15.

[6] Ibid., pp. 8–9.

[7] Bernard Lewis, *The Arabs in History* (New York: Harper & Row, 1966), pp. 131–143.

[8] Lenczowski, op. cit., p. 27.

[9] Ibid.

[10] Ibid., p. 35.

[11] Ibid., p. 46.

[12] See George Antonius, *The Arab Awakening* (New York: Putnam, 1965.)

[13] Lamb, op. cit., p. 15.

[14] From a statement issued by the Arab Higher Committee of Palestine, Feb. 6, 1948; quoted in Lenczowski, op. cit., p. 405.

[15] Ibid., p. 410.

Chapter 11
Monarchs and Military Strongmen

Political institutions in the Middle East vary from place to place, but authoritarian patterns are the rule. Authoritarianism is etched into Arabian history and political culture—witness the survival of feudal monarchies in Saudi Arabia and in the Persian Gulf sheikdoms as well as more modern hereditary monarchs in Jordan and Morocco. At mid-century most Arab nations were still monarchies.

Political traditions in the Middle East are also characterized by extremism and violence (implicit in the concept of jihad, or holy war). The militancy and zeal that Westerners associate with the region's politics are rooted in religion; Islam, for example, has a history of conflict, conquest, and conversion going back some thirteen centuries (see Chapter 10).

These turbulent spirits and combative energies are not always directed against outsiders, as the Iraqi invasion of Kuwait in August 1990 attested. In fact, xenophobia is no greater among Arabs than among other groups in the world. Like other peoples, Arabs are intensely nationalistic, and Arab nations, like the nations of Western Europe (or Africa, or Asia) have fought among themselves. Ostensibly, they have fought over religion or other differences, but no doubt also for reasons that were primordial, particularistic, or patriotic. Their history of internecine warfare is captured in the following passage:

> The very first anecdote usually told to students of the Middle East is the story of the scorpion and the frog that one day find themselves on a riverbank. The scorpion asks the frog to carry him across to the other shore.
>
> "Don't be ridiculous," answers the frog. "If I let you on my back, you'll sting me."
>
> But the scorpion points out that he cannot swim and if he were to sting the frog in midriver, "we both would drown."
>
> So the frog, persuaded by the logic of the argument, allows the scorpion to climb on his back, and they set out into the river. When they reach the middle, however, the scorpion stings the frog and the paralyzed amphibian starts to sink beneath the water. "Why did you do that?" he croaks. "Now we'll both die."
>
> "Oh, well"—the scorpion sighs, shrugging his carapace—"after all, this is the Middle East."[1]

A certain turbulence has been present in domestic politics throughout the region, as well. This may help to explain why fallen monarchs have typically been replaced by strongmen or "popular tyrants." For example, Barry Rubin has argued:

The contemporary Middle East is a stronghold of modern dictators, men whose energy, cleverness, and ruthlessness have enabled them to master their countries. Muammar al-Qadaffi in Libya, Khomeini in Iran, Hussein in Iraq, and Hafez al-Assad in Syria constructed populist, repressive regimes able to tame some of the world's most turbulent and violent political systems. To stay atop the tiger, they must have an ideology acceptable to their cultures, a party and mass organizations furnishing a wide base of supporters, and an energetic secret policy to break up antigovernment conspiracies.[2]

Rubin pointed out that Middle East dictators "must also dominate the economy and control the army" and contended that they are, if anything, "more ambitious" than their counterparts in other Third World regions, "since they claim to have discovered a proper ethical and political system for the entire region or even the whole world."[3]

The Logic of Arab Politics

Some in the West have the notion—reinforced, for example, by the seemingly bizarre behavior of Qadaffi—that Arabs are irrational and that chaos is their natural condition. On the contrary, most Arab rulers *are* rational; that is, "they act in accordance with domestic and regional needs, rather than behave as the West might think proper." At the same time, however, they "face very exacting demands from Islam and Arab nationalism and are simultaneously manipulators and prisoners of the power symbols of these politics."[4] For example, anti-Zionism is a powerful unifier, but it also locks governments into positions that see peace talks with Israel as synonymous with selling out. Many Arab leaders accused Anwar Sadat of doing just that when Egypt signed a peace treaty with Israel in 1979.

In the 1930s nationalism began to eclipse Islam as a force shaping Arabs' identities and goals. This movement, which stressed Arab unity, was fueled by two external forces: European imperialism and Zionism. Before World War I the main motive for unity was anti-imperialism; during the interwar years, that merged with anti-Zionism; and after the Palestine War (1948–1949) the primary motive was hatred of Israel, although anti-imperialism remained strong.

Yet Arab unity is like the weather: Every Middle East leader likes to talk about it, but no one has been able to do anything about it. Many attempts have been made to merge Arab nations—Nasser was always trying, and Qadaffi has tried as well. All efforts have failed. One reason Israel dominates the Middle East despite being isolated and outnumbered is that Arab states have so often been preoccupied by quarrels among themselves. Even the Palestinians, with a passionate cause to unite them, have fought each other, and splinter groups have left the Palestine Liberation Organization (PLO), thus dividing and weakening the Palestinian movement.

Moreover, the quarrels have sometimes turned into open hostilities. Iraq's aggression against Kuwait comes immediately to mind; the civil war in Lebanon is also easy to recall; and the Iran-Iraq War made the 1980s the bloodiest decade in modern Arab history. But there have also been tensions between Iraq and Syria, Syria and Jordan, Egypt and Libya, Libya and Tunisia, Libya and Chad, and the PLO and Syria.

Sadat's decision to make a "separate peace" with Israel shut Egypt out of the Arab League (only Sudan backed Egypt). This illustrates one major verity of the region's politics: Arab states all agree that Israel is the enemy, but they have long been split over strategies for opposing Israel. Some are radical, "rejectionist" states (Iraq, Libya, Syria); others are more moderate (Egypt, Jordan, Saudi Arabia). Even the "moderates," however, distrust and detest Israel.

The Arithmetic of Instability

The turbulence of Arab politics in the 1950s and 1960s, when new nationalist regimes were struggling to consolidate their power, can be demonstrated with a few statistics. During the three decades following the Egyptian Revolution, no fewer than fifty-five "unscheduled" transfers of power occurred in Arab nations. These included coups, revolutions, and assassinations. (Not counted in this figure are "scheduled" changes, which took place in accordance with constitutional procedures.) As shown in Table 11-1, thirty-six transfers took place before 1969, with a sharp decline thereafter, suggesting that Arab leaders had learned techniques for staying in power.

In the Near East and North Africa alone (that is, excluding the Persian Gulf), Arab states experienced two-dozen coups during the 1950s and 1960s. Syria averaged one coup about every two years. Iraq had coups in 1958, 1963, and 1968.

After a coup in Libya in 1969 brought Qadaffi to power, the internal politics of most nations stabilized considerably, despite the repercussions of the Iranian Revolution. With the exception of Sudan, the coup in Libya brought about the only change in regime (as opposed to a leadership change) in the Arab world in the 1970s and 1980s.

In sum, coups, attempted coups, coup plotting, and rumors of coups dominated the region's politics during the 1950s and 1960s. The military took charge in one Arab country after another. Where the military did not take charge, an

Table 11-1 "Unscheduled" Leadership Changes in Arab Nations, 1954–1983 (coups, revolutions, assassinations)

Period	1954–1958	1959–1963	1964–1968	1969–1973	1974–1978	1979–1983
Power transfers	11	15	10	6	8*	5

*Five of these changes occurred in North Yemen and South Yemen, which went through tumult during this period.

anachronistic form of authoritarianism—hereditary monarchy—was able to persevere. Jordan, Morocco, Saudi Arabia, and the oil-rich Persian Gulf ministates of Bahrain, Kuwait, Qatar, Oman, and the United Arab Emirates are cases in point. Western-style democracy made inroads only in Israel, where it is not fully extended to the original Arab population.

Modern Arab Regimes

The new military regimes of the 1950s and 1960s stressed nationalism, Pan-Arabism, and socialism. They were outspokenly critical of the West, imperialism, capitalism, and, above all, Zionism. Egypt, Algeria, Syria, Iraq, and the PLO all looked to the Soviet Union for economic and military aid; after 1969 Libya and South Yemen did, too (the latter became a Soviet client-state in the 1970s). The reason these regimes all embraced the Soviet Union had less to do with ideology (indeed, they typically persecuted their own Communists) than with *realpolitik*. The United States supported the old order and Israel, while the USSR backed modern dictatorships and was at best cool toward Israel.

Once in power the strongmen combined Arab traditions with modern authoritarian techniques. Nasser set the standards for using symbols, propaganda, and charisma to manipulate the masses. He has since been emulated by Assad (Syria), Hassan (Iraq), Boumedienne (Algeria), Qadaffi (Libya), and others. But Arab rulers have given autocratic tactics and methods a new wrinkle. For example, the leader's inner circle is typically reinforced with friends, relatives, and others who have special ties to the leader. In Syria the ruling clique are mainly members of Assad's Alawite Muslim minority. In Iraq most of the ruling elite are from the Sunni Muslim minority, and many come from villages around Tikrit. In Libya, Qadaffi relies on loyal confederates from his own religious group and home territory.

As military officers who themselves have plotted against a previous ruler, these new dictators know well the dangers of a coup, and they have figured out how to prevent them. Typically, they purge any officers who have ties to the former regime or to competing parties, factions, interests, or ideologies. They also tightly control military promotions and rotate or transfer officers so that no one can count on the loyalty of his units. Trusted officers are placed in key positions, thus giving the military a stake in the regime's success—and shared responsibility for any failures. Finally, multiple means of intelligence are created, not only to stamp out dissent but also to keep an eye on each other.

In modern Arab dictatorships a single party is at the center of a web of mass organizations (unions, youths, students, teachers, women, peasants, and so on). The party is an extension of the leader, who uses it to control the society and reward the faithful, in part through patronage appointments in the bureaucracy, schools, mass organizations, industry, and armed forces. Examples include the Baath in Syria and Iraq, the Islamic Republican party in Iran, and the people's committees in Libya.

With this background we turn now to look again at Israel and Egypt. Israel is the only multiparty democracy in the Middle East, while Egypt is an authoritarian state with a dominant party (other parties play only minor roles). Later sections of this chapter will examine two special cases: Saudi Arabia (a traditional monarchy, one of the last) and Iran (a theocracy—also a rarity in the modern world).

Case Studies: Israel and Egypt

Israel and Egypt have been at the center of the Middle East conflict for four decades. The first three major wars after 1949— in 1956, 1967, and 1973—were fought primarily between these two countries (see Chapter 10). In fact, Egypt's claim to Arab leadership was based mainly on its belligerency toward Israel. But after Egypt signed the 1979 peace treaty with Israel, the political face of the Middle East *as a region* changed drastically. Even so, the internal politics of the Arab states were largely unaffected.

In Israel the peace treaty was a major event—potentially momentous—but it was offset by the rise of Khomeini's Islamic fundamentalism, which posed a new threat to the stability of the region. The Iranian Revolution sparked a new outpouring of extremism in the Middle East. The main targets were "Satan America" and, of course, Israel. Although an oppressive siege mentality continues to pervade Israel's political life, the state has functioned as a parliamentary democracy since its stormy beginnings in 1948. Palestinians in Israel, however, have not enjoyed the fruits of civil liberty.

Israel

Israel's multiparty system is unique in the Middle East. For reasons that are probably rooted in the nation's endemic insecurity, Israel has no written constitution. (Such a document would complicate matters, for example, when martial-law measures are deemed necessary.) The state does, however, have statutory laws that define basic rights, election procedures, voting qualifications, military service obligations, and the like. The Law of Return (see Chapter 10) is unique: It provides that any Jew has the right to immigrate to Israel and become an Israeli citizen at any time. In effect, Jews living in other countries have dual citizenship. In this sense Israel is a true Jewish homeland.

Israel's government is similar to the British parliamentary system. The Knesset (parliament) consists of 120 members elected for four-year terms by proportional representation. The party that has the most seats in the Knesset or that can form a coalition chooses a prime minister and Cabinet to run the government. The prime minister is accountable to the Knesset and can be forced to resign by a vote of no confidence. Instead of Britain's symbolic monarchy, Israel has a ceremonial president.

For the first thirty years David Ben-Gurion's Mapai (Labor) party dominated Israeli politics. But the Labor party rarely had a clear majority (since proportional representation has encouraged party proliferation), and so unstable coalition governments have been the rule.

After the Yom Kippur War in 1973 the Labor party was challenged by opposition hardliners (for example, the Likud bloc), who charged that Israel had suffered heavy casualties because the Labor government of Prime Minister Golda Meir had been caught with its guard down. Labor's economic policies were also called into question after runaway inflation forced the government to adopt an unpopular austerity program. In 1977 the right-wing Likud won more seats than Labor, and Menachem Begin, a veteran of the struggle to create the Israeli state, became prime minister. Since Likud lacked a clear majority, Begin made concessions to smaller parties in order to form a governing coalition.

Ironically, it was the hardliners' victory that made the peace treaty with Egypt possible. In Israel as in the United States, a conservative leader can often act more boldly in foreign policy than a liberal leader can, because a liberal's patriotism may be more easily impeached. (Hence, it was Richard Nixon, the crusading Cold Warrior, who initiated rapprochement with the People's Republic of China and signed the first strategic arms limitation treaty with the Soviet Union.) An unabashed Zionist, Begin succeeded where all predecessors had failed: Egypt, which had spearheaded the Arab campaign to ''drive the Israelis into the sea,'' agreed to recognize Israel's right to exist within secure and defensible borders. In return, Israel agreed to give the Sinai back to Egypt.

As noted in Chapter 10, sharing the 1978 Nobel Peace Prize with Begin did not enhance Sadat's popularity at home. But it did make Begin a hero in Israel. The national euphoria helped him and Likud win reelection in 1981.

Celebration gave way to anguish when Israel invaded Lebanon the following year. The Likud-led coalition was starting to unravel in 1981; after the invasion, during which Lebanese Christian militias committed atrocities against civilians in Palestinian refugee camps, while the Israeli army apparently turned a blind eye, Begin narrowly survived a no-confidence motion in the Knesset (by a single vote). The invasion caused a furor in Israel—and elsewhere—because it appeared to violate Israel's own precept that self-defense is the only justification for war. Although the invasion was provoked by PLO border raids from Palestinian bases in southern Lebanon, the Israeli army did not stop there. In June 1982 it encircled Beirut and then called in the Israeli air force. The strategy was to drive the PLO out of Lebanon. Massive bombing achieved the goal, and the PLO agreed to evacuate the city.

Israel won this battle but not the war. Prime Minister Begin found himself in the middle of a political maelstrom. Depressed by events in Lebanon and the death of his wife, Begin retired in 1983. There was still peace with Egypt (although President Mubarak had withdrawn the Egyptian ambassador to Israel), but now Israel itself was deeply divided. Even the military was split. Some high-ranking officers resigned, and many soldiers refused to fight. Meanwhile, the high cost of the war strained the economy and added to growing domestic unrest. Finally, the Arabs had a new cause célèbre, and opinion had turned sharply against Israel even in the West.

The economic and political fallout of the Lebanon invasion made it necessary to seek a new popular mandate. But the 1984 elections were ambiguous: Labor won the most votes but failed to win a majority of the seats in the Knesset. Both Labor and Likud scrambled to form a coalition government, but neither succeeded. These two odd bedfellows then worked out a so-called government of national unit—a first in Israeli history. The two parties agreed to alternate in power, with the leader of the Labor party serving as prime minister for two years and then handing over the government to the Likud leader. Under this arrangement Shimon Peres (Labor) became prime minister in September 1984 and was succeeded by Yitzhak Shamir (Likud) in October 1986.

The attempt at a national unity government was not entirely successful. In the 1988 elections both Labor and Likud lost votes to parties on the far left and far right. The center in Israel was thus further weakened, and the trend toward fragmentation and polarization of the electorate continued. Labor won the largest number of votes, ''but only a nationalist bloc could act as an effective pivot of a viable coalition.''[5] The upshot: Likud's Shamir ''was able to form a viable government on the basis of another national unity coalition with Labor; his alternative, partnership with the religious and the non-religious right, was abandoned because of the preconditions of the religious right.''[6]

If the 1988 elections had a political red flag, it was the tendency toward extremes and the fragmentation of the electorate. As the decade ended, consensus seemed ever more remote. Professor Avner Yaniv of Haifa University in Israel summed up the situation:

> More than anything else, the country needed a clear electoral decision that would facilitate a strong government. But the number of parties and the lists [statements of political intent] in the campaign indicated that this was not to be. Almost 30 lists obtained enough signatories to qualify. The total number of eligible voters was 2,840,000. The necessary minimum for a Knesset seat was thus little more than 23,000 valid votes. Half the lists that obtained enough signatures to qualify therefore stood a reasonable chance of winning enough votes to claim a seat in the next Knesset.
>
> Thus, in addition to Labor and Likud, the two broadly based contenders for national leadership, there were more than 20 single-issue lists standing for anything from the expulsion of the Arab population of the West Bank and Gaza to the drastic reduction of the income tax, the establishment of orthodox Judaism as the law of the land, the rights of senior citizens, and Israel's recognition of the PLO.[7]

Chapter 12 will consider Israel's problems and prospects in the 1990s and beyond. In Egypt the problem of a fragmented electorate has not surfaced; one party continues to dominate the political scene.

Egypt

Modern Egypt's founding father, Gamal Abdel Nasser, created a one-party state in the 1950s. First he outlawed the Wafd party, despite its heroic role in the struggle for Egyptian independence. Having survived an assassination attempt by the Muslim Brotherhood in the mid-1950s, he retaliated by breaking up the organization, ignoring its popular appeal (membership was estimated at around 2 million). He also outlawed the Egyptian Communist party, despite his close ties with the Soviet Union. The Arab Socialist Union (ASU) became the sole embodiment of Nasser's will—all opposition parties were outlawed, disbanded, or driven underground. By definition, all parties other than the ASU were "opposition." A populist dictator par excellence, Nasser's subliminal message to the masses was always, "He who is not with me is against you."

After Nasser's death in 1970, his personalistic one-party dictatorship was continued under President Sadat, but with certain cosmetic changes. For example, Sadat abolished the ASU and allowed several new parties to organize; meanwhile, the former power elite of the ASU formed the National Democratic Front—headed by Sadat. Many observers believed that Sadat was even more autocratic than Nasser.

In fairness, Sadat took a number of significant steps to broaden human rights in Egypt. According to George Lenczowski:

> Sadat . . . launched a thorough policy of "de-Nasserization" in virtually every field of public policy. In the domestic political process Sadat inaugurated an era of liberalism that contrasted with the police methods used in the last years of Nasser's presidency. Egyptians found travel abroad easier than it had been. Citizens began to move and to express their opinions with much greater freedom. Censorship over the Egyptian press was formally removed, and editorials espousing various points of view began to appear even though the newspapers continued to be owned by the ASU. . . . On his part, President Sadat did not cease to castigate what he called the old centers of power, composed of influential dignitaries in the intelligence and ASU organizations, who, according to him, exercised arbitrary power and were guilty of many abuses.[8]

Despite some movement toward pluralism within the ruling party, the Egyptian National Assembly was little more than a debating society. For all Sadat's lip service and outward show of respect, the Assembly continued to be a rubber stamp. This hypocrisy galled many Egyptians, especially those with university degrees and white-collar jobs. Nasser, they reasoned, made no bones about his authoritarian style; but Sadat pretends to be a democrat. That this cynical view extended beyond a single group or class was made apparent in October 1981: Sadat's assassination seemed to cause greater concern in the West than in Egypt.

In keeping with the precedent set after Nasser's death, Vice-President Hosni Mubarak succeeded Sadat (who had been vice-president under Nasser). Under Mubarak, Egypt's one-party system has been modified to the extent that several other parties have been legalized. The first multiparty elections since 1952 were held in 1984, with no surprises. Mubarak ran unopposed and was easily reelected to a full six-year term as president, and the ruling National Democratic party won nearly three-fourths of the seats in the National Assembly. Although the elections appeared to be free and open, appearances can be deceiving. For example, one rule required that parties receive at least 8 percent of the popular vote to be awarded any seats in the legislature, which made things difficult for new parties. Only the New Wafd party was able to qualify.

In 1987, four opposition parties contested the Assembly elections. The New Democratic party won by a landslide (with 70 percent of the vote), but 17 percent of the electorate voted for a coalition consisting of two socialist parties and members of the Muslim Brotherhood (running as independents). The New Wafd party gained ground as well, garnering nearly 11 percent of the vote. A prominent newspaper editor in Cairo proclaimed that "the one-man system is over"— wishful thinking, perhaps, but a sign of changing times.[9]

The rise of Islamic fundamentalism challenged Egypt's single-party system for two reasons. First, in 1952 Nasser led a secular and nationalist revolution; bent on modernization, he was contemptuous of Islamic law and tradition.[10] Anwar Sadat was no less confrontational in dealing with Khomeini-style Islamic fundamentalism. Thus Egypt was a natural target for groups ranging from the Muslim Brotherhood (which Nasser had crushed) to followers of the Ayatollah, who viewed Sadat as a traitor.

Second, Sadat had made peace with the enemy, Israel. This move was risky because it offended both Arab nationalists and Islamic zealots. The group that carried out Sadat's assassination in 1981 fit both descriptions.

Mubarak's strategy for dealing with the Islamic tumult has been subtle, whereas Sadat's was crude:

> By gradually shifting its posture toward the religious opposition from indiscriminate confrontation to selective accommodation, the Mubarak government has . . . isolated and discredited the extremist fringes of the Islamic movement, allowing the state security forces to hunt down and crush remaining pockets of armed resistance. It has [also] allowed the . . . moderate mainstream of the Islamic movement to compete more openly in the political system and in the economy. Several groups that Sadat claimed were trying to tear the country apart have already developed a strong interest in expanding Egypt's multiparty capitalism.[11]

In sum, Mubarak has made concessions both to democracy and to Islam. Although his democratic reforms have been largely symbolic, they uphold the principle of pluralism as embodied in competing parties and free elections with meaningful choices. He continues to fit the Egyptian (and Arab) model of a quasi-civilian strongman; like Nasser and Sadat, he earned his spurs as a high-ranking military officer. Egypt remains essentially a highly centralized, one-party authoritarian state with a populist president who personifies the spirit of the nation—or claims to do so. In Nasser's case the claim was not without foundation; in Sadat's, it was hollow. Mubarak probably falls somewhere between the two. He seems to be respected and has restored trust in the government, but he has not attained the exalted status accorded to Nasser.

The next chapter will evaluate Egypt's prospects for peace, stability, and economic development. Suffice it to say that Egyptian government has weathered four turbulent decades and is nearly intact. Changes that have been made are more in the nature of fine-tuning than restructuring. On the one hand, the survival of the system demonstrates that it has been congruent with Egyptian political culture; on the other, changes in the nation, the region, and the world since the early 1950s raise questions whether the present political system can function satisfactorily for long.

Saudi Arabia and Iran: Divergent Paths to the Past

Feudal monarchies are an oddity in the modern world, but they are not nearly so ''old fashioned'' in the Middle East as they would be in Europe or North America. After World War II most of the Middle East was ruled—insofar as self-rule existed in the region—by kings. Many of these monarchs were deposed during the 1950s and 1960s; the last to fall was King Idris I of Libya in 1969.

Monarchs have survived in Jordan and Morocco, but in both cases they have pushed modernization while making concessions to political pluralism. In contrast, the old-style monarchies in Saudi Arabia and the Persian Gulf sheikdoms have been impervious to political change from within. The Iranian Revolution is the obvious exception, but Iran is not an Arab country, and the Shah had created a dictatorship quite different from the conservative monarchies of Arabia. And in Kuwait the emir was ousted by the Iraqi army of Saddam Hussein, not by a coup or revolution.

Saudi Arabia

As noted in Chapter 10, Saudi Arabia is a great desert peninsula surrounded by the Red Sea, the Arabian Sea, and the Persian Gulf. It is isolated and insulated geographically, culturally, and politically. Nearly three-fourths of its population of 16 million people live in urban areas, an unusually high figure for the Middle East, and only 1 percent of its land is arable. So immense and uninhabitable is the Arabian Desert that no defined boundaries separate Saudi Arabia from its neighbors on the Arabian Peninsula.

Beneath the barren desert, however, lies a gold mine—''black gold,'' that is. Saudi Arabia's crude oil reserves are the largest in the world, between 165 and 170 billion barrels. The Saudis demonstrated their ability to affect regional and global balances of power in the 1970s, when they spearheaded an oil embargo following the 1973 Middle East war.

Saudi Arabia combines antiquity with youth. The modern state dates only from the eighteenth century. At that time Muhammad ibn-Saud (hence the name *Saudi*), the ambitious leader of a nomadic tribe, sought the moral support of Abd al-Wahhab, a famous religious scholar who lived near the village of Riyadh. Ibn-Saud promised to protect al-Wahhab (whose opponents wanted him dead) in exchange for Allah's blessing. Thus was born the Wahhabi movement, an Islamic crusade based on the alliance between two powerful leaders, one secular and one Sunni.

Saudi kings institutionalized the Wahhabi tradition based on the strict moral code practiced by the Prophet Muhammad in Mecca and Medina (both located in Saudi Arabia). This code is still the basis for Saudi law and social behavior. Indeed, the Ministry of Public Morals Enforcement is one of the most important cabinet portfolios; its police patrol the streets, making certain that women wear veils at all times, that there is no eating or drinking during the month of Ramadan, and that Saudi society remains strictly free of alcohol and drugs. To Western eyes, observance of Islamic strictures is particularly oppressive for women (for example, they are not allowed to drive cars). Religious leaders play a strong role in setting public policy; because they view movies as purveyors of evil, Saudi Arabia has no movie theaters.

A Family Affair   The father of the Saudi state literally and figuratively is Abd al-Aziz ibn-Saud. He grew up in exile in Kuwait, where his father had fled in the 1890s after the Rashidis, a rival tribe, seized Riyadh. In 1902 ibn-Saud and a small band of followers crossed the desert, scaled the city's walls at night, and surprised the sleepy Rashidi rulers at daybreak. The people of Riyadh rallied behind the future Saudi king and drove the Rashidis out of town.

For the next thirty years ibn-Saud endeavored to regain the Saudi ancestral lands. He eventually succeeded, using both diplomatic and military skills, and in 1932 he aptly named the state "Saudi Arabia"—it was *his* country. It still is: The Saud family owns and operates it. Today the Saudi "royal family counts more than 5,000 princes and princesses among its numbers, each of whom occupies a privileged position."[12] Thus, there is a prince or princess for every 2,000 commoners.

The Saudi System   Besides reclaiming Saudi territories, ibn-Saud's other major aim was to build a durable political order under an absolute monarchy. The basis for the Saudi system was to be the Wahhabi interpretation of Islamic law; there was thus no place for a written constitution. Political parties and any kind of organized dissent or opposition were prohibited.

Ibn-Saud was not the aloof patriarch one might imagine. In fact, he added a democratic touch to his regal duties. Every day he held a *majlis* (public assembly) in Riyadh at which any citizen could express a grievance, ask a favor, or present a petition. His subjects often addressed him by his given name, Abd al-Aziz. Ironically, the Saudi people had easier access to their ruler than did the Egyptians or the people in any other country in the region.

When ibn-Saud died in 1953, he was succeeded by Crown Prince Saud, his eldest son. Saud was ill-suited to rule, and soon the country was on the verge of bankruptcy. The royal circle feared a coup, possibly instigated by radical Arab nationalist regimes in the region (perhaps Egypt or Syria), whose leaders disdained feudal monarchies. The senior princes decided that Saud should step aside in favor of ibn-Saud's politically adept second son, Faisal. In 1964 Saud abdicated.

The power of a Saudi king, then, is not as absolute as it might appear. Senior princes are regularly consulted about policy. Important decisions are apparently made by consensus, but decision making is shrouded in secrecy. New policies and laws are issued by fiat, and no reasons are ever given publicly. To do so would suggest that royal authority depends on popular approval rather than on heredity. Archaic as this system might seem to Westerners, it has been surprisingly stable in a region where turmoil is the norm.

The Future   King Faisal (1964–1975) was a forward-looking ruler who modernized Saudi society as far as possible within the confines of strict Islamic culture. For example, Faisal introduced education for females and drew up the first development plan for the nation. He was also active and generally constructive in regional politics, mediating in the Yemen civil war and taking a relatively moderate stance on the issue of negotiations with Israel. Also, it was under Faisal that Saudi Arabia (and OPEC) imposed the 1973 oil embargo on the West, demonstrating the Arab world's capacity to disrupt the global economy. The embargo discomfitted the industrial democracies and created strains between the United States and its NATO allies (plus Japan), which all depended on Persian Gulf oil. In the final analysis, Faisal was more anti-Communist than anti-Zionist. (He equated communism with revolution, and he did not see Israel as a threat to the Saudi monarchy.) The best evidence of this was his close and cordial relationship with the United States.

Ironically, Islamic radicalism threatened the Saudi monarchy more than communism or any other secular *ism* has. The threats have come from both Sunni and Shiite communities. In November 1979 fanatical Sunni Muslims seized the Great Mosque in Mecca. Saudi security forces quashed the uprising, but only after a battle that left many dead on both sides. The incident sent shock waves through Riyadh and beyond. Its timing—given that the Iranian Revolution was in full swing and followers of the Ayatollah Khomeini had seized the American embassy a few weeks earlier—gave reason to suspect that Iran was involved. Although it was not, the event was no less troubling to the Saudis, who feared that the Ayatollah was unleashing a tempest in the Middle East. His brand of Islamic revivalism was catching fire elsewhere and had spilled over from the Shiites to ultrarightists among the Sunnis.

The Saudi government responded with a two-pronged policy: More funds were directed to the minority Shia community in Saudi Arabia, and the Saudis sought accommodation with Iran. This policy worked until the summer of 1987, when demonstrations by Iranian pilgrims to Mecca turned violent. Panic ensued, and blood flowed. Khomeini angrily called for the overthrow of the Saudi monarchy, and the Saudis expelled the Iranian ambassador. Again, the political regime showed no signs of cracking.

One key to the stability of the Saudi system is its wealth. As Monte Palmer has pointed out:

> Saudi Arabia and the oil sheikdoms are unique. They can pursue a policy of buying political support by distributing the vast wealth derived from their oil reserves. At the present time, there is enough wealth to support both massive royal families in luxury and a reasonable distribution of the state's wealth to the masses. Indeed, a trade-off exists in which the citizens of the state can prosper economically but are denied political rights. Few states, however, can afford this luxury.[13]

During the 1970s, when the oil price peaked at $34 per barrel (it was $3 per barrel before the 1973 embargo), the oil bonanza benefited the Saudis most of all. They were awash in oil revenues and had more money than they dared to invest in domestic development:

> The Saudi leaders are, with some justification, wary of any type of economic growth that would lead to the emergence of labor unions, political parties, and other political manifestations likely to threaten the regime. Accordingly, the Saudi government has pursued a careful policy of gradual growth. Policies of income distribution are favored over industrial capacity. Education is free, and many students are paid for attending school. Health care and housing are also subsidized by the state. In most instances, to be a Saudi citizen is to live well. Limited industrialization has been initiated by the government and operates under strict government supervision. Labor unions, strikes, political parties, a free press, and similar institutions are strictly forbidden. This is not to say that the Saudi elite is opposed to economic growth. It is, however, opposed to economic growth that poses a threat to the political regime. If one or the other must be sacrificed, it will most surely be economic growth.[14]

The outbreak of war between Iran and Iraq was another windfall for the monarchy. As world oil production plunged, the Saudis took up the slack, raising their production to over 10 million barrels a day. The economic boom transformed Saudi society. Gleaming high-rises sprang up; shops were filled with imported goods; oil refineries, petrochemical plants, steel mills, cement works, and related industries sprouted almost overnight in settlements that, for centuries, had changed very little. Along with industrial development came new schools and hospitals, airports and seaports, roads and power plants.

But the oil boom of the 1970s was followed by an oil glut in the early 1980s. Saudi Arabia was able to weather this storm far better than oil-producing debtor nations (such as Nigeria, Mexico, and Venezuela), but the reversal of fortunes had to be unsettling to people who were unaccustomed to belt-tightening.

Saudi Arabia's oil wealth is a mixed blessing in another sense. With such a valuable asset and a small population, the Saudis have every reason to be paranoid. Many nations that dwarf Saudi Arabia in demographic terms envy Riyadh's riches, as the Iraqi threat to the Saudi oil fields during the Persian Gulf crisis of 1990 made so clear. As a result, the Saudis devote about one-third of annual government spending to defense. Maintaining a state-of-the-art military (especially air force) is a financial drain even for the Saudi monarchy. Nonetheless, vulnerability to invasion prompted Riyadh to invite a massive U.S. troop presence onto the Arabian Peninsula in 1990 as a deterrent to Saddam Hussein. This defense, even though endorsed by the U.N., itself posed a threat to the Saudi government, because it acknowledged the vulnerability of the monarchy and because it humiliated many Arabs to have military forces from pro-Israeli Western governments (especially the United States) on Arab territory.

Iran

In physical area, Iran is about twice the size of Egypt and three-quarters as large as Saudi Arabia. As in those two countries, much of Iran's land is arid and uninhabitable. Most Iranians (numbering about 53 million) are concentrated in northern and northwestern Iran. This Caspian Sea area is semitropical, with an average annual rainfall of 80 inches. An elaborate system of underground conduits—some of them thousands of years old—helps to sustain the large rural population. (All water resources were nationalized in 1967.) Although rapid migration to cities has occurred, nearly half the population is rural—a factor that is politically significant in Iran, because rural dwellers cling tenaciously to Islamic tradition. Not surprisingly, the countryside was a stronghold of support for Khomeini.

Iran was once the core of the ancient Persian Empire. Dating back to the eleventh century B.C., the empire's vast territory encompassed many ethnic groups. Modern Persians, whose language is Farsi, constitute about 63 percent of Iran's population. In northwestern Iran, Azeri Turks are the largest minority group; other Azeris live across the border in Soviet Azerbaijan, where they are the majority. Since their ancestors once ruled Persia, Azeris have a strong sense of national identity, and they have long sought autonomy from Iran's central government in Teheran. Together, Turks and Baluchis constitute about 18 percent of the population.

Kurds, who live mostly in the mountains along Iran's border with Turkey and Iraq, form the second-largest minority group (about 3 percent of the population). They have waged an intermittent war for a separate Kurdish state. (There are also Kurdish minorities in Turkey, Iraq, and Syria.) A *modus vivendi* (temporary compromise) was honored during the Pahlavi era (1925–1979), but it collapsed along with the Shah when Kurdish leaders decided that Khomeini's regime was a threat to Kurdish political and cultural autonomy.

Iran also has an Arab minority (about 3 percent) who, like the Baluchis, are Sunni Muslims. Non-Muslim minorities include Armenians, Jews, Assyrians,

Zoroastrians, and Bahais. The last group is the largest non-Muslim minority in Iran and was persecuted ferociously by Khomeini's government.

Despite its ethnic and religious diversity, Iranian society is held together by strong cultural bonds. Its language, the Shiite sense of community, and a nationalism made fervent by the glories of Persia's ancient past all contribute to Iran's remarkable social cohesion.

From Persia to Iran   Beginning in the eleventh century B.C., the Persian Empire encompassed nearly all the Middle East. Following the Persians, the Sassanid kings (A.D. 226–641) controlled an area almost equal in size until the seventh century, when Arabs defeated them and introduced Islam into Persia. The Shia sect, a purist splinter group, took root there (see Chapter 10), but its adherents were in the minority for several centuries. The Arab rulers were Sunni Muslims who regarded the Shias as a subversive lunatic fringe; to escape persecution, the Shias adopted a practice called *tagiya* (concealment), hiding their beliefs.

In the sixteenth century the Safavids won control of Persia. The first Safavid ruler, Shah Ismail, made Shiism the state religion and invited all Shiites to move there. A great migration of Shiite Muslims flowed from all over the Middle East. Although the Safavids soon lost Persia to the (Sunni) Ottoman Turks, Shiism remained the predominant religion.

In the nineteenth century the Qajars (Turkish) ruled, and Iran's modern borders were defined by treaties with Great Britain, Russia, and the Ottoman Empire. The Qajar *shahinshah* (''king of kings'') enjoyed great pomp and ceremony but under European influence made concessions to commercial interests. The foundations of a modern educational system were laid, and a small intellectual elite—children of the aristocracy—developed. These became the nucleus of future opposition to the shah, whose dealings with foreigners were, they believed, bankrupting the country. The Shiite holy men—mullahs—agreed, and to this day they oppose all Western intrusions into Iranian life.

In the 1890s, this ferment exploded into mass rebellion when the shah gave a fifty-year tobacco monopoly to a foreigner. In 1905 it erupted again in the Constitutional Revolt (a kind of dress rehearsal for the 1979 revolution). The test of strength between ruler and ruled lasted many months and involved considerable bloodletting. In the end the shah was forced to grant a constitution which created an elected *Majlis* (parliament) that, at least in principle, could check the throne's power. The once-absolute monarch conceded that ''absolute'' was obsolete. Or was it?

The Pahlavi Era   After World War I, Iran had no government for a time. Russian and British forces partitioned the country. An extraordinary series of events allowed the clever military commander Reza Khan to set up a new ruling ''Pahlavi'' dynasty. Reza Shah Pahlavi was a visionary leader who ruled with an iron fist. Following the example of Ataturk in Turkey, he set about modernizing and secularizing Iranian society. He abolished traditional dress, including the veil and the fez, and brooked no criticism from the mullahs. Resentful of British interference, Reza Shah favored Germany. In 1941 the British and the Russians occupied Iran. After the war Reza Shah abdicated in favor of his son and went into exile.

When Muhammad Reza Shah Pahlavi ascended to the Peacock Throne, he was only 22 years old. His prime minister, Muhammad Mossadegh, was experienced and popular, and his popularity was enhanced in the early 1950s when he led an effort to nationalize the oil industry (jointly operated with the British) following a dispute over royalties. In 1953 Mossadegh and the Shah had a falling out. The Shah left the country but returned after Mossadegh was overthrown (allegedly with CIA complicity).

Now with U.S. backing, the Shah consolidated his power and resumed the modernizing policies of his father. In 1962 he announced the White Revolution, a six-point program that included land reform, nationalization of industry, voting rights for women, profit-sharing for workers, and a literacy campaign in rural areas. This modernization plan was extremely unpopular among landowners and religious leaders, but the only outspoken critic was Ayatollah Ruhollah Khomeini, Iran's leading religious scholar. Thus began a vendetta between the Shah and the Ayatollah that continued until 1979, when Khomeini—exiled to Paris for years—returned in triumph as the monarchy crumbled.

The Shah's rule had grown increasingly repressive, and during the 1960s and 1970s Iran became a police state. The hated SAVAK (secret police) maintained an elaborate network of informants, and Iranian jails teemed with the Shah's presumed enemies. Meanwhile, the Iranian economy surged ahead, lubricated by oil profits. The Shah sought and received the most advanced U.S. arms, including combat aircraft. His regime appeared to be impervious to the political instability that plagued the Middle East. Visiting Teheran in 1977, U.S. President Jimmy Carter told the Shah, "Under your leadership [Iran] is an island of stability in one of the more troubled areas of the world."[15]

But the situation steadily deteriorated into violence and revolution. Had the Shah acted swiftly and decisively, he surely had enough force to crush the opposition. For whatever reason, however, he did not crack down. The crisis snowballed until its momentum could not be stopped. In January 1979 the Shah and his family fled from Iran.

The Theocratic State   In 1979 the Shah and the Ayatollah went through Iran's revolving door at the same time but in opposite directions. Khomeini's return from Paris (while the Shah traveled first to Cairo) occasioned a tumultuous national celebration; he was the nation's undisputed leader by acclamation. In April he announced the formation of the Islamic Republic of Iran—the authentic Islamic republic, he said, ever since the time of the Prophet Muhammad.

Khomeini set about creating a theocracy, a government guided by the mullahs and based on strict interpretation of the Koran. Islamic law would thus be the law of the land. Religious leaders would serve in the Majlis and actively direct the nation's political life. The Council of Guardians was created to act as a kind of supreme court, using the Koran, not the Constitution, as the highest law. Many of

Iran's eighty thousand or so clerics became the "local political agents" of the Islamic Republican party:

> Every province and city has a cleric who serves as Khomeini's personal representative. Mullahs lead the Crusade for Reconstruction, which organizes volunteers for building roads, schools, and houses (its achievements are among the revolution's proudest boasts), and the Foundation of the Dispossessed, a powerful money-disbursing agency. The Ministry of Islamic Guidance, headed by a cleric, controls censorship and publishing, and local mosques give clearances to students wishing to attend a university. Political loyalty is a major criterion in determining who can teach or study in higher educational institutions. Such a large apparatus will not be easily dismantled or overthrown.[16]

Iran's Constitution and its elected president and legislature notwithstanding, ultimate authority became vested in the "Supreme Legal Guide"—the Ayatollah—responsible only to God:

> There were neighborhood Komitehs, reminiscent of equivalent local watchdogs in Cuba, Nicaragua, Libya, and Ethiopia. To some extent the network of loyal local clerics replaced that of deeply rooted party. The mosques became centers for military recruitment, administration of the rationing system, indoctrination, and control. The regime's Islamic Republic party (IRP), more a collection of factions claiming allegiance to Khomeini than a centralized cadre party, still performed the function of organizing supporters and choosing leaders.[17]

The first years of Khomeini's rule were chaotic. As the revolution took root, the country entered a period of internal instability and international isolation. Relations with the United States—for Khomeini's followers the "Great Satan"—reached a low point with the seizure of the U.S. embassy in Teheran in November 1979. Fifty-two Americans working in the embassy were held hostage until January 1981. It was the defining act of the Khomeini revolution, and one that would leave the country diplomatically isolated for the next decade.

Internally, Khomeini launched a reign of terror; thousands of enemies of the Islamic state—intellectuals, former officials, military officers, and political figures—were arrested, tried before revolutionary tribunals, and executed. Khomeini's main opposition came from the Mujahideen-i-Khalq, which advocated an Islamic socialist republic and opposed undue interference in government by the mullahs. The Mujahideen fought fire with fire, carrying out a series of bombings that killed some Khomeini confederates, including the newly elected president. (Khomeini had already dismissed the first president, Bani-Sadr.) In 1983 the regime crushed the Mujahideen organization.

One other party warrants attention. From 1979 to 1984 the Tuden, a Marxist (and pro-Soviet) party, collaborated with the regime. Khomeini may have appreciated the Tudeh's efforts to undermine the Shah in the decades before the revolution. He may also have wanted to avoid provoking Moscow, having already antagonized the other superpower. But the alliance was uneasy and unnatural, and in 1984 the members of the Tudeh's central committee were arrested and jailed.

During all this instability, Iraq had invaded Iran. One of the bloodiest wars of attrition in modern history, the Iran-Iraq War drained the economies of both countries and caused appalling carnage and suffering. It disrupted oil supply lines in the Persian Gulf and spread an ominous cloud over the entire region.

It also gave new meaning to the idea of "implacable foes": Khomeini and Iraqi President Saddam Hussein turned the war into a combination of jihad and personal vendetta. Although the Ayatollah said that Iran would never make peace until Saddam Hussein fell, in July 1988, he stunned Iran and the world by deciding to quaff "the bitter drink of poison" and accept a cease-fire with Iraq.[18]

Khomeini's regime had painted itself into a corner. It could not continue the war without powerful foreign friends, which it lacked; and it could not quit the war without victory, which it failed to achieve. The war and the revolution were thus linked. Some observers believed that the survival of the Islamic Republic itself depended on who won the war. When the fighting stopped in August 1988, there was no clear winner or loser. Iran had nearly defeated Iraq several times, despite being badly outgunned, but it had dissipated and squandered its energies and had sacrificed thousands of its young in a war that ended in stalemate.

Within a year of the war's end, on June 4, 1989, the Ayatollah died, leaving a bitter legacy. He had inspired the nation to shed Western influence, which in the minds of his followers had eroded the Islamic essence of Iran's ancient proud culture. In doing this, he had also presided over a pariah state that was identified with terrorism abroad and human rights violations at home. Khomeini's demise raised the inevitable question: Can the Islamic Republic survive without the bearded patriarch who personified it?

After the Ayatollah   The turmoil of the Islamic Republic's first decade diverted attention from the fact that Iran's prerevolutionary political institutions were left largely intact. New parallel structures such as the Council of Guardians and the Revolutionary Guard were simply grafted onto the old system. As time passed the Majlis came to play an increasingly prominent role, and the 1985 presidential election—while not the free-for-all that elections often are in the West—was nonetheless contested by opposition candidates. (Even so, a former prime minister who spoke out against the war with Iraq was not allowed to run.) Ali Khamenei was elected to a second term as president in 1985, and in the summer of 1989 he was also named to succeed Khomeini as Iran's supreme religious leader.

Ten years of revolution and war had made a shambles of Iran's economy. Each month of the war with Iraq had cost an estimated $250 million. In 1976 unemployment jumped from fewer than 1 million to nearly 3 million, inflation rose steadily, and the budget was strained beyond its limits. Agriculture was disrupted by the revolutionary upheaval, but a more settled political environment and a bumper crop in 1985 cut Iran's food imports sharply. Besides saving $500 million in foreign exchange outlays, this greatly improved the nation's self-sufficiency.

The war was most damaging to the economy because it severely cut Iran's foreign oil sales. The United States and its NATO allies boycotted Iranian oil during the hostage crisis, and some of Iran's other customers refused to pay the new steep prices ($37 per barrel, compared with $17 a year earlier). Iran's best customer, Japan, sought alternative supplies and did not buy any oil from Iran in 1981–1982. Worst of all, Iraq bombed Iranian oil fields, refineries, and ports. Raids against the Kharg Island terminal cut Iran's export capacity by one-third and crippled the Abadan refinery as well as other important links in Iran's oil infrastructure.

Throughout the turbulent 1980s the Islamic Republic somehow managed to stay afloat and even to keep the oil flowing, though at greatly reduced levels compared with prewar output. During the later years of the decade Iran also began to end its diplomatic isolation, signing natural-gas agreements with the Soviet Union, for example. And shortly after Khomeini's death in June 1989, Hashemi Rafsanjani, the Majlis speaker, even suggested that the United States should help in freeing Iranian hostages held in Lebanon, implying that Iran might be willing to reciprocate.

The passing of Khomeini provided the opportunity for less xenophobic voices to emerge in Iranian politics (for example, Rafsanjani, who by Western standards is considered a pragmatist interested in repairing relations with the West in return for economic aid). According to W. Scott Harrop, "Ideology will surely remain a factor in Islamic Iran's foreign policy . . . [but] Iran's pressing economic and social ills demand that its international environment be "normalized," a fact working against the most xenophobic of the remaining radicals."[19]

A comparison between the Islamic Republic under Khomeini and the People's Republic of China under Mao Zedong is too tempting to ignore. China enjoyed its greatest economic success after the passing of Mao, who was indispensable in overthrowing the old order but a disaster as the architect of a new one. The same might be said about the Ayatollah Khomeini. If the new leaders can set the Islamic Republic on a steady, pragmatic course, the country should have a bright future. The nation certainly has great natural assets and an energetic people. The task is to channel those virtues to achieve national reconstruction and international reconciliation.

CONCLUSION

The political systems of the Middle East are authoritarian in nature and range in type from personalistic military or civilian dictatorships to hereditary monarchies. The only partial exception is Israel, which has evolved a two-tiered system: Jewish citizens enjoy broad civil and political rights that are denied to Palestinians in the occupied territories. Chapter 12 explores the obstacles to peace in the Middle East, including the Palestinian issue.

STUDY QUESTIONS

1. How is Egypt ruled? Has the Egyptian political system changed much since the overthrow of the monarchy? Since the death of Nasser? If so, what are the significant changes?

2. How is Israel ruled? Is it a theocracy? A democracy? A police state? What are the salient characteristics of Israeli politics? What issues dominate the political scene? Which party or parties control the Knesset and the government? Why?

3. How is Saudi Arabia ruled? What is the basis of legitimacy in the Saudi system? What role does religion play? What threats (internal or external) most concern the rulers?

4. How is Iran ruled? Why was the Ayatollah Khomeini so powerful? How did Khomeini's ideas about Islamic law and ethics shape Iranian politics, and with what consequences? Is Iran changing again now?

SUGGESTED READINGS

Ansari, Hamied. *Egypt: The Stalled Society*. Binghamton, N.Y.: State University of New York, 1986.

Bakhash, Shaul. *The Reign of the Ayatollas*. New York: Basic Books, 1984.

Bianchi, Robert. "Islam and Democracy in Egypt," *Current History*, February 1989.

Chafets, Ze'ev. *Hard Hats and Holy Men: Inside the New Israel*. New York: Morrow, 1987.

Cudsi, A.S., and Ali Dessouki (eds.). *Islam and Power*. Baltimore, Md.: Johns Hopkins, 1981.

Dekmajian, H. Hrair. *Islam in Revolution*. Syracuse, N.Y.: Syracuse University, 1985.

Fuller, Graham E. "War and Revolution in Iran," *Current History*, February 1989.

Palmer, Monte. *Dilemmas of Political Development*. Itasca, Ill.: Peacock, 1989.

Rubin, Barry. *Modern Dictators: Third World Coup Makers, Strongmen, and Populist Tyrants*. New York: McGraw-Hill, 1987.

Springboard, Robert. *Mubarak's Egypt: Fragmentation of the Political Order*. Boulder, Colo.: Westview, 1989.

Yaniv, Avner, "Israel Comes of Age," *Current History*, February 1989.

al-Yassini, Ayman. *Religion and State in the Kingdom of Saudi Arabia*. Boulder, Colo.: Westview, 1985.

NOTES

[1] Barry Rubin, *Modern Dictators: Third World Coup Makers, Strongmen, and Populist Tyrants* (New York: McGraw-Hill, 1987), p. 201.

[2] Ibid., p. 200.

[3] Ibid.

[4] Ibid., p. 202.

[5] Avner Yaniv, "Israel Comes of Age," *Current History*, February 1989, p. 102.

[6] Ibid.

[7] Ibid.

[8] George Lenczowski, *The Middle East in World Affairs* (Ithaca, N.Y.: Cornell University, 1980), p. 562.

[9] Jane Friedman, *Christian Science Monitor*, Apr. 7, 1987.

[10] See Robert Bianchi, "Islam and Democracy in Egypt," *Current History*, p. 93.

[11] Ibid., p. 94.

[12] Monte Palmer, *Dilemmas of Political Development* (Itasca, Ill.: Peacock, 1989), p. 314.

[13] Ibid., p. 314.

[14] Ibid.

[15] Mohammed Reza Pahlavi, *Answer to History* (New York: Stein & Day, 1980), pp. 152–153.

[16] Rubin, op. cit., p. 243.

[17] Ibid., pp. 242–243.

[18] Graham E. Fuller, "War and Revolution in Iran," *Current History*, February 1989, p. 81.

[19] W. Scott Harrop, "Iran's Foreign Policy Realists Take Charge," *Christian Science Monitor*, June 21, 1989, p. 19.

Chapter 12
Beyond the Arab-Israeli Conflict?

The Middle East is truly a region of paradoxes. Its sun-baked barren deserts and withering heat disguise the richest oil reserves in the world. Arab nations share a religion, a language, and a cause (Palestine); yet unity has evaded them. Arab culture is permeated by the strict moral codes of Islam; yet the region's history has been one of conflicts, crusades, and cruelties. Modern Arab nationalism is a reaction against Western capitalism and ''imperialism''; yet Marxism has made few inroads, and communist parties have been outlawed nearly everywhere.

The region's prospects are intertwined with its problems—war and the search for peace. This is painfully evident in war-torn Lebanon and in the West Bank and the Gaza Strip, where the intifada has kept tensions high between the Palestinians and the Israelis since 1988. Conflict keeps raising alarms—most recently in 1990, when Iraq invaded Kuwait and the world stood at attention yet again.

Clearly, there is not one ''Middle East conflict'' but many. Whichever example we consider, however, the most general and enduring conflict has been that between Israel and the Arab world. For that reason, and because the future of the Middle East hinges on it, this chapter pays close attention to issues related to the Palestinians. We also examine how the rivalry between superpowers has contributed to the region's problems, and then we focus on the outlook for Israel and Egypt. Finally, the chapter views Lebanon as a tragic metaphor for the Middle East and concludes with a note about Iraq as a major challenge to the region's status quo.

The Arab-Israeli Conflict

As just noted, the phrase *Middle East conflict* is really a semantic device to describe the de facto state of war—the permanent crisis—that has characterized relations between Arab nations and Israel. In fact, the ''conflict'' involves a long series of contentions rooted in the Palestinian dispute. In essence, the problem is that Palestine is now called Israel; ''the Palestinians'' are Arabs who lived in Palestine before the 1948 war (see Chapter 10). But most Jews who make up the majority of Israel's population are ''returned Jews.'' Their ancestors had fled from Palestine in ancient times and lost physical contact with the *place.* As a result, the concept of the Promised Land became an abstraction, but a powerful one kept alive during the Diaspora by religious symbols and sacred texts that through the centuries have connected Jews everywhere in a community of believers which transcends the boundaries of politics and geography.

For Arabs whose ancestors had lived there since the twelfth century B.C., Palestine was anything but an abstraction. Whereas to the Zionists of Europe Palestine was a homeland, to the Arabs of Palestine it was *home*. They had been born there; it was the place of family, friends, and all things familiar. Most of all, it was the piece of earth they possessed. The centuries had given them an ironclad claim: Palestine belonged to them, individually and collectively. To the Palestinians, the Zionists were interlopers whose leaders were Europeans, after all. From this point of view, Zionism was just another form of imperialism.

It is no mere coincidence that Jewish determination to make the abstraction of a Promised Land real was steeled during the 1930s and 1940s. Until then, the concept of a homeland may have been abstract, but the genocide of the Holocaust changed that. Jews had long been persecuted in Europe, but Hitler's "final solution" exceeded any atrocity so far perpetrated by one group against another.

These brief comments reveal the deep tragedy of the Palestinian dispute: Both sides believe they are fighting for their national survival. For both nations, it is a life-and-death struggle, and so "their leaders have been willing to use any means, including terrorism."[1]

American journalist and author David Lamb has aptly called Palestine "the twice-promised land." His book *The Arabs* summed up the issue succinctly:

> In the midst of the Beirut siege, when Israel was pounding the hell out of the Palestinians, Bill Barret, the Middle East correspondent for the *Dallas Times Herald*, received a telex at the Commodore Hotel from his editor in Texas. The message, which was in effect a request for a story, read: "Who are these Palestinian people, and why don't they just go home?"
>
> Whether intended or not, there was brilliance in that telex. In twelve words, the editor had cut to the marrow. He had boiled the most complex of Middle East issues into the simplest of terms—land. The Palestinians couldn't go home because they had no home. Their land had been promised by the British after World War I to two peoples, the Jews of Europe and the Arabs of the Middle East. When it came time to fulfill that promise, the former got a state, the latter got dispossessed. And neither has known a day of true peace since.[2]

The Palestinians

An estimated 4.5 million Palestinians live in the Middle East. The population of Israel is also about 4.5 million, excluding the occupied territories. About 700,000 Arabs live in Israel proper, and another 1.3 million are in the Israeli-controlled West Bank and Gaza Strip. Thus, if Israel were to annex these occupied territories outright, its Arab minority would be about 2 million. The rest of the Palestinians live in neighboring Arab states, some of them in refugee camps.

The Palestinians "as a people [are] the most literate, industrious and best-educated Arabs in the Middle East."[3] Most Palestinian children attend primary school, and proportionately more receive a higher education than is true of Arabs as a whole. In addition:

They are middle class and politically conservative . . . secular and less conservative than other Arabs. (About 12 percent of the Palestinians are Christian.) They wear Western-style clothes, have only one wife and speak English. They run newspapers in Jordan, banks in Lebanon, the civil service in Kuwait, construction companies in the United Arab Emirates. Within their ranks are poets in Syria, millionaire traders in Saudi Arabia, insurance brokers in London, importers in Los Angeles and professors at leading universities in the United States and Europe.[4]

In Israel, Arabs face many obstacles and do not enjoy equal opportunities, despite having equal rights in theory. David Shipler, the *New York Times* bureau chief in Jerusalem from 1979 to 1984, gave a glimpse of this double standard:

A drive down a country road between a Jewish and an Arab town is a journey between privilege and neglect. In the Arab villages, there are no public swimming pools, no neat parks, and often no sewerage systems. The narrow streets are some-times unpaved, often surfaced poorly, and pitted with potholes. Schools have little science equipment, much scarred and broken furniture, and so many pupils that some classes have to be held in rented rooms. In many areas, the government has con-fiscated land in such tight rings around the villages, and has barred the issuance of building permits for new houses, that the communities have no place in which to expand. Arabs frequently build without necessary permission, thereby risking their future if authorities should decide to have the illegal houses demolished.[5]

Roots of the Intifada

The Palestinian issue was exacerbated when Israel seized the West Bank and the Gaza Strip after the 1967 war. This action created a new category of Palestinians: those living in Israeli-occupied Arab territory. Unlike Arabs within Israel's pre-1967 boundaries, these Palestinians have no legal rights. So far, no consensus has been reached about what to do with the occupied territories. The "hawks" insist that Israel must retain control of the West Bank and Gaza; the "doves" con-tend that conquered lands will ultimately have to be given up as part of a larger peace plan.

One of the most controversial issues involves the Israeli policy of creating settlements in the occupied territories. The policy goes back to 1967, when the Labor government established the first Jewish settlements in the West Bank in order to defend Israel's new eastern border with Jordan. Between 1976 and 1977, without official approval, the ultra-right Gush Emunim (Bloc of the Faithful) set up a number of settlements. The Begin government (1977–1983) supported the settlement policy for "the integrity of the whole Land of Israel"; Ariel Sharon, in charge of the policy, called the settlements "the strongest answer to the establish-ment of a second Palestinian state." (Israel's hawks view Jordan, with more than a third of all Palestinian refugees, to be the first.) Begin said Israel was "creating facts"—meaning that settlements in the territories would, in effect, colonize them. Under this settlement policy, Israel had taken over more than half the West

Bank and the Gaza Strip by the mid-1980s, and the number of Jewish settlers had quadrupled, to 42,500.

Terrorism in the territories became a daily fact of life. Both Arabs and Jews were victims as well as perpetrators in violence ranging from rock throwing to car bombings to stabbings to shootings. Palestinians who were accused of terrorist acts could be detained indefinitely without trial or were tried by military courts without counsel or the right of appeal. The Israeli army deported suspects and often dynamited their homes. But Jewish suspects were not prosecuted or were given light sentences.

In addition, Arab newspapers were censored, and Arab universities were periodically shut down (for disseminating ''hostile'' or ''nationalist'' ideas). The situation deteriorated until, in December 1987, it erupted in Gaza in the *intifada*, the Palestinian uprising. Frequent clashes occurred between Israeli security forces and Palestinian youths, armed with little more than sticks and stones:

> For the first time, the Palestinians showed both a willingness to die for their cause and a significant degree of self-restraint. . . . [Israeli] soldiers were ordered to avoid fatalities and instead to resort to a tactic of ferocious beatings. When this policy led to a worldwide uproar it was abandoned, and the world press was soon barred from access to the territories. The Israeli emphasis then shifted to a combination of curfews, searches, spot raids, covert penetration of Palestinian groups and unidentified sabotage, economic pressures, the exile and (reportedly) assassination of political leaders by undercover elite troops.[6]

The intifada posed a double threat to Israel. First, it might spark another war with Israel's neighbors. Second, even if it did not lead to larger conflict, it eroded Israel's support in the United States and Western Europe, where public opinion was becoming increasingly critical of Prime Minister Shamir and the Likud-led government.

Superpower Rivalry

Although conflict is endemic to the Middle East, outside powers—especially the United States and the Soviet Union—have also played a role. The Cold War rivalry between East and West has had a negative impact in at least three ways.

First, the superpowers have viewed the region as an arena in which to compete for divergent goals. Two constant U.S. aims have been to maintain access to Middle East oil for itself and NATO allies (plus Japan) and to protect oil supply lines. So Washington has sought stability above all and has backed Israel and, to a lesser extent, moderate Arab regimes—to the point of alienating more conservative Arab states. For its part, the Soviet Union has long viewed Persia (Iran) and Turkey as falling within its proper sphere and has jealously guarded its position in the Black Sea area. Protecting its access to the Mediterranean through the Bosporus and Dardenelles straits is also a vital Soviet objective. In the mid-1960s the Soviet navy acquired a global reach and began to challenge the United States in the Persian Gulf and the Indian Ocean. The Kremlin has backed those Arab states whose unrelenting intention has been to ''drive the Israelis into the sea.'' To

Moscow, Israel is a bastion of American power and influence in the Middle East; to Washington, Arab leaders like Libya's Qaddafi and Syria's Assad are troublemaking terrorists (more precisely, "state sponsors" of terrorism).

A second negative impact of the superpower rivalry is the introduction of vast sophisticated arsenals into the region. The United States has given or sold billions of dollars in arms to Israel, Saudi Arabia, Jordan, and Iran (before 1979). The United States has also supplied major aid to Egypt since 1979. Similarly, the Soviet Union has provided weapons and aid to Egypt (before 1973), Syria, Libya, and Algeria, among others. The Soviet Union has also supplied weapons to Iraq (as has the United States) and to both sides in the Persian Gulf War. Other powers have been involved, too: France supplied Iraq, and the People's Republic of China sold Sidewinder missiles to Iran. Examples of arms-trafficking in the region are easy to cite.

A third negative impact is that rivalry has made the superpowers unwilling or unable to pressure their client states in the Middle East to come to the negotiating table with serious peace proposals. The Soviet Union has insisted on an international peace conference, while the United States has backed Israel's position that any such conference is premature until Arab states recognize its right to secure, defensible borders.

The ascendency of Gorbachev in the Soviet Union and the Iraqi invasion of Kuwait in 1990 led to the first major shift in superpower rivalries in the Middle East. Gorbachev seemed genuinely interested in a peaceful settlement of the Palestinian question. In 1990 diplomatic relations between the USSR and Israel, broken in 1956, were restored. When Iraq invaded Kuwait in August 1990, the Soviet Union aligned itself with the United States, supported U.N.-backed sanctions, and cut off arms sales to Iraq. These changes were only first steps, but they were early signs that traditional superpower rivalries could be changing after more than four decades.

The Missing Peace

The 1979 treaty between Egypt and Israel was hailed as a major step toward lasting peace in the Middle East. In accordance with the treaty Israel and Egypt exchanged ambassadors, and Israel returned the Sinai to Egypt. The United States underwrote the agreement, making generous new commitments of military and economic aid to both signatories. A decade later, relations between these former foes were cold but correct. One crucial item was missing however—resolution of the Palestinian issue.

As provided in the treaty, Egypt and Israel began talks in May 1979 aimed at bringing "full autonomy" to the West Bank and Gaza. The intent was to complete arrangements for free elections in the occupied territories and to define the powers of a Palestinian "self-governing authority" within a year. But the talks foundered on such issues as security, land, water, Jewish settlements, and Jerusalem. The last issue was the most emotionally charged: On July 30, 1980, the Knesset made

Jerusalem the undivided capital of Israel, even though Arabs and the United Nations consider East Jerusalem to be occupied territory.

There the matter has rested, and no progress has been possible on the Palestinian issue. Frustrations have mounted until the occupied territories gradually became tinderboxes ready to ignite. Since December 1987 the Palestinian intifada has kept the world's attention on the impasse.

In December 1988 the Palestine Liberation Organization, led by Yasir Arafat, made a peace initiative on its own; it renounced terrorism and implicitly recognized Israel's right to exist. In return, the United States established low-level diplomatic contacts with the PLO. The Israeli government then announced a plan for elections in the occupied territories, but Prime Minister Shamir's hardline pledges about the peace process put the election plan in doubt. Throughout 1989 Shamir continued to place obstacles in the path of peace talks—for example, Israel would talk only with non-PLO Palestinian leaders, the Arabs in Jerusalem could not take part in proposed West Bank elections, the intifada would have to stop before talks could start, and so on.

Israel: From Crisis to Crisis

Israel has come far since 1948. It not only has survived among hostile neighbors but also has won several wars. The peace treaty with Egypt has reduced the threat of a two-front war, for it seems unlikely that other Arab states will attack without Egypt's involvement. But in the Middle East "crisis" is chronic; it continues in the occupied territories, in southern Lebanon, and in the minds of Arab leaders in Libya, Syria, Iraq, and the PLO. The 1982 invasion of Lebanon haunts many Israelis who had never doubted the moral basis of Israel's foreign policy or its justification for military action. A siege mentality—resulting from five wars in four decades, from the intifada, and from constant terrorist threats—hangs in the air. There is, then, no peace in Israel.

Nor is there prosperity. After twenty-five years of impressive achievements, Israel's economy began to sputter during the OPEC oil embargo in 1973. Israel's small size and limited natural resources make it vulnerable to economic pressures and reprisals. After the embargo, which led to worldwide recession and inflation, Israel's GNP growth rate dropped to zero (from an average of 9 percent a year between 1950 and 1976—comparable to rates in Japan, South Korea, and Taiwan). Inflation and trade deficits plagued Israel during the 1980s, reflecting increased dependence on foreign oil after the return of the Sinai wells to Egypt; rising defense spending throughout the 1970s; and deregulation of the economy after 1977.

Endless crises take their tolls on a nation—emotionally, physically, economically, and politically. From 1980 to 1984 inflation in Israel ran over 100 percent annually. In 1985 it skyrocketed to 800 percent and forced the national unity government, then headed by Shimon Peres, to declare a three-month state of emergency. Peres ordered an 18.8-percent devaluation of currency (the shekel), a temporary wage-price freeze, a $360-million cut in subsidies, a 3-percent pay cut for civil servants, and increased income taxes (already the highest in the world). Thousands of government workers were cut from the public payroll (previous Labor governments had created a huge bureaucracy employing two out of three Israelis). The powerful Israeli union, Histadrut, called a one-day nationwide strike.

In 1985–1986 inflation forced the government to keep the shekel artificially high, and exports suffered. The economy bounced back in 1987, but growth was halved—to a dismal 2 percent—the following year. Belt-tightening continued during the late 1980s, and everyday life was a struggle for average Israelis. It was difficult to make ends meet, there was little time for relaxation, and the nation was sullen and polarized. A sense that prosperity was slipping away, maybe forever, had surfaced. With pessimism came a ''brain drain,'' as talented young people left Israel for opportunities abroad. And if young people were leaving, would Jews from other nations want to emigrate to Israel? Or would they, like so many Soviet Jews, go to the United States instead?

As a welfare state (social programs equal one-third the GNP every year) with high defense outlays (about one-fourth the budget), Israel typically operates on a deficit. This is eased by four main factors—donations from abroad (especially Jews in the United States), reparations from West Germany for World War II, massive foreign aid (mainly from the United States), and borrowing from foreign banks. In the mid-1980s Israel's foreign debt reached $24 billion, equal to its GNP, and interest totaled $4 billion.

In agriculture, Israel has ''made the desert bloom'' through sophisticated technology and by diverting water from the Jordan River. Half its farmland is irrigated, and the nation is close to food self-sufficiency (90 percent). Israeli kibbutzim (communes) have helped to achieve this impressive agricultural record, but agriculture accounts for only about 6 percent of the GNP and cannot ensure prosperity by itself.

Israel's manufacturing sector is mostly small-scale, except for its aircraft industry. The Cabinet scuttled a major project, the largely U.S.-financed Lavi jet fighter, in August 1987 by a one-vote margin. Cancellation meant the loss of several hundred jobs, but it was argued that expanding industries like electronics would create new jobs and ease the 7 percent unemployment rate in the late 1980s.

Egypt: Subsidized Stability

Egypt's economy remains precarious. Agriculture is the most important sector, accounting for 30 percent of national income, but arable land is limited, and population growth tends to cancel out any gains. Cotton and sugar cane are the main crops. Output increased during the 1980s because of better control over irrigation by means of the Aswan Dam, expansion of land devoted to cash crops (especially cotton), and improved planting methods. But the dam has not boosted the economy as much as Egyptians hoped. The goal was to offset population growth and achieve a measure of food self-sufficiency by reclaiming vast tracts of desert with the abundant waters of the Nile River. But costs have been much higher than expected, and the prolonged drought in the Sahel and the Sahara Desert has imperiled Egypt's sole water supply. In 1987 Lake Nasser reached its lowest level, and there was not enough water to run the Aswan power station, which supplies 20 percent of Egypt's energy.

Egypt has sizable reserves of natural gas and oil (4.5 billion barrels in 1983). New oil discoveries have been made in the Western Desert and the Gulf of Suez. The nation also earns foreign currency from Suez Canal tolls and user fees, tourism, and remittances from roughly 4 million Egyptians working elsewhere (especially in Saudi Arabia and other Persian Gulf states). Finally, U.S. foreign aid helped significantly in the 1980s; Egypt received $2.7 billion in 1986 alone.

President Mubarak's government has sought to reduce dependence on imported goods by encouraging expansion of manufacturing, especially of consumer goods. Incentives include a ten-year tax exemption and the remission of customs duties on machinery for manufacturing. Foreign investors have shown interest in setting up assembly plants in Egypt to take advantage of the abundant labor supply.

The 1979 peace treaty with Israel has been a mixed blessing for Egypt. Other Arab nations ostracized Cairo for a decade, and the treaty also caused political tremors inside Egypt, culminating in the assassination of President Sadat. Egypt was readmitted to Arab councils only since 1989. But from an economic standpoint the treaty has paid off. It has brought billions in U.S. aid and has created cordial relations with the West generally, which encourages tourism. (The pyramids, of course, are among the world's most famous attractions.) Finally, the treaty has made Egypt a more attractive "risk" to foreign investors, who naturally dislike political instability.

Public subsidies are a way of life in Egypt. For example, the government pays high prices to producers of food staples and holds down the costs to consumers. That makes both groups happy, but it diverts resources into consumption rather than investment. Similarly, Egypt built a massive bureaucracy under Nasser and Sadat in order to create jobs for educated youths who otherwise had few career opportunities. The government pursues such policies for at least two reasons. First, "Nasserism" was and is a socialist philosophy that blends populism and nationalism. Second, subsidies and jobs are ways to mollify the population in the face of lagging economic development. They are a kind of bribe, an agreement whereby government and citizens each accept the others' inefficiency.

President Muburak is making an effort to get the economy moving, to wean society from its addiction to subsidies, and to create real jobs by starting new industries. In November 1986 he fired his entire Cabinet and assembled a new team of highly qualified technocrats. Egyptian business leaders and foreign investors seem to have confidence in this new Cabinet, and there are signs of progress as well as reasons for optimism. But prosperity will come slowly—in increments—if at all.

Lebanon: Metaphor for the Middle East

North of Israel and west of Syria, Lebanon is a once-lovely little country on the Mediterranean Sea. Its narrow coastal plain contains Beirut, the capital, and a few miles east rises a rugged mountain range, Mount Lebanon. Beyond this lies a fertile valley where most of the country's wheat is grown. Further east still, the snow-capped mountains of the Anti-Lebanon Range jut skyward, separating Lebanon from Syria.

Mount Lebanon, the nucleus of the modern Lebanese state, has been a natural buffer against frequent invaders en route to some other object of imperial conquest. If Lebanon's misfortune was that it happened to be on the way to other places, its main advantage was its seaports, which gave Syria, Jordan, and other inland areas access to Europe via the Mediterranean.

Lebanon's origins as a nation-state can be traced to the sixteenth century. The Ottoman Turks, who eventually conquered most of the Near East, left Mount Lebanon in the hands of powerful local families—both Maronite Christians and Druze—who became the building blocks of modern Lebanon. Maronite dominance and the fragmented nature of Lebanese society date from this early period.

Lebanon was a social and political mosaic long before the civil war of 1975–1976. Its religions include twenty-one Christian sects and five Islamic; Maronite Christians, Druze, and Sunni and Shia Muslims are most prominent. Equally diverse is the feudal social system in which families and clans form intricate networks. Each is headed by a *zaim* ("boss"). Zaims had private armies, and family feuds were often violent. The rivalries were reinforced by religious animosities.

A particularly bitter rivalry developed between Maronites and Druze, and in 1860 a bloody civil war broke out between them. The British and the French intervened after the Druze massacred 12,000 Christians and drove another 100,000 from their homes in a single month. After World War I, Lebanon was made a French mandate. Maronite leaders persuaded France to create a separate Lebanese state in 1920 (rather than combining Lebanon and Syria, as France had intended). The nation that emerged was much larger than the Mount Lebanon territory, which set the stage for Lebanon's current predicament, for it contained areas in which both Sunni and Shia Muslims predominated.

In 1943 Maronite and Sunni leaders formed the National Pact, whereby the Christians foreswore alliances with nations outside the region and the Muslims agreed not to seek a merger with the Arab world. It was further agreed that the 6:5 Christian/Muslim representation in the legislature would be extended to all public offices. Historically, Christians have outnumbered Muslims in Lebanon, but after the war Muslim communities grew faster because of an influx of refugees and higher birth rates.

Lebanon emerged from World War II as an independent but hardly unified nation. Its political system was based on a preexisting constitution that, though representative, favored the Maronites. An unwritten rule ensured that the president would always be a Maronite.

Lebanese society is thus, at best, a loose confederation of religious communities and patron-client networks. Nonetheless, except for a civil-war "dress rehearsal" in 1958, these groups coexisted in relative peace within a political system that always teetered on anarchy. It was undergirded by little more than a bargain struck during World War II and sealed with a handshake. The National Pact itself was never even put in writing.

Perhaps one reason why this precarious arrangement worked as well and as long as it did was that economic prosperity gave everyone a stake in political stability. Per capita incomes rose steadily between 1950 and 1974; Lebanon compared favorably in this regard with some of the oil-producing Arab nations, even though Lebanon has no oil. Its flourishing economy was a monument to free enterprise. Basic social and even financial services were provided by the extended family rather than by the state. Fortunes were made in real estate and construction, spurred by millions of tourists attracted by the mild climate, scenic mountains, and sandy beaches. Foreign banks and corporations set up Middle East headquarters in Lebanon because of its location, educated labor force, absence of government regulation, and communications and transportation links. But most of all, they were attracted to Lebanon because it was one of the few stable areas in the region.

The illusion of tranquility was shattered in 1975, when a ferocious civil war broke out—ironically sparked by the presence of a non-Lebanese group, the Palestinians. Many Palestinian war refugees had fled to Lebanon after 1948 and were absorbed into Lebanese society as well as business, banking, journalism, and higher education. But a second wave of Palestinian refugees arrived after the 1967 war, and unlike the earlier group these ended up in refugee camps. They were stateless persons who had no homeland and, lacking passports, could not leave Lebanon to go anywhere else.

When the PLO was expelled from Jordan in the early 1970s, it moved its headquarters to Beirut, and refugee camps in Lebanon became natural PLO strongholds. Then the PLO began conducting raids against Israeli settlements from southern Lebanon, and Israel retaliated. Step by step, Lebanon was drawn into the Middle East conflict. The civil war erupted between Christians and Muslims after a bus filled with Palestinians was attacked by a group connected to the militant Maronite Phalange party.

The civil war brought to the surface the many conflicting interests and goals that had been contained for thirty years by the National Pact. Maronites wanted to rid Lebanon of Palestinians; Sunni Muslims wanted full equality with Christians; Shia Muslims and Druze wanted a larger voice in government.

In 1976 a cease-fire was arranged, and the Arab League asked Syria to enforce it. Syria had always had special interest in Lebanon, which is vital to its trade and communications with the outside world. Israel also had a special interest, particularly when the PLO began using southern Lebanon to attack Israeli settlements near the border. Israel countered by establishing control over this area.

Thus, what had begun as a civil war over Palestinians in Lebanon—which, in turn, resulted from the establishment of Israel—soon developed into a confrontation that directly involved Syria and Israel and indirectly entangled other Arab nations, the superpowers, and, in 1978, the United Nations Interim Force in Lebanon. But no force could keep the peace in a country that had come unglued. Feuding Lebanese factions fought relentlessly, and blood flowed. Some 300,000 Lebanese fled to northern cities from the Israeli-occupied south, and Beirut became an urban battleground.

In 1982 Israel decided to force the issue, invading Lebanon in June, surrounding Beirut, and driving PLO guerrillas out of Lebanon. Maronites and Shia Muslims in south Lebanon applauded the PLO exodus, but the Israeli presence was equally undesirable. Furthermore, many PLO guerrillas slipped back into Lebanon or established new camps under Syrian protection in the Bekaa Valley. Israel's control of Beirut gave Maronite militants (the Phalange) an excuse to take revenge against Palestinians, who were defenseless without the PLO. In September 1982 Christian Phalangists entered refugee camps in West Beirut and massacred hundreds of people, mostly women and children. The action outraged world opinion and sent shock waves through Israel's government, whose apparent complicity led shortly thereafter to Prime Minister Begin's resignation.

After the Israeli invasion Lebanon remained fractured by fratricidal warfare. Different parts of the country and capital were controlled by different factions. Syria controlled the Bekaa Valley, and Israel held southern Lebanon. Phalange leader Bashir Gemayel was elected to head a "government of national reconciliation"—a misnomer, since it lacked both legitimacy and authority, was never national in scope, and could not hope to effect reconciliation. President-elect Gemayel's reputation for ruthlessness had earned him a raft of enemies, and he was assassinated by a bomb that destroyed the Phalange party headquarters before he could be sworn in; Parliament then elected his older brother, Amin Gemayel. Israeli troops left Lebanon in June 1985, but Israel kept a "security zone" along its northern border to guard against future attacks.

Ironically, Israel's invasion of Lebanon may actually have helped pave the way for Iran's inroads there. According to R. K. Ramazani:

> The effects of the Iranian Revolution combined with the aftermath of the Camp David Accords and Egyptian-Israeli peace treaty to give rise to an unprecedented alliance between Syria and Iran. Iran's new access to Lebanon through Syria effectively shortened the distance between Iran and Lebanon. The alliance also diminished Syria's resentment over Iranian influence in Lebanon, especially after the Israeli invasion. The invasion, which was prompted in part by the Iranian Revolution, provided a unique opportunity for the Khomeini ideological crusade against the "twin evil" of America and Israel.
>
> . . . the invasion presented an extraordinary opportunity for the Iranian revolutionaries to try to export their Islamic revolution to Lebanon. The ideological appeal of the Khomeini regime could have found no more fertile soil in which to flourish than in the sense of victimhood festering among the Shia masses in Lebanon.[7]

Foreign intervention in Lebanon has only worsened and complicated an already impossible situation. Besides old rivalries between Christian Phalangists and Sunni Muslims, the situation has led to new rivalries, such as that between Shia Muslims and the PLO. Shiite radical groups like Amal, Hezbullah, and the Islamic Jihad—some linked to Iran—have carried out kidnappings and other acts of violence, while cease-fires and endless conferences have led nowhere.

Israel's departure from Lebanon left Syria in the unenviable position of being "an external power, enjoying partial hegemony and struggling with the tasks of keeping public order, effecting political reform, reconciling the diverse interests of its allies and . . . advancing its own interests."[8] Syria's attempts to cut the Gordian knot of deadlock proved fruitless. In February 1987 it sent 7,000 troops back to Beirut in another effort to bring safety and stability to the battle-scarred city.

As soon as Iraq and Iran negotiated a cease-fire, President Saddam Hussein's thoughts turned to revenge against other enemies, including Syria. The following passage captures the sense in which Lebanon had become a convenient, all-purpose battlefield for the pursuit of regional rivalries:

> Beyond an intensification of the propaganda warfare, Iraq's determination to penalize Syria has already been translated into actual policies in Lebanon. Iraq provided Syria's main Lebanese adversary, the Lebanese Forces, with new weapons and financial aid with a view to encouraging the Maronite militia to stand up to Syrian pressures. . . . Iraq intends to return to the Lebanese arena from which it was practically absent during the last eight years [i.e., during the Persian Gulf War].[9]

Lebanon is thus a caldron in which the region's many rivalries and hatreds boil. Here's a short list of ingredients: Syria versus the PLO; Christian Phalangists versus Sunni Muslims; Syria versus Israel; Israel versus the PLO; Syria versus the pro-Iranian Hezbullah (Shiite Muslims); and Lebanese Forces (Christians) versus Syria. In this tumbling free-for-all, the Lebanese forces have sometimes cooperated with the PLO and Hezbullah against Syria's President Assad, whom many Maronites view as the main threat to Lebanon's independence as well as their own privileged position.[10]

In September 1988 Amin Gemayel stepped down as Lebanon's president when his term expired, leaving the highest office vacant, and political stalemate prevented Parliament from electing a successor. Two prime ministers, a Maronite and a Sunni, were eventually named, but the government had no president. Before stepping down, Gemayel had designated the commander of the Christian army, Michel Aoun, as the interim head of government; but the Sunni prime minister rejected this appointment and established a rival government in West Beirut. Syria imposed a land blockade on Aoun's forces in March 1989, and four months later it added a sea blockade (and sank a Maltese oil tanker to underscore its resolve), charging that Iraq had given General Auon Soviet-made missiles.

At the beginning of this decade Lebanon was nominally independent but faced serious questions about how long the "government" could survive. As far back as 1966 an American scholar offered this premonition about the country: "Lebanon is too conspicuous and successful an example of political democracy and economic liberalism to be tolerated in a region that has turned its back on both systems."[11]

The Iraqi Challenge

In August 1990 Iraqi President Saddam Hussein ordered his army into Kuwait, surprising his neighbors and the world. Tactically, the invasion was brilliant: Within hours Iraq seized control of Kuwait and forced the ruling emir to flee. In one fell swoop Saddam grabbed an extremely valuable parcel of the Middle East, enlarging the considerable oil reserves already under his control and serving notice that Iraq had arrived as a great power in the region.

Iraq's "sudden" appearance in this new guise was not entirely a shock. For years Saddam had been reputed to entertain nuclear ambitions. That was one reason why Israel had bombed Iraq's nuclear reactor near Baghdad in 1981— a humiliation that stung Saddam and many of his Arab admirers. In the years following, Iraq fought fiercely against Iran, using its arsenal of chemical weapons and newly acquired ballistic missiles. By 1990 Baghdad boasted a million-man army equipped with thousands of Soviet-supplied tanks and missiles captured from Iran. Its invasion of Kuwait, then, was the culmination of a drive for hegemony that had been under way for many years.

Iraq's annexation of Kuwait put the world on notice and raised a greater threat: that the next goal was the Saudi oil fields. To deter any further action by Iraq, the United States sent a massive force to the Persian Gulf—its largest deployment since the Vietnam War. But the United States was not alone in condemning Iraq. In voting for a total embargo against Iraq, the United Nations Security Council expressed the consensus of the international community that Baghdad's aggression against Kuwait could not go unpunished. Despite the active involvement of the international community, it was above all the military might of the United States that confronted Iraq. In no small measure, the future of the Middle East—the regional balance of power, and perhaps more—hinged on the outcome of this confrontation.

CONCLUSION

There is not one "Middle East conflict" but many. The ongoing Arab-Israeli conflict itself is multifaceted. In addition, throughout the 1980s war ravaged Iran and Iraq, and there have been tensions between Syria and Iraq, Egypt and Libya, Libya and Tunisia, Morocco and Algeria, and many, many others. Yet the Middle East is not the only region where war and revolution have destabilized governments, torn at the social fabric, and ravaged economies. In Part V we will see that Asia has also endured great violence in this century.

STUDY QUESTIONS

1. In what sense is the Middle East an area of paradoxes?
2. What are historical sources and contemporary manifestations of Arab-Israeli enmity? Why has peace between these two groups been so elusive?
3. What is the intifada? How did it start, and why? What do Palestinians want? What do Israelis want? Who's right, and who's wrong, in your opinion?
4. How and why did Egypt and Israel sign a peace treaty in the late 1970s, what were the terms of the treaty, and where do relations between these two former foes stand at present? Will Egypt and Israel continue to live in peace? (Analyze the situation from the standpoint of both countries.)
5. Is Israel an economic success or not? Is it doing better, about the same as, or worse than it was doing twenty years ago? What are its most pressing economic and social problems now?
6. Is Egypt's economy still developing, or has it stalled? What are Egypt's major obstacles?
7. In what sense is Lebanon a metaphor for the Middle East? Can Lebanon be saved, or is it too late? (Give reasons for your opinion.)

SUGGESTED READINGS

Farah, Tawfic E. *Pan-Arabism and Arab Nationalism: The Continuing Debate.* Boulder, Colo.: Westview, 1987.

Luciani, Giacomo, and Ghassan Salambe, eds. *The Politics of Arab Integration.* London: Croom Helm, 1988.

Smith, Charles D. *Palestine and the Arab-Israeli Conflict.* New York: St. Martin's, 1988.

Quandt, William B, ed. *The Middle East: Ten Years after Camp David.* Washington, D.C.: Brookings, 1988.

Yehoshafat, Harkabi. *Israel's Fateful Hour.* New York: Harper & Row, 1988.

NOTES

[1] David Lamb, The Arabs: Journey Beyond the Mirage (New York: Vintage Books, 1988), p. 200.

[2] Ibid., p. 199.

[3] Ibid., p. 201.

[4] Ibid.

[5] David Shipler, *Arab and Jew: Wounded Spirits in a Promised Land* (New York: Penguin, 1987), pp. 443–444.

6 Avner Yanev, "Israel Comes of Age," *Current History*, February 1989, p. 101.

7 R. K. Ramazani, *Revolutionary Iran* (Baltimore, Md.: Johns Hopkins, 1986), p. 175.

8 Itamar Rabinovich, *Current History*, February 1989, p. 80.

9 Ibid., pp. 77–78.

10 Ibid., p. 103.

11 Charles Issawi, "Economic Development and Political Liberalism in Lebanon," in Leonard Binder, ed., *Politics in Lebanon* (New York: Wiley, 1966), pp. 80–81.

CHINA

Area: 3,691,521 square miles
Population: 1.1 billion
Density per square mile: 298
Language: Chinese (Mandarin, Cantonese, local dialects)
Literacy rate: 77%
Religions: Nonreligious (59%), folk religions (20%), atheist (12%)
Monetary unit: yuan
GNP: (1988) $350 billion; $320 per capita

JAPAN

Area: 143,574 square miles
Population: 123 million
Density per square mile: 857
Language: Japanese
Literacy rate: 99%
Religions: Shintoist, Buddhist
Monetary unit: yen
GNP: (1988) $1.8 trillion; $15,030 per capita

INDIA

Area: 1,229,737 square miles
Population: 833 million
Density per square mile: 658
Languages: Hindi and English (official), 12 other languages recognized by Constitution
Literacy rate: 36%
Religions: Hindu (83%), Muslim (11%), Christian (3%), Sikh (2%)
Monetary unit: rupee
GNP: (1987) $246 billion; $290 per capita

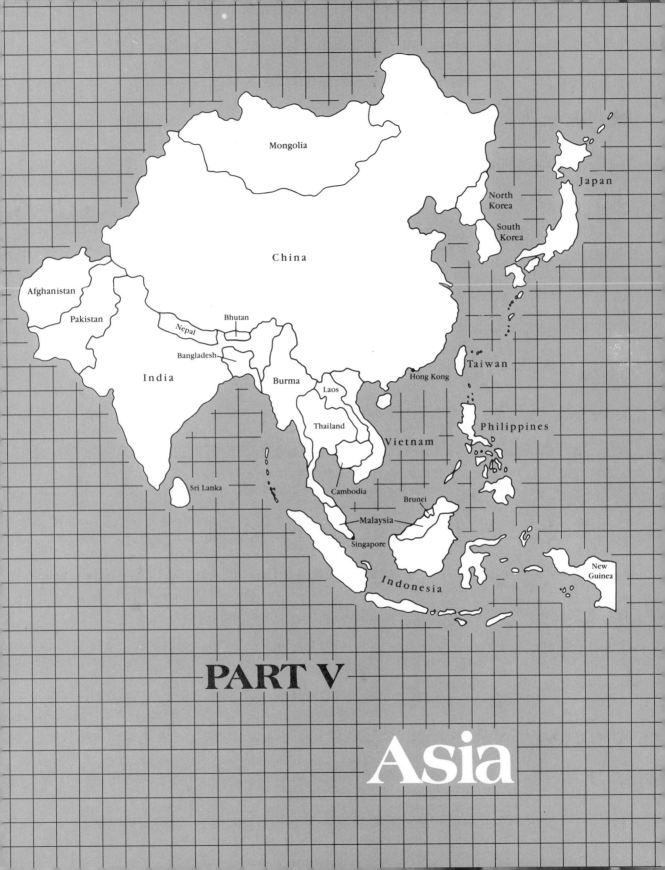

Mongolia

China

Afghanistan

Pakistan

Nepal

Bhutan

Bangladesh

India

Burma

Laos

Thailand

Cambodia

Sri Lanka

Malaysia

Singapore

Brunei

Indonesia

Vietnam

Hong Kong

Taiwan

Philippines

North Korea

South Korea

Japan

New Guinea

PART V

Asia

Chapter 13
Civilizations and Empires

If you could start a chain of fast-food restaurants anywhere in the world, Asia would seem to be the place to do it. Why? Because 60 percent of the earth's inhabitants live there. Asia is huge—it covers 30 percent of the globe—but its demographic rather than geographic mass is what makes Asia a colossus. As far as that fast-food franchise is concerned, a closer look would reveal that wealth in the world is grossly maldistributed, and most of Asia has been left out of the equation. Relatively few people would be able to afford your food. Several Asian nations— led by Japan—are now in the process of redressing the global economic balance in Asia's favor, however. In fact, according to some prognostications, the twenty-first century might belong to Asia.

Asia encompasses the following countries and regions, some of which are in the Middle East (see Part IV) and the western Pacific: Afghanistan, Bangladesh, Bhutan, Brunei, Burma, Cambodia, Hong Kong, India, Indonesia, Japan, Laos, Malaysia, the Pacific regions of Melanesia and Micronesia, Nepal, North Korea, Pakistan, the People's Republic of China (PRC), the Philippines, Polynesia, Singapore, South Korea, the Soviet Union (see Part III), Sri Lanka, Taiwan (the Republic of China on Taiwan, or ROC), Thailand, and Vietnam. In terms of population and geography, these nations range in size from mainland China and India, with a combined population of nearly 2 billion (about 40 percent of the world's population), to Brunei, with a population of 240,000 (about the size of Lincoln, Nebraska).

Of the six regions explored in this book, Asia is the most difficult to treat as a single region because of its size and diversity. On the basis of history, geography, cultures, and languages, one can identify five overlapping subregions: East Asia (particularly mainland China); South Asia (India, Pakistan, and Sri Lanka); Northeast Asia (the two Koreas, North China, and the Soviet Far East); Southeast Asia (Vietnam, Laos, Cambodia, Singapore, Brunei, Thailand, Malaysia, and Indonesia); and the Pacific Rim (most notably Japan, Taiwan, the Philippines, and the South Pacific island chains of Polynesia, Micronesia, and Melanesia.)

On the basis of region alone, Asia can be divided into three subsystems: East Asia (mainland China, North and South Korea, Taiwan, and Japan); Southeast Asia (Vietnam, Laos, Cambodia, Thailand, Malaysia, Singapore, Brunei, Indonesia, and the Philippines); and South Asia (India, Pakistan, Bangladesh, Sri Lanka, Burma, Nepal, and Bhutan). However, some countries do not fit easily into any of these three (for example, the Philippines, Myanmar, and Afghanistan).

Regional subsystems can also be drawn on the basis of political economy. For example, the New Industrial Countries (NICs) are anchored in East Asia (especially South Korea, Taiwan, and Hong Kong); the Newly Exporting Countries

293

(NECs) are primarily in Southeast Asia (Indonesia, Malaysia, Thailand, and the Philippines); the Marxist-Leninist Countries (MLCs) are in Indochina (Vietnam, Cambodia, and Laos); and the Basic Needs Countries (BNCs) are in South Asia (India, Pakistan, Bangladesh, and Burma). But this schema is also far from perfect. For example, Singapore is a NIC, but it is located in Southeast (rather than East) Asia. Also, it is not clear where mainland China and Japan fit in. The former is an MLC in transition to a market-oriented NEC, while Japan is one of the most advanced nations in the world. (This political-economic model of Asia is discussed further in Chapter 15.)

Any attempt to draw clear boundaries around regional subsystems in Asia is beset by problems. For example, mainland China is so prominent in Asia—geographically, historically, culturally, and politically—that it cannot but intrude into other subregions. Even in South Asia, where India is clearly dominant, the People's Republic of China has territorial interests. China's influence on the language and culture of neighboring or nearby nations is very evident in Korea, Vietnam, and Japan.

Some patterns are distinctive to Asia or to large parts of it, however. First, until the mid-twentieth century no nation in Asia had direct experience with democratic rule. None had any indigenous democratic or republican institutions. There was no tradition of "natural rights," morally or philosophically. Authoritarianism of one kind or another, in most cases dynastic in nature, was the basis of all political traditions.

The archetypal Asian political system was that of Imperial China, long described by Western historians as "oriental despotism" and generally thought to be a pattern repeated, with local variations, throughout Asia. In reality there were any number of oriental despotisms, such as one can identify a variety of African or European despotisms. Notwithstanding, it is true that China, Korea, Japan, Vietnam, Cambodia, and India all had hereditary autocratic rulers who governed through centralized administrative systems embedded in hierarchical societies. Moreover, these rulers were the products of advanced civilizations with complex writing systems, a class of scholars and scribes, monumental architecture and public works (especially roads and irrigation systems), and impressive religious and philosophical traditions.

To survey Asian politics, we again will choose a few countries as case studies. The choices are based on the size and importance of the countries as well as on the extent to which they represent the region's patterns. We must, then, take account of China—presently called the People's Republic of China (PRC). The PRC's large, industrious population and its technological ingenuity, cultural prowess, and imposing geopolitical traits have long thrust it onto Asia's center stage.

India, with the second-largest population in the world, is the dominant power in South Asia. Although India is a leading candidate to join the world's "nuclear club," it faces daunting problems related to overpopulation, regional and communal strife, vulnerability to natural catastrophe, pervasive poverty, and excessive regulation of the economy.

Finally, Japan—democratically governed and economically ascendant—is Asia's greatest success story in the postwar period. It is tempting to view Japan as an exception to the trends and patterns in the rest of Asia. Until recently it was common to regard Japan as better reflecting the West than the East, at least economically and politically. Indeed, the Trilateral Commission, a private foreign-policy interest group founded by David Rockefeller in 1973, consists of representatives from the United States, the European Community, and Japan. But today Japan is no longer an isolated example of ''Western'' technology in an Asian setting: South Korea, Taiwan, the British colony of Hong Kong, and Singapore are all important producers of ''high-tech'' exports, and in the 1980s even mainland China began moving toward an export-oriented model of development.

Physical Environment and Population

Stereotypes of Asia often revolve around size and scale—teeming masses of people and vast expanses of desert, mountains, rivers, and jungles. The images are partly figments of the imagination and partly fragments of the truth. In geographic area as well as population, Asia *is* gigantic. It is nearly twice as large as North America, the second-largest land mass. And, as noted already, three-fifths of all people on earth live somewhere in Asia (two-thirds of them in China and India).

Environment

Because of its enormity, Asia has every kind of climate, from the frozen tundra of Siberia to the steamy jungles of Indochina and the tropical lowlands of Indonesia. In between lie temperate zones, which encompass northern China, Korea, Japan, and Taiwan; a massive desert in western China and the semiarid plains of Soviet Central Asia; the high plateaus and snowy Himalayan wilderness of Tibet, Bhutan, and Nepal; and the huge ''subcontinent'' of South Asia with the Great Indian Desert in the northwest and the semitropical Deccan Peninsula in the south.

The topography, too, offers great variety—mountain ranges, fertile river valleys, coastal lowlands, and flowing plains. Much of Asia's deep interior is either sparsely inhabited or not inhabited at all. In fact, this is a striking regional feature: Asia supports over half the world's people, but much of its surface is mountain, desert, or jungle terrain that challenges human life. Mainland China, for example, has more than a fifth of the world's population, and yet two-thirds of its territory is uninhabitable.

We might expect an abundance of natural resources in so vast and diverse a territory, but Asia is not particularly well endowed in this respect. Only mainland China, Indonesia, and the tiny kingdom of Brunei produce much oil, and none is a major oil producer. (Indonesia's reserves are estimated at about 9 billion barrels, about a third of Venezuela's reserves and a small fraction of Saudi Arabia's.) Japan, the region's richest nation, imports all its petroleum. Malaysia produces 35 percent of the world's tin and rubber, and Indonesia exports various raw materials. In general, however, no Asian nation is blessed with extraordinary mineral resources.

Human beings are Asia's most abundant resource—a point not to be dismissed. Japan has proved that natural resources are less vital to economic development than human resources are. Although burgeoning populations have been a liability for many Asian nations, South Korea, Taiwan, Hong Kong, Singapore, and the PRC have harnessed their human potential and have made impressive economic gains in recent years. In contrast, India and Indonesia have failed to do this, while nations like Bangladesh, Burma, Vietnam, Laos, and Cambodia are among the most stagnant nations economically.

Population

Extraordinary efforts to control the population explosion in the People's Republic of China brought the rate of increase down to 0.8 percent by the mid-1980s, but it rose to 1.4 percent in 1989. In India, such efforts have been desultory, and the annual growth rate is 2.2 percent. Other populous Asian nations also face demographic pressures, especially Indonesia (2 percent), Malaysia (2.5 percent), Vietnam (2.6 percent), Bangladesh (2.8 percent), and Pakistan (2.9 percent). The most highly developed nations have the lowest growth rates: In 1989 Japan's was the lowest (0.5 percent), followed by Taiwan (1.1 percent) and Singapore (1.2 percent).

Overall, the fastest-growing populations are in Africa, not Asia. (Kenya's growth rate in 1989 was a staggering 4.1 percent!) But the population *base* is so large in Asia that even moderate growth will keep the region's demographic trend-lines climbing rapidly well into the twenty-first century. Statistical projections for Asia are truly alarming. The region's population in 1990 was estimated at 3.057 billion (the last two digits alone represent more people than in France or Great Britain), and during the decade the population will grow by about 486 million, to 3.543 billion. By 2020 Asia's population is projected to reach 4.466 billion—as many people as were on the entire globe in 1980.

Such data indicate the dimensions of the challenge Asia faces. Even Japan, with its booming economy, has a quality-of-life problem on its hands: Its population is stable, but 123 million Japanese are now living in a country about the size of Montana. In the late 1980s, 35 percent of Japan's population lived on 1 percent of the land; the nation as a whole had a population density per square mile of 857 people. The Tokyo-Yokohama urban area had over 25 million people in the mid-1980s, while the Osaka-Kobe-Kyoto area had 13.6 million. If projections hold, Tokyo-Yokohama will be at nearly 30 million by the year 2000, and the population of Osaka-Kobe-Kyoto will exceed 20 million. Social unrest, political instability, and a deteriorating quality of life loom large unless Japan can find ways to soften the impact of its urban population growth.

Economic Development: The Three Faces of Asia

Levels of economic development vary widely from one part of Asia to the next. Japan has one of the most highly developed economies in the world, and in the late 1980s it rivaled the Soviet Union for second place. Based on gross national product (GNP), only the United States ranked above Japan. (If trends continue, Japan will surpass the United States in GNP by the year 2015.) In qualitative terms, Japan's high-tech multinational corporations, strong currency, thriving financial institutions, huge trade surpluses, and status as a major creditor all make it an economic superpower.

Following in Japan's footsteps are Asia's "four little dragons"—South Korea, Taiwan, Hong Kong, and Singapore. They have adopted strategies patterned on the Japanese model: (a) accelerated industrialization; (b) export promotion; and (c) heavy protectionism. All four nations and Hong Kong are now mass-consumption societies and exporters of high-tech manufactures as well as other, more traditional goods. Besides exporting cars, motorcycles, electronic equipment, and the like, Japan has become a major international financial market. South Korea has also begun exporting cars and, along with Taiwan, is producing many other consumer products that compete directly with Japanese exports. By the mid-1980s, South Korea's per capita income had climbed above $4,500; Taiwan's hovered around $6,000; and Singapore's exceeded $8,000. Japan's was $21,820.

Elsewhere in Asia, countries undertaking basic economic development (road building, mining, steel fabricating, electric power generation, and so on will have all they can do to keep pace with population growth. The poorest Asian nations had abysmal per-capita income levels in the mid-1980s: Vietnam ($180), Burma ($179), Bangladesh ($113), and Cambodia ($100).

Economic statistics do not necessarily give an accurate picture of conditions in a given area. For example, the People's Republic of China, Sri Lanka, and the Indian state of Kerala have a low per-capita GNP by Western standards, and the number of people living in poverty is still rising; but other indicators—infant mortality, life expectancy, literacy, nutrition, and employment—show significant gains.[1] These may be more meaningful measures of development than standards based on money and income.

Some experts argue that the greatest need in the most poverty-stricken developing countries is for more and better jobs. How, they ask, can overpopulated, undercapitalized nations advance economically unless they can put their most abundant resource—human beings—to work? And how can they create good jobs without capital and without markets, both domestic and foreign? Finally, how can they afford to produce for domestic consumption unless people have jobs and incomes so that they can translate their needs into demand? A large population creates the *potential* for demand-driven economic growth, but only if the great majority of people have significant purchasing power.

Thus, from the standpoint of political economy, Asia presents three faces to the world: One is affluent and technologically sophisticated; another is impoverished and tradition bound; and a third is in transition.

Historical and Cultural Patterns in Asia

Asia provided the setting for several ancient civilizations. During the past several millennia, empires flourished in China, India, and Indochina. An urban civilization with an as-yet undeciphered writing system evolved in the Indus Valley (in the northern part of South Asia) and was possibly ruled as a single empire from 3000 to 2500 B.C. It had geometric cities with underground sewers and huge granaries. Bronze was used, and graphic arts were highly developed. This early civilization was probably already in decline when Aryan invaders from the north overran it, around 1750 B.C. The invaders spoke an Indo-European language from which the modern languages of Pakistan, north India, and Bangladesh descend. An Aryan civilization spread from the west as far as the Ganges valley by 500 B.C.

To some extent, Asia is analogous to Europe with respect to dissemination of culture. Just as the cultures and languages of Western Europe were, in many cases, heavily influenced by Greek and Roman civilizations, so those of South, East, and Southeast Asia were influenced by Chinese and Indian civilizations. And just as Russia was insulated by physical, cultural, and linguistic barriers from European intellectual and spiritual movements (such as the Renaissance and the Reformation), so India was somewhat protected from Chinese influence by a physical factor—the Himalayas, the world's highest mountain range.

China's cultural and political influence explains some of the similarities among Asian nations. For example, the imprint of the Chinese writing system is clearly evident in the written languages of Vietnam, Korea, and Japan. Confucianism (an ethical system emphasizing the family and respect for authority) spread well beyond the borders of Imperial China. The Chinese system of centralized administration was imitated by Japan, Korea, and the Vietnamese kingdom in Indochina that gradually displaced the great Khmer Empire (A.D. 600–1300). Indeed, China dominated the Vietnamese culturally and politically for a millennium.

The religions of Asia also show cultural influences. India is the cradle of several religions, including two of Asia's three greatest religious traditions—Buddhism and Hinduism. Buddhism spread from India to China and from there to Japan. In the process it also found its way to Southeast Asia. Hinduism spread across India to Ceylon (Sri Lanka), Malaysia, and Indonesia. Islam, the third great religion, is prevalent in much of South and Southeast Asia. In fact, more of the world's Muslims live in Afghanistan, Pakistan, India, Bangladesh, Malaysia, and Indonesia than in the Middle East.

Cultural grandeur is common throughout Asia. In every part of the region, magnificent shrines, temples, palaces, and gardens can be found that bear witness to the greatness of bygone ages. Without doubt, many Asian societies have enviable records of economic prosperity and political stability. The notion that Asia is destined to be forever poor and benighted flies in the face of the region's historical remnants and cultural artifacts.

Politically, the past reveals striking patterns. First, *empire-building* has been a dominant motif throughout Asia for well over 2,000 years. Early examples include the Asoka Empire in India (250 B.C.), followed by the great Moghul

Empire (discussed later). In China the Han Empire was prospering from 200 to 100 B.C.—the first of many dynasties that dominated East and Southeast Asia until the second half of the nineteenth century. In Indochina the Khmer Empire (A.D. 1000-1250), under Hindu god-kings, controlled vast territories and built the monumental Angkor Wat temple center (1113-1150). Japan was first united under the house of Yamato sometime between the second and fourth centuries. From the late sixteenth century until the Meiji Restoration (1868), Japan was ruled as one nation by the Tokugawa shogunate. In World War II the Japanese attempted to establish an Asian empire that would have included, among other countries, Korea, China, Taiwan, Vietnam, Laos, Cambodia, Malaysia, Indonesia, and the Philippines. Asian history is thus a story of empires and imperialism.

Second, Asia's indigenous political institutions and traditions are rooted in dynastic *authoritarianism*. Its characteristics include the concentration of power in a single potentate who claims to rule by divide authority. In Japan the emperor was worshiped as a god; in China autocrats ruled with the mandate of heaven; the Khmer rulers were Hindu god-kings; and the Moghul emperors of India based their legitimacy on the teachings of Islam. Dynastic rule is an integral element in this pattern, and the great empires of Asia were created and maintained by royal families. Power was passed from one male heir to the next (in the absence of a male heir, an empress did occasionally ascend to the throne). There were, however, some variations in the dynastic pattern. In China a merit-based civil service system was established, and in Japan administrative positions were reserved for the feudal nobility.

Labor regimentation for large-scale construction projects was another characteristic of dynastic authoritarianism. The flood control and irrigation systems of China and Vietnam, the ancient Angkor Wat temple center in Cambodia, and the famous Taj Mahal in India are examples of this use of conscript labor to build on a grand scale. Centralized administration for political control, law enforcement, and tax collection was also typical of Asian autocracy. For example, during the eighteenth century, the golden age of the Qing dynasty, a cadre of only 20,000 civil servants governed a population of 300 million. (At lower levels, officials depended on the cooperation of local "gentry" or on the greed of nonofficial functionaries to get things done.) Finally, advanced methods of food production, as epitomized by the Chinese system, allowed Asia to sustain relatively large populations in premodern times.

None of these characteristics—religion-based authoritarianism, centralized administration, labor regimentation, and advanced agriculture—was unique to Asian political systems. Yet the pattern of highly centralized authoritarian rule reinforced by effective administrative control radiating to the periphery of the political system made it possible to mobilize peasants for massive public works. That pattern was typical of Asian rule until recent times; with some modifications, it also fit the Maoist regime in mainland China until the mid-1970s.

A third facet of Asia's traditional political culture is the prevalence of *patron–client relations*. This pattern of sociopolitical relationships is based on factors that are informal, affective (reflecting friendship or familiarity), and particularistic (excluding all but kinfolk or members of some in-group) rather than on formal, cognitive, and universalistic factors. In other words, traditional Asian society values personal relationships of mutual trust and loyalty more than it values organizational ties based on abstract values. The natural setting for patron–client relations is the village, whereas the city is the natural setting for impersonal, formalistic ties (such as political parties, civic associations, and trade unions).

Higher levels of economic development are generally associated with greater urbanization, and vice versa. Thus one might expect patron–client networks to be eroded by the social changes that typically accompany modernization. The case of Japan, however, casts doubt on this proposition. As Chapter 14 reveals, the Japanese have assimilated traditional patterns of patron–client relations into the democratic process, resulting in a distinctive "patron–client democracy."[2] In short, they have managed to combine Western form with Japanese substance.

Finally, *colonialism and neocolonialism* directly affected nearly every Asian nation. (The term *neocolonialism* refers to economic domination and the alleged exploitation of former colonies by industrially developed nations like the United States, France, and Great Britain.) Historically, Asian colonization of other Asians antedated the arrival of European powers in the region. In the nineteenth century, Europe established its dominance throughout most of Asia. India was among the first to be colonized, and China was the last (and even then it was only semicolonized). Only Japan escaped full or partial colonization by a European power. It did so by adapting more quickly than the other nations to the Western challenge. Again, Japan's genius has been to absorb Western technology and imitate Western institutions while keeping the essence of its own culture intact.

The British colonized present-day India, Pakistan, Sri Lanka, Burma, Tibet, Singapore, Malaysia, and Hong Kong. The Dutch colonized Indonesia while the Portuguese colonized Macao. And the French colonized present-day Vietnam, Cambodia, and Laos. (Thailand was never colonized; Korea was controlled by China and then by Japan following the Sino-Japanese War of 1895.)

There is much debate over the effects of colonization. Some stress the benefits that it brought to the colonies, and others maintain that its burdens far outweighed any benefits. One school argues that the cumulative effects of colonialism have been to impede economic development in the Third World by creating a dependency that is as deleterious to the former colonies as it is advantageous to the West:

> Dependency theorists point out that during the nineteenth-century industrialization of the West, there were no already developed nations whose economic power could effectively control or manipulate the paths of development. . . . Japan, the one Asian nation that successfully industrialized in the late nineteenth century, did so by first fighting off Western imperialism and by prohibiting foreign investment from coming into Japan; in current jargon, it "delinked" itself from the world capitalist system in order to independently develop its economy from internal sources and under leadership of a native entrepreneurial class. Only then did Japan join the European powers in imperialist exploitation of China and Southeast Asia.[3]

Others argue just the opposite—that the nations of Africa and Asia that have developed most rapidly did so by absorbing Western capital and technology, thereby developing export-oriented industry and aggressively entering foreign markets. In this view, nations that responded to colonialism by withdrawing into isolationism and pursuing self-reliance in economic development fared the worst.

Without attempting to assess the impact of colonization on Asia here, there can be little doubt that most Asians today do not wax nostalgic about colonialism. Whatever its overall effects on Asian economic development, its political effect in most cases was to inflict a degrading foreign dominance on proud, more-or-less independent, and in several cases once-powerful nations (even empires).

Decolonization also left an indelible imprint. The struggle for independence was the crucible in which the nations and governments of the Asian subcontinent took form. India and Pakistan, for example, separated into two states after the British left. Pakistan was originally divided into "East Pakistan" (now the independent state of Bangladesh) and "West Pakistan." It was a geographical and cultural anomaly—the two parts being situated on opposite sides of India, separated by nearly 1,000 miles and by differences in ethnicity, language and other factors.

The British were much involved in these arrangements, but they were long gone in 1970, when East Pakistan demanded autonomy and West Pakistan refused. Their confrontation led to a bloody war in which India—West Pakistan's archrival—became heavily involved. The independent new nation of Bangladesh emerged, along with another bitter legacy: the Indo-Pakistani conflict. An unintended consequence of the way the subcontinent was decolonized, that conflict still smolders.

Bangladesh is not the only example of secession in Asia. In 1965 Singapore quit the newly formed Confederation of Malaysia. But Singapore's independence, unlike that of Bangladesh, was achieved without bloodshed. More recently, several groups in India have sought unsuccessfully to secede, at considerable cost in human lives.

The political division of Indochina was another legacy of decolonization. The French did not leave Vietnam gracefully in 1954. Communist leader Ho Chi Minh led the nation in a war for independence that ended with the defeat of the French at Dien Bien Phu on May 5. At the Geneva Peace Conference later that year, Vietnam was divided temporarily into North and South, with the understanding that national elections would occur within two years. Western powers reneged on the agreement when it became obvious that Ho Chi Minh and the Communist party would win. The resulting civil war escalated into international dimensions and, after two decades, finally ended on April 30, 1975. Ultimately, North Vietnam unified the nation through military action and also colonized Laos and Cambodia.

The forgoing examples make it clear that colonialism and decolonization have left scars throughout Asia, especially in the subcontinent and Indochina. Decolonization only accentuated the artificiality of cultural and ethnic "bonds" in most Asian nation-states, and conflicts inevitably followed independence. Since 1945 wars have been an integral aspect of Asian life—pitting Indians against Pakistanis, North Koreans against South Koreans, Vietnamese against Cambodians, and Chinese against Russians, Vietnamese, or Indians. To some extent the wars can be attributed to actions taken (or not taken) by Western powers during the decolonization process, which occurred too hastily. Politically and psychologically the colonial experience will affect Asia for many years to come.

Case Studies: People's Republic of China, Japan, and India

Geography, physical environment, resources, levels of economic development, and history vary greatly among the three countries examined here. Each is distinctive, and yet each represents features found in other parts of Asia.

People's Republic of China

In area, the People's Republic of China (PRC) is the third-largest country in the world, after the Soviet Union and Canada. It is the largest nation in Asia and claims an area of 3.69 million square miles (including Tibet and Taiwan, which the PRC considers a province). The mainland's long coastline extends from the mouth of the Yalu River in the northeast to the Gulf of Tonkin in the South. The PRC's total boundary length is over 17,000 miles; its boundary with the USSR alone is 3,500 miles long.

China may be divided crudely into a lowland portion in the east, composing 20 percent of the territory and 90 percent of the population, and mountains and plateaus in the west. The inland topography rises to plateaus in central China and Mongolia. Beyond these lie the high plateaus of Tibet and the great mountain ranges, most notably the Kunluns and the Himalayas. China has several great rivers that flow eastward toward the Pacific. These include the Amur River in the north, the Yellow River (China's second longest), and the Yangtze River in the south (the longest). Northern China is in a major earthquake zone; in July 1976 a quake measuring 8.2 on the Richter scale hit the city of Tangshan (90 miles east of Peking), killing an estimated 650,000 people.

Most of mainland China lies in the temperate zone, but the country's climate varies greatly along with the topography. Northern areas are colder in winter and have shorter summers than southern areas. Rains are heaviest in the south and southeast, ranging from 80 inches a year in Guangzhou (Canton) to about 25 inches a year in the north and northeast. In the northwest (the Gobi Desert), rainfall averages about 4 inches a year.

Natural Resources and Population   The PRC is fairly well endowed with natural resources, including oil reserves of nearly 20 billion barrels, iron, coal, lead, and a variety of other minerals (including tungsten, antimony, mercury, manganese, molybdenum, potash, phosphates, and tin). The great rivers make hydroelectric power abundant. China is a major producer and exporter of silk and has again achieved food self-sufficiency, even though only about 11 percent of its land area is arable.

China's population reached 1.1 billion in 1989 and has an annual growth rate of 1.4 percent. This is up from the early 1980s, when the government made a major effort to stabilize the population. Despite early success in these efforts, it looks doubtful that the goal of holding the population to 1.2 billion at the turn of the century can be realized.

U.N. estimates of the age structure in China suggest that fully one-third of the population is 14 or younger. This large youthful segment, combined with the elderly age group, means that working adults (roughly 60 percent of the population) must support a significant number of dependents, either directly or through tax-supported government programs. Incidentally, China is one of the few countries in which males outnumber females; a traditional preference for male babies has led even to female infanticide.

The population is distributed very unevenly in the PRC. Much of the mainland is too high, too hot and dry, or otherwise too rugged and barren to support large numbers. As a result, 94 percent of the population is crowded onto about 45 percent of the land, mostly in eastern and southeastern China. About 70 percent of mainland China's people live in a dozen densely populated provinces (Anhui, Fujian, Guangdong, Hebei, Henan, Hubei, Hunan, Jiangsu, Liaoning, Shandong, Sichuan, and Yunnan) and three cities (Beijing, Shanghai, and Tianjin).

The largest ethnic group by far is the Han (94 percent of the population), who predominate in the densely populated parts of China but remain a minority in Inner Mongolia and Tibet. There were fifty-five recognized ethnic minorities totaling about 67 million in the early 1980s. These minorities have an importance disproportionate to their numbers, because they are located in the strategically sensitive border zones to the south, southwest, west, and northwest.

Various Chinese dialects are spoken, but Mandarin is the official language. Written Chinese is a highly refined form of calligraphy; it consists of thousands of ideographs—characters that represent concepts as well as words. There is no Chinese alphabet.

China's Heritage   China's origins go back to the Xia (Hsia) dynasty (about 2200–1700 B.C.). The Shang dynasty (about 1766–1122 B.C.) ruled over the Yellow River valley for several centuries and left records cast in bronze or inscribed on tortoise shell and bone. Historians believe the Shang were conquered by the Western Zhou (Chou) dynasty (1122–771 B.C.), which established a flourishing feudal agricultural society. In 771 B.C. the Western Zhou abandoned their capital at Xi'an and founded a new capital farther east at Luoyang (Loyang). This new Eastern Zhou dynasty (770–249 B.C.) produced the great philosophers Kung Fu-tse (Confucius) and Lao-tse. (Coincidentally, the golden ages in China and Greece overlapped.)

Between 475 and 221 B.C. the great Qin (Ch'in) dynasty emerged. Shi Huangdi (Shih Huang Ti), the first Qin emperor, ended the feudal fragmentation of China, organizing it into a system of prefectures and counties under central control. It was during the reign of Shi Huangdi (246–210 B.C.) that work was begun on the Great Wall as a defense against nomadic Mongolian tribes. During this period the Chinese developed an elaborate irrigation system in the fertile valley of the Yellow River and began cultivation in the Yangtze valley. Supported by a system of intensive farming, which nonetheless did not prevent frequent famines, China's population grew to an estimated 40 million.

The Qin were displaced by the Han dynasty (206 B.C.–A.D. 220), followed by the three kingdoms (Wei, Shu, and Wu). From the fourth century on, a succession of northern and southern dynasties ruled China. The empire was reunited under the Sui (589–618) and Tang (618–907) dynasties. Under the Tangs, especially Emperor T'ai Tsung (627–649), China reached its zenith as the cultural and commercial center of Asia. Poetry and painting also flourished, particularly under Emperor Hsuan Tsung.

A period of partition under the Five Dynasties (907–960) was followed by the Song (Sung) dynasty (960–1279), which is notable for its achievements in literature, philosophy, and science. The Song rulers saw the invention of movable type, gunpowder, and the magnetic compass. Beginning in the twelfth century, incursions by Mongol and Tatar tribes forced the Chinese to abandon their capital and move it to a new, safer site. In the thirteenth century the Mongols under Genghis Khan (Temujin; 1162?–1227) subjugated all of China. The Great Canal, begun under the Sui and Tang dynasties, was completed during the reign of Kublai Khan (1279–1294), the first ruler of the Mongol, or Yuan, dynasty (1280–1368). No doubt impressed by Chinese language, culture, and technology, the Mongols accommodated to the ways of China rather than attempting to displace or destroy them.

After nearly a century of foreign rule and domestic turmoil, the Mongols were supplanted by the native Chinese Ming dynasty (1368–1644). During the reign of Cheng Tau (1403–1424), the heyday of the Ming dynasty, the capital was moved to Beijing. It was during this period that Europe discovered China: The Portuguese arrived in 1516, followed by the Spanish in 1557, the Dutch in 1606, and the English in 1637.

The Ming dynasty was overthrown in 1644 by invaders from the northeast—the Manchus, who established the last imperial dynasty, the Qing (Ch'ing; 1644–1911). The Manchus proved to be effective administrators as well as warriors. As ruling conquerors they nonetheless adopted Chinese culture, laws, and administration. At its peak the Manchu dominion extended to all of China proper, Manchuria, Mongolia, Tibet, Taiwan, and Turkestan—a far-flung empire of 300 million people.

Because it was remote, self-sufficient, and aloof, China was not penetrated by Europeans until the nineteenth century. At the end of the 1800s only one Chinese port, Ganzhou (Canton), was open to foreign merchants, and trade was tightly restricted. British demands for increased trade and Chinese anger over illegal opium imports from British-controlled India led to the "Opium War" (1839–1842), which China lost. The Treaty of Nanjing (1842) forced China to open five major seaports and to cede Hong Kong to Great Britain. At midcentury the prolonged and bloody Taiping Rebellion, aimed at overthrowing the Manchus, reduced southern China to ruins. A second war with Britain (1856–1860), joined by France, opened another major port to foreign trade. From this point forward, the empire was supine, and series of "unequal treaties" resulted in territorial losses to Russian and

Japan. (After the Chinese-Japanese War of 1894–1895, Japan annexed Korea.) In 1898 Britain, France, and Germany all "leased" major ports in Shandong, the concessionary terms dictated by the Europeans. In 1900 the Boxer Uprising, an antiforeign movement, was crushed by the joint intervention of British, French, German, American, Russian, and Japanese troops, Thus, at the turn of the century, China's humiliation was complete, but its nightmare was far from over.

As China went into eclipse, Japan, the land of the rising sun, was emerging. Like China, Japan has a long history of cultural and political achievements.

Japan

The Japanese archipelago is located off the eastern coast of the Asian continent and has a total area of 145,851 square miles, about the size of Montana. Japan is divided into five districts—Honshu, Hokkaido, Kyushu, Shikoku, and Okinawa. Each consists of one main island and many smaller surrounding islands. The principal island is Honshu, where Tokyo is located. In turn, Honshu is divided into five territorial-administrative units.

Like Great Britain, Japan is an island nation near a large continental land mass, but the similarity ends there. Japan is geophysically very different from the British Isles. Composed of the upper portions of a vast, mostly submerged mountain range in the Pacific, much of Japan's terrain is steep and rugged. Over 70 percent of the land is mountainous. Twenty-five mountains have peaks nearing 10,000 feet; the highest is the majestic Mount Fuji, at 12,388 feet. Of Japan's nearly two hundred volcanoes, thirty are still active, and earthquakes are a constant threat. One of the world's worst recorded natural disasters was the Kanto earthquake of September 1, 1923, when a third of Tokyo and most of Yokohama were devastated and more than 140,000 people perished.

At first glance Japan appears to suffer from severe natural disadvantages. Most of its terrain is unsuitable for cultivation, and its mineral resources are negligible. Only about 29 percent of the land area is flat, and these plains lie mostly along the seacoast, where Japan's population and largest cities are concentrated. The 13 percent of land that is arable is also found in the plains. As a result, urban development and rural agriculture compete intensely for the same scarce real estate.

The climate varies from north to south. Most of Japan is fairly humid and normally gets abundant rainfall. Two major ocean currents—a warm one from the south and a cold one from the north—affect weather patterns. Typhoon season runs from May through October, and several storms sweep through the islands each year. In addition, the ecological balance is threatened by environmental pollution related to Japan's large and highly concentrated population.

With 123 million people in 1989, Japan's population is the seventh largest in the world; it is fifth in terms of population density, with 857 people per square mile. In terms of density per unit of arable land, however, Japan ranks first, having about 8 persons per acre. As noted, the population is distributed very unevenly; 4 out of 5 people live on the island of Honshu, while only 5 percent live on Hokkaido.

Japan's Homogeneity   In terms of culture, language, and ethnicity, Japan is one of the most homogeneous nations. The spoken language is unique to Japan, but the written language was borrowed from the Chinese. Japan's religions are Buddhism and Shinto. The latter is a native religion involving worship of natural spirits; it developed under the influence of Confucianism and eventually grew into an instrument of nationalism. After the Meiji Restoration in the nineteenth century, Shintoism became the state religion. It was taught in schools, and all Japanese were required to belong to a state Shinto shrine. State religion was abolished after Japan's defeat in World War II, but Shintoism remains an integral element of Japanese culture.

Buddhism is often considered Japan's most important religion. It was introduced from China and Korea during the sixth century and spread rapidly. Its influence can be seen throughout the nation's fine arts and social institutions. Japan's temples and gardens, its unique tea ceremony, and such arts as flower arranging (*ikebana*) are all derived from Zen Buddhism.

Confucianism also has been significant in shaping Japanese religious, cultural, and social institutions. One offshoot of Confucianism, a cult known as Sokka-Gakkai, controlled the third-strongest political party in Japan (Komeito) until a 1970 law required strict separation of politics and religion.

The Origins of Modern Japan   Mythology holds that Japan's emperors descended from the sun goddess and that Emperor Jimmu Tenno ruled all of Japan in 660 B.C., but there is no evidence of this legendary empire. Emperor Hirohito, who died in 1989, was a direct descendant of the house of Yamato, which established hegemony over Japan during the first centuries after Christ. Contacts with mainland China during the fifth century led to wholesale cultural borrowing: The Japanese imitated or directly adopted Chinese industrial arts, script, medical texts, and calendar; they even embraced Buddhism. Japanese rulers also copied China's political administration with one notable exception: They did not adopt the Chinese merit system, preferring to apportion power on the basis of heredity. The imperial capital was established at Kyoto in 784, where it remained until 1868.

During the twelfth century, powerful military clans arose outside the capital. Yoritomo, leader of the Minamoto clan, set up a military regime at Kamakura in 1192 and forced the emperor to recognize him as the shogun. Thus began the famed Japanese shogunate—a feudal form of government based on hereditary land ownership, vassalage, and military prowess—that lasted for seven centuries. The emperor remained as a figurehead, but political power was held by the shogun of the dominant military clan.

Isolated from Asia by the Sea of Japan, the nation developed a strong military tradition in which rival feudal lords (*daimios*) conducted nearly continuous civil war until the sixteenth century. During this era the Japanese professional warrior class (*samurai*) evolved. This was also when Japan had its first contacts with Europe: Portuguese traders arrived in southern Japan in 1542, followed six years later by St. Francis Xavier, who introduced Christianity. Spanish, Dutch, and English traders followed close behind.

In 1590 the long period of civil war finally ended when Hideyoshi Toyotomi, a peasant who rose to supreme power, pacified and unified the country. He was followed by another great clan leader, Ieyasu Tokugawa, who was appointed shogun in 1603 and consolidated the Tokugawa shogunate, which ruled Japan until the Meiji Restoration in 1868. The Tokugawas moved the capital to Edo (now Tokyo) and closed Japan to all foreigners except Chinese and Dutch traders (who were restricted to Nagasaki). They also banned Christianity. Under Tokugawa rule, Japan enjoyed 250 years of unaccustomed peace and internal order—which encouraged the flowering of culture.

Japan's insularity ended abruptly with the arrival of Commodore Matthew C. Perry and his American fleet of "black ships" in 1853. The following year Perry extracted a treaty of peace and friendship between the United States and Japan, and similar treaties soon followed with Russia, Great Britain, and the Netherlands. The forced opening of Japan to foreigners led to a decade of turmoil. In 1868 samurai from several southern clans forced the Tokugawa shogun to abdicate, thus restoring the emperor (named Meiji) to power. With the Meiji Restoration, Japan embarked on a modernization drive that brought it to preeminence in Asia by the end of the century.

Spurred on by a new elite of modernizing samurai, Japan industrialized rapidly. It also abolished feudalism, establishing a modern army and navy, universal military conscriptions, and compulsory education. State-led economic development based on imported technology propelled Japan into the twentieth century. The new Constitution in 1889 set up a bicameral legislature, the Diet. The reforms created a parliamentary system in theory but not in practice: The new civilian cabinet, headed by a prime minister, was responsible only to the emperor.

Japan's ascendancy at the turn of the century was signaled by spectacular victories over China (1895) and Russia (1904–1905). As a result Japan began to acquire the elements of an Asian empire. The victories gave Japan the territories of Formosa (Taiwan), part of southern Manchuria, and the southern half of Sakhalin Island, as well as railway and port rights in Manchuria; China also recognized Korea's independence, which led to a Japanese protectorate in 1910.

Although Japan's participation in World War I was limited, it was one of five chief powers at the treaty signing in Versailles, and at the 1921–1922 Washington Conference it was recognized as the third-ranking naval power in the world. The economy advanced rapidly during the 1920s, and Japan was transformed from an agricultural to an industrial nation. Industry was organized into huge combines (*zaibatsus*) controlled by families of samurai who had spearheaded modernization fifty years earlier. In 1925 universal suffrage for male voters injected democracy into the system, and political parties arose for the first time. But when Emperor Hirohito ascended the throne in 1926, the military seized the initiative and swept the political parties aside; in 1931, still acting independently of the Tokyo government, the military invaded Manchuria. Japan had embarked on a course of military adventurism and latter-day empire-building that ended in the atomic tragedy of Hiroshima and Nagasaki fourteen years later.

India

The Republic of India is the world's most populous democracy and the second-largest country in Asia (only China is bigger). About one-third the size of the United States, India's territory encompasses most of the Asian subcontinent, which it shares with Pakistan, Nepal, Bhutan, Burma, and Bangladesh.

The southern half of India is bounded by the Bay of Bengal to the east, the Indian Ocean to the south, and the Arabian Sea to the west. In the north the Himalaya Mountains insulate India, climatically and politically, from the rest of Asia. India shares borders with Pakistan on the northwest; with the disputed territory of Jammu and Kashmir, China, Nepal, and Bhutan on the north; and with Burma and Bangladesh on the east. Between the northern mountains and the southern peninsula lies a fertile lowland framed by the Ganges and Brahmaputra rivers. A slender coastal plain edges the Arabian Sea, and a wider one lies along the Bay of Bengal. These five surface features—the mountains, the Ganges floodplain, the peninsula, and the two coastal plains—have shaped India's economic and political history for thousands of years.

India's spectrum of climate types reflects its varied topography, ranging from the arid Rajasthan Desert in the west, to the rain-drenched Khasi Hills of Assam in the east, to winter snowfalls in the northern mountains and Kashmir valley, to scorching spring dust storms in the Deccan Peninsula to the south. Monsoon winds govern the weather patterns, dividing the year into four seasons: rainy (southwest monsoon, June–September); moist (retreating monsoon, October–November); dry cool (northeast monsoon, December–March); and hot (no monsoon, April–May).

India is not exactly rich in minerals but does possess sizable deposits of iron, coal, bauxite, manganese, mica salt, and gypsum. Oil reserves are small (about 4 billion barrels) but not insignificant. As in China, India's huge population is the most abundant "natural resource" and represents both problems for the present and potential for the future.

India's population in 1989 was 833 million, with an annual growth rate of 2.2 percent and a density per square mile of 658 people. In 1921 the population of the subcontinent had stabilized at around 250 million, but since then it has more than tripled. A falling death rate, not a rising birthrate, was the cause of this population explosion. By the 1980s the death rate had dropped to about 12.3 per 1,000 people, because of improvements in health care, nutrition, and sanitation. The birthrate invariably drops more slowly. In India it sank sharply during the 1970s, reduced by an aggressive program of family planning, contraception, and sterilization; but it still stood at 33.3 per 1,000 people in 1981. The net result is that India's annual population increase is the largest in the world, exceeding even the PRC's.

The burgeoning population means that the age structure in India is skewed toward youth. In 1980 more than 40 percent of the population was 14 or younger, while only 3 percent was 65 or older. Thus, 57 percent of the population had to support hundreds of millions who were too young or too old to work. The challenge of providing jobs for millions of new workers every year strains the nation's political, economic, and social systems.

Despite nuclear power and modern steel mills, India remains a traditional society in many ways. Some three-fourths of the population live in rural areas, most in one of the nearly 600,000 villages that have fewer than 10,000 residents (78 percent of villages have fewer than 1,000 people). When observers contemplate rural life in Third World countries, they often think of India, where people typically are born, live, and die in the same village.

India's Diversity Tremendous ethnic, cultural, and religious diversity is perhaps India's most striking feature. Ethnically, India is one of the most complex societies to be found. Linguistically, it is one of the most fecund, giving birth to 1,652 languages and dialects (according to census data). Officially, there are 211 distinct languages, and the 14 that represent the largest ethnolinguistic groups are recognized by the Constitution. About 90 percent of people speak at least one of these fourteen regional languages.

The two principal languages are Hindi and Urdu. Hindi is spoken by 22 percent of the population (mostly Hindus), and Urdu is the primary language of India's Muslim population. Hindi is written in Sanskrit, while Urdu is written in Arabic-Persian script and contains many Arabic and Persian words. Other northern Indo-Aryan languages are Assamese, Bengali, Gujarati, Kashmiri, Marathi, Oriya, Punjabi, Rajasthani, Sanskrit, and Sindhi. In the south the languages are of Dravidian origin; examples include Telugu, Tamil, Kannada, and Malayalam. Some 15 million Indians also speak English, the language of government, diplomacy, education, science, communications, and industry.

Language has played a major role in the drawing and redrawing of India's internal boundaries, and efforts by the central government to make Hindi the national language have met with stiff resistance. In some cases, linguistic differences have magnified cultural and religious rivalries. The Punjab, formerly a province but now two separate states, is a case in point. Punjabi-speaking leaders (mostly Sikhs) demanded that the region be divided. The result was the creation of Hariana, the part of the former territory that is inhabited primarily by Hindi-speaking people. (The "new" Punjab, of course, is the part inhabited by Punjabi-speaking people.) Many other examples of the interaction between linguistics and politics can be cited.

India is also the birthplace of several religions, including Hinduism and Buddhism. Hinduism can be traced back to 1500 B.C. The Buddha (563?–483? B.C.) taught in the sixth century before Christ, when Jainism, another distinctively Indian religion, also appeared. Finally, Sikhism, a monotheistic Hindu sect, was founded in the sixteenth century and is now dominant in Punjab. Originally an effort to reconcile Muslim and Hindu doctrine, Sikhism evolved into a militant sect that violently opposes Islam.

About 83 percent of India's population is Hindu, and about 11 percent is Islamic. Even though Hinduism is preponderant, India's Islamic population is second only to Pakistan's. Buddhism has died out in India; there are actually more

Christians (4 percent) than Buddhists (3 percent). Religion-based violence—between Hindus and Muslims, Sikhs and Muslims, Sikhs and Hindus, and so forth—has been a recurring problem since India's independence in 1947. Indeed, distrust rooted in religious differences led to the creation of a separate Pakistan in 1947, and the unresolved Indo-Pakistani conflict is a legacy of that partition.

India's caste system is *pre*scribed by Hinduism but *pro*scribed by Indian law. A clearer case of conflict between religion and state would be difficult to find. In Hindu doctrine, every baby is born into one of four castes, or classes—*Brahman* (priests and scholars); *Kshatriya* (warriors and rulers); *Vaisya* (artisans, shopkeepers, farmers); and *Sudra* (farm laborers and menial workers)—or is an "Untouchable." These four castes, in turn, are divided into as many as three thousand subcastes (*jatis*) based on occupation, geographic location, and other factors. The 1949 Constitution abolished discrimination based on caste (especially the concept of untouchability), but the system is so ingrained in India's culture that outlawing it has had little effect.

India's Heritage: Splendor Amid Poverty   The Indus valley is one of the oldest continuously inhabited regions in the world and was civilized before the Aryans (Hindus) began invading it from the northwest (2400–1500 B.C.). A thousand years of instability followed. Small states and larger kingdoms were established in various parts of the subcontinent as a steady procession of would-be conquerors struggled for power. During this long period, enduring patterns of village and family life evolved, as did the caste system.

When Alexander the Great invaded in 326 B.C., the region already had a population of 30 million, two-thirds of whom lived in the Ganges Basin. A new Aryan dynasty followed under Chandragupta, who subdued most of northern India and established the Maurya Empire; his successor, the great Asoka (273–232 B.C.), unified all of India. Asoka converted to Buddhism, and his rule brought outstanding administrative, legal, and cultural achievements. Many of India's most impressive ancient Buddhist stupas, pillars, and temples date from this time. After Asoka, invaders from the northwest again overran India, and the empire disintegrated into separate kingdoms again. Caste Hinduism now prevailed over Buddhism, which almost completely vanished from the land of its origin.

Although Brahmanic states have been present in peninsular India for a long time, genuine Hindu kingdoms first appeared there only after the fourth century, and Hindu Rajput princes did not reach the height of their power until A.D. 700 and later. Descendants of these rulers retained power and influence until well after the British arrived in the seventeenth century. Magnificent Hindu structures dating from long before the time of Christ can be found throughout the peninsula, and many of them are still places of worship.

The Hindu epoch was followed by a long period of Muslim rule no less glorious or grandiose. Muslim invaders began streaming through the northeast mountain passes during the eighth century; in the early eleventh century, Mahmud of Ghazni led seventeen forays into Hindustan within three decades. The first Muslim sultan (king) of Delhi held sway during the thirteenth century, and Muslim power reached its pinnacle under the Moghuls, during the sixteenth century. Babur, who invaded the Punjab in 1526, was the first of the Moghul despots to proclaim himself emperor of India, a title he thought he had earned by defeating the Afghan sultan of Delhi. Babur's grandson, Akbar (1556–1605), actually ruled at least the Ganges Basin, and he was the first Muslim emperor to attempt creating a national state by seeking alliances with Hindu kings. Art and literature flourished under Akbar, even though he himself was illiterate. His successors were no less illustrious. Shah Jahan and Aurangzeb were especially renowned and left legacies of splendid palaces, fortresses, mausoleums, and gardens. The Taj Mahal epitomizes the grandeur of the great Moghul rulers, but it is only one among many dazzling works of architecture from this period. Under the despotic rule of Aurangzeb (1658–1707) the frontiers of the Moghul empire were pushed to new limits, but his repressive policies prompted armed revolts, and the empire began its decline.

During the eighteenth century, one form of alien rule replaced another as the British reduced India to a colony through the agency of the British East India Company. (The company itself was brought under British government control in 1784; the first British governor-general was appointed in 1786). After the Indian army revolted in the so-called Sepoy Mutiny (1857–1859), which one scholar called "the most dramatic event in nineteenth century India," the British Crown abolished the powers of the East India Company and assumed direct control over India in 1858. Long the object of imperialistic designs, India was the "crown jewel" of the British empire until independence was achieved in 1947.

CONCLUSION

There is no single Asian civilization; instead, there are several distinctive civilizations—Indian, Chinese, Thai, Khmer, and others. Japan's rich culture was greatly influenced by China but in many ways is unique. Except for the spread of Islam across much of South and Southeast Asia, Asian cultures and civilizations are homegrown—that is, they cross-fertilized one another but borrowed little from non-Asian societies before the Western intrusion around the middle of the nineteenth century. Chapter 14 will look at the political systems of Asia, again focusing on China, Japan, and India.

STUDY QUESTIONS

1. To what extent is China a victim of circumstances, such as scarcity of natural resources, overpopulation, unfortunate geography, and, in general, a harsh environment?
2. How has geography influenced Japan's cultural and political development? What features of contemporary Japanese society can be traced to Japan's unusual physical environment (topography, land scarcity, resources, and climate)?

3. What are the salient characteristics of Indian society and culture, and how do such factors as ethnicity, religion, and language constrain or facilitate the political process?
4. How do the historical experiences of China, Japan, and India compare in terms of (a) empire-building, (b) forms and methods of rule, (c) foreign intrusion, and (d) sociocultural unity or diversity?

SUGGESTED READINGS

Chien-nung, Li. *The Political History of China, 1840–1928*. Standford, Calif.: Stanford University, 1956.

Embree, Ainslee. *India's Search for National Identity*. New York: Knopf, 1972.

Isaacs, Harold. *Scratches on Our Minds*. Westport, Conn.: Greenwood, 1973.

Reischauer, Edwin O. *Japan: The Story of a Nation*. New York: McGraw-Hill, 1990.

Snow, Edgar. *Red Star Over China*. New York: Grove, 1973.

Steinberg, David Joel, ed. *In Search of Southeast Asia*. New York: Praeger, 1971.

Wolpert, Stanley. *A New History of India*. New York: Oxford, 1989.

NOTES

[1] Rushworth M. Kidder, "The North-South Affluence Gap," *Christian Science Monitor* (special report entitled "Agenda 2000"), July 25, 1988, p. B7.

[2] Nobutaka Ike, *Japanese Politics: Patron–Client Democracy* (New York: Knopf, 1972).

[3] John Nagle, *Political System Performance in Three Worlds* (Chicago: Nelson-Hall, 1985), p. 230.

Chapter 14
Change and Continuity

Although Asia's political traditions are authoritarian, its current political institutions defy easy generalization. Old-fashioned autocratic rule has generally disappeared, except for the hereditary monarchies still found in Nepal, Bhutan, and Brunei. Most Asian governments today are authoritarian, although its precise form varies widely from one country to the next.

Constitutional democracy has also made significant inroads. Although clear-cut cases of popular rule are few, two of Asia's three major powers—India and Japan—are thriving democracies. Sri Lanka, an island state off the southeast coast of India, is also a democratic republic. Since early 1986, when the corrupt dictator Ferdinand Marcos was overthrown, the Philippines have turned to democratic rule as well. Prosperous Singapore is a parliamentary democracy in form, but one figure, Prime Minister Lee Kuan Yew, has long dominated the political system. Most recently, South Korea has moved cautiously toward democratic rule. Finally, Taiwan has continued under one-party rule, making only symbolic gestures toward a truly representative form of government.

In the late 1980s six Asian nations, not counting the Soviet Union, were Communist-authoritarian—the Peoples' Republic of China, the Democratic People's Republic of Korea (North Korea), Afghanistan, Vietnam, Cambodia, and Laos. Of these, only China's and Vietnam's communism resulted from revolution; the other four had it imposed from outside. Among these four, only North Korea was independent during the 1980s; Cambodia and Laos continued to be dominated by the Hanoi-based Communist rulers of Vietnam; and Afghanistan's Communist government depended heavily on the Soviet Union for military and economic aid. In the spring of 1988 Mikhail Gorbachev pledged to withdraw all Soviet troops from Afghanistan beginning that summer, and they were gone early in 1989, after a decade of intervention.

Other Asian nations—predominantly in South and Southeast Asia—displayed a variety of authoritarian political structures in the 1980s. Indonesia was ruled by military strongman General Suharto, who had been in power since the overthrow of Sukarno in 1965. Malaysia was governed by a hybrid system of federalism, parliamentary democracy, and traditional monarchy. Thailand's government mixed parliamentary rule and hereditary monarchy; although the military staged a coup in 1976, civilian rule was eventually restored. Until 1988 Burma had been ruled for twenty-six years by military strongman U Ne Win, who stepped down as leader of the Burmese Socialist Program party in July 1988. Subsequent guerrilla insurgencies and violence resulted in the overthrow of the civilian government by a junta led by General Saw Maung, who abolished the parliament and renamed both the party and the country itself (Burma is now officially the Union of Myanmar).

Since its inception in the late 1940s, Pakistan has mixed authoritarian practices with democratic promises. A 1977 coup made Pakistan a virtual military dictatorship under General Mohammad Zia ul-Haq. Zia dismissed the prime minister and dissolved the parliament in May 1988, promising that "free, fair, and independent elections" would follow in November, but political repression continued. In August 1988 Zia was killed in a suspicious airplane crash, and in November Benazir Bhutto—the popular daughter of former President Zulfikar Ali Bhutto, who had been executed by Zia in 1979—was elected to succeed Zia, becoming the first female prime minister in Pakistan's history.

The Impact of War and Revolution

Today's Asian governments arose through revolution and war. Politically speaking, World War II was the most important event in modern Asia. Japan's attempt to unite most of East and Southeast Asia as a new "Greater East Asia" empire ended in defeat at the hands of the U.S. military in World War II.

Japan's Constitution, in effect since 1947, was prepared under the watchful eye of General Douglas MacArthur, U.S. proconsul in Japan after World War II and, literally, the architect of Japanese democracy. So Japan's current political system was imposed from outside, a consequence of losing the war. Because the Japanese Constitution was modeled on Western principles and imposed by the U.S. occupation, Japan was melded into America's postwar military-strategic system in the western Pacific. It meant that Japan would provide bases for U.S. forces; that the United States would be Japan's chief trading partner; and that Japan would not again threaten neighbors or fall prey to extremism. Indeed, the Constitution prohibited two alleged causes of Japanese aggression: military forces and emperor worship.

World War II also set up mainland China's modern political evolution to communism. When Japan invaded and occupied much of China during the early 1930s and 1940s, the Chinese Nationalist government of Generalissimo Chiang Kai-shek was discredited. The only Chinese military successes against the Japanese were those of Mao Zedong's Communist guerrilla forces. After Japan's withdrawal, Mao's forces continued to wage a guerrilla war, but now the enemy was the Nationalist government rather than the Japanese. This civil war lasted until 1949, when Mao's Communists drove Chiang's Nationalists (known as the Kuomintang) off the mainland. Chiang took his rump government to the island of Formosa (Taiwan), where his successors continue to monopolize political power. Mao took China, setting up the highly authoritarian Communist state that continues to rule, even as communism elsewhere has been forced to make accommodations.

India's present political system is a result of the largely nonviolent national independence movement led by Mahatma Gandhi. In this case World War II played an indirect role: The British were too weary and preoccupied with domestic reconstruction after the war to resist Indian demands for self-rule. In fact, Great Britain dismantled nearly all its colonial empire after the war. In Asia, Burma and Sri Lanka (formerly Ceylon) were granted independence in 1948; Malaya, the senior partner in the Malaysian confederation, became self-ruling in 1957.

The creation of parliamentary-style democracy in India reflects the strong British influence. At the same time, however, India's extreme diversity, noted in Chapter 13, made democracy as necessary as it was difficult. Lacking a federal republic that might accommodate its myriad disparate interests and groups, India probably would be ungovernable except by a highly centralized police state. In this sense, by establishing popular self-rule, the founders of independent India made a virtue of necessity.

Pakistan was an afterthought in Great Britain's rush to decolonize. When Pakistan's Muslim chieftains—led by Muhammad Ali Jinnah, head of the Muslim League—objected to becoming part of a Hindu-dominated greater India, the British took the course of least resistance and allowed Pakistan to become a separate dominion. Much of the conflict that has plagued the subcontinent since India and Pakistan became independent has derived from the national boundaries drawn in 1947.

War and revolution were closely related to the decolonization process elsewhere in Asia as well. Despite the urgent tasks of reconstruction at home, the French clung tenaciously to colonial possessions in Indochina. The Vietnamese, led by Ho Chi Minh, waged a protracted ''national liberation war'' against France (emulating Mao's guerrilla strategy and tactics) and emerged victorious in 1954. It took another long struggle—this one, a civil war against the U.S.-backed Saigon regime in the south—and two more decades to reunite Vietnam under Communist rule. The Hanoi government quickly consolidated its control in the south and in 1979 invaded and conquered Cambodia, thereby ousting the bloody, pro-Chinese dictatorship of Pol Pot.

After World War II Korea was divided into north and south sections along the 38th parallel (line of latitude on a map). This temporary expedient became permanent after the Korean conflict (1950–1953) ended in a draw. North Korea, the territory controlled by Soviet troops in August 1945, was set up as a Communist state under the personal dictatorship of Kim Il Sung. South Korea became a pro-U.S., anti-Communist military dictatorship thinly disguised as a democracy. Following widespread protests and rioting in 1987, military strongman Chun Doo Hwan agreed to permit direct popular election of the next president. Roh Tae Woo, a civilian who strongly criticized Chun's government, was elected. But the military held veto power over policy formulation, and mass demonstrations, often violent, kept the country on the brink of civil war. Although reunification is the declared intention of both Korean governments, the prospects for it remain very dim.

Indonesia and Thailand are unusual, for different reasons. Before the war Indonesia was the only major Dutch colony in Asia. After the Japanese withdrew from Indonesia, a war for independence ensued, much as in Indochina. When the Netherlands quit the fight in December 1949, Sukarno—the architect of Indonesia's liberation struggle—took over the reins of government and ruled as a dictator until his overthrow in 1965. The leader of that coup, General Suharto, has dominated Indonesian politics ever since.

Thailand was never colonized. Although Japan occupied it in 1941, after the war Thailand returned to self-government. During the American war effort in Vietnam, Thailand allowed the United States to use a major air base, and in general it has pursued a pro-Western foreign policy. Since the 1980s Thailand has been ruled as a parliamentary democracy with a somewhat fragile multiparty coalition.

Patterns and Trends in Asia

There is no specifically Asian model of democracy. Although the governments of Japan and India are patterned after the British parliamentary system, they both deviate from it in important ways. For example, the British two-party system has no counterpart in Asia. As we shall see, Japan's ruling Liberal Democratic party has dominated its politics and government since the mid-1950s; similarly, India's Congress party—now the Congress-I party—has ruled India for most of the years since independence. Thus, ascendancy by a single party rather than regular alternation in power by two or more parties, seems to be one aspect of Asian democracy.

If there is no Asian model of democracy, neither is there an Asian model of authoritarianism. Most authoritarian governments in Asia are modern in form. That is, they have at least a patina of popular rule and stay in power with a mixture of modern and traditional methods (the modern include control over mass media, public education, and welfare-state benefits; tradition includes political patronage, corrupt practices, and police-state repression).

The most common form of government in Asia is military dictatorship (as in Pakistan and South Korea before 1988, Burma, and Bangladesh). Taiwan and Indonesia are civilian authoritarian regimes that were established by military strongmen (Generalissimo Chiang Kai-shek and General Suharto). The military continues to dominate politics in both countries. Regimes of this type, found throughout the Third World, might be termed "civilitary"—a hybrid in which the leader is a civilian president but the military has a primary role in government.

Another pattern is Marxist-Leninist government (as in the People's Republic of China, Vietnam, Cambodia, Laos, and North Korea). And some regimes are best described as mixed democratic-authoritarian (including South Korea since 1988, Malaysia, Singapore, and Thailand during the 1980s).

Since the 1970s there has been a gradual but discernible trend in Asia toward democratization and greater respect for human rights. This has been evident in a variety of settings, including the People's Republic of China, the Philippines, and South Korea. Exceptions can be found, of course, and the trend itself can be reversed. Nor does it ensure the budding of democracies around the region, for Western-style democracy and Asia's patron–client tradition are certainly strange bedfellows, even if Japan is evidence that they are not necessarily incompatible.

In terms of political economy, Asia shows movement away from central planning and state intervention and toward greater reliance on market forces. This is not simply a move toward laissez-faire economics, however. Instead, it involves an alliance between the state and private enterprise for the purpose of coordinating public and private investment, attracting foreign capital, and developing foreign markets. Again, Japan's success appears to be influential, and similar arrangements have produced impressive results in South Korea, Taiwan, Hong Kong, and Singapore.

Politics in the People's Republic of China, Japan, and India

World War II unleashed massive forces that transformed the political map of Asia as it did Europe's. Within two years of war's end India was independent, and Pakistan—formerly part of British India—sprang into being as a rival state on the subcontinent. Within four years the U.S.-backed Nationalist government of Chiang Kai-shek was driven from the Chinese mainland by the People's Liberation Army of Mao Zedong. Meanwhile, a democratic constitution was imposed on Japan, which soon embarked on a new era. Across Asia, European power was receding, and the two superpowers—the United States and the Soviet Union— filled the power vacuum.

The United States established a massive military presence in Japan and the Philippines and Mao's Communist forces controlled all of China, although they were isolated and needed foreign assistance. Stalin waited until the Chinese civil war was decided and then offered economic aid to Mao in return for his allegiance. In Korea, a Soviet-installed Communist government ruled north of the 38th parallel, while a U.S.-backed anti-Communist regime ruled in the south. This uneasy arrangement exploded in the Korean War (1950–1953) after North Korea invaded South Korea. (The United Nations condemned the invasion, and, the Soviet Union being in absentia, the U.N. voted to intervene on the side of South Korea.)

The French tried to hold on in Indochina, and a slow-motion "liberation war" unraveled until Ho Chi Minh's forces delivered a knockout blow in the 1954 battle of Dien Bien Phu. Both superpowers sought a toehold in South Asia, but India's great post independence leader, Prime Minister Jawaharlal Nehru (1947–1964), chose a policy of nonalignment—that is, friendly relations with both, obligations to neither.

China Under Communist Rule

In 1911 a plan to relinquish control over a Chinese railway to European interests precipitated the downfall of the Manchu dynasty. Following a brief period of republican rule under Sun Yat-sen, a strongman named Yuan Shikai took power. Yuan died in 1916, whereupon warlords ruled in Beijing. Meanwhile, Sun Yat-sen, having consolidated his Nationalist party (kuomintang), set up a government in the south at Guangzhou (Canton). China endured forty years of turmoil until the Chinese Communist takeover in 1949 unified and pacified the country.

The Chinese Civil War

Although the Beijing regime joined the Allies in World War I, it was not rewarded at the Versailles Peace Conference: The powers refused to accede to Chinese demands for an end to all foreign "extraterritorial" privileges. (Some foreign rights were abolished at the Washington Conference in 1922; also, Japan and Great Britain agreed to evacuate the Shandong Peninsula.)

Following the death of Sun Yat-sen, Chiang Kai-shek, the Nationalist party's new leader, succeeded in unifying part of the country. The Kuomintang was founded on Western democratic principles, but it evolved into an instrument of Chiang's dictatorial power. In 1927 he tried to destroy the Chinese Communist party; its remnants fled to southern Jiangxi Province and set up a rural "soviet," gaining valuable experience in governing. Following repeated Nationalist attacks, the Communists again took flight, embarking on their arduous and legendary "Long March" during 1934–1935. Moving north and gaining recruits along the way, they eventually arrived in Shaanxi Province and, now under Mao's firm leadership, set up headquarters at Yenan.

Japan's military leaders watched with keen interest as the Chinese civil war dragged on. In 1931 Japan occupied Manchuria, China's industrial heartland. (Recall that Japan had won control over Korea at the turn of the century, following a war with China.) The Japanese kept up the pressure in northern China, and in July 1937 war broke out. This conflict merged into World War II, and Japan soon occupied much of the mainland. Chiang, forced to abandon the Nationalist capital at Nanjing, took his government to the southwestern hinterland, beyond the reach of Japan's armies. Meanwhile, Mao's guerrilla forces stood their ground in the northwest and fought the Japanese invaders to a stalemate.

Time was on Mao's side: After 1945 Japan was occupied by American forces under General MacArthur, and it was forced to evacuate China. Now the United States became the nemesis of the Chinese Communists. After Japan's forced departure, the Chinese civil war had resumed with fury. Despite massive U.S. support, the Nationalists could not mount an offensive, and in 1949 the Communists won a near-total victory. Chiang Kai-shek took refuge on the island of Formosa (Taiwan), where he set up a rival regime and pressed an increasingly absurd claim that this was the legitimate government of all China. Meanwhile, on October 1, 1949, Chinese Communists—still led by Mao Zedong—proclaimed the People's Republic of China and made Beijing its capital.

The People's Republic of China

After 1949 the Maoist regime quickly consolidated power and launched an aggressive program of industrialization and collectivization, getting significant though limited economic aid from the Soviet Union. In 1957 Mao proclaimed the "Hundred Flowers Campaign," an invitation to the country's professionals and intellectuals to criticize the political system. This was followed by an antirightist campaign against those who previously had attacked the system. In retrospect it appears as though the Mao-induced tumult was a prelude to the "Great Leap Forward," one of history's most ambitious experiments in social transformation.

In the Great Leap, launched in 1958, Mao attempted to catapult China into full communism—ahead even of the Soviet Union. Khrushchev had denounced the "crimes of Stalin" at the Twentieth Party Conference in 1956. His daring move led directly to unrest in Eastern Europe, particularly in Hungary and Poland. Mao observed these events with chagrin, and he decided that the Soviet Union had strayed from the revolutionary path. Communist China, he vowed, would show the way; the Great Leap was an effort to do it.

Although Mao claimed to be a good Marxist-Leninist, he added his own twist to things, much as Lenin had done. But Maoism stood Marx on his head. Mao asserted that human will could overcome all material obstacles, and he placed leadership above economics as the driving force in society. In Marxist terms, Mao viewed the superstructures—a revolutionary party, inspired leadership, mass-mobilizing ideology—as being more important than the economic base. The Great Leap Forward was designed to prove that the power of revolutionary will could reshape society. The Maoist model was the antithesis of Stalinism: Mao sought to harness the "hurricane force" of the people and thus prevent a privileged entrenched elite from taking root in the PRC.

Mao's experiment in mass-mobilization turned out to be a great leap backward and downward, rather than forward. It enlisted some 70 million peasants into a bizarre undertaking that, among other things, involved a futile attempt to produce steel from backyard furnaces. Meanwhile the fields went unattended, even though agriculture had been reorganized into huge communes where all individual work was replaced by group work and where every aspect of private life was collectivized. Life in the communes was regimented to the point of militarization. For example, food was prepared in communal kitchens, meals were eaten in mess halls, and men and women slept in segregated barracks.

The scale of impending disaster was not apparent, as overzealous cadres—anxious to please Chairman Mao—vied with each other by falsifying production figures. When the dimensions of the debacle became clear, leadership was split between utopians (Mao's supporters), who stressed social and moral perfection, and pragmatists, who favored economic efficiency. Marshal Pen Dehuai, the defense minister, denounced the Great Leap Forward, and Mao insisted that he be replaced by Marshal Lin Biao, who extolled the virtues of "Mao Zedong thought." Lin even advocated that a "people's army" be trained to perform domestic revolutionary tasks, rather than a traditional Soviet-style army led by professional officers and trained solely for combat.

Although such infighting was concealed, the dire consequences of the Great Leap Forward became increasingly obvious as the PRC plunged into an economic abyss. The period from 1960 to 1962 was labeled the "three bitter years," as production dropped sharply and famine stalked the countryside. Chairman Mao retreated from daily management of domestic affairs, which were now handled by Liu Shaoqi, Deng Xiaoping, and Zhou Enlai. Between 1962 and 1966 this trio spearheaded the PRC's economic and political recovery while Mao concentrated on foreign affairs and conducted ideological warfare against the Soviet Union.

The PRC's Cultural Revolution

In 1966 Mao Zedong reasserted his leadership by launching the "Great Proletarian Cultural Revolution"—an even stranger campaign than the Great Leap Forward. Mao apparently was troubled by the decline in revolutionary élan among party cadres, the masses, and especially youth. He believed that the only way to keep the revolution alive was to infuse the next generation with the kind of spirit that had sustained the Communist revolutionaries through the Long March and the years of struggle with the Kuomintang. The only way young people could learn the meaning of revolution was to experience it firsthand; otherwise, Mao feared, they would become complacent and elitist. It followed that what was needed was nothing short of a new revolution—one created by Mao himself to purify the party ranks and "educate" the next generation.

Mao's shock troops were the Red Guards, mostly high school and university students inspired by a little red book containing the "Thoughts of Chairman Mao." The Red Guards regarded this pocket-sized publication as their catechism, and Mao as their hero. Directed by a group of zealots who later were condemned as the "Gang of Four," the Guards stormed the bastions of authority, waving the book in the faces of their teachers as they dragged them into the streets, hung insulting signs around their necks, and paraded them for the masses to ridicule.

At first, intellectuals got the brunt of Red Guards' fury, but soon others in authority—including party and state officials—came under scrutiny. At the height of the Cultural Revolution, no one who previously had held a position of authority was safe from the rampaging students. In the meantime, Mao purged the party leadership, including Liu Shaoqi (once designated as his successor) and Deng Xiaoping (secretary general of the Central Committee since 1954). Few senior leaders survived the Cultural Revolution unscathed. Mao's aim was to remove entrenched elites "who had taken the capitalist road." The Cultural Revolution thus set the party against itself and ushered in a decade of fierce infighting and polarization.

Having destroyed the party and state machinery, Mao turned to the only organization still intact—the People's Liberation Army (PLA). As early as 1967 he had denounced two key leaders of the Cultural Revolution. By 1968 the Red Guards had divided into factions and were engaged in armed struggles against each other—not, presumably, what Mao had in mind. Having unleashed a tempest, he had little choice but to ask the army to restore order, and the PLA thus became the dominant force in the new "three-way revolutionary committees" (made up of party cadres who had somehow escaped the purge, the masses, and the army). The Red Guards, having fallen from grace, were sent to the countryside to work in the fields alongside millions of educated young Chinese who had been conscripted earlier in this manner.

By 1969 the country lay in ruins. The entire educational system had closed down, the party was demolished, factories were operating languidly or not at all, food production and distribution—only recently restored after the confusion of the Great Leap Forward—were disrupted again, and it was unclear who was in charge. Estimates of the death toll run as high as 2 million (no one can say). Having caused such calamity, Mao now called for a reconstruction of the party. As a border war between the PRC and the Soviet Union broke out along the Amur and Ussuri rivers in the northeast, the Ninth Party Congress met and elected a new Central Committee dominated by the army. In addition, a new constitution was promulgated; among other things, it named Lin Biao, the PLA's leader, as Mao's heir apparent.

Rather than clarifying the situation, the Ninth Party Congress led to another prolonged power struggle. The principal antagonists were Mao's wife Jiang Qing (a prominent member of the Gang of Four), Lin Biao, Deng Xiaoping, and Zhou Enlai (a brilliant politician and the one moderate who remained in Mao's inner circle throughout various purges). In 1971 Lin allegedly tried to stage a coup that involved an attempt to kill Mao. In the official version, Lin died in a plane crash as he tried to flee the country. After his death the role of the PLA was limited, and two factions fought it out for five years. On one side were the pragmatists, led by Zhou Enlai and the politically rehabilitated Deng Xiaoping; on the other were the radicals, led by Jiang Qing (presumably with the aging Mao's blessing).

Zhou died in January 1976, leaving Deng without a shield from attack by radical Maoists. In April of that year rioters in Tiananmen Square expressed sympathy for Zhou and, by extension, Deng. Although the incident was evidently spontaneous, Deng was condemned as the instigator and once again was stripped of his official posts. Hua Guofeng, the little-known minister of public security, was named premier and first vice-chairman. Mao's death in September 1976 set the stage for a showdown between his widow, Jiang Qing, and Hua. When Jiang and three associates (the Gang of Four) tried to oust Hua, he had them arrested, tried, and imprisoned. Finally, the Cultural Revolution was history.

The Third Plenum: Practice over Theory

Hua Guofeng assumed the top two posts in the party and state, but he and his cohorts were relative newcomers who owed their rise to the Cultural Revolution. By spring 1977 Deng Xiaoping had returned to center stage, and a low-key power struggle ensued between Deng and Hua, who retreated into the sanctuary of "Mao Zedong thought." In sharp contrast, Deng stressed practice over theory, expressing his view in a now-famous metaphor: It does not matter whether the cat is black or white, as long as it catches mice. The new tug-of-war between Hua and Deng was only the latest expression of what had become a perpetual battle between two conflicting tendencies within the Chinese Communist party.

The culmination came in 1978 at the third plenum of the Central Committee, when Deng and his "practice group" emerged clear winners. The plenum sharply criticized the "whateverist faction" that slavishly mouthed Maoist slogans, stamped out the vestiges of the Cultural Revolution, and adopted a new formula: "emancipating the mind" by making "practice the sole criterion of truth." The third plenum was thus a watershed in the PRC's history: From then on, practical policies that could be measured by economic results were given priority over revolutionary actions without any focus or attainable aims.

Before and immediately after the third plenum, a movement for democracy took place. Perhaps to underscore the break with the legacy of the Cultural Revolution, party leadership relaxed controls over free expression. Public debate and open criticism of the government, past and present, suddenly appeared. Huge posters—*tatze pao*—bearing democratic slogans and displayed on Democracy Wall in the center of Beijing, attracted much attention. At first this popular agitation was useful to Deng, but soon it turned into an embarrassment that provoked a crackdown. The regime then issued four guidelines for political discussion, stressing the primacy of the socialist road, the dictatorship of the proletariat, the vanguard party under the banner of Marxism-Leninism, and "Mao Zedong thought."

The third plenum had nonetheless produced important changes in leadership and policy. Two rising young stars, Hu Yaobang and Zhao Ziyang, were made full members of the Politburo. The history of the party was revised, and some distortions of the past were corrected. Mao was still presented in a positive light, but he also was criticized for creating a cult of personality and for leftist tendencies during his last twenty years. In particular, the Cultural Revolution was denounced as a prime example of Mao's reliance on theory over practice, but such schemers such as the Lin Biao faction and the Gang of Four were blamed for the worst excesses. The latter were tried and sentenced to life in prison. (Jiang Qing and Zhang Qunqiao were sentenced to death, but this was commuted to life imprisonment. Lesser figures in the Cultural Revolution were shown no such clemency.)

The PRC's Political Reconstruction

China's economic reforms will be discussed in Chapter 15; they were accompanied by legal and administrative reforms aimed at normalizing the country's politics. Reformers enacted many new laws, decrees, and regulations, including the Criminal Law and the Law of Criminal Procedure. They also promulgated a new constitution in 1982, but the civil rights it ostensibly protects are vitiated by a vague law against "disruption of the socialist system." Nonetheless, by the late 1980s, the PRC's political and legal systems had functioned for the longest period ever.

In February 1980 the Secretariat of the Central Committee was resuscitated with Hu Yaobang as the new secretary general. Hu and Zhao Ziyang were elected to the powerful Standing Committee of the Politburo. Daily affairs of government are handled by the Secretariat and by senior officials of the State Council. At Deng's insistence, lifelong tenure of top party leaders was abolished. Equally important, the party was enjoined to take a hands-off approach to state administration, that is, to stop interfering in executive management. This was in keeping with the new emphasis on pragmatism and professionalism in economic matters.

Hua Guofeng was gradually eased out of politics between 1980 and 1982. In April 1980 he was replaced as premier by Zhao Ziyang; slightly more than a year later he was replaced as chairman of the Chinese Communist party by Hu Yaobang, and as chairman of the military affairs committee by Deng Xiaoping. In September 1982 Hua was removed from the Politburo. These changes confirmed the ascendancy of moderates, and especially of Deng himself.

Further restructuring resulted in 1982 in the abolishment of the position of chairman (Mao's title), the purging of Maoist remnants, and the restoration of the office of head of state (or president). In June 1983 Li Xiannian was elected president by the National People's Congress. Normalization of politics was now complete.

Major changes in party leadership occurred in September 1985, when the party held its first national conference in forty years. Ten elder members of the Politburo retired at this time, making room for six new younger ones. In addition, five new members were appointed to the Secretariat, and ninety-one were added to the Central Committee (fifty-six full members and thirty-five alternates). Sixty-four of the new recruits were "younger people," around age 50. In general, the changes represented another victory for Deng Xiaoping, who wanted to rejuvenate and professionalize top leadership—an aim that was directly related to his commitment to modernizing the economy.

The twelfth Central Committee plenum, held in September 1986, sought to bring party ideology into line with the new pragmatism in management. One resolution adopted at this meeting called for greater freedom of expression. It also reaffirmed the "open door" in foreign policy, especially in trade and investment. Finally, it defended the reforms against attacks by conservative critics within the old guard.

During this period Deng also restructured, streamlined, depoliticized, and professionalized the army; older officers were retired, and promotion was made dependent on merit (in particular, on outstanding performance in military academies). The armed forces were cut by 25 percent (1 million), and military regions were reduced from thirteen to seven. Above all, Deng and his confederates redefined the army's organization and mission to exclude domestic functions; the focus of the military was now clearly on national defense. China's government was thus reclaimed in full by Deng Xiaoping and the new civilian leadership.

The Four Modernizations: The PRC's Economic Reforms

The reform movement in the PRC has had little to do with political change. Rather, it has been aimed at the "Four Modernizations"—of agriculture, industry, science and technology, and national defense. The most impressive early results came in agriculture. Between 1979 and 1981 the rural economy was completely switched from collectivized production to family farming. The PRC quickly became a net exporter of grain and cotton, despite its own enormous population. Due partly to the disruptive effects of the Great Leap Forward and the Cultural Revolution, China had long been a net importer of food, feed, and fiber.

The present farm system operates on a few simple principles. Land owner-ship continues to be public rather than private, but peasants lease the farmland for fifteen years or more. Beyond a certain quota that must be delivered to the state each year, peasants are free to grow anything they wish. Many specialize in various agricultural services and participate in profit-making peripheral enterprises. In just a few years, peasant incomes doubled under this ersatz free-enterprise system. And the rural economy became more diversified and more specialized, the proportion of the population directly dependent on agriculture (roughly 80 per-cent in the late 1970s) began to decline.

These impressive gains have not been matched in the industrial sectors. Eco-nomic reforms in industry were introduced more cautiously. At first industrial managers were allowed to market only a small amount of the output that exceeded their targets; the rest continued to go to the state. The emphasis during this phase was on redressing imbalances between agriculture and industry, and between heavy industry and light industry, while allocating more resources to consumption and less to accumulation.

In October 1984 the country moved beyond these halfhearted industrial reforms. New arrangements aimed to decentralize industrial decision making—that is, to dismantle the system of central planning. In all but a few "strategic" industries, taxation replaced quotas as the means of giving the state its due. Managers were given more discretion in making decisions about production, mar-keting, and investment, although the degree of flexibility was ambiguous. Instruc-tions from above were to be replaced by guidelines. Profit was to be replaced by plan fulfillment. The state would not withdraw entirely but would seek to control the operation of the market.

Not surprisingly, the most fragile and most difficult adjustments related to prices and wages. Under central planning, great distortions occurred. Prices reflected the government's priorities rather than marketplace realities. Wages were set by the state, and labor had no means of organizing to improve pay, benefits, work conditions, and the like. Switching to a system in which prices and wages can respond to market forces is bound to be destabilizing, both economi-cally and politically. The state must relinquish some control over the economy; at the same time, workers' hopes for higher wages and a better life can lead to a "revolution of rising expectations." Thus, in a previously controlled society, even purely economic reforms are risky politically.

The consequences of reduced control were evident in several of China's reform-related problems. For example, enterprises and local governments tended to overspend on construction projects. Left to their own devices, managers did not introduce new technologies as fast as leadership expected or hoped. Other, older problems could not be solved by economic reforms. For example, energy shortages and the outmoded transportation system continued to hamper industry. Unused plant capacity and supply bottlenecks were the telltale signs of these two flaws in the economic infrastructure. Even so, the nation's industrial output grew considerably after 1978, and in the early 1980s China's leaders set the optimistic goal of quadrupling the gross domestic product by the year 2000. As the decade ended, it appeared as though this optimism was warranted.

The PRC's System of Government

For all the reforms of the past decade, the PRC's governing structures have remained essentially intact. After Mao's death, personal rule was replaced by institutionalized rule, but the institutions look and function such as they were intended to ever since the founding of the regime in 1949.

Although the 1982 Constitution is the fifth one since 1949, formal government structures continue to be based on the Stalinist model—a dual hierarchy of party and state organs radiates from the center outward and downward through regional levels, to local units of administration. In theory, at least, the party formulates and coordinates policy, and the state bureaucracy implements it. (The ubiquitous local party committee monitors the implementation of party policy.) Under "dual rule," adopted in 1956, state organs are responsible both to the next-highest level of state administration and to the similar level of party organization. In practice, this has meant that managers on any given level have had to serve two masters. It is easy to imagine that such a setup can become stultifying, can stifle initiative, and can demoralize middle- and lower-level bureaucrats, whose efforts are so essential to success.

The genesis of Communist China's approach to administration was the long civil war, when necessity dictated that party, state, and army be fused into an efficient instrument of mass-mobilization. This tradition of "guerrilla administration" has continued to some extent and is reflected in the peculiar blend of civil and military functions, on the one hand, and party and state functions, on the other. This is one of the trademarks of Chinese communism. While it has always been discernible, it was taken to new extremes during the Cultural Revolution. Party and state organizations from provincial levels on down were dissolved and replaced by so-called revolutionary committees representing the PLA, "revolutionary mass organizations," and "revolutionary state and party cadres." Separate party organizations were reestablished in 1971, but state administration remained in the hands of revolutionary committees until 1979. The 1980s gave new impetus to the separation of party and state.

The party is the supreme repository of institutional power in the "new" Communist China, as it was in the "old" one. It was built on Lenin's principle of "democratic centralism" (see Chapter 8) and was patterned after the USSR's Communist party. In theory, the highest-level policy-making body is the National Party Congress, which usually convenes every five years to elect a Central Committee of roughly 350 members (only 60 percent of whom can vote). In turn, the Central Committee elects the Politburo, which has about twenty members. Although the Chinese party appears to be almost identical to its Soviet counterpart, one difference is that the Chinese Politburo is *not* the most powerful decision-making body. This distinction is reserved for the Standing Committee, an inner circle of six or seven leaders who decide economic priorities, formulate defense and foreign policies, and direct the pursuit of these policies. The Secretariat administers the party's daily affairs and is also chosen by the Central Committee.

The general secretary heads the Secretariat and is the highest-ranking party official. In contrast to the Soviet Union, China's top leader does not necessarily hold any particular title. Deng Xiaoping, for example, was clearly the most powerful leader in the PRC after 1978, but during much of the 1980s he did not hold any of the highest formal positions in either the party or the state. He was, however, chairman of the powerful Central Military Commission, which was set up by the 1982 Constitution to supervise the armed forces.

The State Council is the chief executive organ of government. It is headed by the premier, who theoretically is appointed by the president with the approval of the National People's Congress (NPC). The president, as chief of state, performs such formal duties as promulgating laws and decrees, ratifying treaties, appointing members of the State Council, and receiving foreign diplomats. Chosen by the NPC, the president serves a maximum of two 5-year terms and acts only on the initiative of the NPC or its Standing Committee. He is assisted by a vice-president, who becomes president if that position is vacated.

The premier heads the State Council (government) and is assisted by a secretary general and two or three vice-premiers (reduced from thirteen in April 1982). The State Council comprises the heads of forty-one ministries, commissions, and agencies (reduced from ninety-three in 1982). The State Council drafts laws for approval by the NPC, supervises the state bureaucracy, devises economic plans, and constructs national budgets.

The 1982 Constitution defined the National People's Congress as the "highest organ of state power." In reality, the NPC is a rubber stamp for the ruling organs of the party and the state. Its members are elected by provincial people's congresses and units of the People's Liberation Army. The term of office is normally five years, and the NPC is supposed to convene once a year. (Because of the upheaval of the Cultural Revolution, the NPC did not meet from 1965 to 1975). As a deliberative body of roughly three thousand members, the NPC is unwieldy; moreover, it meets for only a few days at a time. Thus it is largely symbolic, despite its exalted status in the Constitution. When the NPC is not in session, its duties are performed by the Standing Committee. With approximately 150 members, the Committee is better suited to act than the NPC itself. In theory, it possesses important legislative, judicial, and executive powers, including the right to nullify laws that it deems unconstitutional. Nonetheless, the Standing Committee's functions appear to overlap with the State Council's and its role in governing is ambiguous.

Although the PRC does not have an independent judiciary, since the late 1970s there has been renewed emphasis on "socialist legality"—a policy that fits the attempt to foster stability, creativity, and productivity. After a short period of liberalization in 1978, the government clamped down on dissent in 1979–1980. Although the Constitution devotes twenty-four articles to "Fundamental Rights and Duties of Citizens" (including freedom of speech, assembly, religion, and privacy), Article 51 introduces a caveat: The exercise of citizens' rights "may not infringe on the interests of the state, of society, and of the collective.'' Politically speaking, then, the more things change in the PRC, the more they stay the same.

Political Reform in the PRC: The Limits of Change

By early 1986 at least part of the PRC's leadership apparently decided that continued economic revitalization—especially in urban industrial sectors—was impossible without some sort of political restructuring. During the first nine months of 1986 numerous articles in the Chinese press advocated greater autonomy for plant managers in making decisions about consumption, production, and research—precisely the areas that the Chinese Communist party apparatus had reserved for itself. Moving in this direction would thus diminish the powers of the party. Some advocates of liberalization went further, maintaining that China's rapid transition from feudalism to socialism had bypassed the capitalist stage altogether. According to this view, China thus lacked the capital accumulation that occurred during the capitalist stage; the only way to make up for this deficiency was to extend the ''open door'' policy further—allow greater competition, give more play to market forces, and even create a stock exchange to raise venture capital!

In 1987 an ideological struggle became evident within party leadership. On the one side were the reformers, presumably led by Deng Xiaoping and Zhao Ziyang; on the other were the conservative ''old guard'' led by such venerable party stalwarts as Peng Zhen, Li Xiannian, and Chen Yun. The struggle appears to have been precipitated by massive demonstrations in December 1986 by students demanding democracy and Western-style freedoms. Since Deng Xiaoping had expressed his intention to retire after the Thirteenth National Congress scheduled for fall 1987, the leadership struggle was, in effect, a succession crisis; the future of the country was at stake.

In January 1987, Premier Hu Yaobang, a protégé of Deng's, was forced to resign, following ''self-criticism'' in which he took the blame for the students' uprisings. Specifically, he confessed to having allowed ''bourgeois liberalization'' (officially defined as ''the negation of the socialist system in favor of capitalism'') to pollute the political environment. It was clear that Hu was the scapegoat, that he had, in fact, been faithful to Deng's wishes. Nonetheless, Deng, the wily veteran of many battles, managed to survive this challenge unscathed—which also ensured the survival of his economic reforms.

Japan: Land of the Rising Sun

As noted in Chapter 13, Japan had little experience with democracy before the late 1940s. Indeed, in many ways Japan's history and culture were antithetical to Western democratic ideas. Today, less than a half-century after its crushing defeat in World War II, Japan is a shining example of democracy and capitalism in Asia. At the same time, it's politics and government reflect Japan's unique cultural heritage.

Japan's 1947 Constitution

The United States was in a commanding position in Japan after World War II. The 1947 Constitution, still essentially unchanged, embodied a firm resolve by the United States never to permit a resurgence of Japanese militarism. The American influence on the Japanese Constitution is glaringly apparent, especially in its preamble:

> We, the Japanese people, acting through our duly elected representatives in the National Diet, determined that we shall secure for ourselves and our posterity the fruits of peaceful cooperation with all nations and the blessings of liberty throughout this land, and resolved that never again shall we be visited with the horrors of war through the action of government, do proclaim that sovereign power resides with the people and do firmly establish this Constitution. . . . Government is a sacred trust of the people, the authority for which is derived from the people, the powers of which are exercised by representatives of the people, and the benefits of which are enjoyed by the people.

The framers of the 1947 Constitution sought to construct an elaborate system of representative government for Japan. Besides a wide range of civil liberties, the Constitution guarantees the right of citizens to an equal education and of workers to organize and engage in collective bargaining.

Article 9 explicitly renounces war and pledges that "land, sea, and air forces, as well as other war potential, will never be maintained." It should be noted, however, that this provision has not prevented the government from building "self-defense forces." Japan has taken this pledge seriously; until recently it spent less than 1 percent of its gross national product on defense. Ironically, this external constraint has given the Japanese a competitive edge in world trade.

Government by Consensus

Japan has a parliamentary form of government. The emperor continues to be chief of state but is a figurehead who performs ceremonial duties. The real chief executive is the prime minister, who is chosen by the majority party in the Diet (parliament). In theory a powerful figure, the prime minister must mollify and mediate among various factions in the majority party to function effectively as the head of the government. The prime minister has the constitutional power to choose the cabinet (consisting of about twenty ministers) and to dismiss cabinet members at will. The Constitution stipulates that only civilians may serve as cabinet members, a provision that is aimed at preventing any recurrence of militarism; in addition, the majority of members, including the prime minister, must hold Diet seats.

The cabinet prepares and submits the annual budget to the Diet, formulates domestic and foreign policies, manages the bureaucracy, negotiates treaties, and reports to the Diet about both national and international affairs. In short, the cabinet heads the executive branch of the government. As in Great Britain, the principle of collective responsibility is observed—all cabinet members are jointly responsible for all policies and decisions of government. In keeping with Japanese tradition, decisions are usually made by consensus; taking a formal vote, especially within the intimacy of a small group, is alien to Japan's political culture. Personal bonds of mutual trust play a major role in virtually all social, political, and even economic transactions. By the same token, the legalism that is so prevalent in Western democracies has been little emphasized in Japan.

The authors of the Constitution intended to place supreme power in Japan's bicameral Diet. This legislature is divided into a House of Representatives (511 members serving four-year terms) and a House of Concillors (252 members serving six-year terms). Under the Constitution, members of each house are elected by universal suffrage from multimember districts in which voters make only one selection from a list of candidates representing various political parties (often five or more). Smaller parties such as the Clean Government party and the Communist party can garner a limited number of seats in the Diet because in, say, a four-member district a candidate can win simply by receiving the fourth-largest vote.

In this type of electoral system, the distribution of votes is crucial. If, for example, the Liberal Democratic Party (LDP) puts up candidates for all seats in a given district and one candidate attracts most of the votes cast for the LDP in that district, strong candidates from smaller parties have a good chance of securing a seat. (Small parties may choose to run a single candidate in order to make every vote count.)

The Constitution declared that popular sovereignty was to be expressed through the Diet, the only institution empowered to make laws. Whereas in the past the prime minister and cabinet had been responsible to the emperor, they were now responsible to the Diet, the "highest organ of state power." Thus, in theory the Japanese parliamentary system closely resembles the British system. For example, the lower house of the Diet can force a government to resign through a vote of no confidence. (Alternatively, the cabinet can dissolve the lower house and call for new elections following a no-confidence vote.) But appearances are sometimes deceiving, for the Japanese have adapted Western institutions to fit their political culture. The result is a unique system that combines the "new" (democratic politics and market economics) with the "old" (political hierarchy, economic conglomeration, and social discipline).

The distinction between formal (constitutional) power and informal (real) power is crucial to understanding any political system, and Japan is no exception. Although formal power is vested in the Diet by the Constitution, the country is actually run by a ruling triad consisting of top bureaucrats, corporate leaders, and Liberal Democratic party chiefs.

Japan's Party System

The Liberal Democratic party (LDP) has dominated Japanese politics in the postwar years, resulting in a *one-party-dominant system*. Although numerous smaller parties have appeared, they have usually been ineffectual. Among them, the Socialist party has come closest to challenging the LDP, but its role has been confined to that of parliamentary opposition.

For over four decades the governing of Japan has fallen exclusively to the LDP. In a constitutional democracy such success usually indicates that people identify the government with progressive economic and social policies and that the society is prosperous. Such is the case in Japan, where the LDP's dominance goes back to the early postwar period. It was the conservatives who implemented the reforms imposed by General MacArthur, and who minimized discontinuities with the past. As the party in power the LDP "controlled a considerable amount of patronage and had the advantage when seeking the support of economic and professional interest groups." It could count on a majority of the rural vote and had access to the resources of the business community. It was also "on intimate terms with the bureaucracy."[1] But these advantages would probably not have been enough to keep the LDP in power had the party not taken one additional step: In the mid-1950s it began building a national organization with mass membership—"a surprisingly difficult thing to do in Japan where, on the local scene, groups based on personal loyalties, often around one individual, were more acceptable than branch units of a national party."[2]

In short, the Liberal Democratic party has succeeded by coopting much of the opposition, satisfying a multiplicity of interests, and seeking broad popular appeal rather than ideological purity. The LDP is thus a classic example of a catch-all party: Instead of depending on a particular social class, it draws support from a wide range of interest groups.

The internal power structure of the LDP becomes particularly crucial during biennial party conferences, at which the party elects its president, who then becomes prime minister by virtue of leading the majority party. In effect, Japan's chief executive is "elected" by a political party. This may seem undemocratic, but Japanese voters do have an opportunity to choose a new majority party at least every four years. (Elections have actually occurred more frequently—every two years, on average.) Moreover, LDP party conferences are nothing like the staged and orchestrated party conclaves traditionally held in Communist China or the Soviet Union. In Japan the outcome of presidential balloting is the result of intense bargaining by factions, each of which has its own leader, its own constituencies to represent, and its own policies to push.

As noted in Chapter 13, Japan has retained elements of its patron–client system. Before World War II Japan had been ruled by powerful heads of factions and cliques who built and maintained power bases by dispensing personal favors and rewards. This aspect of the political system has endured, although in less-pronounced form. Perhaps the most important vehicle for perpetuating the patron–client tradition has been the LDP itself.

Because the LDP is the chief party, and because it embraces an assortment of political interests, powerful faction leaders have emerged within the party's organization. To considerable extent, they wield the power of political life and death over their followers; they "feed" their factions with money and influence obtained through personal support groups (*koenkai*). When the political fortunes of party leaders rise and fall, the faction leaders act as power brokers, deciding who will become prime minister and which cabinet post will go to whom. By contemporary Western standards this system may seem neither open nor democratic, but by Japanese standards it is remarkably Americanized. Even so, the "paradox of Japan's being an open society made up of closed components" continues to set Japanese democracy apart from its counterparts in the West.[3]

Despite LDP dominance, Japanese voters do not suffer from a dearth of party choices. Besides the Socialists (JSP), there are the Democratic Socialists (DSP) and the Communists (JCP). There is also a Clean Government party (Komeito), which is the political offshoot of the Value Creation Society (Sokagakkai), one of Japan's new religions. A ruling by the Japanese Supreme Court prohibits sponsorship of political parties by religious organizations. This forced the Komeito to sever formal connections with the Sokagakkai, but the public continues to identify the party with the religion that spawned it.

The LDP typically gets around 46 to 48 percent of the popular vote; its nadir was in 1976, when it received less than 42 percent. The Socialists usually capture about 20 percent of the remaining votes, and the other minor parties get 10 percent or less. The electoral system tends to magnify the Liberal Democratic plurality enough to give it a clear majority in the Diet, partly by gerrymandering districts to favor farmers, who traditionally support the LDP. (Gerrymandering occurs when one party succeeds in drawing electoral district boundaries in irregular ways, to dilute the strength of opposition parties or to concentrate its own votes and win more seats than it otherwise would.)

Stability and Prosperity in Japan

Despite occasional riots and demonstrations—and even violent outbursts in the Diet—Japan's democratic government has been remarkably stable. This is especially impressive considering that Japan's political traditions before 1947 were generally authoritarian. Economics has played a key role, for Japan's economic revival after World War II was little short of miraculous.

A close alliance between political and business elites was one major reason for Japan's postwar prosperity, but a drive to penetrate foreign markets and massive infusions of American aid during the Korean War were also crucial. Within two decades the cooperation of government, business, and labor—an alliance that has become a trademark in Japan—produced huge advances in industry and technology. Japan is now an economic superpower, despite "the loss of 52 percent of Japan's prewar territories, the return of 5,000,000 persons to a country about the size of California, the loss of 80 percent of Japan's shipping, and the destruction of one-fifth of her industrial plants and many of her great cities."[4]

India: Democracy Amid Diversity

Although also a democracy like Japan, India is beset by chronic economic problems. The country appears to be singularly ill-prepared for democracy:

I have the impression that when we talk so confidently of liberty, we are unaware of the awful servitudes that are created by the ancient enemies of mankind: the servitude of poverty when means are so small that there is literally no choice at all; the servitude of ignorance when there are no perspectives to which the mind can open because there is no education . . . the servitude of ill-health which means that the expectation of life is almost too short to allow for any experience of freedom. . . .[5]

Such doubts about the suitability of democracy within the Third World seem especially germane to India, a nation of 833 million people encompassing a bewildering array of groups that differ in culture, ethnicity, language, and religion.

India's Drive for Independence

India's quest for self-rule can be traced back to the nineteenth century. Great Britain had originally ruled India indirectly, through Indian intermediaries and allies, but in doing so it introduced various institutions that the British found useful, including property laws and notions about the nature and functions of government. British influence meant that Indians who were chosen for service (in minor roles) in colonial administration were sent to England to receive a "proper classical education." Thus, a familiarity with Western concepts of equality, liberty, social justice, and representative democracy spread and gained currency among India's English-speaking elites, who included merchants, landlords, public officials, doctors, lawyers, and teachers—all with common interests that transcended caste, religion, or region. After 1885 they began to meet annually in a conference called the Indian National Congress, the seed from which the independence movement would later spring.

The British relinquished power in India gradually and with great reluctance. World War I strained Great Britain's resources, and London conceded that it would be necessary to transfer power, but not sovereignty, to Indian hands. Beginning in 1919 the National Congress, led by Mahatma Gandhi, conducted nationwide campaigns of civil disobedience (*satyagraha*, or passive resistance) to British rule. Three periods of confrontation (in 1919–1922, 1929–1932, and 1942) alternated with periods of participation by the Congress, first in a power-sharing arrangement known as "dyarchy" and, after 1935, in provincial self-government.

The last thirty years of British rule saw the National Congress grow steadily in stature and strength, evolving into a major force in Indian politics. It was, at once, a mass movement, a political party, and an alternative government.

The rise of the Congress, however, created a schism between Hindus and Muslims. The latter came to regard the Congress as hardly less inimical to Muslim interests than the British themselves were. Bloody communal riots occurred during the 1940s, in the twilight of British rule. When the British quit India after World War II, they chose the easy way out and partitioned the subcontinent.

The most contentious issue involved the future of Jammu and Kashmir. Located between India and Pakistan, Kashmir was partitioned between the two countries in 1947, but both claimed the entire territory. Kashmir was ruled locally by a Hindu maharaja, but the population was predominantly Muslim, and this majority sought union with Pakistan; the maharaja, however, favored merger with India. So the situation was volatile from the start, and hostilities erupted almost immediately between India and Pakistan. Major wars occurred in 1947, 1965, and 1971. Meanwhile, within India itself violence between Hindus and Muslims was a recurring problem.

The Indian Constitution

Although India gained independence from Great Britain in 1947, it took nearly three years to complete the writing of the new Constitution. Reflecting the complexities of Indian society, the Constitution was extremely long and intricate, containing not one list of power but three: a Union List, enumerating powers of the central government; a State List, reserving certain powers to provincial governments; and a Concurrent List, spelling out the powers to be shared by both. India's diverse society and sprawling geography necessitated not only a federal model but also specific delineation of how power would be parceled out among national, state, and local levels.

The division of power is spelled out in painstaking detail. The Union List contains ninety-seven items covering national defense, the armed forces, atomic energy, foreign affairs, transportation, communications, banking, currency, insurance, the regulation of industry and mining, income taxes, customs duties, and other areas. Enumerated in the State List are sixty-six items of primarily local interest: legal administration, public health and sanitation, education, agriculture, forests, fisheries, burials, duties on alcohol, and a variety of taxes (especially land taxes). The Concurrent (or joint) List contains forty-seven items that fall into gray areas: marriage and divorce, contracts, bankruptcy, civil suits, trade unions, social security, labor welfare, price controls, and so on. Although states may pass laws about these matters, the Constitution stipulates that, where concurrent powers are concerned, national law prevails over state law.

Indian Federalism: Overcoming Language Barriers

The Indian federal system divides the country into twenty-three states and eight union territories and strongly favors the central government to counterbalance the centrifugal tendencies inherent in India's cultural and linguistic diversity.

Because language has been a source of civil strife, India's states were demarcated along linguistic lines. In 1956, when the Indian Federal Union was reorganized and the number of states was reduced, all but two newly created states were based on regional language patterns. English, a vestige of colonization, has remained the language of privilege and power. Although the 1949 Constitutional Assembly specified that Hindi would be the universal language after 1965, regional opposition was so violent that the timetable had to be abandoned. Rather than one national language, then, India has adopted a three-language formula; schoolchildren learn to read and write their native tongue but also study English and Hindi.

India's Central Government

Independence leaders were well aware of the dangers in India's cultural diversity. Thus, they designed a highly centralized democratic system, despite its federal form.

The powers of central government are epitomized by elaborate constitutional provisions covering several states of emergency. First of all, a national state of emergency can be declared in cases of imminent war or revolution. (Under this provision, Prime Minister Indira Gandhi, when faced with a challenge to her political authority, suspended the Constitution in 1975 and assumed dictatorial powers for a period of nineteen months.) In addition, through a special declaration of emergency, central government can take over any state that is threatened with a breakdown of law and order. Finally, if a state becomes financially insolvent, central government can declare an economic emergency and can step in to run the state's affairs until the situation is under control.

The legislature, called the Federal Parliament, is divided into two houses. The upper house, known as the Council of the States (*rajya sabha*), has considerable legislative power, although in budget matters it only has the power of delay. Far more powerful is the House of the People (*lok sabha*), modeled after the British House of Commons. An interesting aspect of the lower house is that it reserves a certain number of seats for groups that were victims of discrimination in the past, including former "Untouchables" who traditionally were treated as outcasts.

As in other parliamentary systems, India's executive is divided. The president, or chief of state, is chosen by an electoral college made up of officials from the Federal Parliament and state assemblies. The prime minister, who performs the usual duties associated with the head of government (such as appointing the cabinet, directing policy formulation, and representing the nation abroad), is elected by the majority party or coalition in the House of the People. Except for the brief period following Indira Gandhi's emergency rule in the mid-1970s and again in 1989–1990, the prime minister has always been the head of the Congress party, which has been the dominant party since independence.

India's Judiciary, Civil Liberties, and Social Rights

India has an independent judiciary that acts as a bulwark against official abuses of human rights. However, during periods of "presidential rule," civil liberties have been suspended, and political opponents have been arrested and jailed. As noted, these emergency powers were used in the mid-1970s, when Indira Gandhi ruled as a virtual dictator for nineteen months. These powers have been used frequently by central government, but usually when instability in a particular state has led to the breakdown of law and order. Normally, India's citizens enjoy the freedoms of speech, press, assembly, religion, and so on.

Of particular interest is a section of the Constitution that sets forth basic "social" rights (as opposed to the more familiar "civil" rights). These can be found in the "directives," of which Article 39 is a prominent part. It stipulates:

The State shall, in particular, direct its policy towards securing

a. that the citizens, men and women equally, have the right to an adequate means of livelihood;
b. that the ownership and control of the material resources of the community are so distributed as best to subserve the common good;
c. that the operation of the economic system does not result in the concentration of wealth and means of production to the common detriment;
d. that there is equal pay for equal work for both men and women;
e. that the health and strength of workers, men and women, and the tender age of children are not abused and that citizens are not forced by economic necessity to enter avocations unsuited to their age or strength.

India's One-Party-Dominant System

Before it broke up in the late 1960s, the Congress party encompassed a variety of interests and was supported by middle- and upper-class nationalists as well as by many members of traditionally lower castes. With the disintegration of the party and the emergence of Indira Gandhi as the eventual successor to her father, Jawaharlal Nehru (1889–1964), a major political realignment appeared likely. What happened, instead, is that one preeminent party merely replaced another, and the basic power structure in India did not change.

A new national party emerged from the former Congress coalition—Prime Minister Gandhi's New Congress (later named the Congress-I for "Indira Congress)." In essence, Congress-I was a reincarnation of the one-party-dominant system, but under Indira Gandhi's personal tutelage. With opposition fragmented and ineffectual, Gandhi was able to retain power despite growing disenchantment with her methods and policies.

When Gandhi declared a state of emergency in 1975, she had many opposition leaders arrested. At the end of martial law in 1977, new elections were announced, and the revitalized opposition parties formed an umbrella organization, led by Morarji Desai, known as the Janata party. This loose-knit coalition won a parliamentary majority and formed a government, but its fragile unity was predicated on little else than hostility toward Gandhi. Lacking consensus or a coherent program, the coalition began to come unglued after only about two years. As India's foreign and domestic problems mounted, the need for a strong leader became more and more apparent. In the 1980 parliamentary elections, the Congress-I party won an overwhelming victory (with only 42 percent of the vote) and again fashioned a coalition that enabled Gandhi to form a government. The Janata party faded into oblivion, and other parties again became a fragmented and ineffectual opposition.

Gandhi's return to power was plagued with misfortune, turmoil, and tragedy. First, her son Sanjay, who won a seat in the lok sabha in 1980, was killed in an airplane crash. Then, in the early 1980s, a resurgence of caste and communal violence threatened Indian society as religious and regional separatism shook the federal structure to its foundations. In Assam and northeast India, hatred against Bengalis and immigrants was expressed in murders, bombings, strikes, and a campaign of civil disobedience. Hundreds of lives were lost in 1982 and 1983. When Prime Minister Gandhi tried to hold new elections rather than prolonging presidential rule, the violence escalated, and New Delhi was forced to make concessions to the militants. Violence also broke out in Kashmir during another election.

The bloodiest outbreaks, however, occurred in Punjab, where a Sikh secessionist movement had been brewing for several years. At first the secessionists represented a small minority, but Punjabi society became polarized as hundreds of people, mostly Hindus, were killed by terrorists. Hindus pressured the central government to intervene. The climax came after an extremist Sikh leader, Jarnail Singh Bhindranwale, turned the Golden Temple of Amritsar into a terrorist stronghold. The Indian army stormed the citadel, killing Bhindranwale and hundreds of his backers and damaging sacred buildings in the process. An army blockade and curfew followed. Sikh troops mutinied in various parts of India, but the ultimate act of retribution occurred in 1984, when Sikh members of Indira Gandhi's personal guard assassinated her.

Gandhi's martyrdom came at a time when her popularity was at low ebb, but the Congress-I and the country rallied around her surviving son, Rajiv, who had entered politics after his younger brother's untimely death in 1980. In the elections of December 1984 the Congress-I won a landslide victory, capturing all but 19 of the 508 seats contested.

Rajiv won early respect for his conciliatory gestures both at home and abroad. But the success of the Congress-I at the national level was not matched in state elections. These defeats undermined Rajiv's credibility, as did continuing communal violence and a resurgence of Sikh separatism. In the summer of 1987 Sikh militants launched a new terrorist offensive, ending hopes of a settlement. Along with these problems, charges of corruption within the government, a damaging conflict over constitutional issues with the outgoing president, and a series of cabinet resignations plagued Rajiv Gandhi's administration and contributed to its downfall in 1989.

The Indian Synthesis

India has traditionally been ruled by charismatic leaders. The great Mahatma Gandhi was the first in a succession of dominant Congress figures. After him, both the Congress and the nation came to be dominated by a new dynasty. Nehru ruled from 1947 to 1964; Indira Gandhi, Nehru's daughter, ruled from 1966 to 1977 and from 1980 to 1984. When she was assassinated and her son Rajiv succeeded her, the tradition of dynastic rule appeared to have returned in a new guise, one adapted to the structures and processes of constitutional democracy. This ability to synthesize foreign and indigenous elements into a new political order is a striking feature of contemporary Asian politics and is visible in Japan and China as well as India.

The presence of firm leadership throughout the postwar period was undoubtedly a key to India's success with democracy. In late 1989 Rajiv Gandhi was forced to step down after his prestige and popularity were damaged by political scandals and social unrest (mainly the festering conflicts in Punjab and Kashmir). His successor, V. P. Singh, was confronted with continuing Sikh terrorism in Punjab and resorted to emergency rule—the same policy for which he had criticized Gandhi. The other immediate challenge for the new prime minister was Kashmir, where a smoldering state of war threatened to burst into flames at any minute in the spring of 1990. By the end of the year, situations like these led to a no-confidence vote, and Singh's government fell. Lacking a strong leader who can bridge the nation's wide social and political gulfs, the prospects for stability in India remain bleak.

CONCLUSION

The political traditions of Asia are distinct from those of Europe and the Middle East. Although both the Asian and Arab ruling systems are authoritarian, Asian societies have displayed a greater propensity to assimilate and adapt certain features of Western society (free elections, market economies, mass consumption, technological innovation). The prospects for such a synthesis are discussed in Chapter 15.

STUDY QUESTIONS

1. What impacts did the outcome of World War II have on political systems in China, Japan, and India?
2. What was China's Great Leap Forward? Was the Cultural Revolution a second "great leap," or was it qualitatively different? Why did Mao believe it was necessary to launch periodic revolutions from above? Is Maoism dead, or does the ghost of Mao continue to haunt the PRC?
3. How is the People's Republic of China governed? What, if anything, changed after Mao's death? How can the uprising in Tiananmen Square in mid-1989 be explained?
4. How does Japan's political system work? How is it similar to Western parliamentary government? How is it different?
5. Given the multiethnic nature of Indian society, how can India function as a parliamentary democracy? What features of other political systems did India borrow? What features are unique to India?

SUGGESTED READINGS

Chang, David Wen-wei. *China Under Deng Xiaoping: Political and Economic Reform*. New York: St. Martin's, 1989.

Hardgrave, Robert L., Jr., and Stanley A. Kochanek. *India: Government and Politics of a Developing Nation*. Orlando, Fla: Harcourt, 1986.

Hrenebar, Ronald J. *The Japanese Party System: From One-Party Rule to Coalition Government*. Boulder: Westview, 1986.

Kohli, Atul, ed. *India's Democracy: An Analysis of Changing State-Society Relations*. Princeton, N.J.: Princeton University, 1988.

Lieberthal, Kenneth J., and Michel Oksenberg. *Policy Making in China: Leaders, Structures and Processes*. Princeton, N.J.: Princeton University, 1988.

Manor, James. "India: State and Society Diverge," *Current History*, December 1989.

Pye, Lucian. *China: An Introduction*. Boston: Little, Brown, 1984.

Reischauer, Edwin O. *Japan: The Story of a Nation*. New York: McGraw-Hill, 1990.

Richardson, Bradley M., and Scott C. Flanagan. *Politics in Japan*. Boston: Little, Brown, 1984.

NOTES

[1] Franz Michael and George Taylor, *The Far East in the Modern World* (New York: Holt, 1964), p. 607.

[2] Ibid.

[3] Robert H. Scalapino and Junnosuki Masumi, *Parties and Politics in Contemporary Japan* (Berkeley, Calif.: University of California, 1962), p. 153.

[4] Michael and Taylor, op. cit., p. 603.

[5] Barbara Ward, *The Rich Nations and the Poor Nations* (New York: Norton, 1962), pp. 158–159.

Chapter 15
Toward the Year 2000—
The Asian Century?

As the twentieth century wanes, Asia stands at a crossroads between its past and future, between tradition and modernity, between nationalism and regionalism. Today's world offers little choice but to modernize or retreat into self-defeating isolationism. The question is not *whether* to change, but *how*. A key issue for many Asian nations is how to manage change so that the economy grows and society prospers without eroding the nation's unique moral, spiritual, cultural, and aesthetic values.

Economic Differences Among Asian Nations

In terms of economic development, one of the most striking features of the Asian landscape is its differentiation. Apart from Japan, which is in a class by itself, Asia can be grouped into several categories: New Industrial Countries (NICs); Newly Exporting Countries (NECs); Marxist-Leninist Countries (MLCs), in which central planning substitutes for market forces; and Less Developed Countries (LDCs). Many LDCs face serious problems arising from unfavorable food–population ratios, land and resource scarcity, natural disasters, and the like. For some the problem is severe. South Asia is home to several of these nations—including India, Pakistan, and Bangladesh—in which meeting basic human needs absorbs virtually all available resources. For lack of a better term, we will call such nations Basic Needs Countries (BNCs).

As noted in Chapter 14, no such classification scheme is perfect. Some countries fit into more than one category. For example, Vietnam is both an MLC and a BNC; India is both a NIC and a BNC; and Indonesia is both a NEC and a BNC. Yet these distinctions illustrate the diversity of developmental stages and strategies found throughout Asia. They also call attention to the possible relationship between economic stages and strategies.

Asia's richest nation, and one of the richest in the world, is Japan, which now ranks second in gross national product (see Table 15-1). More important, Japan's economy has been the most dynamic in the industrially developed world. In fact, it has been so dynamic that it is a source of friction between Japan and its trading partners, especially the United States.[1]

Nor is Japan the only prosperous country in Asia. The Republic of Korea, Taiwan, Hong Kong, and Singapore—the "Four Little Dragons"—have shown remarkably economic vitality in recent years (see Table 15-2). These New Industrial

Table 15-1 Comparison of Leading Economies (percent)

	GNP increase 1987	GNP increase 1988	Unemployment rate	Inflation rate
United States	2.75	2.75	6.25	4.0
Japan	1.5	4.25	3.0	0.75
France	1.5	2.0	10.75	3.25
Great Britain	3.75	3.5	10.75	3.0
West Germany	1.5	2.25	8.0	0.75

Source: Associated Press.

Countries (NICs) are not only emulating Japan but also exporting to Japan. They are producing a variety of consumer goods at lower costs than the Japanese. The "import invasion," still in its infancy, represents an incipient challenge to Japan—one that is potentially as formidable as the challenge which Japan has posed to the United States since the 1960s. As one observer has written:

> Economists and industrial planners say the onslaught of imports, as it broadens, will eventually force Japanese companies to lower their exorbitant domestic prices. That would squeeze their profits and confront more and more of them with the same hard decisions that American companies faced: to close down domestic factories and move many operations abroad.[2]

Taiwan's economic miracle contrasts sharply with the troubled economic history of mainland China since 1949, when the revolution catapulted the Chinese Communist party to power. Today the economy of tiny Taiwan is ten times richer than that of the giant on the mainland. Taiwan is bustling with economic activity of all kinds. Per capita GNP is about $5,000, and consumer goods—including television sets, refrigerators, washing machines, and automobiles—are available at affordable prices. Taiwan's economy not only is industrialized but also has absorbed new technology like a sponge; the result is

Table 15-2 Growth in Selected Asian Economies (percent per year)

	1970–1983	1985	1986
China	7.8	12.3	9.3
Hong Kong	8.7	−0.5	7.2
Indonesia	7.1	—	2.3
Malaysia	7.7	−1.0	0.5
Singapore	8.9	−1.8	1.9
South Korea	7.1	5.0	12.0

Source: Associated Press.

prosperity built on a foundation of massive exports. Taiwan is the world's twelfth-largest trader and the fifth-largest trading partner with the United States. In 1988 its foreign exchange reserves were more than $75 billion. By contrast, the People's Republic of China faced chronic foreign exchange shortages during the 1980s.[3]

Just as Japan has set an example for Asia's NICs, they, in turn, have set an example for other Asian nations. Indonesia, the Philippines, and Thailand all improved their external trade position vis-à-vis Japan in the mid-1980s, particularly in agricultural and fishery products. Among the ASEAN states alone, this export surge cut the annual combined trade deficit in half between 1984 and 1986. (ASEAN stands for the Association of Southeast Asian Nations; its members are Indonesia, Malaysia, the Philippines, Thailand, and Singapore.) Because the economic prospects for these developing nations are tied so closely to rising exports, several states in Southeast Asia are being called Newly Exporting Countries. If Japan's model works elsewhere in Asia—as it has so far in South Korea, Taiwan, Hong Kong, and Singapore—today's NECs may reasonably aspire to become tomorrow's NICs.

The Marxist-Leninist countries in Asia include North Korea, the People's Republic of China, Vietnam, Laos, and Kampuchea (Cambodia). Vietnam dominates Indochina politically, but its overall economic performance has been dismal. Only massive infusions of aid from the Soviet Union since the mid-1970s have kept the overextended Hanoi regime going. The PRC has shifted its economy from near-total reliance on central planning to something like free-market conditions, especially in the agricultural sector. As noted earlier, mainland China has achieved food self-sufficiency since it instituted market-oriented reforms beginning in 1979. North Korea remains an unreconstructed Stalinist state with a self-reliant economy, but until the PRC's recent economic resurgence it was probably the most economically viable Marxist-Leninist state in Asia (not counting the Soviet Union).

Demographic Characteristics in Asia

The Basic Needs Countries include India, Pakistan, Bangladesh, and Burma. Their per capita incomes are among the lowest in Asia (and in the Third World generally), and their population growth rates are among the highest. Indeed, the population explosion has been a pattern throughout Asia and is a major obstacle to net gains in economic growth (that is, annual GNP growth minus population growth).

In Pakistan, for example, the annual population growth rate averaged more than 3 percent in the mid-1980s, while the GNP per capita was well below $400. To improve at all, Pakistan's economy would have to grow more than 3 percent a year. However, the average annual growth rate for South Asia as a whole from 1980 to 1985 was only 2.2 percent. In India, the picture is hardly less bleak. At 2 percent, India's annual population growth rate is below Pakistan's, but its population base is much larger. At current growth rates, their populations will double in about twenty-five years.

Burma and Bangladesh are even poorer. Their per capita incomes are around $200, and population growth rates are high (2.3 percent in Burma and 2.8 in Bangladesh). To make matters worse, in 1988 Burma was racked by violent political turmoil, while Bangladesh was hit by floods that left millions homeless, cost countless lives, overwhelmed relief efforts, and reduced the nation's chronically stagnant economy to ruins.

Troublesome as Asia's population growth may be, Asians are not as prolific as their counterparts in sub-Saharan Africa and Central America, where growth rates were higher (3.2 percent and 2.9 percent, respectively, during the 1980s). On the other hand, Asia's population growth is spectacular compared with Europe's, which averaged a mere 0.3 percent from 1980 to 1985, and with Japan's, which was a modest 0.7 percent in the mid-1980s. To understand the implications of these statistics, consider the time it takes to double the population at a constant growth rate. At 0.5 percent annually it takes 139 years; at 1 percent it takes 70 years; at 2 percent it takes 35 years; and at 3 percent it takes a mere 23 years.

Other demographic characteristics also have important implications for Asia's future. There are generally more males than females in Asian society, whereas in industrially developed nations females typically outnumber males. The reasons are related to culture as well as to economic factors. Deaths associated with frequent pregnancies, poor female hygiene and health care, and the tendency to favor male over female babies are all factors. Some of these problems arise from poverty; others are related to the lower social status of females in many LDCs.

In societies with rapidly growing populations the age composition changes dramatically. As the number of babies born each year rises and the infant mortality rate drops, the population gets younger. In most Asian societies in the mid-1980s, the proportion of children younger than 15 years old was at least 40 percent of the population. The comparable figures for industrial democracies were 22.3 percent in Europe, 22.6 percent in North America, and 23.6 percent in Japan. Implications for LDCs are enormous. First, more health services are needed both for childbearing women and for infants. A large proportion of the very young in Asia suffer from malnutrition, a problem that is likely to worsen as the number of infants increases. Those who survive this crisis will constitute the future labor force; since malnutrition at an early age affects physical and mental development, it also has an impact on later productivity and on health care needs. As preschool populations grow, governments generally have to increase education expenditures, which diverts resources from other development projects that could improve the standard of living.

A second problem for LDCs is that the larger proportion of children puts a greater burden on productive adult members of society. This can be expressed as a dependency ratio: the number of dependents (under age 14 and over age 65) in relation to the economically productive population (between 15 and 64). Except for Japan, dependency ratios are generally higher in Asia than elsewhere, especially in industrially developed countries. In addition, high unemployment typically hits young adults hardest, and Asia is no exception. When unemployed young adults (15 to 24 years old) are considered, the dependency ratio worsens considerably.

Third, the prospects are dim at best for the vast majority of Asia's youth (again excepting Japan and, to a lesser extent, the NICs). Adolescents and young adults are typically rebellious, and students everywhere are loathe to accept the status quo, even if it is favorable. Education without opportunity can be dangerous, especially for societies that are beset by problems which they cannot address, much less solve. Will Asian youth accept their plight? Or will anger and frustration boil over—as it already has in Communist China, Burma, and South Korea—thus further impeding economic growth and development? How can Asia's overpopulated and ''underdeveloped'' nations end this vicious circle?

Finally, the demographic conundrum affects not only Asia's poorest nations but also its richest. Dependency ratios come into play at both ends of the age spectrum. As life expectancy increases and the birth rate comes down, the proportion of elderly pensioners also rises. This problem is only beginning to have an impact in most of Asia, but it is already being felt in Japan, one of the fastest-aging countries in the world. But in the future it is the PRC, with its billion-plus population despite its policy of promoting one-child families, that faces the heaviest burden in Asia as the birth rate drops and life expectancy climbs.

The Challenges of Modernization

Economic development and population control pose major challenges for most of Asia. Both, in turn, encompass a host of interrelated—or even reciprocal—problems. For example, if unchecked population growth affects future economic prospects, underdevelopment also puts obstacles in the path of population control. Education is one essential ingredient in any formula for reducing the birth rate. It is no coincidence that societies with low birth rates also have high literacy rates. By the same token, affluent societies whose governments can afford to provide a wide range of social services, including pensions and medical care for the aged, typically have lower birth rates. In contrast, the poor and needy in developing countries cannot rely on government to provide for them in their old age—having a large family is the only form of ''social security'' available. Hence, what appears to be irresponsible behavior for society as a whole may be entirely rational behavior for individuals.

Large families make sense in societies where wage-earning jobs are few and farming or running a small business is a family affair. Children, especially males, ensure that the head of the household will have help with the arduous labor needed to eke out an existence in an agrarian society where plots of land are too small and capital too scarce to permit the use of modern farm machinery.

This incentive to have large families will not change unless most Asians can become wage earners—they must be able to get jobs with fair compensation and the kind of benefits that are taken for granted in industrial nations. At present, ''developing Asia'' (except for Japan and the NICs) is predominantly agrarian: Roughly 70 percent of the population engages in subsistence farming. Many of the others survive by working, often on a seasonal basis, for subsistence wages. They earn barely enough to stay alive and have no money for anything but bare necessities—no savings, and little or no "social security."

The developing countries of Asia have half the world's population but only 10 percent of its wealth and production, and their share is actually shrinking. When Gunnar Myrdal, the renowned Swedish economist, published his book on Asian economic development in 1968, he entitled it, *Asian Drama: An Inquiry into the Poverty of Nations.* In stark terms Myrdal pointed out that Asia has the worst poverty in the world. U.N. statistics support this conclusion: Several of the world's least developed countries (including Afghanistan, Bangladesh, Laos, and Nepal) are in Asia.

Endemic poverty translates into massive unemployment. No one knows for certain how many of Asia's working-age adults are actually unemployed (most official figures greatly understate the problem), but the figure is probably in the range of 15 to 20 percent. Worse still, *under*employment is much higher than actual unemployment in most of developing Asia. In reality, perhaps half the working-age population needs jobs.

Whatever their relative levels of development, Asian nations face the challenges of continuing to modernize, of integrating traditional methods of production with new technologies, and of adapting to regional and global competition without losing their cultural identities along the way. In other words, Asia must learn to *manage* change rather than be swept along by it. Change is inevitable; its pace and direction will either be dictated by chance or be molded by concious choice.

Lacking such choice in the form of public policies, Asia may or may not reap the benefits of modernization, but it will definitely experience most of the burdens. What burdens? A glance at advanced industrial societies reveals part of the answer: pollution, traffic congestion, overcrowding, rising crime, and the like. Less obvious, perhaps, is the moral and spiritual erosion that has accompanied modernization as the family has given way to the cult of the individual, as values and virtues have been reduced to materialism, and as affluence has brought not leisure but a rat race of "keeping up with the Joneses."

Japan may be illustrative. Affluent and admired, many Japanese now search for the spiritual and cultural values that were subordinated in the climb up the global economic ladder. Although Japan is an Asian society, it has responded to the challenges of modernization with extraordinary resourcefulness and ingenuity; it has adapted to a changing world much more rapidly than its neighbors. It is in a class by itself—in Asia and beyond.

Japan: The Perils of Success

It may seem as though Japan has no serious economic or social problems—at least compared with the rest of Asia. But Japan's very success has created problems. A few of these are essentially internal, while most are, to a significant degree, external. But even the problems that appear to be domestic in nature have an international dimension, because Japan's economy is so thoroughly enmeshed with the global economy.

From Domestic to Foreign Markets

Japan's economic miracle really began in the mid-1950s. From then until the first oil crisis of 1973–1974, Japan did not rely heavily on exports to sustain its accelerating economic growth; on the contrary, it was expansion of domestic markets that energized Japan's economy. Exports grew rapidly, but so did imports of raw materials and fossil fuels. (Japan still imports virtually all of its oil and gas.)

The oil crisis brought dramatic changes to Japan. Its economic growth rate fell from 10 percent to 4 or 5 percent annually, which led automatically to a reduction in imports. The energy crisis also led to conservation efforts. At the same time, leaders of government and business—always closely linked in Japan—began looking to foreign markets as a way to cope with sluggish domestic demand.

Other trends also pushed Japan toward an export orientation during the 1970s and 1980s. For example, Japan's heavy industries such as steel, shipbuilding, manufacturing, synthetic textiles, automobiles, petrochemicals, and home appliances—once the engines of Japanese economic growth—became depressed (as they did in the United States). Foreign competition, especially but not exclusively from Asian NICs, contributed to the decline of heavy industry. Japan turned increasingly to high-technology industries. Meanwhile, many Japanese consumers took to saving rather than spending.

According to Robert S. Ozaki:

> Japan, with the second largest economy in the world, has become a nation that exports too much and imports too little, much to the dismay and frustration of deficit-prone countries, especially the United States. Enormous trade surpluses, instead of being spent in Japan, have found their way abroad as capital investments. For 1986, Japan's trade surplus was $102 billion, of which $52 billion was charged to the United States, and the net capital outflow from Japan amounted to $144 billion. In contrast, in the same year the United States ran a trade deficit of $134 billion and absorbed a $57 billion net capital inflow from abroad. In 1985, Japan became the world's largest creditor nation, while the United States, the richest country on earth, became the world's largest debtor nation, with net external liabilities of $107 billion.[4]

Ozaki and others argued that Japan is now a major source of "disequilibrium," not only for the United States but also within the world economy as a whole. "Translated into an obligation on the part of Japan," Ozaki wrote, "this means that Japan is expected to alter the internal properties and structure of its economy fundamentally to make it an equilibrating (rather than disequilibrating) force . . . commensurate with its weight and strength in the world." Given the nexus between Japan's prosperity and global economic stability, Ozaki believes "it has become imperative that Japan 'internationalize' its economy to a far higher degree than it has already achieved."[5]

Japan's critics cite the need for a wide range of internal economic reforms: (a) Further deregulate the banking system and money markets to end Japan's policy of low interest rates and thus attract overseas assets back into the country; (b) put an end to agricultural protectionism (especially for rice); (c) break up state-supported monopoly arrangements in the distribution system, which make it difficult for foreign manufacturers to penetrate Japanese markets even without tariffs, import quotas, and other barriers; (d) actively combat unfair trade practices of enterprise groups that discriminate against foreign firms; (e) do away with closed bidding for government contracts, which traditionally go almost exclusively to a handful of Japanese construction firms; and (f) generally tighten the interpretation of antimonopoly laws, thus further opening Japan's economy to free-market forces and foreign competition.

Besides such structural changes, critics say that Japan must reverse its economic policies. As the trade imbalance with the United States became increasingly lopsided, these critics say, Japan should have instituted tight money policies to push interest rates up and keep capital at home, and expansionary fiscal policies —especially tax cuts—to encourage imports and absorb more domestic production internally, thus reducing exports). Instead, Japan did just the opposite, while the United States blithely implemented ''Reaganomics,'' that is, the very mix of policies that Japan should have been putting into effect.

The political economy of U.S.–Japanese relations is debatable, but one thing is clear: Japan can no longer afford to pursue a strategy of economic growth without regard for its impact on the United States, Asia, and the rest of the world. For both economic and political reasons, Japan faces pressure from the international community to make major policy adjustments that may require sacrifices. For example, developing nations have amassed foreign debts totaling $1.3 trillion. Meanwhile, as noted, Japan has become the leading creditor nation, and it is inevitable that governments and international agencies will look to Japan for leadership, soft loans, and debt relief, much as they once looked to the United States as benefactor and backbone of the international monetary system.

Moreover, Japan's affluence raises the expectations of free-flowing foreign aid, and there are signs that Japan recognizes this. In 1987 Japanese public and private assistance to developing countries surged more than 40 percent, to over $20 billion.[6] Not surprisingly, most Japanese foreign aid goes to Asian countries; in 1987 the three main recipients were Indonesia ($707 million), China ($553 million), and the Philippines ($379 million). And these significant amounts are dwarfed both by Japan's trade surpluses and by the magnitude of developing Asia's domestic problems. The goal of Japan's expanded program of economic and technical assistance is to get its total overseas development assistance to around 3.5 percent by 1993—an amount that probably will not satisfy the rising expectations of developing Asia.

The Consequences of Trade Imbalance

Far more troublesome for Japan is the growing chorus of criticism, led by the United States, directed at what many consider to be unfair trade practices. For example, the United States has demanded that Japan lift its strict quotas on beef and citrus fruit, and rice-producing countries are demanding that Japan end protectionist policies that prevent imported rice (and other foodstuffs) from entering Japanese markets. In many instances, "tariff rates are roughly equal to those of other industrial nations, [but] they are spiked with special tariffs in industries that are considered vulnerable to foreign competition."[7]

The Japanese are, in fact adept at devising nontariff barriers. For example, a tariff of 20 percent on foreign cigarettes is only the tip of the protectionist iceberg; imported tobacco products can only be sold by 10 percent of Japan's 250,000 tobacconists, and importers are allowed to advertise only in English-language publications. Such nontariff barriers are common in Japan.

Restrictions like these are especially upsetting to foreign competitors because Japan has so aggressively developed foreign markets for its own exports. According to David Brock:

> Examples of the dynamics of the Japanese trade thrust are by now the stuff of legend among foreign competitors. The Ministry of Finance backs industries in which it perceives high demand by directing the allocation of development funds to private companies through the banks it controls. Support originally went to textiles, then switched to automobiles, steel, electronics, semiconductors and now to financial services. To do this, the Japan Development Bank draws on Post Office savings accounts, which, thanks to an exemption from taxes and generous interest rates, have grown to a sum greater than the assets of the 10 largest American money center banks combined. (Japanese law forbids any private bank to pay a higher rate on savings than the Post Office.)[8]

During the early years of Japan's export push, the Ministry of Finance also allowed up to 80 percent of a company's export earnings to be exempt from taxation; later, depreciation allowances pegged to export earnings were substituted for tax exemptions, but the net effect was the same. At the same time, the Ministry of International Trade and Industry, which is charged with promoting the nation's thriving export industries, "targets countries and markets to be penetrated [and] can also bring together large producers into one company to achieve economies of scale—a practice U.S. antitrust law would prohibit." Finally, critics maintain that the Japanese "are willing to go to extreme lengths, subsidizing vulnerable items in foreign markets by raising domestic prices and shielding home markets."[9]

Whether this view of Japanese economic policies is accurate or not, it is widely held, and not only in the United States. It creates an image problem that Japan can ill-afford to ignore. Even Japan's admirers in the West point to the Japanese challenge. For example, in February 1988, Norman Cousins, former editor of the *Saturday Review*, wrote an article arguing that Japan, not the Soviet Union, poses "the greatest single threat to American capitalism." Cousins reasoned as follows:

> Many Americans have allowed themselves to believe that high military spending is essential for high employment and prosperity. Japanese economists see a direct connection between the absence of fat military budgets and their booming economy.

Again, their notions are quintessentially capitalistic: multiply capital by good investments—investment in human intelligence which in turn is converted into acquisition of raw materials and the processing of those materials into new and better products that can command the world's markets and that can return more capital to continue and expand the same process.[10]

If Japan's diplomatic relations are strained, if the international economy founders, and if nations in jeopardy blame Japan—if any or all of these things happen, the consequences for Japan's future could be dire, for Japan is one of the most export-dependent nations on earth. The source of its economic vitality is also the source of its greatest vulnerability.

Nowhere is this vulnerability more evident than in the area of energy. Japan has imported virtually all its fossil fuels since the early 1950s. Before the 1973 oil crisis, its rapid economic growth was fueled by "the relatively stable postwar petroleum regime, managed by the large oil firms and protected by American diplomatic and military strength."[11] Since 1973 Japan has tried to reduce its dependence on imported oil by conserving energy and diversifying its sources, but imported oil still supplies 60 percent of Japan's energy needs, and 70 percent of this oil comes from the Persian Gulf. Two trends—the oil glut and the appreciation of the yen—alleviated the immediate problem in the 1980s, but things have changed in the 1990s. Energy security is an unresolved issue in Japan, and critics believe it must be faced head on.[12]

The Old Order Versus New Challenges

Politically, Japan does not face the kind of instability that plagues many Asian governments. Like the Imperial Chinese whose statecraft they imitated, the Japanese have an extraordinary record as institution builders. "They invent or borrow from others, adapt, refine, but never so rigidly that the rules obstruct rather than facilitate the achievement of their objectives."[13]

This high degree of institutionalization lends stability and predictability to Japanese politics. The postwar predominance of the Liberal Democratic party (LDP) appears likely to continue, even though opposition parties are protected by law, and national elections are free and fair. The choice of Noboru Takeshita to succeed Yasuhiro Nakasone as LDP president and prime minister in the fall of 1987 came as no great surprise to those familiar with Japanese politics. The party president is chosen by bargaining among faction leaders within the national Diet, not by party rank and file or by individual LDP Diet members. Typically, the faction leader with the best record (measured by cabinet, Diet, and party posts held) wins. In elevating LDP Secretary General Takeshita to the party presidency and ensuring his "election" as prime minister, the LDP followed unwritten rules of tradition and precedent.

Similarly, Takeshita's cabinet was selected in accordance with well-established unwritten rules whereby posts are distributed according to factional strength, seniority, and other factors. As a result, the integrity of the process of forming a cabinet was reaffirmed, and the cohesion of the party was maintained, despite its factional substructure. Policy considerations do not seem to play a major role in the distribution of cabinet posts, which perhaps reflects the extent to which policy making has been institutionalized (and depoliticized).

Public policy in Japan displays remarkable continuity from one government to the next. Nakasone accomplished several major administrative reforms begun by his predecessor, Zenko Suzuki. These include privatization of three major public enterprises (tobacco, the telegraph and telephone, and railways); revision of pension and health insurance laws; tax reform; and changes in relations between central and local governments. But Nakasone also left many troublesome policy issues for Takeshita to address.

In sum, Japan faced several domestic and foreign policy challenges at the end of the 1980s. First, extreme land scarcity has produced runaway realty inflation in metropolitan areas, which makes it urgent to devise new land-use policies. Most unusual is the idea to go underground—to construct office complexes under cities. Another sign of the times is the fact that many Japanese now regard Tokyo's high-rise landscape as a "concrete desert."

Second, further tax reforms to reduce huge budget deficits and alleviate the burden of personal income taxes are badly needed. Income taxes claim as much as 80 percent of the gross personal income of wealthy Japanese. Without tax reform, Japan could face a "brain drain" in the 1990s, as well-educated professionals emigrate to search for better living arrangements elsewhere.

Third, Japan's relations with the United States are increasingly strained, a situation in which Japan has much to lose and little to gain. Economically, the United States is far and away the most important foreign market for Japan. Militarily, the U.S. presence in the western Pacific provides the security umbrella that Japan needs to hold defense expenditures far below those of the other industrial democracies. And strategically, the close alliance between the United States and Japan keeps any other power from establishing a toehold in the Pacific Basin.

Fourth, Japan cannot rest on its economic achievements, for the Asian NICs are gaining ground, and the European Community is moving toward economic unification. In addition the United States and Canada—the world's largest trading partners—have entered into a free-trade agreement. Japan's access to foreign markets could become increasingly limited. If the trend toward regionalization of trade is occurring elsewhere, it obviously would be in Japan's best interests to promote economic cooperation in Asia. Any such policy, however, involves long-range planning and coordination.

Ironically, Japan's stable political system could become a liability if its entrenched forces of business and government deter policy changes. In that event, the long era of LDP dominance—a period of extraordinary domestic peace and prosperity—could end. The party most likely to succeed the LDP is the Socialists, who enjoyed a brief surge in popularity in 1989 but subsequently faltered. At the same time, however, the LDP was shaken by an influence-peddling scandal that led to Takeshita's resignation. Can the party be assured of continued election victories?

Whatever happens domestically, Japan has little choice but to redefine its role in Asia and the world. As it does so, it will be walking through a political mine field. For example, there has been growing clamor in the United States over the cost of maintaining U.S. forces in the western Pacific. Critics ask why the United States should continue to defend Japan while Japan enjoys massive trade surplus with United States. In response to such pressures the Tokyo government increased military spending 5.2 percent in 1988. If military pensions are included, defense spending in that year came to $40 billion, or 1.5 percent of GNP—putting Japan in third place in military spending (behind only the United States and the Soviet Union).[14]

Clearly, Japan has the potential to be a military as well as an economic superpower, which makes the rise of Japanese nationalism in the late 1980s especially noteworthy. In the fall of 1988 this trend was accentuated by the grave illness of Emperor Hirohito, whose reign of more than sixty years encompassed the rise of Japanese militarism in the 1930s; the achievement of Japanese supremacy in Asia during the early years of World War II; Japan's abject defeat at the hands of the United States in 1945; the adoption of Western-style democratic rule during the U.S. occupation; and the resurgence of Japan as an economic colossus after the mid-1950s. The outpouring of affection for the stricken emperor—the most important symbol of Japan's political heritage—demonstrated that the vast majority of Japanese people remain emotionally attached to traditional values. Yet there was also protest and disaffection for the past surrounding the November 1990 ceremonies to crown Emperor Akihito.

Communist China: Change and Continuity

Noted scholar A. Doak Barnett assessed China in the mid-1980s:

> A decade has passed since the death of Mao Zedong. During these years, China has embarked on a course of reform that Deng Xiaoping has called a ''new revolution'' and Premier Zhao Ziyang asserts represents ''an extensive, profound and sustained transformation'' of the country's economic structure. In a 180-degree change of direction from Mao's last years, the Chinese have moved rapidly from ideological dogmatism toward eclectic pragmatism, from extreme totalitarianism toward liberalized authoritarianism, from a command economy toward ''market socialism,'' and from autarkic isolationism toward international interdependence. These trends signal a major new stage in China's long march toward modernization.[15]

China Opens Its Doors to Trade

As part of the reform effort—which was put on hold at the end of the 1980s—Beijing had adopted an open-door policy. The PRC more than doubled its foreign trade, primarily with the West, during the Sixth Five-Year Plan (1981–1986). Under Deng Xiaoping's pragmatic guidance, the PRC reversed its long-standing ban on foreign loans and direct foreign investment and began eagerly seeking both. By the end of 1985 Beijing had borrowed more than $10 billion from abroad.

The decision to seek direct foreign investment—absolutely taboo when Mao was alive—was even more remarkable. Deng's most controversial and innovative step was the creation in the 1970s of Special Economic Zones (SEZs), which were intended not only to attract foreign capital but also to stimulate exports and improve access to modern technologies and management methods. Although obstacles to foreign companies remained formidable, the new policy had attracted over $5 billion of investment by 1985.

In 1986 Beijing took several steps to lure more capital into the country. For example, the government's "22 Provisions to Encourage Foreign Investment" offered various incentives including preferential tax treatment, priority access to supplies at guaranteed prices, and soft loans for export-oriented or technologically advanced projects. But these new measures did not remove bureaucratic obstacles, legal impediments, distorted prices, and political uncertainties, and so foreign investment continued to lag behind expectations. In 1987 a total of 2,230 foreign investment deals worth $3.6 billion were approved; in 1985 the peak 3,000 contracts worth $6.3 billion had been signed. According to one expert, "Japanese businessmen do not regard China as a particularly attractive investment site (particularly when Hong Kong and other Asian NIC opportunities are taken into account)."[16]

Beijing also hoped to attract capital from Taiwan, and it set up an SEZ in Guangdong province to accommodate it. But Taiwanese firms have invested only small amounts in mainland China, so far. If the two Chinese governments move toward rapprochement, however, Taiwanese investment in the SEZs could rise sharply.

In the absence of massive infusions of foreign investment (which remains unlikely, especially after the Tiananmen Square massacre in 1989), the PRC's best hope for prosperity is boosting exports. It is common knowledge in Asia that Japan's economic growth in the 1970s was export driven; indeed, the Japanese example probably played a role in inducing the PRC to adopt an export-oriented open-door policy after Mao's death. As a result, the PRC's two-way foreign trade totaled $82.7 billion in 1987—an increase of 118 percent over 1980. Meanwhile, the number of organizations permitted to engage in foreign trade had grown from 16 to over 1,200 by mid-1988.

Even so, Beijing's foreign economic policy has fluctuated between market-oriented policies and central planning. In 1984, when reform was encouraged, fourteen cities were opened to foreign trade and investment; shortly after, however, opponents of radical reform forced a cutback in the number of coastal SEZs. Trade liberalization resurfaced in 1987–1988, only to be put on hold again the next year. Two factors worked against reforms: inflation and political instability. Inflation jeopardized price reform (the core of any move toward a market economy), and the student-led democracy movement in Tiananmen Square in June 1989 threatened the very core of the political system—the legitimacy of the Chinese Communist party's power monopoly.

Another major development before 1989 was the emergence of a legal framework to regulate foreign commerce. A wide array of laws had been promulgated over the decade; a new law on joint ventures was added as recently as 1988. And in 1986 Beijing had applied for membership in the international General

Agreement on Tariffs and Trade (GATT; at the time, four other Communist countries were members—Czechoslovakia, Poland, Romania, and Yugoslavia).

Beijing became a major arms supplier in the 1980s. Weapons sales in 1987 amounted to roughly $2 billion, making the PRC the fourth-largest arms supplier to the Third World (behind the Soviet Union, the United States, and France). According to the Congressional Research Service, China sold $5.3 billion worth of arms between 1983 and 1986—an amount that loomed large in the PRC's trade statistics, for it represented a jump of 167 percent over the previous three-year period.

Although China's principal trading partners are Asian, Western Europe and the United States have accounted for significant shares in recent years. From 1979 to 1986 China's two-way trade was apportioned as follows: Japan, 24.9 percent; Western Europe, 22.6 percent; Hong Kong, 21.6 percent; The United States, 11.8 percent; all others, 19.2 percent. It is noteworthy that just Japan and Hong Kong accounted for nearly half of China's two-way trade. But these data conceal three important trends: (a) Chinese-Soviet trade showed signs of revival in the mid-1980s; (b) trade with South Korea and Taiwan began to climb sharply in the late 1980s; and (c) the PRC gradually shifted away from being an exporter of primary products.

Despite these positive signs, China's foreign trade remained modest at best, compared with such major commercial nations as Japan and the United States. Indeed, the PRC's trade figures paled even in comparison with the NICs. For instance, tiny Taiwan's two-way trade in 1987 was nearly $5 billion more than the PRC's ($87.5 billion to $82.7 billion), and South Korea's total was $83.4 billion. One scholar summed up China's predicament this way:

> If Chinese exports are to lead Chinese economic development, they will have to compete with the other export-oriented economies of the Pacific, economies in which skillful exploitation of world technology trends is a key factor. For instance, Taiwan is now the world's third largest producer of personal computers (PC's), after the United States and Japan, and South Korea is number four.[17]

Finally, China's trade balance was a problem. From 1985 to 1987, for example, its trade deficit rose over $30 billion. Along with rising inflation, the trade shortfall undermined economic reform and allowed the hard-liners, who favored tight controls on the economy and society, to regain ascendancy.

The PRC's bid to be "export-led" appears to have foundered. At the peak of the reform campaign only about 6 percent of the labor was in exporting industries, and exports accounted for about 15 percent of the nation's output (compared with 55 percent in Taiwan and 37 percent in South Korea).[18]

Beijing's Roller-Coaster Reforms

The PRC's open-door policy was one facet of market-oriented reforms launched in the late 1970s by Deng Xiaoping. These reforms prefigured Mikhail Gorbachev's much-touted restructuring campaign in the USSR and may have inspired it. The original intent was to decentralize economic decisions and allow market forces to determine prices, profits, and investments. But the drive for marketplace efficiency turned into a roller-coaster ride that ended in disaster.

The PRC's shift toward market principles was most dramatic in agriculture, where average annual productivity more than quadrupled during the early 1980s, compared with the previous quarter-century. During the years of the Sixth Plan the average annual increase in agricultural output exceeded 8 percent, and the increase in rural per capita income was nearly 14 percent. This success resulted primarily from one factor: The Beijing regime decided to allow private farming. This great leap means that peasants now manage their own land, decide what to plant, and sell only a portion of their crops to the state. They dispose of their net produce, after taxes, in any way they choose. Moreover, individual households have a guaranteed land tenure of at least fifteen years. Legal ownership is the foundation of generating investment, but Chinese culture has never given it the prominence that the West has. The success of market reforms in agriculture are the best (and only) insurance Chinese peasants have that the Communist party will not return to collectivization.

Of far-reaching importance was a land-use policy that separates public ownership of land from the private right to use it. In practice, once a farmer has the right to use land, the state cannot take it away. Furthermore, land-use rights are transferable, meaning that they can be kept in the family. In an effort to curb the loss of farmland (about 400,000 hectares a year in the mid-1980s), fees are now charged for nonfarming purposes. In urban areas the sale of land-use rights

> will become a vehicle by means of which local government can raise investment funds; at the same time it has created a real estate market in which long-term leases can be bought and sold, mortgaged and passed from generation to generation. In December, 1987, the right of use for 8,500 square meters of land was publicly auctioned for Y5.25 million (about $1.4 million) in Shenzhen. Since then, sales of land rights have been conducted in Shanghai and several other major cities.[19]

In industry, decentralization and a shift from bureaucratic strangulation to economic regulation spearheaded the PRC's reform efforts. The number of major industrial products subject to central planning was halved, from 120 to 60. For a time Beijing claimed that by the end of the Seventh Plan (1986–1990) the number would be reduced to "a few vital commodities"; but the pace of reforms slackened after the student revolt in December 1986, and a short-lived campaign against "bourgeois liberalization" left the future of the entire reform movement in doubt. The doubt was dispelled after the June 1989 crackdown, which prompted a purge of market-minded reformers and a revival of totalitarianism.

Although central planning remained the rule in industry, leadership gave lip service to allowing managers greater decision-making authority and stronger incentives to operate efficiently. Indeed, the regime's plan to switch enterprises to a sink-or-swim system of managerial autonomy by 1990—on hold through most of 1987—was reactivated after the Thirteenth Party Congress in October 1987. Reforms were given a boost in 1988, when leadership announced its intent to implement market-oriented reforms, including an overhaul of price and wage systems and an end to commodity-price subsidies. But this decision, too, was reversed after June 1989.

In sum, several key elements of a free-market economy were instituted. In the first place, it was now possible for Chinese enterprises to go bankrupt, and in the fall of 1986 a factory in Shenyang became the first bankruptcy in the PRC's history. Second, a small securities market was opened in Shenyang. (The regime had long inveighed against the old Shanghai stock exchange as a symbol of the evils of capitalism.) Thus, before December 1986, Zhao was at least willing to depart from Communist orthodoxy in the realm of economics.

In April 1988 Beijing adopted a long-awaited Enterprise Law, which stipulated that ownership of an enterprise is separate from its management. Had this law been enforced, managers could either be appointed by the government or elected by workers (like the system of workers' councils in Yugoslavia). Under this law, managers or directors would become legal representatives of enterprises and would be responsible for performance. Enterprise managers would have broader decision-making authority, including the right to determine management structure, to negotiate contracts with foreign firms, to change products in response to the market, and to hire and fire workers. But the old system has remained in force despite the new law—a sterling example of how laws mean little without a constitutional tradition.

In the fall of 1988 Beijing reimposed economic controls intended to curtail the role of the free market and local decision making. The government also froze the prices of basic foods, agricultural supplies, and raw materials; curbed the proliferation of private traders; and cut back capital spending by localities. In other words, leadership again put economic restructuring on hold. The reasons for retrenchment in 1987 were primarily political; in 1988 they were primarily economic. The inflation rate was running at about 50 percent, causing widespread discontent. At the same time, the new flourish of capitalism was leading to corruption involving officials at all levels.[20]

The zigzag pattern of market reforms underscored the political obstacles that continued to delay China's economic resurgence, and as the 1980s drew to a close the status of modernization was in doubt. Despite major gains, the PRC was still among the poorest nations in terms of per capita gross national product, as Zhao himself noted in a speech to the party congress on October 25, 1987. Roughly 80 percent of China's teeming population was rural and used hand tools rather than machines to make a living. Illiteracy remained high, affecting one-fourth of the population. And the disparity between rising expectations and disappointing results threatened the stability of the system and eroded the credibility of the reforms themselves. Finally, the crushing of student protest in Tiananmen Square in 1989 was a reminder of the perils of reform in a society based on coercion. Given the highly centralized nature of China's political system, everything depends on the qualities of its leaders. After the Tiananmen uprising the ouster of Zhao Ziyang, the PRC's leading reformer, cast a dark shadow over the future of reforms.

It is noteworthy that Zhao had provided sweeping ideological justification for economic reforms at the Thirteenth Party Congress. He argued that China was still in the "primary stage of socialism" and would remain there until the middle of the next century. Given its low level of economic development, Zhao argued, the nation's primary task was to spur economic growth. Anything that achieved that was good, he said, no matter how it squared (or did not square) with Communist orthodoxy.

Zhao also had called for political reform, including a clearer division of labor between party and state; further delegation of power to local levels; administrative streamlining and increased efforts to combat bureaucratism; an overhaul of the personnel system aimed at creating a professional civil service; fixed terms of office for party and state officials; a wider role for the masses in governing; further democratization of elections and representative bodies; and a strengthening of the legal system. All these goals, of course, threaten party and state officials.

Zhao's progressive policies were reason enough for hard-liners to purge him at the first opportunity, but the persistent economic problems also contributed. In the fall of 1988 "a decisive shift in power" away from Zhao Ziyang in favor of more cautious reformers like Prime Minister Li Peng and Politburo economist Yao Yilin was reported in the Western press.[21] That shift turned out to be a harbinger of repression and retrenchment.

The tragedy of Tiananmen Square was set in motion in May 1989, when 100,000 students and workers staged a march in Beijing to demand democratic reforms. The protest continued throughout May and coincided with a visit by Soviet leader Mikhail Gorbachev—the first Chinese-Soviet summit in three decades. As the protest movement gathered momentum, demonstrations were mounted in at least twenty other cities, and Beijing declared martial law—to little avail.

Army troops began to enter Beijing with tanks and armored personnel carriers on June 3. They brutally attacked the demonstrators in Tiananmen Square, outside the Great Hall of the People, crushing the revolt, killing and injuring hundreds (possibly thousands), and arresting hundreds more. Security forces later rounded up as many as 10,000 dissenters, and at least 31 were tried and executed. The bloody crackdown and death sentences were all too reminiscent of the "bad old days" of totalitarian rule.

The Chinese Communist party's Central Committee ousted Zhao Ziyang later in June, allegedly for fostering "counterrevolutionary rebellion." The hard-liners also replaced other leaders, including propaganda chief Hu Qili, but they spared many lower-level officials who were sympathetic to reform. The new Politburo launched a drive against official corruption, a move that reminded many of the Maoist rectification campaigns of the past. In September Deng Xiaoping, the aging architect of reform, reappeared after a three-month absence from public view and admonished that Beijing would not abandon its commitment to communism; but he also said that the PRC would maintain an open-door policy with the West and would continue to implement economic reforms.

Changing of the Guard: New Reforms Ahead?

The leaders who grabbed power in 1989 represented the old guard, the veterans of the Long March, now in their seventies and eighties. They were Mao Zedong's comrades-in-arms who had always believed that politics is a struggle for power (a "class struggle"), and it was natural for them to perceive Tiananmen Square as a battleground between the forces of good and evil. But their ouster of Zhao Ziyang and other reformers may have been a "last hurrah." These aging revolutionaries will soon be gone, and the next generation has no personal memory of the Long March, guerrilla warfare, and the struggle against Chiang Kai-shek. Just as reform in the Soviet Union has come from a generation with no roots in early Stalinism, so is it possible that new leaders with no roots in Maoism will push the PRC to economic and even political reforms.

Whether or how new reforms might be launched is impossible to predict, and economic reforms may not be accompanied by political pluralism in the PRC, as they were in Eastern Europe. Although the student-led democracy movement was suppressed, its spirit was not necessarily extinguished. In Poland, for example, although Solidarity was silenced for years, the movement was not destroyed. It went underground, and resurfaced with vengeance in 1988–1989. In the PRC students revolted in December 1986 and met with repression; less than three years later they again took to the streets. Although they represent a relatively small movement within the PRC's enormous population, they constitute a mass movement in absolute terms—any force with more than a million dedicated followers is, by definition, a mass movement.

Strong economic incentives will continue to move the PRC toward both a free-market economy and a pluralistic political system. Internally, the evidence in Asia as in Europe suggests that free enterprise, democracy, and prosperity are interrelated. Externally, Japan and the West will continue to be wary of commercial ties with repressive left-wing regimes. Not only governments of industrial democracies will keep such regimes at arm's length, but private sectors also will refuse to invest in major projects.

In particular, good relations with the United States will be crucial. Although the strategic importance of close Chinese-American relations has diminished along with the Cold War, there are lingering mutual interests in countering any expansionist designs the Soviets may entertain. Beyond strategic considerations, the PRC stands to benefit from easy access to U.S. markets and its investment community. In addition, the PRC's relations with Japan and other prosperous neighboring states depends partly on its relations with the United States. (The web of economic ties is so extensive that Japan and Asian NICs are reluctant to antagonize Washington.)

Normalization of Chinese-Soviet relations is likely to continue during the 1990s as the two countries move beyond ideological dogmas of the 1960s. At the same time, however, renewal of their brief alliance during the early 1950s is unlikely because of historical mistrust, competitive rather than complementary economic situations, and a strategic rivalry based on common boundaries stretching across thousands of miles.

In addition, China has become less important strategically to the United States as the perception of a Soviet threat recedes. This by-product of East-West rapprochement reduces Beijing's bargaining power; the West risks less in shunning the PRC if its domestic methods of rule are not acceptable. Ironically, even the Soviets must now be more cautious in dealing with a repressive PRC government—or face accusations of hypocrisy.

In sum, at the end of the 1980s Beijing's domestic reforms were stalling, and the nation was diplomatically isolated. Aging leaders were bent on resisting demands for democratic reform, but its embers continued to glow. One scenario for the future is that of civil war; another is continuation of the PRC's totalitarian system. Between these extremes is a full range of possibilities, from peaceful transition to pluralism (which seems unlikely) to a non-Communist brand of authoritarianism that can accommodate freedom within bounds.

India: Development or Disintegration?

That India can be so poor and yet remain a relatively stable democracy is a marvel that rivals even the magnificent Taj Mahal. The durability of democracy attests to the coercive power of India's central government, to the resolution of strong leaders like Jawaharlal Nehru and Indira Gandhi to preserve the union, and to the success of a single national political party in integrating the nation's extremely diverse society. Finally, Indian democracy has survived despite a burgeoning population that would strain any nation's resources.

Economic Gains and Losses

In recent decades India's economy has grown at about 3.0 to 3.5 percent annually, well below targets but above the dismal 1.0 percent it grew during the first half of this century. When population growth (2 percent in 1989) is taken into account, per capita gains have been only slightly above 1.0 percent a year—a sluggish pace that nonetheless has raised per capita GNP by a third since 1947. The causes of India's economic plight run the gamut and include "inadequate demand, poor economic management, a decline in public-sector investment, high capital-output ratios, an increasingly hostile global economic environment, overregulation, high cost production, low productivity, and rapid population growth."[22]

A striking feature of India's development has been its failure to achieve a steady pattern of high growth. The golden decade of development was from 1956 to 1966, and it has not been matched since. India remains a very poor country with a per capita income of $290 in 1987. Recent trends have been somewhat encouraging, with an average overall growth rate of 5.5 percent between 1980 and 1985, but the economy's performance continued to fluctuate widely, ranging from 3.6 percent to 7.6 percent during that period.

In an effort to stimulate the economy, the government of Rajiv Gandhi announced budget hikes totaling 12 percent for 1989. To counteract the effects of a three-year drought, the budget called for a 40-percent increase in agricultural expenditures, including a 20-percent increase in food and fertilizer subsidies. The government predicted that the economy would grow between 6 and 8 percent in 1989—an outcome that Gandhi fervently desired leading up to national elections. But this flush of optimism came on the heels of a year in which growth was expected to be no more than 2 percent, reflecting a decline of 7 to 10 percent in agricultural output.[23] Thus the year-to-year fluctuation in performance that has long characterized India's economy has continued.

Although nearly 80 percent of the population is rural, India has more industrial infrastructure than most developing countries. Coal production has increased fourfold; steel production is up to about 11 million tons a year; and oil production has increased from 28 percent of consumption in the 1960s to about 70 percent in the 1980s. India's major basic industries besides coal mining and electricity generation are those producing steel, cement, and chemicals, including fertilizers needed for wheat, rice, and other grains. By the 1980s India was producing a wide array of industrial and capital goods, from traditional textiles to heavy machinery and transport equipment. Much of India's heavy industry is in the public sector. In addition, there is a diversity of light, or consumer, industries; those who have the money to do so can buy all kinds of Indian-made consumer goods. In general, the growth and diversification of its industrial economy in the 1980s made India a candidate for inclusion among the New Industrial Countries.

All these gains, however, could not alleviate India's economic and social problems. The persistence of widespread poverty continues to challenge the government and mar its record. Income distribution continues to be very uneven, and millions of people endure living on income below the national average and below the recognized poverty level (they have just enough money to maintain a nutritional intake of roughly 2,000 calories per day). Estimates in 1975 put the number of Indians living below the poverty line at 277 million, or 46 percent of the population then. Estimates in the 1980s indicated that the proportion of Indians living in poverty may be stabilizing at around 40 percent.

One tragic irony of underdevelopment in so populous a country as India is that so much of its most abundant resource—people—is wasted:

> One of India's most serious problems is unemployment. Unemployment increased from 3.5 million in 1961 to an estimated 20.6 million in 1978 (16.5 million rural; 4.1 million urban). The 1980s has seen an increase rather than a decrease in these unemployment levels. The number of unemployed grows yearly at an accelerating rate, for each year a larger number of young people enters a labor market that is not expanding fast enough to absorb them. Among the unemployed are increasing numbers of university-educated men and women, often highly trained engineers and technicians, who are unable to find work in an industrial sector that continues to operate substantially below capacity. The urban unrest generated by deepening unemployment, especially among the young, is compounded by the deteriorating economic position of the lower middle classes . . . .[24]

Underemployment is even more prevalent than unemployment. Because social services are generally not available in India, people need some form of compensated work in order to survive. But demand for full-time jobs far exceeds supply. In rural India between 5 and 10 percent of adult males may be unemployed, but underemployment pushes that figure up to the range of 20 to 25 percent.

The problems of unemployment are exacerbated by India's many "sick" industries. The state owns and operates such capital-intensive industries as steel, coal, and mining, and most industrial expansion is financed by state-owned banks. The state also tightly regulates the private sector. The legacy of all this intervention is bitter: In 1986 India had "an astonishing 130,600 money-losing concerns that the government (would not) allow to close down for fear of increasing unemployment."[25] The contrast between this picture and the vibrant economies of Japan, South Korea, Taiwan, Hong Kong, and Singapore suggests that India will have to restructure its economy—as has been happening in the Soviet Union and Communist China—or fall even further behind in the region.

Despite socialist slogans, official policies continue to subsidize inequities and sustain the caste-sanctioned structure of inequality in India. The nation's considerable economic achievements "have not been secured without social costs, as evidenced in the wide regional and individual disparities in income." At the same time, changes accompanying economic development—notably improvements in education, transportation, and communication—have "brought a new awareness of poverty to the Indian masses and a sensitivity to the widening gap that separates them from the rich."[26]

Thus, although India has made considerable progress, it still has far to go to improve life for the vast majority of its citizens. Individual well being depends on accelerated economic growth accompanied by a lower birth rate. Both parts of this equation continue to present problems, and there are no simple solutions: "Although there are many who see India poised for a great leap forward, . . . there remains a variety of old dilemmas which may produce less than the expected results."[27]

Communalism and Regionalism in India

In addition to poverty and extreme inequality, India will continue to be plagued by problems associated with communalism and regionalism. Violence between Hindus and Muslims is a constant possibility. In 1982, for example, there were over four hundred recorded instances in which 238 people died. Similarly, in 1984 Hindu-Muslim rioting occurred throughout the year in Hyderabad. In Bombay an alleged insult to the Prophet touched off the worst communal fighting since partition; deaths climbed to 230 before the army quelled the violence. In Kashmir, civil war between Hindus and Muslims threatened to break out as recently as the spring of 1990.

Tensions between Hindus and Sikhs are also high, especially in Punjab, where terrorism has been common. After Indira Gandhi's assassination by two

Sikh security guards in October 1984, anti-Sikh riots in New Delhi and elsewhere left 2,717 people dead. Sikh separatism has simmered for nearly a decade in Punjab, and has reached the boiling point. Poverty is not the cause: With a per capita income nearly twice as high as the rest of India, Punjab is the richest state. Rather, the conflict is ethnic. Sikhs constitute about 52 percent of the population in Punjab, but the balance is shifting. Sikhs have been emigrating out, while Punjab's flourishing agriculture has drawn Hindu laborers into the state. Thus Sikhs have felt an increasing need to protect their culture, religion, and language. The violence escalated in 1983–1984 and ultimately led to the assassination of Indira Gandhi and subsequent reprisals by Hindus against Sikhs.

Separatism is a problem elsewhere in India as well. In the northeast—geographically isolated and strategically vulnerable—rebels have carried out a desultory insurrection since 1947. Tribalism and secessionism combine to produce an extremely volatile situation in the states and territories of this region. Attempts by New Delhi to placate the various groups—for example, by creating the states of Nagaland in 1963 and Mizoram in 1972—have not succeeded.

In Assam the "foreigner" issue rather than tribalism is the source of political turmoil. In particular, the immigration of Bengalis from neighboring Bangladesh has alarmed the Assamese, who fear that they may become a minority in their own state. That may already have happened. Religion is a factor, too: Bengalis are Muslim, while Assamese are Hindu. Also, unlike Punjab, the northeast is impoverished and has felt neglected by New Delhi. The slogan "Assam is not India's colony" indicates how economic grievances are part of the tensions, which are likely to boil over occasionally for a long time.

Will India come apart at the seams? At least one British expert, James Manor of Sussex University, thinks such talk is "nonsense":

> First of all, the massive coercive power of the central government is more than capable of preventing secession. And, second, regional separatist movements seldom develop much momentum, because social and cultural heterogeneity within regions means that there is insufficient solidarity at that level to fuel separatism.[28]

In addition to center-periphery tensions, conflict continues to smolder between India and Pakistan over the issue of Kashmir. Distrust between the two nations has exacerbated problems in Punjab, where India frequently accuses Pakistan of trying to stir up trouble. India and Pakistan have fought three wars since partition—in 1947, 1965, and 1972. Communalism is again a factor: Pakistan is a Muslim nation, and India is Hindu dominated (although Muslims in India constitutes 11 percent of the population and number 85 million). In 1990 ethnic tensions in Kashmir again raised the danger of a war between India and Pakistan.

India has a history of troubled relations with other neighboring states, too. From 1959 to 1962 India and China fought a major border war. More recently, India opposed Sri Lanka in 1987 over its handling of an insurgency by Tamils. Rajiv Gandhi also sent troops to the Maldives Islands at the request of the government to thwart a coup led by foreign mercenaries, and India has feuded with Nepal over its relations with China. India has also quarreled with Bangladesh over the continuing flow of illegal poverty-stricken immigrants into India, particularly in the volatile northeast.

India's Uncertain Future

India's democracy is clearly beset by a host of domestic and international problems. Underlying all its problems is the "population bomb" that has yet to explode, despite dire predictions. External assistance remains essential if India is to avoid catastrophe, but in recent years U.S. foreign aid has been cut. Beginning in 1947 it has amassed to $12 billion, but in 1987 U.S. aid came to a mere $24 million. Although India's economy has grown, foreign aid until recently financed 20 to 30 percent of the government's economic development projects.[29]

The future perils India faces reflect its weak position in the international economic system. Indeed, "India's vulnerability to the flux of the world market, to the erection of trade barriers against its manufactured goods, and to monetary revaluations imposes overwhelming constraints on its development capacity."[30] Political stability in developing nations is often fragile, and the two superpowers have a common interest in promoting cohesion and prosperity in India, which otherwise could plunge the subcontinent into turmoil. India's most famous modern poet, Rabindranath Tagore (1861–1941), stated the situation as clearly as anyone ever has:

> Power has to be made secure not only against power, but against weakness; for there lies the peril of its losing balance. The weak are as great a danger for the strong as quicksand for an elephant. . . . The people who grow accustomed to wield absolute power over others are apt to forget that by so doing they generate an unseen force which some day rends that power to pieces.[31]

CONCLUSIONS

Compared with other regions, Asia has experienced remarkably uneven rates of development, with some countries (led by the Japanese model) achieving the fastest economic growth and others continuing to lag far behind. The success of Japan and the New Industrial Countries may spur similar successes elsewhere in the region. Leading candidates to join the ranks of the NICs are Thailand, Malaysia, and Indonesia.

STUDY QUESTIONS

1. Have Japan, China, and India dealt successfully with the problem of managing change so that the economy grows and society prospers without eroding the values that define what it means to be Japanese, Chinese, or Indian?

2. How and why has Japan achieved such spectacular economic success? What is the link between Japanese politics and economics? Can the Japanese model of political economy be copied? Why or why not?

3. In what ways do China and India face similar challenges in building a modern, competitive economy? In what ways do their challenges differ? How has each responded to their challenges? Which country, in your opinion, has the better chance of succeeding, and why?

4. If political instability threatens Japan, China, or India in the 1990s, what forms might it assume, what might cause it, and what might it mean for the society where it occurs? For the region? (Analyze the situation in each country separately, and then compare their prospects.)

SUGGESTED READINGS

Chang, David Wen-wei. *China Under Deng Xiaoping: Political and Economic Reform*. New York: St. Martin's, 1989.

Frankenstein, John. "Chinese Foreign Trade in the 1980s," *Current History*, September 1988.

Fukui, Haruhiro. "Japan's Takeshita at the Helm," *Current History*, April 1988.

Hardgrave, Robert L., Jr., and Stanley A. Kochanek. *India: Government and Politics of a Developing Nation*. Orlando, Fla.: Harcourt, 1986.

Harding, Harry. *China's Second Revolution: Reform After Mao*. Washington, D.C.: Brookings, 1987.

Manor, James. "India: State and Society Diverge," *Current History*, December 1989.

Nathan, Andrew J. *Chinese Democracy*. Berkeley and Los Angeles: University of California, 1986.

Ozaki, Robert S. "The Japanese Economy Internationalized," *Current History*, April 1988.

Perkins, Dwight. *China: Asia's Next Economic Giant?* Seattle: University of Washington, 1986.

NOTES

[1] See, for example, Robert S. Ozaki, "The Japanese Economy Internationalized," *Current History*, April 1988, pp. 157–160, 178.

[2] *Asian Wall Street Journal*, July 25, 1988, p. 1.

[3] John Hughes, "Taiwan's Miracle," *The Christian Science Monitor*, July 22, 1988, p. 12.

[4] Ozaki, op. cit., p. 157.

[5] Ibid., p. 158.

[6] *Asian Wall Street Journal Weekly*, Sept. 19, 1988.

[7] David Brock, "Fortress of Mercantilism Still Wary of Competitors," *Insight*, July 18, 1988, p. 17.

[8] Ibid.

[9] Ibid.

[10] Norman Cousins, "Japan Is the Real 'Threat' to the US," *Christian Science Monitor*, Feb. 25, 1988, p. 14.

[11] G. John Ikenberry, "The Irony of State Strength: Comparative Responses to the Oil Shocks in the 1970's," *International Organization*, Vol. 40, No. 1, (Winter 1986), p. 105.

[12] Shigeko N. Fukai, "Japan's Energy Policy," *Current History*, April 1988, pp. 169–172, 182–184.

[13] Haruhiro Fukui, "Japan's Takeshita at the Helm," *Current History*, April 1988, pp. 173–175, 185–186.

[14] *The Economist*, Vol. 306, No. 7534, Jan. 23, 1988.

[15] A. Doak Barnett, "Ten Years After Mao," *Foreign Affairs*, Vol. 65, No. 1 (Summer 1986), p. 37.

[16] John Frankenstein, "Chinese Foreign Trade in the 1980's," *Current History*, September 1988, p. 274.

[17] Ibid., p. 258.

[18] Harry Harding, *China's Second Revolution*, Washington, D.C.: Brookings Institution, 1987.

[19] David Wen-wei Chang, *China Under Deng Xiaoping: Political and Economic Reform* (New York: St. Martin's, 1989), p. 254.

[20] Edward A. Gargan, "China Reigning in Economy's Shift to a Free Market," *New York Times*, Oct. 17, 1988, p. 1.

[21] Ibid.

[22] Robert L. Hardgrave, Jr., and Stanley A. Kochanek, *India: Government and Politics of a Developing Nation* (Orlando, Fla.: Harcourt, 1986), p. 329.

[23] Anthony Spaeth, "New Indian Budget Hikes Spending by 12%, Increases Aid to Farmers," *Asian Wall Street Journal Weekly*, Mar. 7, 1988, p. 12.

[24] Hardgrave and Kochanek, op. cit., p. 328.

[25] *Asian Wall Street Journal*, Vol. 10, No. 10 (Mar. 7, 1988), p. 1.

[26] Ibid.

[27] Ibid., p. 329.

[28] James Manor, "India: State and Society Diverge," *Current History*, December 1989, p. 429.

[29] Stephen R. Weisman, "U.S. in India: Less Aid, Less Influence," *New York Times*, Apr. 21, 1988, p. 4.

[30] Hardgrave and Kochanek, op. cit., p. 361.

[31] *Aspects of Our Foreign Policy: From Speeches and Writings of Indira Gandhi* (New Delhi: All-India Congress Committee, 1973), p. 72.

ETHIOPIA

Area: 472,432 square miles
Population: 49.8 million
Density per square mile: 105
Languages: Amharic, Galligna, Tigrigna
Literacy rate: 35%
Religions: Ethiopian Orthodox (40%), Muslim (35%), traditional (15%)
Monetary unit: birr
GDP: (1987) $5.7 billion; $130 per capita

KENYA

Area: 224,960 square miles
Population: 24.3 million
Density per square mile: 107
Languages: English, Swahili, several others among 40 ethnic groups
Literacy rate: 59%
Religions: Protestant (38%), Roman Catholic (28%), traditional (26%), Muslim (6%)
Monetary unit: Kenyan shilling
GDP: (1987) $8.1 billion; $370 per capita

SOUTH AFRICA

Area: 471,440 square miles
Population: 38.5 million
Density per square mile: 82
Languages: English, Afrikaans, Xhosa, Zulu, other tribal languages
Literacy rate: 99% (whites), 60–70% (blacks)
Religions: Dutch Reformed (40%), Anglican (11%), Roman Catholic (8%), other Christian (25%)
Monetary unit: rand
GDP: (1987) $81 billion; $2,360 per capita

NIGERIA

Area: 356,700 square miles
Population: 115 million
Density per square mile: 323
Languages: English, Hausa, Yoruba, Ibo
Literacy rate: 30%
Religions: Muslim (47%), Christian (34%), Animist (18%)
Monetary unit: naira
GNP: (1987) $78 billion; $720 per capita

BOTSWANA

Area: 231,800 square miles
Population: 1.2 million
Density per square mile: 5
Languages: English, Setswana
Literacy rate: 59%
Religions: Christian (48%), traditional (49%)
Monetary unit: pula
GDP: (1985) $905 billion; $880 per capita

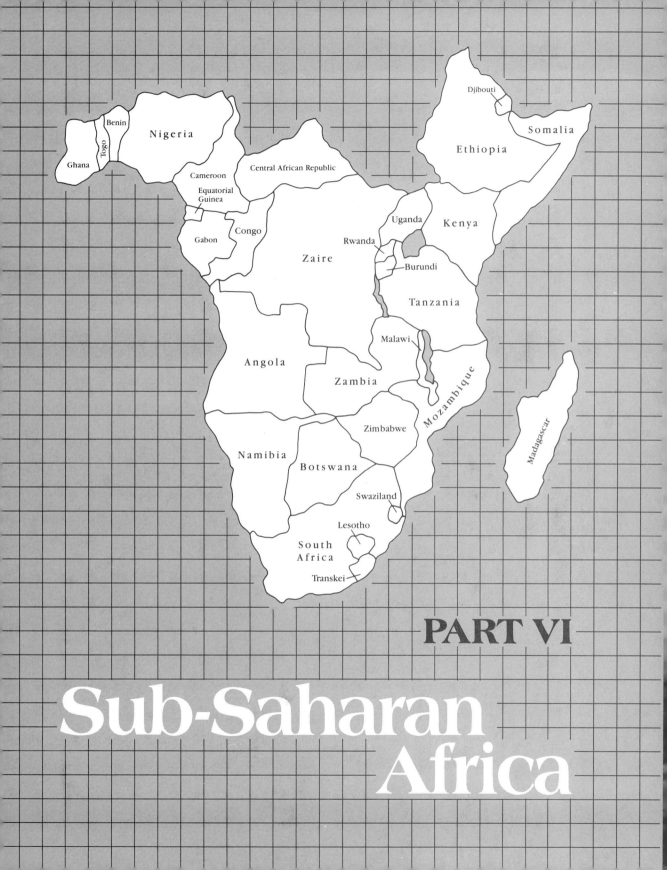

Ghana

Togo

Benin

Nigeria

Cameroon

Equatorial
Guinea

Gabon

Congo

Central African Republic

Zaire

Angola

Namibia

Botswana

Zimbabwe

Zambia

Malawi

Mozambique

Tanzania

Rwanda

Burundi

Uganda

Kenya

Ethiopia

Djibouti

Somalia

Madagascar

Swaziland

Lesotho

South
Africa

Transkei

PART VI

Sub-Saharan Africa

Chapter 16
The Legacy of Colonialism

Sub-Saharan Africa shares a continent with some of the countries regarded as the Middle East or the Arab world: Egypt, Libya, Tunisia, Algeria, and Morocco. The rest of the continent is often divided into East Africa and West Africa (especially when the emphasis is on colonialism) and Southern Africa.

In all, sub-Saharan Africa comprises forty-six separate and independent nation-states: Angola, Benin, Botswana, Burkino Faso (formerly Upper Volta), Burundi, Cameroon, Cape Verde, Central African Republic, Chad, Comoros, Congo, Côte d'Ivoire (the Ivory Coast), Djibouti, Equatorial Guinea, Ethiopia, Gabon, Gambia, Ghana, Guinea-Bissau, Kenya, Lesotho, Liberia, Madagascar, Malawi, Mali, Mauritania, Mauritius, Mozambique, Namibia, Niger, Nigeria, Rwanda, São Tomé and Príncipe, Senegal, Seychelles, Sierra Leone, Somalia, South Africa, Sudan, Swaziland, Tanzania, Togo, Uganda, Zaire, Zambia, and Zimbabwe. In most cases, these states are artificial, the legacy of colonialism. Their borders—drawn by the great powers of Europe for convenience—in some cases arbitrarily divide ethnic groups into two or more "nations"; in other cases they combine several incompatible ethnic groups into a single state.

The very idea of the nation-state is foreign to Africans. Indeed, Western students of Africa can easily be misled by their own idea of what a "country" is. In the context of Africa, a country is not necessarily an aggregation of people whose primary allegiance is to a single state. Rather, it is a state or government recognized by other states or governments as having a legitimate claim to rule a certain territory and population, even though those native inhabitants may reject the claim or view it with indifference.

Physical, Cultural, and Political Variations

A major geographic feature of sub-Saharan Africa is its relationship to the world's largest desert, the Sahara. Some 3.3 million square miles in area and 3,000 miles long, the Sahara stretches from the east coast to the west coast and forms a formidable natural barrier between the Arab world to the north and Black Africa to the south.

Below this vast desert, five great rivers—the Nile, the Congo, the Niger, the Zambesi, and the Orange—are found. Together they flow a total distance of 12,500 miles and boast a basin area of 4.1 million square miles. These mighty rivers played

The author gratefully acknowledges the help of Admasu Shunkuri in drafting Chapters 16, 17, and 18.

a significant role in the political and cultural patterns during Africa's precolonial era, for centuries serving both as natural boundaries and as barriers against foreign intrusion. Ironically, during the nineteenth century the same waterways were important conduits for Africa's colonization by European powers.

The ancient Greeks, who claimed the first European contact with this part of the world, called the region Ethiopia (''land of the burned faces''). During the eighteenth century, European explorers and geographers, revealed similar ignorance of the indigenous cultures and peoples and branded sub-Saharan Africa the ''Dark Continent.'' In reality, the peoples of this region are no more monochromatic than they are homogeneous. Furthermore, the continent can hardly be called dark, for nature has endowed sub-Saharan Africa with an abundance of sunlight. And according to recent archeological data, sub-Saharan Africa may very well have been the birthplace of homo sapiens, the cradle of the first human civilization.[1]

Within the sometimes featureless landscape of sub-Saharan Africa lies great diversity of historical and cultural experiences and significant physical variations, which have helped shape the region's traditions and institutions. Sub-Saharan Africa comprises 9.4 million square miles, or 80 percent of Africa's land mass, and more than 70 percent of Africa's population. With forty-six sovereign states, the region accounts for nearly one-third of votes in the United Nations General Assembly. (Although African nations do not always vote as a bloc, they do see eye-to-eye on such issues as apartheid in South Africa, reform of the international economic order, and decolonization.)

The countries of sub-Saharan Africa vary in ethnicity and languages, regime types, natural resources, climate and topography, population size, and forms of foreign contact; they also differ in the number, intensity, and roots of their political conflicts. While all these factors differentiate them from each other, geography has probably influenced their diversification the most.

The region is a mosaic of distinct ethnic groups and cultures—most experts set the number at more than a thousand. Ethnic composition ranges from essentially homogeneous countries (such as Botswana, Lesotho, Seychelles, and Swaziland) to extremely heterogeneous ones (Cameroon and Chad each have 200 groups; Tanzania has 130 groups, and Zaire has 80). Most sub-Saharan countries have from two to five distinct ethnic groups, and this diversity is matched by great variety of religions and languages. The resulting sociocultural fragmentation is compounded by the presence of non-African religions and languages—the former include Islam and Christianity; the latter, English, French, Spanish, Portuguese, and Afrikaans (in South Africa—a language derived from seventeenth-century Dutch).

Geophysical variation among these countries is most observable as differences in size. They range from tiny Seychelles (175 square miles) in the Indian Ocean to the giant-sized Sudan (967,500 square miles), nearly four times the size of Texas. The total land area of the smallest five countries is only 2,054 square miles, while the largest five countries comprise 2,857,656 square miles.

The size of a nation is not necessarily a clue to the size of a nation's population, in Africa or elsewhere. Nigeria, for example, is about twice the size of California and, with 115 million people in 1989, has roughly 25 percent of the region's total population. In contrast, Sudan is three times as large as Nigeria but has only about 5 percent of the region's population. In 1989 Nigeria's population density per square mile was 323; Sudan's was only 25.

Geography has influenced the development of sub-Saharan nations in various ways. Some countries are landlocked, while others have long seacoasts. Proximity to oceans (or distance from them) shaped these nations' histories, especially regarding foreign intrusion and domination. Not surprisingly, countries blessed with propinquity to oceans were also cursed by being the first to be conquered and colonized. Often they were also the last to gain independence, partly because their harbors and ports made them strategically valuable.

Regarding variations in resources, the countries of West Africa, along the Atlantic coast, are generally richer in minerals than are the highlands of the interior, where agriculture and livestock are the basis of local economies. Location, size of territory and population, and natural resources have shaped relations among the region's states. Thus Mali, Mauritania, Nigeria, and other nations of West Africa have called for economic and military solidarity against the Republic of South Africa; but Malawi, Mozambique, and Botswana—aware of the costs of antagonizing their powerful neighbor—have been more cautious and conciliatory. For similar reasons South Africa has enjoyed generally good relations with the West, for it offers the following natural advantages: major seaports, vast mineral wealth (including some used in modern weapons), and access to one of the world's most important maritime and naval routes.

Patterns of government and politics also vary throughout sub-Saharan Africa, but there are common threads. For example, upon independence the nations of the region sought to adopt or adapt the forms of government that colonial powers had established earlier. But the grafting of foreign models onto African cultures and the neglect of African traditions led to neither peace nor stability. Since independence almost all forty-six states of the region have experienced political violence, including assassinations, massacres, coups and coup attempts, revolts, insurgencies, and civil wars. To many experts, the chronic instability and conflict have resulted from the artificial boundaries created by the European powers. At present nearly two-thirds of the states are under military regimes, and most of the civilian governments—whatever their specific form—display strong authoritarian tendencies. It is this predominance of dictatorship and one-party rule, more than any other factor, that gives the region a monolithic veneer. In nonpolitical aspects of national life the states differ greatly, not only reflecting different circumstances and constraints but also creating the possibility that their futures will be more divergent than their pasts. As for the past, scholar Basil Davidson has written:

> For most of Africa, the effective time-span of history, in so far as it can now be understood, reaches back over about two millennia, and is divided from prehistory—along a line that is always faint and sometimes arbitrary—by the development of iron-working and cultivation, as early populations dispersed and spread through the plains, hills and forests south of the Sahara. . . .

It is the Negroes, evolving a thousand languages and cultural variants over the past several thousand years, who have been responsible for the peopling of Africa with most of its modern inhabitants. Almost certainly they were dominant among the Late Stone Age pastoralists of the Saharan regions before the area began to become dessicated around 2000 BC; thus they formed or helped to form the early populations of Pharaonic Egypt and other peripheral areas along the Nile.[2]

The long history of Africa's social and political evolution cannot be recounted in detail here—only its contours can be traced. Civilization is always cumulative, a process of accretion spanning many centuries, at once differentiating and ordering human existence. A principal aim of civil (or political) society is to enable communities to cope with nature. This interaction of invention and environment, however, is only part of the story. The interaction of self-contained social groups—often with different rituals, languages, and customs—is hardly less important. As our case studies later in this chapter will illustrate, ethnic particularism and interethnic conflict have often gone hand in hand in Africa.

Foreign Intrusion and Conquest

In all the culture and history of African politics, nothing has been more significant than European imperialism. But what explains the origins and patterns of colonial rule in Africa? Why did European conquest of this vast region occur in so short a time? Geographic considerations and ethnic rivalries in Africa as well as Europe's accumulating wealth and advancing technology were major factors.

A History of Foreign Domination

Africa's geography—its size and surface features, climate, resources, and strategic importance—led to a paradox: Although physically remote from the principal power centers in Europe, North America, and East Asia, Africa is surrounded by water and thus can be reached easily via the maritime "highways" that connect the continents.

For centuries Africa was viewed by outsiders with curiosity, awe, and greed. Before the modern era, however, foreign intrusions were hindered by African geography. Although the regularity of Africa's coastlines put its perimeter within reach, the interior was made impenetrable by rugged terrains, high mountains, hot and rainy seasons, unnavigable rivers, swamps, jungles, and tropical rain forests —and the vast, forbidding Sahara Desert. Such natural defenses were unmatched.

By the second century Arab merchant caravans moved along the coast of the Sahara and East Africa, and various Islamic crusades in the seventh century spread Islam among Africans along the trans-Saharan trade route. Although Romans gained a foothold on the Mediterranean coast of Africa as early as the second century, Europe's intrusions were rare and sporadic until the eighteenth century. Thus, as Africans of the interior were adapting to their environment—cultivating land, herding cattle, inventing implements, and building societies and kingdoms

—coastal African societies were trading goods and establishing ties with foreign traders, explorers, and missionaries. In this manner Africans themselves served unwittingly as the "Trojan horse" that gave Europeans entry to the African interior. Coastal Africans befriended foreigners, guided and protected them through the dangers of terrain and hostile interior inhabitants, repaired their ships, and gave them food and shelter. In the final analysis, neither geography nor terrain—which had impeded and deterred foreign intruders—could prevent the encroachment that culminated in colonization of the continent by European powers in the last decades of the nineteenth century.

European explorers began sailing along and probing Africa's coasts between 1450 and 1497. Portugal, under the leadership of Prince Henry the Navigator, sponsored many seafaring expeditions. In 1486 Diaz rounded Cape Horn at the southern tip of Africa, and in 1497 Vasco de Gama was the first European to reach India by this route. The Portuguese successes attracted other European naval powers. Propelled by the new mercantilist ideology, the balance of influence in Africa shifted from Arabs to Europeans and set the stage for later arrival of Christian missionaries seeking converts, even in areas dominated by Islam. A host of other highly destabilizing changes accompanied the European influx.

From 1795 to 1930 European geographers and missionaries took it as their duty to explore the African interior and to map and settle the continent. Europeans flocked to Africa during the latter half of the nineteenth century, searching for riches and adventure. Missionary societies came to fulfill the "Great Commission," which European political elites solemnly declared to be Christendom's benevolent duty (the "White Man's burden," in Rudyard Kipling's famous phrase). In the end these activities fostered Europe's colonial domination over African culture and politics—and helped create some of the region's most intractable problems.

By mid-nineteenth century, Europeans had established colonies and were vying for hegemony. Their rush for overseas territories was propelled partly by the Industrial Revolution and the need for cheap labor, raw materials, and new markets. In early 1885 this rivalry reached its culmination at the Berlin Conference, where European powers divided up Africa. By the end of the century nearly all of the continent was under European colonial rule.[3] By 1914 only Ethiopia and Liberia were self-governing, and even today South Africa remains under white minority rule (discussed later). Only recently, in December 1988, did South Africa give Namibia full independence—seventy-four years after Germany surrendered the country to South Africa.

Cultural Legacies

As prominent Africanist Ali Mazrui has pointed out, most of Africa has a "triple heritage": African, Islamic, and Western.[4] These overlapping traditions are manifested most clearly in the prominence of externally derived religions (Islam, Christianity) and languages (Arabic, English, French, Portuguese) in Africa. Like Mazrui himself, most Africans who have a secondary education or more are likely to speak three languages—an ethnic language, a national language, and Arabic or one European language.

Religion and Politics   Islam is the majority religion in thirteen sub-Saharan African countries and virtually the only religion in Mali, Somalia, Mauritania, and Djibouti. There are about 250 million African Muslims, and large Muslim communities can be found in Nigeria, Ethiopia, and Sudan. Christianity is the major religion in eighteen countries of the region.

Recently, the Islamic nations have exhibited greater religious activism than the predominantly Christian ones. No doubt this phenomenon is related to Arab militance over the Palestinian issue and to other turbulent events in the Middle East, including the Iranian Revolution, which replaced the secular Western-oriented regime of the shah with a fundamentalist Islamic theocracy. This event gave rise to a volatile political climate that witnessed a sharp increase in Islamic religious fervor not only in the Arab world but also in certain African countries. For example, Nigerian Muslims have made pilgrimages to Mecca in greater numbers than any other nationality has.[5] In 1981 Nigeria, which is half Muslim, sent more pilgrims to the Islamic Holy City than even Pakistan, which is 97-percent Muslim and almost equal to Nigeria in population. Islam is also significant in Nigeria's politics: Since independence, five out of seven of Nigeria's heads of state have had a Muslim background. Moreover, the influence of Islam transcends national politics in Africa: Nineteen of forty-five members of the Organization of Islamic Conference are from sub-Saharan Africa, and Nigeria is being considered for classification as an Islamic state and OIC member.

Some scholars question whether Africans who embrace Christianity are as devout as their Muslim counterparts.[6] Studies have shown that, while European and American missionaries were most aggressive in evangelizing, they did not teach their religion within the contexts of local African traditions. Mission Christianity, according to John Mbiti, isolated new members from their roots without rooting itself in their culture. Moreover, to most converts, mission Christians as role models were often indistinguishable from other Europeans, because their lifestyles were identical. Then, too, some locals converted to Christianity for opportunistic reasons, such as gaining employment in mission projects or wanting to appear ''modern.'' Indeed, a self-conscious preference for modernity sets Africans who were educated in mission schools apart from most other Africans.

While the mission legacy produced its own kind of new elites, it is also true that some of these elites did not always comply with the philosophy of the missions. This philosophy discouraged higher education and secular pursuits in politics or the sciences. Some mission students, such as the late Jomo Kenyatta (the ''George Washington'' of Kenya), even came to resent their missions: ''When the Europeans first came to Africa, they told us to shut our eyes and say amen. With our eyes shut, they took our land and we got the Bible.''

Kenyatta was a gifted public speaker, thanks in part to his mission background. As W. H. Taylor noted in a study of Nigeria, the missions succeeded most in teaching such things as interpersonal relations and verbal self-expression.[7] If the missionaries avoided politics, their students often applied religious lessons to political and social analysis, and they used their verbal skills to persuade and politicize people. It is probably not coincidence, therefore, that many of Africa's most illustrious independence leaders had an early affiliation with mission Christianity.

Traditional religions continue to predominate in fourteen sub-Saharan countries. Unlike Christianity or Islam, which are monotheistic theologies, indigenous African religions espouse a multiplicity of divinities and spirits. Thus, for the Oromos of Ethiopia, Abdari represents a universal deity in whom all spirits and nature are unified and in whose name ancestral gods and nature divinities are called upon to perform miracles and fulfill needs. The Yoruba of Nigeria have Ashe or Arisa, the god of all power who can make all things happen. The Yoruba also can call on 1,700 other divinities and spirits for specific needs and occasions.[8] Traditional religions have survived in many parts of the region, a fact that African leaders, who are most likely to be Muslims or Christians, must not ignore.

The Languages of Politics   The linguistic legacy of colonialism on African political culture is no less striking than the impact of imported religions. Non-African languages have both united and divided the societies of Black Africa. Thus, if the classification of a country as Anglophone, Francophone, and Lusophone has provided a sense of group identity, it also points to one of the country's most intransigent problems—deciding which language should be the official one. The conflict often pits English speakers against French speakers. Either English or French is used as the ''lingua franca'' (universal or diplomatic language) in business or official matters in all but nine or ten countries. Portuguese is spoken officially in five countries, and Spanish, Arabic, Italian, and German are each spoken in a few. (The absence of a language used throughout the region is considered by some Africanists to be a major reason why efforts to launch a Pan-African movement have failed.)

Despite the spread of Islam in Africa, Arabic is spoken by the majority in only five nations of the sub-Sahara. There are several reasons for this: (a) Being merchants by tradition, Arabs found it more ''cost-effective'' and profitable to learn local languages than to teach Arabic to Africans. (b) The postslavery Arabs stressed the egalitarian tenets of Islam and therefore did not try to foist Arabic on African Muslims.[9] (c) Arab settlers came to sub-Sahara in trickling numbers and thus did not play an imposing role in local politics and government. (d) Europeans were the principal colonizers and power brokers, and Africans had compelling reasons to learn European languages. However, Arabic is the language of Islam. Thus, even where Arabic did not become the local vernacular or the language of governments and schools, Islam has made Arabic part of the African psyche, and its influence cannot be discounted.

To capture the kaleidoscopic character of African societies, some scholars talk about ''Africanity'':

Those with a superficial knowledge of black Africa see it as a monolithic culture in which everyone lives, feels and thinks alike [but] those who know it really well detect beneath the diversity a large cultural unity. . . . The cultural unity of the diverse African people—the sum of all the component parts that give the various societies of traditional Africa their common characteristics—is known as "Africanity."[10]

Diversity gives rise to some contradictions. In a number of sub-Saharan countries, cultural pluralism and social cleavages have become the wellsprings of conflict leading to bloody rebellions and massacres (for example, recent ethnic violence involving the Tutsi and Hutu in Burundi). In some countries—Senegal, Tanzania, Zambia—statesmanship has contained ethnolinguistic tensions. But where group affinity is stronger than national identity (as in Ethiopia, Nigeria, Sudan, Somalia, Uganda, and Burundi), ethnic and religious tensions have erupted in full-scale civil wars.

Finally, where imported or imposed cultural differences have been sources of conflict, indigenous religions and languages have sometimes ameliorated civil strife. In fact, African leaders who recognize the unifying force of indigenous culture occasionally have politicized local traditions in order to gain legitimacy or to galvanize popular support for particular policies.

Deprivation and Militarization

Some experts view the prevalence of civil strife in sub-Saharan Africa as further legacy of foreign intrusion and domination. Deprivation and militarization are two prominent features of this.

From their earliest contacts with Africa, foreigners discovered no legends or ways of life—nothing intangible—that engaged their interest. They did, however, find resources they coveted (ivory, gold, diamonds) and lands and peoples they could enslave and colonize. In the process they deprived Africans of dignity, land, and natural wealth and denied them the fundamental right to self-determination. On African soil, Africans were obliged to learn foreign languages, take foreign names, and worship foreign deities. Many suffered loss of self-esteem and knowledge of self-worth. Some resolved their "identity crisis" by fully assimilating foreign norms and values; others resolved it by rejecting foreign ways. During most of this century the societies of sub-Saharan Africa have been torn by conflicts between "rejectionists," who demand independence and liberation, and "assimilationists," who would acquiesce to continued foreign domination.[11]

Even the religions that were brought to Africa have contributed to hostilities. In a book entitled *Things Fall Apart*, Nigerian novelist Chinua Achebe has illustrated how the presence of mission Christianity created tension among Africans when the converts denigrated the unconverted as "pagans" and the unconverted maligned the converted as traitors who fraternized with foreign gods. In the same vein, Jomo Kenyatta, in *Facing Mount Kenya*, explained how colonial religions disrupted the utility of Kikuyu sociopolitical institutions. During colonization and the later struggle for independence, some Africans fought on the side of the Europeans with whom they shared a religion and benefits such as jobs and social status. When postcolonial sub-Saharan governments saw and feared the factionalizing effects of the new religions, they persecuted local converts, closed many mission operations, and restricted missionaries to teaching only government-approved subjects.

In the postindependence period, sub-Saharan Africa has struggled to overcome the lingering effects of economic and military domination, otherwise known as "neocolonialism." The economic legacy of colonialism limited Africa to producing raw materials for Europe and to consuming finished products imported from overseas, often with borrowed capital or "foreign aid." For all its long association with Europe, sub-Saharan Africa's average per-capita gross domestic product is a paltry $450. All of Africa accounts for only 1 percent of world industrial output, but Africa is still supplying significant amounts of raw materials to markets of the industrial north. To describe this relative deprivation another way, the sub-Saharan countries, which make up almost 30 percent of U.N. membership, together cannot afford to contribute even 1 percent to the U.N. budget.

Militarization constitutes yet another legacy of foreign domination. Sub-Saharan countries, despite widespread poverty, spend huge sums of money importing military hardware from former colonial powers. Not only do such arms purchases divert foreign exchange earnings and domestic revenues from indigenous economic development, but they also nurture tendencies toward militarism among national groups.[12]

The legacies of colonialism have provoked and prolonged conflicts among sub-Saharan countries. The long duration of wars for liberation (or independence)—which lasted for nearly two decades in Angola, Mozambique, and Zimbabwe—is partly attributable to foreign influences. When Angola finally won independence from Portugal in 1974, the Soviet-backed Popular Movement seized power in most of the country, touching off a civil war. The Soviets used Cuban troops as a proxy army to defend the Marxist regime, while the United States and South Africa backed Joseph Savimbi's guerrilla forces (known as UNITA—the National Front for the Total Liberation of Angola).[13] South Africa sent troops across the southern Angola-Namibia border in June 1981, killing 300 people and occupying several towns. South African forces withdrew the following September, but the war raged on until the late 1980s.

The independence struggle has given way to civil war in other places as well. In Mozambique an insurgency during the 1980s took many lives and left a wake of economic devastation. The U.S. State Department estimated that 100,000 people died in 1987 alone. (The combined death toll in Mozambique and Angola during the 1980s is estimated at 745,000.) Struggles for majority rule in South Africa, and for independence in Namibia—both against the same white minority regime—have continued for more than two generations.

Indigenous Economic and Social Problems

Although colonialism and neocolonialism have contributed to deprivation and militarization, foreign intrusions cannot be blamed for all the socioeconomic problems that seem so endemic in sub-Saharan Africa. There are also internal causes, such as mismanagement of resources, natural calamities (especially drought), and above all the absence of a spirit of compromise and civic responsibility that transcends group animosities.

During the 1960s sub-Saharan Africa enjoyed an average annual economic growth rate of 3.4 percent, which deteriorated to 0.5 percent in the 1970s and plunged to −2.4 percent in the 1980s.[14] African leaders have raised expectations, but the promises remain unfulfilled.[15]

National unity in many countries is impeded by military coups, border conflicts, abuses of human rights, hordes of refugees victimized by famine and violence, and a continuing brain drain.[16] In Uganda alone, hundreds of thousands lost their lives under the successive regimes of Idi Amin and Milton Obote. The carnage was the result of Amin's personal dictatorship, his bloodthirsty style of rule, and the legacy of brutality he left when he fled the country in 1979. One tragic consequence of continuous turmoil in sub-Saharan Africa is the fact that today there are approximately 5 million African refugees (more than six times as many as in 1960).

Among the most intractable problems facing sub-Saharan Africa is the population explosion. The rate of population growth for the region as a whole is about 3 percent, the highest in the world. Given a population of about 385 million in 1985, the region will have 600 million people by the year 2000, and another 18 million babies will be born in that year alone.[17]

The region will thus be squeezed in a deadly vise as the population gets younger and the carrying capacity of the land gets ever more fragile. According to estimates, 80 percent of Ethiopia's population will be under age 40 in the year 2000, and over 50 percent of Kenyans will be age 30 or younger.[18] In both nations the majority of the population by the year 2000 will be school-aged youths who will represent a burden on society and government in terms of food, shelter, education, and job opportunities. This demographic time bomb means that the political systems of sub-Saharan Africa—many of which have already proved unstable—will come under increasing stress.

Case Studies: Four Nations of the Sub-Sahara

Ethiopia, Kenyan, Nigeria, and South Africa are the four sub-Saharan nations highlighted in this chapter. One of the only African nations to escape colonization, Ethiopia is now ruled by a Marxist-style military dictatorship. Neighboring Kenya is a former British colony and potentially a leader in East Africa. Nigeria, also a former British colony, is potentially a leader in West Africa. Finally, South Africa, unquestionably the most powerful nation south of the Sahara, is ruled by a white minority government under a highly oppressive system of racial discrimination known as apartheid. As such, it is an anachronism that represents the vestiges of European colonialism in Africa.

Ethiopia

Long known as the ancient kingdom, Ethiopia traces its origins to the Aksumite dynasty (450 B.C.), whose capital was the city of Aksum. The Solomonic dynasty, the fourth in Ethiopian history, lasted from 1270 to 1974, when it was overthrown by a military coup following a mass revolt.[19]

    The essential features of Ethiopia's political and cultural history include the establishment of an enduring dynastic monarchy, the acceptance of Christianity (the Coptic Church dates from the fourth century), and the evolution of the written languages of Geez and Amharic. These elements gave Ethiopian political life a sense of tradition and continuity. As historian Arnold Toynbee pointed out, however, geography also played a major role in Ethiopia's political and cultural evolution. In fact, Ethiopia's national anthem credits the nation's continuity and independence to the natural defenses provided by the mountainous landscape. But the natural defense also contributed to Ethiopia's isolation. "Encompassed on all sides by the enemies of their religion, the Ethiopians slept near a thousand years forgetful of the world by whom they were forgotten," wrote Edward Gibbon in *The Rise and Fall of the Roman Empire*.[20] So the price of Ethiopia's independence has been isolation and obscurity. Just as the nation's long history and rugged terrain have contributed to its extraordinary continuity, so have they obstructed its path to modernity.[21]

    In addition to its geographical defenses, Ethiopia's romantic image and embrace of Christianity earned sympathy for it in the West and served to restrain foreign aggression and intrusion. Indeed, many Europeans who were surprised by Ethiopia's victory over Italy in 1896 were also outraged by Fascist Italy's invasion of Ethiopia in 1936. Many Europeans and Americans saw Ethiopia as a Christian nation under attack by a totalitarian aggressor. But despite Ethiopia's proud history and rich heritage, it is one of the world's most underdeveloped countries.[22]

Ethnic Groups and Statehood   Ethiopian politics before the twentieth century was dominated by rivalries among ethnic kings and princes, who raised armies to extend or defend their territories. The appearance of tranquility in Ethiopia thus often concealed a turbulent internal reality. During the nineteenth century, when the rest of sub-Saharan Africa was being carved up by European powers, Ethiopia was the scene of a domestic scramble for feudal "colonies"—a drama that set the stage for the secessionist movements of the present.

    By a complex process of colonial-style military conquest, ethnic assimilation, and political-administrative integration, Ethiopia grew into a state twice the size of Texas. It ranks third in Africa both in physical size and in population (about 50 million); only Nigeria and Egypt outrank it. One mark of Ethiopia's importance in Africa is the fact that Addis Ababa, the capital city, is the headquarters of the Organization of African Unity. The U.N. Economic Commission for Africa is also located there.

The population comprises three major ethnic groups: Oromos, Amharas, and Tigris-Eritreans. (Some argue that Tigris and Eritreans have undergone political differentiation over the past century, but in our view that does not change their classification as one group.) In addition, dozens of other minorities have their own customs and languages. Among the three major groups the Oromos are most numerous (58 percent), and the Amharas and Tigris are about equal in number (20 percent each). Because of the varied patterns of internal conquest and migration during the seventeenth and eighteenth centuries, ethnic settlements in Ethiopia are dispersed. The Oromos, whose internal migrations were extensive, have a substantial presence in nine of Ethiopia's fourteen provinces. The Amharas, who have dominated Ethiopia's politics for a century, made their home in the central highlands and also are found in metropolitan centers of other regions. The Tigris-Eritreans stayed close to home in the provinces of Tigre and Eritrea (the latter became a province of Ethiopia only in 1962).

In sum, Ethiopian society is not as homogeneous as it may first appear. Nor has Ethiopia's social history been one of peace and harmony. Ethiopia's past illustrates that continuity is not always the same as stability. In fact, the national integration of modern Ethiopia really began only around the turn of the century, during the reigns of Menelik II and Haile Selassie.

National Integration   Emperor Menelik II, who ruled from 1889 to 1913, was the first to launch a campaign for national unification. He did so by methods that paralleled European colonial practices: Menelik conquered some of the ethnic nobility and enticed others into cultural assimilation through language (the teaching of Amharic) and religion (the Orthodox, or Coptic, Church). Menelik's successor, Emperor Haile Selassie, built on this foundation during a rule that lasted half a century (1923–1974). As just noted, Eritrea became part of Ethiopia in 1962. When Selassie was overthrown in 1974, ethnic tensions still ran high, and ethnic particularism had not yet given way to nationalism.

Each of the principal ethnic groups dominated at one time or another. The Tigris identify with the origin of the Ethiopian Empire at Aksum; the Amharas replaced the Aksumite dynasty and ruled for the longest time; and the Oromos also had their period of greatest influence. Before the Amhara conquest they had developed sophisticated sociopolitical institutions—the Gada system—by which the people chose and changed leaders every eight years. The Oromos had rivaled and replaced the Amhara rulers during half of the eighteenth century; as the majority ethnic group, they resent being consigned to second-class citizenship. The close association of ethnocultural identity and political power on the one hand (the Amharas have long been dominant), and the alienation of less-dominant ethnic groups on the other, have combined in an explosive admixture that threatens the survival of the modern Ethiopian state.

Like most autocrats, Haile Selassie used a combination of coercion and persuasion to stay in power for fifty years. He was a no-nonsense ruler who knew how to use both the carrot and the stick. If he could be charming to friends, he could also be ruthless to enemies.[23] In ethnic affairs he would punish dissidents within a particular group, reward and elevate others who were loyal within the same group, and use patronage to divide and conquer potential opponents.[24] Selassie alone controlled this intricate system of rewards and punishments.

For all his authoritarian ways, Selassie did seek to integrate and modernize Ethiopian political life.[25] In 1931 the Emperor promulgated the first formal Constitution defining the role of the nation's most basic institutions, including the bureaucracy, the nobility, and the Coptic Church. He also professionalized the police, armed forces, and state administration, which was organized under centralized ministries for the first time. In 1955 he directed reform of the judicial system and regularized tax and revenue collections, putting them on a cash basis.

Selassie's political reforms were little more than window dressing. He set up symbolic elections and allowed local constituencies to elect delegates to the Chamber of Deputies, which assembled but did not really legislate. He later created the office of prime minister as another symbolic gesture to separate the monarchy from daily operations of the government. All these "reforms" were designed to placate critics; in reality, Selassie clung to absolute power and encouraged a lavish cult of personality.

On the positive side, Selassie left a legacy that included international recognition of Ethiopia's borders. On the negative side, he left the nation divided and disaffected. As Chapter 17 will show, Selassie's dethronement in 1974 was one step toward revolutionary terror and turmoil. Fifteen years later, Ethiopia's political life has still not entirely stabilized.

Kenya

During the course of Europe's scramble for Africa in the late nineteenth century, Kenya fell under British colonial rule until 1963, when it became independent. Although Kenya is a large country (nearly the size of Texas), its northern portion —about three-fifths the land mass—is arid. The English language and the Anglican Church made a lasting imprint on the nation, but Kenya's recent history is also a product of tradition, geography, and other factors. Swahili is the principal indigenous language. Over two-thirds of the population is Christian (38 percent Protestant; 28 percent Roman Catholic). The remainder are Muslim (6 percent) or embrace a traditional native religion.

Kenya illustrates the multiethnic character of so many sub-Saharan African nations. With a total population of about 24 million, Kenyan society is composed of some forty ethnic groups, including the Kikuyu, Luo, Luhya, Kelenjin, and Kamba. In addition, there are Asians, Arabs, and Europeans. The Kikuyu constitute the largest group in Kenya, roughly 21 percent of the total; the Luo comprise about 13 percent.

Kenya has the highest population growth rate in the world (4.1 percent in 1989), and over half the population is 14 years of age or younger. This demographic trend has overwhelmed the country's steady but unspectacular economic growth. With a per-capita income of $370 in 1987, Kenya has struggled to meet the many challenges of development since independence. From 1965 to 1985 Kenya's per-capita economic growth amounted to a paltry 1.9 percent per year. Nor is income evenly distributed; the top 10 percent of the population enjoy over 45 percent of total income.

The Arabs, who were the first foreign arrivals, came down the east coast of Kenya during the seventh century. Although they made forays into the interior in search of slaves, ivory, gold, and iron, they were primarily interested in controlling trade routes, and they built cities (or city-states) along the coast as well as in Tanzania and Mozambique. Much later, around 1500, the Portuguese arrived and forcibly displaced the Arabs, only to be ousted by them again in the seventeenth century. Then the Arab sheikdom of Oman controlled the Kenyan coast until the British took control in the late nineteenth century. Although the Arab influence is longer standing, the British influence may well prove longer lasting. Before the twentieth century, foreign influence in Kenya was generally confined to coastal areas—a pattern that occurred elsewhere in Africa as well.

Kenya became a British crown colony after World War I, in 1920. The country gave Great Britain a foothold in East Africa. In World War II, joint British-Kenyan forces launched a successful offensive against Italian positions in Ethiopia and Somalia. After the war a nationalist movement emerged.

During the colonial period, native Kenyans relied on trade unions to express their political interests.[26] As part of this tradition, the Kenya African Union (KAU) was founded in 1944. Destined to become Kenya's largest mass organization, with 100,000 members, the KAU played an active role in the independence struggle. In the late 1940s, a charismatic Kikuyu leader named Jomo Kenyatta spearheaded Kenya's drive for independence from Great Britain.

Early in 1952 the Mau Mau, a secret society bent on expelling all whites from Kenya and purifying Black Africa, launched a terror campaign against Europeans and Africans who were friendly to them. The Mau Mau were mainly Kikuyu, the largest of Kenya's ethnic groups and the dominant force north of Nairobi, the capital. In October the colonial government proclaimed a state of emergency, and the British sent troops. A bloody guerrilla war ensued and lasted several years (1952–1956). Over 10,000 Mau Mau fighters were killed, and some 2,200 were captured. The Mau Mau themselves killed an estimated 2,800 people.

Until the Mau Mau rebellion, Kenya's political experience was largely devoid of violence. The Mau Mau guerrilla movement took far more Kenyan lives than British (only 38), but it demonstrated the Kenyan desire to be free of colonial domination and the inevitability of independence. London responded to the Mau Mau challenge in several ways. First, it launched a military campaign that resulted in heavy casualties. Second, it arrested many of the KAU members, charged them with participating in the Mau Mau movement, and sentenced them to long jail terms. Jomo Kenyatta, who had been president of the KAU since 1947, was imprisoned for seven years (1954–1961). Third, colonial authorities made a conciliatory gesture, allowing eight Kenyan representatives to serve in the colonial Legislative Council, including Oginga Odinga, Tom Mboya, Ronald Ngala, and Daniel arap Moi, all members of the KAU who became national leaders in postindependence Kenya.

The Mau Mau uprising faded after February 1956 following the capture of several of its leaders, but the violence showed how strong nationalist feelings were in Kenya. The British arranged for elections to the Legislative Council (parliament) in March 1957, granting a limited African franchise based on educational qualifications. The eight Africans who were elected refused to serve, demanding instead a universal franchise and free primary education for all.

In 1960 the KAU was reconstituted as a full-fledged political party—the Kenyan African National Union (KANU). At this time the realities of multiethnic politics in Kenya became painfully apparent. KANU membership was dominated by the Kikuyu and Luo ethnic groups. Fearing that such an alliance would ignore the interests of their own ethnic groups, Ronald Ngala and Daniel arap Moi left KANU and formed the Kenyan African Democratic Union (KADU).

In February 1961 the British allowed a general election to be held within the framework of a parliamentary system. KANU and KADU contested the election, and KANU won a parliamentary majority. KANU leadership decided to delay the choice of a party president until Kenyatta was released in October 1961. As chief of the majority party, Kenyatta became Kenya's first prime minister upon independence in 1963 (In 1964 Kenya proclaimed itself a republic, with Kenyatta as president.) In the euphoria of the moment, KADU was voluntarily dissolved, and most of its members joined KANU. The unity, however, was short-lived.

After independence, the government made an effort to replace ethnic particularism with Kenyan nationalism. As part of this effort, Kenyatta moved away from party pluralism, which only exacerbated ethnic rivalries. Culturally, Swahili was championed over English; Kenyatta himself downplayed and criticized English as a colonial language and spoke it sparingly. He coined the slogan *Kenya Na Kanu* (''Kenya and KANU'') to emphasize national unity and the fact that all ethnic and other groups were encompassed by a single political party.

A major threat to Kenya's political stability was the ethnic clash between the Kikuyu, led by Kenyatta, and the Luo, led by Mboya and Odinga. The first Kenyatta government was based on a delicately balanced coalition in which the Luo and other ethnic leaders were given key roles in government. The arrangement soon broke down, however, and Odinga split from KANU in 1966, forming his own party called the Kenyan People's Union (KPU).

The assassination of Mboya in 1969 led to an outbreak of ethnic violence after a Kikuyu was charged with the crime and executed. Kenyatta then banned Odinga's party. In the elections that year KANU was rebuffed by the voters, although Kenyatta, the only candidate for president, was reelected. Concluding that a competitive multiparty arrangement would not work, Kenyatta moved to establish a one-party system with a strong executive (some of Kenyatta's critics considered him a virtual dictator).

Despite persistent instability, Kenyatta remained president until his death in 1978. His successor, Daniel arap Moi, has followed in Kenyatta's footsteps, ruling with a firm hand and at times resorting to measures that many regard as brutal and repressive.

Nigeria

Nigeria has great potential and great problems. With one-fifth of Africa's population—115 million people—it occupies only 3 percent of the continent's land mass. Its tropical climate is uniform throughout the country, but its geography can be divided into two main zones, savanna and rain forest. It also has areas of mangrove swamp in the extreme south, especially in the delta of the Niger river and in highlands in the east.

Problems posed by the tsetse fly, for which science has found no solution, illustrate the interplay of geography, environment, and economic development in Nigeria. Where the tsetse fly thrives, cattle and horses cannot survive. This has far-reaching implications for agriculture and transportation, and thus for the diet and living standards of Nigerians. As one noted Africanist has written:

> Equally important are the implications for conquest: the tsetse fly and forest stopped invading cavalry as man could not. The hills and mountains provided refuge; so too did the swamps and creeks far to the south, which must have been as unfathomable to African outsiders as they were to the succession of European explorers trying to solve the great geographical mystery of the Niger.[27]

Nigeria's geographic diversity is matched by ethnic and cultural diversity. Nearly four hundred separate languages are spoken, giving testimony to the cultural richness and deep-rooted identity of many subgroups. Evidence of iron smelting dates back to 900 B.C., and bronzes were produced as early as the ninth century.

Over centuries, a variety of political systems evolved, including states, confederations, and empires. Some politics were localized and relatively democratic (although they were far less institutionalized than modern constitutional democracies). Most developed internally and without major foreign intrusions until the nineteenth century. Northern traders crossed the Sahara Desert during the tenth century and introduced Islam. European traders did not appear until the sixteenth century and did not venture beyond the Niger Delta until the eighteenth century. Only during the late nineteenth century was the full impact of British expansionism felt. Earlier in the century Islam had spread through the north, contained only by the rugged terrain.

British Rule   The British drew the boundaries of the country that came to be called Nigeria after 1914. They were late arrivals on the scene and made the mistake of trying to impose uniform administrative and political structures throughout the territory. But what worked in the north did not work in the south. The decision to divide the country initially into two parts, northern and southern, rather than four or more was, in retrospect, a major blunder. This north-south division reinforced a psychological split: British-educated southerners in the coastal east and west believed they were "more fit" to rule than northerners, who were Islamic and supposedly insular—two traits that earned them the scorn of many in the south.

The trauma that the Great Depression in the 1930s brought upon European economies had repercussions on the colonies as well. Nigeria was a source of export revenue for beleaguered Britain, which no doubt intensified Nigerians' desires to cast off British rule. Even so, Nigeria did not become independent until 1960.

World War II was the catalyst of decolonization throughout Asia and Africa. Before the British left Nigeria, they divided it into three regions (bifurcating the south into east and west). Each region was dominated by a distinct ethnolinguistic group: the Hausa in the north, the Yoruba in the west, and the Ibo in the east. In 1967 the government, then under military control, replaced the regions with twelve states.

The Politics of Particularism   As just noted, three major ethnic groups—the Ibo, the Yoruba, and the Hausa—have dominated Nigerian politics. The most popular and most charismatic political figures during and after the drive for independence were usually identified with one of these three groups. (For example, Nnamde Azikiwe, or Zik, was an Ibo, and Chief Abafemi Awolowo was a Yoruba.) In addition, there are several other sizable groups, including Nupe, Edo, Ijaw, Tiv, Fulani, and Kanuri.

Ibos, Yorubas, and Hausas each provided the base for a political party, resulting in a three-party system. During the 1950s, when independence was negotiated, there were two main sources of tension: the north-south split and the resentment of minority groups in each of Nigeria's administrative-territorial subdivisions. Violence has erupted at times and has smoldered beneath the surface even in periods of apparent tranquility.

In Nigeria, as elsewhere, the British did not foresee—and subsequently did little to resolve—the issues of ethnic politics that they had helped to create. Thus, within a few years after the British left, Nigeria was convulsed by one of the bloodiest civil wars in modern African history. A vital political lesson to be drawn from Nigeria's turbulent past is that a multiparty system in an ethnically fragmented society—particularly when that society faces enormous economic challenges—is likely to be unworkable.

Nigeria's political experience since independence will be detailed in the next chapter. Briefly, at its inception Nigeria was hailed by outsiders, especially, the British, as a "model of democracy." But that was not to be, at least not without tribulation. Following the first national elections in 1959, and independence shortly thereafter, a coalition government was formed. But its stability was threatened from the start. After a series of political crises, the military staged a coup and assumed power in January 1966. This coup was only the first in a series, for in Nigeria democracy has vied with dictatorship. So far, the latter has prevailed most of the time.

South Africa

Nowhere has the colonial legacy been more tenacious and invidious than in South Africa. Afrikaners—the dominant white minority of Dutch descent—claim that, when their ancestors arrived during the seventeenth century, the southern tip of Africa was largely uninhabited. They claim to have been the first to settle it.

In truth, when the Dutch East India Company set out to establish a way station on the Cape of Good Hope in 1652, the expeditionary force of 200 men encountered an indigenous group called the Khoikhoi, whom they enslaved. The Khoikhoi (called Hottentots by whites) were eventually wiped out by smallpox, and the Dutch colonialists then imported slaves from the East Indies and Madagascar. The Khoikhoi, Dutch, Malay, and others produced the mixed-race group now known as Cape Coloreds, who in time were classified by Afrikaners as a distinct inferior group. (Coloreds are not to be confused with blacks, a majority group that ranks below them in the apartheid system.)

The Dutch farmers (or Boers) who immigrated to what is now South Africa pushed outward from the Cape colony. Many Boers settled only long enough to exhaust the soil and then moved on. As they penetrated into the interior, they encountered another indigenous group, the San. The Boers shot the San, whom they disdainfully regarded as savages and thieves and called "Bushmen."

It was not until the late eighteenth century that the Boers met a serious challenge from indigenous Africans—the Xhosa. As Dutch settlers moved north along the Indian Ocean coast, Africans were moving south to escape population pressures as well as tribal wars and slave raiding (mainly by the British). In the ensuing Kaffir wars, which lasted over a century, the Boers subdued the Africans, but not without high death tolls on both sides.

Reverberations from the napoleonic wars in Europe were felt as far away as South Africa. When France occupied the Low Countries (Netherlands) in 1795, the Dutch asked the British to take over the Cape and keep the French out. The British gladly obliged, but then decided to stay themselves; in 1814 the Netherlands ceded South Africa to Great Britain, thus giving legal force to what was plainly a fait accompli.

The "Great Trek"   The Dutch in the Netherlands could accommodate themselves to the loss of South Africa more easily than the Boers could. The British takeover turned the tables: Now it was the Afrikaners who were forced to live under rules made by "foreigners." For example, the British insisted that everyone be equal before the law, regardless of color or creed, and in 1834, to the dismay of many Boers, slavery was abolished. Two years later the Boers, convinced that the British wanted to destroy their way of life, began the "Great Trek." Between 1836 and 1838 about twelve thousand Dutch farmers and their families headed out in search of new frontiers. Afrikaners venerate these stouthearted forebears much as Americans honor the pioneers. Like those who settled the American frontier, the *voortrekkers* (Dutch pioneers) set out in caravans, endured tremendous hardships, and occasionally fought battles with Africans, drawing their wagons into a circle called a *laager*. One ill-fated group vanished. When the Zulus massacred 570 Boer settlers in 1838, the Boers retaliated by killing 3,000 Zulus (an event chillingly portrayed in the British film *Zulu*). In general, the voortrekkers' dealt with Africans much as the pioneers dealt with Native Americans. They used persuasion, force, or fraud to push native inhabitants off the land. The very idea of owning land was alien to Africans, as it was to many Native Americans.

The voortrekkers' destination was the fertile province of Natal on the eastern coast facing the Indian Ocean. But in 1843 the British annexed Natal, outraging the Boers and prompting them to undertake another great trek. This time they moved northeast—inland—and established two small republics, the Transvaal and the Orange Free State. Once again ensconced in their own enclaves, the Boers shared South Africa with the British in an uneasy but peaceful coexistence until 1867, when diamonds were discovered in the Transvaal.

The Boer War   With the discovery of diamonds in 1867 and gold nine years later, the British began pouring into the two Boer republics. So many ''outlanders'' rushed into the Transvaal that they soon outnumbered Afrikaners two to one. The Transvaal government, headed by Paul Kruger, attempted to undercut the British by disenfranchising them—a favorite Boer tactic.

The British in the Cape colony looked covetously at the Transvaal and the Orange Free State. Sir Cecil Rhodes, the founder of Rhodesia (and of the Rhodes scholarships to Oxford), conspired with the British high commissioner, Alfred Milner, to provoke Kruger into declaring war; their ultimate goal was to annex the Boer republics.

The ensuing war, from 1899 to 1902, was bitter and bloody. In the end the British prevailed, but at great moral and material loss. The Boers fought valiantly; the British resorted to drastic measures, what today would be considered abuses of human rights (such as putting Boer families in concentration camps, where some 26,000 women and children died of typhus). When the Boers finally sued for peace in 1902, the British had won the battle but lost the war. Guilt-ridden and dispirited, London extended full political rights to the defeated Boers, who eventually converted their demographic advantage over the British into full control of the country.

The Ascent of the Afrikaners   The British allowed the Boers of the Transvaal and the Orange Free State to be self-governing, which helped usher in a brief era of goodwill. In 1910 the Union of South Africa was proclaimed, finally knitting the four colonies into a single nation-state. World War I produced new strains on British-Afrikaner relations: Although South Africa's foreign policy was dictated by Great Britain, many Afrikaners were sympathetic to the Germans, and a German colony was next door to South Africa. When the British pressured the South African government in Pretoria to jointly invade South-West Africa (now Namibia), many Afrikaners opposed Pretoria did it anyway. Similarly, many Afrikaners opposed South Africa's entry into World War II.

Anti-British sentiment also had economic causes, for the British dominated industry and commerce, while the Afrikaners were primarily farmers. When the

Depression disrupted world trade and precipitated a collapse in farm prices, many Afrikaners, now desperate, streamed to cities for jobs. Against this backdrop, Afrikaners became mobilized and radicalized. They set about creating the infrastructure for a new Afrikaner state and society—cultural associations, schools and universities, insurance companies, and political parties.

The National party was founded in 1914 as the vehicle of Afrikaner self-assertion. At the time of its founding the party was moderate and conciliatory toward the British. But in the 1930s, under the leadership of Daniel Malan, it became a militant instrument of Afrikaner nationalism. The doctrine of white supremacy—the cornerstone of apartheid—was thus formed during the world-wide depression between the two world wars. Students of history will note that the South African system had its origins in the same turbulent era of racial superiority as Nazi Germany, Fascist Italy, and other extreme right-wing regimes and movements.

The Nationalists did not simply build a party; they launched a movement. With persistent patience they spread the ideology, of white supremacy, using the poignant image of the circled wagons in a *laager*: Anyone who resisted the movement was breaking the circle and aiding the enemy. In 1948 the National party won the general election—what the Afrikaners had lost by the bullet they now recaptured by the ballot. Spurred by their tragic history, they now dug in, building a fortress state prepared to meet all challenges with force.

CONCLUSION

Politics and government in sub-Saharan Africa are conditioned by such factors as geography, ethnic diversity, culture, and especially colonialism. The image of Africa as a wonderland of exotic jungles, wild animals, and primitive tribes is a Hollywood creation. The other familiar image of poverty and famine, gives the impression that Africa is a wasteland. The reality is that Africa is neither a wonderland nor a wasteland. Only the most progressive, far-sighted leadership can solve the region's formidable socioeconomic problems.

STUDY QUESTIONS

1. How has geography influenced economic and political development in sub-Saharan Africa?
2. What role did colonialism play in shaping African politics?
3. How does the historical and cultural context of politics differ among Ethiopia, Kenya, and Nigeria? Are there any striking similarities?
4. Compare the experience of the Boers (Afrikaners) with that of early pioneers in the United States. What is the relevance of this history to the current situation in South Africa? Does it justify apartheid?

SUGGESTED READINGS

Davidson, Basil. *Africa: A History of a Continent*. New York: Macmillan, 1972.
Davidson, Basil. *Africa South of the Sahara*, 17th ed., Lanham, Md.: Europa, 1988.
Fanon, Franz. *The Wretched of the Earth*. C. Van Markman, trans. New York: Grove, 1968.
Mazrui, Ali A. *The Africans*. Boston: Little, Brown, 1986.
Mbiti, John S. *African Religions and Philosophies*. London: Heinemann, 1969.
Meredith, Martin. *In the Name of Apartheid: South Africa in the Postwar Period*. New York: Harper & Row, 1988.

NOTES

1 See, for example, Alan Walker and Mark Teaford, ''The Hunt for Proconsul,'' *Scientific American*, Vol. 260, No. 1, January 1989, pp. 76–82.

2 Basil Davidson, *Africa South of the Sahara*, 17th ed. (Lanham, Md.: Europa Publications, 1988), p. 4.

3 See, for example, Frantz Fanon, *Black Skin: White Masks*, C. Van Markman, trans. (New York: Grove, 1967); T. Walter Walbank, *Contemporary Africa: A Continent in Transition* (New York: Van Nostrand, 1956), pp. 107–110; Basil Davidson, *Africa: A History of a Continent* (New York: Macmillan, 1972), pp. 275–293.

4 Ali A. Mazrui, *The Africans* (Boston: Little, Brown, 1986); for a critique, see Hailu Habtu, ''The Fallacy of the Triple Heritage Thesis: A Critique,'' *Issue*, Vol. 13, No. 1 (1984), pp. 26–29.

5 Ali Mazrui, ''The Semitic Impact on Black Africa: Arab and Jewish Cultural Influences,'' *Issue*, Vol. 13, No. 1 (1984), pp. 3–8.

6 See, for example, John S. Mbiti, *African Religions and Philosophies* (London: Heinemann, 1969), pp. 75–91.

7 W. H. Taylor, ''Missionary Education Reconsidered: The Nigerian Case,'' *African Affairs*, Vol. 83, No. 331 (1984), pp. 189–205.

8 Mbiti, op. cit., pp. 75–91.

9 Davidson, op. cit., pp. 143–144.

10 George Balandier and Jacques Marquet, eds., *The Dictionary of Black African Civilization* (New York: Leon Amiel, 1974), p. 3; see also Jacques Marquet, *Africanity: The Cultural Unity of Black Africa* (New York: Oxford, 1972).

11 See Franz Fanon, *Black Skin: White Mask* (New York: Grove, 1967), C. Van Markmann, trans.; and *The Wretched of the Earth* (New York: Grove, 1968), Constance Farrington, trans.

12 See John D. Rusk, ''Warfare and Human Rights in Angola and Mozambique,'' *Africa Today*, Vol. 34, No. 4 (1987), pp. 33–44.

13 See John Stockwell, *In Search of Enemies* (New York: Norton, 1978).

14 *World Development Report*, 1987, p. 171.

15 Peter Robbs, ''Privatization in Africa,'' *Development International*, March–April 1987, pp. 27–30; Salim Lone, ''Africa Moving Rapidly on Reforms,'' *Africa Recovery*, Vol. 1, No. 1 (February–April 1987), pp. 14–17.

16 K. Matthews, ''The OAU and the Political Economy of Human Rights in Africa,'' *Africa Today*, Vol. 34, Nos. 1 & 2 (1987), pp. 85–96; for more on refugees and the brain drain,

see the special series in *Issue*, Vol. 22, Nos. 1 & 2 (Spring 1982); and Vol. 9, No. 14 (Winter 1979).

[17] *New York Times*, Aug. 21, 1988, p. E-3.

[18] *World Development Report*, 1987, p. 17.

[19] For a detailed discussion see John W. Harbeson, *The Ethiopian Transformation: The Quest for a Post-Imperial State* (Boulder, Colo.: Westview, 1988), pp. 22–59.

[20] Quoted in Paul H. Brietzke, *Law, Development and the Ethiopian Revolution* (London: Associated University Press, 1982), pp. 13–15.

[21] Ibid., pp. 15–16.

[22] Mulatu Wubneh and Yohannis Abate, *Ethiopia: Transition and Development in the Horn of Africa* (Boulder, Colo.: Westview, 1988), pp. 3–4.

[23] Leonard Mosley, *Haile Selassie, The Conquering Lion* (Englewood Cliffs, N.J.: Prentice-Hall, 1965), p. 7.

[24] Ryszard Kapuscinski, *The Emperor* (New York: Harcourt, 1983), pp. 28–33ff.

[25] Wubneh and Abate, op. cit., pp. 17–23.

[26] See Bethwell A. Ogot, *Historical Dictionary of Kenya* (London: Scarecrow, 1981).

[27] Jean Herskovits, *Power and Democracy in Africa*, Foreign Policy Association, Headline Series No. 257 (January–February 1982), p. 8.

Chapter 17
Endemic Authoritarianism?

Civil and religious government is allowed to be the principal cause which affects (and even forms) the character of nations. Climate, diet, occupation, and a variety of other less considerable causes contribute their share to the general effect. It is not, however, by abstract reasonings alone, on the separate or combined influence of those causes, that the character of a nation can be ascertained; but actual observations on their genius and conduct must also be attended to.

These observations were made in the eighteenth century by a Swedish civil servant named C. B. Wadstrom, who became fascinated with Africa as a result of reading and hearing about it from Europeans who had been there. His curiosity got the best of him: In 1787—while Hamilton, Madison, and the other Founders of America were meeting in Philadelphia to forge a constitution and a new nation—Wadstrom set sail for Africa. For a year he traveled around Africa, making observations about what he called the ''character and disposition'' of the Africans (much as Alexis de Tocqueville would do in America a half-century later).

What Wadstrom learned about Africans was contrary to what he had read about them in the works of European contemporaries. Rather than the stereotypes of primitive, wild people, he found Africans to possess many civil and cultural virtues. Returning to Europe, he wrote *An Essay on Colonization* which included the following impressions of Africans:

Their understandings have not been nearly so much cultivated as those of the Europeans; but their passions, both defensive and social, are much stronger. No people are more sensible of disrespect, contempt, or injury, or more prompt and violent in resenting them. They are also apt to retain a sense of injury, till they obtain satisfaction, or gratify revenge. In this they resemble other imperfectly civilized tribes, and even the more refined Europeans, in whom that benevolent religion, which teaches forgiveness of enemies, has not yet produced its full effect.[1]

As the quotation opening this chapter clearly shows, Wadstrom was concerned with the critical matters of comparative politics and anthropology. He stressed that forms of government and culture can tell more about a society than such factors as climate or diet. In that light he showed that his contemporaries did not write the whole truth about Africa, because their method was fallacious; consequently their conclusions were self-serving and tended to rationalize Europe's exploitation and colonization of Africa.

Today's scholars face similar problems in studying foreign societies, and Wadstrom's precautions are still relevant. One's perspective and selection of material are crucial elements in trying to comprehend the complexities of other peoples' social and political systems.

Clashing interests and festering conflicts are the stuff of politics in sub-Saharan Africa as in most places, and they shape the region's political patterns. As we examine the political structures of sub-Saharan Africa, remember that the nation-states of this region are almost all newcomers, having gained independence only since World War II. We will focus on two principal issues—political unity and economic self-reliance—because they provide an essential background for understanding contemporary Africa.

Independence and Its Aftermath

As noted in Chapter 16, the political systems of contemporary sub-Saharan Africa were formed in the crucible of colonialism and, later, in the process of decolonization. From the Berlin Treaty (1884–1885), parceling Africa among the European powers, until the middle of this century, all of sub-Saharan Africa with the exception of Ethiopia and Liberia was under colonial rule. In most cases the rule was direct foreign rule or "trusteeship"—a status somewhere between legal sovereignty and complete subjugation.

In some countries nationalist guerrillas attempted to resist European colonizers, but such efforts proved futile.[2] The balance of power favored Europeans, who had professional armies and superior weapons and were adept at using a divide-and-conquer strategy, playing rival ethnic groups against each other and hiring African mercenaries to fight rebellious African nationalists. For example, the Fante fought against the Asante resistance in West Africa, and the Baganda of Uganda allied with the British, who gave them special treatment.

Long-standing ethnic rivalries in Africa made it relatively easy for the British and other colonial powers to pit African against African. In addition, the rich European intruders had the wherewithal to entice segments of the native population into alliances. Human frailties are not confined to any one culture or region, and the complicity of Africans in their own subjugation testifies to this. The interethnic conflicts and violence associated with European colonialism in Africa set the stage for the region's internal instability today.

World War II ushered in a new epoch in the history of sub-Saharan Africa. The international system collapsed, and new global alignments and a new "bipolarity" emerged. The Cold War (and anticommunism) replaced colonialism as the West's obsession, and world opinion turned against colonialism. What had been an international status symbol at the turn of the century became an anachronism. In the new international arena, the rules had changed; indeed, the game itself had changed. The U.N. Charter enshrined the principles of self-determination and noninterference, and the African struggle received new moral impetus.

The cracks in the structure of colonialism became increasingly apparent with time. Among the new factors in world politics was the spontaneous combustion of "national liberation movements" throughout the colonized world (later called the "Third World"). The economic and political costs of maintaining overseas empires for war-torn European nations preoccupied with their own recovery and reconstruction were now prohibitive. The three former Great Powers of Europe—Great Britain, France, and Germany—were superseded by two superpowers, the United States and the Soviet Union. The Eurocentric balance of power itself was replaced by a global balance in which the nations of Western Europe— once colonial overlords—were no longer even autonomous or self-reliant.

In this "brave new world" Africans found ready allies among emerging socialist revolutionary states such as Cuba, China, and the Soviet Union. The radical anticapitalist and antiimperialist ideology of these states struck a responsive chord among Africans, for whom capitalism and imperialism meant exploitation. When Europeans conscripted Africans to fight in World War II, they probably did not realize that they were also preparing colonial peoples for armed resistance against their oppressors.[3] Meanwhile, the United Nations provided a new forum for all nations seeking liberation, and Articles 1 and 2 of its Charter obligated member-states to support the cause of self-determination everywhere.

Sudan became the first sub-Saharan country to obtain independence (1956), followed by Ghana (1957) and Guinea (1958). In 1960 seventeen new sub-Saharan nations gained independence, bringing the total to twenty-two; by the end of 1965 the number had climbed to thirty. And while African nationalists deserve credit for pushing the pace of decolonization, larger historical forces also played a crucial supporting role.

The momentum of decolonization, which seemed so irresistible in the beginning, was broken in the regions farther south of the equator. In southern Africa the Portuguese in particular clung tenaciously to the colonies of Angola and Mozambique. Protracted civil wars had to be fought before Angola, Mozambique, and Namibia (formerly ruled by South Africa) won independence. Elsewhere, however, colonial powers bowed out gracefully, but perhaps too quickly. In fact, the speed and ease of independence helped create the weak governments and fragmentation that afflict the region.

The Elusive Ideal of African Unity

Of the three principal time periods in African politics (precolonial, colonial, and postcolonial), it is the last period, since 1960, that has received the most attention. It was a new era of self-rule, but it also brought the imposing challenges of nation-building. The postcolonial period has been a search for unifying political philosophies and administrative systems, as well as models of economic development, that can foster national integration and regional cooperation. The region's experiences since independence have revealed a colonial "hangover" that works against African unity and self-reliance.

One of the most persistent problems is that the prevailing model of state administration incorporate colonial forms of hierarchy and authoritarianism. These are alien to Africa's tradition of direct access and communication between the people and their leaders.[4] Thus, Africans have been faced with the need to choose. Should they return to traditional modalities, adopt colonial institutions, or try to combine the two into a unique African blend (much easier said than done)?

First Stirrings: The Early Conferences

After independence, African leaders had to walk a tightrope—trying to act independent and negotiate the best terms for self-rule, on the one hand, and having to operate within the constraints of continuing economic dependency, on the other. Many African leaders had returned from the battlefront, prison, or exile, and they suddenly had to master political skills, such as administration and persuasion. They attended conference after conference, searching for answers to common problems; they met in Accra, Addis Ababa, Algiers, Cairo, Casablanca, and Monrovia. They also went to non-African capitals and met with leaders of other developing nations, comparing notes and sharing ideas.

The Bandung Conference in 1955 was the first time all thirty-eight of the developing countries met to discuss common problems. The attendees promised to cooperate by sharing information, especially pertaining to economic and political development. A series of such conferences ensued and became institutionalized during the 1960s and 1970s in such forms as the Non-Aligned Movement (NAM) and the Group of 77.

The NAM was launched at the Bandung Conference as an alternative to choosing sides in the East-West conflict. It thus helped focus attention on the North-South conflict: the tension resulting from maldistribution of wealth between northern industrial democracies and southern developing nations. The Group of 77, formed in 1964, is the largest caucus group in the United Nations. It has grown to over 120 members—all of them developing countries—and is the major means by which the developing South has pressured the industrial North to fund a New International Economic Order (NIEO). The goal is to bring about greater global equity by redistributing resources (principally in the form of foreign aid and trade concessions) between North and South.

The issue of African unity topped the agenda at these early regional gatherings. In the realm of economics, African leaders optimistically forged a consensus in favor of self-reliance. (Chapter 18 will examine the obstacles they encountered in seeking unity and self-reliance.) Thus, the postcolonial challenges were new. Although the struggle for political independence was over (except in southern Africa), the struggle for economic independence was about to begin. Meeting in Accra in 1958, the first All-African People's Congress declared that, although the political domination of colonialism had ended, the economic domination of neocolonialism continued.[5] Kwame Nkrumah, Ghana's premier and a participant at the meeting, wrote a book, *Neo-Colonialism: The Last Stage of Imperialism*, in which he elucidated the main features of neocolonialism and asserted it was incompatible with economic development in the African context.[6]

The tenets of African unity and self-reliance assumed two main policy forms: Pan-Africanism and African socialism. This incipient ideology can be seen, above all, as a rejection of the West. If European imperialists had carved up Africa,

Africans would come together in bold new patterns of regional integration; if the West had a love affair with capitalism, Africa would opt for socialism.

Nkrumah's Vision

Pan-Africanism emerged when Ghana and Guinea gained independence, in 1957 and 1958, respectively. Nkrumah was a leading advocate of African unity, but his views were not particularly original. In fact, they were based on the writings of African descendants like Edward Blyden, George Padmore, Marcus Garvey, and W. E. B. Dubois, who had lived, traveled, and taught in the United States, Europe, and the West Indies.[7]

Nkrumah became acquainted with the works of these black intellectuals as a visitor to Europe and the United States. He was captivated by the idea of promoting a collective African consciousness.[8] What Nkrumah had in mind was not only the political and economic unification of sub-Saharan Africa but also the solidarity of all Africans worldwide.[9] His was a vision of revolutionary "black power" on a global scale; in effect he was saying, "Africans of the world, unite!" In Nkrumah's quasi-Marxist world view, Africans were the proletariat, and Europeans were capitalist oppressors.

But many of Nkrumah's contemporaries thought his concept of African unity, for all its intellectual and emotional appeal, was too idealistic or too radical. As a result, the unity movement broke into factions early in the 1960s. The more radical, or Casablanca, group wanted immediate political unity; the more conservative, or Monrovia, group preferred to start with socioeconomic and cultural cooperation. Sensitive to Africa's cultural and political fragmentation, they spurned the idea of Pan-African unity at a moment in history when sub-Saharan states were faced with basic nation-building tasks, including the inculcation of a sense of national identity.[10]

The Organization of African Unity

Various groups continued to hold unity conferences in Acra, Brazzaville, Casablanca, and Monrovia between 1958 and 1963, when a third faction emerged, taking a position midway between radicals and conservatives. The setting was a 1963 conference in Ethiopia's capital, Addis Ababa, at which thirty-two independent states agreed to establish the Organization of African Unity (OAU). Patterned after the United Nations, the OAU Charter adheres to the basic U.N. principles of noninterference in the internal affairs of member-states, respect for the territorial integrity of member-states, human rights, and peaceful settlement of disputes.[11] Although the idea of having an OAU standing army was proposed by Nkrumah and was debated at Addis Ababa, the majority of participants opposed this measure. Since then, no OAU member-state has openly engaged its troops in a regional conflict that did not directly affect it. But in the 1980s Libya did send troops into Chad in an effort to influence the outcome of a civil war there; Libyan forces also helped Tanzania defeat Idi Amin in the Ugandan civil war after Tanzania and Uganda, traditional foes, invaded each other's territory during 1978–1979.

Today the ideal of African unity is a distant hope at best. The OAU has played a useful role in settling a number of conflicts among member-states, and it acts as a moral restraint on aggression. It has also helped newer members through the critical early stages of independence and has used its influence to pressure South Africa to grant Namibia independence and to end apartheid. But human rights abuses, hunger, and other deprivations continue to be common throughout the region.

Like people elsewhere, Africans have taken to nationalism much more readily than to regionalism (or Pan-Africanism). Julius Nyerere of Tanzania, a founder of the OAU, has lamented that the idea of Africa has faded since the days of the early conferences: "At that time we saw Africa and we talked about Africa, today we are more Tanzanian than African, and Kenyans are more Kenyan than African." [12]

Indeed, Africans are too preoccupied with national problems to put much emphasis on distant ideals like African unity. According to one interpretation, nationalism and the nation-state are legacies of colonialism; thus Africa's predicament, including fragmentation, is external in origin. [13] Others say that Africa has had time to put its house in order and that, whatever the causes of Africa's current problems, only Africans can solve them.

In any event, the OAU still holds annual conferences of African heads of state as well as conferences of foreign ministers and ministers of economics and finance. Yet there have also been at least seventy coups and military interventions since 1963, and the OAU—founded in the name of African unity—has devoted most of its energy and resources to mediating the many conflicts arising from African disunity and civil wars.

Sub-Saharan Development and Self-Reliance

A fundamental choice facing the newly independent states of sub-Saharan Africa was whether to adopt the Soviet model of central planning and collective farming, the Western free-market model, or a composite African model based on local traditions and methods. A fourth alternative was to design a new model tailored to fit Africa. Meeting the challenge of economic and political development necessitated a series of interconnected policy decisions about strategies, resources, and procedures.

Most African nations have chosen neither the Soviet model nor Western-style capitalism—both models, though starkly different, are European. Emerging from the experiences of colonialism, war, and the struggle for independence (which was often relatively peaceful), they opted for a model based on self-affirmation and self-reliance. In other words, they wanted to be masters of their destiny, for obvious historical and psychological reasons. They stressed cooperative social values and relations in which the members of society work and produce for the good of the whole and the state acts as the agent of society, protecting and promoting the freedom and well-being of the individual. The debates over policy, both domestic and foreign, were almost always undertaken within the context of shared assumptions about the need for socialist self-reliance.

African Socialism

Self-reliance, as discussed here, is an integral part of an ideology known as African socialism. This ideology draws on the traditional system of the extended family, whose members are expected to work for the common good and share benefits and burdens equally.[14] African socialism has been espoused by such prominent "independence" leaders as Kwame Nkrumah and Leopold Senghor in West Africa and Julius Nyerere, Tom Mboya, Oginga Odinga, and Kenneth Kaunda in East Africa. In their views one finds a unifying thread that recognizes the imperatives of material progress but puts human development above accumulation of capital; social well-being is given priority over industrial growth.

For Nkrumah the starting point was affirmation of the African personality, enriched by Africa's traditions and its heritage of cultural pluralism, including Islamic and Christian values. As he put it:

> With true independence regained, however, a new harmony needs to be forged, a harmony that will allow the combined presence of traditional Africa, Islamic Africa and Euro-Christian Africa, so that this presence is in tune with the original humanist principles underlying African society. Our society is not the old society, but a new society enlarged by Islamic and Euro-Christian influences. A new emergent ideology is therefore required, . . . which will not abandon the original humanist principles of Africa.
> . . . Such a philosophical statement . . . will give the theoretical basis for an ideology whose aim shall be to contain the African experience of Islamic and Euro-Christian presence as well as the experience of the traditional African society, and, by gestation, employ them for the harmonious growth and development of that society.[15]

Leopold Senghor of Senegal struck a similar chord in arguing that the African outlook is humanist and that Africa must build on this foundation. He used the concept of "negritude" (his term) to encompass the sum total of cultural values of blacks everywhere. In his article "Negritude: The Humanism of the 20th Century" he expanded this idea of an African personality to include any action and principles necessary to enhance the cultural development of people who have been deprived of identity and self-esteem by the inhumane experiences of slavery or colonialism.[16]

For Julius Nyerere the essential ingredient of self-reliance is less psychological and more social and political in nature. It is intimately tied to the broadening of human freedom:

> If the purpose of development is the greater freedom and well-being of the people, it cannot result from force. . . . By orders, or even by slavery, you can build pyramids and magnificent roads, you can achieve expanded acreage of cultivation, and increases in the quantity of goods produced in your factories. All these things, and many more, can be achieved through the use of force; but none of them results in the development of people.[17]

The method of self-reliant development envisaged by Nyerere is cooperation between society and state, but starting with the smallest unit, the individual: "In order to maintain our independence and our people's freedom we ought to be self-reliant in every possible way and avoid depending upon other countries for assistance."[18]

As president of Tanzania, Nyerere devoted himself to thinking, speaking, and writing about self-reliance and socialism in the African context. Like Gandhi and Mao, Nyerere stressed the necessity of a national work ethic and moral character. He asserted that true development comes from indigenous resources—the land and the people (both abundant in Tanzania)—not from capital and technology (both scarce), and not only in Tanzania but throughout sub-Saharan Africa. Thus in 1967 Tanzania issued the Arusha Declaration, a socialist program of development known as *ujamaa*, or familyhood.[19]

The expression of African socialism began introspectively in Kenya. Tom Mboya and Oginga Odinga defined what self-reliance and socialism came to mean there. Although they differed on the details, they agreed that Kenya's economic development should be based on indigenous resources and values. Mboya wrote:

> When I talk of "African Socialism," I refer to those proved codes of conduct in the African societies which have, over the ages, conferred dignity on our people and afforded them security regardless of their station in life. I refer to universal charity which characterized our societies and I refer to the African's thought processes and cosmological ideas which regard man, not as a social means, but as an end and entity in the society.[20]

Another advocate of socialist self-reliance for Africa is Kenneth Kaunda, President of Zambia. His humanist approach to economic development contrasts sharply with Western capitalist views, which stress the profit motive, that is, self-interest. "I have a passionate belief in the worth and possibilities of man," Kaunda wrote, "and I expect him someday to achieve a perfection."[21]

Although this vision may seem over idealistic and naive to Western observers, it authentically expresses African values, which tend to be group oriented rather than individualistic and are not tied to Western logic and pragmatism. In fact, Kaunda is not a utopian dreamer; on the contrary, he emphasizes the work ethic and the need to modernize. The way to prove one's worth, he says, is with "a spade or a sickle."[22]

In the following passage, Kaunda synthesized hard work, humanism, and modernity into a philosophy of African economic development:

> Modern Africa is no place for the uncommitted. Life here demands cool nerves, perpetual optimism and great faith in human possibilities. Those who live with their bags mentally packed are of all men the most miserable. They are like hypochondriacs, taking their temperature and feeling their pulse every hour to see whether they are still fit. They are blind to the positive aspects of independence. They do not notice the immense nerve and dedication of our people—their gritted-teeth determination to make Zambia great—because they are utterly preoccupied with the search for cracks in the foundation. They magnify every isolated incident into a full-blown calamity. Every loose stone heralds an avalanche, every gust of wind a tornado. They wish to feast upon the fruits of our prosperity but will slink off at the first sign of adversity.[23]

Neither Communism nor Capitalism

In sum, Africans have embraced a world view that is neither communistic nor capitalistic, neither revolutionary nor conservative. Rather, it reflects Africa's cultural diversity and unique historical experience. As one African scholar observed:

> One could put together a symmetrical pattern of one to seven cleavages, and then take a leap to fifty and beyond. The symmetry in the form of an inverted pyramid begins with one continent, Africa; two permanent [cultural-geographic] parts, the Arab North and black South; three religious systems, African traditional religions, Christianity and Islam; four dominant international languages, English, French, Arabic and Portuguese; five external hegemonic systems competing for influence or profit within Africa, Western Europe, North America, the Soviet bloc, China and Japan; six political traditions partly fed by those five hegemonic systems and partly in opposition to those systems, liberal capitalism, socialism, nationalism, conservative traditionalism, militarism and Pan-Africanism; seven combat traditions, the warrior tradition, the jihad, passive resistance, guerrilla warfare, revolutionary terrorism, modern conventional warfare, and prospects for a nuclear option first in South Africa and later elsewhere in Africa.[24]

In this mosaic of social, cultural, and historical diversity can be seen the need for an African synthesis. As we have noted, the principal elements of this have been self-reliance, socialism, and Pan-Africanism (which has remained a distant ideal). Self-reliant socialism, in the African context, is predicated on the values of social equality and harmony and has provided a conceptual framework for development strategies and policies. It may seem as though self-reliance and African unity are contradictory aims, but the African notion of self-reliance does not imply autarchy at all. On the contrary, most African leaders advocate equitable interdependence. (What they mean by "equitable" will be discussed in the next chapter.)

Political Patterns in Sub-Saharan Africa

As noted earlier, politics and government are conditioned by geography, history, culture, and the physical environment. Into this contextual tapestry, the sub-Saharan countries have woven a variety of political patterns, including military dictatorship, civilian authoritarianism, and even constitutional democracy.

Christian Potholm, a scholar and student of African politics, has developed a useful classification of African political systems, identifying two basic regime types: polyarchal and authoritarian. He subdivided the polyarchies (another term for representative democracy) into single-party and multiparty forms, and grouped the authoritarian regimes into civilian oligarchies and military praetorian forms.[25] Potholm distinguished one form from another by looking at such characteristics as the extent to which there is electoral competition, the level of demonstrable support for law, and the protection of civil liberties by government. Obviously, the values embedded in these criteria are more likely to be found in polyarchies than in authoritarian systems.

It is, however, mistaken to conclude that polyarchal systems are all equally liberal or that authoritarian systems are all equally repressive. Potholm recognized that significant differences exist within classifications; hence, he did not talk about a single type of system in each category but about a polyarchal and authoritarian "spectrum."

The Polyarchal (Democratic) Spectrum

Multiparty States   On one end of the spectrum of African polyarchies are multiparty systems, found in Botswana, Gambia, and Senegal. Other countries also claim to be multiparty democracies. Sudan, for example, has nearly thirty political parties. But Sudan has not sustained a viable competitive system of parties and elections; instead, changes of government have been brought about by military coups (most recently in June 1989, for the fifth time), and Sudan's authoritarian rulers have never felt constrained by party leaders or democratically elected legislatures. In fact, the last coup in Sudan dissolved the Constitution, the Parliament, and all political parties.

In truth, only Botswana, Gambia, and Senegal have had free and fair elections involving multiple candidates for the office of president as well as seats in the national legislature. Africa's three multiparty states have several other features in common. They each have a unicameral legislature and a national chief executive who is also head of state and holds the title of president. Periodic elections are held by universal suffrage, and candidates seeking legislative office or the presidency conduct free-wheeling campaigns. Presidential and legislative terms of office are consistently fixed in all three countries: five years in Gambia and Senegal and four years in Botswana. There is no limitation on reelection. In Gambia and Senegal the president is directly elected by a simple majority of the popular vote. The president of Botswana is indirectly elected by a simple majority of the elected members of the legislature. In each country the vice-president is appointed by, and serves at the pleasure of, the president.

In the first elections held after independence, the party leader who was most instrumental in blazing a trail to independence was usually able to carry his party to victory. Subsequent elections in Africa's multiparty states have generally favored incumbent parties. While minor parties have managed to win some legislative seats, they have not been able to muster parliamentary majorities or to force the leading party into parliamentary coalitions or to capture the presidency. As shown in Table 17-1, recent elections bear out this pattern of success for the party of independence.

In recent elections, opposition parties have made modest inroads in all three countries. For example, after the 1988 election, the Democratic party of Senegal had a total of seventeen legislative seats, nine more than in the 1983 election, while the majority party lost eight seats. Also, in 1988 President Abdouf Diouf was elected by a majority of 73 percent—11 percent fewer votes than he received

Table 17-1 Dominance of Majority Parties in Recent Elections

Country	Year	Majority Party	Seats Won
Botswana	1984	Democratic party	29 of 34
Gambia	1987	People's Progressive party	31 of 36
Senegal	1988	Socialist party	103 of 120

Sources: Facts on File, Keesing's Contemporary Archives, and World Factbook.

in 1983—while the candidate of the Democratic Socialist party garnered 26 percent of the popular vote, almost double the party candidate's 1983 total.

Single-Party States   Single-party states are the other half of Potholm's polyarchic spectrum. Yet it must be noted that some single-party states do not fit into this spectrum. If none of the attributes of constitutional democracy is present—free and fair elections involving competitive parties, the rule of law, and respect for civil liberties—then the political system belongs in the authoritarian spectrum.

Like the multiparty states, single-party polyarchies in sub-Saharan Africa have a unicameral legislature and a chief executive, or president, who is both head of state and head of government. Periodic elections are held for members of the National Assembly, and legislative seats are contested by several candidates in each voting district. In many single-party states, candidates must be party members and must receive party approval to stand for election.

Kenya, Sierra Leone, Tanzania, Zambia, and Zimbabwe are all examples of single-party polyarchies. At independence, each of these countries had multiple parties, but they later switched to constitutional one-party systems.

In this type of system, the ruling party typically nominates only one candidate for president, and the nominee must receive a majority of votes in the party's central committee (whose members may vote either "yes" or "no"). In Kenya the president is elected indirectly by the National Assembly. Although party approval and confirmation are requirements for the presidential candidate, they are not always needed for candidacy in legislative contests. Thus in Ethiopia's first legislative election in 1987, some 2,250 candidates contested the 835 seats, and some were nominated by mass organizations (although the great majority were handpicked by the Marxist Workers Party of Ethiopia). Tanzania's most recent general election was held in 1985; President Ali Hassan Mwinyi received a 92-percent "yes" vote—a suspiciously large share. At this "election" Tanzania's ruling party approved 238 candidates who contested 156 legislative seats.

Zambia's United National Independence party nominated 532, 766, and 790 candidates to contest 125 seats in the general elections of 1973, 1978, and 1983, respectively. The large numbers of nominees, however, were not matched by voter turnout, which averaged less than 40 percent. Those who went to the polls unseated nearly 50 percent of incumbents in each election.[26] The combination of low turnout and high votes against incumbents suggested that Zambians were less than satisfied with the system. But results of the 1988 election seemed to belie this: More than 50 percent of the electorate cast ballots, and President Kaunda was reelected by a resounding 95.5-percent "yes" vote, a much higher approval rating than in the previous elections.

In Sierra Leone the last legislative election was held in 1985. The aptly named All People's party approved 335 candidates to contest 105 elective seats. The party typically offers at least three contestants for each seat, a common practice among one-party states in sub-Saharan Africa. Thus one-party systems are more democratic than they may at first appear to Western observers.

Why is single-party polyarchy more popular in sub-Saharan Africa than multiparty democracy, which is prevalent in Western Europe? First, mindful of the recent colonial past, Africans have sought to avoid imitating European political institutions, preferring instead to develop their own models and methods of governing. Second, the fragmentation of many African states that resulted from the drawing of political boundaries by European colonial powers made it necessary to mitigate conflict and unify the nation. Obviously, this task is complicated by the existence of competing parties, which tend to perpetuate and institutionalize society's divisions. Third, a single "umbrella party" that encompasses a variety of interests may be more appropriate for the level of development in many sub-Saharan states; a multiparty system places a premium on compromises and coalitions—a luxury that many developing countries can ill afford.

The Authoritarian Spectrum

Authoritarian regimes may be military or civilian in character, and they may be autocratic (rule by one) or oligarchic (rule by a few). In sub-Saharan Africa, the most common forms of authoritarianism are civilian oligarchies and military praetorian regimes, to use Potholm's terminology. These terms will be defined below, but first some words of caution are in order.

In the first place, it is often difficult to distinguish between a single-party polyarchy and an authoritarian regime. For example, authoritarian regimes may have political parties, and they may hold elections. The key is not whether parties and elections are present but whether they are politically meaningful. If parties are merely symbolic and elections are nothing more than rituals, there is every likelihood that the political system which sponsors them is authoritarian.

Second, not all authoritarian regimes are equally brutal and repressive, although many certainly are both. Terms such as "benevolent dictator" and "enlightened despotism" suggest what Aristotle taught long ago: Monarchs (or their nonhereditary counterparts) *may* be high-minded and humane. But students of history cannot help but note that instances of enlightened despotism are rare. As Lord Acton observed long ago, "Power tends to corrupt and absolute power corrupts absolutely.'' The history of the twentieth century offers little to contradict this assertion.

Third, in the African context it is important to note that some authoritarian regimes claim to be transitional, while others are well entrenched and more-or-less permanent. The former, often called ''provisional'' governments, are likely to follow a military coup.

Entrenched Authoritarian Regimes Zaire, Somalia, Malawi, Guinea, and Côte d'Ivoire are examples of authoritarian government in Africa. Authoritarian traits, as Potholm suggested, include the absence of electoral competition, repression of civil liberties, intolerance for dissent, and arbitrary rule. These regimes have remained relatively unchanged for a quarter-century or longer under the same leader. As the leaders reach old age, it becomes appropriate to describe their regimes as gerontocracies (rule by the aged)—in fact, Potholm called them ''gerontocratic authoritarianism.''

Authoritarian rulers in Africa come to power in various ways: by rising through the ranks a step at a time, by a military coup, or by promotion from the traditional hierarchy. Once in power, they employ age-old techniques of governing; they enforce compliance by means of accommodation, coercion, and cooptation of critical elites and the masses. Accommodation may involve the use of government programs to revive indigenous cultures and traditional values, thus neutralizing popular aspirations for liberalization and modernization. Symbols of nationalism are exploited to negate any social or political ideas that might challenge the policies of the rulers. President Mobutu Sese Seko of Zaire, for example, changed the Belgian Congo to Zaire, Leopoldville to Kinshasa, and other European names to Zairean names; he also changed his own name (from Joseph D. Mobutu) and urged his people to do likewise. Recalling the evils of colonialism is a common device used by such leaders to instill patriotism.

Elections are manipulated and modified in ways designed to mollify the people without giving them a real voice. Thus, Zaire, Somalia, and Malawi have periodic elections, but the elections are tainted; for example, mandatory voting is likely to involve an element of coercion. The last time President Mohamed Siad Barre stood for reelection in Somalia (1986), he received a 99.9-percent ''yes'' vote. Similarly, President Félix Houphouët-Boigny received 100-percent approval in his 1988 reelection in Côte d'Ivoire. When President Mobutu was reelected in 1984 (his present term runs through 1991), he was approved by 99.6 percent of the votes. For all practical purposes, Hastings Kamuzu Banda of Malawi, Mobutu of Zaire, and Houphouët-Boigny of Côte d'Ivoire are presidents for life.

The practice of cooptation is entwined with carrot-and-stick methods in a strategy of divide and rule. The ruler's cabinet is frequently reshuffled, and various privileges and perquisites are give to bureaucratic functionaries in the civil service and armed forces and to business and economic elites, so that their long-term interests rest with the status quo. To the extent that longevity and continuity have resulted, the leaders develop an intricate network of patron–client relationships in a type of authoritarianism that may be called either "personalistic" or "gerontocratic." In time, the authoritarian rule of a single strongman and his cronies can become self-legitimizing; in effect, the state becomes the patrimony of an autocratic or oligarchic leadership. One danger is that as the leader ages the system can become increasingly ossified—the presidents of Malawi, Somalia, and Côte d'Ivoire are now in their eighties.

Another danger in personalistic authoritarian regimes, including gerontocracies, arises from the absence of orderly procedures for succession. Who will replace the existing leader, and how? Such questions are especially important in a political system that concentrates power and authority in the hands of a single individual. The political climate can become heavy with uncertainty, especially if the leader is very old, becomes ill, or is the target of an assassination attempt. At such times the possibility of a succession crisis looms large, and political stability may give way to chaos and confusion.

An illustration or two may help make the point. Sékou Touré ruled Guinea for twenty-six years (1958–1984), and his regime was widely regarded as harshly authoritarian. He died without making any provision for succession. (Often personalistic rulers are reluctant to name an heir-apparent for fear of creating a rival.) His death left a power vacuum that has since been filled by the military. To cite another example, Emperor Haile Selassie of Ethiopia was dethroned after forty years of authoritarian rule; his ouster was followed by a bloody revolution. If history is any guide, Malawi, Côte d'Ivoire, and Somalia may be facing similar succession crises.

Provisional Authoritarian Regimes   Provisional regimes are self-consciously transitional and usually look ahead to a time when they will give way to either one-party or multiparty constitutional government. Such regimes are usually run by the military because, typically, the military has staged a coup. In sub-Saharan Africa the military almost always proclaims its goal to be corrective—to rescue the nation from economic malaise or mismanagement, to defeat the forces of subversion or national disintegration, or to stamp out official graft and corruption. Even the names these provisional regimes give themselves are instructive: the Committee for National Redemption (Burundi), the Provisional National Defense Council (Ghana), the National Resistance Movement (Uganda), and the (now dissolved) Provisional Military Administrative Council (Ethiopia).

At first military juntas almost always claim to be temporary. Although some provisional military regimes *have* kept faith and returned the government to civilian control, many others have not. Since independence in Ghana, Nigeria, Sudan, and Uganda, military takeovers have occurred repeatedly. In Ghana, for example, Flight Lieutenant Jerry Rawlings led a successful coup in 1979. (The fact that a mere lieutenant could overthrow a government suggests that political life in some parts of sub-Saharan Africa is capricious and that political authority is precarious. Any ruler with true legitimacy cannot be cast aside so easily. Rawlings returned the government to civilian rule in 1980, warning that the military would step in again if the politicians failed to govern effectively. In 1981, alleging corruption and mismanagement, Rawlings led a second coup, returning the country to military rule. He has remained in power as of this writing.

Structures and Functions of Government

Governmental process basically involves the formulation, implementation, and adjudication of rules. These functions correspond roughly to the legislative, executive, and judicial branches of government. No modern polity can operate well without such a division of labor. And although societies of sub-Saharan Africa are still engaged in political development, they already display many institutional elements, including structural differentiation and functional specialization, that are associated with modern political systems.

Lawmaking and Legislatures

Within the countries discussed in this chapter the legislatures have several similarities. First, most sub-Saharan political systems, including authoritarian regimes, have a formal legislative body variously called the "Parliament," "constituent assembly," or "national assembly." In Ethiopia colonial language permeated least, and the legislature is called the Shengo.

Election to the legislature carries great prestige both for the members themselves and for their families and friends. One reason may be that African legislators typically do not have to compete with lobbyists for the government's attention. Lacking organized interest groups, which are so prevalent in the West, legislators in Africa often carry a greater share of responsibility not only for lawmaking but also for focusing on special-interest issues, articulating them, and fashioning the various demands into coherent policy. Indeed, one theory argues that the prevalence of single-party polyarchy or authoritarian regimes in Africa reflects distaste for interest-group politics, which many Africans view as alien and divisive. In African legislatures issues tend to be debated on their merits, and relatively little attention is paid to special interests.

Legislatures in sub-Saharan Africa tend to be unicameral. (Zimbabwe is an exception.) The routes to the legislature vary, but the main avenue continues to be direct appointment by the chief executive. Sometimes elected members can appoint additional members to represent professional organizations, traditional chiefs, and trade associations. Such appointed legislators have earned recognition in their field or have demonstrated support for the ruling party. Some legislatures include consultative chiefs as ex officio members, as in Botswana, Sierra Leone, and Zambia.

As elaborate as legislative debates often are, the independence of the legislature is diminished by constitutional advantages given to the chief executive, who can veto legislation, dissolve the parliament, and appoint a number of legislative members who are then in his debt. In Zaire, President Mobutu can bypass the legislative assembly altogether, making laws by personal fiat or in consultation with his ministerial council.

The Chief Executive

In their executive branches these political systems reveal one of the ambivalences of the triple heritage discussed earlier: The head of state is adorned with traditional powers but holds a title typically found in modern Western systems. Thus the chief executive usually has the title of president but does not have presidential constraints. In fact, presidents in sub-Saharan Africa often have powers that befit an emperor.

Generally speaking, the chief executive is both head of state and head of government; executive powers and duties are defined broadly and often vaguely. The ambiguities are deliberate and are used to stretch presidential prerogatives as far as necessary. The president is always male and is expected to be fatherly, personable, and charismatic. When these expectations are met, the national leader commands popular respect and even adulation; often he will be given lofty titles bespeaking awe and deference. For example, Premier Nkrumah of Ghana was called *Osagyefu* ("Savior"), President Kenyatta of Kenya was addressed as *Mzee* ("Wiseman"), and former President Nyerere of Tanzania is revered as *Mwalimu* ("Teacher"). The titles engender both intimacy and legitimacy; at the same time, however, the constitutions of many countries give leaders nearly absolute power.

Compared with American presidents, African chief executives are not constrained by checks and balances or separation of powers. Not only do many African chief executives have the power to appoint members of the legislature (an unthinkable breach of the separation of powers in the United States), but they also can dissolve the parliament without risk of impeachment or electoral defeat.

Chief executives in sub-Saharan Africa are chosen in several ways. In Botswana, Kenya, and Zimbabwe the president is elected by the legislature. In Senegal and Gambia the people directly elect the president by secret ballot from a slate of candidates nominated by competing parties. In some one-party systems a single candidate is nominated by the party congress and, as noted earlier, the people simply cast a "yes" or "no" vote. The third method is military intervention followed by the establishment of a provisional or caretaker government (which, as we have seen, has a way of becoming permanent). When the military intervenes, the leader of the coup usually becomes the "acting" president.

The terms of office range from five years in most sub-Saharan countries to seven years in a few. The president of Zimbabwe serves a six-year term; the presidents of Gabon, Sierra Leone, and Zaire serve seven years and then must get their popular mandate renewed. None of the countries has a constitutional limitation on the number of consecutive terms that the president or members of parliament may serve.

In Africa's single-party states the president heads the party, and his renomination and reelection are virtually guaranteed. President Kenyatta of Kenya died in office at the age of 88. A geriatric President Senghor of Senegal resigned in 1980 for reasons of advanced age and failing health. President Julius Nyerere of Tanzania is the rare case of a one-party president who departed from office with grace and style: In 1985 he stepped down because, he said, it was time to inject new dynamism into the political system. (Nonetheless, he retains the powerful position of party chairman.)

Case Studies: Ethiopia, Kenya, Nigeria, Botswana, and South Africa

The following discussion begins with Ethiopia, a Marxist military dictatorship that appears to be in transition between a traditional authoritarian monarchy and a single-party political system. Next we look at Kenya, a single-party polyarchy; then at Nigeria, in transition between a military dictatorship and a Western-type parliamentary democracy; followed by Botswana, one of the region's only authentic constitutional democracies. Finally we examine South Africa, where the region's only surviving white-minority regime presents a dual system: democracy for the white minority and tyranny for the black majority.

Ethiopia

Ethiopia's recent political history begins with the overthrow of Emperor Haile Selassie in 1974. The years before the coup were marked by growing unrest in the form of labor strikes, student demonstrations, and rumors among military officers and bureaucrats. Some of Selassie's detractors sought political change, but most were motivated by bread-and-butter issues—deteriorating economic conditions that brought sharply escalating prices and scarcity of consumer goods. The situation was the worst for people living in Tigre and Wollo provinces in the north. In 1973–1974 a severe drought struck northern Ethiopia; 3 million people were affected, and some 400,000 died of starvation. News of the famine shocked the world. Amid press reports of an official cover-up, critics charged massive bureaucratic ineptitude.

The government's inattention to warning signs of drought and the bureaucracy's failure to respond in a timely manner fueled a popular uprising in 1974. Militant student and labor groups, who felt vindicated in their long-standing opposition to the government, staged protests as public confidence in the imperial rule plunged to a new low. In this radicalized and revolutionary atmosphere, the old order crumbled and fell. What began as a popular revolt ended in a military coup.

The military moved onto center stage gradually, almost imperceptibly. Officers at first prefaced their demands for salary raises and perquisites with pledges of allegiance to the emperor. The government placated the officers, legalized the labor unions, and temporized with the students. Two commissions were formed—one for national security and another to investigate official corruption.

The emergence of the military as the revolutionary vanguard took Ethiopia's intellectuals and other elites by surprise. The armed forces had never been in the forefront of opposition to imperial rule; indeed, the officers were traditionally drawn from elites who were auxiliaries of the ruling class.[27] In the early stages of the revolution, the populace associated the military with the political hierarchy. Apparently, some officers, particularly younger ones, became caught up in the groundswell as students, teachers, and workers took to the streets.

In mid-1974 each division of the Ethiopian army sent three representatives to the capital, Addis Ababa, to discuss the future of the country. This led to the formation of the Provisional Military Advisory Council (PMAC), known in Amharic as the *Derg* (''committee'').[28] From this point forward the army assumed leadership of the revolution; in fact, the Derg was a military junta in which a junior officer, Major Mengistu Haile Mariam, played a prominent role. Firmly in command, the junta deposed Haile Selassie on September 12, 1974.

In November the Derg arrested sixty top government officials. Later that month a shakeup occurred within the military junta, and the titular head, General Aman Andom, was reportedly killed in a shootout while resisting arrest. The internal power struggle continued for several years before Colonel Mengistu—having dispatched two more rivals within the leadership—became the undisputed strongman in late 1977. (By this time Mengistu had promoted himself from major to colonel.)

From 1974 to 1979 there was internal opposition to the military junta. Various groups in society claimed the right to direct the revolution. Besides the ruling PMAC, the two principal civilian groups were the Peoples' Revolutionary party (EPRP) and the All-Ethiopian Peoples' Socialist Movement (MEISON).[29] The EPRP and MEISON gained wide support among intellectuals, workers, and peasants representing major ethnic groups. Both entities were Marxist-Leninist, and both represented a cross-section of the population. But the groups differed on strategy and tactics: The EPRP advocated and waged armed struggle against the PMAC and its civilian sympathizers, whereas MEISON sought to make peace with the PMAC and to persuade military leaders to relinquish power. The military junta used MEISON to help it wipe out the EPRP, then crushed MEISON itself. With MEISON gone, the last civilian opposition vanished or went underground.

During its turbulent first years in power the Derg established a reputation as one of the most repressive regimes in the Third World.[30] When troubles mounted—violent uprisings, blood coups, war with Somalia—and relations with the West deteriorated, Mengistu turned to the Soviet Union for economic and military aid. Moscow, in turn, arranged to have Cuban troops airlifted to Ethiopia to prop up Mengistu's embattled regime. At this point Ethiopia faced an astonishing array of internal and external challenges. Besides the urban opposition just mentioned, there were secessionist movements in Eritrea and in Tigre; and in 1977 Ethiopia fought a war with Somalia in the Ogaden, the huge eastern region of Ethiopia populated mainly by Somalis and thus claimed by Somalia.

In 1979 the PMAC created the Commission to Organize a Worker's Party of Ethiopia (COWPE). For Mengistu the Commission had two advantages: It bought time by temporarily quieting popular demands for a political party and a return to civilian rule, and it gave the Derg control over the formation and precise character of the new party. In 1986 the Commission finally unveiled its plan for a one-party socialist state. The new party was named the Workers Party of Ethiopia (WPE), and the new state became the People's Democratic Republic of Ethiopia.

Early in 1987 a national referendum was held regarding a new constitution. The government claimed a turnout of 96 percent, and it was no surprise that 81 percent voted "yes"—the alternative was a continuation of Mengistu's personal dictatorship. It also seems likely that many voters had been intimidated by a decade of political repression.

The Shengo, an 835-member national legislature, was seated on September 9, 1987, and the PMAC was formally dissolved. The legislature's first acts were to elevate Colonel Mengistu to the presidency and to approve his nominees for the Council of State and the Council of Ministers. Thirteen years after Emperor Haile Selassie was deposed, Ethiopia had finally gotten a constitution. Beneath the trappings of civilian rule, however, the "new" government bore striking resemblances to the old, and Ethiopia's one-party state was patterned after the Soviet model rather than on any African model. If Mengistu had gone looking for a more pluralistic one-party system, he could have found one right next door, in Kenya.

Kenya

President Jomo Kenyatta had smooth sailing for a short period following independence in 1963, but soon the KANU coalition (described in Chapter 16) began to come unglued. Oginga Odinga and other leaders to the left of Kenyatta became disenchanged with his attempt to blend capitalist and socialist policies. This ideological tension radiated down to the rank and file in KANU. Kenyatta and Odinga had a dramatic falling out. Odinga, a vice-president of KANU, became a shrill critic of the party's economic programs, which, he charged, pandered to the rich. Kenyatta retaliated by abolishing the position of vice-president, hoping to isolate Odinga or at least to neutralize him within the party.

Odinga's response was to organize a rival political party, the Kenyan People's Union (KPU), which rendered Kenya a two-party state once again. In the 1966 elections Odinga's party won 30 out of 158 seats in the legislature. Thereafter, Odinga and the KPU became increasingly strident in their opposition to Kenyatta's policies. The assassination of Mboya in 1969 precipitated an outbreak of ethnic violence. Kenyatta, blaming the KPU, ordered Odinga and his disciples jailed. He then banned Odinga's KPU party. Kenyatta subsequently persuaded some KPU members to return to KANU and contest the 1974 election.

It now became clear that occasional acts of repression were merely tactical; Kenyatta's strategy was to coopt the opposition. In retrospect the 1974 election appears to have been a turning point. Kenya became a one-party polyarchy, as many former KPU leaders accepted the offer of "amnesty" and returned to KANU to resume their careers in public service. Even Odinga, after several stints in prison, rejoined KANU as a life member in 1980.

Given Kenya's ethnic diversity, the switch to a single-party arrangement had a major impact on internal politics. Kenyatta had surmounted the KPU challenge by skillfully using the carrot and stick and by merging the two chambers of parliament into a single chamber, which facilitated presidential control. To diffuse ethnic tensions, Kenyatta popularized his "unity in freedom" (*harambee-uhuru*) slogan; chose as his vice-president Daniel arap Moi (from one of Kenya's ethnic minorities, the Kelenjins); and championed a nonethnic African language, Swahili, as the official tongue. Swahili is the lingua franca of Africa; as such it is the logical choice for use as an official, national language in a multiethnic country such as Kenya.

After 1970 KANU was the only functioning political party in Kenya. Despite persistent charges of corruption and abuses of power by the regime, Kenya under Kenyatta's one-party system achieved a high degree of political stability, which was accompanied by steady economic growth. In 1982 a constitutional amendment officially made Kenya a single-party system.

When Kenyatta died in 1978, at age 88, he was peacefully succeeded by Vice-President Daniel arap Moi, in accordance with the Constitution, which calls for a new election after a ninety-day waiting period. Playing on Kenyans' reverence for Kenyatta, Moi capsulized his campaign in a single Swahili word, *nyayo* ("footsteps"), a clever way of promising to follow Kenyatta's course faithfully. He underscored this continuity by naming a vice-president from Kenyatta's Kikuyu ethnic group.[31]

The orderly transition from Kenyatta to Moi meant that Kenya's one-party polyarchy had survived a major test. Although Kenya encountered serious political and economic problems in the 1980s, its democratic processes, limited though they are, have survived. Elections continue to offer the voters choices—not between parties but among several candidates. Elections in 1983 and 1988, for example, had as many as 900 candidates competing for 158 seats in the National Assembly. Although incumbents are still frequently defeated, the number of ousted incumbents has been steadily declining, which raises concerns that Moi has rigged elections or intimidated voters.

Nigeria

Nigeria represents the military variant of African authoritarianism. But also clearly present in Nigerian politics is a tendency toward federal democratic republicanism, not unlike that found in the United States.

Since gaining independence from Britain in 1960, Nigeria has oscillated between civilian and military rule. Civilians were in charge for a total of ten years; from 1960 to 1966 and from 1979 to 1984. For the other twenty years, five military regimes have ruled. Thus Nigeria has experienced two years of military rule for every year of civilian rule.

The civilian regimes came to power by means of ballots, while the military regimes assumed power by using bullets (or threatening to do so). Military coups have been a fact of political life in Nigeria. Though regime changes have been frequent and unscheduled, their avowed objectives have been remarkably constant: to eliminate official corruption, foster good government, and improve the quality of life; and to establish a pluralistic political order based on the consent of the governed. It is fair to say, however, that these lofty aims have so far eluded Nigeria.

The First and Second Republics   The first republic was short-lived, lasting only from 1960 to 1966, when it was toppled by a military coup led by Colonel Yakubu Gowon (who, in turn, was ousted in 1975 for failing to curb corruption and restore civilian rule). No sooner had the military government seized power than a crisis arose that imperiled the very survival of Nigeria as a nation-state.

From 1967 to 1970 Nigeria was plunged into civil war when the Eastern Region (more commonly known as Biafra) seceded. The war pitted the Ibos (the majority population in Biafra) against the politically dominant Yoruba. With casualties exceeding 1 million—many Biafrans starved to death despite international relief efforts—the secessionists capitulated in January 1970. To the victors' credit, the Ibos quickly reintegrated into national life, but distrust among the regions persists.

The second republic came into existence in 1979, when General Olasegun Obasanjo, who took charge after the 1975 coup, kept his promise to restore civilian rule. Following national elections General Obasanjo returned power to the victors—a new president and parliament—in accordance with a highly acclaimed democratic constitution. The election itself was vigorously contested by several national parties, including the Unity Party of Nigeria (UPN), Peoples' Redemption party (PRP), Greater Nigerian Peoples' party (GNNP), and the National Party of Nigeria (NPN).

The NPN candidate, Shehu Shagari, narrowly won the initial presidential contest to become the first and last president of the brief second republic (1979–1984). No sooner had Shagari been reelected than charges of economic mismanagement and corruption were leveled against his government. In a now-familiar pattern, Shagari was ousted by the military, and many of his cabinet members were put on trial and barred from public life. Nigeria once again reverted to military rule.

The Military Regimes   In Nigeria as elsewhere, the armed forces intervene, promising to restore public confidence in government, eradicate corruption and mismanagement, and improve living standards. In addition, they typically promise to restore civilian rule, and they give lip service to democracy and human rights even while violating them.[32] Like Gowon and Obasanjo before him, the present head of Nigeria's government, General Ibrahim Babangida, has pledged to reinstitute civilian rule and free elections under a new constitution by 1992. But Nigeria's coup-prone politics of the past caution against undue optimism. Perhaps the safest bet is that Nigeria will continue to be in transition for the indefinite future, a nation in search of a viable political system that can satisfy the aspirations of the Nigerian people for a stable and responsive government.

In the meantime Nigeria's military rulers will continue to wear two hats as soldier-politicians. Instead of a legislative assembly to debate policy and pass laws, there exists a Supreme Military Council to issue edicts and proclamations. Thus, as the search for a political model continues, the promised 1992 national election remains Nigeria's best hope for a third chance at civilian democratic self-rule.

Botswana

Botswana is an anomaly in many ways. Nearly the size of Texas, it has a miniscule population of 1.2 million, with a population density of about 5 per square mile. The people are mainly ethnic Tswanas, and the national language is Setswana (English is the official language). Only a minority of the people have adopted a foreign religion; more than half hold to indigenous beliefs. Located in southern Africa, Botswana is landlocked. Its main industry is tourism. The Kalahari Desert spreads over the southwest. Only 2 percent of the land is arable, but 70 percent of the population depends on agriculture for its livelihood. Nearly 90 percent of Botswana's imports come from neighboring South Africa, with which it is linked in a customs union; most of its exports—consisting mainly of live cattle, meat, and such minerals as coal, copper, nickel, and diamonds—go to Western Europe and the United States.

Unlike many African nations Botswana does not have a problem with over-population. Its tiny economy has grown at a respectable rate of 8 to 9 percent annually, and its per capita GNP in the mid-1980s was $880—modest enough, but higher than most in the region. It has been politically stable, no doubt reflecting its ethnic homogeneity, relative isolation, and lack of strategic importance.

Formerly a British colony, Botswana became fully independent in 1966. It is democratically governed, Western oriented, and greatly influenced by South Africa. Independence and multiparty democracy were attained relatively smoothly in Botswana. From 1885 to 1966 Bechuanaland (now Botswana) was a British protectorate. In 1958 the British permitted the formation of legislative councils, which consisted of thirty members: ten elected whites, ten colonial officers, and ten Botswanans, including the man who later became the first president—Sir Seretse Khama.

Seretse Khama was the son of a traditional chief of an ethnic group known as the Bamangwato; he was the first in line to succeed his father when he was sent to study in England. Meanwhile, his uncle, Tshekedi Khama, was regent of the chief-dom.[33] But Seretse Khama returned home in 1948 married to a white British woman named Ruth Williams, which put his hereditary claim and political acceptability into question. His regent uncle objected to the marriage as a breach of custom, and the British government as well as the white regimes in Rhodesia (now Zimbabwe) and South Africa opposed the marriage because of its political implications.

Although Khama's marriage was a major hurdle, in the final analysis it did not prevent him from a distinguished political career. Yet he had to overcome obstacles both in Botswana and in England. For example, the British arranged a visit to England by Khama in 1950, and then they barred him from returning to

Botswana until 1956. But Khama eventually did return, and in 1958—still married to Ruth Williams—he was elected to the Legislative Council.

With just two years of experience in the Legislative Council, in 1960 Botswanans formed their own Botswanan People's party (BPP), facing not only the issue of independence but also a controversy over which group of South African Black Nationalists to support (whether to take the path of accommodation or militant nationalism). When the BPP opted for accommodation and supported the multiracial program of the African National Congress (ANC), the militant faction of the BPP decided to back the more radical Pan-African Congress. This rift led disenchanted BPP members to form a second party, the Botswana Independence party (BIP). It was in this climate that Seretse Khama seized the opportunity to form a new, moderate party, the Botswana Democratic party (BDP).

In preparation for Botswana's independence an election was held in 1965 to decide which party—BPP, BIP, or BDP—would be entrusted to govern the new nation. The outcome was a resounding victory for Khama's BDP, which won twenty-eight of thirty-one seats. Since Botswana's new Constitution called for a British-style parliamentary democracy, Khama became the first prime minister.

Shortly thereafter, another party, the Botswana National Front (BNF), was created when one hereditary chief withdrew from the BDP. Led by Bathoen II, chief of the Bangwaketse, this party is Marxist and advocates radical redistribution of wealth. The BNF is now one of four opposition parties in Botswana and has won several seats during each of the last three parliamentary elections—four out of thirty-four seats most recently. No other opposition party can claim equal success.

Botswana has been a model republic since its inception in 1966. Free elections, competitive parties, open debates, respect for civil liberties, and political stability all combine to make the country an island of democracy in a sea of authoritarianism. In the late 1980s one needed only to contrast the political calm in Botswana with the turmoil in the surrounding countries of southern Africa to appreciate Botswana's achievement.[34]

Why has Botswana succeeded where the others have failed? First, Botswana enjoys a high level of ethnic and sociocultural homogeneity. Nearly 95 percent of Botswana's people are ethnic Tswanas; over half practice indigenous religions; and up to 80 percent speak Setswana. Second, Botswana's wealth of diamonds and copper provides the wherewithal for economic development and foreign trade. Third, the nation's homogeneity helps minimize internal tensions, while geographic and demographic constraints limit external ambition. Finally, Botswana's preoccupation with South Africa helps induce political cohesion. Botswanans fear that their country is too small and too near the storm centers of regional conflict—a fear that is strongly reinforced by South Africa's periodic raids on Botswanan territory.

South Africa

South Africa is synonymous with apartheid. An Afrikaans word, *apartheid* simply means "apartness," and it refers to the legally required, forced separation of racial communities in the Republic of South Africa. One way to understand the apartheid system is to look at the legal structure that supports it. In all, some 350 laws have been passed to implement apartheid. Here are a few of the most important ones:

- Land Act (1913): Prohibits Africans from acquiring land outside their native reserves
- Mines and Works Amendment Act (1926) (also known as "Color Bar" Act): Prohibits Africans from skilled work in the mines
- Group Areas Act (1950): Outlaws racially mixed residential areas; specifies which races live where
- Native Building Workers' Act (1951): Extends the earlier mining color bar to skilled construction trades
- Natives Act (1952): Requires all Africans over 16 to carry a passbook specifying where they may live and work
- Native Laws Amendment Act (1952): Prohibits most Africans from remaining in urban areas for more than 72 hours
- Separate Amenities Act (1953): Segregated virtually all public transportation, facilities, and accommodations, including beaches (led to "Whites Only" signs that have now disappeared)
- Riotous Assemblies Act (1956): Outlaws protest gatherings
- Separate Universities Act (1959): Prohibits nonwhites from most universities except by special permission
- General Law Amendment Act (1963): Lets police hold anyone considered suspicious for renewable 90-day periods (later reduced to renewable 14-day periods) without trial or legal recourse
- Bantu Homelands Citizenship Act (1970): Makes all Africans citizens of their tribal homelands (*bantustans*) and deprives them of South African citizenship (the apogee of apartheid)

As the forgoing list suggests, apartheid has evolved through a steady accretion of laws and amendments. The cumulative effect is to create a comprehensive and highly institutionalized system of racial discrimination.

The popular usage of apartheid and its elevation to a nationalist ideology for the dominant Afrikaners dates back to the campaign and election of 1948, when the present Nationalist party came to power. The main agenda in that early political campaign was to find a workable solution for the ethnic and race issues that had bedeviled South Africa since the founding of the Union in 1910. Having won the election, the Nationalist party sought to fulfill its campaign pledge to keep the races separated. To this end, the new government designed a set of social policies based on the permanent separation of whites, blacks, coloreds, and Indians. The "homelands"—areas reserved for different black ethnic groups—were part of this policy. The overriding purpose was to exclude all nonwhites from positions of power and privilege.

In reality, South African has a dual system of government, complete with two separate sets of rules. For the whites—Afrikaners and British—the system functions as a constitutional democracy. Historically, free elections (for whites only) were contested by multiple parties, and voters cast secret ballots for the candidates of their choice. From 1910 to 1984 the British "Westminster model" operated: Following national elections the majority party in the all-white House of Assembly chose a prime minister (in practice, the leader of the white majority party), who then formed a government.

In 1984 South Africa instituted a new constitution, which had been approved by two-thirds of the electorate (still whites only) in a national referendum the previous year. The Constitution provided for a new three-chambered Parliament: the House of Assembly (whites, 178 seats); the House of Representatives (coloreds, 85 seats); and the House of Delegates (Indians, 45 seats). Thus the legislature now includes colored and Indian representatives, but it continues to exclude the black majority. Furthermore, the white minority remains firmly in control: The three houses meet separately, and the colored and Indian chambers cannot override the white chamber.

Perhaps more significant is the adoption of a presidential mode to replace the traditional parliamentary model. The president is elected indirectly by the Electoral College consisting of the three chambers of Parliament. Under the new system the president can dissolve Parliament on any number of grounds. In the event of a parliamentary deadlock—a definite possibility under the new tricameral configuration—he can rule in consultation with the President's Council, a purely advisory body that he appoints. In a crisis the president can proclaim martial law. So broad are the president's powers that some critics view the new system as a potential dictatorship.

Despite the appearance of change, apartheid and white minority rule in South Africa remained largely intact during the 1980s. But the decade also brought growing domestic and foreign pressures on the government of President Botha. It was a sign of the times that an opinion poll taken in South Africa in 1986 showed nearly three-fourths of whites and a solid majority of blacks believed apartheid would be abolished within ten years.[35]

In 1989 President Botha stepped down and was replaced by F. W. de Klerk, who vowed to end apartheid. In early 1990 de Klerk promised to allow peaceful protests, and in February he freed Nelson Mandela, who had been imprisoned since the 1960s for his antiapartheid activities as a member of the African National Congress. Mandela's release was a symbolic gesture designed to show de Klerk's earnest intent to bring about peaceful accommodation between whites and blacks and to set the stage for negotiations. In March 1990 de Klerk announced that he would enter into talks with leaders of the African National Congress.

CONCLUSION

Authoritarian rule is common throughout sub-Saharan Africa, but not all governments of the region are equally repressive. Ethiopia under Mengistu is one of the worst from the standpoint of human rights violations; Kenya was one of the best under Kenyatta, but there are persistent reports of political persecution by Kenyatta's successors. In Nigeria, promises of democracy by the military rulers have not been fulfilled. In general, the governments of sub-Saharan Africa, whether civilian or military, have not been efficient or effective. Is there hope for Black Africa? This question is the focus of Chapter 18.

STUDY QUESTIONS

1. What factors influenced the early economic development of African countries? To what extent do these factors remain in force today?
2. Why is one-party polyarchy more common in sub-Saharan Africa than multiparty systems like those in Europe?
3. Comparing Ethiopia, Nigeria, and Kenya, where would you most want to live if you happened to have political ambitions? Where would you least want to live? Why?
4. What is apartheid? How has it changed in recent years? Do you think it is on the road to extinction?

SUGGESTED READINGS

Baker, Pauline. "South Africa on the Move," *Current History*, May 1990.

Clapham, Christoper S. *Transformation and Continuity in Revolutionary Ethiopia*. Cambridge: Cambridge University, 1988.

Falola, Toyin, and Julius Ihonvbere. *The Rise and Fall of Nigeria's Second Republic: 1979–1984*. London: Zed, 1985.

Hull, Richard W. "United States Policy in Southern Africa," *Current History*, May 1990.

Mazrui, Ali, and Michael Tidy. *Nationalism and New States in Africa*. London: Heinemann, 1984.

Miller, Norman N. *Kenya: The Quest for Prosperity*. Boulder, Colo.: Westview, 1984.

Parker, Frank J. *South Africa: Lost Opportunities*. Lexington, Mass.: Lexington, 1984.

Potholm, Christian. *The Theory and Practice of African Politics*. New York: University Press of America, 1985.

St. Jorre, John. *A House Divided: South Africa's Uncertain Future*. Washington, D.C.: Carnegie Endowment for International Peace, 1977.

Tangri, Roger. *Politics in Sub-Saharan Africa*. London: Heinemann, 1985.

Wubneh, Mulatu, and Yohannis Abate. *Ethiopia: Transition and Development in the Horn of Africa*. Boulder, Colo.: Westview, 1988.

Zartman, William I., ed. *The Political Economy of Nigeria*. New York: Praeger, 1983.

NOTES

[1] C.B. Wadstrom, *An Essay on Colonialization* (London: Darton and Harvey, 1794), pp. 9–10.

[2] Examples of such resistance during the early years of this century include the Asante rebellion in the Gold Coast; the Baoule and Samori rebellion in the Ivory Coast, 1901–1917; and the Maji-Maji rebellion in German East Africa; see Ali Masrui and Michael Tidy, *Nationalism and New States in Africa* (London: Heinemann, 1984), pp. 116–132.

[3] Ibid., pp. 13–15.

[4] Christian Potholm, *The Theory and Practice of African Politics* (New York: University Press of America, 1985), pp. 34–36.

[5] Ali Mazrui, *Towards a Pax Africana: A Study of Ideology and Ambition* (Chicago: University of Chicago, 1967), pp. 74–75.

[6] Kwame Nkrumah, *Neo-Colonialism—the Last Stage of Imperialism* (New York: International, 1966), pp. 239–259.

[7] See Manning Marable, *W. E. B. Dubois, Black Radical Democrat* (Boston: Twayne, 1986), pp. 99–120; see also Mazrui and Tidy, op. cit., pp. xii–xvi.

[8] Basil Davidson, *Africa: History of a Continent* (New York: Macmillan, 1972), pp. 294–297.

[9] Mazrui and Tidy, op. cit., pp. 21–23.

[10] Amadu Sesay, et al., *The OAU After Twenty-Five Years* (Boulder, Colo.: Westview, 1984), pp. 1–13, Chap. 3.

[11] Roger Tangri, *Politics in Sub-Saharan Africa* (London: Heinemann, 1985), pp. 17–25.

[12] *African Recovery*, May 25, 1988.

[13] Mazrui and Tidy, op. cit., pp. 373–374.

[14] See especially William Friedland and Carl G. Rosenberg, Jr., eds., *African Socialism* (Stanford, Calif.: Stanford University, 1964) pp. 250–258; and Tom Mboya, *Freedom and After* (Boston: Little, Brown, 1963), pp. 164–178.

[15] Kwame Nkrumah, *Consciencism* (London: Heinemann, 1966), p. 70.

[16] Wilford Curtey and Martin Kilson, eds., *Independent Africa: A Reader* (New York: Random House, 1979), pp. 179–192.

[17] Clyde R. Ingle, *From Village to State in Tanzania: The Politics of Rural Development* (Ithaca, N.Y.: Cornell University, 1972), p. 99.

[18] J. K. Nyerere, *Uhuru Na Moja: Freedom and Unity* (New York: Oxford, 1973), p. 247.

[19] Ibid., p. 232.

[20] Quoted in Friedland and Rosenberg, op. cit., p. 251.

[21] Colin Morris, *A Humanist in Africa (Letters to Olin Morris from Kenneth Kaunda)* (New York: Abingdon, 1966), p. 19.

[22] Colin Legum, ed., *Independence and Beyond: A Collection of Speeches by Kenneth Kaunda* (London: Nelson, 1966), pp. 18–19.

[23] Morris, op. cit., p. 63.

[24] Ali Mazrui, *The African Condition: A Political Diagnosis* (London: Cambridge University, 1980), p. 92.

[25] Potholm, op. cit., especially Chaps. 5 and 6.

[26] C. Chikulo Bornwell, "The Impact of Elections in Zambia," *Africa Today*, Vol. 35, No. 2 (1988), pp. 37–41.

[27] See Robert D. Grey, "The Petite Bourgeoisie in the Ethiopian Revolution," in Irvin Leonard Markovitz, ed., *Studies in Power and Class in Africa* (New York: Oxford, 1987), pp. 118–129.

[28] For a chronology of events see Raul Valdes Vivo, *Ethiopia's Revolution* (New York: International, 1978), pp. 115–124; and Deirdre Griswold, *Eyewitness Ethiopia: The Continuing Revolution* (New York: World View, 1978), pp. 43–49.

[29] Mulatu Wubneh and Yohannis Abate, *Ethiopia: Transition and Development in the Horn of Africa* (Boulder, Colo.: Westview, 1988), pp. 3–4.

[30] Thomas Magstadt, "Ethiopia's Great Terror," *Worldview*, April 1982.

[31] Abel Ndumu, "Seven Years of Nyayo," *Africa Report*, November–December 1985, pp. 51–53.

[32] Toyin Falola and Julius Ihonvbere, *The Rise and Fall of Nigeria's Second Republic: 1979–1984* (London: Zed, 1985), pp. 248–256.

[33] For a discussion of Botswana's political history, see Jack Halpern in *Africa South of the Sahara, 1989*, 18th ed. (Lanham, Md.: Europa, 1988).

[34] Sheila Rule, "In Botswana, a Democracy in Full Voice," *New York Times*, July 31, 1988; and Blaine Harden, "A Lesson for Africa: Democracy Works," *Washington Post*, Apr. 24, 1988.

[35] *New York Times*, Aug. 3, 1986, p. 1.

Chapter 18
Development and Dependency

No one familiar with Africa disputes the fact that the sub-Saharan nations, with few exceptions, face daunting economic and political challenges. The most pressing need is for effective policies aimed at stabilizing population growth and boosting food production. It is this food/population imbalance, not simply population growth itself, that is the crux of the problem.

The evidence of deprivation has at times been shockingly apparent. Pictures of emaciated children in Ethiopia and Sudan in the mid-1980s flashed on our television screens during the evening meal. The famine resulted from the combined effects of continuous warfare and a disastrous drought that struck much of the region in 1984–1985. It took countless human lives and put an estimated 30 million people at risk of starvation.[1] In addition to Ethiopia and Sudan in East Africa, Angola and Mozambique in southern Africa were also extremely hard hit. In the summer of 1986 these four nations contained 80 percent of an estimated 18 million Africans still endangered by famine.[2]

The drought that triggered Africa's worst famine in memory was a grim reminder of the region's fragile economic and political condition. The challenges facing sub-Saharan Africa are further illustrated by these startling facts:

- ☐ The region's forty-six nations have 450 million people from 1,000 ethnic groups speaking more than 800 languages.
- ☐ If present population growth continues, the region's population will double in twenty-three years.
- ☐ From 1972 to 1987 per-capita food production in the region fell in all but one year.
- ☐ Health and education standards in the region are the worst in the world, including the Third World.
- ☐ Of every 100 children born in the region, 20 die before their fifth birthday.[3]

Besides drought and famine, disease is a major killer in sub-Saharan Africa, where doctors, hospitals, clinics, and medications are frequently unavailable even to the gravely ill. Inadequate health care has always been a major problem in developing countries, but in the 1980s a new specter—acquired immune deficiency syndrome (AIDS)—stalked Africa. A disease for which no cure is known, AIDS is thought to have originated in Africa. Recent predictions hold that the epidemic might wipe out a quarter of the region's population. The social, moral, political, and economic impact of such a catastrophe is incalculable.

417

Garden of Eden in Decay?

In his Reith Lecture series for the British Broadcasting Corporation, professor Ali Mazrui took a different approach to describing Africa's condition. Mazrui used a powerful metaphor that no doubt shocked some of his British audience:

> It is as if I were a doctor and Africa came to me and asked for a comprehensive medical examination on the eve of a particular anniversary. The most important century in Africa's relations with Europe is the century from the 1880s to the 1980s. It was in the 1880s that the Conference of Berlin was held to agree on the terms of the European partition of Africa. It was in the 1880s that Egypt was occupied, that the Nile Valley was scrambled for, and that the repercussions for the rest of the continent were released. It was in the 1880s that the map of Africa began to acquire more decisively the different flag colours of the occupation powers of Europe. Let us assume Africa has come to my clinic for varied medical tests on the eve of the hundredth anniversary of Europe's rape of the body and her possessions.[4]

Mazrui proceeded to diagnose Africa's condition in terms of multiple maladies, most of which he asserted were caused by European colonialism and economic dependency. Mazrui characterized Africa as a "garden of Eden" in decay—the first habitat of mankind, but the last to be truly habitable.[5]

The Global Response

In May 1986 the United Nations convened a special session devoted solely to Africa's predicament, the first such meeting about the economic problems of a single region. The heads-of-state delegation of the Organization of African Unity (OAU) carried with it a detailed relief and recovery plan totaling $128 billion, which included a plan calling for $45.6 billion in external aid over a five-year period (primarily coming from industrial nations—an increase of 130 percent). In addition, the OAU plan asked Western creditor nations to forgive debts estimated to be as high as $55 billion over the same period.[6]

With the exception of Canada, Denmark, and the Netherlands, the donor nations—led by the United States—resisted making specific commitments. Even without foreign aid, African leaders made it clear the recovery program would not "go back into the cooler." According to Bolaji Akinyemi, then Nigeria's minister of external affairs, "We are not seeking to make Africa a charity case."[7] Akinyemi pointed out that more than 70 percent ($82.5 billion) of the resources needed under the recovery plan would be provided by Africans themselves. Although the special session helped focus world attention on Africa's plight, the results were inconclusive, and many Africans were disappointed.

That the special session was called at all, however, suggested that the world can no longer ignore Africa. The drama of a continent's teetering on the brink of collapse was given wide coverage in the world press. Pictures of skeletal children barely clinging to life appeared in newspapers and magazines; emaciated mothers unable to nurse their dying babies stared with hollow eyes into television cameras.

People were shown traveling to relief camps with empty bowls in search of a few scoops of grain. Around them, the drought-striken land offered no hope.

To make matters worse, Africa's economies staggered under a massive burden of foreign debt estimated at $200 to $300 billion. Interest payments alone consumed about half the region's foreign exchange earnings.[8] Thus Africa was being squeezed in an economic vise: The drought devastated agricultural production (which is still the foundation of most sub-Saharan economies), while the debt sapped export revenues (which were also reduced by the drought).

Foreign governments and various humanitarian agencies responded to this crisis. Creditors considered debt relief in various forms; celebrities turned their talents to fund-raising efforts. Pop recording artists got together and made a worldwide hit of Stevie Wonder's song "We Are the World," and the proceeds were donated through an organization called "USA for Africa." In July 1985 a seventeen-hour rock concert, "Live Aid," was broadcast on radio and television to 152 countries and raised $70 million; participants included Joan Baez, David Bowie, Phil Collins, Bob Dylan, Mick Jagger, Elton John, Tina Turner, The Who, and Led Zeppelin. Irish rock musician Bob Geldof was the principal organizer. He had earlier organized a British all-star rock group, "Band Aid," to record a famine-relief song, "Do They Know It's Christmas?"[9] Public international relief efforts were also extensive. At the peak of the crisis, in 1985, official emergency aid reached an estimated $3.4 billion. In all, some 1 million persons were said to have been saved.[10]

One upshot of the crisis was to accentuate the failure of African nations to achieve the goals discussed at the beginning of Chapter 17. Julius Nyerere, former president of Tanzania and a long-time champion of African socialism and self-reliance, has criticized fellow African leaders for reacting to the crisis of the moment but failing to engage in longer-term problem solving:

> Virtually all African governments are now almost entirely occupied with crisis management—that is with searching for foreign capital even to maintain the very minimum administrative and economic structures, and with keeping the economy running somehow. In the process, we have ourselves begun to believe that all Africa's problems are the result of Africa's mistakes, Africa's incompetence, and its political and economic venality. We are apologetic and demoralized in the face of the rest of the world.[11]

But Nyerere failed to mention the role of African socialism itself in either causing or failing to prevent the region's economic distress. Another omission is the definition of "self-reliance." What does it mean? Autarky? Interdependence in some sort of Pan-African economic grouping? Neither alternative has been realistic at any time since decolonization following World War II. Ironically, heavy borrowing from the West—hardly consistent with self-reliance—has led to sub-Saharan Africa's most pressing economic problem: a mountainous foreign debt.

Among Africa's most agonizing issues is the refugee problem. As pointed out earlier, dependency theorists argue that the militarization of African society is one consequence of European colonialism. In turn, a consequence of militarization has been the creation of refugees. In the 1980s the problem of refugees reached crisis proportions as war and revolution joined drought and famine to produce a tidal wave of displaced and destitute souls.

Famine, Conflict, and the Refugee Problem

Africa is a war-torn region. The persistence of armed conflict, both domestic and international, has been a stubborn fact of life for many sub-Saharan countries since the early years of independence in the 1950s. Hardly a country in the region has not been involved in a civil war or a border war. The civil wars in Ethiopia and Sudan have continued for more than a quarter-century. The 1967 war in Biafra took a heavy toll, as did the Congo crisis from 1960 to 1964. In the 1970s Tanzania backed Ugandan rebels and successfully overthrew dictator Idi Amin. A territorial dispute between Ethiopia and Somalia erupted in war in 1978 and came close to engaging the superpowers. In Angola civil war raged from 1975 to 1988 and was internationalized when Cuban troops intervened on the side of Angola's Marxist government and South African troops buttressed Joseph Savimbi's UNITA rebels. This thumbnail sketch by no means exhausts the conflicts that have plagued the region and that continue to sap its resources while undermining cooperation.

Border conflicts, civil and ethnic strife, and chronic political instability have taken tremendous tolls. The human cost can be measured not only in casualty figures but also in the rising tide of refugees. Of the estimated 12 million refugees worldwide in the late 1980s, nearly half of them were Africans fleeing from wars, persecution, and hunger.

During the 1980s Africa's refugee problem most directly affected thirteen nations. Estimates by the wire services and news media suggest that these countries together host between 4 and 5 million refugees. But there are no refugee figures for Kenya and Botswana, which are adjacent to two of sub-Saharan Africa's trouble spots. Why would hundreds of thousands of Ethiopians flee to neighboring Sudan and Somalia, but none at all go to neighboring Kenya? Kenya shares borders with several countries that have produced large numbers of refugees (Rwanda, Uganda, and Somalia, as well as Ethiopia). Similarly, Botswana is next to Mozambique, Angola, and South Africa—all of which have produced significant numbers of refugees—but Botswana has reported receiving none.

It is conceivable, then, that hundreds or even thousands of refugees are in Kenya, Botswana, and other countries where none are counted. Some governments may not publish refugee figures for fear of arousing domestic opposition or antagonizing the regimes from which the refugees are fleeing. One cause of tensions between Uganda and Kenya, for example, is that Ugandan troops sometimes cross the Kenyan border to pursue Ugandan refugees. Similarly, South Africa frequently threatens Botswana for accepting black South African refugees. In some cases, the desire to maintain friendly relations or to respect treaty agreements would act as a restraint on accepting refugees (or on publicly disclosing their presence).

For some unknown reason, there are no reports of refugees in West Africa. Similarly, Mozambique and Rwanda, whose nationals make up 31 percent (1.15 million) of the region's refugees, do not claim to host any refugees themselves. On the other hand, Malawi, Swaziland, Tanzania, Zambia, and Zimbabwe do not contribute to the flood of refugees, but together they host about 34 percent (1.25 million) of the total.

Four nations account for more than three-fourths of all sub-Saharan refugees: Ethiopia (30 percent), Mozambique (26 percent), Angola (11 percent), and Sudan (10 percent). These are the four countries that have suffered the double adversity of war and famine. Yet another dimension of the refugee problem is seldom mentioned. In 1988 more than 13 million Africans were displaced and living in temporary settlements. Because these victims of war and famine had not crossed any international border, they were not counted as refugees.

Among the internally displaced groups, black South Africans (28 percent) and Angolans (16 percent) are affected most seriously. Taken together, the number of refugees and displaced persons in sub-Saharan Africa during the late 1980s was in the range of 17 million.

Although there is no good way to quantify the human and economic costs of conflict and famine, the costs are readily apparent. Refugees suffer physical deprivation, indignities difficult to imagine or exaggerate, and loss of self-respect. Their home governments are plunged into debt and are forced to turn outside for help, often losing independence in the process (Ethiopia and Angola come readily to mind). Host governments must bear burdens of conflict and mismanagement that are not of their own making. Their delivery systems for education, health, housing, sanitation, and the like can easily be overwhelmed but cannot be rapidly expanded. Even food reserves are often not available, and, once again, external dependencies are created.[12] It is easy to see how internal conflicts can spill over, giving rise to border tensions and international conflicts. There is a vicious cycle in which conflict begets conflict. The upshot is to perpetuate the militarization of African politics.

Some sub-Saharan countries deserve credit for attaining a high degree of political stability and for providing shelter for refugees—among them are Botswana, Kenya, Malawi, Tanzania, Zambia, and Zimbabwe. What kind of domestic backlash might ensue in these countries remains to be seen; clearly, they cannot continue to accommodate an influx of refugees without severe stress to themselves. A presentiment of what might happen did occur in West Africa during the late 1970s and early 1980s, when a failing economy induced the Nigerian government to order the forced expatriation of thousands of guest laborers and refugees from neighboring Ghana.

Roots of Despair: The Sub-Saharan Economic Crisis

Earlier we noted that in May 1986 an emergency session of the U.N. General Assembly was called to consider ways of ameliorating the economic crisis in sub-Saharan Africa. Toward the end of 1987 the U.N. secretary general, Javier Pérez de Cuéllar, issued a study which concluded that Africa's economic situation was not improving—indeed, that it may have gone from very bad to worse. The study also concluded that industrialized nations had not fulfilled their promises to provide some $9 billion in additional foreign aid and to take steps to make it easier for Africa to compete in world commodity markets.

The 1980s: Decade of Decline

During the first half of the 1980s Africa's combined gross domestic product (GDP) dropped steadily. Net exports were negative in every year except 1985, when exports barely exceeded imports. In 1982–1983 the trade deficit amounted to $23 billion—a huge sum for a region with a total annual GDP of about $150 billion. Meanwhile, the exploding population helped plunge the region into a severe debt crisis: In 1986 Africa's external debt was roughly equivalent to its GDP. Worse still, the debt was climbing toward $200 billion, 440 percent greater than export earnings, and the price of manufactured imports kept rising (20 percent in 1986–1987).[13]

To meet this crisis the African nations were to raise $82.5 billion under the plan adopted by the U.N. General Assembly in June 1986, while the industrial nations pledged $9 billion annually for five years. In addition, yearly debt-service requirements were projected at $14.6 billion, bringing the total external financing needs to about $24 billion. Despite good intentions, the net inflow of external funds amounted to only $18 billion—a decrease in real terms over the 1985 level.[14]

According to the secretary general's report, "Serious initiatives have yet to be taken by the international community . . . to respond to the increasingly tightly entwined debt, commodity, and resource-flow problem in Africa." The net flow of resources was said to be "grossly inadequate" to compensate for Africa's drastically reduced export revenues and mounting debt-service obligations. Moreover, industrialized nations had not delivered on their promise "to deal urgently with commodity issues." On the contrary, the report asserted that there had been almost no effort to stabilize the prices of raw materials (commodities and minerals), Africa's major exports.

By contrast, the report noted that no fewer than twenty-eight African nations had adopted at least some of the recommended reforms. For example, more than four-fifths had created price incentives to boost agricultural production and rural development; two-thirds had taken steps to improve internal distribution; and more than two-thirds had allocated at least 25 percent of total investment to agriculture (as the plan recommended). Furthermore, there had been movement toward privatization as public-enterprise subsidies were being curtailed in many countries and laws affecting investment and business were being liberalized.

The report also noted the downside of these economic reforms. They had adversely affected immediate social well-being (health, education, and employment) and had probably contributed to political instability. "Africa's margins of maneuver to implement the program of action are being reduced." Finally, "The human and social consequences are unacceptable," said the secretary general.

This sentiment was echoed by many African leaders including Zambia's President Kenneth Kaunda, who warned of the dangers of adopting ''painful economic reforms . . . often at tremendous economic and social cost and in the face of serious political risks, which in many a country have threatened the very foundations of social cohesion and political stability.''

Zambia is a kind of microcosm of the dilemma facing Africa. The Zambian government reduced urban food subsidies and raised farm prices in compliance with the 1986 U.N. blueprint. The idea was to cut deficit spending and encourage greater agricultural output, which it did. On the one hand, food production jumped 15 percent, and manufacturing rose 5 percent; on the other, food prices also rose, quite predictably, sparking urban riots that left at least fifteen people dead and forced Kaunda to rescind the offending measures.[15]

Tanzania encountered another kind of pitfall: It increased cotton production by 75 percent in 1986 but actually earned less from this principal export than in 1985. There were two reasons, both arising from external sources. First, world cotton prices fell sharply in 1986; second, Tanzania devalued its currency to comply with the rules of the International Monetary Fund (IMF). The Tanzanian case illustrates how dependent many African nations are on world commodity prices. Cotton is Tanzania's major export, and commodity prices on the world market often fluctuate greatly. At the same time the IMF extends credit on easy terms to finance international trade. Many countries in the developing South experience chronic hard-currency shortfalls and depend on IMF loans to purchase imports, especially manufactures from the industrial North. As a consequence they are often at the mercy of external forces—one reason why ''neocolonialism'' is still a factor in sub-Saharan Africa.

The Demographics of Black Africa's Decline

Many observers contend that Africa's economic ills are caused, above all, by overpopulation. In the West government officials and scholars accept this argument almost on faith, and it does appear plausible. Africa's population growth rate is the highest in the world, and the region has also been hardest hit by food shortages. Thus a strong prima facie case can be made for the view that population growth is the root cause of deprivation and decline in Africa.

But is this argument accurate? Djibril Diallo, chief spokesman of the U.N. Office for Emergency Operations in Africa, objected to it:

> Of all the myths about Africa prevailing in the West, none is propagated with more vigor and regularity than the notion that overpopulation is a central cause of African poverty. The recent famine has given propagators of this myth fresh ammunition with which to press home their argument.
>   . . . the overpopulation myth is particularly harmful because it preempts deeper probing into the complex causes of underdevelopment.[16]

Djibril argues that acceptance of this myth in the West actually complicates efforts to launch family planning programs in Africa: ''After centuries of foreign domination, many Africans are deeply suspicious of any campaigns designed to alter the way they live and behave." He gave a clear example of how sensitive the issue of population control can be in the multiethnic context of African society:

> Just as the Kenyan government was concluding careful negotiations with the United States Agency for International Development to launch a major marketing drive for contraceptives in the rural areas, children in the central highlands areas suddenly stopped taking their free milk drinks at school. The reason became clear a few days later when a man appeared in court charged with spreading the rumor that the milk had been treated with contraceptive chemicals. The implication behind the rumor was that the authorities wished to reduce the population increase of the ethnic groups living in the region.[17]

Several points merit consideration. First, a double standard is often applied by experts who stress the link between food supply and population size. Japan, Switzerland, and the Netherlands are not self-sufficient in food and have relatively little farmland, and yet they are not charged with being overpopulated. By contrast, "Africa has more arable land per capita than any other developing region." Under the right conditions, Chad alone could feed the whole Sahel—an area that stretches westward from Chad to the Atlantic Ocean across most of the northern sub-Sahara. Second, Africa's average population density is only 16 per square kilometer, much lower than China's (100 per square kilometer) and India's (225). Nonetheless, China and India have both made impressive strides toward food self-sufficiency. According to Djibril, "In their quest for appropriate solutions to their own food predicaments, more and more Africans are making their way to India to study breakthroughs there."[18]

But even Africans who criticize the critics do not argue that family planning is not needed in many sub-Saharan countries—only that it is not a panacea. No one familiar with Africa's recent history and current predicament can doubt that the outlook is bleak.

Reasons for Underdevelopment in Africa

Scholars have long debated the causes of Africa's economic and political problems, and a variety of theories has emerged. One view holds that European colonial powers intentionally blocked the region's development.[19] Another view (espoused by Ali Mazrui and Julius Nyerere, among others) stresses the debilitating but unintentional consequences of colonial exploitation. A variation on this theme has been offered by Adebayo Adedeji, general secretary of the U.N. Economic Commission for Africa, who indicts colonialism for changing Africa's agricultural priorities from food production for local consumption to export crops like cocoa, coffee, and tea—for which prices are set by demand in foreign markets.[20]

More introspective African playwrights blame certain African traditions for creating resistance to social change and progress.[21] They also accuse political elites of abusing power and lacking the vision needed to lift Africa out of deprivation.

Western development theorists sometimes draw on social psychology and cultural anthropology to explain why some societies achieve development more easily than others. This perspective focuses on variations among societies with respect to informal rules, behavioral norms, lifestyles, and expectations.[22] Other development theorists, as noted in Chapter 3, draw on political economy—more specifically, on incentives theory, which looks at the presence or absence of formal rules, legal structures, and contractual relations that undergird commercial activity, define rewards and punishments, and reinforce the work ethic.[23]

Some African societies exhibit a kind of family-centered particularism which breeds social attitudes that are inimical to individual success and economic development. For example, the Oromos and the Amharas of Ethiopia are very self-conscious about how others perceive them. Given this tradition, a person does not become too ambitious, because individual achievement can bring social stigma (called *yiluntabis*). To ignore this norm is to be ostracized as greedy or as an overachiever. This social ethic is prescribed in maxims: "He dies alone who eats alone," and "Death in a crowd is glory." In principle the morality of cooperating and sharing is good, but in practice the taboo on individualism both constrains competition and stifles personal aspirations.

If change-resistant customs like this applied in many parts of traditional Africa, so were colonialism and certain nonindigenous socioreligious practices equally detrimental to personal growth and national self-reliance. Colonialism undercut Africans' sense of personal efficacy; at the same time it introduced individualism into a society that traditionally had stressed collective, community values. The colonial white man was the *Bwana*, or master-benefactor, who brought new values and behavioral norms. By the same token, non-African religions, particularly Protestant, were often at odds with African belief systems and seemed self-contradictory. On the one hand missionaries taught that sinners had direct access to the Savior (the equality of all God's children); on the other hand these same missionaries often behaved in a condescending manner.

In addition, as colonial administrators and missionaries dispensed food, medicine, and education, they also created a socioeconomic environment conducive to low self-esteem and dependence. Ironically, colonizers cast themselves in the role of givers and cast Africans in the role of receivers. This ascription of roles became an important factor in shaping African politics. When a society's self-image is premised on foreign standards and largesse (as in colonial subjugation), a habit of uncritical receiving, which is detrimental to economic development, may evolve.

The benevolence of colonial administrators and the charity of missionaries thus were mixed blessings. While religious altruism encouraged generosity, it also bridled individual initiative and desire for worldly possessions. Indeed, in some places religion was a barrier to economic development. An example was the land monopoly of the Ethiopian Orthodox Church, which for many years laid claim to one-third of the land. Nearly every other day of the week was designated a religious holiday for one saint or another, and Orthodox believers would observe some of these days—at least one of them most ceremoniously. Thus, able-bodied persons were encouraged to roam the streets and visit homes asking for charity in the names of saints. Since religion sanctioned such beggary, peasants who accepted the primacy of spiritual over material values shared their meager food in hopes of heavenly rewards.

With respect to education, students in church-sponsored schools studied humanities rather than science, engineering, and technology, which churches spurned as too materialistic and worldly. Therefore, even in the selection of curriculum and career the new religions discouraged the attitudes and orientations associated with free enterprise in the West. The Orthodox, Roman Catholic, and Protestant churches also encouraged tithing and the belief that it is more blessed to give than to receive. The value conflicts are clear: Such moral and religious lessons may counteract greed, but they also teach that goodness is inversely related to wealth and possessions.

Another factor deserves mention here: African socialism. The search for an alternative to the Western capitalist model of development has made entrepreneurship suspect throughout much of Africa. Only a new social ethic that encourages individual initiative is likely to spur an era of progress and rapid economic growth in this region. Such a sea-change in attitude will probably not occur in the grass-roots level unless it is fostered by African leaders—the same ones who for decades have rejected Western values while embracing ''dependency theory'' to explain Africa's problems.

Dependency Theory Revisited

Frequent and disruptive coups, revolutions, secessionist movements, civil wars, and disenfranchisement since independence point to the weakness of political institutions in sub-Saharan Africa and support the view that political and economic development are linked. As noted in Chapter 3, theories to explain chronic economic instability abound. One approach that has gained attention in recent years, especially among Third World development scholars, is dependency theory.

Theotonio Dos Santos has defined dependency as ''a situation in which the economy of certain countries is conditioned by the development and expansion of another economy to which the former is subjected.'' Dos Santos argues that interdependence gives way to dependence, ''when some countries (the dominant ones) can expand and can be self-sustaining, while others (the dependent ones) can do this only as a reflection of that expansion which can have either positive or negative effect on their immediate development.''[24]

Dependency theory and the concept of neocolonialism gained currency during the late 1950s and early 1960s, after the U.N. Economic Commission for Latin America published a study by Raul Prebisch.[25] Originally conceived as an explanation for the consequences of Latin America's economic exploitation by the United States, the dependency perspective eventually came to be seen as especially applicable to Africa and Asia. Its relatively benign interpretation of colonialism has attracted many scholars from the United States and Europe, widening its acceptance and application to the entire Third World.

The concept of dependency transcends economic and political realms; it includes social and psychological attitudes and behaviors of dominant and dependent nations toward each other. Dependency connotes a relationship that is not equal or reciprocal.[26] Although the ties between the center (developed) and periphery (underdeveloped) can be negative or positive, the gains for the periphery are, at best, indirect. According to Dos Santos:

> Trade relations are based on monopolistic control of the market, which leads to transfer of surplus generated in the dependent countries to the dominant countries: Financial relations are from the viewpoint of the dominant powers based on loans and export of capital, which permit them to receive interest and profits, increasing their domestic surplus and strengthening their control over the economies of other countries. . . . The result is to limit the development of their internal market and their technical and cultural capacity as well as the moral and physical health of their people.[27]

James Caporaso stressed the role of transnational ties between foreign and local capitalists, restricted development choices, and distortions in the domestic economy caused by the incorporation of the less developed nations into the world market system. Caporaso's theory stresses ''asymmetries'' in relations between the center and periphery:

> Structural asymmetries are the basis for power, i.e., these asymmetries provide the resources to affect others by depriving them of the desired exchange of goods. When one actor supplies another with large amounts of important goods which cannot be easily replaced at tolerable costs, that actor is in a position to influence the dependent actor.[28]

As a consequence, domestic economic structures are distorted, and development policies are responsive to external market conditions rather than to internal needs. For Africans, poverty and despair are inherent in this system, Caporaso argued, because the power to improve their plight is outside their own societies.

Thus, dependent development exists where a given nation can take only limited initiatives and has limited access to such vital resources as capital and technology, which are externally controlled. According to many dependency theorists, who are heavily influenced by the turn-of-the-century writings of J. A. Hobson and V. I. Lenin, underdevelopment is perpetuated by the workings of the world capitalist systems.[29]

A. G. Frank argued that:

> Underdevelopment, no less than development itself, is the product but also part of the motive power of capitalism. Capitalist development everywhere has been a fundamentally contradictory development based on exploitation and resulting simul-

taneously in development and underdevelopment. Additionally, the growth and expansion of European mercantilism of the 16th century led to the development of a single, integrated capitalist system of worldwide scope. Associated ever since the beginning with the growth of powerful states, the expansion of mercantilism-capitalism led to the development of a metropole and, related to it through ties of commerce and force, of a periphery. Variously related to each other through colonialism, free-trade, imperialism, and "neocolonialism," the metropole exploited the periphery in such a way and extent that the metropole became what we today call developed while periphery became what we now call underdeveloped.[30]

In sum, the economies of underdeveloped countries not only have become "asymmetrically" integrated with those of industrially developed nations but, in this view, also have become permanently unequal partners in the global system. Not surprisingly, dependency theorists tend to be anticapitalist and usually advocate socialism as the cure for underdevelopment and the transformation of the international economic order. They reject the existing system of foreign trade, aid, and investment as a capitalist web that ensnares developing nations and holds them in economic bondage.

Development Theories in African Perspective

There is at least some truth in almost every theory of development, but none is without flaws. For example, traditional evolutionary theory, which seeks to explain development in terms of internal causes, largely ignores the effects of colonialism and neocolonialism. Dependency theory, on the other hand, blames underdevelopment on external causes, particularly colonialism and capitalism, but ignores internal factors.

The evolutionary theory often prescribes a laissez-faire policy and softpedals the need for concerted state action. Its bias in favor of security and stability places the highest priority on maintaining the status quo, even though social progress and economic development sometimes require radical change. Dependency theory recognizes the need to correct the structural distortions associated with neocolonialism, but it often seeks to do this through revolution. As the case of Ethiopia shows, revolutions may be indiscriminate, destroying both negative and positive elements of the old order and impeding rather than facilitating development. This is especially so if the revolution does not have popular support and if the new regime feels compelled to squander its resources on repression and efforts to legitimize itself.

For Africans, the development debate is far from academic. Development policy in the region has been entangled in an ideological rivalry between socialism and capitalism, between anticolonialism and pro-Western anticommunism. Peter Berger, a keen observer of this conflict, suggested that one viable strategy for developing nations may be to pursue "selective socialism" or "selective capitalism."[31] Berger further suggested that both capitalism and socialism should be seen

as means to an end and should be measured by the same yardstick: Does this approach help or hinder the achievement of society's goals?

Another weakness of most development theories is their failure to give due consideration to physical environment, as opposed to history, culture, social psychology, and politics. Geography has played a major role in shaping Africa's history and politics; it is also a barrier to economic development in most of the region.

The Sahara Desert, for example, extends across North Africa to the Atlantic Ocean. Spanning some 3.5 million square miles, it is the largest desert in the world—the contiguous United States would fit easily into the Sahara. Yet this arid region is inhospitable to habitation and is unsuitable for agriculture or animal husbandry. In much of sub-Saharan Africa the alternation between blazing heat and floods frequently causes drought during the planting seasons, eroding the soil and destroying crops. To cite but one example, Sudan had barely recovered from two years of drought when, in August 1988, six times as much rain fell in just two days as fell in all of 1987. The country was inundated and came to a standstill for weeks. Floods destroyed 100,000 homes and left 1.5 million people homeless.[32]

Such catastrophes have impeded development and the prospects of many African countries. Floods, volcanoes, and earthquakes occur suddenly and—unlike such human problems as corruption and political instability—are not susceptible to public policy. No amount of statesmanship can influence nature's course.

Although theories of development can help diagnose Africa's economic and political ills, they cannot change the prognosis in the short run. Perhaps a better understanding of the causes of African poverty and underdevelopment will lead to wiser policies and brighter prospects over time. Meanwhile, it must be recognized that there is no one African Polity, only African polities; no one African Problem, only African problems; no one African Solution, only African solutions.

African Democracy: Wave of the Future?

At the beginning of the 1990s there were signs that the trends toward democracy and respect for human rights in Latin America and Eastern Europe were also having an impact in sub-Saharan Africa. In Niger, Côte d'Ivoire, Benin, Gabon, Cameroon, Kenya, and Zaire, opponents of authoritarian government pressed for democratization.[33]

In Benin, for example, President Mathieu Kerekou renounced Marxism in late 1989 and called for talks with the democratic opposition. In March 1990 he resigned and transferred power to a non-Communist prime minister. Meanwhile, in Niger in February 1990 government security forces responded to the demands of professionals and government workers for better pay by shooting demonstrators. Following this outrage President Ali Saibou fired his cabinet ministers and promised to introduce democracy. In Côte d'Ivoire doctors and teachers went on strike against the government's new austerity program. President Houphouët-

Boigny closed the schools for the year, and protesting students demanded multiparty elections and the president's resignation.

Such developments were only straws in the wind, and it is doubtful that they portend far-reaching changes of the kind that occurred in Eastern Europe in 1989. As we have seen, authoritarian rule is deeply rooted in Africa. In one sense, a discussion of whether multiparty democracy is likely to come to the region begs the question: Is political pluralism a viable model in multiethnic societies? Given the region's instability, a premature move toward democracy raises the possibility of a slide into civil strife and social chaos that could end tragically, as it did in Nigeria in the late 1960s. Otherwise put, democracy is not a panacea for Africa's ills; in some cases it may only exacerbate existing problems.

Case Studies: Ethiopia, Kenya, and South Africa

Ethiopia

Fifteen years after the overthrow of Emperor Haile Salassie, Ethiopia was one of the most beleaguered and embattled nations in sub-Saharan Africa. Ethiopians had suffered enormously from famine and oppression, and most lived hand to mouth, with little or no security against future calamities. Constant reports of gross human rights violations had sullied Mengistu's reputation nearly everywhere in the world. Secessionist movements in Tigre and Eritrea provinces continued unabated and had resulted in military defeats for government forces in 1989. In mid-1989 some Western analysts suggested that the downfall of the Mengistu regime was imminent.[34]

As noted earlier, Ethiopia under Mengistu became a Soviet client-state in return for massive subventions from Moscow—between 1977 and 1989 Soviet aid to Ethiopia exceeded $11 billion. But then something quite unexpected happened: Mikhail Gorbachev instituted reforms at home and changed Soviet priorities abroad. One upshot was a waning of Soviet largesse.

Ethiopia thus had little choice but to look to the West for help. The U.S. government, however, viewed Mengistu with revulsion in view of his human rights abuses. To become eligible for U.S. aid, the Bush Administration said, Mengistu would have to stop "brutalizing" his people, halt the forced resettlement of peasants, reform Ethiopia's collectivist economic policies, and seek a negotiated cease-fire with rebel forces in Tigre and Eritrea.[35] Thus, as the 1980s drew to a close, the Mengistu regime, still Stalinist, was sinking, and its lifeline (to Moscow) also appeared to be in jeopardy.

The new Constitution did little to alter the basic nature of Mengistu's dictatorship. Nor did it make any real concessions to ethnic groups that long felt excluded from the political process. Although some observers held out hopes that the system might open up somewhat in the 1992 elections, such hopes had little foundation.

In 1986 Foreign Minister Goshu Wolde resigned in protest, declaring, "I cannot, in good conscience, continue to serve a Government whose short-sighted and rigidly doctrinaire policies are leading the country and the people into misery and destruction." Wolde described how he had "recently watched, with helplessness, as my country slipped further and further into authoritarianism and absolute dictatorship, with the inevitable consequences of intolerance and repression."[36] On May 17, 1989, an abortive coup took place. These two events demonstrate that even within the ruling elite (Wolde was a member of the Communist party's Central Committee), corrosive doubts about the direction of the country were undermining Mengistu's position.

Has Ethiopia's revolution achieved anything positive? Arguably, yes. Before the revolution two-thirds of the land belonged to the feudal aristocracy and the Orthodox Church. Ethiopian society was divided into two social classes—landed gentry and landless peasant farmers. Now the aristocracy has been dispossessed, but agriculture is collectivized. Thus, although the land is no longer in the hands of the few, it is still not in the hands of the many.

Also, educational opportunities are now apparently available to many more youngsters than was true under the feudal system. Since the revolution in the mid-1970s the literacy rate has quadrupled, by some estimates. Claims of this kind, however, are nearly impossible to verify, since the government is so secretive.

On the negative side, the economy has stagnated since the revolution, and the physical quality of life has not improved; if anything, it has gotten much worse for many people. The spiritual quality of life has also worsened: Freedom of speech, movement, and assembly are sharply restricted, and according to the Constitution even religious freedom "may not be exercised in a manner contrary to the interest of the state and the revolution." What good is land reform if it does not lead to an increase in food production and agricultural productivity? And what is the point of a "People's Democratic Republic" if the people are not allowed to exercise democratic freedoms?

Of course, not all of Ethiopia's troubles can be blamed on the government. Nature has not been kind in the past decade; several droughts have caused crop failures and famines. But even natural calamities have been exacerbated by the endless cycle of war and repression.

Is the Constitution only a sham? It was, after all, approved in a national referendum—the first in Ethiopia's 2,500-year history. The people elected 835 "legislators" from a field of 2,250 candidates. To be sure, the legislature is a rubber stamp, but the exercise of electing and convening it does set a precedent that may at some point become significant. The tickets have been paid for; now the Ethiopian people are waiting for the curtain to go up.

Kenya

During the 1980s the Moi government survived strong criticism of its human-rights record, a coup attempt, student unrest, and a high-level scandal. The scandal involved Charles Njojo, a popular and ambitious Kikuyu politician who was in charge of law enforcement and internal security. Njojo was accused of colluding with foreign governments, including South Africa. The "Njojo affair" faded after a judicial commission cleared Njojo of any wrongdoing; but it left nagging doubts about the integrity of the people around the president.

More troublesome was a coup attempt by the Kenyan air force support troops in 1982. The coup failed, but it sent shock waves through the government. Several thousand air force personnel and civilian suspects were detained and put on trial. Although twelve airmen received the death sentence, most of the others were granted amnesty.

Student demonstrations and protests against alleged mismanagement of the economy and violations of civil liberties led to the closing of Kenya's universities at times, and a small band of agitators known as *Mwakenya* became a nuisance to internal security forces.[37] In the 1980s the world press put Kenya in the spotlight, as critics accused Moi of trampling on human rights.

Despite these rumblings, Kenya's one-party system is highly resilient and is not likely to collapse soon. KANU's membership has actually increased in recent years (although the main reason seems to be that civil service employees are now required to be members of the party).[38]

In 1988 the government introduced a controversial primary election system known as queuing. A month before the general election voters were asked to select legislative nominees by (literally) lining up behind the candidate of their choice. The candidates with the most "votes" proceeded to the general election.[39] Also in 1988 the number of elective seats in the National Assembly was raised from 158 to 188. The new election method, the added seats, and the defeat of incumbents combined to produce many new legislators in the Assembly (roughly one-third of the membership), but only at the expense of electoral controversy, allegations of voting fraud, and a spate of lawsuits.

At the end of the 1980s many critics decried what they viewed as a tendency toward presidential dictatorship in Kenya. Several disturbing signs pointed toward this. For example, in the fall of 1988 the National Assembly, without debate, unanimously passed a constitutional amendment giving the president nearly unlimited power to fire judges. This endangers the independence of the judiciary by making judges subject to political pressures under threat of dismissal. The same amendment also extends from twenty-four hours to fourteen days the period during which police can hold suspects before bringing them to court. That this amendment was approved unanimously and that the National Assembly acted as a rubber stamp raised questions about the future of polyarchy in Kenya.

The situation was alarming to Moi's critics because the president was becoming increasingly intolerant of opposition and was resorting to the tactics of a demagogue. The government had taken to attacking elements in society that it viewed as disloyal, including church leaders, lawyers, and students. The wealthy Asian business class—only about sixty thousand in number but in control of 70 percent of the urban retail sector and much manufacturing—also felt persecuted.

In addition, the government had launched a vitriolic campaign against foreign journalists, the British Broadcasting Corporation, and Amnesty International ("an agent of imperialism"), among others.[40]

Worse still, persistent reports of arbitrary detentions and torture made the assault on the judicial systems and the legal profession seem particularly ominous. According to one close observer writing in early 1988:

> Eleven people are detained without trial under Kenya's Public Security Act, while more than 80 have been jailed in connection with a secret anti-government movement known as Mwakenya, which was uncovered in court, and both Amnesty International and the American Lawyers Committee for Human Rights have published evidence that many were tortured into pleading guilty.[41]

Plainclothes officers of the dreaded Special Branch, Kenya's secret police, enforce the unwritten rules against criticism of President Moi as well as the laws against sabotage and sedition.

Critics also charge that Mwakenya has been used as a kind of hobgoblin: "The clampdown on criticism, including the fear that one may be branded a Mwakenya member for expressing disloyal thoughts, has prevented any real opposition from emerging."[42] Whether true or false in this case, the fact remains that populist tyrants in Africa and elsewhere have frequently used such tactics to stifle opposition.

In this regard it is noteworthy that President Moi also accused Libya of trying to destabilize Kenya's political system, and that several Moi detractors were convicted of spying for Libya. In addition, tensions with neighboring Uganda reached the boiling point in December 1987, when fighting broke out between Kenyan police and Ugandan soldiers at Busia, the main border crossing between the two countries. Again, these actions are consistent with a pattern of rule that combines populism and authoritarianism.

It would be a mistake to conclude that President Moi has no popular support. Despite all the controversy, the 1988 general election gave him a renewed mandate. In 1993, when his third five-year term expires, Moi will be 70 years old; he will have served as many years as Kenyatta did, and he will still be young enough to stand for reelection. He may choose to follow the examples of Nyerere (Tanzania) and Senghor (Senegal) and step down, but he has shown no signs of losing either his vigor or his grip.

It is worth recalling that Kenya has long had a reputation for economic vitality and political tolerance. In February 1989 the U.S. State Department maintained that Kenya "remains one of Africa's success stories both in terms of economic growth and political stability."[43] Another observer noted that "The country feeds itself, has avoided the conflicts and bloodshed which plague its neighbors, and has enjoyed steady expansion while other countries have sunk deeper into poverty."[44] All these accomplishments are as impressive as they are rare in the sub-Saharan region.

Although Kenya continues to face daunting tasks of economic and political development, it is relatively better off than any of its neighbors. Compared with the situations in Sudan and Ethiopia, conditions in Kenya seem bearable. (Somalia, Uganda, and Tanzania seem worse-off, too.) When Moi stumps in the villages, he stresses bread-and-butter issues—roads, schools, clinics, and the like. He points out how much better things are in Kenya than in neighboring countries, and he promises that, so long as he has the support of the *wananchi* (ordinary citizens), living standards will continue to improve. Thus, while the political scene may appear bleak to outsiders, the economic picture could be much worse, in the minds of many Kenyans.

Kenya and Ethiopia are a study in contrasts. Kenya's economy is viable enough to give the government a glow of legitimacy, even though by Western standards its methods are not always acceptable. On the other hand, Moi's excesses pale in comparison with Mengistu's atrocities. Whereas Mengistu has been preoccupied with containing Ethiopia's rebels, Moi's greatest challenge may be to contain Kenya's population growth, which remains the highest in the world. In the long run, economic growth, however steady, may not be able to outstrip Kenya's demographic liabilities. Unless the economy continues to grow and the government continues to deliver on its promises of a better life, pressures will inevitably build. So far, Kenya has coped remarkably well—so well, that most Kenyans probably expect things to keep getting better. Therein lies the challenge for Moi and his successors.

South Africa

In early 1989 President Botha, in ailing health, stepped down as head of the ruling Nationalist party, but he stayed on as president. Botha was succeeded by F. W. de Klerk, a hard-liner on apartheid who had long opposed and obstructed proposals to mitigate discrimination against blacks. Embittered and isolated within his own party, in August 1989 the autocratic Botha resigned the presidency after more than a decade in power. Botha detested de Klerk but could not block de Klerk's elevation to the presidency.

When de Klerk took power, South Africa was a country in crisis. The African National Congress (ANC), which for years had directed the armed struggle against the Pretoria government from its headquarters in Lusaka, Zambia, intensified its campaign of violence and terrorism in the 1980s. Botha had made some important concessions before 1985; he scrapped laws outlawing sex and marriage between different races, extended rights to black trade unions, gave blacks property rights for the first time, and abolished the hated Pass Laws used to control the influx of blacks into South African cities. Botha had seriously contemplated far-reaching reforms in the apartheid system during the mid-1980s, but he succumbed to pressures from the right wing within his party and instead gave a defiant speech warning the world not to push South Africa too far.

The international reaction was swift and damaging. A spate of economic sanctions and diplomatic protests left Pretoria isolated and ostracized from the international community. Foreign banks called in their loans early, multinational firms quit South Africa, and the value of the rand plummeted. These external pressures appear to have precipitated the deep economic recession into which the country sank during the last half of the decade.

Economic troubles were accompanied by intensified political pressures at home and abroad. Botha was ultimately defeated by a wide array of opposition forces. His successor, de Klerk, could see the handwriting on the wall: Negotiate with the black majority (and protect white interests insofar as possible), or risk a convulsive end to white rule in which Afrikaners might lose everything. In February 1990 de Klerk not only released Nelson Mandela from prison (where he had languished since 1961) but also legalized the ANC and invited thousands of ANC exiles to return to South Africa and take part in seeking an accommodation between blacks and whites. With Mandela as the ANC's recognized leader, direct talks were set for April—an unprecedented occurrence in itself.

But a negotiated settlement in South Africa will not come easily, for several reasons. First, the extreme right within the Nationalist Party is increasingly popular among ordinary Afrikaners who fear that their way of life is endangered. Hardliners will try to block concessions to blacks at every turn. Second, it is not clear who, if anybody, can claim to speak for all of South Africa's blacks. The movement is divided and disposed to self-inflicted wounds (for example, in the spring of 1990 Mandela admitted that the ANC had tortured some of its own members who were accused of disloyalty). Third, a bitter legacy forged by years of brutal repression will continue to jeopardize any attempt at a peaceful solution.

To his lasting credit, Botha did eventually facilitate negotiated settlements to the protracted wars in Angola and Namibia. At the beginning of the 1990s, however, the black majority and the white minority confronted each other with no idea about how to share power. The possibility of civil war hangs over South Africa; the nation needs unprecedented leadership and vision to bring about peaceful change.

Afterword: Some Requisites of Change

Since Africa's problems are so pervasive, solutions must transcend ethnic and partisan politics. Some argue that Africans may need to change their attitudes toward themselves, each other, and the outside world; adopt a new outlook and take charge of their own destiny; and recognize that in a properly ordered society, power, position, privilege, and status are based on achievement, not ascription. In this view, the region's psychology of dependence needs to be broken.

Africa can certainly borrow from the West without, in the process, losing touch with its own history and culture. For example, Africa may need to assimilate the Western and Asian work ethic. Ironically, self-determination for Africa will, to some degree, require emulation of the West. Japan certainly has demonstrated that it is possible to imitate Western technology and even the Western work culture without abandoning one's own traditions, customs, and moral and spiritual values.

At the same time, Africans may rediscover their indigenous values of social responsibility and compassion; to do so, in some cases, they may need to set aside narrow familial particularism. It may also be necessary to exercise greater discretion in accepting foreign aid, to avoid perpetuating dependency.

Corruption and coercion have been prevalent in postindependence Africa, and its leaders can set an example by abjuring self-indulgence and placing public interest above personal gain. This is true everywhere, of course; all politicians, priests, and officials are obliged to remember that power and authority are a public trust. Many governments in Africa and elsewhere would be money ahead, literally and figuratively, to rely less on coercion and more on consent.

Finally, political regimes can bring about a revolution of attitudes and expectations only by ensuring opportunities to all members of society. Trust, accountability, and a spirit of fair play between governments and citizens, between citizens and one another, and among governments are essential.

CONCLUSION

As the colonial era fades from memory, the governments of Black Africa will not be able to blame continuing poverty, oppression, and the lack of social progress solely on the West. Despite the unresolved debt crisis, the rhetoric of dependence and neocolonialism already has a hollow ring in much of Africa south of the Sahara.

STUDY QUESTIONS

1. In what sense is Africa a "garden of Eden in decay"?
2. How do scholars explain Africa's economic and political problems? Which theory makes the most sense to you, and why?
3. Compare Ethiopia and Nigeria in terms of social diversity, political stability, and economic development. Which country has the better future prospects?
4. What are the major problems facing Kenya today, and what obstacles stand in the way of solving them? Is more democracy the answer? Less democracy?

SUGGESTED READINGS

Baker, Pauline. *The United States and South Africa: The Reagan Years*. New York: Ford Foundation–Foreign Policy Association, 1989.

Berger, Peter, and Bobby Godsell, eds. *A Future for South Africa: Visions, Strategies, and Realities*. Boulder, Colo.: Westview, 1988.

Berger, Peter, and Bobby Godsell. "South Africa on the Move," *Current History*, May 1990.

Giorgis, Dawit Wolde. *Red Tears: War, Famine and Revolution in Ethiopia*. Trenton, N.J.: Red Sea, 1989.

Mazrui, Ali. *The African Condition: A Political Diagnosis*. London: Cambridge University, 1980.

McGowan, Patrick J., and Dale L. Smith. "Economic Dependency in Black Africa: An Analysis of Competing Theories," *International Organization*, Winter 1978.

Rosenblum, Mort, and Doug Williamson. *Squandering Eden: Africa at the Edge*. San Diego: Harcourt, 1987.

Sampson, Anthony. *Black and Gold: Tycoons, Revolutionaries, and Apartheid*. New York: Pantheon, 1987.

Wubneh, Mulatu, and Yohannis Abate. *Ethiopia: Transition and Development in the Horn of Africa*. Boulder, Colo.: Westview, 1988.

NOTES

[1] *USAID Highlights*, "The President's Initiative to End Hunger in Africa," Vol. 4, No. 3 (Summer 1987).

[2] Mary Anne Weaver, "UN Plans for Africa," *Christian Science Monitor*, June 3, 1986, p. 1.

[3] Data supplied by the United States Agency for International Development (AID).

[4] Ali A. Mazrui, *The African Condition* (London: Heinemann, 1980), pp. 1–2.

[5] Ibid., pp. 6–9.

[6] *UN Chronicle*, Vol. XXIII, No. 4 (UN Special Session on the African Crisis, August 1986), pp. 7–20; and *Africa Report*, May–June 1986.

[7] Mary Ann Weaver, op. cit.

[8] *UN Chronicle*, August 1986, pp. 7–20.

[9] Ibid., p. 21; and "We Are the World," *Africa Report*, July–August 1987, pp. 40–41.

[10] *UN Chronicle*, February 1987, p. 47.

[11] *Africa Recovery*, Vol. 2, No. 2 (June 1988), p. 9.

[12] See, for example, Sheila Rule, "Refugees Tax Already Desperate Malawi," *New York Times*, July 18, 1988, p. 1A.

[13] Ted Morello, "UN's Africa Recovery Program Fails to Make Dent in Crisis," *Christian Science Monitor*, Nov. 6, 1987, p. 14.

[14] Ibid.

[15] Ibid.

[16] Djibril Diallo, "Overpopulation and Other Myths about Africa," *Christian Science Monitor*, Apr. 22, 1986, p. 15.

[17] Ibid.

[18] Ibid.

[19] See Walter Rodney, *How Europe Underdeveloped Africa* (Washington, D.C.: Howard University, 1974); and Samir Amin, *Imperialism and Unequal Development* (New York: Monthly Review Press, 1977).

[20] *UN Chronicle*, Vol. XXII, No. 2 (1985), p. 7.

[21] See, for example, Chinua Achebe, *Arrow of God* and *Things Fall Apart* (London: Heinemann, 1958); T. M. Aluko, *The Gab Boys* (London: Fontana, 1969); Ola Rotimi, *The Gods Are Not to Blame* (London: Oxford, 1971); and Ayi Kwei Armah, *The Beautiful Ones Are Not Yet Born* (Boston: Houghton Mifflin, 1968).

[22] Talcott Parson, *The Social System* (New York: Free Press, 1951); and ''Evolutionary Universals in Society,'' in T. Parson, ed., *Socialization Theory and Modern Society* (New York: Free Press, 1967).

[23] See, for example, Seymour Martin Lipset, ''Some Social Prerequisites of Democracy, Economic Development and Political Legitimacy,'' *The American Political Science Review*, 53 (March 1969), pp. 69–105.

[24] Theotonio Dos Santos, ''The Structure of Dependence,'' *American Economic Review*, 60 (May 1970), pp. 231–236.

[25] Lois Eugenio DiMarco, ed., *International Economics and Development: Essay in Honor of Raul Prebisch* (New York: Academic, 1972), pp. 1–34.

[26] See, for example, James A. Caporaso, ''Introduction,'' *International Organization*, Vol. 32, No. 1 (Winter 1978), p. 6; ''Dependence, Dependency, and Power in the Global System: A Structural and Behavioral Analysis,'' *International Organization*, Vol. 32, No. 1 (Winter 1978), pp. 13–43, 121–125; Patrick J. McGowan and Dale L. Smith, ''Economic Dependency in Black Africa: An Analysis of Competing Theories,'' *International Organization*, Vol. 32, No. 1 (Winter 1978), pp. 179–235; and R. Dan Walleri, ''Trade Dependence and Underdevelopment: A Causal Chain Analysis,'' *Comparative Political Studies*, Vol. 11, No. 1 (April 1978), pp. 94–121.

[27] Dos Santos, op. cit.

[28] Caporaso, ''Dependence, Dependency, and Power,'' p. 28.

[29] Immanuel Wallerstein, *The Modern World System* (New York: Academic, 1974), pp. 67, 301; Immanuel Wallerstein, ed., *World Inequality: Origin and Perspectives on the World System* (Montreal: Black Rose, 1975), p. 16; Celso Furtado, ''Development and Stagnation in Latin America: A Structuralist Approach,'' *Studies in Comparative Development*, Vol. 1, No. 11 (1965); and Samir Amin, *Imperialism and Unequal Development* (New York: Monthly Review Press, 1977), pp. 12–15.

[30] Ander Gunder Frank, *Capitalist Underdevelopment* (New York: Oxford, 1976), pp. 94–95.

[31] Peter Berger, *Pyramids of Sacrifice: Political Ethics and Social Change* (New York: Anchor, 1976), Chaps. 5, 6.

[32] ''Nigeria: The Thought of Lt. Gen. Obasanjo,'' *Africa Currents*, No. 10 (Winter 1977–78), pp. 12–14.

[33] See, for example, Robert M. Press, ''Africans Join Protests for Multiparty Rule,'' *Christian Science Monitor*, Apr. 11, 1990, p. 1.

[34] See E. A. Wayne, ''Ethiopian Regime Looks West for Helping Hand,'' *Christian Science Monitor*, May 8, 1989, p. 1.

[35] Robert M. Press, ''Reforms May Be Doing More Harm Than Good.'' *Christian Science Monitor*, May 8, 1989, p. 1.

[36] ''Ethiopia's Foreign Minister Quits,'' *New York Times*, Oct. 28, 1986.

[37] *Weekly Review*, Nairobi, Feb. 12, 1988, pp. 4–6.

[38] Todd Shields, ''Kenya,'' *Africa Report*, Vol. 33, No. 3 (May–June 1988), pp. 47–49.

[39] *Weekly Review*, Nairobi, Feb. 12, 1988, pp. 16–18; and Apr. 1, 1988, pp. 4–26; also see Shields, op. cit.

[40] Linsey Hilsum, ''The Dynamics of Discontent,'' *Africa Report*, Vol. 33, No. 1 (January–February 1988), pp. 22–26.

[41] *Weekly Review*, Apr. 1, 1988, p. 24.

[42] Ibid.

[43] Current Policy No. 1148, U.S. Department of State, Bureau of Public Affairs, p. 4.

[44] Todd Shields, *Africa Report*, November–December 1988, p. 50.

MEXICO

Area: 761,600 square miles
Population: 86.7 million
Density per square mile: 114
Languages: Spanish, Indian languages
Literacy rate: 88%
Religion: Roman Catholic
Monetary unit: peso
GNP: (1988) $173 billion;
$7,253 per capita

BRAZIL

Area: 3,286,470 square miles
Population: 151 million
Density per square mile: 45
Languages: Portuguese, Spanish, English,
French
Literacy rate: 74%
Religions: Roman Catholic (88%),
Protestant (6%)
Monetary unit: cruzado
GNP: (1987) $313 billion;
$2,130 per capita

ARGENTINA

Area: 1,072,067 square miles
Population: 32 million
Density per square mile: 30
Language: Spanish
Literacy rate: 94%
Religion: Roman Catholic
Monetary unit: austral
GNP: (1987) $77 billion;
$2,360 per capita

VENEZUELA

Area: 352,143 square miles
Population: 19 million
Density per square mile: 54
Languages: Spanish, Indian languages
in interior
Literacy rate: 88%
Religion: Roman Catholic
Monetary unit: bolivar
GDP: (1987) $47 billion;
$2,520 per capita

Mexico

Cuba

Dominican Republic

Jamaica

Belize

Haiti

Puerto Rico

Virgin Islands

Honduras

Guadeloupe

St. Lucia

Guatemala

Barbados

El Salvador

Nicaragua

St. Vincent

Trinidad and Tobago

Costa Rica

Venezuela

Panama

Colombia

Guyana

Ecuador

Surinam

French Guiana

Peru

Brazil

Bolivia

Paraguay

Uruguay

Chile

Argentina

PART VII

Latin America

Chapter 19
The Spanish Conquest and Its Aftermath

Latin America acquired its name from the Latin-derivative languages spoken there (Spanish and Portuguese). Geographically, Latin America encompasses Mexico and Central America, South America, and the region known as the Caribbean. It includes thirty-four sovereign states ranging in size from Brazil, larger than the contiguous forty-eight United States, to the tiny island of Barbados, about one-tenth the size of Rhode Island. The actual "Latin" states—those in which Spanish or Portuguese is the principal language—number only twenty. All of these except Brazil, colonized by Portugal, were once under the colonial rule of Spain.

Central America comprises seven independent nations: Belize, Costa Rica, El Salvador, Guatemala, Honduras, Nicaragua, and Panama. (Mexico, usually considered a part of Central America, is historically and geographically separate from it. Central America together with Mexico is sometimes called "Middle America.") Two years after they broke from Spain, in 1823, Guatemala, Honduras, El Salvador, Costa Rica, and Nicaragua formed the United Provinces of Central America. This union lasted until 1838. Since then, repeated attempts to restore the union—some twenty-five in all—have failed.

With a land area of nearly 6.9 million square miles, South America is the world's fourth-largest continent. (North America's land mass is about 9.4 million square miles.) South America has some of the highest mountains in the world (the Andes), the largest rain forest (the Amazon Basin), and some of the oldest advanced civilizations (like the Incan). South America's multiplicity of native Indian cultures complements its geographic diversity.

The Caribbean consists of hundred of islands in a chain running from northern South America to southern Florida. The southernmost islands are Trinidad and Tobago; the northernmost are the Bahamas. Cuba is by far the largest of these islands. Some, like Cuba and the Dominican Republic, are Spanish speaking, whereas in others the primary language is English, French, or Dutch. The Caribbean islands are culturally diverse and only tenuously connected by strands of history or commerce to the rest of Latin America. These islands are often called the "West Indies." Geographer David Lowenthal aptly characterized the difficulty of generalizing about this subregion:

> Alike in not being Iberian (Hispanic), the West Indies are not North American either, nor indeed do they fit any ordinary regional pattern. Not so much undeveloped as overdeveloped, exotic without being traditional, they are part of the Third World yet ardent emulators of the West.[1]

Although language is a common denominator throughout most of Latin America, the region as a whole is a diverse mixture of nations and cultures. The stereotypes suggested by words like *mañana* (putting things off until tomorrow) and *machismo* (making a display of male virility) greatly oversimplify Latin American culture. Spain, Portugal, England, France, Italy, the Netherlands, Africa, and indigenous peoples have all contributed to the cultures of the region.

Nor do experts agree on the extent to which Latin America comprises a unity. Some, like Chilean historian Claudio Veliz, argue that the Iberian (Spanish and Portuguese) inheritance is an essential part of life in Latin America. Others, like U.S. political scientist Lawrence Graham, demur. In Graham's view, "What is clear is that generalizations about Latin American cultural unity are no longer tenable." He noted, correctly, that nationalism is a powerful force in the region, and that "one of the effects of nationalism has been to . . . lead growing numbers of individuals within the region to identify with their own nation-state before they think in terms of a more amorphous land mass called Latin America."[2]

Certainly, stereotypes are inimical to an understanding of Latin America, and generalizations are hazardous. Indeed, every state in the region has distinctive features. But recognition of the differences should not obscure the fact that Latin America also has a common heritage rooted in the historical influence of Spain and Portugal and thus in the cultures of the Mediterranean. This European—and particularly Iberian—connection has not resulted in carbon-copy cultures, but with few exceptions it has profoundly influenced the development of culture.

Land, Population, and Resources

As we have seen throughout this book, the physical environment influences the history of nations and regions in many subtle and not-so-subtle ways. None of these influences is more basic than that of geography.

In Latin America geographic factors have often hindered economic development and impeded state-building, that is, the spread of the state's administrative and political institutions, popular recognition of the state's legitimate authority, and growth of a sense of citizenship as evidenced in identification with the state's symbols, aims, and interests. Throughout much of the region the progression from local to national loyalties, so essential to state-building, has been blocked by physical barriers—mountains, jungles, and sparsely inhabited plains. In Bolivia, for example, most Indians (the majority of the Bolivian population) appear to identify themselves not as "Bolivians" but as members of a tribe, village, or region. The same can be said of the native populations in Guatemala and Peru, among other places.

The Land

The most important aspect of Latin America's geography is also the most obvious: its location in the Southern Hemisphere. This fact is significant for a host of climatic, political, economic, diplomatic, and cultural reasons. Generally speaking, the climate is warmer and wetter than in North America. The vast rain forests of South America's Amazon Basin, for example, are enormously important from an environmental standpoint and have no counterpart in the north. Among other factors, temperature, rainfall, and altitude make South America a world apart, environmentally, from North America. Geographic diversity *within* Latin America is hardly less striking.

South America   The continent of South America divides quite naturally into three main parts: the northern Andean countries of Venezuela, Colombia, Ecuador, Peru, and Bolivia; the Southern Cone countries of Argentina, Uruguay, Paraguay, and Chile; and Brazil (almost the entire eastern half of the continent). The small states of Guyana, Suriname, and French Guiana, situated on Brazil's northern frontier, are part of South America in geography only: Guyana was a British colony until 1952, Suriname was a Dutch possession until 1975, and French Guiana continues to be administered by France.

   The majestic Andean Mountains, with peaks reaching nearly 23,000 feet in Chile and Argentina, stretch all the way from Venezuela in the north to the tip of the Southern Cone. This massive mountain range cuts South America into east and west and divides the narrow coastal plain from the rest of the continent. These mountains, along with the Amazon jungle, also divide some countries (Venezuela, Colombia, Ecuador, Peru, Bolivia, and Chile) into separate regions—again, with important political, economic, social, and cultural consequences. To cite one example, Colombia's three major cities—Bogotá, Cali, and Medellín—are situated in deep valleys and isolated from each other by mountain ranges. Not surprisingly, Colombians have thus developed a strong sense of regionalism.

   From the standpoint of demographic settlement, South America appears to be a "hollow" continent. Most large urban centers are coastal, and there is relatively little interior development. Latin America has few interior cities to match in size or significance such inland U.S. cities as Chicago, Detroit, Minneapolis–St. Paul, and St. Louis.

Middle America   The Andes are justly famous. Less famous is the chain of volcanic mountains that extends from Mexico through the land bridge linking the continents of North and South America. These mountains have influenced the history of Middle America in several ways. As barriers to communication, for example, they have complicated the process of national integration. Because their terrain is difficult or impossible to cultivate, they have also impeded economic development. Mexico amply illustrates the problems associated with such a forbidding landscape. The mountains that constitute the "spine" of Middle America rest atop major fault lines. Volcanic eruptions and earthquakes have reduced thousands of villages and nearly every major city in this region to rubble and ash at one time or another. In recent years massive earthquakes have devastated Mexico City in the north and Managua, the capital of Nicaragua, in the south. Disastrous floods are also common, because of heavy rains from May to October, and along the coast hurricanes are a familiar threat.

A kaleidoscope of microclimates and environments, Central America can be divided into four geographic subregions: northern Guatemala and Belize (an extension of Mexico's Yucatán Peninsula); the Caribbean coasts of Guatemala, Honduras, and Nicaragua; the Pacific volcanic region; and the Costa Rica–Panama isthmus. The cultural and political history of Central America is anchored in the highlands and Pacific plains because these areas are the most hospitable to habitation.

Population Patterns

The people of Latin America are as diverse as the land. Except for the West Indies, descendants of the Spanish (or Portuguese) colonial rulers are the nucleus of a social and economic elite throughout most of the region. At the bottom of the socioeconomic order is Latin America's large and culturally differentiated Indian population. By and large the Indians of Latin America have clung tenaciously to traditional values and beliefs and have resisted ''modernization'' schemes drawn up by urban elites, who remain foreigners in their eyes. Attached to a particular locality and oriented toward village and family, native inhabitants still do not view themselves as, for example, Guatemalans, Nicaraguans, or Peruvians. They typically live in rural poverty, often remote from the center, and are victims of benign neglect at best and of governmental abuse at worst.

The elites are European or Europeanized, urban in outlook, university educated, and sophisticated. They typically live in affluent neighborhoods, preferably in capital cities. They constitute the professional class—politicians, businesspeople, bureaucrats, lawyers, doctors, engineers, academics, and the like. The cities are also home to absentee landlords—the scions of ''old money'' for whom land ownership is not only a source of wealth but also a status symbol and proof of pedigree, which seems so important to many Latin elites.

The Latin ''Melting Pot''   South America displays a three-layered ethnic pattern of Spanish (or Portuguese), Indian, and *mestizo* (mixed Spanish/Portuguese and Indian). The ''melting pot'' effect of ethnic commingling is most dramatic in Chile, which is 95-percent European and Spanish-Indian; it is least evident in Argentina and Uruguay, which are overwhelmingly Spanish-European. Indians are most prevalent in the Andean countries of Bolivia, Peru, and Ecuador, a reminder of the Incan civilization that once flourished in these areas. (For example, over half the population of Bolivia is classified as Indian.) In Venezuela and Colombia, Spanish and Indians are outnumbered by mestizos, who constitute about 60 percent of the population. Mestizos are a major segment of society in most of Latin America. Generally there is little or no stigma attached to mixed-blood (or *pardo*) origin, and mestizos, unlike Indians, are prominently represented among social, political, and economic elites.

In Central America a similar pattern holds, with one notable exception. Here *ladinos* are a major element in the population. The word is derived from Latin and refers to anyone who has been latinized. Beyond that general definition, *ladino* means different things in different places. In Guatemala it is synonymous with mestizo; in the rest of Central America it refers to Indians who have adopted European culture.

Initially, ladinos were caught between two cultures and rejected by both. They looked Indian and acted "white." But they excelled as entrepreneurs and, as such, became agents of social change, modernization, and national integration. Today ladinos are the local leaders in Guatemala, Nicaragua, Honduras, and El Salvador.

Urbanization, Migration, and Poverty Since the Spanish Conquest, culture in Latin America has been inseparable from city life. This bias against the harsh, remote, and "uncivilized" world beyond the city gates permeates the thinking of the elites and middle class who dominate Latin society and define its values. Latin culture is highly social—networks of families and constant interaction with friends and neighbors are the norm. In fact, there are more cities of over half a million in Latin America than in the United States, although the United States is far more advanced industrially. (Urbanization and industrialization are often viewed as inextricably entwined.)

In recent decades Latin America has been the scene of major population shifts from the countryside to the cities. This migration cannot be explained by cultural factors or by the lure of bright city lights alone. Rather it is driven by land scarcity, population pressure, insurgency, rural poverty, and the promise of a better life. The last factor turns out to be an illusion for most migrants.

The cities of Middle America have been particularly hard hit by the influx of people from impoverished rural areas. The population of Mexico City, for example, has climbed to astronomical levels (17 to 18 million in 1987) and continues to grow at an alarming rate. The government's capacity to provide essential services such as running water, electricity, sewage disposal and treatment, garbage removal, street maintenance, neighborhood schools, or even fire and police protection is overwhelmed. Living conditions in the shantytowns that have sprung up on the outskirts of mushrooming urban centers like Mexico City are wretched by any standards.

In Central America, El Salvador has experienced the most intense population pressure. There is simply too little land, and the landholdings are too large to accommodate a population that is growing at a rate of 2.7 percent a year—the highest rate in Central America. Most of the land is devoted to export crops—primarily cotton and coffee—or to cattle raising. Thus it is little wonder that land reform has been a burning issue in El Salvador and that a rural insurgency has torn the country asunder in the last decade. Nor is the problem of land scarcity in El Salvador likely to be resolved: Even if agrarian reforms were entirely successful (which is highly unlikely), there would still be too little land to go around.

Thousands of Salvadorans migrated to Honduras in the 1960s in search of land or jobs in commerce and industry. By the end of that decade, some 75 percent of all foreigners in Honduras were immigrants from El Salvador. The resulting tension was a contributing cause in a two-week war between the two countries in 1969.

Depopulation of the countryside is also taking place in South America. Peru and Bolivia provide striking illustrations. In both cases, people from the impoverished highlands, facing famine, have fled to cities. In the case of Peru, natural disasters and a vicious guerrilla war in the southern Andes (especially in Ayacucho province) have played a role as well. At present, 6 million people, or roughly one-third of Peru's population, live within the environs of Lima, the capital. Most newcomers have no money, no education, no job, and therefore no choice but to become squatters, settling in squalid suburban communities that Peruvians euphemistically call *pueblos jovenes* ("new towns").

Although population movement is not equally acute everywhere in Latin America, it is pervasive throughout the region. Where the grass looks greener on the other side of the border, immigrants (and refugees) flock to neighboring countries. Venezuela has had an immigration problem somewhat analogous to that of the United States vis-à-vis Mexico. Since the early 1970s, when Venezuela experienced an economic boom driven by oil exports, Colombians have been "invading"—crossing the border illegally—in search of high-paying jobs.

Thus, population movement poses serious problems for many governments in Latin America. If the trend reflected positive marketplace conditions—economic growth and labor shortages—this geographic mobility would be healthy. Unfortunately, in contemporary Latin America it reflects negative conditions—poverty, hunger, insurgency, and despair.

Natural Resources

In general, Latin America is not resource rich, but neither is it resource poor. Mexico and Venezuela are both significant petroleum producers and exporters. Chile is blessed with over a quarter of the world's copper deposits, about half the iodine, and a great variety of other minerals. Brazil has extensive iron deposits and produces large quantities of crude steel. Brazil and Colombia also have precious gemstone deposits. Colombia, for example, produces 90 percent of the world's emeralds, and Brazil has diamond mines. Both countries produce gold.

In addition to mineral and gemstone deposits, Latin America has rivers that produce hydroelectric power, and Brazil has the world's largest rain forest, which, among other things, produces an extremely important resource: oxygen. Brazil's rain forest has become the focus of worldwide attention, because destruction of this vital asset is occurring at an alarming rate (hundreds of thousands of miles of jungle vegetation are disappearing each year). The tropical rain forests of South America (and of sub-Saharan Africa) generate not only oxygen but also exports worth billions of dollars a year. Vast tracts of jungle forest are also being destroyed by burning to create farm and grazing land. The destruction contributes to a phenomenon only recently recognized, the "greenhouse effect" (a global warming that occurs when heavy concentrations of carbon dioxide and other chemicals in the atmosphere trap the sun's heat).

Much of the devastation is the result of government policies aimed at encouraging Brazil's land-hungry peasants (70 percent of the rural population is landless) to resettle in Amazonia, a "land without men for men without land." This serves to sidestep the politically delicate issue of land reform (0.7 percent of the farms occupy 43 percent of the cultivated land area). Brazil's disappearing rain forest provides a clear illustration of the tensions between environment and development in the Third World. It suggests that, in a conflict between the two, the environment is likely to lose unless something is done to change the public's perceptions and policy maker's priorities.

Latin America has long been a major food producer. Although some states in Central America have been labeled derisively as "banana republics," they are also important producers of such export crops as cotton, sugar cane, and coffee. The same holds true for South America. For example, coffee accounts for 50 percent of Colombia's annual legal exports, although Brazil produces the most coffee. Argentina is a leading producer and exporter of beef and feed grains.

Colombia, Bolivia, Peru, and Ecuador are the world's leading coca producers and supply most of the cocaine sold in the United States. Although coca may not be considered a "commodity" by many observers, the fact remains that it is the major export crop for several countries in Latin America. Coca plants are extremely hardy, grow in a variety of climates and at different altitudes, and yield by far the highest income for the peasants who cultivate them. Of course, drug traffickers profit the most. The value of South America's illegal drug trade is invariably estimated in billions of dollars.

The illegal drug industry poses serious political and social problems for the Andean countries. Cracking down on coca cultivation is tantamount to threatening the livelihood of many peasants in the remote and impoverished highland regions where most of the crop is grown. In Peru, for example, government workers who eradicate coca crops have been attacked and even murdered; coca growers have rioted on occasion. At the same time there is considerable domestic and international pressure on governments to combat the drug kingpins who build empires complete with armed contingents, processing labs, air fields, and transport systems. Faced with the prospect of extradition for trial in the United States, the Medellín drug cartel in Colombia has waged a campaign of terror aimed at intimidating politicians, judges, and other government officials. Drug lords have also infiltrated the courts, the bureaucracy, the police, and even the armed forces, using bribery and extortion to neutralize the government.

Latin American Development and Dependence

Lenin's 1916 essay entitled "Imperialism: The Highest Stage of Capitalism" sets forth a thesis about the economic causes of nineteenth-century imperialism. Lenin characterized the processes of advanced capitalist development as follows:

1. The concentration of production and development of capital to such a high stage that monopolies come to dominate economic life.
2. The merging of bank capital with industrial capital; the resulting "finance capital" gives rise to a powerful "financial oligarchy."
3. The export of capital becomes more important than the export of commodities.
4. The internationalization of monopoly capitalism; world markets are shared for mutual profit.
5. The territorial division of the entire globe by the greatest capitalist powers is consummated.[3]

Lenin argued that imperialism could generate higher profits for monopoly corporations by exploiting cheap Third World labor and pirating natural resources. Part of these profits, in turn, could be used to coopt or buy off potentially militant, unionized workers in the West (Lenin called them the "labor aristocracy").

Closely related to this line of analysis is the leftist view that Western-based multinational corporations (MNCs) have, in effect, created a new kind of colonialism, "neocolonialism," by substituting multinational corporate economic domination for former political-administrative control. The MNCs allegedly manipulate Third World governments, coopting leaders, exploiting elite fears of leftist revolution, buying off the military with arms aid, and interfering in domestic politics. An oft-cited case in point is Chile from 1970 to 1973. The United States undertook a covert operation in Chile—in conjunction with U.S. corporate interests—to destabilize the government of the popularly elected socialist president, Salvador Allende. According to one critic:

> MNCs have attempted, through privileged links to the State Department, the CIA, and the Pentagon, to undermine policies and overthrow regimes that threaten their interests (to make and repatriate profits to shareholders). The MNC would of course prefer not to have to "get tough" in order to assure a favorable investment climate; but in fact it does get tough when its profit margins are at stake, and it can call in some pretty powerful friends to help it get its way.[4]

This vehement criticism of Western governments, banks, and corporations—including such U.S.-dominated world organizations as the International Monetary Fund (IMF) and the World Bank—has recently been echoed in the writings of the so-called dependency theorists. Dependency theory amounts to "a new explanation for the growing gap between rich and poor nations and for the inability of even the best-suited candidates for development (mainly in Latin America) to produce anything like the healthy industrial growth pattern of the Western powers in an earlier era."[5] The genesis of this school of thought, which has been extremely influential among Latin American political and intellectual elites, is instructive:

> Special hopes and much publicity had been given to the Alliance for Progress, a United States-sponsored investment and aid program of the 1960s, the goal of which was to achieve a breakthrough to sustained and independent economic development for at least several Latin American nations. The spectacular failure of the Alliance. . . led to a thorough critique of conventional Western models. . .which spelled out a

general "do it like we did it" approach. This critique in turn led to a new theory of dependency, which accounted for the failure of Western-style development to appear in Latin America and also predicted that real development would not appear as long as the dependency syndrome lasted.[6]

Significantly, dependency theory was "invented" by a group of Latin American economists (Dos Santos, Sunkel, Cardoso, Casanova, and Frank). It has since been applied by others to Africa and Asia as well. No doubt this theory has some merit. At the same time, it is a whitewash of the extremely inequitable conditions that Latin socioeconomic elites have both created and perpetuated. In this light, it is a self-serving rationalization for homegrown inadequacies and failures.

It is difficult to generalize about development in Latin America because the picture changes considerably from one state to the next and even from one part of a given state to the next. Many Latin American nations have achieved a great deal politically, economically, socially, and culturally. But there is still much to be done throughout the region to create decent living standards for the multitudes who live in poverty and who have little hope of ever escaping its deprivations.

Political History and Culture

Many studies dealing with the development of Latin American political institutions begin at the wrong point: the story of the Spanish Conquest or even the independence movement in the early nineteenth century. The Spanish could not begin building new institutions until they displaced, destroyed, adapted, or assimilated the entrenched Indian cultures and, indeed, civilizations that they found already in place.

Latin America's Original Civilizations

The Incas, Mayas, and Aztecs were the three most advanced Indian cultures in the Americas. The Inca Empire stretched 2,000 miles along the high mountains and plateaus of the Andean range in South America. It was based in what is now Cuzco (Peru), north of Lake Titicaca. From Cuzco, the Inca monarch, or Sapa Inca, controlled a highly centralized empire.

When the Incas expanded their territories, conquered peoples were fully integrated into their political system and even had to learn the Incan language, Quechua. The empire had extensive transportation and communication systems (roads, supply posts at regular intervals, and runners) as well as an advanced water system of aqueducts, irrigation ditches, and reservoirs.

Incan agriculture was innovative and efficient, and the administrative system was highly sophisticated, penetrating as far down into society as the family structure itself. The Incas had been established at least 400 years by the time Francisco Pizarro arrived in the 1520s.

The Mayan civilization, anchored in the Yucatán Peninsula of present-day Mexico, had existed for at least 1,000 years before Hernán Cortés came and conquered (1519–1521). The Mayas, like the Incas, were architects. They built large stone temples, developed an accurate calendar, and had a writing system (something the Incas did not have). The Mayas also surpassed the Incas in mathematics and astronomy. Religion was a vital part of Mayan life, and priests actually ruled for a time, turning the Mayan political system into a kind of theocracy.

In contrast to the peace-loving Mayas, the Aztecs were aggressive and often attacked weaker neighbors. Entering Mexico in the 1200s, they too were empire builders, making alliances with tribes that they could not easily subjugate and collecting tribute wherever possible. They worshipped various deities and practiced human sacrifice. The pictorial writing system they developed was less advanced than that of the Mayas. Their administrative system was also inferior, but they excelled in architecture and sculpture, building immense religious pyramids and a capital city, Tenochtitlán, which was an engineering marvel. Situated in the center of a large lake, the fortress city, adorned by imposing temples and statuary, could be reached only by three causeways. It supported a population of 60,000 families.

Many other less advanced Indian tribes inhabited the Americas. Millions of Native Americans lived within territorial and cultural boundaries etched into ''maps'' that had guided their ancestors, and governed their way of life, for centuries. One thing all the indigenous peoples had in common was that they did not want to be liberated, converted, conquered, or enslaved. But there was no stopping the Iberian juggernaut borne by the winds from an alien world.

The Spanish Conquest

Christopher Columbus arrived in the New World in 1492 while on a quest for the king and queen of Spain to find a new route to the ''Indies.'' The first Spanish settlements were established in the Caribbean, where the colonists had little difficulty subduing native Indian populations and subjecting them to a slavery-based tribute system. Attempts to gain a foothold on the mainland were less successful, however, as the more advanced Indians savagely attacked and killed some of the first explorers and slave-catching parties.

Spain had only recently become a unified state under Ferdinand and Isabella after a long war to oust the Moors. As a consequence, a generation of Spaniards knew no other life than that of war. Unfortunately for Native Americans, many Spaniards became soldiers of fortune and journeyed to the New World in pursuit of adventure and riches.

Hernán Cortés first conquered Cuba, then cast about for another challenge. He set sail for the mainland in February 1519 with eleven ships and six hundred men—against the governor's orders. Following two years of bloody battles, Cortés finally conquered the Aztecs. Although once a rebel, Cortés was vindicated by his triumph and became Spanish proconsul in Mexico. The Spanish built Mexico City on the ruins of Tenochtitlán, the great Aztec capital.

Cortés sent armed expeditions into other parts of Mexico and Central America. In 1523–1524 an expeditionary force led by Pedro de Alvarado defeated the Mayas. A second empire had fallen.

The conquest of the third empire—the Incan—took longer, even though it was aided by internecine strife among the Incas themselves. Francisco Pizarro set out from present-day Panama in 1524 to explore South America. Having discovered the wealth of the Incas, he sought and received permission from the Spanish court to conquer and colonize the "new" continent. Pizarro's charging horsemen and thundering artillery terrified the Incas, who, despite a great advantage in numbers, panicked and fled.

From that point on it was just a matter of time before Spain colonized the Andean Empire of the Incas plus the northern and southern parts of the continent that are now Colombia and Venezuela (in the north) and Paraguay, Uruguay, and Argentina (in the south). Meanwhile, the Spanish were also colonizing Central America. (After some excursions into North America in the 1540s, Spanish explorers reported that nothing there would attract settlers.)

Spanish Colonial Rule

Colonizing Latin America proved to be more difficult than conquering it. The Conquest brought chaos to areas where organization had once flourished. Now Spain had to build new institutions on the ruins of those it had destroyed. Nor was governance Queen Isabella's only concern; converting the Indians to Christianity was a high priority from the outset.

The Spanish needed laborers to build their cathedrals and cities and to work on their plantations, and so they conscripted the Indians. The *encomienda* system was designed to compel the Indians to do what supposedly was in their own best interest: to work for pay while learning the Christian religion. Indian laborers were organized by villages, where an *encomendero*—who supervised work, religious instruction, and welfare—had virtually unlimited authority. He also collected all fruits of the land and labor he managed.

Had the system worked the way it was intended, the Indians' dignity and freedom would have been respected. But flagrant abuses occurred. Many of the encomenderos were petty tyrants. The Indians, forced to do grueling work, became slaves. The hard labor killed many conscripts, especially in the Caribbean islands, where native populations were totally wiped out. (They were replaced with slaves from Africa, which is why blacks now make up the majority of the population throughout much of the Caribbean.)

In most of Latin America, Indians remained the primary labor source, particularly in the high elevations to which they were adapted. In these areas the Spanish divided villages into sections and forcibly drafted about one-seventh of the males to work in the mines or elsewhere until another section relieved them. Laborers were supposed to be paid, and there were limits on the distance they could be taken from home. But abuses were common, and Indians were frequently overworked and poorly fed, housed, and clothed. Many died in the mines of Peru and other areas.

Despite efforts of the Spanish Crown to protect Indians' rights and prevent their exploitation, the colonists always prevailed. The encomienda system lasted well into the eighteenth century, when it was finally outlawed. By this time, however, colonial overlords had imposed Spanish culture, including Christianity, on the Indians, leaving a legacy of hatred and prejudice that remains a major cause of civil strife in parts of the region (such as Peru and Guatemala).

Nor did exploitation of the Indians end with the demise of the encomienda system. Ironically, the natives were forced to help destroy their own empires and build a new one. Persecuted and proselytized, they found their cultures, languages, and identities threatened with extinction. That cultures are often more resilient than political systems is evident in the fact that the Spanish Empire is long gone, but some of the Indian cultures have survived. For example, in Peru 30 percent of the people still speak no Spanish; they speak Quechua, the language of the Incas.

The basic problem inherent in Spanish rule involved the desire of the Crown to maintain direct control over its colonial empire while its proconsuls had to make decisions and react to conditions "on the ground." (Communications between the colonies and the royal court took months under the best of circumstances.) To deal with this, a viceroy system was eventually established whereby an official appointed by the Crown exercised full authority within a designated territory. The viceroys (and captains-general) had the responsibility to enforce laws, collect taxes, administer, spread Christianity, and, most important for them, command the Spanish army within their jurisdiction.

Besides being inefficient in structure and practice, the colonial administration of the Spanish Empire became corrupt to the core. True, some Spanish officials served with honor and distinction, but these were the exceptions. More often, unqualified people of poor character curried favor with the Crown in order to get a colonial post in the Americas. By the end of the sixteenth century, office-seekers simply bid for positions that literally went to the highest bidder. Political favors, promotions, the legal system, tax collection—all had their price. Property ownership came with no guarantees of permanence, and even inspectors were not above bribe-taking. In the words of one historian:

> Corruption was universal and in most cases unpunished. The public treasury was defrauded in countless ways, and justice or more frequently injustice was for sale in the courts.[7]

The Role of the Church   Under the Spanish colonial administration a special relationship between church and state developed. Catholicism had been the official religion in Spain since the days of the Roman Empire, and the Spanish Crown was determined to export the "one true faith" to the New World. To this end, the Spanish excluded all foreigners and non-Catholics from the colonies.

With an almost homogeneous Catholic population in colonial Latin America, the Catholic Church became very powerful, controlling baptisms, weddings, registration of births and deaths, religious processions and festivals, holidays, and charities. It built and managed the schools, hospitals, asylums, missions, and cemeteries and operated its own system of civil and criminal courts. The Church amassed great wealth, receiving 10 percent of the taxes as well as bequests of money and land from the estates of the rich. It also controlled much of the banking system, held many mortgages on personal property, and was a large landholder. In addition, Church revenues were tax exempt.

The power of the Church reached its zenith during the Spanish Inquisition during the sixteenth century. The Spanish Crown established tribunals in Lima in 1570 and in Mexico City in 1571; the tribunals punished heretics and other religious offenders by property loss, imprisonment, exile, or even death—sometimes by burning. Other repressive measures included press censorship and even book burning.

The power of the Church was eventually perceived as a threat to the state. In 1767 Charles III expelled the Jesuits—a Roman Catholic religious order founded in 1534 that had played a leading role in the colonial phase of the Spanish Inquisition—from Spain and the colonies. The Spanish Crown won this battle, but it was only the beginning of a long struggle between Church and state in Latin America. This conflict pitted liberals (who wanted to reduce Church power and enact religious reforms) against conservatives (who supported minor Church reforms but generally aligned themselves with the clergy).

The Church-and-state dispute lasted far beyond the period of Spanish rule (from about 1500 to the 1820s) and became particularly important in Mexico, Central America, Colombia, and Ecuador. The liberals, who eventually won out, instituted religious reforms that abolished many of the Church's privileges. Years of struggle, however, were largely for naught:

> In most instances . . . all that the people obtained from the expensive, bloody, and prolonged conflict was a little more freedom in religion—in which they were not seriously concerned, since they were content to remain Roman Catholics—and somewhat broader opportunities for education.[8]

In the end the Church retained its religious monopoly and much of its prestige, but its power and wealth were curbed.

Control of Trade   Despite the tension between the Church and the Spanish Crown, religion was one instrument of Spanish imperial rule. Another was a crude form of mercantilism—the unabashed plundering of the region's natural resources. Spanish indifference to the material well-being of the colonies contrasted sharply with the Crown's solicitude for the spiritual welfare of the Indians. Spain actually discouraged economic development in Latin America, concentrating instead on extraction and export of raw materials, particularly gold and silver. Surprisingly, the Crown never took full advantage of the potentially profitable cash crops such as sugar, indigo, and cacao.

Besides neglecting economic growth in the colonies, Spain also imposed severe trade restrictions on them. Only two Spanish ports, Seville and Cádiz, were allowed to carry on trade with the colonies, and all imports had to pass through New Spain (Mexico) or Peru. Tough restrictions also governed trade among the colonies themselves. Lone ships sailing between Spain and the New World would often be captured by foreign powers or pirates. Thus, after 1550, almost all trade was done in fleets of merchant ships or convoys sailing under the protection of the Spanish navy.

With so many restrictions and dangers, goods imported to Latin America became exorbitantly expensive, and illegal trade networks developed. The Portuguese and French smuggled goods into the Spanish colonies with the aid of corrupt Spanish officials. Brazil often served as the entry point for illegal goods.

Piracy declined during the eighteenth century, and the convoy system was eventually abandoned. In 1778 Spain lifted most trade restrictions on the colonies. By this time, however, Spain had been drained by wars and had lost its naval supremacy to the British. Its ill-conceived attempt to monopolize Latin American trade had actually diverted profitable commerce into illegal channels.

Class Conflict   Spanish colonial administrators also had to deal with tensions among newly developing social classes. Of particular concern was the animosity between creoles (New World descendants of the Spanish) and *peninsulares* (immigrants from Spain). The Crown persisted in giving preferential treatment to "pure" Spaniards whose ties to Spain were most direct; creoles greatly resented such discrimination.

The mestizos were the next-ranking class in the Latin American caste system. Intermarriage between Spanish and Indian came about partly because few Spanish women immigrated to the New World. Mestizos were not accepted as equals by the creoles, although some white fathers succeeded in conferring upper-class status on their children of mixed blood.

Next in rank came the *mullatos* (mixed Spanish and African blood) and *zambos* (mixed African and Indian blood). Both groups held lower status than the mestizos, but none of the mixed races suffered from open discrimination. The lowest classes were the Indians, free Africans, and African slaves, in that order. Members of these groups faced discrimination in education, employment, and other areas.

Class conflicts thus became a natural part of the evolution of Spanish rule in Latin America. Spanish imperial policy was flawed and generally unenlightened from start to finish. Having discovered the New World by accident, the Spanish Crown did not know what to do with it. By the time it finally decided that its highest priority in the colonies was to keep other powers out, the Spanish conquistadors had already destroyed three native civilizations. Overlooking Latin America's long-range economic potential, Spain adopted a short-range policy of exploitation that, in simplest terms, emphasized extraction at the expense of cultivation. Meanwhile, the Spanish left the "Indian problem"—as well as the social and cultural development of the colonies—to the Roman Catholic Church, which itself exploited the Indians and resented every intrusion of secular authority.

The Spanish colonists could accept the sad state of affairs in Latin America out of blind loyalty. But a new class of "native" Latin Americans was emerging to challenge colonial rule. One of the most urgent tasks of the new states would thus be to fill the "legitimacy vacuum" that the Spanish left as a legacy.

Independence and Self-Government in Latin America

The conquest of Spain by Napoleon and the abdication of Charles IV at Bayonne in 1808 undercut the authority of the Spanish proconsuls in the colonies. Most of the colonists, even the rising creole and mestizo classes, had no desire to exchange Spanish tutelage for French. Latin America's turbulent independence movement grew out of the confusion and disarray that followed Spain's fall. (By contrast, Brazil—a Portuguese colony—made a peaceful transition to independence. This probably accounts for the relative stability that has characterized Brazil's political development, in sharp contrast to that of other Latin American countries.)

Simón Bolívar, the most famous of Latin America's early liberators, led an abortive revolt against Spanish rule in the summer of 1811; two years later he captured Caracas, the capital of Venezuela, and earned the title of Liberator. After the defeat of Napoleon in 1815, however, Ferdinand VII ascended to the Spanish throne and sent a force of 10,000, which crushed the revolution. Some other early insurrections met with similar results. But the virus of revolution spread like an epidemic, and Spain could not contain it.

The conflict pitted not only Spain against the colonies but also colonist against colonist. In fact, the independence struggle has often been characterized more as a series of civil wars than as "national liberation wars" against Spain. As the ranks of revolutionaries swelled, a nearly equal force of colonists who were loyal to Spain rose up to defend the Crown's interests. Much of the fighting took place between royalist and revolutionary forces, a division that continued into the early postindependence period.

Independence from Spain was achieved in the mid-1820s. But the newly independent states soon encountered many of the same problems the Spanish had had in establishing stable systems of government. The first turbulent decades after independence were marked by power struggles in which *caudillos* ("men on horseback," or strongmen) played a prominent role in many countries. Brazil and Chile enjoyed relatively stable government, but other countries—notably, Argentina, Mexico, Colombia, and Venezuela—were torn by civil war. Freed from the commercial restrictions imposed by Spain, Latin America (particularly Argentina, Brazil, and Chile) became more actively involved in international trade. However, Middle America and much of South America sank into a deep torpor. In general, the period from 1820 to 1870 brought little prosperity to the region, and the population remained predominantly rural, illiterate, and poor.

Beginning in about 1870 Latin America entered a second phase of its modern development, as international capitalism expanded and opened up new markets around the globe. Latin America's exports consisted of foodstuffs and raw materials for which demand was rising in Europe's rapidly industrializing nations (as well as in the United States, later). Many Latin American nations, enjoying an unprecedented export boom, could now finance imported manufactured goods. Transport and urban life were modernized. Argentina's economic development was especially rapid during this period. In other countries, too, national leaders saw export-driven growth and foreign capital as the keys to progress.

The new economic vitality stimulated social change. Cities grew, literacy spread, and a middle class evolved. At the same time a new urban proletariat (and labor movements) also sprang up, especially in countries where a surge in exports created domestic markets for consumer goods that could be manufactured locally. Social diversification accompanied urbanization during the early stages of industrial development—with important consequences for political life. The state became better organized. As new social groups (especially the industrial labor force) emerged to challenge traditional land-owning elites, the stage was being set for future domestic tensions and power struggles.

A major change in hemispheric relations occurred with the rise of the United States as a great power. The emergence of the "colossus to the north" was dramatically evidenced in the Mexican-American War (1846–1848), the Spanish-American War (1898), and the thinly disguised seizure of Panama (1903). Numerous military interventions during the first three decades of the twentieth century confirmed the new patterns of power and influence in the Western Hemisphere.

The worldwide depression of the 1930s followed by World War II greatly disrupted the international economy and ushered in the third phase of modern Latin American history. The export-driven economies of the region saw their foreign markets dry up. Without export earnings, the Latin nations could not service their overseas debt and were soon cut off from foreign financial markets. Every country except Argentina and Haiti defaulted. The crisis led directly to greater state intervention in the economy, and "import-substituting industrialization" became a prominent strategy.

World War II brought a new surge in the region's exports that, in turn, helped finance industrialization. By 1960 Argentina, Brazil, and Mexico had become the leading industrial nations in the Third World, with Chile and Colombia trailing behind. The smaller nations, however, remained dependent on agriculture and mining. All the while, the role of the state—particularly in banking, market development, and industry—continued to grow.

As industrialization advanced, the process of social differentiation was also accelerated. The middle class and organized labor gained political power, although truly pluralistic multiparty systems did not develop (except, partially, in Chile). Broad-based populist coalitions ruled for extended periods in some countries—for example, in Brazil under Getúlio Vargas and in Argentina under Juan Perón. In Mexico one-party rule became entrenched.

From the 1930s to the 1960s Latin America displayed a variety of political systems, including civilian democracies and military dictatorships. Whatever the specific disposition, however, the shadow of the caudillos and the possibility of a coup were ever present.

Political Culture

Perhaps one of the most important ways the past impinges on the present politically is through its power to shape the values, perceptions, and predilections of a nation or, as in Latin America, of an entire region. The colonial experience gave Latin America a unique moral unity that was reinforced by the pervasive influence of the Roman Catholic Church and the dissemination of the Spanish language. Colonial administration was staffed at the highest levels by Crown-appointed peninsular officials through the Council of the Indies at Seville. (After their tenure top officials were subject to the *residencia*, an evaluation of their performance in office.)

When the Spanish Empire crumbled in the 1820s, a struggle developed between liberals, who were generally associated with republicanism and anticlericalism, and conservatives, who wanted to preserve the privileges of the traditional elites and saw defense of the established Church as one way to do it. Liberals also came to be identified with demands for local autonomy, whereas conservatives favored a strong, centralized state. The role of Napoleon in weakening the Spanish monarchy and destroying its mystique in the colonies was significant: Napoleon himself became a kind of model for the fledgling Latin American republics, and military prowess became the principal source of political legitimacy. Hence, the military caudillo was institutionalized throughout the region in the first half-century after independence.

Caudillismo was highly personalistic—it depended on the personality of the leader. Simón Bolívar, liberator of Venezuela, Colombia, Ecuador, Bolivia, and Peru, epitomized this phenomenon at an early stage. Unlike Bolívar, however most caudillos were pragmatic military figures who cared little about ideas, ideals, or ideologies. Constitutions were used to legitimize power seizures rather than as constraints on power wielders. Venezuela, the first country to draft a constitution (1811), has since had no fewer than twenty. Historically, law has been subordinated to order, and order has been a function of military rather than civilian leadership. Thus one trademark of Latin America is a prominent military role in domestic affairs *even when civilian rule is in effect.*

Localismo—a strong identity with a particular geographic area—is another salient feature of Latin American politics. Typically, caudillos asserted their local dominance first and only then, if at all, challenged existing rulers. The extent of a caudillo's power depended on his personal charisma, which in turn reflected his military exploits, machismo, and local reputation. If he could recruit a large enough personal army, he had a fighting chance of toppling the current strongman (who may or may not have come to power by similar means). More likely he would be content to rule his "fiefdom" as one part of a larger and relatively loose-knit political system based on local patron–client networks.

Local political bosses were not universally loved. In fact, they were often called *caciques* in Hispanic Latin America (or *coronels* in Brazil). These terms are still used, and they have a pejorative connotation, implying a panoply of corrupt practices.

Militarism and localism were thus deeply embedded in the culture and even, to some degree, in the geography, which isolated small areas and made communication difficult. As discussed previously, the Andean mountains cut South America into east and west and are seldom crossed by car or train even today. Tropical jungles are also a barrier in large parts of both Central America and South America. In Argentina extensive flat grasslands (pampas) provide an excellent environment for grazing; isolation there arises from the distances between haciendas or communities. In general, geographic isolation in Latin America reinforced tendencies toward local particularism and created barriers to political integration. This helps to explain why civil and (more recently) guerrilla wars have been so much a part of the region's history.

Hostility toward the United States, or *anti-yanquismo*, also permeates Latin American politics. This sentiment is expressed in literature as a rejection of North American materialism and in politics as a radical, sometimes revolutionary, brand of left-wing extremism. The Cuban Revolution (1959)—which signaled Cuba's break with the United States—might have become a symbol throughout the region had it not been for Castro's clumsy attempts to "export revolution" (that is, to subvert governments in Latin America). After Che Guevara, a revolutionary compadre of Fidel Castro, was killed in Bolivia in 1967, fear of communism caused a chain reaction of military coups and repressive countermeasures that wiped out any threat of revolution in most places; the anti-Americanism that helped spawn it, however, was left intact.

Patterns of Military Rule

There are several identifiable patterns of military intervention or involvement in Latin American politics. In some countries the military has often ruled in coalition with civilian leaders, as in Brazil and Uruguay. In other countries military and civilian rulers have tended to alternate in power, as in Peru and Ecuador. In still others the military is entrenched in the political system, but military rule, when it occurs, is unstable; Argentina and Bolivia are examples. Personalistic rule by a general-turned-president is yet another familiar pattern, and recent examples include Panama under Noriega, Chile under Pinochet, and Paraguay under Stroessner. Finally, in a number of Latin American countries the military plays a key role but has not actually ruled for many decades (this is the case in Venezuela, Colombia, Mexico, and Cuba). Costa Rica is a genuine exception to the militarism found throughout the region: It has no standing army.

Until the 1960s most military dictatorships fit the personalistic caudillo model to the extent that their legitimacy depended heavily on the prestige and personal authority of a single individual. During the 1960s and 1970s the military in many Latin countries entered into a limited partnership with civilian politicians, holding elections or plebiscites without giving up real power. During the 1980s the military stepped back (except in Panama, Chile, and Paraguay) and let the politicians grapple with growing domestic problems.

The United States and Latin America:
An Interventionist Tradition

The United States is viewed with a mixture of admiration and resentment in Latin America—admiration for U.S. military prowess, power, and prestige but resentment for the "big stick" diplomacy (interventionism) that has so often overshadowed U.S. efforts to be a good neighbor. The foundation of U.S. foreign policy toward Latin America was laid in the 1820s with the enunciation of the Monroe Doctrine, which declared the Western Hemisphere off limits to the Great Powers of Europe. In retrospect, the United States was replacing Spain as the dominant external power in Latin America: The promulgation of the Monroe Doctrine coincided with the crumbling of the Spanish Empire in the New World. The only time the European powers violated the U.S. ban on interference from outside the hemisphere was in Santo Domingo and in Mexico during the 1860s, a time when the U.S. Civil War momentarily placed the Monroe Doctrine in limbo.

The United States engaged in a series of conflicts in Latin America. It made Mexico relinquish Texas in 1836, and after the Mexican-American War (1846–1848) it came away with Texas and the entire southwest (California, Nevada, Utah, and most of New Mexico and Arizona). Half a century later the United States acquired Cuba, Puerto Rico, Hawaii, and the Philippines in the Spanish-American War (1898). In 1903 President Theodore Roosevelt cast a covetous eye on the Isthmus of Panama, wrested the desired territory from Colombia, and built the Panama Canal.

Since then there has been no waning of U.S. interest or intervention in Latin affairs. The U.S. government sent marines into Nicaragua and Honduras in 1912 (and kept a military presence in Nicaragua until the late 1920s) and entered the Dominican Republic and Haiti in 1915–1916. President Wilson also sent a military expedition headed by General John J. Pershing into Mexico in 1916 after Pancho Villa conducted a raid against a border town in New Mexico. U.S. troops stayed in Mexico for nearly a year. Although Villa was his adversary, the president of Mexico opposed the U.S. military action; the venture accomplished little more than to solidify Mexican sentiment against U.S. interventionism. The fact that Mexico was sympathetic to Germany in World War I illustrates the intensity of anti-U.S. feeling in Mexico during this period.

After World War II the United States intervened in Guatemala against the Arbenz government (1953), attempted to overthrow Fidel Castro in Cuba (1961), sent marines into the Dominican Republic to stop a leftist takeover (1965), armed the Nicaraguan *contras* against Daniel Ortega's Sandinista regime (1980s), invaded Grenada (1983), and overthrew Panamanian dictator Manuel Noriega (1989). In addition, the United States supported Great Britain against Argentina in the Falklands War (1982).

But "big stick" diplomacy is only one side of U.S.–Latin American relations; the "good neighbor" policy is the other. After World War II the United States created the Organization of American States (OAS) to provide a multilateral framework for hemispheric collaboration. During the early 1960s President John F. Kennedy launched the Alliance for Progress aimed at fostering economic cooperation and development in Latin America. More recently, the Reagan Administration sponsored the Caribbean Basin Initiative to promote prosperity, trade, and free enterprise in the Caribbean.

Today the United States is Latin America's major trading partner. Moreover, U.S. aid and investment have played a key supporting role in Latin development efforts. U.S. banks, encouraged by the government, made billions of dollars in loans available to Latin America during the 1970s, as did banks in other Western countries; the result was a foreign debt that topped $400 billion at the end of the 1980s. The United States and the International Monetary Fund have agreed to debt relief and rescheduling schemes in a number of cases, but the price Latin debtor states have had to pay is high: unpopular austerity programs that create severe strains on recently established democratic institutions.

Case Studies: Mexico, Brazil, Argentina, and Venezuela

This section looks closely at four Latin American countries: Mexico, Brazil, Argentina, and Venezuela. The first three, especially, represent the region's political patterns and trends. Venezuela did, too, until the late 1950s, when it adopted a democratic constitution and elected its first president. Since then Venezuela has evolved a stable political system in which power has been transferred peaceably every five years to elected leaders. Mexico has also had a relatively stable government for many years, but its political system is dominated by a single party, the Institutional Revolutionary party (PRI).

Mexico

Under Spanish rule Mexico was known as New Spain, a fitting tribute to the flagship colony of Spain's New World empire. Upon independence in 1821 Mexico had the largest population in Latin America and produced two-thirds of the world's silver. Mexico City was not only the largest city in Latin America but also its cultural center. Despite these advantages, the new nation of Mexico got off to a troubled and turbulent start.

Mexico's first two constitutions were short-lived. The first election (1829), fittingly enough, was nullified when the losing party, refusing to accept the outcome, revolted and ousted the victorious party, with help from the military. Thus precedent was set at an early stage: Elections must be held for the sake of appearances, but the outcome is not sacrosanct. If the results are not satisfactory, resort to violence rather than submit; better yet, manipulate the elections to ensure the desired results.

The greatest figures in Mexico's political history before the Revolution of 1911 are Antonio López de Santa Anna, Benito Juárez, and Porfirio Díaz. Santa

Anna, the first durable leader after independence, came to power in a revolt (1829) and dominated the political scene for the next twenty-five years. He dissolved Congress and discarded the Constitution. He was a tough-minded pragmatist, but his rule was destined to coincide with one of the greatest humiliations in modern Mexican history.

In 1835 settlers in Texas revolted against Mexico City. They defeated the Mexican forces the following year and captured Santa Anna, who was forced to sign a treaty granting Texas its independence from Mexico. In 1838, after several foreign powers accused Mexico of offenses against their nationals, France sent a fleet to Veracruz and demanded restitution in the form of a large cash payment. The fighting that followed is known as the "Pastry War" because France claimed a baker's shop had been ransacked. Britain mediated the dispute, and Mexico paid the claim.

The worst was yet to come. In 1845 the United States annexed Texas despite a warning from the Mexican government that such a move would be considered an act of war. Mexico attacked but again lost. Disgraced, Santa Anna stepped down and went into exile. Mexico signed the Treaty of Guadelupe in 1848, which officially made the territory that now comprises Texas, New Mexico, Arizona, Nevada, Utah, and California part of the United States. For Mexico the loss of this vast region was traumatic and humiliating. (Santa Anna returned from exile in 1853 and resumed his former role as dictator until a revolt forced him to flee in 1854, ending one of many unhappy chapters in Mexico's history.)

Since independence there had been a struggle between liberals and conservatives in Mexico. The conservatives, who identified with the Church and landed aristocracy, were in the ascendancy in the 1820s. Under Santa Anna pragmatism eclipsed ideology (Santa Anna and many of his contemporaries switched sides opportunistically). With the end of the Santa Anna era, the liberals, who sought to reduce the power and wealth of the Church and extend civil rights to previously disenfranchised groups, gained the upper hand. Led by a caudillo named Juan Álvarez, the new liberal government embarked on major reforms: the *Ley Juárez* (Juárez Law) of 1855, which stripped the Church and military of judicial powers and established equality before the law, and the *Ley Lerdo* (Lerdo Law) of 1856, which abolished all corporate landholding. The Ley Lerdo dealt a heavy blow to the Catholic Church, which, along with villages, was a major "corporate" property owner. The new reforms and sundry individual liberties and protections were enshrined in the Constitution of 1857.

The conservative reaction led to the War of the Reform (1857–1860), in which the Church excommunicated those who swore allegiance to the new Constitution and a chain reaction of uprisings in defense of "religion and rights" occurred. A full-scale civil war more violent than anything since the independence struggle raged for several years. The liberals finally won and elevated Benito Juárez, one of Mexico's most famous statesmen (and an Indian), to the presidency. Juárez, who had been imprisoned by Santa Anna in 1853 but later played a crucial role as architect of the liberal reforms under Juan Álvarez, ruled Mexico during the turbulent 1860s.

The civil war took a heavy toll in blood and treasure. To sustain the war effort, the government had seized foreign assets, for which reparations were now demanded. Since the United States was unable to enforce the Monroe Doctrine during its own Civil War, Britain, Spain, and France launched a joint expedition to seize Veracruz, Mexico's capital at the time, and, in effect, hold it for ransom. France's dictator, Napoleon III, saw a golden opportunity to extend his domain with a deft move on the international chessboard: He installed Maximilian, brother of the Austrian monarch, as Mexico's new emperor! It was a bizarre plan bound to fail, but not before Mexico was once again subjected to a humiliating foreign intervention.

Maximilian's brief reign (1864–1867) gave the conservatives a chance to regain the upper hand. But after the European powers withdrew, the liberals deposed and executed him. The liberal victory brought Juárez (and the Juáristas) back to power.

Mexico's economy was in a shambles, and the public treasury was empty. The government had defaulted on its international loans and had amassed a sizable internal debt as well. The liberals took to quarreling among themselves. In 1872 Juárez was elected to a fourth term, but he died soon after. Four years later Porfirio Díaz, irked at Juárez's successor for seeking his own reelection, staged a classic caudillo-style military coup. Thus began the longest period of personal rule in Mexican history, from 1876 to 1911.

The *Porfiriato* (as Díaz's rule was called) represented the triumph of pragmatism over ideology and ushered in a period of accelerated economic development. Díaz ruled as an enlightened dictator, placing prosperity ahead of liberty. Elections were rigged, and opposition was coopted or crushed. "Plenty of administration and no politics" was a popular Porfirian slogan. Díaz stressed the creation of a state-energized market system as the key to economic revitalization. Always the pragmatist, he refused to let *anti-yanquismo* or nationalism interfere with his development strategy. He attracted foreign capital by allowing foreign investors to develop—and profit from—mining ventures, railways, and commercial agriculture.

Mexico's economic recovery under the Díaz dictatorship is the bright side; there was a dark side as well. In rural areas the rich got richer as enterprising landlords gobbled up smallholders' lands, and protest was smothered by local *jefes politicos* (political bosses) loyal to the Porfiriato. The result was rising agrarian discontent. In the cities, too, the burgeoning middle class, educated and prosperous, resented being excluded from the political process. During the waning years of the Díaz dictatorship, the surface tranquility was deceiving: Underneath an upheaval was in the making.

The revolution that began in 1910 did not end until 1917. It was a volcanic event that left Mexican society in a shambles. Francisco Madero was the leader of the Mexican Revolution. Although he came from a family of landowners, Madero was a proponent of political and agrarian reform. He wrote a widely circulated book urging Mexican voters to reject Díaz in the 1910 election. During the presidential campaign Díaz jailed Madero for allegedly fomenting a revolt. Díaz won the election and then released Madero, who fled to Texas and proclaimed a revolution against Díaz. Madero subsequently returned to Mexico, organized a military force, and in May 1911 captured Ciudad Juárez, the largest city in Chihuahua. Faced with a civil war that would pit society against the state—and the many (peasants, the rising middle class) against the few (administrative officials, the landed aristocracy, the Church's hierarchy)—Díaz resigned.

A popular hero, Madero was elected president of Mexico in November 1911. He had little time to savor his triumph, however. The very next year two simultaneous revolts broke out, one led by Emiliano Zapata in the south, the other led by Pancho Villa in the north. In 1913 the commander-in-chief, General Victoriano Huerta, overthrew Madero and assumed the presidency. Madero was killed, allegedly during an attempted escape as he awaited trial for treason.

The Mexican Revolution did not die with Madero, however. Civil war ravaged the country for several more years before Venustiano Carranza emerged as victor and president. In 1917 Carranza promulgated a new constitution, one that built on the liberal foundations of the 1857 Constitution. It prescribed an impressive array of reforms in government, education, labor, and land tenure. For example, the Constitution prohibited presidential self-succession; embraced the principle of universal compulsory education as a responsibility of the state (rather than the Church); created a labor code that guaranteed workers the right to organize, strike, and bargain collectively; expropriated all property of religious orders; and restored communal lands to the Indians. Although such measures may seem bland today, in 1917 they were radical. The Constitution reduced the role of the Church in the nation's political life. By secularizing Mexican society, it sought to undercut the moral authority of the power elite, whose legitimacy depended on the Church, and at the same time to remove a major impediment to modernization.

Scintillating in theory, the 1917 Constitution was never fully observed in practice. In 1920 Álvaro Obregón, a caudillo from the state of Sonora who had earlier defeated Pancho Villa, came to power following the overthrow and assassination of President Carranza. His successor, Plutarco Elías Calles, dominated Mexican politics for a decade. The "Sonoran Dynasty" pared down the army and drastically reduced the military budget. It sought the support of urban workers and land-poor campesinos as a counterweight to the military, which unsuccessfully revolted three times (1923, 1927, 1929).

Sonoran policies combined conservative and liberal elements. Moderate land reform and anticlericalism coexisted with a preference for a strong centralized state, a capitalist economy, and a placid, productive society. In many respects Sonoran rule resembled Porfirian rule. For example, foreign investment was encouraged, although it was more closely regulated than during the Díaz dictatorship. Although the 1920s brought economic progress, the progress was sometimes accompanied by violent social and religious strife.

A civil war over the issue of Church rights raged for three years (1926–1929). In 1928 Obregón was elected to a second term as president but was assassinated by a Catholic fanatic before his inauguration. It was this act that prompted former President Calles to spearhead the formation of the National Revolutionary party

(PNR), the precursor of the Institutional Revolutionary party (PRI), which has dominated Mexican politics since 1946. By further institutionalizing civilian rule, the PNR in effect demilitarized the political system.

The PNR helped Calles maintain his dominance until 1934, when Lázaro Cárdenas, a Calles protégé, was elected president but proved to be too independent and too radical for his mentor. The power struggle was won decisively by Cárdenas (Calles was sent into exile), and a period of genuine agrarian reform began. A populist at heart, Cárdenas transferred 17 million hectares of land from individuals to communities. The *ejidos* (communal lands) could be farmed individually or collectively—despite his populism, Cárdenas was not a dogmatic ideologue. The campesinos were further assuaged by the removal of unpopular local bosses, who were replaced by reformist *politicos* attuned to Cárdenas's controlled rural revolution.

Cárdenas also courted organized labor. In 1936 the Confederation of Mexican Workers (CTM) was founded and became an integral part of a newly constituted official party. Cárdenas pleased labor by arbitrating generous wage settlements, nationalizing the railways, and expropriating foreign oil companies (1938). Cárdenas thus was instrumental in building a broad farm-labor coalition and paving the way both for Mexico's economic resurgence after 1940 and for what is now called the "institutionalization" of the Mexican Revolution—a euphemism for one-party rule.

From World War II to the present, Mexico has undergone substantial economic development. With the PRI monopolizing power and setting priorities, the government was able to launch a modernization drive with single-minded determination. The results were extraordinary: Industry surged ahead of agriculture, and manufacturing displaced mining as Mexico's economic engine. Between 1940 and 1965 the economy grew fivefold overall, and agricultural output quadrupled; the population doubled. Mostly fortuitous events kept the bubble from bursting until the 1980s, although warning signs were apparent at least a decade earlier.

During the 1970s, as the population grew at an alarming rate of 3 to 4 percent a year, urbanization went out of control; despite advances in agrotechnology, food self-sufficiency came to an end. The impact of the population explosion was cushioned for a time by the 1973 oil embargo, which was a bonanza for Mexico. But it was merely the calm before the storm: The oil glut of the early 1980s plunged debt-ridden Mexico into the worst economic crisis since the Great Depression, one so severe and destabilizing that it undermined the foundations of Mexico's political system. These developments are explored in the next two chapters.

Brazil

Portugal's colonial claim to Brazil dates back to the middle of the fifteenth century, but the first settlement was not established until 1530. Phillip II of Spain extended his authority to Portugal in 1581, and —after a war between the Spanish and the Dutch—the Dutch dominated Portugal for a time. This period coincided with the heyday of the Dutch West India Company, which effectively controlled

Brazil after overcoming some resistance by Portuguese settlers. The Dutch opened up trade with Brazil, but the colonists continued to revolt, eventually with Portugal's aid. The ensuing war ended in 1654, and the Dutch abandoned claims to Brazil in 1661.

Portugal's interest in Brazil was desultory at best. In 1695 gold was discovered, and diamonds were found in 1729. Settlements had been confined to the coast, but the gold rush sent a flood of fortune seekers into the interior, and towns sprang up there. In contrast to its status in the Spanish colonies, the Catholic Church in Brazil was poor and thus less influential politically. During the 1700s Britain helped Portugal hold Brazil in return for trade privileges.

When Napoleon invaded Portugal in 1807, the royal family took refuge in Brazil. This happenstance helped reverse Brazil's status as a benighted colonial backwater. Under direct rule of John VI, the Portuguese monarch, Rio de Janeiro became the capital of Portugal, and a colonial culture blossomed, complete with schools, libraries, newspapers, and banks. The king returned to Portugal in 1821, but his son, Prince Pedro, stayed in Brazil.

Back in Portugal the ruling council tried to enact restrictions that were harmful to Brazil. When Pedro was ordered to return to Portugal, he refused, and with the rallying cry "Independence or Death" he declared himself emperor of Brazil on October 12, 1822. Brazil thus became independent without bloodshed or upheaval—a peaceful transition to self-rule that contrasts sharply with the turbulence of Spanish America. Pedro I ruled until 1831, when, having lost a short war with Argentina and alienated Brazilians in various ways, he abdicated in favor of his 6-year-old son.

An unstable triumvirate-style regency began after Pedro I departed, and it became a single-headed regency in 1835. The Parliament met in July 1840, ousted the regent, and pronounced the boy-emperor, age 14, old enough to rule. The coronation of Pedro II, who reigned for the next half-century, ushered in a period of stability and economic development. The Brazilian monarch was a pragmatist who mediated between liberals and conservatives, courted both, genuflected to neither, and used his "moderating power" under the Constitution to handpick prime ministers and thus manipulate his made-to-order bipartisan governments. Although he jealously guarded his royal prerogatives, Pedro II protected freedom of the press and public debate.

During the 1850s the emperor's failure to stop the clandestine slave trade eroded Brazil's special relationship with Britain, and so Brazil formed an alliance with the United States that persists to the present. Pedro's obduracy in prolonging a war with Paraguay (1864–1870) caused disillusion within the officer corps, and this was one reason for the demise of the monarchy.

Although slavery was repugnant to Pedro II, he knew that abolishing it would be disruptive. In 1888, while he was visiting Europe, his daughter, Isabel, pushed through a bill that abolished slavery without compensating slave owners. The latter were infuriated and withdrew their support for the monarchy. In November 1889 the military revolted. The emperor was forced to abdicate and was sent into exile. There was no single cause for the coup. Even accident played a role: The aging monarch was dying of diabetes, and Isabel was unpopular. More important, however, was that the monarchy as an institution had become arthritic and inflexible in the face of social change—which, ironically, it had done much to foster.

The empire was replaced by a republic. General Deodoro da Fonseca headed a coalition government in which Ruy Barbosa was the outstanding figure. Barbosa drew up a constitution patterned after the federal government of the United States. The first five years, however, were characterized by power struggles among oligarchies controlling different states. For the winner, the prize would be control of the national government. After 1894 three civilian presidents, all from São Paolo, brought a period of peace and prosperity to Brazil—the "golden age" of the first republic. Coffee, rubber, sugar, cacao, and tobacco became Brazil's chief exports. During the early 1900s the country produced three-fourths of the world's coffee, but overproduction hurt prices. Brazil experienced a brief post–World War I boom followed by a sharp recession.

In 1922 a group of radical young army officers, the *tenentes* (lieutenants), rebelled; in 1924 another army revolt occurred, but loyal troops suppressed it and established martial law. The first republic collapsed in 1930, a casualty both of the Great Depression, which devastated Brazil's export-dependent economy, and of an increasingly chaotic political system. The military's power seizure was designed, in part, to preempt civil war in Brazil. Fractious rivalries among the politicos themselves—not military treachery—are what finally doomed the republic.

The 1930 revolution put Getúlio Vargas in the presidential palace, and he remained there until 1945. He managed to get elected president in 1933 (the first time Brazilians had ever been allowed to vote by secret ballot), but it was several years before Vargas could consolidate his position. In 1937 he suspended the Constitution rather than relinquish the presidency. From that point on he ruled as a relatively benevolent dictator, banning political parties, censoring the press, and creating a corporatist state (the *Estado Novo*, or "new state") in which business, labor, landowners, and bureaucrats were fused in common cause. Vargas tried to develop a manufacturing industry but with meager success; Brazil remained dependent on agricultural exports.

Brazil sided with the United States and the Allies in World War II and even sent troops to fight on the Italian front. After the war Vargas agreed to free elections, but the military was not taking any chances: Believing that Vargas would not give up power without a fight, the generals carried out a successful coup and established a democratic republic that lasted until 1964.

The most important figure during this period was President Juscelino Kubitschek, who took office in 1955 vowing to give Brazil "Fifty years' progress in five." During his tenure industrial production rose by 80 percent, and economic growth averaged 7 percent a year. Brazil became self-sufficient in auto production and created an international airline. Kubitschek's most flamboyant project was the building of a new capital city, Brasília, in the interior of the country on a site that was previously desolate. Unfortunately, Kubitschek's profligate spending (financed partly by international borrowing) led to debt-servicing problems and spiraling inflation. The resulting disillusionment brought a surprise winner in the 1960 election—an independent candidate named Jânio Quadros.

Quadros had a reputation for integrity and competence; for reasons that remain unclear, however, he resigned within seven months. Vice-President João Goulart was just the opposite of Quadros: incompetent and politically inept. As the economy declined and inflation soared, Goulart pursued a quixotic, vaguely leftist course that antagonized not only the military but also the wealthy and middle classes. In the spring of 1964 the military staged a coup that had widespread civilian support, especially in the press. More than two decades were to pass before civilian rule was restored.

It gradually became apparent that what appeared to be just another military coup was, in fact, a revolution. The military junta proceeded to centralize power, drive the traditional parties into the political wilderness, and ruthlessly rid Brazil of subversive leftist elements. Newspaper editors were harassed, all signs of dissent were suppressed, and opponents were arrested. Torture and death squads were the junta's gruesome trademarks.

Old-guard politicians were muzzled, but the military called on civilian technocrats to engineer Brazil's economic recovery. Chief among these was the finance minister, Antonin Delfim Neto, who worked a short-lived "economic miracle" during the early 1970s by obtaining new loans, retiring old debts, and attracting foreign investment. Thus reinvigorated, the economy grew at an annual rate of 10 percent, inflation dropped to respectable levels (15 to 25 percent), and Brazil finally began exporting manufactures.

But the oil crisis spoiled Brazil's economic recovery. The economy slowed, and inflation rose sharply. After 1974 the military regime, now headed by Ernesto Geisel, a pragmatist, moved to ease the repressive political measures still in effect. His successor, João Baptista Figueirédo, continued on this course, allowing an independent trade union movement to develop and lifting the ban on free-standing political parties. This process culminated in 1985 with the election of a civilian president.

Argentina

Although Argentina's rolling plains and pampas region were ideally suited for agriculture and cattle grazing, the Spanish paid it little attention. Europe was not interested in agricultural products, and Argentina did not have mineral wealth to match that of Mexico and Peru.

In some ways this benign neglect turned out to be advantageous. The process of social diversification was delayed in Argentina because economic development lagged behind that in other parts of Latin America. As a result, the class conflicts that typically accompany rapid social change were absent. Also, the Catholic Church never became as entrenched in Argentina as it did, for example, in Mexico. Argentina thus avoided the religious strife that ripped the social fabric in some nations of the region.

Argentina's stability, abundant land, and temperate climate made it attractive to European immigrants, who began arriving around 1810. A great influx of Spanish and Italian immigrants lasted through 1930, boosting the population and transforming the nation's character. (Argentina's population rose from 1.2 million in 1852 to approximately 8 million in 1914.) Wild and lawless *gauchos* (cowboys) had roamed the plains earlier, but the new cattle-raising settlers created a more structured and sedentary society. The gauchos' way of life also changed as they were integrated into the routines of the large ranches. Argentina's economy began to develop on the foundation of large-scale ranching and meat processing.

When Argentina declared its independence from Spain in 1816, it was a collection of "United Provinces" and regions, including not only present-day Argentina but also Bolivia, Paraguay, and Uruguay. The hope of keeping the entire viceroyalty of the River Plate together was soon abandoned, and attention turned to uniting the provinces of Argentina in fact as well as name. The various parts of the new nation were controlled by caudillos.

The first political issue to be settled was whether Argentina's structure should be federal (decentralized) or unitary (centralized). Buenos Aires favored a unitary system because this would give the capital power over the provinces. But caudillo rulers in the provinces favored a federal system because they wanted to retain a large measure of independence from Bueno Aires. The issue sparked an ongoing civil war that finally ended in 1835, when Juan Manuel de Rosas, a provincial leader, defeated the forces of Buenos Aires and became its governor. With Buenos Aires under his control, Rosas dominated the entire country, creating an extensive domestic spy system and terrorizing opponents. Rosas appears to have been a demagogue of the first order. Although he ruled Argentina as a ruthless dictator, his motto was "Long live the Argentine Confederation; death to the savage unitarians."

In 1852 Justo José Urquiza defeated Rosas in the battle of Monte Caseros and became chief executive of the Argentine federation. Buenos Aires refused to join. National unification was not achieved until a decade later, following another civil war between Buenos Aires and the federation. Urquiza withdrew from politics after the indecisive battle of Pavon (1861), whereupon Bartolomé Mitre, the governor of Buenos Aires, gained the ascendancy and persuaded the caudillos in the provinces to make Buenos Aires the national capital for five years.

During the 1860s Argentina entered a lengthy period of stability and steady economic growth. With agricultural exports leading the way, profitable farming and ranching continued to take precedence over industrial development. The large landowners were the predominant economic interest, and they enjoyed far greater political influence than any other class. New political parties emerged during the 1890s, but it was not until 1912 that an electoral reform law created a genuine multiparty system. As a result of the new law, Argentina's first popularly elected president took office in 1916. World War I brought the economic boom to an end in 1913, but the economy bounced back during the 1920s. By this time Argentina had become the most prosperous nation in Latin America.

The Depression threw Argentina's export-oriented economy into a tailspin and led to a military coup that ended fourteen years of representative democracy. A coalition of several parties (the *Concordancia*) held power until 1943, when the army staged another coup. The outbreak of World War II disrupted world trade once again and thus dealt another blow to Argentina's beleaguered economy.

For the remainder of the war Argentina was ruled by the military. It was during this interregnum that Colonel Juan Domingo Perón, then Minister of War and head of the Secretariat of Labour and Social Welfare, began his ascent to power. Because the Peronista movement is still a force in Argentine politics, the rise and fall of Perón himself—a story that spans a thirty-year period—is discussed in the next chapter. Suffice it to say that Perón's overthrow by the military in 1955 was the first in a series of coups over the next two decades. Not until 1983, following a nightmarish reign of terror, would the government be returned to civilian control.

In sum, Argentina did not suffer the disruptive and destabilizing effects of Church-state conflict that divided Mexico during its early history. Nor did it suffer the humiliating foreign interventions, military defeats, and losses of territory that marred Mexico's debut as an independent republic. Unlike Brazil, it did not have the advantage of a unifying monarchy during the greater part of its first half-century of independence. Instead, it had to struggle longer and harder with the problem of political intergration than Brazil did. Mexico, however, faced similar nation-building problems—how to stitch separate regions into a tightly knit union. In all three countries the military played a major role in politics. The main difference between Mexico, on the one hand, and Brazil or Argentina, on the other, is that Mexico managed to demilitarize the political process in the twentieth century. The same cannot be said of Brazil and Argentina.

Venezuela

Venezuela is twice the size of California, but much of its land is unsuitable for farming. Vast plains (*llanos*) form a sparsely populated region that has had little economic importance. The Orinoco River, stretching 1,600 miles, drains 80 percent of the country. Political and economic power is concentrated in two coastal cities, Caracas (the capital) and Maracaibo (the center of the oil industry).

More than four-fifths of Venezuela's population (between 19 and 20 million) is urban. Venezuela is a relatively large country in area, but its population is smaller than Mexico's (about 87 million) and Argentina's (about 32 million). Compared with Brazil's area and population (151 million), Venezuela is dwarfed. Yet Venezuela's strategic importance is second to no country in South America, because of its location and natural resources. It is next door to one of the world's vital strategic chokepoints, the Panama Canal, and the country is blessed with major oil deposits.

Venezuela's economy has been dependent on oil since the 1930s, and until recently oil exports have provided excess foreign reserves. These were not, however, used to diversify the country's industry or develop its agriculture.

Because most of Venezuela's wealth has been concentrated in cities, rural areas have been depopulated, and the rural labor force has been depleted. Thus, since the 1950s Venezuela has been forced to import food. Its balance-of-payments picture was rosy, however, until the 1980s, due to large oil revenues. The oil glut of the early 1980s plunged Venezuela into a debt crisis.

Geographic and economic factors give Venezuela a special place in the strategic calculations of the West, especially of the United States, and the country's domestic politics have reinforced this. Venezuela's recent political experience is a sharp departure from its authoritarian past, which we will examine next. (Chapters 20 and 21 will cover Venezuelan politics after 1958.)

Formerly part of Gran (Greater) Colombia, Venezuela became a separate entity in 1830, following the death of the Liberator, Simón Bolívar. The disintegration of Bolívar's political system coincided with economic depression and financial insolvency.

During its early years as an independent republic, Venezuela was guided by General José Antonio Páez, a comrade-in-arms of Bolívar and a caudillo in his own right who had recruited rebellious *llaneros* (settlers from the grassy plains of the interior) to the revolutionary cause. Páez recognized the need for Venezuelan independence when the Liberator's popularity began to wane. It was Páez who led Venezuela's separatist movement in 1830, setting up a government and calling for a constitutional convention. The separation was accomplished with almost no bloodshed, since Colombia's government in Bogotá could not muster any resistance.

Páez became president in 1831 and stepped down at the end of his term in 1835, having survived a rebellion in 1831. Páez was reelected in 1839 and played a prominent role in various political struggles during the next twenty-five years before going into exile in the United States for a final time in 1863. The other dominant figure in Venezuela's turbulent politics was José Tadeo Monogas, who, with his brother's help, ruled Venezuela as a virtual dictator until Páez led an army revolt and ousted him in 1861. Another authoritarian figure, Guzmán Blanco, monopolized politics from 1873 to 1888.

Venezuela's most notorious and durable caudillo was Juan Vicente Gómez, who seized power in 1908. Gómez, who ruled the country for twenty-seven years, was a venal tyrant whose contributions to Venezuela's development, such as improving schools and roads, were overshadowed by corruption and cronyism. He kept the army under tight control, banned private firearms, and set up a spy network to squelch revolution at its source. Gómez was not only shrewd but also lucky enough to rule when Venezuela's great oil deposits around Lake Maracaibo were discovered. Oil-export revenues made it possible to pay off the nation's foreign debt as well as line the pockets of Gómez, his family, and his friends.

The death of Gómez in 1935 ended the dictatorship. Another general, Eleazor López Contreras, was elected president in 1936. Contreras promulgated a new constitution, which limited the president's term to five years. When leftist parties won a decisive victory in the 1937 legislative elections, Contreras arrested many of their leaders (including newly elected congressmen) on charges of Communist subversion. Most of these leaders were exiled, and most left-wing organizations—including the militant Federation of Students, which had led the opposition to Gómez—were banned.

Although Contreras suppressed radicalism, he also instituted a far-reaching program of social reform aimed at mollifying poor rural and urban workers and stopping the spread of subversive ideas, especially communism. In 1941, against the backdrop of World War II, Venezuela held elections as prescribed in the Constitution. The winner, Isaías Medina Angarita, continued the policies of his predecessor until October 1945, when he was overthrown in a military coup. Rómulo Betancourt, the popular leader of *Acción Democrática* (the Democratic Action party, a left-of-center party known simply as AD), became the provisional president. A year later elections for a constituent assembly gave AD a majority. Rómulo Gallegos, well-known novelist and AD founder, became Venezuela's first popularly elected president in 1947, and AD received an overwhelming majority of the vote for the assembly.

In 1948 Colonel Carlos Delgado Chalbaud staged a successful coup; he was assassinated in 1950. Then a military junta ran the country until 1954, when Colonel Marcos Pérez Jiménez became the provisional president. Jiménez ruled Venezuela as a traditional caudillo, but his overthrow in 1958 set the stage for a new era in Venezuelan politics. Before 1958 Venezuela fit the Latin American stereotype of the "praetorian" regime in which the military is dominant and governments change hands more often by coups than by elections. Since 1958 the picture has changed dramatically, as Chapter 20 will reveal.

CONCLUSION

The countries of Latin America still bear the imprint of the Spanish Conquest, but the United States has long since replaced Spain as the dominant external power in the region. The military juntas that have traditionally ruled throughout most of Latin America often enjoyed the support of the United States since World War II, provided that they had the proper anti-Communist credentials. In the 1980s one South American government after another switched from dictatorship to democracy. Why and how are questions taken up in Chapter 20.

STUDY QUESTIONS

1. What is "Latin culture"? Is it reflected in Latin political traditions and institutions? If so, how?
2. Compare and contrast political development in Mexico, Brazil, Argentina, and Venezuela. What role did the military play in the history of these countries? How did the world wars and the Great Depression affect political development in these countries?

3. Does Latin America have abundant natural resources? Fertile farmland? Climatic conditions conducive to agriculture? Should Latin America be poor? (Suggestion: Use the case studies as focal points in developing a thoughtful response.)

4. What do you think it means to be Mexican, Brazilian, Argentine, or Venezuelan? Do Mexicans see the world much differently than Argentines? Brazilians? Venezuelans? What similarities and differences would you expect among citizens of these four countries?

SUGGESTED READINGS

Burns, E. Bradford, *Latin America: A Concise Interpretive History*, 3rd ed. New Brunswick, N.J.: Prentice Hall, 1982.

Burns, E. Bradford. *A History of Brazil*. New York: Columbia University, 1980.

Hopkins, Jack W., ed. *Latin America: Perspectives on a Region*. New York: Holmes & Meyer, 1987.

Lowenthal, Abraham F. *Armies and Politics in Latin America*. New York: Holmes and Meyer, 1976.

Meyer, Michael C., and William L. Sherman. *The Course of Mexican History*, 2nd ed. New York: Oxford, 1983.

Scobie, James R. *Argentina: A City and a Nation*, 2nd ed. New York: Oxford, 1971.

NOTES

[1] Quoted in Paul B. Goodwin, Jr., *Latin America*, 3rd ed. (Guilford, Conn.: Dushkin, 1988), pp. 81–82.

[2] Ibid., p. 3.

[3] See V. I. Lenin, *Imperialism: The Highest Stage of Capitalism* (New York: International, 1969), p. 16.

[4] John D. Nagle, *Comparative Politics: Political System Performance in Three Worlds* (Chicago: Nelson-Hall, 1985), p. 229.

[5] Ibid., p. 230.

[6] Ibid.

[7] Dana Gardner Munro, *The Latin American Republics: A History* (New York: Appleton, 1950), p. 81.

[8] J. Fred Rippy, *Latin America: A Modern History* (Ann Arbor, Mich.: University of Michigan, 1958), p. 185.

Chapter 20
Caudillism, Coups, and Constitutionalism

Latin America differs from North America in many ways, but no difference is more striking than the two regions' political traditions. As we are about to see, however, politics changed dramatically in Latin America during the 1980s, as one country after another switched from military to civilian government based on popular election. Indeed, democratization is a major theme in this chapter and the next one. Yet the Latin tradition has been authoritarian, and that is the model we will describe—mostly in the past tense. Obviously, any such description is bound to oversimplify Latin politics, and readers are forewarned.

The Authoritarian Model

Throughout Latin America authoritarian regimes, often dominated by or dependent on the military, have restricted civil liberties and have paid little more than lip service to free elections. In most cases dictators or military juntas were closely linked to an entrenched economic elite, and the most common method of replacing a government was through a military coup d'état (literally, a "stroke of state").

Dictators and juntas sometimes held elections, but these were seldom either free or fair. More often the government banned opposition parties and jailed their leaders; muzzled the press; harassed, threatened, and intimidated voters; stuffed ballot boxes; manipulated voter-registration rolls; bought votes; and—if all else failed—falsified election returns.

Corruption has been rampant in Latin American politics. Election fraud, bribery, and extortion have all been pervasive. Worse still, political violence both from governments and their opposition have afflicted many Latin American societies. Among the egregious examples of recent government repression are Guatemala, Nicaragua, Argentina, Chile, and Brazil. From the standpoint of human rights abuses, the most notorious case is probably Argentina's "dirty war" (1976–1982) against leftist subversion; some six thousand people have vanished (and are called, simply, "the disappeared").

Although torture, death squads, and fear characterized Argentine politics during the civil war, similar political factors can also be cited in El Salvador, Guatemala, and Peru, to name but three Latin countries. In Argentina repression came in response to a leftist insurgency threat (the Monteñeros). The same has occurred elsewhere. Earlier in the 1970s, for example, a military junta seized power in Uruguay after the civilian president asked for help in fighting urban

475

guerrillas (the Tupumaros). In both cases repressive policies probably had played a role in bringing about the insurgencies; in turn, the insurgencies prompted the governments to increase their repression. Thus in Latin America power struggles between ruling oligarchies and disaffected leftist groups have led to violence on both sides.

Insurgencies are a fact of political life in many Latin American countries. During the late 1980s guerrilla groups were engaged in ''armed struggle'' against governments in Guatemala, El Salvador, Colombia, Chile, Peru, Nicaragua, and Ecuador. The persistence and magnitude of insurgencies have varied from country to country. In Venezuela, Uruguay, and Argentina guerrillas have been defeated, for now. In Colombia, where several insurgent groups are active, kidnapping and other terrorist acts occur regularly. In Peru a vicious Maoist guerrilla movement, *Sendero Luminoso* (''Shining Path''), has been terrorizing the countryside and the capital since 1980; some ten thousand people have been massacred by either guerrilla or government forces. In sharp contrast Mexico has not had a civil war or insurgency since the Revolution of 1910, but that raged for seven years and cost over a million lives.

Latin Democracy: The Domino Effect

Until recently, to speak of Latin American democracy was almost a contradiction in terms. Excluding the Caribbean nations, three notable exceptions were Costa Rica, Colombia, and Venezuela. Costa Rica is a small neutral country with no army whose former president, Oscar Arias Sánchez, was awarded the Nobel Peace Prize in 1987 for his Central American peace plan. Colombia is a troubled nation with a violent history that nonetheless has managed to function as a two-party constitutional democracy since the end of a civil war (1946–1958) known as *la violencia* (''the violence''). Venezuela is an oil-rich nation with a democratic political system which resembles that of the United States (including the federal structure).

A growing number of other Latin nations began converting to civilian democratic rule during the late 1970s, and for a decade Latin dictatorships toppled like dominoes. In South America the new democracies include Brazil, Argentina, Uruguay, Peru, and Bolivia. In Central America the nations of El Salvador, Honduras, Nicaragua, and Guatemala have instituted fragile, embryonic democratic processes, although their military leaders are waiting to see whether the civilian governments will falter. Mexico remains a mixed regime, half democratic and half authoritarian; although elections occur every six years, the ruling Institutional Revolutionary party (PRI) has always won, although by decreasing margins recently.

Most elections in these countries have been free and unfettered. Candidates have had access to the media and have been allowed to campaign without interference. Political rallies are no longer treated as subversive. Elections have been intensely competitive.

Exceptions to the democratization trend in Latin America during the 1980s were Nicaragua and Panama in Central America; Paraguay and Chile in South America; and Cuba in the Caribbean. In these countries the peaceful transfer of power via free competitive elections has remained a distant dream of liberals. But in 1989–1990 Nicaragua, Panama, and Chile moved toward popular self-rule—albeit along very different paths.

The following sections examine the contemporary political systems of Mexico, Brazil, and Argentina—three countries that fairly well represent Latin America's political traditions and institutions. Since two of them, Brazil and Argentina, have recently switched from military dictatorships to civilian democratic rule, we can investigate that trend. Together, these three countries have a larger population than that of the United States (about 270 million to about 249 million in 1989), and their combined land mass exceeds the United States by nearly 1.7 million square miles. Since population growth in these countries is higher than in the United States, the demographic gap will increase. Finally, we will also look briefly at Venezuela as an exception to traditional Latin authoritarianism.

Mexico

Chapter 19 explained that Mexico's political system originated in the Revolution of 1910 and that its 1917 Constitution was forged in a protracted and violent struggle. Recall that the Mexican Revolution was a class struggle—not between ''proletariat'' and ''capitalism''—but between the wealthy landed aristocracy and impoverished peasants who, for all practical purposes, were serfs in a semifeudal order. Indeed, the convulsive, extreme nature of the struggle cannot be fully understood without understanding the extremes that spawned it—extreme inequality, extreme poverty, extreme injustice, and extreme indifference to mass suffering. Such was the legacy of General Porfirio Díaz (1876–1911), Mexico's last and most infamous military dictator.

The long and bitter fight against a tyrant who ruled with an iron fist for thirty-five years (about the average life expectancy for the Mexican underclass in that dark age) produced a generation of revolutionary leaders who were determined to create a just social order. The Constitution of 1917 was the instrument designed to achieve that lofty aim.

The Constitution of 1917

In theory Mexico is a federal republic comprising thirty-one states and the Federal District (around Mexico City, the capital). The Constitution of 1917 assigned legislative power to a bicameral National Congress, elected by universal adult suffrage (that is, all nationals who are 18 or older and have ''an honorable means of livelihood''). The Senate (upper house) has sixty-four members (two from each state and the Federal District), serving a six-year term. The Chamber of Deputies (lower house) has four hundred members directly elected for a three-year term. Three hundred seats are filled from single-member districts, and nearly all are traditionally won by the majority party—the Partido Revolucionario Institucional (PRI). In 1986 the number of seats reserved for minority parties was increased from one hundred to two hundred, to be allocated under a scheme of proportional representation.

Executive power is given to the president, directly elected for a single, non-renewable six-year term. He appoints the Council of Ministers (cabinet), whose members head various government departments, as well as other senior military and civilian officers. The Constitution of 1917 also created an independent judiciary. The federal Supreme Court has twenty-six members including a chief justice. Supreme Court justices, who must be native born, are appointed by the president with Senate approval. The thirty-one state governors are popularly elected for a six-year term; like the president they can never serve again. Under Article 76 of the Constitution, the president can ask the Senate to remove the governor of any state in which law and order has broken down.

In sum, the Constitution of 1917 set up a federal democratic republic in which powers are clearly separated among three branches of government. The Constitution also enshrined the aims of the Revolution of 1910 by mandating radical land reform, drafting a labor code, and sharply curtailing the power of the Catholic Church. Its provisions dealing with religion, education, and the exploitation of mineral wealth reflect the long struggle against dictatorship, the Church, large landowners, and "economic imperialism."

On paper the Mexican Constitution—drafted the same year that the October Revolution occurred in Russia—is a scintillating document. Supposedly it was Lenin's Soviet regime that put workers on a pedestal, but Mexico's founders outdid even the Bolsheviks in this area. Article 123 of the Constitution, for example, deals with labor rights. Its provisions include an eight-hour workday, a general minimum wage, a twelve-week leave for pregnancy (half before and half after the birth), two extra rest periods each day for nursing mothers, equal pay for equal work regardless of sex or nationality, profit sharing for workers, double pay for overtime, and appropriate compensation for job-related injuries or diseases. This list of workers' rights sounds impressive today; in 1917 it was ground breaking.

The leaders of a party in power often pretend that things are better than they actually are. Nowhere is the contrast between appearance and reality sharper than in the difference between the formal workings of Mexico's government (the Constitution) and its informal workings (the system).

The System in Mexico

"Effective suffrage, no reelection"—this was democracy in a nutshell for Francisco Madero, president of Mexico from 1911 to 1913. Half of this formula— no reelection—has been put into practice. The idea behind the one-term rule was to prevent dictatorships like that of Porfirio Díaz. The rule also prohibits the members of Congress, state legislatures, and municipal councils from serving two consecutive terms, again to ensure that leadership does not become self-perpetuating and oligarchic. But almost every rule can be circumvented. In Mexico this rule is "observed" in a formal sense; informally, however, the system is a game of musical chairs in which majority-party (PRI) politicians rotate from one position to another.

Although this system's reality is different from the intent of its authors, Mexico has enjoyed seventy years of political stability. For the entire period the government has been controlled by one party, the PRI, which in turn has fashioned a powerful coalition of government, party, labor, industrial, and agrarian leaders.

The president is the key figure in the system. To become president a politician must have previous experience as a cabinet member and must be male, youthful and physically vigorous, and able to mediate between the left and right wings of the PRI. The party's inner circle, headed by the incumbent president, chooses the nominee, who is always elected. In effect, the outgoing president picks his successor. There is no vice-president; if necessary the Congress chooses an interim chief executive. Since 1946 every president of Mexico has been a civilian.

Although the Constitution gives Congress extensive power to make laws, in reality the president dominates the legislative branch. He can introduce legislation directly into both houses and can set the legislative agenda. He also can veto legislation but has never had to do so because no law that was opposed by a sitting president has ever been enacted!

The president can also issue decree laws in most areas of public policy. For example, Mexico's income tax was created by decree; only years later did Congress get around to enacting it formally. Presidential decrees have created cabinet ministries, government departments, public corporations, and major public works projects. The budget, family planning, and nuclear energy are all areas in which policy—later to be rubber stamped by Congress—has been effected by presidential fiat.

The most important cabinet officer is the *secretario de governacion* (minister of internal affairs), who supervises intergovernmental relations, liaison with Congress, elections, voter and party registration, immigration and emigration, motion-picture production, radio and television air time, the federal police, and federal prisons. Other key cabinet positions include planning and budget, finance, commerce and industry, public enterprises, foreign affairs, and labor. President José López Portillo (1976–1982), for example, had been the finance minister; President Miguel de la Madrid Hurtado (1982–1988) was previously planning and budget minister.

Since the Congress is totally dominated by the PRI, it debates the form rather than the substance of legislation. Floor debates are often vigorous but have little effect. Criticism of government policies is frequently voiced by opposition party leaders, but even this is softened by the media, which pander to the all-powerful PRI-dominated state. Seniority is not an issue in Mexico's Congress for two reasons: Committees do not wield real power in a legislature that is dominated by the executive branch, and members cannot hold consecutive terms.

The judiciary is independent, but judges owe their jobs to a highly politicized patron–client system. Since 1929 every Supreme Court justice has belonged to the PRI. Although corruption is endemic throughout the government, justice is frequently served anyway. The major restraint on presidential power is the writ of *amparo* (relief), by which federal judges can protect citizens from violations of their constitutional rights by stopping the offending government agency from taking action until the Supreme Court has ruled on appeal. The Court may halt official action, compel officials to carry out constitutional obligations, or force judges to specify or clarify the charges against a defendant in a criminal case. Some 5,500 writs of amparo were issued against the president or cabinet ministers between 1917 and 1980; the Supreme Court ruled against the government in about a third of these cases.

The PRI's control extends to the thirty-one states as well. Although governors *are* popularly elected, the PRI inner circle—dominated by the president—decides whose name will be on the ballot. Nomination is tantamount to election; since 1929 every state governor has been a member of the PRI. In all but six states, governors' terms do not coincide with presidential elections, which means that each new president inherits twenty-five governors who were chosen by his predecessor. As mentioned earlier, the president can direct the Senate to remove a governor. Since 1964 presidents have exercised this prerogative only about once per term; before 1964 it was used far more frequently.

Mexico presents a sterling example of what political scientists often call a "one-party-dominant system." Although regular elections are held, the PRI always wins control of the government. The federal government sets the rules governing the creation and operation of political parties. These rules are fairly liberal, but parties must obtain at least 1.5 percent of the national vote to retain legal status. The fact that there were no fewer than nine parties represented in Congress in 1985 suggests that, in a purely formal sense, the right of free association is respected and that minority parties do not have to overcome insurmountable obstacles.

The PRI monopolizes the non-Marxist center-left on the political spectrum. Since 1933 the party has developed six-year plans for the economy; a plan then becomes the basis for the government's program. As its name suggests, the PRI claims to be the permanent custodian of an ongoing and institutionalized revolution. It embraces welfare-state policies (even though the state lacks resources to turn rhetoric into reality), state ownership of major industries, and individual or communal ownership of land. Two fundamental principles of the party are "no reelection" and the right of all workers (including public employees) to strike.

In foreign policy the PRI stresses Mexico's independence from the superpowers and Western Europe. Distancing itself from "Yanqui" imperialism is a major motif; to this end the PRI is sympathetic to left-wing "anti-imperialist" regimes in Latin America (notably in Cuba, Nicaragua, and Peru). The fact that Mexico lost about half its total area to the United States in the Mexican-American War (1846–1848) accounts for some of the tension that characterizes relations between these two "distant neighbors"—a term coined by journalist Alan Riding.[1]

Minority parties run the gamut from conservative to collectivist. On the right is the Partido Democrata Mexicano (PDM), which advocates reprivatization of the economy, reduction of welfare programs, an end to the PRI patronage system, and a ''union of Church and state.'' Another right-of-center party is the Partido Accion Nacional (PAN), which in the 1980s became a serious challenger to PRI control in parts of Mexico, especially in Chihuahua, Durango, Hermosillo, and Ciudad Juárez.

On the far left there has been an array of Marxist parties, including the pro-Soviet Communist Party of Mexico (PCM), also known as the Unified Socialist Party of Mexico (PSUM); a Trotskyite party called the Revolutionary Part of the Workers (PRT); and several other socialist and workers' parties. The PRI could not have wished for a better ''divide-and-conquer'' scenario.

Mexico's 1988 Presidential Election

A challenge was mounted on the left in the 1988 presidential election when a new populist party, the Democratic National Front (FDN) led by Cuauhtemoc Cárdenas (whose father, Lázaro Cárdenas, was one of the most popular presidents in modern Mexican history), forged an alliance with the Mexican Socialist Party (PMS). The PMS was created the previous fall when six leftist parties formed a coalition led by Herberto Castillo. Castillo stepped aside to clear the way for Cárdenas to run against the PRI candidate, Carlos Salinas de Gortari. Cárdenas, a disaffected former PRI leader, had forged his party in 1987 out of more than fifteen center-left groups.

The alliance between the FDN and the PMS was thus an untested merger made up of two equally untested coalitions. Although PRI candidate Salinas was declared the winner by a slim margin (amid allegations of massive ballot-box fraud and some indications that Cárdenas may actually have polled the most votes), the fact that the left managed to unite even temporarily was unprecedented and may portend a significant new development in Mexican party politics.

The attempt to unite the left followed in the wake of labor unrest. Until recently government and organized labor worked hand in glove, but economic difficulties have led to serious friction between the PRI and the Confederation of Mexican Workers (CTM). Independent labor unions made rapid gains and for the first time appeared to pose a potential challenge to the traditional PRI-CTM domination of the political system.

The Decline (and Fall?) of the PRI

A deepening economic crisis formed the backdrop to this growing domestic disaffection with the PRI. A monstrous external debt, mounting budget deficits, skyrocketing inflation, massive unemployment, a sharp decline in consumers' purchasing power, the plummeting peso—these were the conditions that greeted the incoming president in 1988. The domestic crisis and its implications are explored in Chapter 21. For now it suffices to say that the future of the PRI and the political system it dominates seemed more uncertain as the 1980s ended than ever before in its history.

Brazil

Just as Mexico's Constitution is far more democratic than its political system, Brazil's movement toward democracy, known as the *aberatura* (political liberalization), is incomplete. Even so, the holding of free elections in January 1985 signaled the end of two decades of military rule and the beginning of a new era in Brazilian political life.

Brazil's motto, *Ordem e Progresso* ("Order and Progress"), has been emblazoned on its flag since the founding of the republic in 1889. These two aims have been paramount ever since. Notice that the motto does not mention liberty or equality; both these democratic virtues are, at best, subsumed under "progress," which significantly comes after "order." In any event, this motto brackets a century of Brazilian history.

In 1977 then-President Ernesto Geisel, who envisioned a gradual and orderly transition to civilian democratic rule, elaborated on the dynamics of progress in Brazil. Democracy, he argued, was the most essential ingredient in the political arena. But democracy could only be achieved "if we raise the standard of living of Brazilians," which, he added, "can only be raised through economic development." Thus it was necessary to recognize the triangular relationship of government, society, and economy (corresponding to democracy, prosperity, and development) if the century-old promise of order with progress was ever to be fulfilled.

Brazil's Recent Political History

In Brazil the concept of progress has always been closely linked with the stabilizing presence of a protective and centralized authoritarian state. In the 1920s disenchanted middle-class groups joined junior military officers (*tenentes*) in opposing an oligarchy representing the interests of entrenched coffee-plantation owners. They believed that the military alone could awaken the nation, unlock its pent-up energies, and spearhead modernization. They wanted to oust conservative politicians who blocked the path of progress. The tenentes' program included labor reforms such as recognition of trade unions, a minimum wage and maximum workweek, and regulation of child labor. It also called for land reform, state ownership of natural resources, and all-out expansion of the public school system. The tenentes faded into history, but many of their ideas were adopted by Getúlio Vargas, who staged a revolution in 1930, established a fascist-style corporatist state, and ruled as a benevolent dictator until 1945, when the generals forced him to resign.

For the next eighteen years Brazil was governed by a parade of civilian presidents. The parade ended abruptly in 1964, when the military—disgruntled by the leftist leanings of President João Goulart and by his failure to curb rampant inflation and official corruption—staged a bloodless coup. The military did not view this intervention as anything ordinary: It was the start of a revolution from above. As if to pick up where the tenentes and Getúlio Vargas had left off, the military launched a major modernization drive. They would have order with progress, but it would come at the expense of freedom and dignity. Strict press censorship was imposed, and egregious abuses of human rights became commonplace.

During the decade following the Revolution of 1964, Brazil experienced what many called an "economic miracle"—growth rates averaged about 10 percent a year. But the benefits went primarily to the upper and middle classes; they did not trickle down to the vast majority of Brazilians who continued to live in poverty. Furthermore, Brazil's development strategy was fundamentally flawed. It stressed industrialization, mechanization, and capital-intensive investment to the neglect of agriculture, appropriate technologies, and public works projects that would benefit the whole nation.

During the 1970s the "miracle" turned into a nightmare for Brazil's military rulers. A worldwide recession triggered by the OPEC oil embargo hit Brazil especially hard. Energy-import prices shot skyward, while the price of agricultural products (about 40 percent of Brazil's exports) fell sharply. Meanwhile, the deteriorating rural economy caused a mass migration into overcrowded cities, which could not provide basic services for the influx. (In 1970 about 56 percent of the population was urban; by 1984 the figure has risen to 68 percent.) Brazil's military rulers were rediscovering the advantages of civilian government.

It took several years to make the transition from military to civilian rule. As the economy continued its tailspin, inflation soared past 200 percent a year by 1984, and workers' incomes plunged by 30 percent. Polls showed that nine out of ten Brazilians favored direct election of the president. Mass protests in the spring of 1984 left no doubt that the polls accurately reflected public sentiment.

In January 1985 Tancredo Neves was chosen as Brazil's first civilian president in twenty-one years. The military had refused to permit direct elections but, to mollify the masses, had chosen Neves, one of its critics within the Brazilian Democratic Movement party, to guide the transition to civilian rule. Meanwhile, the Congress—in defiance of the military—voted unanimously that henceforth the president would be directly elected.

Before he could be inaugurated, Neves fell gravely ill and died, following a series of operations. His successor, Vice-President José Sarney, had earlier been named acting president, and now he took office under unenviable circumstances. Paradoxically, Brazil's authoritarian tradition as embodied in the Constitution vests extraordinary powers in the chief executive, giving the new president an impressive array of tools for the job.

But President Sarney was unable to turn the economy around. Bloated budgets contributed to galloping inflation (in 1988 consumer prices climbed 692 percent). In November 1989 Fernando Collor was directly elected to the presidency. The transfer of power from one civilian chief executive to another was a remarkable event, given Brazil's recent history. Collor promptly initiated spending cuts and market-oriented reforms, including a liberalized trade policy that pleased the United States and the International Monetary Fund.

Brazil's Constitution and Government

The 1969 Constitution, amended by presidential decree in 1977 and 1978, made Brazil a federal republic comprising twenty-three states, three territories and the Federal District (Brasília). The president is the linchpin in the system. He is the supreme commander of the armed forces, issues decrees and regulations, sets the budget, proposes legislation, and appoints cabinet ministers. A legislative majority in the hands of the opposition does not block presidential action. Any measure introduced by the president automatically becomes law, even without congressional approval. In addition, the president can intervene in any of the twenty-three states without consulting Congress, and he can declare a state of siege and rule by decree.

Under the 1969 Constitution the president served a six-year term and was chosen by an electoral college comprising the members of the Congress and delegates from state legislatures. In May 1985 Congress approved a constitutional amendment that provided for direct election of the president by universal suffrage. The 1988 Constitution incorporated those changes and set the president's term at five years.

Brazil's Congress is bicameral, and except for one-third of senators, is elected directly. Members of the Chamber of Deputies (lower house) are elected for four-year terms, while Senate members are elected for eight-year terms. The number of deputies is based on population. Congress has the formal power to approve legislation as well as budgets, taxes, and treaties. As noted earlier, however, the preponderance of legislative power is vested in the president.

Political Liberalization in Brazil

The Amnesty Bill and the Party Reform Bill of 1979 set the stage for Brazil's political liberalization. The former allowed hundreds of political exiles to return; the latter once again legalized political parties, provided they were not ideological and did not target a single class. Thus, the Communist party was outlawed, and a labor party was expressly forbidden. (The ban on Communist parties was lifted in 1985.)

The prohibition against a workers' party reflected the regime's preoccupation with order and its awareness that the crippled economy—along with the mass discontent it engendered— could be profoundly destabilizing. This situation was alarming, in part because government and labor in Brazil had long enjoyed a relationship of mutual trust and dependence. Organized labor expected the state to protect its interests; demands for democracy were secondary. If the government, whether authoritarian or democratic, could deliver on promises of benefits to the workers, labor would support it. The government's failure during the 1970s and early 1980s to protect workers in conditions of economic crisis severely strained this long-standing compact. Faced with hyperinflation, surging food prices, and massive unemployment, labor defected in 1983, joining the rising chorus of voices demanding direct elections and civilian rule. After 1985 President Sarney sought to placate organized labor, which remains a potent force in Brazilian politics.

Labor militancy was not the only challenge facing Brazil's embattled rulers. Emboldened by the Party Reform Bill, new parties sprang up. In Brazil party organizations are notoriously weak and often personalistic, and coalitions tend to be fragile and shifting. From 1965 to 1979 there were only two legal parties—the pro-Government ARENA party and the opposition Brazilian Democratic Movement (MDB) party. The former was reconstituted as the Social Democratic party (PDS) in the early 1980s; by then the MDB had become the PMDB (its founders simply added the word *party* to the official name). As the 1985 elections approached, political maneuvering intensified. A dissident faction of the right-wing PDS split away to form the Liberal Front party (PFL), which subsequently entered into a coalition with the center-left PMDB. The coalition, known as the Democratic Alliance, challenged the PDS in the electoral college and won. José Sarney was the PFL's candidate; when the coalition was formed, Sarney was given the number-two spot on the ticket. As noted, Tancredo Neves, the PMDB candidate, headed the winning ticket but did not live to serve. Thus, as the leader of a small splinter party, Sarney became Brazil's first civilian president in over twenty years.

In addition, the Democratic Labor party (PDT), the Brazilian Labor party (PTB), and the Party of Workers (PT) merit brief attention. All three are center-left, non-Marxist, pro-labor parties. The PDT favors welfare-state policies and considers itself a social democratic party. The PTB and PT both stress the need for further democratization of the political process.

There are also a dozen or so smaller parties that are legally registered but have negligible impact. The two most important are the Communist Party of Brazil (PCB) and the Socialist Party of Brazil (PSB). In part because the left is so fragmented in Brazil (as elsewhere in Latin America), the probability of any serious challenge from this side of the political spectrum is, at best, low.

One measure of Brazil's gradual march toward democracy is the number of political parties that now contest elections. Before 1979 there were just two official parties. In the 1982 elections there were five parties; in 1986 there were more than a dozen, and no fewer that eleven of these won at least one seat in the national Congress. The proliferation of parties is at least a crude gauge of the liberal democratic reforms that have taken place in Brazil during the 1980s.

Liberalization was advanced in the spring of 1985 when Congress legislated several significant changes in the electoral system. First, as mentioned earlier, it abolished the electoral college and stipulated that in the future the president would be elected by direct popular vote. Second, it required direct election of mayors in all municipalities and state capitals. Third, it enfranchised illiterates (nearly a quarter of the population), thus expanding the electorate by 20 million voters. Fourth, it abolished the "party loyalty" rule, which obligated members of Congress to vote the party line and penalized party defectors. Fifth, it eased the establishment of new parties and, as noted, legalized Communist parties.

None of these changes obviates the fact that democracy in Brazil is plagued by economic ills and social inequities, but the steps so far are impressive, especially given the country's authoritarian tradition. Brazil's weak cultural and historical foundations for democratic institution-building may be insurmountable. Time alone will tell.

Argentina

When Raúl Alfonsín was sworn in as president of Argentina in December 1983, it marked the end of an era of extraordinarily repressive and brutal military dictatorship. The Argentina that President Alfonsín inherited was a nation in chaos. The economy was hurtling downhill like a runaway locomotive, the political system had been unhinged by an ignominious defeat in the Falkland Islands War, and the society was sullen and seething from the atrocities of Argentina's former military rulers.

A Coup-Prone Past

Like Brazil, Argentina has a history of military intervention in the political process as well as some limited experience with democracy and civilian rule. Argentina's first president to be freely elected by direct popular vote was the head of a reformist party: Hipólito Irigoyen. He was elected in 1916 and remained in office until 1922. Elected to a second term in 1928, he was removed two years later by an army coup, and the nation's first military regime was established. In 1932 civilian rule was restored; this time it lasted about a decade before the military again staged a coup.

After World War II the nation's most famous political figure, Colonel Juan Perón, was elected president (February 1946). Perón extended the franchise to women in 1947, and he founded the Peronista party in 1949. His second wife, Eva ("Evita") Duarte de Perón, was widely admired and extremely popular, especially among Argentina's industrial workers. Perón was reelected in November 1951. (Eva Perón died the following year at the age of 33. The personality cult that soon developed around her memory became a rallying point for the Peronista party and the nation's poor.) As president, General Perón stressed extreme nationalism and social progress through an alliance between the state and organized labor. His attempt to secularize Argentina and to legalize divorce led to conflict and confrontation with the Roman Catholic Church, which excommunicated him. In 1955 he was ousted by a military coup and went into exile in Spain.

In 1973, having returned to Argentina after eighteen years in the political wilderness, Juan Perón was once again elected president of Argentina—this time with more than 60 percent of the popular vote. During the years of Perón's enforced absence Argentina had been plagued by political instability and a pervasive sense of drift. Many Argentines viewed Perón as a national savior; for these believers, his return was a "second coming" in more ways than one. But he died in

1974, leaving it to his politically ambitious third wife (and vice-president), Isabel ("Isabelita") Martínez Perón—whose official position was a thinly veiled effort to capitalize on the "Evita" cult—to work the miracle his death had left undone.

But the miracle was not to be. Economic problems forced Isabel Perón to adopt unpopular austerity measures. The resulting discontent, coupled with spiraling inflation, prompted the military to intervene once again. Following the 1976 coup by the armed forces, a three-headed junta was set up, and Lieutenant General Jorge Videla was sworn in as president.

Argentina's "Dirty War"

During the 1970s a left-wing guerrilla group, the Monteñeros, carried out violent acts against the government. A particularly heinous deed was the kidnapping and killing of General Pedro Aramburu, a former president. The military regime that took power in 1976 reintroduced the death penalty for abduction, subversion, and terrorism as part of a major offensive against the guerrillas. The anti-insurgency campaign succeeded; unfortunately, this "success" came at the expense of human rights. For two years the regime waged a "dirty war" against subversion. People were arbitrarily arrested, imprisoned, tortured, and murdered by the security forces, who were given a blank check to do whatever was necessary to crush the insurgency. Thousands of people the junta suspected of disloyalty simply disappeared. The odious methods epitomized by Argentina's "disappeared ones"—estimates go as high as thirty thousand—met with outrage in the United States and elsewhere. (Argentina was a prime target of President Jimmy Carter's human rights crusade.)

The "dirty war" succeeded in destroying the insurgency, but it created an international furor. In 1978, after armed opposition had been quashed, the government eased its repression. Pressures for political liberalization mounted, and in 1981 the government made overtures to political parties as a prelude to eventually restoring democracy. A coalition of five parties, the so-called *Multipartidaria*, importuned the military junta to hold general elections. But tensions between the government and society were exacerbated by the rapidly degenerating economic situation.

The Falkland Islands War

To divert attention from domestic problems, the government, now headed by Leopoldo Galtieri, manufactured an external crisis. Argentina had long claimed sovereignty over nearby British islands that Argentines called the Malvinas and the British called the Falklands. When negotiations failed, Argentina invaded the islands, and a short but ferocious naval war with Great Britain ensued. The British administered a humiliating defeat to Argentina in general and to the military junta in particular.

Huge demonstrations against the government were followed by mass strikes and social chaos. The military rulers tried to stem the protest with renewed repression, but the embattled regime was now bankrupt morally and politically. In early

1983 the government announced that both general and presidential elections would be held at the end of October.

The Peronist party, which had never lost an election it contested, was the favorite to win again in 1983. But Raúl Alfonsín, the leader of the Radical party, pulled an upset by garnering 50 percent of the vote; his Peronist opponent could muster only 39 percent. (A decade earlier, Perón himself had won over 60 percent of the popular vote, to the Radical party's 24 percent.) Despite this setback, the Peronists were far from dead. They won control of the Senate and of many provincial legislatures and governments. The Radical party managed a slim majority in the Chamber of Deputies and captured over half the provincial governorships.

President Alfonsín was confronted by two critical issues: the economy, which was in a nosedive, and the "dirty war," whose perpetrators had mostly gone unpunished. Both issues were explosive. In 1983 inflation was soaring (to over 400 percent), the gross domestic product was falling, and capital flight—a barometer of domestic investors' opinion about the future—was estimated at $2 billion.

The question of how to punish former military rulers and their henchmen for the atrocities committed against Argentine citizens during the "dirty war" was, in some ways, more explosive than the economic situation. Alfonsín was perched on the horns of the proverbial dilemma: Given the armed forces' propensity to revolt, any move against the military raised dangers of a coup; but given the public anger, any attempt to downplay the "dirty war" would provoke a groundswell of indignation. If he lost control of the situation, Alfonsín either would have to ask the security forces to intervene (shades of the dark past) or would have to wait for the army to stage another coup (in the name of law and order, of course). Either way, he would lose—and so would the cause of democracy in Argentina.

President Alfonsín managed to finesse the situation by steering a middle course. The former military rulers were tried, and some were convicted; their sentences ranged from $4\frac{1}{2}$ years to life imprisonment. Although many Argentines thought the government had been too lenient, the military brooded, and rumors of coup plotting circulated. Nor did the matter end with the trial of the highest authorities. Several hundred lower-ranking officers were also implicated in atrocities, and the president courageously promised that they also would be brought to justice.

Argentina's Constitution and Government

With the return to civilian rule in 1983, the principles of Argentina's original Constitution, drafted in 1853, were restored. The "Declarations, Rights and Guarantees" gave the Roman Catholic religion "State protection," but guaranteed "freedom of religious belief" to all. It also granted freedom of association and expression; made everyone equal before the law; protected citizens against arbitrary arrest, ex post factor laws, and unwarranted search and seizure; enshrined property rights ("no one may suffer expropriation"); and expressly prohibited confiscation of property as a judicial remedy or penalty.

Argentina's political-administrative system comprises the Federal District, twenty-two provinces, and the national territory of Tierra del Fuego. Executive power is vested in the president, who is the chief of state, head of government, and commander-in-chief of the armed forces. The president "issues the instructions and rulings necessary for the execution of the laws, and himself takes part in drawing up and promulgating those laws." He also appoints judges of the Supreme Court and other tribunals, ambassadors, top-echelon civil servants, senior officers of the armed forces, and, of course, his cabinet ministers. All but the latter require Senate approval.

The president and vice-president run on a single ticket and are indirectly elected for a six-year term. Members of the electoral college are chosen from each province, the Federal District, and the national territory, with each region having twice as many electors as it has representatives to the national Congress. Candidates must be at least thirty-years old and Argentine Catholic by birth.

The Constitution gives the president broad executive powers, including the right to introduce and veto legislation, conduct foreign affairs, and suspend citizens' constitutional guarantees by declaring a state of emergency. The president is not eligible for immediate reelection.

American students will recognize many parallels between the constitutions of Argentina and the United States. Even the method of choosing presidents is similar. The U.S. Electoral College is a reminder that American presidents also are elected indirectly. One big difference, however, is that although Argentina's Constitution dates back to middle of the nineteenth century, it has been inoperative during most of its existence.

One key to popular self-government is a freely elected legislature. In Argentina, lawmaking power is vested in a bicameral Congress, comprising the Chamber of Deputies (254 directly elected members, chosen for four years and eligible for reelection) and the Senate (46 members, chosen by provincial legislatures for nine-year terms, with one-third of the seats being renewed every three years).

Argentina's Congress has powers similar to those of the U.S. Congress, including the power to regulate foreign trade, fix import and export duties, levy taxes, contract loans, regulate debt and the currency system, and determine the budget. Congress also approves or rejects treaties, authorizes the president to declare war or make peace, and sets the strength of the armed forces. Legislation relating to taxes and the draft must start in the Chamber of Deputies, the lower house. Impeachment procedures are like those in the United States: The lower house decides whether there are grounds for a trial, and, if so, it is then conducted in the upper house (Senate), where a verdict is rendered.

Most bills may be introduced in either house, and both houses must approve a bill for it to become law. Traditionally, legislative initiative was primarily a presidential prerogative; now, however, Congress is more assertive than in the past, a development that President Alfonsín encouraged. As in the Congress, proposed legislation is referred to standing committees for preliminary action before it goes to the full chamber for final vote. Unlike its U.S. counterpart, the Argentine Congress does not use conference committees to resolve differences. Instead, bills must be sent back and forth between the two chambers until agreement is reached. Finally, a presidential veto can be overridden by a two-thirds vote of both houses.

The fact that the Constitution makes Congress an equal partner with the president is highly significant in this regard. Logically, a strong legislature goes hand in hand with a strong party system. In a true democratic republic, political parties often operate most effectively and purposefully through the legislative branch. The reverse is also true: The legislative branch operates best when political parties function to articulate and aggregate interests within the larger society. When the system provides incentives for parties to compete vigorously, they tend to flourish; and when parties flourish, a president cannot afford to ignore them. Such a system requires that the chief executive be a skilled mediator and conciliator.

In a country beset by internal problems, there are pros and cons to this type of system. Since in Argentina the president is indirectly elected, he does not have the same sort of popular mandate as a directly elected president such as in Mexico. This fact, combined with the relatively powerful role of Argentina's legislative branch, might weaken the moral authority and credibility of the chief executive in a time of trouble. But in Argentina a countervailing force is at work: Argentines tend to revere their elected presidents. Far more than in the United States, the fortunes of political parties hinge on the presence or absence of charismatic personalities. Hence, personal popularity (*personalismo*) was the primary source of Juan Perón's power. The same was true of President Alfonsín, until the economic crisis forced him to step down in June 1989.

Venezuela

Thanks to its large oil reserves, Venezuela became Latin America's most prosperous country during the 1960s. No doubt this happy coincidence helped stabilize the government and solidify popular sentiment in favor of Venezuela's fledgling democracy. The reason is simple: A thriving economy tends to give an aura of legitimacy to the existing political order.

The impetus for Venezuela's turn toward democracy in the late 1950s came, in part, from the country's powerful labor movement, which was (and is) closely allied with Acción Democrática (AD). It was not only organized labor that opposed military rule, however; so did Venezuela's highly organized and politicized university students, the middle class, and business leaders, most of whom supported the center-right Social Christian party. Thus, a broad consensus in favor of civilian rule and political accountability had developed in Venezuela. In addition, the United States—Venezuela's most important trading partner, arms supplier, and source of military training—was quietly pressuring the military to relinquish power to civilian politicians.

As noted in Chapter 19, before 1935 Venezuela experienced long periods of authoritarian rule including that of José Antonio Páez (1830–1846 and 1861–1863), Gúzman Blanco (1870–1888), and Juan Vicente Gómez (1908–1935). These dictatorships alternated with shorter periods of unstable democratic rule. Venezuela's mixed tradition of democracy and dictatorship results in a political culture characterized by respect for authority and pride in democratic institutions.

The evolution of Venezuela's constitutional democracy dates back to the death of Gómez in 1935. The process was interrupted by the military regime of Marcos Pérez Jiménez (1948–1958); with the exception of this ten-year dictatorship, Venezuela has been democratically ruled for well over half a century.

Rómulo Betancourt is the dominant political figure in recent Venezuelan history. His democratic convictions were solidified during the Gómez dictatorship, which he actively opposed. Always an opponent of military rule and a long-time advocate of political reform, Betancourt founded the Democratic Action (AD) party in 1941. As mentioned, AD is one of Venezuela's two major parties, and it typically has more success at the polls than its archrival, the Social Christian party.

As AD's top leader, Betancourt was elected president in 1958 and headed a government in coalition with three other parties. In 1963 another AD leader, Raúl Leoni, was elected president. Thus, Betancourt and Leoni governed Venezuela for the first crucial decade after the Pérez Jiménez dictatorship. With the help of large oil-export revenues, they managed to restore the nation to financial health after Pérez Jiménez left the economy in a shambles and the country heavily in debt. Two other "Adecos" have been elected to the presidency, Carlos Andrés Pérez (1973–1978 and 1988–present) and Jaime Lusinchi (1983–1988). Nonetheless, Betancourt remained the preeminent leader of AD until his death in 1981.

Betancourt was not only the leader of a political party but also a major contributor to the founding and consolidation of Venezuela's current political system. As a theoretician, he was an incisive exponent of democratic principles. As a politician, he practiced what he preached. U.S. President John F. Kennedy, who served at about the same time as Betancourt, once characterized himself as "an idealist without illusions." The same could be said of Rómulo Betancourt.

Venezuela's Constitution and Government

Under the present Constitution, promulgated in 1961, Venezuela is a federal republic divided into twenty states, one Federal District (Caracas, the capital), two territories, and seventy-two "Federal Dependencies" in the Caribbean. The main outlines of the system originated in party agreements and tacit understandings on moderate reform and reconciliation among key elites (including military leaders) during the period from 1957 to 1961. Since the adoption of the Constitution there has been vigorous competition between government and opposition parties, and the nation has witnessed five peaceful transfers of power via free and fair elections.

The president is both head of government (chief executive) and head of state (chief diplomat). He has the right to declare a state of emergency and thus to restrict or suspend constitutional guarantees, but, significantly, he must have the approval of Venezuela's Congress. The president has the usual complement of executive powers: He appoints high-level civilian and military officials, initiates legislation, serves as commander-in-chief of the armed forces, and plays a key role in the budgetary process.

Although the Constitution does not place great constraints on presidential power, the vitality of Venezuela's pluralistic society and the strength of both real and potential opposition are an imposing deterrent to arbitrary presidential rule. Effective governance in Venezuela requires intraparty and interparty coalition building, compromise, and persuasion. Party leaders constantly court the country's well-organized interest groups and pay careful attention to public opinion. Moreover, presidents can serve only one five-year term and must wait ten years before running again. In 1988 Carlos Andrés Pérez became the first president ever to be elected to a second term (Rafael Caldera Rodríguez tried but failed).

Although the military is not a threat to civilian rule now, the armed forces are a check on presidential power. Labor unions, corporate industry, the press, and factionalism within the ruling party also limit the chief executive. Finally, according to Article 150 of the Constitution, the Senate can authorize a court martial (that is, impeachment) of the president.

The president is directly elected by a plurality of the total votes cast. He must be Venezuelan by birth, at least thirty years of age, and a layman. There is no vice-president; if a president dies in office or becomes incapacitated, a new election is held as soon as possible. In the interim a caretaker presidency is set up as provided in the Constitution.

Both houses of Venezuela's Congress are elected by popular vote on the basis of proportional representation. The Senate has 50 members, and the Chamber of Deputies has 201. Congressional elections coincide with the presidential election, and deputies and senators serve five-year terms, like the president.

From a structural standpoint, Venezuela's Congress closely resembles that of the United States. In practice, however, party discipline is stronger (in part because the two major parties are hierarchical, tightly organized, and truly national in scope). The power of party delegations (*fracciones*) in Venezuela's Congress is not offset by powerful standing committees, as in the United States.

Although Venezuela's Congress has a variety of powers, its main function is to consider and sometimes rebuff presidential initiatives. It becomes an initiator itself—and a major player in the all-important "battle of the budget"—only when the president's party is in the minority. This is always a possibility in a non-parliamentary system, because the chief executive is elected separately, rather than being automatically elevated to the top position by virtue of leading the majority party.

By approving legislation, the Congress legitimates policy. By debating current issues, it invigorates the political process and provides a safety valve to release pressure without threatening stability. Finally, the Congress is a highly visible showcase of pluralism and tolerance, which are essential values in any liberal democracy.

Parties, Legitimacy, and Stability in Venezuela

Unlike most other Latin American countries, Venezuela has highly organized political parties that do not depend entirely on the personality of a particular leader for their viability. Voting is obligatory, but the high turnout in Venezuelan elections is largely the result of (a) grass-roots party organizations that mobilize supporters, (b) the perceived benefits of voting, and (c) a supportive civic culture, in particular, a citizenry that prides itself on responsible participation.

Venezuela's two major parties are Democratic Action (AD) and the Social Christian party (COPEI). As noted earlier, AD dominated the political scene for the first decade after the return to democratic rule in 1958. Since the election of Social Christian leader Rafael Caldera Rodríguez in 1968, the two parties have alternated in power, and there has been a widely observed propensity for voters to chastise the party in power at the polls.

Both AD and COPEI are moderate parties; AD is center left and COPEI is center right, although on social-welfare issues the parties are quite similar. Calders founded COPEI in 1946; he was a leader of a Catholic student movement that opposed the direction of Betancourt's reforms. In the 1978 election—the last time COPEI won—the party focused on such mundane issues as educational reform and the need for broadened participation in the democratic process. A third issue revolved around the "promoter state," which in practical terms meant a slight tilt toward the private sector without diminishing the role of the public sector. The party's candidate, Luis Herrera Campíns, also promised to improve social services and reduce inefficiency in government.

The presidency of Herrera Campíns (1978–1983) was a fiasco from which COPEI could not quickly recover. The oil glut of the early 1980s hit Venezuela's oil-dependent economy with the force of a sledgehammer. In some respects Herrera Campíns was Venezuela's Herbert Hoover: Both had the misfortune to become president when their countries were teetering on economic disaster. The difficulties for Herrera Campíns arose partly because COPEI did not win a majority in Congress, and so he headed a minority government. But the main problem was the declining economy. After growing at a rate of 4 to 5 percent a year during the 1970s, the economy actually shrank by 1.7 percent in 1980. Escalating external debt, falling oil revenues, and rising import costs forced the government into unpopular economic adjustment. In 1983, a presidential election year, the economy contracted nearly 6 percent, opening the door for AD to recapture control.

COPEI's constituency has been the Catholic Church, the Federation of Chambers of Commerce, and university students. Its internal problems reflect a generation gap: Caldera, the grand old man, continues to dominate the party and resist changes, while younger leaders are eager to renovate the party and overcome the stigma associated with Herrera Campíns.

Democratic Action is a highly centralized party comprising several powerful groups, including the orthodox faction, the labor faction, and the left-leaning, development-oriented, "statist" faction. Each faction has its own leaders and agenda. The orthodox faction sees itself as the custodian of the Betancourt tradition. The labor faction is anchored in the powerful Confederation of Venezuelan Workers (CTV) and is headed by Manuel Penalver. The left wing of AD is the power base of the current president, Carlos Andrés Pérez. Formally, the party is run from the top down through the National Executive Committee; informally, it is run by a small inner circle known as the *cogollito*.

The balance of forces within AD thus reflects a mixture of policy preferences. In general, AD advocates rapid economic development, gradual nationalization of oil production, a full-fledged welfare state, and close ties to the Western alliance (and specifically the United States). The party also stresses the need for economic diversification and balanced growth based on adequate investment in both industry and agriculture. Finally, AD's leadership tends to be moderately anti-Communist, reform minded, and benign in its attitude toward free enterprise.

The great majority of Venezuelan voters cluster around the middle of the political spectrum. The expectations of left-wing parties—particularly the Movement Toward Socialism (MAS)—have repeatedly been disappointed (most recently in 1983, when MAS, with an articulate and appealing candidate, failed once again to capture even 10 percent of the vote).

Political campaigns in Venezuela are long and costly; per-capita campaign expenditures are estimated to be the highest in the world. In 1983 total campaign costs were estimated at nearly $250 million, considerably higher per capita than the cost of the 1984 U.S. election. Venezuelan presidential candidates begin maneuvering for the next election almost the morning after the last one, partly because the constitutional ban on self-succession always makes the president a "lame duck." Campaigns go on for two or more years, and it is hardly an exaggeration to say that politics is like a national sport.

The future of Venezuela's democracy will be assessed in Chapter 21. But considering the past and present, it is fair to say that the political system has functioned in accordance with constitutional norms, that Venezuela has been politically stable, and that the government enjoys popular acceptance and thus legitimacy. A major reason for this success has undoubtedly been the existence of two moderate and durable political parties, both of them committed to perpetuating the system as well as to gaining power. Another reason is that popular consensus favors constitutional democracy. Opinion polls and elections have demonstrated repeatedly that Venezuelans want neither a military dictatorship nor a Marxist revolution.

Why did democracy take root in Venezuela but not in Guatemala or, until recently, in Argentina? As suggested earlier, the winds of fortune favored Venezuela. First, the military faced growing popular resistance during the 1950s in the form of mounting social unrest, mainly labor strikes and student demonstrations. The fear that instability might get out of hand helped turn the military against Pérez Jiménez and set the stage for democratic reforms. Second, when the military decided to let civilians take charge in 1958, a statesman of extraordinary stature—Rómulo Betancourt—happened to be available. He guided Venezuelan democracy through its infancy, and his international prestige and popularity at home kept military coup-plotting in check. Third, the 1960s coincided with the oil-driven economic boom. That the move to democracy was associated with the economic upturn greatly enhanced the credibility of the new constitutional system. Finally, Venezuela's oil reserves and U.S. strategic interests in South America fostered a special relationship between the two countries. No doubt the senior military officers responsible for the 1958 coup (many of whom were trained in the United States) were well aware of the importance Washington attached to constitutionalism and the rule of law.

CONCLUSION

During the 1980s Latin America went through a remarkable political metamorphosis, from military to civilian rule. In many cases this transformation was accomplished without bloodshed or social upheaval. Chapter 21 looks at the prospects for economic development and social progress, on which the fate of Latin American democracy hinges.

STUDENT QUESTIONS

1. How is Mexico ruled? Is the Mexican political system democratic or authoritarian? Is it repressive or tolerant of dissent? Is it a multiparty or one-party system? Are the leaders civilian or military?
2. How is Brazil ruled? What is the role of the military? How, when, and why did political change come to Brazil? Is the chief executive directly or indirectly elected? President or prime minister? Civilian or military? Constitutionally strong or weak?
3. How is Argentina ruled? What is the role of the military? How and why has this role changed? What is Peronism, and is it a threat to Argentine democracy at present?
4. Compare and contrast Venezuela's democracy with that of the United States. (Include the executive and legislative branches, the political party system, and other relevant features.)

SUGGESTED READINGS

Black, Jan Knippers. *Sentinels of Empire: The United States and Latin American Militarism*. New York: Greenwood, 1986.

Loveman, Brian, and Thomas M. Davies, Jr. *The Politics of Antipolitics: The Military in Latin America*. Lincoln, Neb.: University of Nebraska, 1989.

Potash, Robert. *The Army and Politics in Argentina*. Stanford, Calif.: Stanford University, 1980.

Riding, Alan. *Distant Neighbors: A Portrait of the Mexicans*. New York: Vintage, 1986.

Wynia, Gary W. *The Politics of Latin American Development*. New York: Cambridge, 1984.

NOTE

[1] Alan Riding, *Distant Neighbors: A Portrait of the Mexicans* (New York: Vintage, 1986).

Chapter 21
Toward a New Order in Latin America?

During the late 1980s two major trends defined the contours of Latin American politics. The economic dynamism of the 1960s and 1970s gave way to an epidemic of debt and decline that weakened the social fabric and threatened the stability of nearly every government in the region. At the same time, the violent forces of revolution and repression that had ravaged the region for nearly two decades were finally subdued in many countries as civilian governments replaced military regimes in Guatemala, El Salvador, Honduras, Ecuador, Bolivia, Peru, Brazil, Uruguay, and Argentina. Add these countries to those where civilians have long ruled—Mexico, Costa Rica, Venezuela, and Colombia—and a pattern becomes clear: The role of the military in Latin America has receded, at least temporarily, and aspirations for popular self-government have achieved unprecedented institutional expression.

In South America this is a particularly dramatic turnabout from the previous period, when military rule and brutal repression were so widespread that only Venezuela and Colombia still had civilian governments, competitive elections, opposition parties, and critical news media. As one observer has noted,

> Throughout South America, a new breed of "bureaucratic authoritarian" regimes snuffed out most political life; banning political parties, repressing trade unions, suspending constitutional guarantees—and institutionalizing torture, "disappearances," and other systematic violations of human rights.[1]

Transition to Civilian Rule

The onset of economic difficulties during the 1970s deepened into a full-blown crisis in the early 1980s and sent the military scurrying for cover. In Argentina the generals, conjured up a war, which they lost. Elsewhere they bowed out more gracefully. Nearly everywhere the key question was not whether the military would relinquish power but precisely when and how. (Two exceptions were Paraguay and Chile, where the dictatorships resisted pressures for change.)

By the mid-1980s the transition from dictatorship to democracy, from military to civilian rule, was well under way. The last country in South America to make this switch was Chile, where General Pinochet was defeated in a plebiscite and so allowed free elections in November 1989. As noted in Chapter 20, Brazil's generals had allowed a civilian president to take charge in 1985. By the early 1990s, then, the main issue was whether the newly chartered governments could

496

consolidate power while having to overcome a daunting array of domestic (especially economic) problems.

Peru was an important test case. There, a charismatic young politician, Alan Garcia Pérez, was elected president in 1985. His victory was impressive for several reasons. First, he was only 36 years old, one of the youngest chief executives in the world. Second, he was the head of the Popular American Revolutionary Alliance (APRA), a left-leaning party with a long history of opposition to the military; no APRA candidate had ever before been allowed to assume the presidency. Third, his election signaled the first time in many decades that power had been transferred by a free election from one civilian president to another, and without fraud or foul play. Fourth, Peru faced excruciating economic difficulties, including runaway inflation, massive unemployment, and a burdensome foreign debt (Garcia vowed to limit debt payments to no more than 10 percent of Peru's export earnings). Fifth, the nation was in the midst of a bloody and protracted guerrilla war.

By the middle of his term, President Garcia's popularity had faded, and the future of Peru's fledgling democracy was in doubt. In 1990—despite the stagnant economy, hyperinflation, and an insurgency that threatened chaos—elections were held. For the third time in a decade the military allowed power to be transferred from one freely elected civilian leader to the next. Alberto Fujimori, the son of Japanese immigrants, defeated popular novelist Mario Vargas Liosa in a runoff election in June. Fujimori promised to adjust Peru's exchange rate to promote exports and to discourage food imports. Whether Fujimori can reverse the country's steady slide into an economic abyss remains to be seen.

In Uruguay, Bolivia, and Ecuador, civilians were in charge, but the military stood ready to intervene at any time. Elections in Ecuador in 1988 transferred power peacefully from a right-wing president (Cordero) to a left-wing one (Borja). In Bolivia a dreadful economic situation and chronic instability dimmed prospects for continued civilian rule. In Uruguay, President Sanguinetti grappled with the nation's economic problems while trying to restore both civilian rule and civilized politics, but he was forced to pay a heavy price—to sweep past human rights abuses under the rug. And in Argentina President Alfonsín had managed to place former military rulers on trial; remarkably, several were sentenced to long prison terms.

Until the late 1980s Chile and Paraguay were authoritarian holdouts. Isolated internationally and facing wide opposition at home, in 1989 the Chilean regime held a ''yes or no'' plebiscite on a new constitution that would automatically renew General Augusto Pinochet's term in office for another decade. (Pinochet had seized power in a military coup in 1973.) Chilean voters rejected the new constitution, paving the way for national elections in November 1989. In Paraguay a military coup led by General Andres Rodriguez ousted aging dictator Alfredo Stroessner, who had ruled since 1954. Rodriguez won the presidency in Paraguay's first multicandidate election in decades, and he has promised to relinquish power to an elected civilian in 1993.

South America's two democratic showcases, Colombia and Venezuela, were not immune from destabilizing forces. Colombia reeled from the combined impact of natural disasters (including a volcanic eruption in the fall of 1985) as well as several insurgencies and illegal drug trafficking. When President Betancur's domestic peace initiative collapsed in 1985, M-19 guerrillas (the Movement of April 19) stormed the Supreme Court building in Bogotá, seized scores of hostages, and executed some of them (including eleven justices) before being killed themselves by security forces.

Venezuela, for some years awash in oil profits, had to adopt austerity measures after world-market oil prices plunged in the early 1980s. A declining standard of living threatened to crack the broad consensus—fueled by "petrol prosperity"—that had undergirded Venezuelan democracy since the late 1950s.

In Middle America, Mexico and Costa Rica were joined by Guatemala, El Salvador, and Honduras in forming a solid majority of countries under civilian rule. But only Costa Rica was an unambiguous case of democracy in action. The turmoil in El Salvador continued, as violence was perpetrated by both the left (the Farabundo Martí National Liberation Front, or FMLN) and the right (security forces and the ARENA party). The death toll in 1987 was estimated at 62,000, and efforts to negotiate a settlement failed.

In Guatemala and Honduras, where democracy had sprouted in the mid-1980s, the military continued to play an important behind-the-scenes role in government, which, in both cases, was headed by an elected civilian. But Honduras remained the poorest state in Latin America (except for Haiti), and Guatemala continued to be plagued by violence and urban disappearances. Elsewhere, democratic Costa Rica was flanked by the area's two remaining authoritarian regimes.

The year 1990 brought dramatic changes in Nicaragua and Panama. In Nicaragua, Violetta Chamorro defeated Daniel Ortega in national elections. Ortega's Marxist-military junta had ruled the country for a decade. In Panama the personal dictatorship of General Manuel Noriega ended when the Bush Administration ordered a military intervention, captured Noriega, and brought him to the United States to stand trial for drug trafficking. El Salvador remained a battleground, but the Central American peace process gained new impetus at the start of the new decade.

Finally, Mexico's pseudodemocratic system, which was remarkably resilient over the years, began to come unglued in the late 1980s. A severe economic crunch compounded by low oil prices and a huge external debt; mounting social problems epitomized by the polluted, crime-ridden, congested, and overcrowded capital; and rising discontent across the entire social spectrum threatened the PRI's six-decade-long domination of the political system. In the 1988 elections the PRI's candidate, Carlos Salinas de Gortari, won by the smallest margin in the party's history. Two opposition candidates—one from the left, the other from the right—made unusually strong showings. When the PRI lost a gubernatorial election in mid-1989, some experts pronounced the PRI-dominated system defunct—perhaps prematurely, but not without good reason.

Throughout the region political stability in the 1990s is a dependent variable. Peace, order, and progress hinge above all on economic performance.

And progress is being hindered in several key countries by enormous foreign debt.

Foreign Debt and Domestic Distress

An article in *The World Today* (April 1987) summed up the situation in many of Latin America's new democracies:

> Democracy has returned at an inconvenient time: elected governments have had to plunge their countries into unpopular austerity so that they can service the foreign debts piled up by the generals and put their internal economies in order. Standards of living, already miserably low, have gone down almost everywhere. There have been demonstrations and strikes against austerity in Argentina, Brazil, Uruguay, Bolivia, Panama, Guatemala, and El Salvador. Yet extremists of left and right are failing to take advantage of what ought to be a splendid opportunity. Elections are regularly won by middle-of-the-roaders (though left-wing parties seem to be on the rise).[2]

The region's total debt was somewhere around $416 billion by the end of the 1980s. Paying off this debt strained the economies of Mexico, Venezuela, Brazil, Argentina, and Peru—the major Latin debtor nations—and, according to some observers, placed debt and democracy on a collision course. Many Latin countries still depend heavily on a single export: copper (Peru), oil (Venezuela and Mexico), bananas (Honduras), coffee (Colombia), sugar (Cuba), and so on. For Colombia, Peru, Bolivia, and to a lesser extent Mexico, another commodity—illegal drugs, mainly cocaine—has become a source of export earnings. In addition, the age-old problem of income maldistribution continues to threaten stability in Latin societies.

The economic picture was not entirely bleak in the mid-1980s. Latin America's combined gross domestic product grew by 3.4 percent in 1986, compared with 2.7 percent in 1985. Interest rates on the region's debt fell from 8.6 percent to about 6 percent. In South America, countries with the best growth rates were Brazil and Peru (toughly 8 percent), followed by Argentina, Chile, Uruguay, and Colombia (5 to 6 percent). Inflation fell from a runaway regional average of 275 percent to 70 percent—still far too high but a giant step in the right direction. Brazil's "Cruzado Plan," Argentina's "Austral Plan," and Peru's "Inti Plan" all brought dramatic short-term reductions in inflation.

Peru was in a tailspin when Garcia took office in 1985, but after a year of shock treatment the economy began to show signs of revival. Such measures as a freeze on prices and exchange rates along with wage hikes produced a surge in consumer spending; factories were working at full tilt for the first time in years. Industrial output, construction starts, and imports were all up sharply, and inflation tumbled (from 183 percent to 63 percent within a year). But by 1990 Peru's socioeconomic problems had returned, including hyperinflation, budget deficits, stagnant output, strikes, and trade deficits.

In some parts of the region even foreign-debt pressures were alleviated. Mexico negotiated a sizable new loan package in 1987; Uruguay signed a multiyear restructuring agreement and obtained new capital from abroad; and Venezuela had earlier succeeded in restructuring its debt. Other countries—including Brazil, Argentina, and Peru—were also maneuvering for international debt relief.

The economic dilemma facing most of Latin America, however, was not likely to be relieved soon. To avoid losing International Monetary Fund (IMF) borrowing privileges and to obtain new loans from the World Bank and from foreign governments and commercial banks, debtor nations were under great pressure to adopt IMF austerity programs. This generally meant budget cuts, constricted money supplies, tax increases, wage restraints—any belt-tightening measure that might restore solvency and stability. But there is a serious downside to this formula:

> Since the debt crisis, the poor in Latin America have got poorer and the middle class has moved down a peg or two; austerity policies have been unpopular. Letting off steam, voters kicked unpopular austerity-minded governments out of office in Colombia (1982), Venezuela (1983), Ecuador (1984), Peru (1986), and the Dominican Republic (1986).[3]

Decade of Decline

Despite hopeful signs, during the 1980s Latin America entered the worst recession in half a century. Production per capita declined about 7 or 8 percent throughout the decade, and real income per capita dropped approximately 10 percent. People's basic needs cannot be translated into effective demand, and so business and industry are hurt by shrinking domestic markets. On the human level, individual hardships are compounded by austerity-induced budget cuts for health, education, social security, defense, and public works, as well as by curbs on state subsidies for food, fuel, housing, and transportation.

In industrial democracies any double-figure jobless rate is generally perceived as a policy failure, one that will cause voters to take reprisals against the party in power. In Latin America, however, it is not uncommon to find 40 percent of the labor force unemployed or underemployed. The combination of unemployment, soaring inflation, and a shrinking social safety net is particularly deadly in developing countries where poverty is endemic and maldistribution of wealth is built into society's structure.

Losing Interest

Exacerbating Latin America's domestic economic problems is the debt burden being borne by Mexico, Brazil, Argentina, and Venezuela. Other countries (Chile, Colombia, Peru, and Ecuador) also have substantial, though much smaller, debt-service obligations. The region's debt–export ratio, a measure of its repayment capacity, deteriorated rapidly in the early 1980s. As a result, over one-third of Latin America's export earnings were devoted to interest payments.

Beginning in 1981 the outflow of funds from interest payments and repatriated profits of foreign firms exceeded the inflow from new loans and investments. In other words, Latin America had a net loss of capital every year. Between 1981 and 1987 the region transferred about $150 billion to industrial democracies—an amount equal to roughly 5 percent of its combined GDP. Interest payments cut deeply into Latin America's savings, and capital flight further reduced domestic investment and consumption. Finally, for the region as a whole, investment shrank by about 25 percent during the 1980s.

The debt crunch thus set up a vicious cycle. Devoting savings to debt service rather than to investment stunted economic growth. Slow growth, in turn, meant debtor nations had to choose between external and internal priorities (that is, loan repayment versus wage concessions, tax cuts, subsidies, and so on). This predicament generated politically charged controversy. For example, in 1985 Peru's President Garcia bitterly denounced the IMF and the United States and announced that Peru would limit its loan repayments to one-tenth of annual export earnings. The IMF withdrew Peru's borrowing privileges, and the United States declared outstanding loans to Peru "value impaired," thus effectively blocking future credit from U.S. commercial banks. Yet Garcia's unilateral "solution" to Peru's debt problem was less drastic than it might have been; there had been fears that Peru might actually default. President Garcia talked and acted like he wanted to lead a debtors' revolt, and his defiance was endorsed enthusiastically by Peruvians.

The political impact of the debt issue was hardly less apparent in other parts of Latin America. The list of countries in which economic ills had led to the downfall or crippling of incumbent governments since the mid-1980s included Mexico, Brazil, Argentina, Peru, Ecuador, Venezuela, and Bolivia. The message from the voters was clear: Provide economic relief, or do not expect any more self-sacrifice. By the end of 1987 eight Latin American countries were substantially in arrears on their external debt payments, and governments were under mounting pressure to take drastic action. Given these volatile circumstances, the danger that a single default might touch off a chain reaction could not be dismissed.

Latin American Foreign Policy

The debt problem has rekindled traditional Latin fears of U.S. domination and has underscored Latin dependence on the United States (in part because the United States plays a key role in shaping IMF policy). But the anti-Yanqui sentiment prevalent throughout Latin America has been insufficient to create regional solidarity. Beyond occasional denunciations of neocolonialism and U.S. interventionism, most Latin states have been careful not to antagonize the United States.

Efforts to promote trade expansion and economic integration have generally failed. The Andean Pact—which includes Venezuela, Colombia, Ecuador, Peru, Bolivia, and Chile—has never borne fruit. Other efforts to form a united front in dealing with the United States have also failed. When President Garcia announced that Peru would repay its debt at its own pace, the leaders of other debtor states did not follow suit and instead distanced themselves from Peru. Brazil, Venezuela, and Argentina all went separate ways in devising debt strategies. Given their combined debt of nearly $200 billion, had these three countries acted together, they would have had real leverage. But acting together is not a strong inclination of Latin American states.

Although the region has had territorial disputes—for example, between Peru and Ecuador, Peru and Chile, and Chile and Argentina—no wars have been fought between Latin states for decades. Instead, governments have been preoccupied with domestic strife, insurgencies, and civil war, as in El Salvador, Nicaragua, Colombia, Peru, Uruguay, and Argentina.

During the 1980s Cuba and Nicaragua were the only pro-Soviet states in Latin America. In 1990 voters in Nicaragua rejected Daniel Ortega, electing the pro-U.S. Violetta Chamorro, a vigorous opponent of Ortega's Marxist policies. And in Peru, where President Garcia frequently railed against U.S. imperialism, a moderate won the 1990 elections. One year earlier, in Argentina, Peronist candidate Carlos Menem was elected president; on assuming office he quickly let it be known that he would abandon the traditional Peronist antagonism toward the United States. In sum, despite the apparent tension in U.S.–Latin American relations, there is little tendency to "gang up" on the United States. The Soviet Union has never made any great inroads in South America, and recent trends seem to favor closer North-South relations in the Western Hemisphere.

Case Studies: Mexico, Brazil, Argentina, and Venezuela

As already indicated, many of the economic and political problems we are about to examine are found throughout Latin America. But the debt crisis is especially acute in these four countries, which together accounted for nearly 75 percent of the region's foreign debt. There are significant differences among the countries as well. For example, Mexico and Venezuela are oil exporters; Brazil and Argentina are not. Venezuela's debt–export ratio is around 3:1, Brazil's is about 4:1, Mexico's is 5:1, and Argentina's is between 6:1 and 7:1. Thus, while Argentina's debt is only half Mexico's and Brazil's, its debt *burden* is heavier.

Mexico

In the summer of 1988 national elections were held in Mexico. In the past, elections have been cut and dried: The PRI won every presidential, senatorial, and gubernatorial race since the party's inception in 1929.

But things were different in 1988. Two opposition candidates ran strong campaigns against the PRI's standard-bearer, Carlos Salinas de Gortari. One, Cuauhtemoc Cárdenas, happened to be the son of former populist president Lázaro Cárdenas (1934–1940); For days after the election the Federal Election Commission was silent. The PRI claimed victory, but did not indicate by what margin. Salinas's predecessor, Miguel de la Madrid Hurtado, had gotten "only" 71 percent of the vote in 1982—a record low. This time it appeared as though the PRI candidate had gotten less than half the votes. More than a week went by without official results; in the meantime, Cárdenas, amidst charges of election fraud against the ruling party, claimed *he* had won. Although the outcome was in doubt, there could be no doubt about one thing: The PRI's monopoly of power was being challenged like never before.

Mexico's Economic Quagmire   Deepening economic crisis formed the backdrop to this growing domestic disaffection with the PRI. During the 1970s the economy—bolstered by high oil prices and easily obtained foreign loans—grew an average of about 8 percent a year. At the beginning of the 1980s, however, the rosy picture clouded over as oil prices fell sharply in response to the glut on the world market. By this time Mexico was well on its way to accumulating a $100-billion foreign debt; at the end of 1982 interest payments alone (about $10 billion in 1987) were devouring 35 to 45 percent of the nation's annual export earnings.

To make matters worse, inflation and unemployment were both sky high. Prices were rising 60 percent a year or more, and unemployment was estimated as high as 45 percent. In 1982 the peso slipped from 12.5 to 48 to the dollar. By 1986 it was devalued to 500 to the dollar. The following year inflation rose to 105 percent, a record high. At the same time the budget deficit soared to 13 percent of gross domestic product.

This crisis forced Mexico's government to take drastic action. Currency controls had been put into effect in 1982, despite periodic promises from the government not to use such controls. Under growing pressure from the International Monetary Fund and foreign creditors, President de la Madrid adopted unpopular austerity measures including reduction of state subsidies for food and fuel. Other spending cuts were also made in an effort to curb the escalating budget deficits.

Finally, Mexico was also hit by a natural disaster in September 1985, when a massive earthquake rocked Mexico City and five states. The greatest loss of life and property occurred in the capital, where deaths were estimated at 7,000 officially but as high as 20,000 by other sources. Some 300,000 people were left homeless, and property damage was estimated at around $4 billion. The government came under scathing criticism for doing too little too late. There were also allegations that international relief funds had been misappropriated by corrupt officials.

Burdens without Benefits   Mexico's economic problems are easily demonstrated with a few statistics. But less visible is the social crisis that preceded and is now aggravated by economic problems. Mexico City's population growth and social ills were noted earlier. With a population of some 17 million (expected to more than double by the year 2020), and rapid urbanization occurring elsewhere in Mexico as well, the government will be under increasing pressure to invest in municipal services, schools, hospitals, roads, housing, and the like—in other words, to *expand* rather than reduce government spending.

The PRI's poor showing at the polls in 1988 no doubt reflected the fact that presidential candidate Salinas also happened to be chief architect of the country's austerity program. How long can the Mexican people accept the burdens of austerity, especially when so few of them shared in the benefits of former prosperity?

Nation-Building: Mexico's Unfinished Business   Mexico is still a developing country, both politically and economically. From a political standpoint, perhaps the most important postindependence task is nation-building, that is, integrating the various parts of the country into a unified political system. In Mexico the difficulties of national integration have been complicated by two considerations: the status of the Indian population and regionalism.

Today the mestizo population greatly outnumbers both Indian and Spanish elements. Nonetheless, distinct Indian tribes or ethnic groups still number more than two hundred and speak some fifty languages and dialects. Indians are often the victims of discrimination in Mexico, and yet many Spanish-speaking Mexicans view them as hindering social modernization, economic development, and political integration.

A greater obstacle to integration is that many Mexicans identify with a specific region more strongly than with the nation itself. One expert has argued that there are actually *five* Mexican nations:

1. Metromex—Mexico City and its environs, "the most powerful nation of the federation"
2. New Spain—the central zone, formerly the colonial heartland
3. Mexamerica—the progressive northern region adjacent to the U.S. border
4. South Mexico—the poor, underdeveloped, predominantly Indian nation between the Metromex and Guatemala
5. Club Mex—the resort areas of both coasts (for example, Cancun, Acapulco, Manzanilla, Puerta Vallarta, and Mazatlan)[4]

One source of regional antagonism is the uneven development within the country. Metromex, a relatively small geographic entity, accounted for one-half of Mexico's industry and 38 percent of its GDP in 1987. Uneven regional development has been accompanied by unequal growth. Metromex again provides the illustration. Besides its wealthy elite, the region's 2 to 3 million government employees, businesspeople, and unionized workers—the middle class—have enjoyed job security and a rising standard of living until recently. But the underclass has suffered true deprivation: Half of Metromex's poor live without running water, 40 percent have no health care, and a quarter have too little to eat.

In the late 1980s Mexamerica had a population of about 38 million, a diversified and relatively dynamic economy, and a burgeoning middle class, many of whom supported the market-oriented National Action party (PAN). The northeast is industrialized, particularly the city of Monterrey. It has close commercial ties with the U.S. border states of Texas, New Mexico, Arizona, and California.

New Spain, actually the colonial center of "old" Mexico, has a population of 30 million. Long the breadbasket of Mexico, it is a traditional PRI stronghold. But it is now overpopulated, undercapitalized, and too heavily dependent on outmoded agricultural methods. Of the young men who went north in search of job opportunities, 80 percent were from this area.

Finally, South Mexico, with a population of about 15 million, is the poorest of these five regions, while Club Mex, with about 1.5 million people, is the newest and richest region. Club Mex comprises the chain of nine tourist resorts along both coasts and is the most artificial region. Its inhabitants are mostly bilingual immigrants from Metromex who have been trained to deal with the international holiday clientele. Club Mex has raised controversy because inhabitants of other parts of Mexico believe the government has devoted excessive investment capital to its development, at their expense.

Thus, Mexico has a wide array of economic, social, and political problems. The question is whether these problems will destabilize and radicalize society before solutions can be found that might, at the very least, alleviate the mounting pressures on the nation's political institutions.

Brazil

Unlike Mexico, Brazil has endured frequent changes in its political and constitutional system during the past half-century. The most recent change occurred in 1985, when the military junta relinquished power to an indirectly elected civilian president. The promised new constitution was completed in 1988, after the Constituent Assembly had considered more than ten thousand proposals. Two critical issues were resolved. First, the Constituent Assembly voted to maintain a presidential system rather than switching to a parliamentary system (despite wide support for the latter). Second, the Assembly drafted a provision signaling that President José Sarney would be allowed to serve through 1990, an important concession because Sarney had promised to honor the four-year-term commitment that Tancredo Nves had made during the 1984 presidential campaign; once in office, however, Sarney changed his mind. The 1988 Constitution set the president's term at five years. Until the issue was resolved, the possibility of military intervention could not be ruled out.

The continuing economic decline was another scenario made to order for a military coup. As one observer noted in early 1988:

> Unlike the Argentine military, the Brazilian armed forces are not a discredited institution; this makes it highly plausible that the military could return to power. Politicians, industrialists and businessmen are known to be reestablishing their old ties with key military men since the politicoeconomic situation began to deteriorate during the second half of 1987. The unions, agrarian reformers and leftist radicals have eagerly pushed for a confrontation, not a conciliation, with the Sarney government and the economic elite.[5]

The Politics of Confusion The confusion of the political situation was nowhere more evident than in the composition and proceedings of the Constituent Assembly. In November 1986 Brazilians elected 559 delegates (*constituintes*) to the Assembly to draft a new constitution. The Brazilian Democratic Movement party (PMDB; see Chapter 20) controlled 307 delegates on paper. In reality, nearly three-fourths of the PMDB's original constituintes came from the extinct ARENA party. As a result of opportunistic party switching and reshuffling that took place after the ban on new political parties was lifted in the early 1980s, party affiliations were neither a reliable guide to political convictions nor even a sure sign of party loyalties. Under the circumstances, it was no wonder that the Assembly gave the appearance of a three-ring circus.

The confusion over the drafting of the new constitution was mirrored in the government, where the majority PMDB was a hodgepodge of right-wing, moderate, liberal, and left-wing politicians. The PMDB was hampered by intense factionalism, and there was some speculation that it might even break up into rival parties. If so, it would not be the first time a Brazilian party had self-destructed in the 1980s: The Social Democratic party (PDS), the descendant of the right-wing ARENA party once headed by President Sarney himself disintegrated in 1985 when its members defected in droves to various other parties. Sarney had virtually no power base of his own. Instead, he had to court PMDB chieftains in Congress and try to ingratiate himself with the electorate by pretending to be a born-again populist. The resulting disarray and drift seemed to invite military intervention.

Brazil's Moratorium   At the end of 1990 Brazil's external debt stood at $115 billion—the largest in Latin America. Negotiations had dragged on for eighteen months with no agreement. President Sarney's economic cabinet had been a revolving door: three finance ministers, two economic planning ministers, and four Brazilian Central Bank presidents. In late February 1987 Brazil suspended interest payments on its huge commercial bank debt (then $67 billion), which amounted to roughly 60 percent of its total foreign debt. It was, in effect, a moratorium, although Sarney refused to use the word—one step away from default. What motivated him to take such drastic action?

Brazil's debt pressures during the late 1980s must be seen against a backdrop of hyperinflation, austerity, bulging budget deficits, and high unemployment. Even in less extreme circumstances the debt burden might have been unbearable. From 1983 to 1986 Brazil had paid interest totaling some $40 billion while imposing austerity measures prescribed by the IMF. (From 1983 to 1985 Brazil's debt payments alone accounted for almost 20 percent of Citicorp's profits.) The country was also enduring a recession and received a little new money from overseas commercial banks. Its trade surplus was $8 billion in 1986; the same year it had to pay $10 billion to service external debt.

Sarney's initial efforts to deal with economic problems, especially inflation, had an Alice-in-Wonderland quality about them. The Cruzado Plan, as it was called, created a new unit of currency, the *cruzado*; it froze wages and prices and abolished indexation (pay hikes pegged to inflation). At first the plan seemed to work, but not for long:

> One month after it was introduced in February 1986, inflation fell to zero. An artificial boom followed as wages temporarily outpaced inflation. Profits soared. The São Paulo stock market doubled in a single month. The unknown Sarney became popular. But by the summer of 1986 acute shortages had appeared. . . . Relative prices became absurd. Typewriters, assuming you could find them, were cheaper than shoes. Meanwhile the Central Bank kept money loose, feeding inflation. By fall inflation was raging. By June 1987 it exceeded 1,900 percent and interest rates were

nearly 30 percent a month. The stock market fell 90 percent in real terms. The country's trade surplus nearly disappeared, despite falling prices and interest rates.[6]

In April 1987 Sarney again changed his economic team and unveiled a new stabilization plan, which called for a ninety-day freeze on wages and prices, forbade automatic wage adjustments, and accelerated currency devaluation to spur exports. These measures achieved at least partial success; Brazil's trade balance improved, and inflation—which had been galloping along at up to 27 percent *a month* for the first half of 1987—came down somewhat.

Slight improvements, however, could hardly offset the effects of previous economic policies. Hyperinflation and unemployment had hit labor and the poor in a way that, among other effects, boosted economic crime rates (especially robbery and shoplifting). Bizarre events suggested the dimensions of social discontent:

> In late May, near São Paulo, hungry people attacked garbage workers and battled them for the garbage. In early June, Rio bus ticket prices were raised by 50 percent, provoking huge downtown riots. . . . The situation has become even worse in . . . Brazil's poorest areas. Each week about 200 buses arrive in São Paolo from [the nation's] northern regions filled with refugees. They survive in makeshift huts, huddled against the city's damp nights.[7]

Changing his mind again, Sarney announced in February 1988 that Brazil would pay $350 million to banks around the world and would cover part of the $850–$900 million in back interest that was due in January. Sarney also agreed to negotiate an austerity program with the IMF. He could not more clearly have signaled his intention to shift from confrontation to conciliation.

Even the defusing of the crisis atmosphere generated by Brazil's 1987 debt moratorium raised doubts about whether President Sarney had a plan or was improvising. It remained to be seen whether he finally would make the deep cuts needed in the national budget. Once before, his economic advisers had urged him to reduce government spending by trimming 300,000 federal jobs; Sarney had refused, expanding the public payrolls instead. Lacking a solid power base, dependent on opportunistic PMDB politicians, and incapable of forging a national consensus, Sarney had not been willing or able to administer the medicine that the economy needed. In the twilight of the 1980s Brazil had neither order nor progress. The generals and the voters demanded both, and they turned to Fernando Collor de Mello, who took office in March 1990.

Argentina

Argentina was a nation in decay when democracy arrived in 1983. The signs were easy to see: a $45-billion foreign debt, eventually rising to $53–$54 billion; an inflation rate of 600 percent a year and climbing; and real income that had fallen below 1970 levels. More than a decade of economic progress had been lost. President Raúl Alfonsín's early assurances that the economy would recover and the standard of living would improve turned out to be dead wrong. Over the next eighteen months the economy's decline accelerated. By June 1985 inflation skyrocketed to an annual rate of 1,900 percent while the GDP dropped by 5 percent during the first half of the year.

The Austral Plan   Faced with the worst economic crisis in Argentina's history, Alfonsín unveiled an austerity program, the Austral Plan, in mid-1985. The program's drastic belt-tightening measures, including a ninety-day wage-and-price freeze and extensive budget cuts, were immediately denounced by Argentina's largest trade union and by the Peronista party. The general public was more receptive, however, and the inflation rate did fall dramatically in the first few months after the plan went into effect. Although the rate climbed again later, it stayed well below pre-austerity levels. In the 1985 congressional elections, Alfonsín's Radical Civic Union (UCR) outpolled the Peronists, 43 percent to 34 percent.

The year 1986 was generally suspicious. Inflation for the year was at 82 percent (still high, but moving in the right direction), and the economy grew by 5.5 percent after shrinking by 4.8 percent the previous year. In April 1987 the government announced with much fanfare that it had renegotiated the country's foreign debt on highly favorable terms. Praise for Alfonsín's economic policies poured in from all directions—most notably from Barber Conable, the World Bank president, who called the Austral Plan ''an excellent program.''

Just when it appeared that Argentina's diseased economy was finally recovering, Alfonsín found himself in a confrontation with the military. The precise circumstances surrounding Argentina's transition to civilian rule made the danger of a military coup greater there than elsewhere in Latin America. The military had relinquished power following Argentina's defeat by Great Britain in the Falkland Islands War—that is, the junta was brought down by the British, not by the Argentines. As Alfonsín himself put it, ''It wasn't exactly the storming of the Bastille.''[8]

The Law of Due Obedience   When Alfonsín took office, a dark cloud hung over Argentina. The military had committed atrocities against thousands of Argentine citizens and had gone unpunished—without atoning, repenting, or even admitting any wrongdoing. This was a delicate issue because military officers were likely to stage another coup rather than permitting politicians to heap scorn on the armed forces. But the public clamored for justice.

As noted in Chapter 20, Alfonsín tried to escape from this trap by placing only a few officers (former junta members) on trial. To prevent the net from being cast too widely, he pushed through Congress a law that set a sixty-day deadline for indictments. Much to the government's chagrin, the courts moved swiftly to indict hundreds of officers.

In April 1987 the crisis came to a head when 150 officers and troops seized an army training facility on the outskirts of Buenos Aires. This was answered by a tremendous outpouring of popular support for Alfonsín and constitutional government. The tension mounted as the army's Second Corps at first advanced, on Alfonsín's orders, and then stopped: No military unit was willing to use force against the mutinous troops. It was a stalemate.

No one knows for certain what deal Alfonsín made with the military, but a settlement was reached. One upshot was the Law of Due Obedience, which granted most officers immunity from prosecution on the grounds that they were simply obeying orders when they committed crimes in the conduct of Argentina's "dirty war" against subversives (1976–1983).

The crisis was resolved, but not to the public's satisfaction. The military had been pardoned for appalling human rights abuses without having expressed even a little remorse. Alfonsín had won the battle with the rebel officers, but many felt that he was losing the war against military tyranny.

Argentina's Economic Relapse Alfonsín's problems with the military were compounded by another economic downturn. By mid-1987 inflation was again surging; from June to August it rose an average of 10 percent a month. Other economic indicators were equally alarming: The budget deficit was much larger than expected, the trade surplus was smaller, the value of the austral was eroding, and foreign currency reserves were seriously depleted.

In the fall elections the Peronists turned the tables on the Radical Civic Union, outstripping the president's party in the congressional races and also winning sixteen of the twenty-two provinces, including the largest one, Buenos Aires, with one-third of Argentina's population. This setback for the UCR had two consequences: First, any hope of a constitutional change before 1989 that would allow Alfonsín to seek a second term was gone. Second, the two largest parties would have to cooperate if the Alfonsín government were to avoid paralysis in 1988 and 1989. The approach of the 1989 campaign, however, seemed to preclude all but the most grudging cooperation.

Peronist candidate Carlos Menem won the May 1989 national elections, and Alfonsín transferred power to him in June, six months earlier than required. Menem received a strong popular mandate, sweeping twenty-three of twenty-four electoral districts and garnering 49 percent of the popular vote (against 37 percent for the UCR's candidate). Even so, his presidency faced formidable obstacles. Inflation was up to 2,000 percent annually, and the country's foreign debt was nearly $60 billion. Having paid no interest on this in over a year, the government somehow had to win the confidence of Western banks and governments as well as the IMF. At a minimum this meant an austerity program complete with spending cuts and tax reform. In addition, Menem surprisingly moved to privatize state-owned companies and deregulate the economy.

Argentina's new free-market reforms were clearly aimed at pleasing the United States and the IMF, whose goodwill and support were necessary for Menem to have any chance of dislodging the economy. Menem lost little time in serving notice that he would abandon the Peronist tradition of keeping the United States at arm's length. In September he became the first Peronist president ever to visit Washington while in office. He also moved toward normalization of relations with Great Britain and vigorously backed U.S. antidrug efforts in South America; he even refused to recognize Noriega's government in Panama. The reasons behind Argentina's new foreign policy were clear. In the words of Peter Hakim, staff director of the Internation-American Dialogue, Argentina's economy was in such bad shape that "it needs debt reduction before it can restructure its economy"—an objective that could not be achieved without the cooperation of the United States.[9]

As in Mexico and Brazil, democracy in Argentina faced several major tests. Putting the nation's economic house in order was one. Keeping the military in their barracks was another. Restructuring the external debt for a second time (after the 1987–1988 relapse) was still another. As Piero Gleijeses has observed:

> For Argentines, their country's straits are all the more painful because they are haunted by a past that the passage of time and a succession of failures have made all the more alluring. There was a time—the first three decades of this century—when Argentina had a strong economy and the sixth highest per capita income in the world; a time when Argentina seemed poised to become the leader of Spanish America.[10]

All that is gone now, and Argentina's democracy hardly seems poised for leadership in the 1990s. Rather, it will be preoccupied for some time with extraordinary economic and political challenges.

Venezuela

Like its neighbor, Colombia, Venezuela has been democratically governed for several decades. But unlike Colombia, Venezuela is not faced with armed insurgency; and although drug trafficking is a concern, it does not threaten the nation's political and social fabric. In the late 1980s the two-party system continued to lend stability and legitimacy to Venezuela's political system, and there were no serious third-party challenges on the horizon. The left-wing Social Action Movement (MAS) had been badly beaten at the polls in 1983, and no other party of the extreme right or left claimed a popular following.

Although Venezuela's democratic consensus did not appear to be threatened, the dramatic drop in oil prices in the early 1980s pushed the economy into a prolonged slump. Growth slowed to a snail's pace or stopped altogether; in 1983–1984 it declined by about 8 percent. Meanwhile, unemployment climbed (officially) from 7 percent in 1982 to nearly 12 percent by the mid-1980s (unofficial estimates put the figure closer to 20 percent). Inflation also threatened to become an issue, although it was relatively low compared with the rate in other Latin countries.

As the economy continued its downslide, Venezuela's foreign debt peaked at roughly $36 billion and became an issue domestically. President Jamie Lusinchi promised to drive a hard bargain with Venezuela's creditors in seeking to refinance the government's share of the debt. An agreement was reached in 1985–1986, but Lusinchi later called for new negotiations to ease the debt service burden further. In the elections of 1988 voters returned a former president to office for the first time in history. Carlos Andrés Pérez became president in 1990.

Ironically, Venezuela's good fortune in finding large oil reserves has also led to problems. Oil accounts for 90 percent of the nation's exports, over 60 percent of revenues, and about 22 percent of GDP. These figures add up to a serious oil dependence problem that has long been present but was accentuated by the sudden drop in prices in the early 1980s. For decades Venezuela neglected to invest adequately in agricultural development and industrial diversification; one consequence is that the country has lost its self-sufficiency in food production. Having to import food—which it could produce domestically—has exacerbated the debt-service burden.

Nonetheless, Venezuela has both political and economic advantages over many other nations in the region. Besides its considerable resources, it has a close relationship with the United States, which has strategic interests in Venezuela's democratic government and can be expected to use its own resources to help Venezuela negotiate the bumpy road ahead.

CONCLUSION

Many Latin American countries have made great strides in recent years toward opening up their political systems to wider participation. For societies traditionally built on privilege and gross maldistribution of wealth and power, democratization is potentially explosive. We have stressed throughout this book that politics and economics are inextricably intertwined. Unless Latin America can put its economy in order, democracy will be meaningless to the majority of the people, who are mired in poverty. And if democracy favors the few while failing to bear fruits for the many, there is the ever-present danger that it will end in tragedy.

STUDY QUESTIONS

1. Is there a Latin American "underdevelopment syndrome"? What patterns are discernible throughout the region? What is the cause of this seemingly pervasive economic malaise? What is the cure?
2. How are the current economic predicaments of Brazil and Mexico similar? How are they different?
3. Would it be wiser to invest in Venezuela or Argentina? Why?
4. In what sense can it be said that there is not one Mexico, but five?
5. Which of the four countries—Mexico, Brazil, Argentina, and Venezuela— is most likely to be plunged into turmoil in the coming years? Which is least likely to face a revolutionary situation? If a regime change does occur in one or more of these states, how do you think it will happen, and with what results?

SUGGESTED READINGS

Casagrande, Louis B. "The Five Nations of Mexico," *Focus*, Spring 1987.

Pang, Eul-Soo. "The Darker Side of Brazil's Democracy," *Current History*, January 1988.

Gleijeses, Piero. "The Decay of Democracy in Argentina," *Current History*, January 1988.

Stallings, Barbara, and Robert Kaufman. *Debt and Democracy in Latin America*. Boulder, Colo.: Westview, 1989.

Wiarda, Howard J. *Latin America at the Crossroads: Debt, Development, and the Future*. Washington, D.C.: American Enterprise Institute, 1987.

NOTES

[1] Abraham F. Lowenthal, "The United States and South America," *Current History*, Vol. 87, No. 525 (January 1988), p. 1.

[2] "Will Latin America Last?" *The World Today*, April 1987. Reprinted in Paul B. Goodwin, Jr., *Latin America*, 3rd ed. (Guilford, Conn.: Dushkin, 1988) p. 120.

[3] Ibid.

[4] This list and information in the following few paragraphs are based on Louis B. Casagrande, "The Five Nations of Mexico," *Focus*, Spring 1987, pp. 2–9.

[5] Eul-Soo Pang, "The Darker Side of Brazil's Democracy," *Current History*, January 1988, p. 22.

[6] James S. Henry, "Brazil Says: Nuts," *New Republic*, Oct. 12, 1987.

[7] Ibid.

[8] See Piero Gleijeses, "The Decay of Democracy in Argentina," *Current History*, January 1988, p. 6.

[9] Linda Feldman, *Christian Science Monitor*, May 23, 1989, p. 8.

[10] Gleijeses, op. cit., p. 5.

Index

513